UNIVERSITY OF BRISTOL
UNIVERSITY LIBRARY
TYNDALL

INTRODUCTION TO THE MODERN ECONOMIC HISTORY OF THE MIDDLE EAST

INTRODUCTION TO

THE MODERN ECONOMIC HISTORY OF THE MIDDLE EAST

BY

Z. Y. HERSHLAG

SECOND, REVISED EDITION

LEIDEN
E. J. BRILL
1980

HC 40.7 HER

ISBN 90 04 06061 8

Copyright 1980 by E. J. Brill, Leiden, The Netherlands

All rights reserved. No part of this book may be reproduced or translated in any form, by print, photoprint, microfilm, microfiche or any other means without written permission from the publisher

PRINTED IN THE NETHERLANDS

To my wife and children

PREFACE TO THE SECOND EDITION

Nearly 15 years have passed since the first edition of this book in English was published. In the meantime, it was followed by a Hebrew version, in Jerusalem, and an Arabic translation, in Beirut. The original publication went out of print and we have been faced with the usual dilemma of reprint *versus* revised edition. Despite the largely historical character of the study, we opted for a revised edition in order to be able to re-check sources, eliminate mistakes and misprints and benefit from the helpful criticism, comments and suggestions of the reviewers of our first edition, as well as have recourse to some additional sources and studies on the subject.

Some of the reviewers of our first edition took exception to the inclusion in the Appendices of certain documents which had been already published elsewhere. We gave a great deal of thought to the criticism, but have finally decided to retain the whole body of Appendices for two reasons: 1. All documents, including those previously published, have been, already for the first edition, thoroughly checked and compared with the originals and, where necessary, adjusted and corrected; 2. We believe that the interested reader will benefit by being able to check, identify and study important subjects through immediate reference to sources constituting part of the volume. In the meantime, two important and very useful volumes of documents and readings were edited by Professor Charles Issawi, namely, on *The Economic History of the Middle East 1800-1914,* in 1966, and on *The Economic History of Iran 1800-1914,* in 1971; these, however, are complementary rather than competitive to our Appendices.

In the course of time I have had the benefit of advice, comments and insights of a great number of colleagues and researchers in private discussions, conferences and correspondence and all their aid is most warmly appreciated.

The help of my assistants Yair Menzly and Yitshak Gal has been of outstanding value, as was that of Mrs. Gabriella Williams and Ruth Parnass in the preparation of the manuscript.

Autumn 1979.   Z. Y. H.

PREFACE TO THE FIRST EDITION

The purpose of this study is twofold, but modest in both respects: 1) To prepare the ground and set up a framework for further, more detailed and comprehensive research into the economic history of the Middle East in modern times, a subject that has been rather neglected among the numerous studies of Middle Eastern history; 2) To investigate the historical background of Middle Eastern society and economy as a starting point for the present author's forthcoming study of the contemporary economic structure of this region.

The present book deals mainly with the period about 150 years since 1800, although incursions had to be made into earlier history for the purpose of a better understanding of a society so deeply rooted in the past. Particular stress had to be laid on socio-political and international aspects which may be particularly helpful in explaining how it arrived at its present institutional and economic structure.

The study falls into two main periods, and, therefore, also in two books in the present volume: the first—until World War I; and the second—the inter-war period. The Ottoman Empire is usually regarded as the backbone of Middle East society in the first period, but two exceptions should be made to this generalisation. First, Persia and Egypt must be dealt with separately: Persia on account of its independent political and economic status; Egypt, owing to its peculiar problems notwithstanding its formal adherence to the Ottoman Empire. Second, the Ottoman Empire during this period hardly admits of a geographic and demographic definition. Complementing its more or less permanent elements of Anatolia, Iraq, the Levant, part of Arabia and eastern Thrace in Europe, tributary States and dependencies fluctuate around the imperial centre, dropping out in succession as they win independence. Hence the statistical and economic data fluctuate with the boundaries of the Empire, Egypt (with the Sudan and south-western Arabia) being clearly excluded, except for the yearly tribute incorporated in the receipts of the Ottoman budget.

The inter-war period is characterised by the rearrangement of the Middle Eastern scene: Turkey (proper), Persia and Egypt emerge as independent States, while mandatory regimes are set up for Syria and Lebanon, Iraq (until 1932) and Transjordan. This determines our treatment of the area during this second period. Palestine, with its particular history and problems, has been left out.

In a forthcoming volume on the Contemporary Economic Structure of the Middle East we hope to deal, against the background of the present historical inquiry, with the basic problems common to the Middle East and backward countries generally;

the interplay between population growth and the availability of economic resources; the main constituents of the existing economic structure; the organisation and methods of production; the distribution of wealth and national income; the focuses of entrepreneurship in the region; and patterns of change in the social and economic structure.

The author is indebted to many of his friends and students who read or with whom he discussed the whole or parts of the manuscript. Among them are: Professor Bernard Lewis and Mr. Vernon Parry of the School of Oriental and African Studies, University of London; Professor David Ayalon of the Hebrew University, Jerusalem; Professor A. N. Poliak of the University of Tel-Aviv; Mr. H. Cohen, Mr. Y. Ben-Porath and Mr. A. Y. Firestone, Jerusalem. None of them shares responsibility for the author's views and the shortcomings of the study.

Mr. A. Y. Firestone, Mrs. Hanna Shmorak, Jerusalem, and Mr. E. N. McMillan, The Hague, kindly dealt with the English version and edition. Mr. J. Lansdorp, Heemstede, prepared the maps and Mr. M. Fisher, Tel-Aviv, took care of the Index.

Mr. Eliahu Elath, the President of the Hebrew University, Jerusalem; Professor C. A. O. van Nieuwenhuize, the Institute of Social Studies, The Hague; the Eliezer Kaplan School of Economics, Jerusalem; the Laura-Julia Foundation, Jerusalem; and Mif'al Hapayis, Israel, are thanked for every assistance and financial help given in the course of our work.

The wholehearted support of the Tel-Aviv University and its Rector, Professor A. Klopstock, was of paramount importance in the final stages of this study.

The following institutions and publishers are offered thanks for their kind agreement to the reproduction of the documents under their copyright or trusteeship: The Trustees of the British Museum, London; The Foreign Office, London; "Current History", Events Publishing Company, Philadelphia; The Publications, Board of the United Nations, New York; The Executive Documents Publications, The Senate of the U.S., Washington.

The Tel-Aviv University, Summer 1963.   Z. Y. H.

Note on Transliteration

Apart from a few Turkish words and names, such as *yeni çeri, Çelebi, Küçük Kaynàrca,* in which modern Turkish spelling has been used, most of the words are spelled in a manner more familiar to the English reader, e.g., *Pasha, shaykh, jizya,* or *kharadj*. The original spelling has, however, been retained in quotations and documents cited or reproduced.

CONTENTS

Preface to the Second Edition VII
Preface to the First Edition VIII

Introduction 1

BOOK ONE
THE MIDDLE-EAST ECONOMY UNTIL WORLD WAR I

Part I. The Decline and Disintegration of the Ottoman Empire

1. The Disintegration of the Political and Military Structure 7
2. Land and Taxes the Focus of the Feudal System—Duality of Centralism and Feudalism 10
3. The Middle Eastern City and the Guilds 18
4. Islam, the Minorities and Socio-Economic Concepts 22

Part II. Attempts at Reform in the Ottoman Empire and Expansion of Foreign Interests

1. Attempts at Westernisation before the Tanzimat 28
2. The Tanzimat 31
3. The Ottoman Land Code 40
4. The Capitulatory System and Its Economic Implications 43
5. The Spread of Foreign Concessions 49

Part III. The Ottoman Finances and Economy

1. Budgets, Banking, and Currency 55
2. The Public Debt 63
3. The Patterns of Production and Services in the Ottoman Economy in the 19th and Early 20th Centuries 71

Part IV. The Economic Development of Egypt in the Nineteenth Century

1. The Rise of Mehmed Ali and his Agrarian Policy: Transition to Cash Crops 81
2. Mehmed Ali's Industrialisation Drive—The System of Monopolies 88
3. A Retrospect of the First Half of the 19th Century 94
4. Prosperity and Depression on the Cotton Market and Penetration of Foreign Capital 99

5. The Growth of the National Debt, "Caisse de la Dette Publique" and "Dual Control" 104
6. The Economic Consequences of Ismail's Rule 110
7. Economic and Political Control by the British 117
8. The Egyptian Economy on the Eve of the First World War 124
9. The Suez Canal 129

Part V. Persia and its Economic Problems in the 19th and 20th Century (until World War I)

1. The Decline of Persia's Economic Resources and Public Finances 140
2. Some Problems of Major Economic Sectors 144
3. Exogenous Causes of Persia's Economic Difficulties: The Competition between the Powers 149
4. Endogenous Causes of Persia's Economic Difficulties: The Social Structure and the Weakness of the Central Government 155
5. Attempts at Reform 158

Book Two

THE ECONOMIC AND SOCIAL CHANGES IN THE INTER-WAR PERIOD

Part VI. The Middle East at the End of the First World War

General Review 165
   A. The Renewed Meeting between East and West 165
   B. The New Political Structure and its Economic Effects 167
   C. Derangement of the Village and Town Structure 170

Part VII. The Economic Development of Republican Turkey

1. From Sèvres to Lausanne - A New Page in Turkish History 172
2. The Economic Development of the Twenties and Its Limitations 179
3. The Causes of the Changes in Economic Policy 186
4. The Nature and Methods of Etatism 190
5. The Five Year Plans 194
6. The Results of the Etatist Policy - A Review 196

Part VIII. Persia between the Two World Wars

1. Political Changes and Social Reforms 203
2. Attempts at Economic Reconstruction 204
3. Formation of State Economy 210
4. Bottlenecks in the Development Process 215

CONTENTS

Part IX. The Egyptian Economy during the Twenties and Thirties
1. Egypt's Post-War Problems and Economic Policy 218
2. Public Financing 223
3. The Agricultural Sector and Agrarian Policies 226
4. Limited Results of Industrialisation and of the Development of Infrastructure 229
5. The Structure and Trends of Foreign Trade 233

Part X. The Economy of the Mandated Territories (Syria, Lebanon, Iraq, and Transjordan) between the Two World Wars
1. Ethnic and Demographic Problems and the Political Structure 236
2. Economic Policy and Reality 241
3. Currency and Public Finances 249
4. Transport and Communications 259
5. The Agrarian Sector 262
6. The Industrial Sector 268
7. The Oil Sector 271
8. Foreign Trade and Balance of Payments 273

Summary 279

Appendices 291

Bibliography 401

Index 412

LIST OF TABLES

I	Budgets of the Ottoman Empire, 1853-1911	57
II	Budgets of the Ottoman Empire by Fiscal Year between 1909 and 1914	59
III	French, German and British Holdings in the Debt of the Ottoman Empire, 1914	67
IV	The Ottoman Empire's Foreign Trade, 1880-1913	79
V	Structure of Turkey's Foreign Trade in 1914	80
VI	Egypt's Budgets for the Years 1821-1840	97
VII	Egypt's Income and Expenditure Budget for the Year 1833 ...	98
VIII	Foreign and Local Capital Investments in Egypt in 1902	104
IX	The Budget of Egypt, 1876	107
X	Investments in Public Works during Ismail's Reign	111
XI	Changes in Economic Values during Ismail's Reign	113
XII	Cost of Living in Cairo and Alexandria in 1877	115

XIII	Burden of Interest on the Egyptian Economy during the Years 1880-1929	122
XIV	The Changes in the Distribution of Landed Property in Egypt, 1896-1916	126
XV	Suez Canal Traffic, 1870-1948	137
XVI	Shortening of Communication Lines by the Suez Canal	138
XVII	Increase in the Credit of the Agricultural Bank of Turkey during the Years 1922-1929	182
XVIII	The Budgets of Turkey during the Years 1930/31-1939/40	192
XIX	Changes in the National Income in Turkey during the Years 1927-1939	200
XX	Changes in the Consumption Level in Turkey during the Thirties	201
XXI	Comparison between Receipts and Expenses of the Persian Budget for the Years 1924/5 and 1938/9	207
XXII	Average Yields in kg per Hectare in 1934/38 (Egypt, Persia, Sudan, Turkey)	209
XXIII	Persia's Foreign Trade, 1939	213
XXIV	Food Consumption in Egypt	219
XXV	The Occupational Structure of the Egyptian Population prior to the Outbreak of the Second World War	223
XXVI	Egyptian Budgets, 1929/30-1937/8	225
XXVII	Distribution of Landed Property in Egypt in 1936	226
XXVIII	Distribution of Crop Areas in Egypt during the Thirties	228
XXIX	Growth of Egyptian Industry, 1927-1945	231
XXX	Productivity of Egyptian Industry (1937) in Comparison with Other Countries	231
XXXI	Structure of Egypt's Foreign Trade, 1913-1935	234
XXXII	Distribution of the Population in the French Mandate Area, 1921-1938	237
XXXIII	Religious and National Distribution of the Population of Iraq in 1919	239
XXXIV	School Network in Iraq in 1936-38	248
XXXV	Development of Main Sources of Revenue of the Iraqi Budget, 1927-1939	256
XXXVI	Government Investments in Iraq in the Years 1927-1939	257
XXXVII	The Budgets of Iraq for the Years 1927-1939	258
XXXVIII	Iraq's Balance of Payments in 1938/9	277
XXXIX	Per Capita Consumption of Food in Egypt, England and the U.S.A. in 1937	284
XL	Average Daily Consumption of Calories in Different Countries in 1938/9	284
XLI	Company Dividends Distributed in Select Countries during 1930-37	286
XLII	Per Capita Savings in 1938 (Comparative Table)	287

LIST OF APPENDICES

Regarding Parts I-III

1. Interpretation of the Distinction between 'Ushr and Kharadj Lands by Abū Yūsuf Ya'kūb 293
2. Treaty of 1454 between Venice and the Ottoman Empire 293
3. Capitulation with France, 1535 295
4. Capitulations between Great Britain and the Ottoman Empire, 1675 298
5. Treaty of Commerce and Navigation between the United States and the Ottoman Porte, 1830 306
6. Imperial Ottoman Firman for the Protection of English Steam Vessels Destined to Navigate the River Euphrates, 1834 307
7. Convention of Commerce and Navigation between Her Majesty and the Sultan of the Ottoman Empire, Balta-Liman 1838 308
8. The Hatti Sherif of Gülhane, 1839 310
9. The Hatti Hümayun by Sultan Abdul Mejid, 1856 311
10. The Ottoman Land Code, 1858 312
11. Treaty of Commerce and Navigation between Her Majesty and the Sultan, 1861 315
12. Decree of 28 Muharrem, 1299 (December 8(20), 1881) 320
13. The Baghdad Railway Convention, 1903 332
14. Ottoman Circular announcing the Abrogation of the Capitulations, 1914   343

Regarding Part IV

15. Second Act of Concession and Specification for the Construction and Management of the Great Maritime Suez Canal, 1856 (with the modifications up to 1875) 344
16. Decree for the Establishment of a Treasury of the Public Debt in Egypt, 1876 348
17. Convention between Great Britain, Germany, Austria-Hungary, Spain, France, Italy, the Netherlands, Russia, and Turkey, respecting the Free Navigation of the Suez Maritime Canal, 1888 350
18. Homestead Exemption Law (Five Feddans Law), 1912 352

Regarding Part V

19. The Grants and Privileges made by Shah Abas (text adjusted by Shah Sefi, 1629) 352
20. Anglo-Persian Commercial Treaty, 1801 354
21. Treaty of Friendship and Commerce between the United States and Persia, 1856 355
22. Concession of the Tobacco Régie in Persia, 1890 358

23. Agreement of May 28th, 1901, between the Government of His Imperial Majesty the Shah of Persia and William Knox d'Arcy 359
24. Convention between the United Kingdom and Russia relating to Persia, Afghanistan and Thibet, 1907 (part concerning Persia only) 362

Regarding Parts VI-X

25. Treaty of Friendship between Russia and Turkey, 1921 363
26. Treaty of Friendship between Persia and the Russian Socialist Federal Soviet Republic, 1921 366
27. Article 22 of the Covenant of the League of Nations 370
28. Select Articles from Mandate for Syria and the Lebanon 371
29. Select Articles of Anglo-Iraqi Treaty (later [in 1924] included in Mandate for Iraq) 371
30. Article 18 of the Mandate for Palestine 372
31. Text of the Chester Concession, 1923 372
32. Soviet Caspian Sea Fisheries Concession in Persia, 1927 381
33. The Red Line Agreement of the Turkish (Iraq) Petroleum Company, 31.7.1928 385

Maps

1. Turkey, Arabia and Persia in 1701, following p. 8.
2. Turkish Railways on the Eve of World War I, following p. 52.
3. Spheres of Influence in Persia, 1907, following p. 160.
4. Egypt during World War I, following p. 128.
5. The Suez Canal in 1917, following p. 136.
6. The Middle East on the Eve of World War II, following p. 272.

INTRODUCTION

The historical reasons and roots of the economic decline of the Middle East and its continued lagging behind modern development have remained controversial, if not enigmatic, to students and analysts of the area.

Attempts to explain the loss of past prosperity have usually focused, rather selectively, on the 'legacy' of *either* the endogenous *or* exogenous factors.

Jacques Weulersse, inquiring into the origins of the protracted backwardness of the Middle East, singled out the year 1516, when the last Ottoman Conqueror, Selim I, perpetuating the Byzantine, Arab and Seljuk heritage he had found in the area, passed on to future generations "même statut de la terre, même hiérarchie sociale, même politique de l'Etat, même rôle de la religion."[1] Acceptance of this view could cast a serious doubt on the contention of structuralist economists that time and not space determine economic development, to which the Middle East would be a remarkable exception. In the opinion of Weulersse and others, not much has changed in the social and economic structure of the region, despite the passage of time, owing to its spatial conditions—provided these are made to include not only the physical, but also the spiritual climate (religion and passive conception of life). Or, perhaps, is Braudel right in attributing an almost transcendental unity to the Mediterranean basin, which to his mind is unconquerable, but rather conquers and changes its would-be conquerors: "Le Proche-Orient n'est pas conquis par les Arabes; c'est lui qui les conquiert, qui les assimile à sa substance. Qui agit avec eux comme ces fleurs avec les insectes assez imprudents pour se loger en elles: elles se referment et les dévorent."[2]

In this case, Islam itself should be regarded as the outcome of the desert and of the caravan cities, a product of its climatic, geopolitic and economic conditions (its fatalistic trait, the element of the *jihad* and the soldiers at the top of the hierarchy, immediately followed by the merchants). This geographical and spiritual climate subsequently also remoulded the conquerors who had come to succeed the Arabs in power, and continued to exert an overwhelming influence on the ruling institutions, social structure and economic performance. To the extent that time *was* a determinant of change, it sowed the seeds of recession rather than of progress. The decline set in when the superiority of the West manifested itself in rapid military, social and economic changes in contrast to the inadaptability of the Orient.

---

[1] Jacques Weulersse, *Paysans de Syrie et du Proche-Orient,* Gallimard, 1946, p. 59.
[2] F. Braudel, *La Méditerranée et le Monde méditerranéen à l'époque de Philippe II,* Paris, 1949, pp. 298-9.

On the other hand, the 'Middle East Question' has been discussed in the past mainly from the point of view of the major Powers, whose nationals had a political or economic stake in the region. And indeed the political and military struggle between Europe and the Ottoman Empire constituted the dominant element in the relations between these two parts of the world, almost throughout the entire period. It is likewise true that what appear to be attempts at social, judicial and economic reform within the Empire mainly came about (mostly on paper only) as the result of Turkish military defeats or of the slaughter of Christian groups which provoked the Powers concerned to demand such reforms. This provides the main explanation for the intensification of the capitulatory regime on the one hand, and the declarations of reforms like that of Hatti Sherif of 1839 and Hatti Hümayun of 1856 on the other. Frequently peace treaties, like the Treaty of Turkman-Chai in 1828, or of Paris in 1856 and of Berlin in 1878, clearly imposed on Persia and the Ottoman Empire, respectively, the duty to expand capitulations and reform the regime. However, the large gap persisting between these "reforms" and actual conditions, and the fact that the multiplication of laws merely served as an expression of anarchy and arbitrary rule,[3] render it necessary to look for the deeper causes within the Empire (or, as the case may be, Persia) itself.

The true legacy of the past has been very complex, with interdependent external and internal, negative as well as positive components. Alongside human and material losses, social and cultural inflexibility, domestic and external oppression, foreign domination and exploitation—some tangible and real values were inherited from the past, such as new irrigation facilities, new crops, certain modern land and water transportation systems, some, formally at least, improved legal and administrative devices, and, last not least, an emerging spirit of national identity and consciousness of the need to bring up the society and its individuals to modern standards.

A comprehensive investigation of interrelated political, social, institutional and economic factors may contribute to a better understanding of the disintegration and decay of an area which had been the cradle of cultures, religions and nations, as well as of the hardly successful attempts at reform. The resulting social and economic phenomena of the East may appear like a mounted cinematographic film, projecting a series of events, sometimes at an ordinary pace, sometimes in slow motion, and sometimes even in inverted sequence, where the hero is seen scuttling back from his target to the diving board, as though time itself was rolling back.

Although the Middle East from time to time came in contact with Western civilisation, many cultural and socio-economic concepts and institutions have persisted which are utterly foreign to the Western spirit, and which embody the specific set of values of this part of the world. There is undoubtedly no little exaggeration in the description of Western observers who put all the blame on the character of the Turks and their approach to economic problems, as will be seen from a discussion of the impact of outside factors. But it is interesting to read the

---

[3] Cf. William Miller, *The Ottoman Europe and its Successors, 1801-1927*, Cambridge University Press, 1934 ed., in part. Chs. VII and X.

opinion of an English doctor who lived in Smyrna (Izmir) during the 'fifties of the 19th century: "It is a fact that while their institutions have improved, their wealth and population have diminished. Many causes have contributed to this deterioration. The first and great one is that they are not producers. They have neither diligence, intelligence, nor forethought. No Turk is an improving landlord. When he has money he spends it on objects of immediate gratification. His most permanent investment is a timber palace, to last about as long as its builder. His only professions are shop-keeping and service. He cannot engage in any foreign commerce, as he speaks no language but his own. No one ever heard of a Turkish house of business, or of a Turkish banker, or merchant, or manufacturer. If he has lands or houses, he lives on their rent; if he has money, he spends it, or employs it in stocking a shop, in which he can smoke and gossip all day long. The only considerable enterprise in which he ever engages is farming some branch of the public revenue. His great resource is service, either that of a private person or of the Sultan. People talk of the place hunting of France and of Germany; it is nothing to that of Turkey. A place closes the vista of every Turk's ambition."[4]

In spite of the industrial revolution in the West, in spite of Napoleon's campaigns and even in spite of the attempts at reforms within the Ottoman Empire during the 19th century, the region has failed to integrate organically within the evolving modern social and economic set-up. Even a fairly optimistic observer, who states that "it is no exaggeration to say that during the last 150 years the Middle East has compressed, in some regions and branches, the process through which Europe passed between the Middle Ages and the end of the nineteenth century", submits that in the Middle East "there were very few signs at the beginning of the present century to indicate that a radical change would occur in the relations between the indigenous and foreign groups, and between the rather inert majority and the more differentiated and economically active minorities."[5] The period between the two World Wars, after the collapse of the Ottoman Empire, indeed marks a considerable turning point in the relations between the West and the Middle East, and in the approach of local authorities to economic and political principles within the oriental society. Moreover, the present, post-war period, one of whose characteristic features is the accumulation of large capital resources in the oil regions of the Middle East, engenders good chances for abolishing some of the factors which have led to the backwardness of the Middle East.

The experience of the past, however, proves that the supply of capital alone is not likely to solve the problem of economic backwardness. Even the increasing readiness of the well-developed industrial countries to offer economic, administrative and technical assistance does not yet afford a guarantee for the success of the efforts at development. Eastern society is loath to accept the leadership and domination of the more advanced part of the world. The sometimes

---

[4] N. W. Senior, *A Journal kept in Turkey and Greece, in the Autumn of 1857 and the beginning of 1858,* London, 1895, pp. 210-211.
[5] Ch. Issawi (ed.), *The Economic History of the Middle East 1800-1914,* The University of Chicago Press, 1966, pp. 7-12.

justified fear of accepting Western civilisation in its full technical, economic and cultural sense is deeply rooted in the consciousness of the East. Changes in technology and economy lead to changes in the social and political regime, in mentality and in religion. If, however, these latter changes, which may be termed changes in the social superstructure, fail to materialise owing to the adherence—particularly on the part of the rural sector—to antiquated modes of life, tribal forms, old consumption habits, the domination of religion and the *'ulema* (the Muslim priesthood)—then the technological and economic innovations will similarly fail to endure. An outstanding example of this phenomenon in the Middle East is the period of Mehmed Ali in Egypt, when a clash occurred between the technical and economic changes introduced and the social and political structure of the country. This clash ended in the defeat of the reforms, even though the *coup de grâce* was administered by outside forces.

In the course of the years the Ottoman conquest lost the impetus which had unified this enormous area during the period of its growth. To a growing extent the latent rifts and dualities have started to reveal themselves, endangering the very existence of this society. The split has sharpened in all the main spheres of life—military, political, administrative, fiscal—although the fellahin, constituting a major part of the population, have remained frozen within their shell. The progressive disintegration of society, especially in its institutional structure, bore within it the seeds of inevitable final dissolution. Changes brought by the First World War in the political structure of the region and consequently also in its social and economic structure produced a considerable social ferment in the area and new economic and social strivings, sometimes gradual, sometimes hectic, within the apparently sealed and impermeable shell of backwardness.

Still, even on the heels of World War II, which opened up new vistas for national and economic aspirations, the Middle East has not yet been able to overcome the various adverse conflicting forces and factors blocking the road to sustained social and economic development.[6]

---

[6] This later, contemporary period is examined in the present author's *The Economic Structure of the Middle East,* Brill, Leiden, 1975.

BOOK ONE

THE MIDDLE-EAST ECONOMY UNTIL WORLD WAR I

PART ONE

THE DECLINE AND DISINTEGRATION OF THE OTTOMAN EMPIRE

1. THE DISINTEGRATION OF THE POLITICAL AND MILITARY STRUCTURE

The changes which took place in the structure of the Ottoman Empire between the 17th century and the middle of the 19th century were a function of the continuous economic decline of this political entity whose production and trade patterns were still based mainly on the rich legacy of the Byzantine and the Arab periods. This decline, taking place at the very time when Western Europe was being swept by a stormy political and economic revolution, widened the gulf between a stationary East that was consuming its capital and a West that was moving quickly toward a growing accumulation of capital and the adjustment of its social and political patterns to new economic needs. Denied local investment and local economic initiative at a time when foreign wars and the Sultans' luxuries swallowed up most of the national income, the Ottoman Empire could not but fall prey to foreign capital and to foreign powers whose political and economic interests did not coincide with its own. Among the consequences of this state of affairs was a continuous tension between the Turkish majority in the Empire and its minorities that inevitably culminated in the persecution of the latter.

When surveying the disintegration of the Empire one must not ignore the role played by the political and economic interests of the Powers, but at the same time one cannot overlook the share of Turkey's own ineffective, corrupt and venal administration which dislocated the economy and exploited it mercilessly without any serious attempt at its fundamental reconstruction. The changes ushered in by the 19th century reflected not only the intervention of external forces but also the play of local interests with a stake in the traditional structure and in reform, respectively.[1]

The internal disintegration of the Ottoman Empire can be traced back to a short time after it had reached the peak of its political and military power, at the end of the 16th century.[2] The year 1580 marks the approximate beginning of a continuous flow of Mexican and Peruvian gold and silver brought to the Middle East by European traders—Spanish, French, Portuguese and others. Soon not only was the

---

[1] Among the private and official testimonies which cast an interesting sidelight on various aspects of the Ottoman regime from what might be termed a field perspective are: The Eastern Question Association, *Papers on the Eastern Question,* London, 1877, pp. 3-47; and N. W. Senior, *A Journal kept in Turkey and Greece, in the autumn of 1857 and the beginning of 1858,* London, 1859, *passim.*

[2] Von Hammer places the beginning of the disintegration at the end of the reign of Suleiman the Magnificent, who withdrew from the deliberations of the government, disregarded the distinctions between the State treasury and the inner treasury and failed to curb excessive spending both at the Sultan's court and on the part of the Viziers and provincial Pashas. Cf. Joseph von Hammer, *Geschichte des Osmanischen Reiches,* Pesth, II, 1834, pp. 348-353.

shortage brought about by the dwindling supply of African gold overcome, but the plentiful stream of American gold sent prices spiralling up and gravely disturbed the old economic order of the Ottoman Empire. Spain in particular, in whose hands lay the keys to the treasures of the Western hemisphere, was in a position to substitute for her former exports of goods the export of gold and gold coins, in great demand in Europe and the Middle East alike. Europe was able to pay for at least part of these imports by selling the Spaniards surplus arms, and many European cities and business houses made fortunes on such transactions in coin and bars. The East, on the other hand, had little to offer but raw materials and a narrow range of products. The supply of goods at home grew short and prices rose.[3] The inflationary process depressed the real value of the Janissaries' pay and the Sipahis'[4] rents—in the latter case, to the extent that they were paid in cash and not in kind. The result was a heavier burden of taxes and exactions on the peasants and the consequent depletion of the main fount of State revenue. While Murad IV (1623-1640) heeded the memorandum submitted to him in 1630 by his counsellor, Koçu Bey, succeeded in reorganising the Empire's foundering finances and even managed to bequeathe a substantial treasury surplus to his successors, his reign was followed by a period of renewed disintegration of the polical and economic structures alike.[5]

This disintegration, in which an appreciable role was unquestionably played by the rounding of the Cape of Good Hope and the consequent diversion of a good deal of the Middle East's through trade to the ocean routes,[6] took on an unmistakable character with the retreat of the Ottoman armies from the high tide of their power in Europe, and especially their defeat under the walls of Vienna in 1683 and the peace treaty of Carlowitz in 1699.[7] With the splendour of past conquests dimmed, the populations of occupied European territories grew more restive, making for increased difficulties for the Ottoman rulers, who lost a good many of their most valuable and lucrative provinces.

A close parallel may be drawn at this point to the later days of the Carolingian Empire, whose disintegration may also be ascribed to the disruption of the central administration and of the national economy. However, the difference in the nature of Eastern and Western feudalism was reflected in the anatomy of the disintegration

---

[3] Cf. F. Braudel, *op. cit.,* Ch. II. As a matter of fact the Ottoman currency was devalued as early as the 1560's, but it is not clear whether this was done to adjust it to the falling price of silver, on which it was based, or whether it can already be interpreted as an indication of the economic decline of the Ottoman Empire.

[4] Sipahi-horsman in Persian. For a further discussion of the Janissaries and Sipahis, cf. below.

[5] B. Lewis, "Some Reflections on the Decline of the Ottoman Empire", *Studia Islamica,* 1958, IX, p. 112. Cf. Ch. Morawitz, *Les finances de la Turquie,* Paris, 1902, pp. 5-10.

[6] Although this process took longer than is generally assumed and in the 17th century Alexandria, Tripoli, Aleppo and Baghdad were still important commercial centres.

[7] For details about this period see C. Brockelmann, *A History of the Islamic Peoples,* London, 1949, pp. 335-343. For the text of the Treaty see *Treaties, & c. between Turkey and Foreign Powers, 1535-1855,* compiled by the librarian and keeper of the papers, Foreign Office, London, 1855, pp. 47-59. Cf. also P. Wittek (*The Rise of the Ottoman Empire,* London, 1938, p. 3) who states: »It was not until the peace of Passarowitz (admittedly a printing mistake—should be: Carlowitz—Z.Y.H.) in 1699 that the slow, gradual process of decomposition began, called "the dismemberment of the Ottoman Empire", although it really concerned only its European possessions.«

process. In Europe the main disruptive push came from the provinces, which sought to crystallise feudal relations into the maximum degree of independence for themselves; in the Ottoman Empire, on the other hand, the central government itself contributed to the disintegration of the Empire. It divided up the tax-collection network among tax-farmers; it resigned itself to the sweeping powers of the local feudal lords; and it recognised the substantial autonomy of the *millets,* the self-governing religious communities which in principle (and mostly in fact) coincided with national communities.[8]

These characteristic elements of feudal Middle East society—office-holding provincial feudal lords, tax-farmers and *millets*—which restricted the power of the central government, were accordingly turned into ruling groups with a stake in the traditional social and economic order though ever more rebellious of the central authority. The Empire's political and administrative disintegration was thus accompanied by the persistence of old social and economic patterns. In the conditions of a typically agrarian society, weakened central authority meant the neglect of land registration and the relaxation of government supervision over it. This distorted landholding patterns to the peasant's disadvantage and exposed him even more than formerly to the exactions of landowners and tax-farmers.

The central government was also constantly engaged, covertly or overtly, in a struggle with the military caste of the Janissaries, which rose to power in the days of the great Ottoman conquests and victories and sought to dictate to the Sultan how the country should be administered. The Janissary infantry,[9] which had become the Sultan's standing army at the end of the 14th century and the beginning of the 15th, were *Kapı Kulları,* i.e. soldier slaves of the Sultan, subject to his direct command through the intermediary of their Agha and paid out of the State treasury—unlike the Sipahi cavalry, which had its place in the feudal hierarchy. As a permanent army close to the centre of power and under its immediate influence, the Janissaries adapted themselves more quickly to the use of firearms. This conferred on them superiority over the Sipahis, who clung to old-fashioned warfare and to cavalry

---

[8] See below, Chapter 4.

[9] The name Janissaries originated in the term *Yeni Çeri,* the New Army, in opposition to the feudal Sipahis of earlier days and to the early 14th century attempt at raising an army among the peasants which had had to be abandoned because of their poor discipline. The Janissaries were recruited from among children kidnapped from local non-Muslim families or captured in military campaigns and prepared for a life of war and Ottoman patriotism. Cf. *Modern History, or, The Present State of All Nations,* by Mr. Salmon, London, 1744, Vol. I, The Present State of the Turkish Empire, Ch. VIII—Treats of the Turkish Forces, or Militia; M. Belin, "Essai sur l'histoire économique de la Turquie, d'après les écrivains originaux", *Journal Asiatique,* août-sept. 1864, p. 273; Joseph van Hammer, *op. cit.,* I, 1834, pp. 376-377; H. A. R. Gibb & H. Bowen, *Islamic Society and the West,* Royal Institute of International Affairs, Oxford University Press, Vol. I, Part I, pp. 58-59, 179.

For a somewhat different explanation of the origin of the Janissaries, cf. David Urquhart, *The Military Strength of Turkey,* 1869, p. 78. Urquhart, who also refers the reader to D'Ohsson, VII, p. 327, says: "The body of Janissaries was recruited from the tribute children, restricted to a thousand a year and taken from the Bosnians, the Greeks (of Morea), the Bulgarians, and the Armenians. This is doubtless an infraction of the institutions of *Mahomet,* which impose on the Rayas the poll-tax in lieu of military service. It would appear, however, that the districts whence they were taken were not at the time incorporated in the Empire. These children might become Mussulmans, but there was no constraint."

tactics. The struggle between the two corps[10] went on through the 16th and 17th centuries, after which the victorious Janissaries took on the Sultan. Their first attempt to impose their authority on him and on his court was made as early as the days of Suleiman, at the beginning of the 16th century.[11] At the end of the same century Murad III embarked on a policy specifically designed to weaken them so that they could no longer impose their will on the Empire.

The fighting tactics of Europe's Christian armies proved superior not only to those of the feudal Turkish cavalry, whose strength had been sapped by internal conflicts, but also to the rigid structure of the Janissary forces, and the Sultan and his entourage grew ever more convinced of the need to reorganise the army. Meantime, however, economic difficulties arose. At the beginning of the 17th century, when the treasury grew bare, arrears piled up in the Janissaries' pay and an open insurrection broke out in 1623-28. The Sultan quelled it by bribing the leaders of the revolt and awarding tax-farming privileges to the Janissaries, whose power thus continued to grow at the expense of the Sipahis. In an attempt to secure fixed pay and economic security, the latter then strove to be included among the Sultan's *kullar,* and many placed themselves at the disposal of the provincial governors, in a relationship that recalled the Roman client.

The Sultan's difficulties in his struggle with the Janissaries were complicated by the fact that they—along with the standing cavalry and artillery—had sold their pay certificates at a discount to the local population and set themselves up in industry and commerce, *inter alia* trading the rations allocated to them by the authorities, in addition to their military duties. The pay certificates became a sort of currency, and those who held them acquired a vested interest in the continued existence of the corps. Thus pressure groups were born that had a stake in preventing far-reaching military reforms.[12] At the end of the 18th century and the beginning of the 19th the struggle between the government and the Janissaries erupted several times into open clashes, and terminated in the destruction of the corps.[13]

2. LAND AND TAXES THE FOCUS OF THE FEUDAL SYSTEM—
DUALITY OF CENTRALISM AND FEUDALISM

In the Middle East as in Europe, land was at the core of the economics of the feudal system,[14] although until the 11th century the principal acknowledgement of suzerainty was the payment of taxes, mainly in cash, which were collected

---

[10] There was a clash between the Sipahis and the Janissaries as far back as 1512, during Selim I's expedition to Asia (Von Hammer, *op. cit.,* I, p. 699).

[11] *Ibid.,* II, p. 43.

[12] Mehmed Esad, *Précis historique de la destruction de corps des Janissaires par le Sultan Mahmoud en 1826,* traduit du Turc par A. P. Caussin de Perceval, Paris, 1833, pp. 98-9, 154-5, 237-8; *Life of Midhat Pasha,* by Ali Haydar Midhat, London, 1903, pp. 17-18; Edward S. Creasy, *History of the Ottoman Empire,* 1878, p. 453, and *passim.*

[13] See below, Part Two, Ch. 1.

[14] Cf. A. H. Lybyer, *The Government of the Ottoman Empire in the Time of Suleiman the Magnificent,* Harvard Economic Studies, Cambridge, Mass., 1913, esp. pp. 100-105.

throughout the country and brought to the central government and with which one single State army was maintained. The grant of fiefs in return for military service was not instituted until 1087, under the Seljuk Turks, by the prime minister Nizam el-Mulk. Later it spread into various parts of the Muslim world, including several provinces of what was later to be the Ottoman Empire and Egypt. The Ottomans granted fiefs in return for military service at the earliest periods of their rule:[15] Othman himself, the founder of the dynasty, was awarded a fief by the Seljuk prince of Asia Minor; he gradually expanded his holdings and after 1286 himself began to confer fiefs on others.[16]

The division between what might be called the fiscal system and the purely feudal one was to a certain extent historical and geographic: the system of awarding fiefs in return for military service took root mainly in Anatolia and the European provinces of the Ottoman Empire, while in the Arabian peninsula, Iraq and Egypt the prevalent practice was to grant domains in return for lump sums and annual tax payments to the Sultan. The main intermediaries between the State and the cultivator were the Sipahis who constituted the chief feudal element in the Empire's complex socio-economic structure.[17]

A feudal hierarchy based on size of fief and seignorial authority emerged in the course of time among the fief-holding Sipahis, beginning with the *Subaşi* at the bottom and going on to *Alay-Bey, Sanjak-Bey* and *Beyler-Bey*.[18] The fief-holders, themselves exempt from taxes, were authorised to collect taxes from the peasants and the local tax-farmers and their revenue determined the number of horsemen which they were expected to furnish to the Sultan.[19] The Sipahi officers were the representatives of the central government in the provinces and supervised land affairs and transactions. The land which they held and which was cultivated by the peasants belonged, however, not to the Sipahis but to the State—only *miri* land, and not *mulk-'ushri,* being given out in fief; and although the Sipahis could transmit their holdings in inheritance to their sons, their holdings returned to the State in the absence of male heirs. The Sipahis' functions and revenues were delimited fairly strictly, at least in theory. This distinguished them from the feudal lords of the

---

[15] M. Belin, *op. cit.,* pp. 271-2; C. H. Becker, "Steuerpacht und Lehnswesen", *Der Islam,* V, Strassburg, pp. 82-91.

[16] M. Belin, "Du Régime des fiefs militaires dans l'Islamisme", *Journal Asiatique,* mars-avril 1870, p. 223.

[17] The reference here is to the feudal Sipahis as distinguished from the "Sipahis of the Porte". The latter were *kullar* in the personal service of the Sultan, like the Janissaries. 'Aini 'Ali, writing in 1609, noted that the Sultan's military and civil administration consisted of over 90,000 men, including 76,000 in the land and regular forces, 2,400 in the naval forces, about 2,000 high officials and army commanders and some 11,000 civil servants. Within the regular army there were nearly 50,000 Janissaries and members of auxiliary units, 8,000 artillerymen and 21,000 Porte Sipahis, Silihars, and others. (The civil payroll includes, among others, 21 Jewish doctors.) M. Belin, "Essai...", *loc. cit.,* pp. 247-259, and "Du Régime...", *loc. cit.,* pp. 224-5.

[18] M. Belin, "Etude sur la Propriété Foncière en pays musulmans et spécialement en Turquie", *Journal Asiatique,* fév.-mars 1862, p. 197.

[19] Under Murad I (1359-1389) fief-holders with a revenue of 120 francs (75 piastres) were expected to furnish one horseman, and an additional horseman was levied for every additional 200 francs of revenue. See Ch. Morawitz (*op. cit.,* p. 123). His data are in aspers, which we have converted into francs.

West, although sometimes they enjoyed certain seignorial privileges in relation to the cultivators and developed a feudal hierarchy based on the size of their fiefs.[20]

At first, as the fief system spread, the central government demanded military service in return for the grant of these domains, but as time went on its main attention turned to securing the maximum tax revenue to the State treasury for financing the standing army and meeting other expenditure. In this context the growing disruption of the central administration necessitated working out new fiscal policies and collection methods.

At the base of the Muslim tax system was the same distinction between conquerors and conquered that operated with regard to land tenure and applied to the Arab conquests as well as to those of the Seljuk and Ottoman Turks. The lands of the conquerors were referred to as *'ushri or 'ushuri* ("tithe-paying") and *mulk* ("property"); the latter name was also adopted for them in the Ottoman Land Law. Their holders, who had full title to them, paid only the tithe on the crop *('ushr)*. The lands of the conquered, on the other hand, were required to pay a tax called *kharadj,* except in Arabia, where the lands were *'ushri* because of the Prophet's qualms about imposing *kharadj* on Arabs.[21] The *kharadj* was either a tax on crop yields, called *muqasama* (generally at a higher rate than the *'ushr*) or a fixed annual land tax *(muwazzaf)* on cultivated and fallow land alike.[22] In the Ottoman Empire land paying *kharadj* was generally referred to as *miri,* and the fundamental title to it was in the hands of the State, in view of the Koranic injunction that all conquered land belonged to the community.[23] Some of these *miri* lands were alienated by leading Turkish citizens who succeeded in building up huge private estates *(çiftlik)*; but under the Ottoman Land Law (Part I, Article 4) holders of such land were required to pay not merely *'ushr* but the same land tax rates as the holders of land which had remained *miri.*[24]

Not only did the conquerors take over vast stretches of land yielding substantial revenue, but the main financial burden of supporting the State devolved on the con-

---

[20] Schematically, this hierarchy went up from landless or small-holding peasants to *timar* holders, *ziamet* holders and large *ziamet* holders.

[21] M. Belin, "Etude sur la propriété", *loc. cit.,* oct.-nov. 1861, pp. 421-13. Cf. our Appendix 1.

[22] The land and tax laws were first compiled in 1566 by the *defterdar* (Chancellor of the Exchequer) Mehmed Çelebi. Cf. Morawitz, *op. cit.,* pp. 3-4; M. A. Ubicini, *Letters on Turkey,* I, London, 1856, pp. 254-5; J. von Hammer, *op. cit.,* II, pp. 340-42; M. Belin, "Etude sur la propriété..." *loc. cit.,* oct.-nov. 1861, p. 404.

[23] Despite this injunction the Muslims left a large part of the conquered countries in the hands of their inhabitants, who paid *kharadj* on it and generally had full freedom to do with it as they saw fit despite the fundamental title vested in it by the Islamic State. Some of them who adopted Islam within a short time of the Arab conquests were even required to pay no more than the *'ushr.* See Khadduri, *War and Peace in the Law of Islam,* Baltimore, 1955, pp. 160-161. According to Islam's commentators all land held by Arabs not converted to Islam is *'ushr* land, while all conquered land held by non-Arab non-Muslims is *kharadj* land. See Appendix 1.

[24] It is important to remember that the connection between the *mulk* (and *kharadji)* lands of the early Muslim conquerors and those of the Ottoman Empire was in the legal sphere rather than in the actual status of the land. Cf. A. N. Poliak, *Feudalism in Egypt, Syria, Palestine, and the Lebanon, 1250-1900,* 1939, pp. 36, 65.

quered, and particularly on the non-Muslims.[25] These *dhimmis*[26] were subjected not only to the *kharadj*[27] (paid by conquered holders whose lands had not been expropriated) but also to a poll-tax called the *jizya*,[28] to which every non-indigent able-bodied free male was liable. The Koran gives no clue to the difference between the *kharadj* and the *jizya*,[29] but later sources indicate that while the former designated any tax, the latter referred specifically to the poll-tax.[30] In time the *jizya* also became a tax for exemption from military service, and on the eve of the Hatti Hümayun decree of 1856 it averaged 30 piastres *per capita*.[31] It was then abolished, however, and replaced by a lump-sum payment for exemption, the *ianei askeriïè*[32] or *bedel*, first at the rate of 5,000 piastres for every 180 men and after 1884 at 5,000 piastres for every 130 men. The Constitution of the Young Turks in 1908 reaffirmed the abolition of the *jizya* and the obligation of military service for all, but the *bedel* exemption tax remained in force until the First World War.[33]

In order to prevent State revenue from shrinking as more and more of the population was converted to Islam, it was decided at an early stage in the history of the

---

[25] Although the legislation of the Tanzimat period nominally did away with this discrimination, in practice it carried on almost until the end of the Empire.

[26] From the Arabic word ذمي, which means (a non-Muslim) enjoying (Muslim) protection: a Christian, Jewish, Zoroastrian or Sabian inhabitant of a country ruled by Muslims. In his discussion of the rights of non-Muslims in Muslim law, Heffening dwells mainly on the concept of *amn* (security, protection) and *musta'min* (the one who benefits from such protection). See W. Heffening, *Das islamische Fremdenrecht*, Hannover, 1925, pp. 9-14.

[27] The word, of questionable origin, had a long history and different uses before the Ottoman period. Only some views on its origins are presented here. According to P. Schwarz's "Origin of the Arab Kharadj (Land) Tax", *Der Islam*, VI, 1916, p. 97, and after him the *Enzyklopaedie des Islams*, the concept of *kharadj* was borrowed by the Arabs from "the language of Byzantine administration, which probably derived it from the Greek χορηγία", which originally meant the equipment, management or financing of a choir, and hence financing generally, the provision of funds, etc. The *Encyclopedia of Islam*, on the other hand, believes that the word *Kharadj* is derived from the Aramaic *hālak*, through the intermediary of the Persians, a theory stated by Hemming in *Orientalia*, IV, 291, 899. Another widespread hypothesis is that the word comes from the Arabic root خرج, meaning: to go out (of the earth); while a less accepted theory traces it back to the Aramaic *kharga*, meaning poll tax. Cf. J. Løkkegaard, *Islamic Taxation in the Islamic Period*, Copenhagen, 1950, pp. 125-6. For χορηγία see H. G. Liddell & R. Scott, *A Greek-English Lexicon*, Oxford, Reprinted in 1958, p. 1999; and Pape, *Griechisch-Deutsches Handwörterbuch*, 1866, II, p. 1342.

[28] From the word جزية, punishment. For the tax itself cf. Abou Yousof Ya'koub, *Le Livre de l'Impôt Foncier (Kitab El-Kharadj)* traduit et annoté par E. Fagnan, Paris, 1921, pp. 37-8, n. (1).

[29] The word *jizya* appears once in the Koran (Sura 9, v. 29) in the sense of a poll-tax paid by a subjugated people. The word *kharadj* too appears once (Sura 23, v. 72) meaning wage or tax. It is interesting to note that the French scientific mission which accompanied Napoleon to Egypt found *kharadj* used in the sense of poll-tax (*Description de l'Egypte*, II, 1818, p. 121; M. Khadduri, *op. cit.*, pp. 187-193). Otherwise it was used there for any ground-rents of the peasants. Cf. A. N. Poliak, *op. cit.*, p. 65.

[30] M. Khadduri, *ibid*.

[31] Gibb and Bowen, *op. cit.*, Vol. I, Part II, pp. 4, 16.

[32] This tax, which brought in only 5,000 piastres in 1855/6, yielded 59,609,000 piastres in 1860.

[33] *Recueil des Firmans Impériaux Ottomans adressés aux valis et aux Khédives d'Egypte, 1597-1904*, Le Caire, 1934, p. xxxix.

Arab Empire that Muslims acquiring *kharadj* land, or holders of *kharadj* land who were converted to Islam, would continue to pay the *kharadj muwazzaf* land tax on it, i.e. that the *kharadj* land would continue to pay *kharadj* regardless of who held it. As time went on, however, many Muslims succeeded in evading this rule and in paying only *'ushr* on such holdings,[34] by having them registered in their name as private land or by bequeathing them as *waqf*.[35]

The tax on *kharadji* land was at first very much higher than on *'ushri* land, amounting in practice to 20-25% of the gross income from it. In time the two types of *kharadj* tax which we noted above—the one on crops and the one on land—were blended into a single crop tax, which the Turks referred to as *'ushr*. The rate, at first lower than 10%, was later raised to 12-12$^1/_2$% of the crop, assessed while standing in the field. In Turkey proper this *'ushr* tax continued in force until its abolition by Kemal Atatürk in 1925.

In addition to the *'ushr* on land, Muslims paid *zakat* (زَكَاة, meaning purity and alms in the sense of purification) considered one of the five pillars of Islam.[36] At first this was not a tax in the proper sense of the word but a contribution expected from the rich for the poor and aimed at bridging inequalities of property and income in the spirit of Islam.[37] The importance and the principles of *zakat* are discussed in the Koran,[38] but the payment rates were evolved by tradition, on the basis of the believer's property in livestock, gold or silver.[39] The impost was collected by the State or the community, which distributed it among the needy. With the passage of time *zakat* in its original form disappeared and in 19th-century Turkey its place had been taken by the *vergi,* more frequently known as *verko,* a sort of property tax (or, as Belin terms it, income tax) imposed on real estate as well as on gold, silver, merchandise, camels, cattle, etc., and payable by Muslims and Christians alike.[40]

While most of the State revenue came from the land and from war booty, which was natural in the warlike agrarian society that characterised the Ottoman Empire during the period of its expansion, the treasury also had other sources of income, among which the main ones were the taxes from crown lands, the *jizya,* tributes from vassal dependencies, customs *(gumrūk),* export duties *(reftiyè)* and excise on

---

[34] Cf. Th. H. Juynboll, "Kharadj", *The Encyclopedia of Islam.*

[35] Beginning in the second half of the 14th century, fiefholders in the Ottoman Empire began to transmit their fiefs to their sons, or even to individuals of their choice in the absence of male heirs. Only in the 16th century, under Suleiman the Magnificent, were steps taken to have heirless fief lands reassigned to the State. Such attempts were taken up again, generally without great success in wresting back such lands for the crown, by Murad III at the end of the 16th century, by Abdul Hamid I, by Selim III toward the end of the 18th century and by Mahmud II in the early 19th century.

[36] The other four "pillars" are: a. The belief in one God and in the Prophet's mission; b. The *salat* (Arabic) or *namaz,* i. e., five obligatory daily prayers; c. The pilgrimage to Mecca; d. Fasting in the month of Ramadan. The holy war *(jihad),* considered by the Koran as one of the foremost duties of a Muslim, was later often regarded as a practical expression of the belief in the unity of God and in the mission of Muhammad.

[37] *Koran,* Sura 9, v. 60.

[38] *Ibid.* Also Sura 2, v. 43 and Sura 9, v. 104.

[39] Mouradgea D'Ohsson, Ignatius, *Tableau Général de l'Empire Othoman,* Paris, 1790, I, pp. 269 ff.

[40] M. Belin, "Etude sur la propriété...", *loc. cit.,* avril-mai 1862, p. 286, n.

mines, salt and rice paddies. These were all imposts originating in the *shari'a,* i.e. the Koran and the other principles of religious law. They were referred to as *hukuki* or *ruzumi.*[41] In addition, there were the taxes imposed by the ruler in virtue of his customary *('urfi)* authority to promulgate decrees *(kanun).* Known as the *tekâlifi 'urfiye,* they included fines, redemption payments, imposts and excise on goods not covered by the provisions of the *shari'a* to this effect.[42]

The changes which tax collection methods underwent influenced the pattern of Middle East society no less, and possibly even more, than the changes in the principles of taxation. There were three main methods of collection: by government officials, by the army and its officers—at first the Sipahis, later the Janissaries and finally the provincial commanders—and by private tax-farmers. While generally speaking these three methods represent three stages of historical development which succeeded one other in the order we have mentioned them, at various periods they were in existence side by side. As we shall see later, this continued to be the case even after the official abolition of the traditional tax-farming system by the decree of Gülhane and the Tanzimat reforms.

In practice this meant the coexistence of two systems. One, the feudal, was based on the grant of land and of the taxes to be collected from its cultivators, in return for which the feudal lord assumed certain obligations, mainly with regard to military service. This type of arrangement was given a particular fillip in the second half of the 16th century, when the position of the *derebeys,* or feudal lords, was greatly strengthened.[43] The other system, fiscal and centralistic, was founded on the maintenance of a regular central army and the collection of taxes for the central government throughout the Empire through the intermediary of officials or tax-farmers.

The grant of landed estates, which was the main pillar of the first system, was also often a feature of the second system, especially where the State tended to give up, of its own free will or under the press of circumstances, the direct management of lands and the collection of taxes from them by its own officials. The latter function was then imposed on fief-holders who were committed in return for their estates to transfer part of the revenues they collected in the provinces to the central treasury, generally in the form of annual payments.

The State officials in charge of collection were generally the district governors and their appointees. Yet these often found it impossible to get together the necessary

---

[41] Three of these taxes, namely the *jizya,* the *'ushr* and the land tax, were sometimes collectively known as *kharadj.*

[42] M. Belin, "Etude sur la propriété..." *loc. cit.,* fév.-mars 1862, p. 198; Gibb and Bowen, *op. cit.,* Vol. I, Part II, p. 2.

David Urquhart gives a simplified and incomplete, but nevertheless instructive and concise summary of taxation in the Ottoman Empire at the beginning of the 19th century, by reducing it to five major heads: ¹) Poll-tax fixed at ten, six and three leonines, or piastres, on adult males not professing Islam; ²) Land tax, one-tenth of the produce, or by assessment; ³) *Nouzouli* and *avarisi,* assessed taxes in towns where the population is not agricultural; ⁴) Customs, three per cent on foreign commerce, export and import; internal transport duties at gates of towns and bridges; ⁵) Excise upon gun powder, snuff, wine, etc. — D. Urquhart, *Turkey and Its Resources,* London, 1833, pp. 86-7.

[43] Cf. Ali Haydar Midhat, *op. cit.,* p. 12.

funds, even with the assistance of local agents and assessors. One of the reasons for the failure of the system of collection through agents was the practice of collecting the tax in kind, i.e. in produce which had to be transported, stored and guarded. Other reasons included arbitrary assessment (which, however, continued to characterise tax collection even when other methods were adopted) and fraud and corruption on the part of the agents.[44]

Thereupon the government resorted to a method that resembled the European feudal system. The provincial army commanders were given estates and the right to collect the taxes designated for the maintenance of the armies in the provinces, which had previously received their allocations from the central government. In return for their fiefs,[45] the commanders undertook to raise, equip and maintain provincial armies and to keep them at the disposal of the central government, but in the social and economic circumstances of the Empire it did not prove much more effective than the system of clerks and officials.

The increasing disruption of central authority made it imperative to turn to a new set-up, especially with regard to those lands that were not held in military fiefs: private tax-farming. This system, which started flourishing in the 17th century,[46] was still in wide application after the first half of the 19th, even though it had formally been abolished by the Tanzimat. Up to the end of the 17th century the contract was generally for a year only, after which it could be renewed or given to some other tax-farmer *(multazim)* but later the practice spread of conferring the privilege on a lifetime basis. The *multazimin* were leased *miri* land and given the authority to collect taxes in a particular district in return for a predetermined payment to the State treasury. The rest of the taxes they took in were theirs, and in the course of time they succeeded in accumulating huge revenues and land holdings of their own.

This system, which had its good points in the short run, could not but redound, in the prevailing social context and under conditions of non-existent administrative supervision, to the disadvantage of the cultivator, to whom the State and the government became identified with the ruthless tax-farmers. The *multazimin* resorted to every means in order to increase their takings regardless of official tax rates and without concern for the peasants or the land. Villagers were reduced to virtual social and economic serfdom as oppression grew heavier, at least until the first attempts of Selim III to subject the tax-farmers to more rigid government control.[47]

---

[44] At a later stage, after the Tanzimat and the establishment of *tapu* land registration offices, the government made another attempt at direct collection, but this time by civil servants. See next section and chapter on Tanzimat.

[45] *ʾIqtaa,* presumably introduced in the period of the Buwayhids, 932-1055 A.D., transplanted to Egypt by Salahaddin in the 1270s, abolished in the 16th century following the Ottoman conquest, and re-created as *ʾuhda* under Mehmed Ali in the 19th century with a partial resemblance only of the original *ʾiqtaa. — Cf.* G. Baer, *Introduction to the History of Agrarian Relations in the Middle East* (Hebrew), p. 10.

[46] And more specifically with the decree of Mustafa II on January 30, 1695.—M. Belin, "Etude sur la propriété...", *op. cit.,* fév.-mars 1862, p. 196 n.

[47] M. A. Ubicini, *op. cit.,* I, p. 281.

There was an intimate connection between this tax system and the turn conditions took in the Middle Eastern village.[48] In the first place, many of the tax-farmers were given land in order to sublease it or to collect the taxes due to the treasury from the cultivators. In time many of these *miri* lands were turned into the private property of the original lessees and managers. Even though the government occasionally endeavoured to prevent this development, the State's active intervention to protect its rights was precluded by the distance of the provinces from the capital and by the growing power of the local strong men. As the central administrative apparatus grew weaker and the provincial governors and landowners grew stronger, the lot of the cultivators on the domain of the army commander or the *multazim*, referred to in both cases as the *muqataa* or the *iqtaa*, grew worse: in addition to his taxes the villager had to pay rent, to supply produce to landowners, officers and agents and to perform without compensation various services exacted from him by the landlord.

In the second place, the dearth of means of payment made for the progressive development of a system of tax payment in kind, based on assessment in the field and on the application of the tax rate to the crop thus estimated.

Thirdly, since the social structure of the village made it difficult for the State or landlord to deal individually with the cultivators, collective responsibility for tax payment developed early in the Middle Eastern village. While opinions are divided on the origin of the communal system of land tenure, or *mushā'*, and the phenomenon that has been referred to as "agrarian communism," there is some ground for the belief that they can be traced back to this collective responsibility.[49]

The cycle of Eastern feudalism, oppression and plunder was closed by another characteristic: landlord absenteeism. This development also occurred in Western feudalism, but in the Middle East it was so universal that it became one of the hallmarks of its retrogressive social and economic structure. The landowner, who resided in town and sometimes even abroad, made no real attempt to improve the land he rented out or to assist the peasants who groaned under the burden of taxes and debts: he was only concerned with squeezing as much as possible out of them. Absenteeism subsists to this day in a large part of the Middle East, contributing heavily to the region's social and economic backwardness.[50]

Throughout all this, the inhabitants and institutions of the Middle Eastern village remained insulated from any outside change, shut in a shell of tradition. The village's stability made for a great deal of homogeneity throughout the region, but it stamped the whole future of Middle East society with its brand of conservatism and backwardness. Through all the invasions the villager remained rooted to his land: he

---

[48] See J. von Hammer, *op. cit.*, II, pp. 343-344.

[49] On the basis of various sources, Heaton avers that collective responsibility for taxes was imposed in the third century in Egypt, where the Romans resorted to it first on a family basis and then on a village basis in view of the wholesale abandonment of the land by poverty-stricken peasants who found the tax burden too heavy. (H. Heaton, *Economic History of Europe*, revised edition. Harper and Brothers, New York, 1948, p. 49.)

[50] On the other hand, in those Middle Eastern countries that have attempted agrarian reform in the 20th century, the task has been rendered easier by the absenteeism of the effendis, who were unable to argue seriously that they were fulfilling any constructive function in the management of their estates or contributing entrepreneurship.

was not drawn to the city, and he did not let his conquerors penetrate into the village. The conquerors were confined to the cities and the regional administrative centres. Two separate arenas of history were thus created—the town and the village. In the former, successive waves of conquerors assimilated each other to a greater or lesser extent; in the latter the local fellah, faithful to his traditions, his way of living, his methods of production and his consumption habits, remained impervious to outside influence, even though the ethnic structure of the village changed in time with the assimilation of a certain proportion of immigrants and nomads.

Since the rural population constituted the overwhelming majority of the population, it is no wonder that the village impressed its stamp on all of Middle East society. The villager, deeply attached to the land, clung to it despite the attractions of city life and the opportunities offered by the beginnings of modern industrial penetration into the Middle East in the 19th century. He preferred the village with its floods and droughts, its depleted and overcrowded land, its misery and hunger. He remained attached to it even if he left it for the city—and there were cases where whole villages were abandoned because of extortionate taxes or plunder by the feudal lords or the nomads in the face of a passive or powerless central government—or even for overseas, and particularly Latin America. Those emigrants who did not return sent remittances of money to the village or otherwise exerted their influence in its favour in faraway lands.

Torpid and unchanging, the Middle Eastern village has withstood the changes, the attempts at reform and the revolutions of the 19th and 20th centuries, and its conservatism brands the whole pattern of Middle Eastern society to this day.

3. THE MIDDLE EASTERN CITY AND THE GUILDS

In the latter days of the Ottoman Empire the urban concentrations of the Muslim world were well past their full flowering and the peak of their influence on Islamic culture which they had reached in the Islamic Middle Ages. Socially the cities were in a different world than the countryside, and their relations with it were largely of an economic nature—the relations between consumer and producer.[51]

The cities grew mainly around the sites of certain fundamental economic and religious institutions. According to Massignon,[52] these were: 1. the Exchange, with the toll-gatherer, the local mint and the auction market; 2. the ware-houses of goods and valuables; 3. the thread and commodities market; and 4. the seminary or university and the mosque.

Although ethno-religious and occupational differentiation within the city's population was pronounced, a substantial measure of solidarity prevailed among the residents, particularly when it came to resisting arbitrary government action or

---

[51] Gibb and Bowen, *op. cit.*, Vol. I, Part I, pp. 276 ff.
[52] Cited in Bernard Lewis, "The Islamic Guilds", *The Economic History Review,* Vol. VIII, No. 1, Nov. 1937, p. 20.

taxation. Generally such resistance took the form of passive disobedience,[53] although there were cases of rebellion or even armed insurrection.

The economic structure of the Ottoman city was largely determined by socio-religious patterns. Most of the Empire's ethno-religious groups, if not all, were represented in each of the larger cities; but they resided apart, in separate quarters each inhabited almost exclusively by members of one group. This division was reflected in the city's economic life, since each of the ethno-religious groups had become associated with certain specific occupations. The Turks were officials and soldiers, the Greeks as well as the Jews engaged in trade and finance, the Armenians were artisans. Within these occupations, there was further specialisation along ethno-religious lines. Certain cities like Smyrna and Salonika, where the Turks were a minority, took on in the wake of this development the overriding character of commercial towns, with the addition of services that are typical of port cities.[54] Trade was largely carried on directly between the customer and the artisan, generally a master in the guild, or in the bazaars, where the various kinds of goods and services were each available in a separate section of the market.

The distinguishing characteristic of the Islamic towns until the 19th century was the organisation of their residents in corporations, termed *asnaf, naqabat* or *tawa'if* in Arabic.[55] These corporations were mainly professional guilds, but while their social functions were on the whole broader than those of the European guilds,[56] their economic power and their control of their professions were less absolute than in the West. The occupations included in this type of corporate organisation comprised not only artisans and merchants but also musicians, male and female singers, wrestlers, dancers, snake charmers and even beggars.[57]

Not only did these guilds round out economic functions with social, political and religious ones—ceremonies and worship under the aegis of the corporation—but the government made use of them by endowing their heads with administrative and tax-collecting functions. There being no city self-government and hence no municipal organisation, the affairs of the city's residents were mostly in the hands of a chief shaykh, or other officer deemed to be representative of the population. He administered them jointly with the police commander and the agha of the Janissaries. The shaykhs who headed the various quarters, and sometimes also the heads of the corporations, were responsible to the chief shaykh, and in some cities

---

[53] This may be compared, though on a smaller scale, to the *bast* in Persia, for which see below in our discussion of that country.

[54] Lucy M. Garnett, *Turkey of Ottomans,* London, 1911, pp. 153-169.

[55] These names were variously in use at different times and in different periods. Occasionally the term *gedik* was used by Turks for a corporation, although it originally meant the right—transferable by sale or inheritance—to engage in a business or occupation. Cf. M. Belin, "Etudes sur la propriété...", *loc. cit.,* avril-mai 1862, p. 264.

[56] Since the cities of the East never reached the degree of community organisation that marked those of the West, the guilds had to take up some of the vacuum and took on functions that were not only professional as in Europe, but supplied the basic framework for the life of the cities as a whole. Cf. Lewis, *loc. cit.,* p. 20.

[57] Gibb and Bowen (Vol. I, Part I, p. 227, n. 2) cite the report of the Egyptian historian al-Jabarti, that in 1718 the Cairo beggars' association presented Ibrahim Bey with a fully equipped horse worth 22,000 paras.

the corporations heads in each quarter were responsible to the shaykh of the quarter.[58]

The origin of the Islamic guilds goes back to the ninth century, when large concentrations of capital made possible the employment of thousands of workers and slaves in fields and plantations in the countryside, and in industry and the crafts in town. The craftsmen and artisans began to organise by trade, and the fullest flowering of the towns, in the 10th and 11th centuries, enabled the guilds to expand their activities. These were given an additional fillip by the social ferment manifested in the liberal and anti-orthodox religious and political movements of the times, movements which infused into the Islamic guilds a social and political colouring that the European guilds never had.[59]

The Islamic guilds went through stormy developments in their millennial history. In 1640 there were 1100 guilds in Istanbul,[60] as against only 35 when the Turks took the city. In time many of the corporations were affected by the economic paralysis and technical backwardness that marked the decline of the Empire, but they continued to occupy an important position until the 19th century.[61]

Most of the guilds were also open to non-Muslims, but in effect the corporations were organised along ethno-religious lines as a result of the characteristic occupational specialisation which we have noted among the various communities. Such occupations as pharmacy and painting, as well as the bulk of the commerce in foodstuffs, were the exclusive domain of Muslims. Banking and trade in gold and silver, on the other hand, were carried on by guilds made up almost entirely of Christians and Jews.

Their Middle Eastern guilds were generally much more democratic than their European counterparts and lacked their rigid and arbitrary structure,[62] although they too had a hierarchy of masters *(usta)*, journeymen *(khalfa)* and apprentices *(çirak* or *mübtedi)*. The shaykh who headed each corporation was assisted by a small council but the final decision was his.

The guilds' functions included professional and trade regulation, fixing fair prices—in conjunction with the government, which often set ceiling prices only—

---

[58] Cf. M. Clerget, *Le Caire,* 1934, pp. 178-187; E. W. Lane, *An Account of The Manners and Customs of the Modern Egyptians,* London, 1860, Ch. IV.

[59] Lewis *(loc. cit.,* pp. 23-30) surveys two theories with regard to the origin of the Islamic guilds. One is that they were an outgrowth of the Byzantine guilds—but Lewis notes pronounced differences in character as well as in structure. The other is Massignon's theory that it was the liberal and anti-orthodox Carmathian movement which encouraged workmen and artisans to unite against all sorts of orthodox injunctions curbing their freedom to build their own lives instead of leaving all decisions to God alone. This would account for the extent to which the Islamic guilds were identified after the Mongol invasions, and particularly in Anatolia, with the *futuwwa,* associations of young men propagating ethical ideals. Lewis believes that, whatever the part of the Carmathian movement in shaping the guilds, it strengthened them and did impart to them a certain anti-orthodox colouring which made them the object of persecution and strict supervision by Sunni (orthodox) rulers.

[60] Another source, the Turkish traveller Evliya Çelebi, compiled in the mid-17th century a list of Constantinople's corporations and guilds and described their structure. He listed 57 sections and 1001 guilds in the city (Lewis, pp. 31-32).

[61] According to J. Bowring *(loc. cit.,* p. 117), 164 corporations operated in Cairo in 1837.

[62] Particularly in the Arab provinces. In Istanbul their organisation was stricter and more centralistic.

keeping trade secrets, and ensuring professional standards and the rigid homogeneity of product styles (as in clothing or shoes). Though formally independent, the corporations were subject to strict State control, exercised until the 18th century through the intermediary of the shaykhs and after that through special officials *(kahyas)* generally appointed by the government. The Janissary aghas and the *qadis*[63] also frequently had an important say in corporation affairs, whose control was often officially delegated to the latter.[64] Daily supervision of the tradesmen's practices, on the other hand, along with the collection of taxes and excise, was in the hands of a special inspector, the *muhtasib,* assisted by a special market militia.

Like the European guilds, the Islamic ones had "patron saints". These were the Prophets of Islam: figures from the Bible such as Adam (patron of the tailors and the bakers), Noah (shipbuilders), or Joseph (clock-makers), or from Muslim tradition, such as Muhammad himself (merchants) or his companion Salman (barbers).

Notwithstanding the important role which the guilds played within the towns, they had no commensurate voice in State affairs or in the life of the country as a whole even at the high point of their development, and in the 19th century they disintegrated rapidly. Some of the guilds were weakened, and ultimately went out of existence, as a result of the decreasing role played by the minorities in the Empire's economic life; others, especially during the reign of Abdul Hamid I, managed with the aid of bribery at the Port to secure monopolistic positions in which they could dictate terms to businessmen. Among these were the guilds of porters and servants.

An important reason for the disintegration of the professional corporations— perhaps the decisive one—was their conservatism. The opposition of their leaders to technical advances and new methods of production was prompted by the desire to maintain their hegemony. However, this proved impossible, particularly in the second half of the 19th century, with the increasing penetration of European interests and the Turks' own efforts to revamp their whole economic life. On the other hand, the guilds and their economic tradition were strong enough to keep the Empire away from the mainstream of the industrial development which was sweeping Europe at the time, and although the corporations were officially abolished in 1860 it was too late for such a step to spur industrialisation, particularly in view of the critical financial, economic and political situation.

The Young Turks, who tried their hand at economic legislation in a number of fields, also attempted to organise producers along professional lines. Professional associations designed to replace the guilds and endowed with very similar functions were recognised under regulations issued in 1910, 1912 and 1915, and the municipal authorities[65] were entrusted with supervising them (under the Turkish Republic, the

---

[63] D'Ohsson, *op. cit.,* II, p. 171.

[64] *Ibid,* IV, p. 228.

[65] Main municipal reforms, aimed at more extensive and modern self-government, started in 1858 for one quarter of Istanbul and in 1868 for the whole of Istanbul, and was followed by the vilayet law intended for the establishment of local elected councils in the provincial cities, with limited fiscal and other powers.—Cf. B. Lewis, *The Emergence of Modern Turkey,* London, 1961, pp. 387 ff.

Law of 1925 delegated this supervision to the Chambers of Commerce and the Ministry of National Economy). Coachmen, boatmen, porters, butchers and other tradesmen were organised in such professional associations, which the Young Turks controlled or influenced through the association leaders. The experiment was not very successful, at least not under the Empire.[66] In addition, the merchants organised an association of their own, which bore a Muslim character and into which non-Turkish Muslims were admitted as well. It was also intended to engage in industry, including exports and imports. Consumer organisations *(milli istihlak)* were set up in the same period in various fields. The Young Turks sought to turn all these associations into active constituents of the nationalist movement. One of the results was that the economic position of the non-Turkish minorities suffered, and it looked as though the interests of European investors might be threatened as well. This was the early origin of the nationalist trends that were to characterise Turkey's subsequent economic development.[67]

The dissolution of the guilds in the 19th century was one of the symptoms of the changes which took place in the structure and the position of the Ottoman towns, and particularly in the Empire's administrative and economic centres. The economic relations with the West were growing closer; transport and communication connections were being established and banking and commercial services developed; the intelligentsia and the officer class, both based in the towns, had spearheaded the reform movement; and the population of the towns and cities grew. All these political, economic and demographic factors brought down the traditional economic and administrative order and new municipal entities arose, which were charged with the responsibility for the provision of services (not always all the services, some of the latter being provided by foreign concessionnaires) and implementing the municipal budget. The development of the cities suffered as a result of the political and economic difficulties which the Empire as a whole was going through, and they lacked the proper industrial base which a modern city requires. But their function as centres of commerce, brokerage, tourism, municipal services and State administration helped the Ottoman towns become, after the war, the focuses of the nationalist movements and the industrialisation programmes of the countries of the Ottoman succession.

4. ISLAM, THE MINORITIES AND SOCIO-ECONOMIC CONCEPTS

We have seen how the character of the Middle Eastern village imparted to the entire region a large measure of homogeneity and did much to obstruct its economic development. The same may be said of the orthodox Islamic character of the Ottoman State, whose influence made itself felt in every domain.

Islam, like the other great monotheistic faiths, claims to be the only true religion, to the point where throughout history holy wars *(jihad)* have been fought in its name

---

[66] O. Mukdim, *Handicrafts in Turkey,* reprinted from the International Labour Review, Geneva, 1955, pp. 18-19.

[67] Tekin Alp (M. Cohen) *Türkismus und Pantürkismus,* Weimar, 1915, pp. 35-40.

against the infidels. But the objective was to make Islam the ruling faith of the world rather than to convert the non-Muslims. Once the Ottoman Empire passed the peak of its power, however, and went over to the defensive, the Islamic social and political order that had crystallised within it found it difficult to co-exist with other faiths. Of course, religious motivations will not suffice to explain such events as the massacres of the Bulgarians, the Greeks, the Assyrians or the Armenians, which must be viewed against their political background and against the rebellions and the unrest which they were designed to quell.[68] This view is corroborated by the oppressive treatment to which the Turks subjected the Arabs, who were largely Muslims, and which reached a climax during the First World War.[69] But whatever the case might be the Powers found it necessary to intervene to an increasing extent to protect the rights, and occasionally the lives, of the religious minorities.

For the Muslim, Islam is an all-inclusive philosophy of life that supplies the answer to every problem by reference to its Koranic principles or to its body of interpretative tradition.[70] Islam's commentators have always stressed its inner harmony and universality that take care of any legal, social, political or economic contingency. According to one contemporary Arab writer, "...Islam has one universal theory which covers the universe and life and humanity, a theory in which are integrated all the different questions; in this Islam sums up all its beliefs, its laws and statutes, and its modes of worship and of work. The treatment of all these matters emanates from this one universal and comprehensive theory, so that each question is not dealt with on an individual basis, nor is every problem with its needs treated in isolation from all other problems."[71]

An important concept in this outlook on life is the necessity to resign oneself to certain facts, such as inequalities in wealth. The Koranic foundation of this approach rests on the idea of predestination (Sura XV, v. 5), even if the latter is intermittently contradicted by elements of free choice. Although, as we have seen, the institution of the *zakat* is designed to moderate these inequalities, its very existence constitutes an acknowledgement of their inevitability. According to Muslim sources God himself has declared that he has given more to some than to others, thus justifying, at least indirectly, the institution of private property; and tradition has it that the Prophet himself and the early Caliphs handed out State land to private individuals.[72]

These concepts of eternal universal solutions and a foreordained fate explain why Islam is not among those faiths—such as Protestantism, for instance—which have promoted economic enterprise. This was accentuated by the ban imposed by the Koran and its commentators on taking interest (though not on paying it), and by

---

[68] Cf. Lucy M. Garnett, *op. cit.*, pp. 141-142. Midhat Pasha claimed that the Powers, and particularly Russia, often resorted to provocation in order to set off Turkish repression that would provide them with an opportunity to intervene. Midhat Pacha, *La Turquie, son passé, son avenir,* Paris, 1878, pp. 15-17.

[69] M. Hartmann, *Der Islamische Orient,* II, 1909, pp. 548-549, gives a good summary of the Turks' attitude toward the Arabs.

[70] G. Young (ed.), *Corps de Droit Ottoman,* pp. 251 and 285.

[71] Sayed Kotb, *Social Justice in Islam,* p. 17.

[72] Cf. Abou Yousof Ya'koub, *op. cit.*, pp. 91-94.

identifying interest with usury,[73] which resulted in the concentration of financial activities in the hands of the minorities, in the subjection of the fellah to usurers (many of whom were Muslims who got around the prohibition)[74], frequently effecting in the fellahin's desertion of villages, in particular on the heels of droughts and following insolvency, as well as in a grave delay in the evolution of an autonomous system of banking and credit.

At the same time, the provisions of the Koran and Islamic law prohibiting the consumption of certain foods and of alcoholic drinks and regulating the dress of the faithful,[75] and, later, of the infidel, had a profound effect on production patterns. Even the consumption of tobacco (first brought to Constantinople in 1605, during the reign of Ahmed I), opium and coffee were subjected at various times to attacks by the strict interpreters of Islam, although these could enlist no Koranic evidence in support of their views and a more liberal interpretation won out in the end. This explains the historical ups and downs in the production and the consumption of these items. The supply and the demand of the various products that were subject to religious restrictions depended, and to a certain extent continue to depend to this day, on the extent to which these restrictions could be moderated.[76] All in all, the character of the dominant religion in the Middle East played an important part in stilling any economic advance in that region, to the point even where commerce, the glory of the Arabs which Muhammad himself had praised so highly[77] and which had constituted the lifeblood of the Islamic Empire in the days of its greatest flowering, was largely concentrated, in the latter days of the Ottoman Empire, in the hands of non-Muslim minorities.

An important role, which had its socio-economic aspects, was played by the emergence of the *'ulema* ("the Learned") as the religious elite of the Muslim world. The scholars of religious law were at first little more than the people's religious and legal counsellors, devoid of any formal standing and subject in every way to the overriding temporal and spiritual authority of the Sultan and Caliph. In the course of time the religious and the judicial functions of the *'ulema* were separated and the judicial branch, the *qadis,* acquired broad power,[78] including the administration of many *waqfs* and the influence that the management of such large properties and revenues conferred on them. We have also noted their authority over professional associations in the towns. All in all, the *qadis* were among the leading officials in the Ottoman Empire, and they also occupied some of the important posts in the State.

It was only natural that differences of opinion manifested themselves to an increasing extent between the Sultan and the *'ulema,* and the decline in the Sultan's

---

[73] Cf. S. B. Himadeh, *Monetary and Banking System of Syria,* Beirut, 1935, pp. 21-22.

[74] Scattered references to usury in general and to the specific role of minorities can be found in El Djabarti, *Merveilles Biographiques et Historiques ou Chroniques,* I, pp. 64-65, II, p. 121, IV, pp. 128-9.

[75] *Koran,* Sura II, verses 275-282; Sura II, v. 130; Sura IV, v. 161; Sura XXX, v. 39.

[76] M. D'Ohsson, *op. cit.,* I, p. 49; II, pp. 100-135 and 120-124.

[77] The order of importance of the various occupations, as handed down by the Prophet, is: 1. army; 2. commerce; 3. agriculture; 4. the crafts, etc.

[78] The main authority was vested in four provincial *qadis,* residing at Adrianople (for European Turkey), Brusa (Asiatic Turkey), Cairo (Egypt) and Damascus (the Arab provinces). *Recueil des Firmans Impériaux Ottomans adressés aux valis et aux Khédives d'Egypte, 1597-1904,* Le Caire, 1934, p. xiv.

authority that we have noted since the end of the 17th century correspondingly boosted the position of the *'ulema*.[79] Along with the Grand Vizier and sometimes the Agha of the Janissaries, the Shaykh ul-Islam or Qadi of Istanbul was the most powerful figure in the Empire after the Sultan.[80] And the *'ulema* as an institution, more so even than the principles of the religion which they expounded, obstructed attempts at social and economic reform which could endanger the status of an elite that they had built up for themselves on the basis of the existing religious, legal and social order.

Our estimate of the place of religion in Muslim society must be qualified by the understanding that among the Turks the position was not the same as among the Arabs. Long before they were converted to Islam the Turks had been governed by a customary code in which their ruler's lawmaking authority played an important role. This authority was carried over into the period of the Ottoman conquests and exercised by the Sultan. The laws thus promulgated grew over the years into a corpus of criminal, civil and commercial-economic regulations that were outside the Muslim religious law or *shari'a* though not openly in conflict with it. They later were codified by the *Mejelle,* in 1869-70, and the other law codes of the Tanzimat period. This development may incidentally explain why the Turks found it easier than the Arabs to build their State along revolutionary and secular lines after the First World War.

The *shari'a* which was sacrosant to Muslims and in practice regulated every aspect of their lives until the issuance of the new codes in the mid-19th century, was not applied to the non-Muslim minorities. These communities were permitted to organise their own religious, social and legal lives. They were known as *millets,*[81] and they enjoyed autonomy within the framework of the *millet* system.

The roots of this system go back to Byzantine days, but the main push in its development was provided by the Islamic way of thinking and by the workings of the Ottoman administration, for which the religious minorities and the foreigners were inferior but tolerated by the true faith and its judicial system. This allowed the various non-Muslim communities to lead their lives autonomously, each in a separate framework. The Muslim majority, under the Caliph, also formed a *millet* of its own,[82] including various national communities such as the Turks, the Arabs, the Kurds, the Albanians, etc. Heterodox Muslim groups such as the Druse, were also nominal members of this *millet*. The Christian churches—Catholics, Protestants, Greek Orthodox, constituted separate *millets,* all according to their particular denominations. The Jews formed a single *millet,* headed by a Chief Rabbi

---

[79] J. von Hammer, *op. cit.,* I, pp. 592-601; M. A. Ubicini, *Letters on Turkey,* Part I, London, 1856, pp. 65-112.

[80] D'Ohsson, *op. cit.,* II, p. 259.

[81] *Millet* is the Turkish form of the Arabic word ملة, which means "national-religious community" (in distinction from the present Turkish use of the word: "nation").

[82] Cf. *De la situation légale des Sujets Ottomans non-Musulmans,* par le Comte F. Van den Steen de Jehay, Ministre Résident de S. M. le Roi des Belges, Bruxelles, 1906, p. 23. The privileges conferred on the various *millets* were defined in the Sultan's firmans and in various decrees whose texts are given in G. Young (ed.), *Corps de Droit Ottoman,* Vol. II, pp. 1-165.

(Haham Bashi) resident in Istanbul, although in practice he was more of a representative than a community head, in view of the non-hierarchic structure of the Jewish congregations, each of which was virtually autonomous.

The autonomy of the *millets* was to all intents and purposes as far-reaching in the legal, administrative, social and educational fields as in the religious domain. They had their own institutions, economic as well as religious and judicial. Each community was responsible for the maintenance of its own institutions, and this situation continued in the second half of the 19th century notwithstanding the Sultan's formal undertaking in the Hatti Hümayun of 1856 that henceforth the State would see to it.[83]

Although the basis of the *millets* was clearly religious and not national or territorial, these well-organised groups often developed a definite political national consciousness and even separatist tendencies. This was particularly true of the Christian *millets,* many of which coincided with ethnic groupings. The separatist tendencies of the *millet* system were strengthened by the capitulations, which gave such Powers as France and Russia the right to protect first the Holy Places, and then specific Christian minorities. In time the *millet* system, with its capitulatory overtones, became one of the main causes of the limitation of central authority and the disintegration of central administration in the Ottoman Empire.[84]

We have noted the identification of minority groups with specific occupations. Their concentration in the fields of crafts, brokerage and other economic services can be traced on the one hand to their being shut out of government and military careers, and on the other to their penchant for economic activity and to the autonomy of the *millets*. This process went on until the last days of the Ottoman Empire, and the Republican regime had to take stringent measures in order to put an end to it.

We have seen how the waxing power of the provincial overlords, the *millet* system and the fiscal methods which put the State treasury and administration at the mercy of the well-entrenched tax-farmers, all combined to weaken the central government of the Ottoman Empire. This disintegrative process, which was accompanied by the emergence of new national entities,[85] could not be halted unless the social and the economic structure of Ottoman society could be fundamentally altered. This structure, in turn, could not be changed without transforming its foundations—the production methods and social relations in the Middle Eastern village and the traditional religious way of thinking of Islam. While the adjustment of Christianity, in particular of the Protestant churches, to socio-economic changes had started as early as the sixteenth century, the hold of religion on the Muslim society survived

---

[83] Ch. Morawitz, *op. cit.,* pp. 167-171. A detailed description of the internal structure of the various *millets* is given in M. A. Ubicini, *op. cit.,* II.

[84] "Chacun des cultes reconnus forme des lois, un Etat dans L'Etat". (Leon Verhaeghe, *Recueil des Rapports des Secrétaires de Légation de Belgique,* T. J. Bruxelles, 1872, p. 334.)

[85] As late as the eve of the War of 1876 with Russia the Ottoman Empire extended over 1,812,048 square miles. By the end of the Balkan Wars in 1914, its area had shrunk to 710,224 square miles. Even after the annexation of the Sanjak of Alexandretta in 1939 the area of Republican Turkey was just 296,500 square miles.

the social and economic revolutions of the West, and has remained strong until recently.[86]

Several comprehensive attempts at reform, designed to strengthen the Ottoman Empire politically and economically, were made during the course of the 19th century. Unfortunately the would-be reformers, to the extent that they were sincere, set too much store by the influence that changes in the legal and institutional superstructure could have on basic economic and political concepts. And even in this superstructure there were domains, such as education, which were neglected by the reforms.

Although throughout the 19th century Egypt theoretically remained a part of the Ottoman Empire, the rule of Mehmed Ali and his successors, and later of the British, rendered the Sultan's hegemony over Egypt purely nominal. The most the Porte ever did was to remind the Khedive periodically, generally under the pressure of the Powers, that certain decisions were subject to the Sultan's approval. We shall have to consider the widely differing histories of Egypt and the Ottoman Empire in separate sections, supplementing them with a section on Persia in order to cover developments in all of what is known today as the Middle East.

---

[86] Cf. H. M. Robertson, *Aspects of the Rise of Economic Individualism,* Cambridge Univ. Press, 1933, p. 165; R. H. Tawney, *Religion and the Rise of Capitalism,* New York, 1947, Ch. IV.

PART TWO

ATTEMPTS AT REFORM IN THE OTTOMAN EMPIRE AND EXPANSION OF FOREIGN INTERESTS

1. ATTEMPTS AT WESTERNISATION BEFORE THE TANZIMAT

While the impact of Europe did not make itself widely felt in Turkey until the second half of the 19th century, in certain respects substantial European influences were at work as early as the end of the 18th. This applies particularly to the military field, where the Sultans early sought to regenerate the Empire's might by having recourse to Western patterns and techniques. Their attempts bred numerous conflicts between the court and the Janissaries, who had attained a position of decisive influence in the political as well as in the military field.[1] Tried and tested in foreign battles, this caste made up the bulk of the professional Turkish army. They and their commanders opposed the raising of a conscript army, the introduction of European training methods and fortification techniques—which in turn implied other structural changes in the army—and particularly any judicial or social reforms that might threaten their positions of power in the Empire.

Selim III, who acceded to the throne in 1789, was not the first Sultan to clash with the Janissaries, but it was during his reign that the conflict took on the character of a life-and-death struggle. Selim, one of the first European rulers to recognise the French Republic, strove to tighten the Empire's bonds with Europe in search of the new Western techniques in military training and organisation, in building fortifications and in the economic field.[2] He established military academies which he staffed with European officers; had Western military texts, particularly French ones, translated and printed in Turkish; ordered English naval training boats for his fleet; repaired the Empire's border fortifications; and set up the famous arsenal of Tophanè. In the field of civil administration he introduced a number of innovations designed mainly to provide more funds for the maintenance of a modern army; he decreed that feudal estates would revert to the Sultan upon the holder's death; and tried hard to impose strict central supervision over the activities of the tax-farmers in the provinces, with the ultimate object of abolishing the tax-farming system and replacing it by collection by government officials.

The Janissaries, who were still powerfully entrenched, sensed the threat that such reforms, in particular the attempt at setting up a regular army (the *nizam jedid*), represented to their hegemony.[3] They combined with the *'ulema,* who were equally

---

[1] The Janissaries' commander, or agha, outranked all the Ottoman State ministers except the Grand Vizier, and sometimes himself occupied the latter post. See J. von Hammer, *op. cit.,* pp. 599, 728.
[2] Cf. Halidé Edib, *Turkey Faces West,* 1930, pp. 63-66.
[3] A. Slade (Muchaver Pascha), *Records of Travels in Turkey, Greece,* etc. New Edition, London, 1854, p. III; E. S. Creasy, *op. cit.,* pp. 457-458; H. von Moltke, *Der russisch-türkische Feldzug in der europäischen Türkei 1828 und 1829,* Berlin 1845, pp. 15-16.

hostile to Selim's reforms, and this coalition, headed by the Shaykh ul-Islam, succeeded in having the Sultan deposed in 1807 and later assassinated.

But the end of the Janissaries could not be long postponed. Selim's successors were determined to push on with his reforms. After the short reign of Mustafa IV, young Mahmud II ascended the throne in 1809. When the Janissaries manifested their opposition to his reorganisation of the army on a modern pattern, he had them liquidated in 1826,[4] and from then on the government's efforts were directed toward building up a conscript popular army on the European, and specifically on the Napoleonic, model. The emulation, in fact, was at times too slavish, failing to take local conditions into consideration. For instance, the substitution of the flat European saddle for the concave one of the Turkish cavalry greatly reduced the effectiveness of the latter. The replacement of flowing dress and turbans by tight-fitting European uniforms and hats was equally unfortunate.

Mahmud's economic policy bore some resemblance to the one which, as we shall see later, Mehmed Ali evolved for Egypt. In an overwhelmingly agrarian economy such as the Ottoman Empire's, the village represented the main source of State revenue if the government was unwilling or unable to mobilise capital abroad but still strove to develop industry and infrastructure, and to maintain a powerful army. Mahmud launched a system of land- and consumption-taxes which impoverished the population to the point where riots flared up. While the riots were ruthlessly put down, little could be done about the fact that more and more tracts lay fallow as a result of oppressive taxes that cramped the peasant's will to work.

Another unfortunate policy was the practice of supplementing State monopolies by awarding other monopolies to the highest bidder. As the only legal purchasers from the farmer, these monopolists depressed prices to the point where it no longer paid to produce such items as silk and opium, which had enjoyed earlier good prices on the export market.[5] The resulting deterioration in the agricultural sector on the one hand and the actual loss of Moldavia, Wallachia and Egypt on the other hand, adversely affected the supply of agricultural produce, causing a particular rise in the prices of cereals, and were an additional factor in the fall in the purchasing power of local currency.[6]

Mahmud was aware of the difficulties of transplanting modern European practices to the feudal soil of the Middle East, but he did not gauge correctly the

---

[4] Mehmed Esad, *op. cit.*, pp. 158-183, and *passim*.—The number of Janissaries in Mahmud's days had been estimated at some 60,000, and their liquidation was only accomplished after minute planning on the part of the Sultan. They were first deprived of their officers, then split up into small groups, and shot after a frontal attack by the regular forces or by resort to terror, followed by mopping-up operations. See A. Slade, *op. cit.*, pp. 136-140. N. W. Senior, *A Journal kept in Turkey and Greece*, 1859, pp. 136-137, claims that the number of Janissaries killed was relatively small, and that European historians have greatly exaggerated the number of victims.

Recueil des Firmans Impériaux Ottomans, loc. cit., pp. 148-150, reproduces the text of Firman No. 471 of 1826 in which Mahmud II explains to Mehmed Ali the circumstances in which the Janissaries were liquidated, ascribing the need for the operation to the threat which they constituted to the Empire.

Cf. also H. von Moltke, *Der russisch-türkische Feldzug*, pp. 16-19.

[5] A. Slade, *op. cit.*, pp. 141.

[6] H. von Moltke, *Briefe über Zustände und Begebenheiten in der Türkei aus den Jahren 1835 bis 1839*, Berlin, 1893, pp. 51-55.

structural, long-term influence of his policies on the economy. His excessive taxes filled the treasury coffers for the time being but wrought havoc with the productive capacity of a large part of the national economy. They dealt a blow to the feudal lords but impoverished the small peasantry even further. This policy was to yield its bitter fruit in the second half of the 19th century, when it became evident that the State's economic and financial resources were drying up.

The liquidation of the Janissaries removed only one obstacle, mainly political and military in nature, to the country's development and the assertion of State authority: the Empire's backward economic and social structure was a far more formidable barrier. The Sultan's struggle with the fief-holders, who had waxed particularly strong in the course of the 18th century in the wake of the near-collapse of central authority, was an uphill fight. It went on long after Mahmud II abolished the fief system, expropriated the fiefs, which were made inalienable State property, and compensated their holders by awarding them life pensions (1831).[7] The result was that the Muslim feudal lords in Greece,[8] Bosnia and Serbia, the Arab Pashas in Syria, Palestine and Egypt—as well as the Wahabis, who were then under Egyptian rule—rose up in arms. Mahmud, who had not had time to train an effective army to take the place of the Janissaries, was constrained to resign himself to the loss of a number of territories—and to opening the Dardanelles under the Treaty of Adrianople in 1829.[9]

Mahmud's reforms did not even last out his reign. He was ultimately forced to give them up along with other projects, and even to return the fiefs to their former holders. His main lasting achievement was in Anatolia,[10] where he did succeed in breaking the hold of the *derebeys* ("Lords of the Valleys") on the land. These powerful families had divided Anatolia's land among themselves, transmitted these estates to their descendants as if they were their private property, and grown into a class of local overlords totally independent of the Sultan to all intents and purposes. Mahmud left some of them in possession of their land, but imposed on them taxes—partly to assert the State's supreme ownership—and the duty to provide him with men in time of war. At the same time he tied them to his fortunes by a system of grants, mainly by forgoing the service that each family head owed him. From then on the State on the one hand and the small peasantry on the other assumed an important role as landowners in Anatolia, imparting to it a special character that made the task of land reform simpler in Turkey after the war than in the other countries of the Ottoman succession, where large private estates predominated.[11]

---

[7] M. A. Ubicini, *op. cit.*, I, pp. 280-281.

[8] In Greece the feudal lords, who had fought Mahmud's expropriatory measures before 1831, profited from the insurrection that culminated in Greece's independence, with the support of the Powers, in 1832. Part of the country, however, remained under Ottoman domination until the second half of the 19th century, and here the fief-holders' struggle against the Sultan continued.

[9] *Treaties, etc. between Turkey and Foreign Powers, 1535-1855,* pp. 539-551. These losses had their good points: they gave the Empire a respite from external wars, and they relieved the Porte from the burden of administering a number of distant and disaffected territories. Cf. M. A. Ubicini, *op. cit.*, II, pp. 110-111.

[10] L. Steeg, "Land Tenure", *Modern Turkey* (ed. E. G. Mears), New York, 1924, p. 238; A. Slade, *op. cit.*, pp. 113-115; E. S. Creasy, *op. cit.*, pp. 529-530.

[11] See below, Part Seven, Ch. 2.

One part of the Empire—Syria and Lebanon—was opened to a good deal of Western influence in the wake of the Egyptian occupation of 1831-1840 under Ibrahim Pasha. This influence made itself felt in the economic domain —particularly in trade—as well as in the cultural field, where it was assisted by missionary activity and the growth of a local class of officials and intellectuals. But in other parts of the Empire the impact of the West was still very limited, except in certain respects. Mahmud II established a few secondary schools, sent 150 students to Europe, opened a medical school, set up a postal service, had pamphlets on disease prevention printed and distributed, forbade the expropriation of private property, and introduced a clothing reform, including a new head-gear, the fez.[12] But the State was not making efforts to impart a new way of life or new ways of thinking to the masses, or preparing the way for deeper social and economic transformations. The reforms, often restricted to official decrees and regulations, were imposed from above—and even as such they did not last.

2. THE TANZIMAT

The age of reform known in the history of Ottoman Turkey as the Tanzimat[13] opened in 1839, the year of Mahmud's death. On November 3rd his son and successor, Abdul Mejid, addressed to the Grand Vizier, Mustafa Reshid Pasha,[14] a letter that was to become known as the Hatti Sherif of Gülhane, the Noble Writ of the Palace of Roses, where it was read out in public as a proclamation.[15]

A large part of the responsibility for the proclamation of the writ lay with the Great Powers, who were concerned with the condition of their nationals in the Ottoman Empire; but the main reforms envisaged in it affected the Empire's own subjects. In his writ, the new Sultan undertook to continue his father's reforms; he granted full religious and judicial equality to all citizens regardless of religion; he declared that military service would henceforth take in all Ottoman subjects; and he promised that taxation would be according to financial capacity and within the limits of the law.

The last mentioned undertaking was a reference to the system of fiefs and tax-farming, whose beneficiaries mulcted the population without any regard for law or

---

[12] Cf. B. Lewis, *The Emergence of Modern Turkey,* Second Edition, OUP, 1968, pp. 101-2.— 100 years later the very same fez was banned by Atatürk as a symbol of ignorance and fanaticism, and replaced by the hat.—*Ibid.,* pp. 236, 267, 410-11;

[13] See E. Engelhart, *La Turquie et le Tanzimat,* Paris, 1884; J. H. Kramers, "Tanzimat", *The Encyclopedia of Islam,* Vol. IV, pp. 656-660; M. A. Ubicini, *Letters on Turkey,* Part I, pp. 27 ff. The word Tanzimat is formed in Arabic from the root نظم "to arrange", "to put in order", and hence, تنظيمات "arrangements", "regularisations", "reforms".

[14] Reshid's influence was prominent in the proclamation of the Hatti Sherif as well as of the Hatti Hümayun of 1856, about which see below.

[15] G. Noradounghian, *Recueil d'Actes Internationaux de l'Empire Ottoman,* Vol. II, pp. 288-290 (correctly 292); N. W. Senior, *A Journal kept in Turkey and Greece,* London 1895, particularly pp. vi-xi. For text, see our Appendix 8.

justice. It constituted a repetition of the attempt of 1831 to do away with this system, but was no more successful than Mahmud's measures. The direct collection of taxes through imperial officials proved a failure and had to be rescinded, the main step backward being taken in 1852.

However, under the pressure of the Powers, the advance was resumed in 1856 in the fields of civil and foreigners' rights as well as in the economic domain. That year a new proclamation was issued, the Hatti Hümayun,[16] among whose undertakings in the economic field were an end to the exploitation of the peasants by tax-farmers and the replacement of the tax-farming system by direct collection; the adaptation of taxation to the requirements of production and trade; and State assistance in the development of banking and other credit institutions.

These were accompanied by guarantees of civil equality and protection for all citizens, and by complementary provisions in the military and religious fields, such as the stipulation that military service would be universal. The latter provision was a repetition of the undertaking of 1839, but apparently it again proved unworkable, for instead of being taken into the army the non-Muslims paid the exemption fee or *bedel* to which we have already had occasion to refer and which represented an important source of State revenue.

To secure the implementation of the reforms proper institutional arrangements were made. The Council of Judicial Ordinances *(Meclis-i Ahkâm-i Adliye)*, set up in 1837, was enlarged by the Hatti Sherif of 1839, and given central controlling power over the *tanzimat*.[17]

In 1861 Abdul Mejid's successor, Abdul Aziz, issued a new writ which confirmed the previous reforms, relaxed certain restrictions on them that were inherent in the old orthodox way of thinking, and among other things spoke in more unequivocal terms of the establishment of banks and credit agencies for purposes of economic development.[18]

Such promises and undertakings were reiterated several times, particularly in the 1870's, under the influence of Young Turk circles,[19] and after the accession of Abdul Hamid II in 1876. This reiteration in itself hints at the extent to which the promises were mainly declarations on paper, made at the behest of foreign powers or under the pressure of internal developments. In addition we also have direct proof of the failure of the various reforms projected by the Tanzimat. One of the outstanding instances was the continuation of the system of tax-farming, the concessions being sold to the highest bidder.[20]

---

[16] For text, see our Appendix 9.

[17] B. Lewis, *The Emergence of Modern Turkey*, p. 106, and *passim*.

[18] M. Belin, "Etude sur la Propriété Foncière", *loc. cit.*, avril-mai 1862, pp. 274-291.

[19] The beginning of the activities of the first Young Turk group is generally given as 1864, year of the establishment of the newspaper "Hürriyet" (Freedom) in Paris. This group included elements which elevated Abdul Hamid II to power. The ruthless reign of the latter and his abjuration of his promises to set up a liberal constitutional system gave the impetus to the formation of a revolutionary new group of Young Turks from 1889 onward. An interesting study of this movement and its development is E. D. Ramsaur's *The Young Turks,* Princeton, 1957.

[20] The Eastern Question Association, *Papers on the Eastern Question,* "Commercial and Financial Aspects of the Eastern Question" by J. Holms, London, 1877, pp. 10-12; N. W. Senior, *A Journal kept in Turkey and Greece, 1859,* p. 43.

Still, one ought not to underestimate the significance of these attempts at reform, for in certain fields they provided a solid beginning of progress, or at least paved the way for more effective efforts in the 20th century.[21] Further, in view of changed political and financial circumstances the proclamation of 1856, in contrast with that of 1839, was followed up by a number of genuine judicial and economic concessions to foreigners.[22] The period of the Tanzimat was one of closer attention to education, although the reformers' efforts were concentrated mainly at the higher levels of schooling. To us this emphasis may seem paradoxical in view of the fact that there was no elementary school network to speak of, whatever schools did exist being affiliated mainly to the *millets*; but it may be more readily explained in the light of the reformers' eagerness to catch up with the West as rapidly as possible. According to official Turkish sources the number of pupils in the country's State schools—elementary and other—added up in 1911 to 1,331,000. However, according to other sources, this figure is greatly exaggerated, and this suspicion would seem to be borne out, *inter alia*, by the negligible share of expenditure on education in the State budget. If we add to this the low standard of instruction which, at the elementary level, was generally limited to religion, we shall appreciate the extent to which education constituted a bottleneck in the country's development. A State Council for Education was set up as early as 1838, but only during the period of the Tanzimat proper, and particularly in the 1860's, was the secondary school network expanded, 1868 seeing the foundation of the Lycée of Galata Seray, which was to become the centre of higher education in the Empire. Of the 4,500 students at the University of Istanbul in 1910 over 3,000 studied law and the humanities, 850 medicine, 500 engineering and 170 mathematics and natural sciences.[23]

The gradual advance in the codification of Ottoman law expressed itself in the promulgation of the Commercial Code in 1850-1, the Land Code in 1858 and the

---

[21] The development of Ottoman law and the regulations that supplemented it can be traced in George Young (ed.), *Corps de Droit Ottoman—Recueil des Codes, Lois, Règlements, Ordonnances, et Actes les plus importants du Droit Interieur, et d'Etudes sur le Droit Coutumier de l'Empire Ottoman*, 7 Vols., Oxford, 1905-06. In his introduction to the collection Young concludes that three categories of law may be distinguished in the Ottoman Empire: "Le premier est droit religieux commun à tout l'Orient Musulman; le second, le droit coutumier et civil, est plus ou moins basé sur le droit religieux, mais ses sources et sa sanction ont été en grande partie laicisées et sa portée est limitée à l'Empire Ottoman; le droit capitulaire est de caractère international et n'intéresse en général que les Communautés Etrangères établies en Turquie".

[22] Cf. G. Pélissié du Rausas, *Le Régime des Capitulations dans l'Empire Ottoman,* Paris, 1902, pp. 108-120.

[23] E. G. Mears, *op. cit.,* pp. 123-125; Halidé Edib, *Turkey Faces West,* pp. 70-71. Education was completely in religious hands—Muslim, Christian or Jewish—until 1846. From then until the end of the 1870's it is interesting that to the extent that the State showed any concern for education it expressed itself in the establishment of a few military and secondary schools—including the attempt to set up a university—and keeping a watchful eye on the books being printed in or imported into the country. The first Minister of Education was appointed in 1856. Elementary education was in the hands of the local communities, which were also responsible for financing it with the support of the parents and, formally at least, the government. It is therefore difficult to get an idea of the total expenditure on education from the State expenditure, which accounted for only $2^1/_2\%$ of the national budget, not including vocational schools of various types.

Commercial-Marine one in 1863-4. The formulation of a Civil Code was then taken in hand. A series of law-compilations had already been published, and had done much to popularise the law and to narrow the scope of arbitrary exercise of authority on the part of judges and officials. A commission headed by Cevdet Pasha was then constituted to codify the Empire's civil law with an eye to the prevailing needs. It filed its report on April 1st, 1869, and its findings became the basis of the new Civil Code, the Mejelle,[24] the first part of which was issued in 1870. This was mainly a collection of civil laws based on the principles of Islam as interpreted by the great Sunni jurisconsult and founder of the school of religious law predominant among the Turks, Abu Hanifa (699-767), but conciliated with modern conditions under the influence of European jurisprudence,[25] and particularly the Napoleonic code, in an attempt to deal with such new problems as modern commercial relations, foreign exchange, associations and companies, title, evidence, etc.

The end of the 1870's and the 1880's saw the promulgation of legislation defining procedure in every sphere of commercial, civil and criminal law. A whole network of tribunals had to be set up alongside the *shari'a* courts to deal with cases under the new civil law,[26] whose codification had helped clear up what cases came under what type of law. The *shari'a* courts—and the *millet* courts for non-Muslims—continued to deal with matters of personal status (marriage, divorce, succession, etc.), the *waqfs* and religious issues; the civil courts concerned themselves mainly with criminal and commercial cases;[27] and the capitulatory tribunals, whose authority was based on international conventions, took up cases specifically concerning foreign nationals. These were generally tried by the respective consular courts and under the law of the countries they represented.

An account of the Tanzimat would not be complete without dwelling on the man who was perhaps their main architect after Reshid Pasha—Midhat Pasha[28] (1822-1884). Midhat was well qualified for his reforming role by a rich store of experience amassed in study and travel in Europe, then in service in various parts of

---

[24] Code Civil Ottoman, *Corps de Droit Ottoman*, Vol. VII, Titre CXIII.

[25] *Ibid.*, Vol. VII, pp. 172 and 176-177. Cf. Abou Yousof Ya'koub, *op. cit., passim;* M. D'Ohsson, *op. cit.*, I, pp. 4-5.

[26] *Law in the Middle East*, ed. by M. Khadduri and H. Liebesny, Vol. I, pp. 292-308.

[27] Commercial and criminal cases involving foreign nationals either in their dealings with each other or in relation to the Ottoman State—were generally brought before mixed courts. The confusion which existed between the jurisdiction premises of the mixed and those of the consular courts led to continual disputes between the local authorities on the one hand and the foreign representatives and governments on the other.

[28] For an account of Midhat's life see the French or English edition of his biography by his son: *Midhat-Pacha, sa vie—son oeuvre*, par son fils Ali Haydar Midhat Bey, Paris, 1908; *Life of Midhat Pasha*—A Record of His Services, Political Reforms, Banishment, and Judicial Murder—delivered from private documents and reminiscences by his son Ali Haydar Midhat Bey, London, 1903. There are also memoirs of his secretary and confidant, A. Clician Vassif Effendi, *Son Altesse Midhat-Pacha Grand Vizir*, Paris, 1909. During the first, "official" period of the Tanzimat it was Fuad and Ali, rather than Midhat Pasha, who ranked among the pioneers of Tanzimat along with Reshid. But Midhat's personality and diversified activities reflect to a larger extent the effort to break up the old legal, political and economic set-up of the Empire.

the Empire such as Syria, Serbia and the Danube Provinces, and finally during a year as President of the Council of State, an advisory body to the Sultan and government. In 1869 he was appointed governor of Iraq.

This backwater of the Empire had enjoyed a great deal of independence under the Georgian pashas of Baghdad and had developed good relations with the West, in particular the British. It succeeded to evade, until the second quarter of the 19th century, efficient intervention of the central Ottoman authorities and ran its own system of arbitrary taxation, customs, corrupted coinage, under conditions of tribalism, widespread robberies and recurrent plagues. Only since the early 1830's, under Ali Riza Pasha, and then in the 1850's, under Mehmed Reshid Pasha, the Ottoman reforms started penetrating also Iraq.[29] Midhat Pasha continued the attempt of Mehmed Reshid to improve irrigation and river navigation but devoted his reforming energy to other endeavours as well. Armed with civil as well as military powers in his capacity as governor, he did not hesitate to launch a frontal attack on the old order in the extremely risky field of land tenure. He ordered the registration of all land in order to put an end to the chaos which had prevailed for centuries in the field of ownership, to establish land rights, and to provide a basis for substituting settlement on land for tribalism, and for social, economic and fiscal reforms.

Registration and categorisation of land ownership, tenure and cultivation—aiming at securing ownership by the state but tenure by the individual cultivator—were expected to produce more equity, better utilisation of manpower and more efficient taxation. Midhat's measures, however, were of very limited duration and only partly successful for a number of reasons. The population, plunged in ignorance and political powerlessness, feared that land registration was a prelude to higher taxes or a census for army purposes. The shaykhs and the landowners took advantage of such apprehensions in order to encourage the peasantry to register the land in their name, and even resorted to terror to achieve this purpose. The State officials, untrained and venal, generally worked hand in glove with the shaykhs and landowners. The reforms envisaged by Midhat foundered on these obstacles, and far from eliminating the backwardness and the dire exploitation that characterised the Iraqi countryside, the land registration strengthened vested interests even more.[30] The conditions of land tenure in Iraq, and the extreme polarisation of landed property in that country, were destined to persist at least until the revolution of 1958.

In other social and economic fields Midhat was considerably more successful. He managed to settle on the land substantial numbers of nomads who had constituted a menace to public security, and particularly to travellers; he improved taxation and tax collection methods,[31] at first at the price of forceful repression but later, after

---

[29] H. S. Longrigg, *Four Centuries of Modern Iraq*, 1925, pp. 77, 212 ff., 280-323.

[30] Cf. Sir Ernest Dowson, An Inquiry into Land Tenure and Related Questions, Letchworth, 1930, p. 18; H. S. Longrigg, *op. cit.,* pp. 298-9; 305-7.

[31] A particularly important reform in this respect was the replacement of the government's share in the date crop by the *jarib* tax, named for a local measure of area roughly equivalent to the acre. This tax, which took soil category and location into account, came to be known in time as a model of fairness, and its implementation incidentally helped determine landholder rights.

the settlement of the nomads, with a good deal of success; he developed an irrigation and navigation network on the Euphrates and the Tigris; raised Iraq's appalling health standards; extended the educational network; and devoted a great deal of attention to the development of the towns by encouraging municipal government and local industry. In his attempt to raise all-around living standards he even streamlined methods of social assistance.

In view of the fact that the only group on which Midhat could lean in his reforming endeavours, beside the Army, was the Turkish officialdom, he strove to raise the standards of education and efficiency among the latter, and particularly to fight corruption within its ranks. But it was a hopeless task. Externally polished and even Westernised to a certain extent, the bureaucracy was rotten to the core, venal and oblivious to the Empire's interests.[32]

A direct line may be drawn from Midhat Pasha's achievements as governor of Iraq to his endeavours as Grand Vizier soon after, first in 1873 and then in 1876. His first tenure soon came to an abrupt end, mainly due to his clashes with the Sultan Abdul Aziz over financial and economic issues. While on paper the Empire's budget accounts indicated treasury surpluses, in actual fact deficits running into millions of Turkish pounds accumulated annually. The office Khedive of Egypt and the governorships of the provinces were bought at the Porte. The ultimate break between the Sultan and his Grand Vizier came over Baron Hirsch's railway concession: Abdul Aziz revoked it and then revised it in 1872, but dismissed Midhat Pasha, following the latter's (successful) request from the Sultan to repay the public treasury his own share in the profits resulting from the concession's revision.[33]

Midhat, who embodied in action the philosophy of the Young Turks, paved the way for the accession of Abdul Hamid II after the death of Abdul Aziz and the deposition of Murad V. The hope that the new ruler would adopt a more progressive policy appeared substantiated when he appointed Midhat Grand Vizier in place of Reshid Pasha on December 19th, 1876, promised to continue in the path of reform (though the wording of his very first declarations to that effect already deviated from some of the economic and legislative principles formulated by Midhat) and announced on December 23rd of the same year that a constitution would be promulgated and representative parliamentary institutions established.[34] Although Midhat was not a member of the commission that was appointed to draft the constitution, he played an important part in staging the plan that was ultimately adopted. This provided for a two-chamber parliament on the French and Belgian model: a Senate whose members were to be appointed by the Sultan and a Chamber of Deputies elected for four years by secret ballot in general elections in the provinces. The Constitution provided for individual freedom and equal rights for all citizens without distinction of race or creed (Articles 8-11 and 17); the independence of the judiciary, which was to deal with civil cases according to the civil and not the

---

[32] Ali Haydar Midhat, *Life of Midhat Pasha,* p. 63; H. S. Longrigg, *op. cit.,* pp. 280-2; 299-300.

[33] *The Times,* 21.8.1888. - I am indebted to Dr. K. Grunwald for his comment on the subject.

[34] *La Constitution Ottomane du 7 Zilhidjé 1293 (23 décembre 1876)* expliquée et annotée par A. Ubicini, Paris, 1877. See particularly p. 9. Murad V had already made the same promises in July of that year.

religious law (Articles 81 and 87); universal elementary education (Article 114);[35] military service for members of all religious communities (implied in Article 17); and the prohibition to raise revenue or disburse expenditure otherwise than as authorised in the official budget (mainly Articles 96-99).

But Abdul Hamid's promises were motivated by the desire to conciliate the European Powers rather than by concern to improve the condition of the Empire's population.[36] Before many weeks had passed Midhat Pasha was exiled—on February 5th, 1877[37] and although he was later allowed to return and appointed at the end of 1877 to the governorship of Syria and in mid-1880 to that of Smyrna, shortly afterwards he was tried for complicity in the murder of Abdul Aziz and condemned to death although the charge was not substantiated.[38] In the summer of 1881 he was instead exiled again, this time to Hedjaz, where he was assassinated on April 26th, 1883.[39]

The infant Parliament too did not survive very long. First convened in March 1877, it held two sessions before being prorogued from February 1878. However, new undertakings to implement the judicial and social reforms that had been decided on, and to protect the rights of the Christian minorities, were made in connection with the Treaty of San Stefano with Russia in March 1878[40] and the Constantinople Agreement with Britain in June of the same year[41] under which Turkey gave up territory in the Balkans, Kars, Ardahan and Batum in the Caucasus, and resigned her control of Cyprus. Similar undertakings followed the Treaty of Berlin of July 13th, 1878,[42] but in practice no attempts at reform were made until the Young Turk[43] revolt of 1908 and Abdul Hamid's deposition in 1909.

Although the coming of the Young Turks to power was signalised by radical policy changes, the new regime's reformatory capacities were handicapped by two factors. The first was the character of the new leaders. Although they were the historical continuation of the movement of the Tanzimat and Midhat Pasha, they were not inspired, like their predecessors, by idealism or intellectualism. The bloody regime of Abdul Hamid II had supervened, illusions had been shattered, revolutions based on the use of force had been staged close to home (Russia in 1905) and had

---

[35] *Corps de Droit Ottoman*, Vol. II, pp. 352-394; Ch. Morawitz, *op. cit.*, pp. 171-178. The provision with regard to universal elementary education appeared singularly impractical in the country's social and economic conditions and fiscal circumstances, not to mention the emphasis of Ottoman educational policy on higher Europeanised education rather than popular elementary schooling.

[36] Cf. Circular of December 26th, 1876 to the foreign representations in Istanbul, reproduced in *La Constitution Ottomane*, pp. 52-56.

[37] *La Constitution Ottomane*, p. 13; *Midhat-Pacha, sa vie—son oeuvre*, p. xix; *Life of Midhat Pasha*, pp. 145-146.

[38] See the reports from the trial in the London "Times", cited in *Life of Midhat Pasha*, pp. 214-223.

[39] In addition to the books of Midhat's son and secretary, his assassination is dealt with in a report of the Ottoman Committee of Union and Progress ("Young Turks") which appeared in Geneva in 1898 under the name *Assassinat de Midhat Pacha d'après les Documents Officiels de la Jeune Turquie*.

[40] G. Noradounghian, *op. cit.*, III, pp. 509-521.

[41] *Ibid*, pp. 522-525.

[42] See in particular Articles 61 and 62 of the Treaty of Berlin in G. Noradounghian, *op. cit.*, IV, pp. 191-192.

[43] The group originally styled itself the Ottoman Committee of Union and Progress.

provided the main inspiration for the young Ottoman officers who took over in Istanbul after 1908. They were experienced and realistic, but they lacked the idealism wich can be a weak point but also a driving force, and this showed in the economic field as it did in the political and social fields.

The second handicap was the international circumstances attending the Young Turk's short rule. The entire period was marked by almost continuous foreign wars and came to a tragic end for the Ottoman Empire in the First World War. The Kemalist movement which followed the war may properly be described as a reaction to the Young Turk's regime rather than as a continuation of it and an attempt to learn from their mistakes.[44]

The failure of the Tanzimat reforms may be attributed primarily to the opposition of the feudal classes—whose existence depended on the traditional economic and social order and who guarded their vested interests jealously—to any legal or political changes that might endanger their position.[45] Every socio-economic order generates its own system of laws and administration which meets its needs and guarantees its smooth operation. It is natural that in a society most of whose members are backward, ignorant, bound by religious tradition and subjected to despotic rule, a secular and democratic constitutional system will not work. If the Ottoman government did agree to certain changes, or even initiated them, this was either motivated by its determination to regain the power it had lost to the feudal classes, or represented temporary concessions to overt or covert external pressure. A typical illustration of this process was provided in 1856, when the Hatti Hümayun proclamation guaranteeing equal rights to the minorities came on the heels of the resolutions of the Paris Peace Conference on this subject.[46] When Abdul Hamid began to suspect that the Young Turks who had raised him to power were seriously contemplating basic changes, he stowed away all their reform schemes and reverted to an autocratic rule that was more ruthless than that of his predecessors. The nation's claim, in any case as reflected in the Young Turk movement, to a share in government decisions for the improvement of its legal, social and economic condition was effectively stymied by a combination of three factors: the Sultan's autocratic tendencies, moderated by his awareness of the need to conciliate the growing power of the Western Powers, as expressed in the Capitulations; the rise of the Ottoman Debt; and the concession system.

Not until the end of the century did the Young Turk circles reawaken to activity, determined to effect their reforms even by armed strength, if need be. When they

---

[44] Cf. Halidé Edib, *Turkey Faces West*, pp. 96-132.

[45] Contemporary sources give countless examples of arbitrariness and corruption in the economic and financial fields at the highest levels of Ottoman administration. Among these sources are N. W. Senior, *A Journal kept in Turkey and Greece, 1857-58*, London 1859; A. du Velay, *Essai sur l'Histoire Financière de la Turquie*, Paris, 1903; Ch. Morawitz, *Les Finances de la Turquie*, Paris, 1902.

[46] Compare in particular Articles 9 of the Treaty of Paris (in G. Noradounghian, *op. cit.*, III, p. 74) with the first articles of the Sultan's writ, whose wording reflects directly the Powers' concern with the condition of the Empire's minorities. On the other hand, one should note Ubicini's point (II, pp. 431-433, citing Palmerston) that Turkey's efforts to stamp out her backwardness in every field aroused the ire of certain Powers, such as Russia, which were looking forward to the early demise of the Ottoman Empire.

did come to power, their efforts in most domains proved unavailing. We have already noted the nearly continuous state of war in which Turkey found itself at that time; this had its ruinous economic consequences.[47] But so did the influence of the West within the country, psychologically as well as commercially and politically. Like most underdeveloped countries down to our day, Turkey began to emulate Western patterns of consumption, including conspicuous consumption, long before it was ready or able to take over modern patterns and methods of production on anything like a comparable scale. Thus neither a solid modern economic foundation nor the legal and social superstructure on which it is built and with which it interacts were able to arise in Turkey.

An additional element of no mean importance that deprived the Tanzimat of their effectiveness was the Ottoman outlook of their framers, and of the Young Turks after them. Any attempt to crystallise a national Ottoman entity out of a Babel of tongues and races that was characterised, in addition, by economic differentiation along national and religious lines, and to do so through reforms which were themselves concessions to the forgeign Powers and to national minorities, was foredoomed to failure.[48] Only after far-reaching territorial changes during the Balkan wars and the First World War, and the political upheaval that followed, did it become possible to effect more successful social and economic reforms.

The Empire's history during the 19th century was thus characterised by two trends: on the one hand continued backwardness and increasing disintegration, and on the other organised attempts to reform the State's political, social and economic structure. Amidst the social and economic quagmire, the beginnings of a fundamental change were manifesting themselves. Technical and economic innovations were beginning to penetrate the region, mainly in the field of communications—railway construction, regular steam navigation services, telegraph and later telephone lines—but also through the erection of a certain number of industrial plants. Liberal political and economic philosophies were also at work, demanding the removal of customs barriers and an expansion of international economic activity. This seemed to open up the prospect of a change in the unilateral character of the capitulatory system, which conferred, as a matter of fact, all the privileges on the West and resulted in the displacement of the weaker and less efficient Eastern producer by his Western competitor.

These processes afforded an additional fillip to Western penetration, which manifested itself in new techniques of finance, production and administration. The character of this penetration, however, was far from being harmonious or co-operative. Faced with the challenge of the West, the economic and political organisation of the traditional agrarian society, already rotten from within, broke down completely, with no viable new social or economic institutions to take its place; and only the minorities, whose economic rise had been actually fostered by

---

[47] For Turkey's wartime economic difficulties, see J. Pomiankowski, *Der Zusammenbruch des Ottomanischen Reiches*, 1928, pp. 319 ff.

[48] Ziya Gökalp, *Türkçülüğün Esasları*, 1939 ed., pp. 37-52 and *passim;* U. Heyd, *Foundations of Turkish Nationalism*, 1950, pp. 71-81.

the conservatism of Middle Eastern society, were in a position to assert themselves, side by side with the foreign interests, whose contribution to the advancement of the local population was entirely incidental.

3. THE OTTOMAN LAND CODE

We have seen how landowners and provincial overlords grew steadily more powerful through the 17th and 18th centuries, and how the disintegration of the old system of land tenure set off a grave social and political crisis, particularly between 1769 and 1839, as the Empire's internal weakness and the State's decreasing capacity to command loyalty resulted in the detachment, *de jure* or *de facto*, of a whole series of dependent territories such as Greece and Egypt.

The authors of the Tanzimat were aware that the Empire's adjustment to this situation entailed a good deal of rethinking of its agrarian policies and accorded it a special place in their codifying endeavours. Vacillating attempts at agrarian reform, originated in 1829, were followed in the Gūlhane proclamation of November 1839, by the abolition of the fief-system and of tax-farming. New tax collectors were appointed, some of whom, as government officials, remitted the takings directly to the State treasury, while the majority paid in an agreed fixed annual sum based on an estimate of the revenue to be raised, but without being awarded any domains or permanent status in the area where taxes had been farmed out to them.[49] The main object of this reform was to do away with the hereditary fief and its appended hereditary tax-farming privileges. A law of 1840 set the tithe throughout the Empire at 10% of the crop; by the end of the 19th century it stood at 12.63% of the assessed gross revenue.

The Ottoman Land Code of 1858[50] contained no overriding legal or economic innovations, but it rendered future development possible by formulating the prevailing property regulations and categories of land tenure; defining the latter as follows in terms of the classification of Muslim religious law:

Mulk land. This term, which comes from the Arabic word for possession or authority, indicated freehold land, *dominium*, held in full title and with all the attendant rights of transfer, sale, mortgage, bequest and creating endowments. These lands included all *'ushri* land—as we have seen, in certain parts of the Empire the word *'ushri* was more widespread than the term *mulk*—and those *kharadj* lands which had become unrestricted private property in the course of time, even if the owners were non-Muslims.

Miri land. Here the residual title was the State's. While the land was in actual possession and use of the holder, he needed the State's formal authorisation to

---

[49] Cf. David Mitrani, "Land Tenure", *Encyclopeadia of the Social Sciences,* Vol. IX, p. 103.
[50] Code de Terres, *Corps de Droit Ottoman,* Vol. VII, pp. 45-83. For an English version see *The Ottoman Land Code,* translated from the Turkish by F. Ongley, London, 1892. See also Stanley Fisher, *Ottoman Land Laws,* Oxford 1919; M. Belin, *loc. cit.,* avril-mai 1862, pp. 291-292 and *passim;* M. Khadduri and H. J. Liebesny (ed.), *Law in the Middle East,* Washington, 1955, Vol. I, p. 181 and *passim.*

transfer it and he was responsible for cultivating it and maintaining its productivity under penalty of forfeiting it if he left it fallow for three years. Such land could be passed on in inheritance not only to the holder's children but also to his parents and, subject to certain regulations and a predetermined order of priority, to other relatives as well if there were no immediate heirs (Article 59); but it could not be otherwise bequeathed. Upon acquiring or inheriting *miri* land the holder had to pay a *tapu*[51] fee in return for the right of tenure. He also had to pay the tithe and other taxes.[52]

Waqf land. In Arabic the word *waqf* means stopping or holding up, the reference being to "frozen", endowed property. *Waqf* land was, as a rule, private land, the revenue from which was devoted by the country's ruler or by a private individual to religious or charitable purposes, the endowment being inalienable and irreversible. Real estate, and even livestock, furnishings or other movable property attached to real property could be *waqf*, but for the purposes of our discussion we shall consider *waqf* land alone.

This topic warrants more extended treatment in view of the momentous role played by the religious endowments in the economy of the Ottoman Empire, due both to the extent of the land affected[53] and to the conditions to which its administration and the use of income from it were subjected under the endowment writ.[54] The ownership of the endowment was vested in the community of the faithful as a whole, but the income was allocated according to the founder's stipulations. The founder also appointed a trustee or trustees to administer the *waqf*; in the absence of such trustees, administrators were named by the *qadi*. This, as we have noted, invested this religious official with a function of considerable economic importance. There were also non-Muslim *waqfs*, supervised by the religious communities in question.

In addition to the purely religious or charitable endowments *(waqf khairi)* dedicated to the maintenance of mosques, hospitals, orphanages, etc., there were also family endowments *(waqf ahli* or *dhurri)* whose income went to the founder's family, or to persons specifically designated by him, and only upon their death reverted to charitable causes stipulated in his writ. Both these main two categories of *waqf* broke down into a number of sub-categories.

A parallel institution, the "quasi-waqf", evolved on *miri* land. Since only freehold land could be disposed of at will, only *mulk* land could really be made

---

[51] The term *tapu*, which was employed before 1858 as well, originated in the Turkish word *tapmak*, meaning rendering homage or fulfilling an obligation connected with the status of vassal. It later evolved to take on the significance of the right to hold land against payment and under the conditions defined above. Cf. M. Belin, *loc. cit.*, février-mars 1862, p. 184.

[52] The *miri* lands were made up of the following main categories: a. fiefs, income from which went to the fief-holders; b. the Sultan's lands, income from which went to the private treasury of the Sultan and his family; and c. the rest of the State lands, held by high officials, tax-farmers and cultivators. Cf. Gibb and Bowen, *op. cit.*, Vol. I, Part I, Ch. V, pp. 235-275 and esp. p. 237.

[53] According to Ubicini, *op. cit.*, I, 159-265, three-fourths of all the land in the Ottoman Empire in the 1850's was *waqf*.

[54] Cf. Charles Morawitz, *op. cit.*, pp. 111-117. Constant conflicts and suits over the *waqf*, and the judges' corruption, gave rise to the expression "Half the *waqf* goes to the judges."

waqf; in the course of time, however, holders of *miri* land too sought out ways of securing their rights and those of their families in it against sequestration and against the limitations imposed on them by its *miri* status.[55] As a matter of fact, it was legally possible to turn *miri* land into an endowment, but this required the authorisation of the *tapu* offices set up to implement the land law. Such authorisation was not readily given, and required bribery, influence in high places and evasion of the law. Even if all this was successful, the "quasi-waqf" was occasionally turned back into *miri* by the authorities.

Owing to the countless legal complexities to which the *waqf* system gave rise, this class of tenure became in practice one of the worst types of absentee ownership: sometimes, in fact no one knew who the owner was. In principle, the limitations imposed by their inalienable character made *waqf* properties impossible to lease and hence difficult to utilise efficiently; practically, they were not only leased, but when the restrictions were relaxed, a substantial part of the properties fell into private hands and was converted into ordinary inheritable land. In Middle Eastern conditions of tenure and cultivation, in both instances the economy suffered, as a result of neglect and inefficiency.

The Ottoman State sought to tighten its control over *waqf* property, first through the Sultan's officials and later through the Imperial Office of Evkaf (*waqfs* in Turkish), until a special Ministry of Evkaf with an extensive bureaucracy was set up in 1840. Although the Law of 1858 redefined the conditions under which a *waqf* could be established and administered, the imperial government never succeeded in neutralising the harmful social and economic effects of this form of tenure. Far from helping to raise national income in general and State revenue in particular, many of the endowments actually piled up deficits which had to be made good by the imperial treasury.[56]

Matruka and Mawwat land. These were the last two categories of land.[57] The former referred to land required for public use: communal pasture, forests not included in endowment estates, roads and byways, and public grounds in the cities. *Mawwat* land, on the other hand, was land that belonged to no one, was uncultivated, uninhabited and removed from any place of habitation. Persons reclaiming and cultivating such wastes could acquire them as *miri* land (Article 103 of the Land Code), but first had to prove to the authorities that they were willing and able to farm them,[58] in which case they were entitled to receive long-term tax exemptions and other benefits.[59]

---

[55] The desire to protect one's property against expropriation or oppressive taxation was often at the root of the wholesale conversion of *mulk* land into *waqf* during the Mamluk period in Egypt, for instance. See M. D'Ohsson, *op. cit.*, I. pp. 307, 309, 315.

[56] Except for Republican Turkey the status of the *waqf* in the countries of the Ottoman succession did not undergo a radical transformation until after the Second World War.

[57] Code des Terres, *Corps de Droit Ottoman*, Vol. VIII, Ch. I, Paragraphs 5 and 6; and Book II, Chs. I and II.

[58] Muslim law and tradition in this respect based itself on the great Sunni jurisconsult, Abu Hanifa, who ruled "He who reclaims dead land gains title to it subject to the Imam's (ruler's) authorisation". Cf. Abou Yousof Ya'koub, *op. cit.*, p. 96.

[59] Numerous controversies have arisen in Muslim law around the subject of reclamation and

The Code of 1858 (following the stipulations of Hatti Hümayun) also attempted to bring about direct relations between the cultivator and the State, in particular in fiscal matters. Tax collection was entrusted to *tapu* officials instead of the tax-farmers and fief-holders, and the law also made it illegal for a *çiftlik* held by a single person to extend over an entire village, except in special circumstances (Article 103). Article 78 granted the right of possession over *miri* or *waqf* land to anyone holding and cultivating such land for ten years without anyone formally raising an objection.

It should be noted that under Article 107 any mines or mineral deposits underlying *miri* land, such as gold, silver, sulphur, coal, gypsum, etc., were the property of the *Beit el-Mal*, or State treasury, and not of the land-holder.

A law promulgated in 1867 extended the right of inheritance with respect to *miri* land to brothers, grandchildren, husbands and wives of deceased holders. Another aspect of the same law was a provision recognising the validity of old *tapu* documents as evidence of title. This favoured the former fief-holders and landlords, who had such old documents or succeeded in acquiring them after the law was promulgated; it worked to the disadvantage of the actual land-holders and cultivators, who remained tenants, sharecroppers or even landless farm workers.

The Mejelle, or civil law code of 1869-70, retained the land categories of the Land Code of 1858. A real attempt to implement the law with regard to the abolition of fiefs and the regularisation of the problems of mortgage, inheritance and the status of State lands was not made until the Young Turks came to power, on the eve of the First World War, beginning in 1910. The Ottoman Provisional Law of Survey and Registration of Immovable Property, promulgated in 1912 (A.H. 1331), laid down principles for establishing and registering *tapu* rights, for a cadastral survey, for an up-to-date Land Register and for reliable tax assessment. This programme was to have been carried out systematically, province by province, but as in the case of a number of other plans projected by the Young Turks, the war came before it ever got off the ground.

4. THE CAPITULATORY SYSTEM AND ITS ECONOMIC IMPLICATIONS

Capitulations were in existence in a variety of countries, ranging from distant China to Persia and Egypt, which to all intents and purposes ceased to be an integral part of the Ottoman Empire at the beginning of the 19th century,[60] but they reached their most extensive development in Ottoman Turkey.

---

acquisition of waste land. Many commentators have disputed the right of non-Muslims to benefit from this traditional privilege. Abu Hanifa accorded it to them, but subject to the ruler's permission. M. Belin, *loc. cit.*, fév.-mars 1862, pp. 171-186.

[60] Dealing with the background of the Ottoman Capitulations one will come across a large number of documents relating to other countries, such as Russia, Poland and even Western European States, which might, if subjected to a comparative study focused on the aspect of capitulations and concessions, yield the conclusion that for a long period international grants of privilege of this type occurred quite frequently in European history as well, particularly in connection with trade and other economic activities. Such a study would probably shed conclusive light on our tentative opinion that the

The word Capitulations is generally traced to the Latin *caput* or *capitulum*, i.e. chapter heading or title, indicating articles of agreement.[61] Such agreements were concluded, among others, between the Sultan of Turkey and other Powers, to whose subjects they granted specific privileges in the Ottoman Empire.[62]

On the face of it, there was therefore no connection between the capitulations and the *millet* system, the former relating to foreign powers while the latter applied to religious minorities within the Empire. But they had an important point in common: the attitude of Muslim law to non-Muslims, which set them apart in most respects from the jurisdiction of the Muslim State and the rights and obligations of the faithful.[63] Some of the seeds of this attitude may also be found in Byzantine law, and in turn in the Roman law from which it originated.[64] A related root of the institution of capitulations was the traditional concept of law as something which an individual carried with him by virtue of his origin or allegiance wherever he went, so that a State was justified in demanding that its laws be applied to subjects residing outside its territorial limits, in the Ottoman Empire for instance.[65] This could not be done, of course, without the agreement of the host country, and the capitulations constituted international legal recognition of this status of conditional extraterritoriality while at the same time affirming the political sovereignty and authority of the host country.

As far as Islamic countries were concerned, the way to such concessions of certain rights to non-Muslims was opened by the Koranic injunction to protect the infidel who seeks protection. The original context[66] made it clear that the reference was to enemies surrendering in battle, but Islam's juriconsults, religious leaders and rulers gradually widened its application to include travellers, traders, foreign envoys and other foreign groups.[67] With the "law of foreigners" taking shape in Arab and then Turkish Islam, the substantial autonomy conferred on local religious minorities

---

capitulations themselves were not among the decisive causes of the disintegration of the Ottoman Empire, but that it was the Empire's growing weakness, which sprang from other causes, that enabled the capitulatory system to assume a degenerated form which proved fatal to the Empire's economic independence. A conclusion along these lines might help redirect the search for the real causes of the Empire's decline from the external factors to which it is today still generally ascribed to internal processes that have not as yet been given their due weight.

[61] Other opinions derive the term directly from an Italian word of the same origin meaning agreement, or from a direct translation of the Arabic صُلْح (sulkh- peace, conciliation). See "Capitulations" in Académie Diplomatique Internationale, *Dictionnaire Diplomatique,* Paris; Abdollah Moazzami, *Essai sur la condition des étrangers en Iran,* Paris, 1937, p. 31.

[62] The Ottoman concepts on which the capitulations were based were the Turkish *ahd name,* meaning treaty, and the Arabic أَمتياز أجنبي or privileges for foreigners.

[63] Cf. Albert Bourgeois, *La Formation de l'Egypte Moderne,* Paris, 1939, pp. 111-112.

[64] Theodor Mommsen, *Gesammelte Schriften,* Vol. VI, 465-468; W. Heffening, *op. cit.,* Ch, IV, pp. 117-124. The latter source also sees an indirect connection between Islamic law and the Jewish Mishna and Talmud on the subject of foreigners.

[65] Cf. M. Khadduri and H. J. Liebesny, *op. cit.,* pp. 309-312.

[66] Sura 9, v. 6.

[67] W. Heffening, *op. cit.,* pp. 28 ff.

was paralleled by the granting of special rights to foreign subjects, both in unilateral declarations by the Porte and in treaties concluded with other States.

Before the Ottoman capitulations, the Crusaders and the Mamluks had granted similar concessions to the Italian trading cities. When the Turks conquered Egypt they conferred capitulatory rights on the Venetians, and later, in 1528, on the French. In a way, these privileges represented a continuation of those stemming from the treaty concluded by the Mamluk sultan of Egypt and Louis IX of France in 1251, the treaty of 1454 between Venice and the Ottoman Empire, and the capitulations conferred on the French by the Circassian Mamluk sultan of Egypt, Qansuh Ghoury, in 1512.

For the Empire as a whole, the first capitulations of modern times were granted by Suleiman the Magnificent to François I of France in 1535, and amended and expanded in 1581 and in subsequent years.[68] Under their terms the Sultan authorised the King of France to maintain an Ambassador at the Porte; allowed French vessels to ply freely between Turkish ports; granted France the right to protect the Christian Holy Places, particularly in the Holy Land; and authorised France's consuls in the Levant to try French subjects residing in Turkey without applying to Turkish courts.

A section of particular importance, which first appeared in the capitulations granted to the Venetians but which was incorporated in all subsequent concessions to other Powers, limited the customs duties levied by the Ottoman authorities on imports from the countries concerned. The Venetians were promised that the tariff on their goods would not exceed two per cent of their value in the Turkish ports where they were imported, and that any rise in this rate would be subject to their consent. While the tariff was subsequently raised on several occasions, this need to secure the Powers' agreement kept the rise slow and gradual, and even at the beginning of the 20th century the duty did not exceed 10-11%, *ad valorem*.[69]

In the course of time capitulations had also been granted to England (1580-83),[70] Holland (1613), Russia (1717), Austria (1718) and Prussia (1740). By the end of the 18th century just about every Eurpean country had been included, except Switzerland and the Papal State. The United States was added to the list in 1818.[71] It should be noted that while in requesting their capitulations the French had been guided largely by political considerations—France's economic interests in the Levant did not become substantial until later, and particularly after Colbert—the English and the Dutch had been impelled primarily by economic motives: the

---

[68] The texts will be found in *Treaties, etc. between Turkey and Foreign Powers, 1535-1855*, pp. 179-230. For a historic analysis of the rapprochement between Suleiman and François against the background of the latter's rivalry with Charles V, see G. Pélissié du Rausas, *op. cit.*, Vol. I. pp. 3 ff. For texts of several capitulations, see our Appendices.

[69] *Corps de Droit Ottoman*, Vol. III, pp. 220-304; Ch. Morawitz, *op. cit.*, pp. 83-86. Treaties concluded in 1861 and 1862 with 13 nations authorised Turkey to impose specific duties on certain commodities, but the vast majority remained subject to the flat *ad valorem* rate, and the subsistence of the two tariff systems side by side was also a continual source of disputes between the Empire and the Powers.

[70] R. Haklyut, *The Principal Navigations, Voiages, Traffiques and Discoveries of the English Nation*, London, 1598, Vol. II, pp. 141 ff.

[71] J. T. Shotwell and F. Deak, *Turkey at the Straits*, A Short History, New York, Macmillan, 1940, pp. 12-13; G. Pélissié du Rausas, *op. cit.*, Introduction.

English Levant Co. and East India Co. were formed in 1581 and 1600 respectively, while the Dutch East India Co. was established in 1602, and in this period England and Holland became the main competitors of the traditional trading interests—the Genoese and the Venetians.[72]

It is also characteristic that while relations between continental Europe and the Ottoman Empire were worsening, culminating in the Vienna campaign of 1683, Britain's rising power and prestige strengthened her position within the capitulatory system. New capitulations—in 1661 and 1675, for example—not only conferred on her extensive additional economic privileges but also invested her with the right, which had previously belonged to the French,[73] to protect the interests of the Dutch and other nationalities.[74]

Originally the capitulations had been favours granted to foreigners by the powerful Sultan as a token of his generosity,[75] or at the most agreements among equals in which the Sultan's superiority was acknowledged. They remained in effect only during the reign of the Ottoman ruler who had granted them, and their intent was to tighten friendly relations, to prevent wrongs from being committed and to foster trade and economic ties. Even when they had the appearance of unilateral grants, they had been, as a matter of fact, negotiated even in the early period, and had stipulated reciprocal rights and obligations.[76] But by the 19th century, in the wake of the Empire's decline, the capitulations had taken the form of agreements that were imposed on the Sultan and that every new Ottoman ruler was forced to recognise and to renew automatically upon his accession.

This was the birth of what was known as the capitulatory system, which opened the gates of the Empire wide to arbitrary interpretations of the capitulations on the part of the Powers and to penetration of foreign interest and influence in the economic and political fields.[77] The low tariff barrier enabled foreign goods,

---

[72] Cf. F. Braudel, *op. cit.,* pp. 339-340.

[73] Although the French did not come to the aid of Vienna, their policy in the mid-17th century was unmistakably anti-Ottoman, and the friendly relations between the two countries were not restored until the 18th century, prevailing until the Treaty of Küçük-Kainàrca.

[74] *The Capitulations and Articles* (between Gt. Britain and the Ottoman Empire), Constantinople, 1663 and London, 1679. Such "right of protection" over other nationals did not, of course, prevent these other nations from having consular representations of their own in Turkey.

[75] The economic provisions of the capitulations in those days, and in fact almost until the end of the 18th century, were aimed at nothing more than raising the status of the foreign nationals to the standard of the Sultan's subjects, who had previously benefited from various privileges denied to foreigners, such as lower export duties.

[76] Cf. G. Bie Ravndal, *The Origin of the Capitulations and of the Consular Institutions,* 67th Congress, 1st Session, Senate, Doc. No. 34, Washington 1921, pp. 34-45.

[77] The extent to which the evolution of the capitulations represented the growing enthralment of the Ottoman Empire to the Powers may be gauged by comparing the capitulations of 1535 with those of 1675 (see both in our Appendices). It may be noted that the capitulations of 1740, for instance, which were among the most significant and far-reaching ever granted, coincided with a ruinous war with Russia, a serious agricultural depression and grave unemployment in Istanbul. Cf. M. Belin, "Essai sur l'histoire économique de la Turquie", *Journal Asiatique,* déc. 1864, pp. 485-486. In tracing the development of the capitulations together with their international aspects, the reader will find the synchronised tables of the dates of Ottoman and European rulers in Noradounghian's collection (*op. cit.,* pp. XVII-XXIII) of great benefit.

sometimes inferior to the local products, to flood Ottoman markets and to deal a serious blow to the productive capacity and competitive ability of local producers, while the markets that were opened to Turkey's raw materials in the developed countries of the West represented only partial compensation for the ruin of prospects for the development of a diversified local industry.[78] In Egypt, for instance, the Powers to whom capitulations had been granted benefited at least until 1800 from import duties of 3-5%, while goods brought in from other countries paid more. In addition, most of the customs revenue flowed into the pockets of the beys to whom the State had farmed it out.[79] Even where the capitulatory clauses were reciprocal, the Turks were unable to exploit this mutuality in view of the widening gap between their backward economy and the quickly developing West. Foreign concessionnaires enjoyed a wide freedom of movement and activity, from which their firms and also their governments benefited. Particular importance attached to the Treaty of 1838 between Turkey and Britain, which not only confirmed all the previous capitulations and other privileges from which British subjects benefited but provided, *inter alia*, for the abolition of the Ottoman monopolies that had been given a particular spur, as we have seen, during the reign of Mahmud II.[80] Even the long-standing ban on the sale of land to foreigners was ultimately abolished under the pressure of the Powers that held capitulations, in the Hatti Hümayun of 1856 and in a firman of 1867 which allowed foreigners to own real property.[81]

The Porte did do its best to insert into the capitulations and commercial treaties all sorts of restrictive provisions enabling it to give some measure of protection to such local products as salt and tobacco, to prevent smuggling, to control the import of arms, and generally to preserve a certain amount of sovereignty for itself in the teeth of attempts at arbitrary interpretation on the part of the Powers. This tendency was particularly apparent in the commercial treaty of 1861 with France, on the pattern of which others were concluded in 1861-62 with Britain,[82] Belgium, Italy, Russia, the United States, Spain, Denmark, Austria and Prussia.[83] The Turks also attempted to get around the capitulatory concessions in all sorts of ways: port and provincial authorities made inordinate assessments of the value of imported goods and exacted various fees and double payments. In order to close such loopholes the Powers found it necessary to reformulate the text of capitulations which were up for renewal.[84] The Porte's insistence on a narrow interpretation of the capitulations also led to an open conflict with the bondholders of the Ottoman Debt, particularly in 1876, after the issuance of an Imperial firman in which the Sultan purposed to fund the Debt and to reduce interest payments unilaterally. The creditors' representatives held that the capitulations and commercial treaties did not

---

[78] E. G. Mears (ed.), *Modern Turkey,* 1924, p. 433.

[79] *Description de l'Egypte,* X, pp. 339-347; 350; 394.

[80] Convention of Commerce and Navigation, etc., 1838, in *Parliamentary Papers,* 1838, L, pp. 289-295. See also our Appendix 7.

[81] *Corps de Droit Ottoman,* Vol. I, pp. 337-341. The Hatti Hümayun proclamation made its promise in this regard contingent on the conclusion of implementary arrangements with the Powers.

[82] See Appendices.

[83] *Recueil des Firmans Impériaux Ottomans, loc. cit.,* p. xxxvii.

[84] *Description de l'Egypte,* X, p. 349. For illustrative texts see our Appendices.

allow the Sultan to make arbitrary decisions with regard to foreigners as if they were his subjects, and that the validity of any arrangement was conditional on their agreement.[85] While formally the Porte did not accept this view, in practice, as we shall see later from the settlement that was ultimately decided, it bowed to the creditors' demands.

The tax policy that ultimately evolved toward foreigners was as follows: while non-Ottoman subjects paid land and livestock taxes and the *'ushr*, under the economic capitulations they were exempt from the *jizya*, from general taxes such as highway taxes and profit levies, from excise, slaughtering taxes and export duties; they also benefited, as we have seen, from low tariffs that could not be raised without the Powers' consent. The Ottoman government waged a long struggle from 1880 until 1907, before the Powers finally consented to an increase: under an agreement signed on April 25th, 1907, with France, Germany, Austria-Hungary, Italy and Russia, the tariff was raised from 8% to 11%, the additional 3% to be collected by the Administration of the Ottoman Public Debt (see Part Three, Ch. 2). Not until the First World War did Turkey raise the rates further, this time unilaterally, and under the Law of March 10th, 1916, the *ad valorem* duties on most imported commodities were replaced by a tariff including a greater number of specific duties than had been agreed upon under the treaties of 1861 and 1862. Implementation of the new system, however, ran up against a number of practical difficulties, and in fact the authorities continued to apply the old one.[86]

In view of the grave economic, judicial and political difficulties created by the capitulations for Turkey, it is no wonder that the Young Turks repudiated them on October 1st, 1914, though this move was not recognised by the Powers. The Powers' opposition, which continued during Atatürk's republican regime, was not based on selfish considerations alone. The Turks' growing xenophobia and their persecutions of various Christian groups, particularly the Bulgars, the Armenians and the Greeks,[87] and the fear that the lives or at least the property of foreign nationals in Turkey would be in danger if the Powers gave up their privileged position, also played a part in this stand. Under the Treaty of Sèvres in 1920 the Sultan was compelled to recognise the continued existence of the capitulations. However, the old regime in Turkey was already dying by then, and when the Treaty of Sèvres was replaced in 1923 by the Treaty of Lausanne, the capitulations were abolished for good. In Sudan the capitulations were abrogated under the Anglo-Egyptian Condominium Treaty of 1899;[88] in Iraq, Palestine, Syria and Lebanon under the Mandates of 1922; and in Egypt under the Montreux Convention of 1937.[89]

---

[85] *La Crise Financière Ottomane devant les Capitulations,* Paris, 1876, particularly pp. 17-20.

[86] Cf. Administration de la Dette Publique Ottomane, *Compte-Rendu du Conseil d'Administration, 1922-1923,* Constantinople, 1924, pp. 27-28.

[87] Which did not prevent the Christians, in turn, from humiliating and persecuting the Jews. Cf. L. M. Garnett, *Turkish Life in Town and Country,* 1904, pp. 187-189.

[88] See specifically Articles 5, 6 and 8.

[89] Cf. J. C. Hurewitz, *Diplomacy in the Near and Middle East,* Vol. I, pp. 216-218, and Vol. II, p. 121; A. H. Hourani, *Syria and Lebanon,* London, 1946, p. 310. In the mandated territories, important elements of the capitulations were retained in the text of the Mandates—see below, Part Six, Ch. 1, and Part Ten, Ch. 2. With regard to Egypt, see Part Nine, Ch. 1.

5. THE SPREAD OF FOREIGN CONCESSIONS

The capitulatory system facilitated the penetration of foreign capital which was granted, particularly in the second half of the 19th century, an increasing number of concessions for the establishment and operation of all sorts of economic enterprises in the Ottoman Empire.

Paricular significance in this regard attaches to the fact that all the big banks in the Empire, with the exception of the Agricultural Bank that was founded in 1889,—the Deutsche Orient Bank, the Deutsche Bank, the Crédit Lyonnais and the Banque Ottomane—were controlled by foreign capital. A specially important role was played by the Banque Ottomane, launched in 1856 by British bankers and reorganised in 1863 with the participation of French financiers. Accorded the exclusive right (along with the Ottoman government itself) to issue currency within the boundaries of the Empire, this bank, which ultimately passed under predominantly French control, exercised until the First World War a profound influence on all aspects of Ottoman life, extending not only into finance but also into transportation and other services.

The other banks were focuses of a similar spread of foreign influence into credit and financing, and thence into investment in services, mining, and commercial enterprises. In time foreign capital took over the control of the Empire's imports and exports, railways, ports, power and water supply and mining. The acquisition of concessions for mines and railways was facilitated by the lifting of the ban on land sales to foreigners in 1867, following strong representations made to the Ottoman government by Powers holding capitulations. Further, it became the practice to grant the holders of railroad concessions a strip of land 2 to 20 kilometres wide on each side of the right-of-way, and the possibilities opened up by the exploitation of this land—particularly when it held mineral riches—were often more important to the concession holders than the railway itself.[90]

Until 1861 the ownership of mines was governed by the principle of Islamic law that mineral deposits belong to the owner of the land they underlie. A study of the relevant legislation, particularly after 1536, shows that the Ottoman State devoted continual efforts to meeting the problems this posed, both with regard to ownership claims and with respect to ensuring uninterrupted production. Where the land was privately owned or leased from the State, the operator paid a tithe on output; where the lease was in the nature of a concession, terms of payment to the State were agreed upon; and where the State itself operated the mines, it collected all the income and paid fixed sums to the managers or officials in charge on the spot. Under the influence of French law, legislation was later promulgated making it possible to collect royalties from the owners of land who operated mines on their properties, as well as from special concessionaires on State land.[91] The important

---

[90] Cf. Robert Anhegger, *Beitraege zur Geschichte des Bergbaus im Osmanischen Reich*, I, pp. 5-20 and passim.

[91] For a balanced and objective view, reference must be made to similar concessions, under similar terms, awarded in other world regions, and even in the industrialising western countries themselves in the later 18th and in the 19th century.

coal mining concession granted to a French company in the Ereğli district in 1896 was made on the basis of these new principles, which were later amended and perfected.

The Empire's coastwise navigation too was soon concentrated in the hands of foreign concessionaires, particularly from the year 1856 onward.[92] In 1883 the government handed over its tobacco monopoly, the Régie de Tabacs, to a joint company set up by the Austrian Kredit Anstalt and the Banque Ottomane with the agreement of the Administration of the Public Debt, to which the tobacco revenues had been earmarked under the Decree of Muharrem of 1881.[93]

A particular importance attached to the Ottoman railway concessions. In 1856 a British company was granted a concession for building a line between Izmir and Aydın, and in the following year an Englishman named Layard was awarded another for a railway to connect the Bulgarian port of Varna with Rusçuk on the Danube.[94] Further concessions were granted for the construction of a number of other lines in Europe, the most important of which, for a railway connecting Vienna with Istanbul, was obtained by the Baron Hirsch in 1869.[95] This was followed by the award of concessions for various lines in Anatolia, particularly Izmir-Kasaba and Mersin-Tarsus-Adana. In 1888 a company sponsored mainly by the Deutsche Bank obtained concessions for railways from Haydar Pasha to Ankara and from Istanbul to Izmir. Organised in March 1889 as an operating company under the name of Société du Chemin de Fer d'Anatolie, this concern then launched protracted negotiations with the government which entered an active phase in 1893 and culminated on March 18th, 1902, in the award of a concession for the "Berlin to Baghdad" railway, i.e. the extension of the existing railways from Konya to Baghdad and the Persian Gulf, a distance of a thousand miles. A special subsidiary was formed for that purpose in 1903 under the name La Société Impèriale Ottomane du Chemin de Fer de Bagdad.

The project of a railway to Baghdad had been conceived by the Germans in connection with their plan for expansion in this part of the world (it was a German engineer, Wilhelm von Pressel, whom the Ottoman government invited in 1872 as consultant to plan a rail network for the Empire). But the Turks themselves had an overriding intrest in such a scheme, and in order to protect the projected railway and to enhance its strategic value they insisted that it be laid out along a difficult mountain route rather than by way of the coastal plain.

The financing of the Baghdad railway project, the cost of which was originally estimated at $200 million, was undertaken by a consortium based on an agreement signed in 1899 by the Deutsche Bank, the Anatolian Railway Co, the Banque Ottomane and the Izmir-Kasaba Railway Co. The Baghdad Railway Company in its final form was set up on March 5th, 1903, with the Germans in control of 60% of

---

[92] *Corps de Droit Ottoman,* Vol. III, pp. 109-116.
[93] A. du Velay, *op. cit.,* pp. 502-515.
[94] *The Times,* January 15th, 20th, 21st, and 30th, 1857.
[95] Cf. Kurt Grunwald, *Türkenhirsch,* A Study of Baron Maurice de Hirsch, Entrepreneur and Philantropist, Jerusalem, 1966.

the capital.⁹⁶ While the scheme reflected the aspiration of Germany's economic interests to break through to the markets of Asia by way of a land route that could compete with the maritime route through British-controlled Suez, the strategic and political significance of the menace the new railroad represented to the British road to India should not be lost sight of either.⁹⁷ This is an excellent illustration of how the new railway being built in the Ottoman Empire served strategic aims—be they a Power's or the Porte's—rather than Turkey's urgent economic needs. As a matter of fact, few efforts were invested in establishing transport connections between the various provinces of the Empire and its administrative centre, or between the various production centres and their markets, even though the original plan for the Baghdad Railway did pay attention to some of those aspects.

Notwithstanding the advantages of all kinds from which foreign investors benefited in the Ottoman Empire, they also attempted to impose on the local government the risk for their own enterprises. The Baghdad Railway Company, for instance, was given free land, free lumbering rights for the construction of the track, and the right to set up various ancillary enterprises that were exempted, along with the railway's own property, income and imports, from all taxes and customs.⁹⁸ Yet in keeping with the principle established in the grant of the Izmir-Aydın concession of 1856, according to which the investors were guaranteed a return of 6% up to a limit of £T. 72,000 a year, the builders of the Baghdad Railway were also given a guarantee that the Ottoman government would make up the difference between a specified income per kilometre of track and the company's actual takings. The government's undertaking to protect investors against loss of profit⁹⁹ had its economic justification, particularly if the government considered the enterprise vital, and in any case it helped attract new investors. But this practice dealt a serious blow to one of the basic elements of profit—risk-taking—particularly since the investors, while unable to realise satisfactory returns on the enterprise itself during the first years of its existence, recouped this in their capacity as partners in profitable supply of equipment or raw materials to these selfsame enterprises, which was generally the case. It was inconsistent for the investors to demand both free initiative and freedom of movement for their capital on one hand and government intervention in their favour on the other, thus impairing efforts towards increasing

---

⁹⁶ The text of the concession is to be found in *Parliamentary Papers,* Cd. 5635, Vol. CIII, 1911, No. 1, in French, an English translation appearing on pp. 37-48. For the main points of the agreement see our Appendix 12. See also *Reports of the Baghdad Railway Company,* 1908; Wilhelm von Pressel, *Les Chemins de Fer en Turquie d'Asie,* Zurich, 1902; Paul Rohrbach, *Die Bagdadbahn,* Berlin, 1902, pp. 6-23; E. M. Earle, *Turkey, The Great Powers and The Bagdad Railway,* London, 1923, pp. 21-23, 59-60 and 70-71; *Politique des Chemins de fer en Turquie Républicaine,* Ankara, 1938; *Corps de Droit Ottoman,* Vol. IV, pp. 120-180.

⁹⁷ Leon Dominian, *The Frontiers of Language and Nationality in Europe,* London & New York, 1917, pp. 257-8.

⁹⁸ See particularly Article 8 of the Baghdad Company concession.

⁹⁹ The concession granted to the Deutsche Bank in 1888 for the operation of the existing Scutari-Izmit railway for a period of 99 years provided, for instance, for a gross annual income of 10,300 francs per kilometre. The investors undertook to extend the line by an additional 486 kilometres to Ankara (Angora at that time), and on this stretch the government guaranteed an income of 15,000 francs per kilometre. Cf. E. M. Earle, *op. cit.,* pp. 31-32 and 52.

the efficiency of their enterprises to ensure a satisfactory return. This objection applied with double force in a backward and capital-starved country whose critical financial predicament was enmeshing it to an ever-increasing degree in vassalage to its foreign creditors.[100]

After the formation of the Administration of the Public Debt, in 1881, foreign concessionaires who did not content themselves with government guarantees of their return could obtain supporting guarantees from this international agency. As will be explained below, the collection of specific Imperial revenues had been delegated under the Decree of Muharrem to the Administration, which earmarked it for the service or repayment of specific debts. Upon the conclusion of the Deutsche Bank concession agreement additional revenues were thus earmarked for meeting the German railway's kilometric guarantee. This process was made possible not only by the pressure of foreign capital for favourable conditions but also by the Turks' own lackadaisical approach to economic activity by foreigners.[101]

The government's own efforts at stimulating capital investment appear to have concentrated mainly on the financing of public overheads and services, and to a markedly lesser degree on producing sectors. The value of establishing and expanding transportation facilities and utilities should not be underestimated: they were destined to be the trailblazers of economic development, opening up new regions to production and trade. This process was the reverse of what had happened in some other countries, where it was production and trade that had spurred the services and public overheads, whose profitability was thus more evident in the short run. All in all, the investment pattern of the Ottoman Empire was determined not only by the investors' profit and security motives and the Powers' political designs, but also by the local government's military considerations and its determination to Westernise. The sources unmistakably bear out E. M. Earle's contention that in the period of Abdul Hamid II at least, the Sultan's military and autocratic preoccupations exerted a decisive influence on his concession grants and on the investment patterns of foreign capital.[102] As a result of this and of the lack of

---

[100] The aggregate annual sum which the government had to pay to the Administration of the Public Debt to cover railway guarantees alone rose from £T. 57,400 in 1889/90 to £T. 1,301,500 in 1903/4, and the total outlay under this head for 1889-1904 was £T. 12,811,300. Between 1889 and 1911 the Anatolian Railway Company alone got over four million Turkish pounds. Cf. D. C. Blaisdell, *European Financial Control in the Ottoman Empire,* Columbia University Press, 1929, p. 3; *Corps de Droit Ottoman,* Vol. IV, p. 118.

[101] In his article on "Capitulations" in E. G. Mears, *op. cit.,* G. Bie Ravndal quotes an official American report on the status of U. S. firms in Turkey which illustrates the total lack of government control over the activities of foreign enterprise: "There is no law in Turkey obliging any foreign bank, banking house or mercantile firms wishing to establish a branch house in Turkey to submit itself to any official or legal formalities"... "Foreign firms conserve their nationality and are governed with regard to their national organization, and to the rights and duties of its members, according to the law of their country". (p. 431). One must parenthetically note that the foreign Powers expanded their influence not only through economic or judicial concessions but also through various cultural and educational activities, particularly missions and schools, in the absence of a real organised official school network. Some 90,000 students attended Turkey's thousand foreign schools before the First World War: about 54,000 were registered in French schools, and the rest were mainly divided among American, British, Italian and German educational institutions.

[102] E. M. Earle, *op. cit.,* p. 23.

local industrial entrepreneurs, the role of the Empire's main, albeit rather modest, industrial entrepreneurship devolved on the government.

The rise of the Young Turks to power in 1908-09 was marked by attempts to regularise the question of foreign investments and economic activities in general, relying on local resources and emancipating the economy from the tutelage of foreign capital.[103] Most of these endeavours, however, were stymied by continued administrative corruption, by the outbreak of the First World War and by further financial entanglements. Nor were the Young Turks unprepared to grant foreign concessions incorporating quite impressive privileges. The famous Chester concession was a case in point. The American rear-admiral Colby M. Chester was delegated by a group of U.S. investors to conduct negotiations for a comprehensive concession under which the group would cover Anatolia with a dense network of railroads, exploit mineral deposits and set up a number of public utilities.[104] The talks began before the Young Turks came to power, but the concession was placed on the Turkish Parliament's agenda in 1911 and it might well have gone through were it not for the pressure of German interests and the outbreak of the Balkan and World Wars.[105]

The Young Turks' attempts to put their economic house in order were spearheaded by the activities of their Minister of Finance, Javid Bey,[106] who was the first to work out a State budget that was worthy of its name, on the European model.[107] Javid availed himself of the assistance of French advisers, notably M. Charles Laurent. Attempts were made to reorganise the customs system, also with the aid of foreign experts, and particularly of Sir Richard F. Crawford. Legislation designed to encourage local industry without taking stringent measures against foreign concession-holders was passed in 1909 and 1913, the latter law in paricular offering to prospective industrialists incentives such as exemptions from land and business taxes and from customs duties on raw materials, building materials and equipment.[108] The war prevented these laws from reaching the implementation stage, but similar ones were enacted in 1923, and in particular in 1927, under the Turkish Republic. On the eve of the First World War, in 1913, foreign investments in the Ottoman Empire—Egypt and investments in the Ottoman Public Debt excepted—added up to 1,686 million francs, or £ 70 million.[109]

---

[103] M. Hartmann *(Der Islamische Orient,* III, 1910, p. 64) cites in this context a statement made on September 14th, 1909, by Ismet Bey, who represented army and middle-class circles. "We want no foreign capital of any kind", he declared, "for otherwise we face the risk of finding ourselves one fine day in the position of hirelings in our own land. We will carry out the improvements and the refurbishments when we have the required funds".

[104] The text of the concession is given in our Appendix 31.

[105] Henry Woodhouse, "American Oil Claims in Turkey", *The New York Times Current History,* Vol. XV, No. 6, March 1922, pp. 953-959. Consideration of the concession was delayed until the 'twenties. See below, Part Seven, Ch. 1.

[106] Javid was of *dönme* stock, i. e. his family were descendants of the Jewish sect of Shabtai Zvi who were outwardly converted to Islam but retained their allegiance to that sect. For an assessment of his achievements, see *Memoirs of Halidé Edib,* p. 345.

[107] See next chapter.

[108] Salty Vitali, *Industriewirtschaft der modernen Türkei,* Verlag Konrad Triltsch, Würzburg, 1934, pp. 46-47.   [109] Cf. Table III below.

In the negotiations for the Treaty of Lausanne the Turks attempted to abolish the foreign concessions, but in vain. The Treaty incorporated a provision recognising an Ottoman ordinance of October 29th, 1914, authorising the grant of concessions to foreigners, and the most the Turks achieved was the Powers' consent to the withdrawal—against payment of compensation—of two new foreign concessions that had not yet been implemented. In practice, however, far-reaching changes in the field of concessions were effected by the nationalisation of the harbours and of the coastwise transport *(cabotage)* that took place in the 'twenties and by the difficult conditions that were created for the operation of concession companies in such fields as commerce, the railways and the services. In the 'thirties the concessions were abolished in these fields as well.

It is difficult to countenance the attempt of certain scholars to describe the economic activity of foreign interests in the Ottoman Empire in terms of spheres of influence, taking a leaf out of the history of neighbouring Persia, particularly after the Anglo-Russian Treaty of 1907.[110] In the first place, in Turkey the foreign interests often got together for specific purposes, as in the case of the Ottoman Bank or even the Baghdad Railway. In the second place, what strikes the observer of the latter-day history of the Ottoman Empire is not the exercise of different influences on different parts of the country but the successive rise and decline of the influence of single States on the Empire as a whole, illustrated by the supremacy of Russia until the Crimean War, then of Britain and France until the early 1880's, and then of Germany until the First World War. At the same time, one must admit that the concentration of the investments of specific countries in specfic parts of the Empire played an important part in the attempt to divide up Turkey that was embodied in the Treaty of Sèvres, although the very fact that the Treaty proved unworkable may be partly ascribed to the weakness of the historic basis for such a division.

---

[110] Cf. Leon Dominian, *op. cit.,* pp. 250-252.

PART THREE

THE OTTOMAN FINANCES AND ECONOMY

1. BUDGETS, BANKING, AND CURRENCY

Continual war,[1] high spending at the Sultan's court, the lack of a clear dividing line between the State budget and the Sultan's spending,[2] the faulty structure of the financial and fiscal systems and the low state of production—all these progressively undermined the Ottoman economy as the 19th century wore on. The national debt grew; so did the gap between the Empire's resources on the one hand and its ambitions and undertakings on the other, until it was no longer possible to bridge it. The construction of palaces,[3] mosques, public buildings and army housing swallowed huge budgets,[4] particularly under Abdul Aziz (1861-76).[5] If Turkey learned something from European financial theory, it was mainly how to print currency and to take loans. Government ministers signed obligations that were heavily discounted; the metal currency was continually debased; plentiful supplies of paper currency were issued; and foreign loans were relied on to an increasing extent.

There were no national budgets to speak of,[6] although some more serious attempts in this direction were made with the onset of the Tanzimat in 1839. The

---

[1] Until the mid-17th century the wars still "paid off" in rich loot and in taxes imposed on conquered provinces and tributary states; but from then on most of the wars were of a defensive character, and in addition to the high cost of maintaining and equipping its armies the Empire frequently had to pay reparations.

[2] The budget of the Sultan and his retinue was first unequivocally set under a special law of September 1855—at 120 million piastres or approximately £ 1 million. M. Belin, "Essai sur l'histoire économique de la Turquie", *Journal Asiatique,* mai-juin 1864, p. 477.

[3] The Dolmabahçe palace alone, put up under Abdul Mejid, cost £ 2,800,000 to build.

[4] According to William Eton's *A Survey of the Turkish Empire,* London, 1798 (quoted in Morawitz, *op. cit.,* p. 14) after the Treaty of Küçük Kaynàrca in 1774 the income of the Ottoman treasury added up to £ 4 million a year (not including *waqf* revenue) and the expenditure on the army, the palace and the harem to £ 3.4 million a year.

[5] Morawitz, *op. cit.,* p. 49. See also L. M. Garnett, *Turkey of the Ottoman,* London, 1911, esp. pp. 61-69.

[6] The information that we can gather from sources in this field is sporadic. Thus we learn that the Ministry of Finance kept regular accounts of income and expenditure in 1572; that an account of expenditure was drawn up in 1609 by Ayni Ali (the original text was published in 1864); that at the end of the 17th century Marsigli found in operation an effective system of financial administration from which he felt European states could profitably learn; that a complete budget of income and expenditure was drawn up by Eyubi Effendi for the year 1660/61; and that short-term attempts were made in the mid-17th century by Murad IV and the two Köprülüs to balance the budget by reducing the army and effecting savings. Cf. M. Belin, "Essai, etc." *loc. cit.,* mai-juin 1864, pp. 447-448, 468-469; août-septembre 1864, pp. 243-244; octobre-novembre 1864, pp. 312-332. One of his sources is Garzoni, *Relazioni Venete,* I, p. 427.

organisation of a Ministry of Finance in 1839[7] resulted in more attention than previously being devoted to establishing budget estimates on a more realistic assessment of revenues and attempts to cut back expenditure, but the success of these efforts was limited, particularly in view of the development that followed the Crimean War. The first budget based on a European model was published in 1861, as an appendix to the financial report of the Grand Vizier, Fuad Pasha.[8] This was the period of the Foster-Hobart mission sent by the British Government to investigate Turkey's financial position and budgetary structure.[9] Budgets continued to be published, though in a faulty form, until the year 1866, after which there was an interruption until 1869.[10] Certain reforms were then introduced when the Administration of the Ottoman Public Debt came into being, but the first earnest attempt to build a modern budget was not made until the eve of the First World War.[11]

In the 1850's the revenue of the Ottoman Government ranged between £ 7 million and £ 10 million a year (at 125 Turkish piastres to the pound sterling) while expenditure varied from £ 7 million to £ 11 million annually. Table I below gives a picture of the budget for 1853/4, derived from data collected by Ubicini;[12] for 1859/60, as put together from various Turkish sources by the mission of Foster and Hobart;[13] and for 1910/11—the Young Turks' first budget after the deposition of Abdul Hamid II.[14] The first two are listed in the table as implemented, and have been converted to pounds sterling at the average real rate of exchange for the period, or 125 piastres to the pound; the Young Turks budget is listed as approved, before implementation, and the conversion rate employed is the real rate of exchange that same year, or 180 piastres to the pound.

It must be remembered that the budget for 1853/4, which even left a small surplus, referred to the year in which the Crimean War began. Immediately after that heavy military expenditure provided the first and most important push to entangle the Empire in foreign debt. But the sources do not supply enough information to make it possible to reconstruct the financial position fully, and there is reason to believe that even before the Crimean War the budgets were not balanced.[15] The steep rise in revenue that can be noted in 1910/11 may be attributed mainly to the increased proceeds from indirect taxation. Here a decisive part was

---

[7] The office of State Minister of Finance was created in 1839; until then the High Treasurer or Defterdar controlled only part of the State funds.

[8] M. Belin, "Essai, etc." *loc. cit.,* août-septembre 1864, p. 269.

[9] *Report on the Financial Condition of Turkey* by Foster and Hobart, London, 1862.

[10] A. H. Layard, *Turkish Budgets and Turkish Finance,* 1869, p. 3.

[11] See *Loi des Finances de 1327,* Constantinople, 1911.

[12] M. A. Ubicini, *op. cit.,* I, p. 266.

[13] *Report,* etc. by Foster and Hobart, pp. 1 and 17.

[14] *Loi de Finances de 1327,* pp. XI-XVIII.

[15] Layard's opinion on the subject is unequivocal, at least as far as the period up to the end of the 1860's is concerned: "Turkish budgets are absolutely worthless as guides either to the government issuing them, or to the proposed lenders for whose enlightenment and security they are supposed in a great measure to be prepared and published" *(op. cit.,* p. 17).

TABLE I

Budgets of the Ottoman Empire, 1853-1911 (in £)

	Revenue		
Source	1853/4	1859/60	1910/11
Tithe	2,200,000	2,844,000	3,800,000
Land & Property Taxes	2,000,000	2,224,000	1,650,000
Poll tax [16]	400,000	477,000	550,000
Customs [17]	800,000	1,591,000	2,600,000
Indirect taxes [18]	1,500,000	2,202,000	6,660,000
Tributes: Egypt	300,000		440,000
Wallachia [19]	20,000	374,000	
Moldavia [19]	10,000		60,000
Serbia [19]	20,000		
	7,250,000	9,712,000	15,760,000

	Expenditure		
Head	1853/4	1859/60	1910/11
Foreign debt service [20]	—	891,000	
Internal debt service [20]	—	687,000	4,630,000
Sultan's court [21]	690,000		
Sultan's family	77,280	1,254,000	280,000
Army and police	2,760,000	3,400,000	6,440,000
Navy	355,000	791,000	930,000
Civil administration	2,070,000	3,184,000	4,630,000
Foreign service	92,000	205,000	140,000
Public works	92,000	78,000	860,000
Subsidies to *waqfs* and Holy Places	115,000	384,000	220,000
Pensions and compensation for expropriated property	404,080	215,000	1,940,000
Subsidies to Banque Ottoman (or other payments)	276,000	—	40,000
	6,932,080	11,089,000	20,110,000

[16] A regulation of 1834 set the poll tax rate at 15, 30 or 60 piastres-depending on the assessee's economic condition—for every non-Muslim adult male (Ubicini, p. 269). In the budgets of 1859/60 and 1910/11, this tax is listed as a tax on exemption from military service: nominally, after the Hatti Hümayun, both Muslims and non-Muslims exempted from service were liable to it, but in effect, since no steps were taken to conscript non-Muslims into the army, it was mainly from them that the tax was levied; and in practice the rates they paid were also higher. Cf. Stratford de Redcliffe, *Turkey,* reprint from *The Nineteenth Century,* June and July 1877, in *Current Discussion,* Vol. I, New York, 1878, p. 96.

[17] Includes import duties and export levies.

[18] i. e. trade licences, stamp taxes, taxes on food brought into the cities, highway and bridge tolls, excise and rent from salt and fisheries, mining concession taxes and postage stamp revenue. The 1910/11 budget includes revenues collected by the Ottoman Public Debt Administration—and, on the expenditure side, payments on account of the Debt.

[19] In 1910/11 those countries no longer paid tribute, but there was still revenue from Cyprus (since 1878), Mt. Athos and Samos.

[20] There must have been some expenditure on this score in 1853/4, even though the steep rise under this heading did take place only later.

[21] While the progressive reduction in the revenue of the Sultans from private sources—their land

doubtless played by the Administration of the Public Debt, which administered a large part of these revenues. The outstanding fact to be noted from an examination of the expenditure budget for the same year is the tremendous rise in the allocation for debt service, which swallowed up 23% of the budget[22] as against 14% in 1859/60.

The second half of the 19th century was marked by a constant rise in the Empire's expenditure, and although revenue rose as well it did not catch up. Layard's survey of the budgets of the 'sixties[23] points out the clear gap between budgetary estimates and execution; between revenue and expenditure; between the promises to balance the budget, or even to pay off the debt, and the constant rise in the debt due to continuous deficits; between the nominal value of the Ottoman loans and the actual price the bonds fetched from investors; and between the plans to allocate a substantial part of the budget to constructive purposes, and the breakdown of the actual expenditure. In addition, there were also considerable differences between official estimates of the most oppressive obligation—the current debt—and more realistic assessments by foreign experts.[24] All this vagueness was another reason why no budgets were published between 1866 and 1869, after which year Turkey, forced to apply in earnest to the international money market, had no choice but to make some attempt at producing the budgetary evidence that had to back up loan applications.

While a certain amount of order was introduced into the Imperial Treasury and into its accounting practices as a result of the intervention of foreign revenue administrations that culminated in the establishment of the Administration of the Public Debt in 1881, fiscal policy and administration continued to be chaotic and to yield annual deficits. As a good example of the difficulties of balancing the budget in that period, one can take the fact that while the estimates for 1897/8 provided for a revenue of £T. 18.5 million and an expenditure of £T. 18.4 million, i.e. a surplus of £T. 100,000, even official summaries show that the effective deficit for the 'nineties averaged out to an annual £T. 1.2 million.[25]

We have mentioned the important part played by Javid Bey in creating a modern budget structure under the Young Turks regime on the eve of the First World War. Yet this period too was marked by yearly deficits, as we have already had an opportunity to see with regard to the 1910/11 budget. The deficts in the budgets as executed were generally even heavier than in the estimates.

---

holdings, special taxes and levies, confiscations of property, the estates of deceased *kullar*, etc.—was already in progress in 1853/4, in that year the expenditure item from the State treasury under this head still reflects only part of the Sultan's actual revenue. The figures for 1859/60 and 1910/11 are more valid in this respect, largely owing to the undertakings given in this regard in the Hatti Hümayun in 1856, but while the entry for 1859/60 still does not cover all expenses of the court, the one for 1910/11 is probably accurate though much lower than the former, owing to the effects of the Young Turk revolution.

[22] The figure would be even higher if other payments on account of the debt, buried in other expenditure entries, were taken into account.

[23] A. H. Layard, *op. cit., passim.*

[24] In March 1868, for instance, the Turkish Minister of Finance estimated the current debt at £ 5 million while foreign experts produced detailed calculations showing that it stood at £ 10 million at least.

[25] *Corps de Droit Ottoman,* Vol. VII, Table facing p. 18.

TABLE II

Budgets of the Ottoman Empire by Fiscal Year between 1909 and 1914 (in £T. million) [26]

	1909/10	1910/11	1911/12	1912/13	1913/14
Estimated income	25.1	29.2	31.6	33.7	33.7
Estimated expenditure	30.5	36.0	41.2	36.9	36.9
Estimated deficit	5.4	6.8	9.6	3.2	3.2
Effective income	?	?	27.3	27.6	29.2
Effective expenditure	?	?	30.0	39.0	35.3
Actual deficit	?	?	2.7	11.4	6.1

To the obstructions that were placed in the way of economic development by external factors, including the low tariff imposed on Turkey by the capitulations, one must add those that were increased by the Ottoman government's own fiscal policy. Constantly under the pressure of heavy expenditure, the government attempted to meet it by every means at its command, external and internal. Thus while the tariff on imported wines and spirits stood at 5 to 10 per cent, local producers were taxed to the tune of 15%. On the other hand, the authorities were unsuccessful in their efforts to increase the treasury income from basic taxes such as the tithe by streamlining collection to prevent the proceeds from flowing into the pockets of tax-farmers and middlemen and by fighting bribery and graft. The government sought to appoint agents who would collect the taxes in cash on the basis of the average of the past five years, instead of the prevailing method of assessment or selling the crop on the spot and collecting the tax rate on it. This scheme too, however, ran up against the opposition of the Administration of the Public Debt and of the railroad concessionaires who had been given kilometric guarantees, for part of the revenue from the tithe was earmarked for them and they feared that the new system might cut into their incomes.[27]

The whole revenue structure was faulty. The *verko*, which next to the tithe had become the government's main source of revenue, not only lacked any progressive elements but was frequently out of all proportion to the payer's income or property since it was set in advance for long periods, sometimes for years. There were thus extreme discrepancies not only between different provinces but also between different individuals, making a consistent tax policy impossible. The collection of the tithe in the second half of the 19th century continued to be in the hands of tax-farmers, who leased it and subleased it, with disastrous results for the fellah and for the government's share of the collections. Even the collection of customs duties was leased out, depriving the treasury of additional revenue, as did the evasion of customs duties, particularly the internal ones.

On the expenditure side, the hope that the increase in government liabilities in the

---

[26] From W. W. Cumberland, "The Public Treasury," in E. G. Mears, *op. cit.*, p. 390. The differences between the figures for 1910/11 and those for the same year in our previous table stem from recourse to different sources and to a different method of calculating the value of the piastre.

[27] Blaisdell, *op. cit.*, pp. 133-146.

'fifties had only been resorted to as a passing emergency measure soon proved vain. Expenditure grew constantly, upsetting the balance of payments and the stability of Turkey's currency. High palace spending, which sometimes reached 15% of the total State expenditure if items not listed in the budget were taken into account, was a heavy burden on the treasury until the deposition of Abdul Hamid II. High army officers and civil officials were paid as much as £ 5,000 to £ 20,000 a year while the masses of low officials had to make do with salaries of £ 6 to £ 60 a year. As a result the high earners became accustomed to a life of luxury and had to maintain it by graft and seeking bribes, while their subordinates had to resort to the same methods in order to earn their bread. Expenditure on education was low, and the activity of foreign missions, *millets* and municipal institutions in this domain was not enough to compensate for this inertia.[28]

Characteristic of the Turkish fiscal system were the differentials between the various provinces. On the eve of the First World War the government's annual revenue ranged from £T. 0.20 *per capita* in Arabia to £T. 1.61 *per capita* in European Turkey, and government expenditure from £T. 0.35 to £T. 1.38 *per capita*, respectively. In some provinces, such as European Turkey and Anatolia, the government's income was higher than its expenditure; in others, like Arabia and Syria, the opposite was the case. One must doubt the wisdom of a fiscal policy that tried to skim off profits from a depressed region such as Anatolia instead of doing its best to channel sums to it for development.[29]

The government attempted to finance its activities and to bolster the Ottoman currency by having recourse to local banks even before a network of foreign banks spread over the Empire in the wave of concessions of the second half of the 19th century. This government motive was behind the founding of the Bank of Constantinople in 1844 by the two Galata bankers, Aleon and Boltazzi, but the bank broke up after less than ten years, upon the outbreak of the Crimean War. Its bankruptcy cost the Ottoman treasury £T. 600,000.[30] The Banque Ottomane, established in 1856 after the Crimean War,[31] was in practice immediately turned into an agent of the government, and after eight years it was awarded, under the name Imperial Ottoman Bank, a special licence that made it something like a State bank. From that time on the State got most of its loans either directly from the Ottoman Bank or through its intermediary. In addition to its credit and currency-issuing activities, the bank was active in the establishment of various economic enterprises such as the Régie co-interessé des Tabacs de l'Empire Ottoman, the Société Minière de Balya-Karaaydın and the Société des Eaux de Constantiople.[32]

---

[28] *Report*, etc. by Foster and Hobart, *passim*. Even under the budget for 1910/11 State expenditure on education totalled barely £T. 500,000 or less than 3% of the total expenditure. *Loi des Finances de 1327*, pp. 83-88.

[29] Cf. E. G. Mears, *op. cit.*, pp. 319-392.

[30] *The Development of National Banking in Turkey*, published by the Press Dept. of the Ministry of the Interior, Ankara, 1938, pp. 4-5.

[31] Preparations for the Bank's establishment were already made before the war, as can also be seen from the expenditure estimates in the government budget for 1853/4 (Table I). The Bank's capital was at first British; in 1863 it became a Franco-British enterprise. Cf. p. 49 above.

[32] *The Development of National Banking in Turkey*, p. 7.

In time a number of smaller banks arose as well, interested mainly in doing business with the government. It soon became evident, however, that the government was not even in a position to meet interest payments, and most of these banks either closed or merged with the Ottoman Bank.

In addition to supplying the government with credit, the foreign banks' main activities consisted, as we have seen in our chapter on concessions, in financing development in the fields of communication and the utilities. This contrasted with a shortage of credit institutions for financing production, and particularly agriculture, the backbone of the Empire's economy. The terms of the traditional creditors in this field, landowners and usurers, were so harsh that cultivators sank deeper and deeper in debt, particularly in view of the extortionate rate of interest: in the Danube Province of the 1850's, for instance, creditors received one para a day for each piastre. Since there were 40 paras in a piastre,[33] this was an interest rate of over 900% per annum. Midhat Pasha, who was then the governor of the province, launched a programme of co-operative credit societies which was also imitated in other provinces, but its success was very limited, mainly owing to the lack of an effective overall economic administration and to the philanthropic emphasis of these societies, which should instead have been organised as business enterprises. Nor were the authorities able to work out ways of seeing to it that the money lent was put to proper use or that it would find its way back to the credit societies. Only on August 15th, 1889, was a Bank of Agriculture set up at Istanbul, with branches all over the country. It operated on a business basis, but in view of the experience of the credit societies it had swung to the other extreme: it had to maintain high liquid reserves and borrowers were required to provide real estate as collateral, something which most of the small peasants found impossible. All in all, very little changed as far as farm credit was concerned until the advent of the Republic.

A steep fall in the value of Turkey's currency took place between 1774, date of the signing of the Treaty of Küçük-Kaynàrca, and 1829, and after a very short period of relative stability depreciation started again in the 'thirties. Von Moltke stated in 1836, that 12 years previously (i.e. in 1824) the value of the Spanish thaler had been 7 piastres while in 1836 it fetched 21 piastres.[34] Thus within a period of only 12 years local currency fell by two-thirds in terms of foreign exchange. Later developments, after Mahmud's II death, complicated still more the currency problem. The issue, in 1839, of the first *qaima,* treasury notes which carried an interest of 9%-12% and bearing no redemption date, fulfilled for the first time a function similar to that of paper currency. Later the interest was reduced, and although it was paid on time the *qaima's* market value fell.[35] In 1842 the use of paper notes became restricted to Constantinople and its suburbs.

In 1844 a new currency system was introduced: the old debased silver currency was replaced by the new *mejidia* and coins of lower denomination. The *qaima,* however, remained in circulation, and the fall in its value undermined the whole

---

[33] *Para* originates from a Persian word meaning part, piece. Cf. M. Belin, "Essai, etc." *loc. cit.,* mai-juin 1864, pp. 447-448.

[34] H. von Moltke, *Briefe,* etc., p. 52.

[35] M. A. Ubicini, *op. cit.,* I, pp. 298-299.

monetary structure. A loan was taken from a British bank in 1858 to buy up the *qaimas* and restore stability to the coin currency, but this operation did not take place until 1862. By 1860-61, when there were £T. 20 million treasury notes in circulation, they were sold against gold at a discount of 50%-60%. In December 1861, when the rate of exchange stood at 110 piastres to the pound sterling, in practice the pound fetched 190 piastres. This deterioration resulted from the recurring spread of the *qaima* as legal tender to all the provinces of the Empire.[36] The government took steps to withdraw the *qaima* from circulation, but in 1862 there were still £T. 10 million in these notes, worth only £T. 4 million in gold pounds. With the aid of another British loan, obtained through the co-operation of British advisers with the Grand Vizier, Fuad Pasha, the outstanding paper notes were withdrawn by the beginning of 1863.[37] However, in the 'seventies there was another decline in the value of the piastre in the wake of Turkey's badly deteriorated financial condition, forcing the government, with the consent of the Administration of the Public Debt, to reorganise the monetary system again in the early 'eighties. This reform, called the Kararname, based the Turkish pound on gold (at 4.40 gold dollars) and divided it into 100 piastres, the silver mejidia being worth 20 piastres.

Since various other coins circulated in the provinces,[38] the piastre assumed an important function as a common denominatory unit in terms of which their value was stated; it also served as an accounting unit for the government and in international transactions. But the relation between the piastre and the gold Turkish pound did not long remain stable: owing to the piastre's depreciation in terms of silver and the depreciation of silver in relation to gold, at the beginning of the 20th century the gold pound fetched 180-200 piastres. In 1900 there were 43 million Turkish pounds in circulation (in gold and silver coins) as against some 18 million half a century earlier.[39]

With the outbreak of war the government's printing of notes soon boosted the volume of currency in circulation until by war's end it reached £T. 160 million in paper notes and £T. 40 million in gold and silver coin. The value of the pound in relation to gold and to foreign currencies declined accordingly. In 1916 the paper pound was worth 60% in Constantinople, and only 10%-20% in the provinces.[40] By 1918-20 the pound sterling fetched an average of 3.50 Turkish pounds, and by August 1921 eight Turkish pounds. When the Treaty of Lausanne was drawn up, the value of the Turkish pound for customs purposes was calculated at 10 to the

---

[36] Stratford de Redcliffe, *Turkey,* in *Current Discussion,* Vol. I, p. 67.

[37] The *qaima* was officially withdrawn in June 1862. *Rapport de S. A. Le Ministre Des Finance à Son Altesse Le Grand-Vezir,* 23 Sept. 1863; Supplement to No. 1896 of the *Journal de Constantinople* of June 15th, 1862; A. H. Layard, *op. cit.,* pp. 6-7.

[38] It was estimated that £T. 12 million worth of foreign coins were in circulation within the boundaries of the Ottoman Empire. Cf. E. G. Mears, *op. cit.,* p. 406.

[39] *Corps de Droit Ottoman,* Vol. V, pp. 1-5. At that time too there was a large amount of foreign coins in circulation—Indian, Persian, Austrian—although the central government had expressly forbidden it. In the Levant, the French franc was widely used in commercial transactions.

[40] Cf. J. Pomiankowski, *Der Zusammenbruch des Ottomanischen Reiches,* 1928, p. 263.

pound sterling.[41] Under the Republic the currency was stabilised—temporarily at least—at 1032 piastres to the pound sterling under the Currency Protection Law of February 25th, 1930.

2. THE PUBLIC DEBT

The heavy taxes and exactions to which the Ottoman Empire's depressed population was ruthlessly subjected—the direct agricultural taxes which made up over 50% of the treasury revenue, the indirect taxes and the arbitrary price system of the monopolies—did not suffice to meet the needs of the public budget and the Sultan's court. The economy was simply incapable of bearing all this expenditure, particularly since it was in the hands of selfish and imcompetent officials and overlords. There was no lack of agricultural and mining resources in Turkey, but in the absence of administrative, managerial and technical skills and planning of the scope and direction of investment, the national product did not grow sufficiently to yield adequate taxes and savings. This made the State increasingly dependent on outside credit for financing its ordinary expenditure.

At the beginning of the 1860's the Empire's public debt was estimated at only two and a half times the country's annual public revenue (in England at that time the debt stood at twelve times the annual public revenue)[42] but even then, before the meteoric rise that took place in the 'sixties and 'seventies, the composition of the debt was unusual in that it was practically all external. Further, a large part of the liabilities were short-term, while the ability to pay of the strained treasury and the corrupt establishment was limited to the extreme.

The State's main creditors had at first been the bankers of Galata, mainly Greeks, Jews, and Armenians, apart from the Jewish *sarrafs* in Iraq, but since the middle of the century European lenders had assumed ever-increasing importance. It may be a coincidence that the Ottoman market—and as we shall see later the Egyptian one as well—opened wide to European penetration precisely at the time when large capital surpluses had begun to accumulate in Europe—but this coincidence proved of historic significance for the fate of the region.

Turkey contracted her first big loan in 1854, in connection with the Crimean War. It amounted to 55 million francs, or £ 2.3 million, and was financed by the London bank of Dent, Palmers and Company, which floated 6% bonds on the market to cover it. Of the sum of 55 million francs only about half found their way into the Imperial Treasury, for the bonds were absorbed at a 20% discount, and other deductions included floatation expenses, the bank's commission and an advance payment on interest. On the other hand, since the interest and the redemption rate were governed by the nominal value of these securities, the banks and the bondholders realised good profits and an excellent return. This situation with regard to foreign loans was to go on at least until 1875. As early as this stage, the revenue

---

[41] See following chapter, and also Administration de la Dette Publique Ottomane, *Compte-Rendu du Conseil d'Administration, 1919-1929,* Constantinople, 1921, p. x, footnote.
[42] *The Times,* October, 12th, 1861.

from Egypt's tribute—an annual £ 282,000—was set aside as a guarantee that the government would fulfil its obligations to the bondholders.[43]

The Powers, and particularly Britain and France, interested as they were in the continued existence and strengthened economy of the Ottoman Empire, were sympathetic to any applications for credit, and after 1855 backed some of the emissions with their own guarantees.[44] But the decisions with regard to investments in Turkey and to loan subscriptions were, at least until 1875, in the hands of the private bondholders and of the banks, which themselves took up part of the issues. The demand for Ottoman bonds was at first quite extensive, but it quickly dropped in the wake of the Turkish government's delay in meeting its obligations; and in 1875, when on the one hand the Empire was beset by a grave financial crisis and on the other the power struggle for influence over the "sick man of Europe" grew in intensity, the foreign interests intervened more decisively, backed less unobtrusively this time by their respective governments.

In the space of the 20 years between 1855 and 1875, Turkey had obtained 12 additional loans, the proceeds of which were used partly to meet obligations arising from loans contracted earlier (interest payments and short-term credit) and partly to cover new expenditure such as the expansion of the fleet, the repression of the revolt in Bosnia and the Sultan's tours of Europe under Abdul Aziz. By 1869 the Empire's debt was already estimated at £ 76 million, of which over £ 12 million were current debt.[45] By 1875 Turkey's liabilities added up to some 5,500 million gold francs, of nearly £ 200 million. Of these only 2,700 million had been actually received by Turkey,[46] the rest going to cover bank premia and various expenses as well as differentials of 20% to 55% between the bonds' nominal value and the discounted value at which they had been absorbed, due to the rapid deterioration of the Empire's position on the money market.[47]

The public debt accounted for the bulk of the aforementioned liabilities, followed by foreign investments in the railroads. The latter were managed by concession-holding firms, but the government guarantees which had been accorded to them, along with the fact that ownership of the lines could be transferred to the government, justified classifying these investments under the heading of liabilities of the Turkish economy. Hence these liabilities had to be paid up, or, eventually, written off when the process of expropriating the concessions began after the First World War.

Principal and interest payments on the debt added up in 1875 to £ 14 million, of which £ 12.5 million were owing to creditors abroad.[48] In the budget for 1875/6, 50% of all expenditure was earmarked for payments on account of the public

---

[43] D. C. Blaisdell, *op. cit.*, p. 48.

[44] Cf. G. Noradounghian, *op. cit.*, II, pp. 445-446.

[45] A. H. Layard, *op. cit.*, p. 16.

[46] A Turkish source, *La Turquie en voie d'industrialisation*, p. 8, estimates the amount actually received by the Ottoman treasury by 1875 at 3,000 million francs, or £ 125 million.

[47] One loan of £ 40 million, granted to Turkey in 1874 through the Ottoman Bank, was taken up by investors at just 43$^1/_2$%. Cf. D. C. Blaisdell, *op. cit.*, p. 37.

[48] Ch. Morawitz, *op. cit.*, p. 51.

debt.[49] Since most of the loans granted to Turkey through the intermediary of the banks carried guarantees by foreign governments, mainly Britain and France, the latter sent their representatives to Turkey in order to supervise the use to which the loans were being put and the arrangements made to repay principal and interest as agreed. Although the Turks did their best to restrict this supervision and the intervention of the foreign representatives as much as possible, largely by not implementing the experts' recommendations, the practice created a precedent for the later large-scale intervention of foreigners in the Empire's finances and in the management of its economy.[50]

The year 1874 was marked by a series of economic difficulties. The crops were poor; floods inflicted widespread damage; epidemics broke out in various parts of the Empire. The government was forced to provide assistance at a time when tax collection difficulties had scraped the treasury till clean. In the succeeding three or four years the rebellions in Herzegovina and Bulgaria, the wars with Serbia and Montenegro and particularly the war of 1877/8 with Russia blew up the serious financial crisis to disastrous proportions. In October 1875 the Ottoman government decided to promulgate a decree under which as of January 1st, 1876, only half of the coupons coming due on external debts would be redeemed in cash, the remainder to be paid in bonds carrying 5% interest that would mature five years later.[51] Within three months it had become apparent that the government would be unable to abide even by this new arrangement, for coupons coming due remained unredeemed. Hardest hit were creditors holding bonds that carried no foreign government guarantees and to whose service no specific revenue, such as the tribute of Egypt, was assigned, their securities being guaranteed only by the treasury's general revenue.

The reaction of the bondholders' representatives to the decree of 1875 was sharp: they charged that it was illegal and contrary to the capitulations.[52] The war with Russia of necessity postponed any decision on the future of the debt; but at the Congress of Berlin in 1878 the creditors' representatives succeeded in having a general plan for funding the Ottoman Debt included in the conference proceedings.[53] After a short time, however, in 1879, Turkey was completely bankrupt and informed the foreign representations that a new settlement would have to be arrived at, for she was not only unable to pay anything on account of principal but also found it impossible to meet even half of her interest payments to creditors.[54]

[49] *Budget des Recettes et des Dépenses, 1875-6,* Constantinople, 1875.
[50] Cf. *Reports of Lord Hobart,* 1863, *passim.*
[51] For text and explanation of the decree see *La Crise Financière Ottomane devant les Capitulations,* Paris, 1876, p. 1, and *passim.*
[52] *Idem,* pp. 4 ff.
[53] *Parliamentary Papers,* Cd. 2136, Turkey, No. 39, 1878, pp. 257-271.
[54] While the Ottoman treasury's revenue had gradually risen from about £ 15 million at mid-century to £ 22 million in 1874, fully 55% of this revenue, or £ 12 million, went to serve the debt. But these were revenue estimates of official budget publications, converted to sterling at the official rate; according to contemporary sources a realistic assessment of the 1875/6 budget was an expenditure of £ 32 million and a revenue of not more than £ 15.3 million as contrary to the official estimate of £ 19.1 million. *Papers on the Eastern Question,* "Commercial and Financial Aspects", by John Holmes, 1877, p. 10.

The budget for 1880/81, doubtless drawn up in an attempt to prove to the creditors just how hopeless the Empire's financial position was, provided for an operating deficit of £T. 6 million[55] plus a current debt of £T. 20 million, yielding a total deficit of £T. 26 million.[56] In view of this situation the creditors obtained from their governments an intervention on a broader scale than similar interventions in the past,[57] and the Powers forced the Sultan to promulgate the "Decree of Muharrem" of December 20th, 1881[58] setting up an Administration of the Ottoman Public Debt[59] and delegating to it the collection of certain government revenues[60] which had been placed in 1880 under the authority of representatives of the creditors and the Ottoman Bank. Turkey had preferred to come to a direct agreement with the creditors' representatives[61] and to set up a special Administration for this purpose, rather than court the risk of the Powers taking matters into their own hands under the resolutions of the Congress of Berlin.[62]

The Administration of the Ottoman Public Debt, whose seat was Constantinople, grouped together representatives of Britain and Holland (one joint representative), France, Germany, Austria-Hungary, Italy, Turkey (which had creditors among its nationals too) and the Ottoman Imperial Bank, which was financed, as we have seen, by foreign capital. Formally these representatives were each appointed by the association of bondholders in his country, but in practice the appointments were made in very close co-ordination with the governments concerned. As a result most of the delegates were experienced not only in finance but also in public administration, and knew how to look out for the interests of their countries. A

---

[55] A revenue of £T. 16 million and an expenditure of £T. 22 million.

[56] *Budget 1880-81,* Constantinople, 1880, pp. 3-4 and *passim.*

[57] As early as 1860, at an early stage in the growth of the Ottoman Empire's indebtedness and in the wake of the Hatti Hümayun's promise of a financial reform, an advisory council of foreign experts—an Austrian, an Englishman and a Frenchman—was constituted into a Higher Council of Finances that supervised the State's financial administration. The representatives of bondholders of the external debt were also co-opted on to the commissions charged with collecting the revenue assigned to the service of these bonds long before the Administration of the Ottoman Public Debt, for which this served as a precedent, came into being. Cf. D. C. Blaisdell, *op. cit.,* pp. 26, 31.

[58] So named for the Muslim month during which it was promulgated. For text, see our Appendix 12. The official text is reproduced in *Corps de Droit Ottoman,* Vol. V, pp. 69-95, and the English translation in *Parliamentary Papers,* Cd. 5736, 1911, Vol. CIII, pp. 672-690. Upon its promulgation the Decree was published in French and English in Imperial Ottoman Debt, *Decree dated December 8/20,* 1881, with Its Annexes, London, Council of Foreign Bondholders.

[59] For the history of the Ottoman Debt see, among others, Ch. Morawitz, *op. cit.,* pp. 225-364; A. Du Velay, *op. cit.,* pp. 421-547.

[60] See below, p. 67.

[61] Most of the investigators of the history of the Debt and its Administration believe that the "Decree of Muharrem" was not a unilateral decree but a sort of agreement between the Ottoman government and its creditors. At the same time, most of them feel that it did not have the character of an international instrument in the sense of a free intergovernmental agreement.

[62] Tracts on Finance, *La Turquie et sa dette,* 1881, p. 10. Incidentally, according to the Treaty of Berlin, Turkey was supposed to pay £T. 35 million to Russia in reparations for the War of 1877. This payment was not included under the "Decree of Muharrem" and only on May 14th, 1882, was a settlement signed in Constantinople between Russia and Turkey, providing for yearly instalments of £T. 350,000. The revenues from the tithe and from livestock taxes in four provinces of the Empire were assigned to these payments. Cf. D. C. Blaisdell, *op. cit.,* p. 91.

Frenchman and an Englishman served alternately as Chairman of the Administration.[63] The "Decree of Muharrem" invested the Turkish government with the authority to supervise the activities of the Administration, but under the Administration's statutes the government representatives had an advisory status only.

The Debt, which had added up to £ 191 million that year, was reduced to £ 106 million[64] in a compromise between the Ottoman government—which demanded that the debt be calculated on the basis of the price actually paid by the original investors in the securities, i.e. at the original discount—and the creditors, who put forward as their minimum claim the price of the securities as listed in the prospectus of issue.

The revenues whose collection was transferred to the Administration so that the proceeds could be applied to the Debt were the income from the salt and tobacco monopolies and taxes and excise on stamps, spirits, the fisheries (partial) and silk. Some of the revenue from provincial tributes, particularly those deriving from the provisions of the Treaty of Berlin, was also to be applied to the service of the Debt. In 1907 all these revenues, which were estimated to constitute one-third to one-quarter of the total State income, were supplemented by the 3% customs surtax added to the former *ad valorem* rate of 8%.[65] If any surpluses were attained over the payments due, 75% of them were to be transferred to the Ottoman treasury. An earlier ordinance, in 1903, had amended the Muharrem Decree mainly in favour of the government. Article 17 of the Muharrem Decree stipulated that all the revenues of the Administration of the Public Debt—and of course all its expenditure as well—would figure in the budget of the Empire.

In time the national composition of the main creditors underwent a change. As we have seen, in 1881 they were the French and the British, but about the turn of the century Germany replaced Britain. By 1914 the French held 60% of the Ottoman debt, the Germans 21% and the British 14%. If we take only the holdings of these three nations into account, they divide up as follows:[66]

TABLE III

French, German and British Holdings in the Debt of the Ottoman Empire, 1914
(in millions of francs)

Debt Type	French		German		British	
	Sum	%	Sum	%	Sum	%
Public Debt	2,454	63	867	22	578	15
Private Enterprises	903	53	553	33	230	14
Total	3,357	60	1,420	25	808	15

---

[63] This arrangement was to be operative for five years under Article Five of the Decree. The argument for it was that France and Britain represented the interest of the main creditors, which was indeed the case at the time the Administration was established.

[64] Ch. Morawitz, *op. cit.*, p. 245.

[65] It should be noted that by collecting this surtax the Administration acted mainly in keeping with the interests of the Great Powers. who desired to direct the revenue from this source to meeting the Ottoman government's obligations in Macedonia.

[66] *Les Intérêts financiers de la France dans l'Empire Ottoman,* juillet 1919, quoted in E. G. Mears, ed., *op. cit.*, p. 357.

The German share in the Empire's finances and economic enterprises began to rise rapidly after the award of the first railroad concession to the Deutsche Bank in 1888 in return for a loan of DM 30 million, equivalent to £ 1 million or £T. 1.65 million. In the five short years following this agreement German exports to Turkey rose by 350%—and her imports from Turkey by 700%.[67] The semi-official explanation tendered by the Germans for this development was mainly economic, but amazingly frank: Germany's population was growing, the country's character was becoming industrial and commercial rather than agricultural, her international contacts were expanding, her dependence on international economic relations was increasing, and she stood in need of an assured supply of raw materials and food along with an assured market for her products.[68]

The highwater mark of this German activity[69] was reached in 1903, with the granting of the Baghdad railway concession. Shortly afterward, when the Young Turks came to power in 1908, and particularly after the deposition of Abdul Hamid II in 1909, they made an attempt at a rapprochement with England and France, but the refusal of these two Powers to grant them an additional loan of $ 30 million after protracted negotiations with Javid Bey resulted in a reorientation toward Germany. The latter quickly provided the desired loan in conjuction with Austria-Hungary.[70]

Two aspects of the operation of the Administration of the Public Debt are particularly worth noting. One is the fact that the State had been divested of part of its sovereign authority—the collection of specific State revenues. Their management was delegated to the Administration, which paid off the creditors directly. This derogation of the State's authority was highlighted by the fact that the Ottoman government's relations with the Administration were not always smooth, owing at least partly to the fact that some of the Administration's members were at the same time directly representing the interests of concession-holders, and particularly of the railroad companies. Be that as it may, we have already noted the Administration's interference with the government's attempts to reform the State budget structure by modifying the principles and collection methods of the tithe.

But at the same time the Administration introduced modern fiscal administration into the Ottoman economy, or at least into part of it, and this was destined to have a definite economic and educational significance. Under its efficient management larger sums were collected than were needed to meet debt payments, creating substantial surpluses. We have noted that 75% of the latter were turned over to the Ottoman treasury: between 1903 and 1920 it collected £T. 11 million in this manner.[71]

Not satisfied with tax collection, the Administration reorganised the marketing of produce in the fields which had been assigned to it. It sought to raise agricultural

---

[67] E. M. Earle, *op. cit.*, pp. 36-37.

[68] Karl Helfferich, *Die Deutsche Türkenpolitik,* Berlin, 1921, p. 7.

[69] The Germans played a central role in reorganising and training the Turkish army from 1882 on. The Ottoman Empire's conscription regulations were also framed under the influence of German advisers.

[70] K. Helfferich, *op. cit.*, pp. 23 ff.

[71] *Compte-Rendu du Conseil d'Administration,* 1919-20, Annexe No. 6.

yields by soil conservation, pest control, the distribution of seeds and seedlings and agricultural counselling.[72] The consequent improvement of farm incomes paved the way for higher tax receipts. Higher export proceeds were another result; so was the development of processing industries in salt and silk, for instance. The Administration's average annual income from the revenues it administered rose from an original £T. 2-2.5 million to £T. 3-3.5 million and then to £T. 4.5 million on the eve of the First World War and to £T. 11-12 million at the beginning of the 1920's.[73] Although this was the time when the Empire's finances—outside the sector controlled by the Administration—were the weakest, foreign banks and other companies began to invest again in Turkey's economy, and particularly in the railway system, on the strength of the Administration's guarantees that if their profits fell below a specified rate of return they would be supplemented out of the Administration's revenues.[74] One aspect of this development was, as we have noted, that after 1888 the Administration could be said to have become the government's agent with regard to implementing the "kilometric guarantees" that were included in the various concessions. This encouraged the expansion of the railway network, although on the other hand it turned the Administration into an interested party in the disputes that occasionally broke out between the government and the concessionnaires over the interpretation of their concession agreements.

Another beneficial result of the Administration's etablishment was the inproved terms from which Turkey benefited on the money market. Her securities, which had been absorbed only at 40% discounts and had to yield 5% to 6% of their nominal value, were purchased after 1881 at 80% to 90% of their face value and the interest rate was reduced to 3% and 4%.[75] The Administration employed about 5,000 persons, of whom only 1% or 2% were Europeans, in its collection and other activities, which were conducted through 700 agencies throughout the Empire.[76]

During the First World War the Administration continued to operate, although its Council no longer represented all the countries: the British and the French pulled out immediately and after Italy's entry into the war in 1915 only Germans, Austro-Hungarians and Turks were left. At the beginning of 1915 this rump Administration, now officially presided over by a Turk, decided to freeze all payments due on account of capital and interest to nationals of the Allied Powers. Upon the victory of the latter, however, and their occupation of Turkey, the Administration was taken over by the British, the French and the Italians: the representatives of the Central Powers had to withdraw[77] under Article 19 of the Mudros Armistice Agreement, which forced all German and Austrian nationals to leave Turkey.

---

[72] *Reports of the Ottoman Public Debt,* London (from 1884 on) particularly 1919-1920, p. 11; Ch. Morawitz, *op. cit.,* pp. 310-311.

[73] *Rapport sur les opérations de l'année 1299* (1883-1884), pp. 1-2; *Compte-Rendu 1919-20,* p. VIII. The substantial fall in the value of the Turkish pound must, of course, be taken into account when assessing this increase.

[74] C. C. Blaisdell, *op. cit.,* p. 3.

[75] *Ibid.,* p. 6.

[76] *Compte-Rendu 1919-20,* p. 27.

[77] *Idem,* p. XI.

During the war the rump Administration had fulfilled an important function in the implementation of Turkey's monetary policy. It played the part of agent and trustee in the allocation of credit from Germany and Austria-Hungary and in guaranteeing £T. 6.6 million in currency notes issued by Turkey at the beginning of the war as a counterpart to Turkish gold deposited in the central banks of Germany and Austria upon the Ottoman Bank's abandonment of its currency-issuing monopoly.[78]

Under the Treaty of Sèvres, imposed on Turkey in 1920 and providing for the establishment of a Financial Commission of the victorious nations to manage Turkey's financial affairs, the future Administration of the Public Debt was to consist only of Englishmen, Frenchman, Italians and representatives of the Ottoman Bank. This body was also to be charged with going over the Administration's wartime transactions and debiting the Turkish government where needed. But as Mustafa Kemal's rule spread in 1919-22 the Administration was progressively deprived of several of its powers and the matter was brought up at the negotiations of 1922-23 in Lausanne along with the whole question of the Ottoman Debt.[79]

The Turkish delegates were successful in eliminating from the text of the final treaty any reaffirmation of the "Decree of Muharrem" or of its amendment of 1903. After wearying and protracted negotiations it was agreed to set the Ottoman Debt at £ 130 million and to impose only £ 84.6 million of it on Republican Turkey, which had lost all its non-Turkish provinces. The remainder was divided among the other countries of the Ottoman succession.[80] Turkey's own indebtedness was to be liquidated in annual instalments of £ 5.8 million, but this arrangement too proved impossible to implement. A new agreement signed in Paris in 1928 was followed in 1933 by a more specific one reducing Turkey's debt to 7 million gold Turkish pounds (i.e. approximately 70 million paper pounds) to be paid off in annual payments of 700,000 gold pounds or 7 million paper pounds.[81] The debt was thus to be liquidated in 1944, although according to a statement made in 1958 by Turkey's Minister of Finance the payments were extended and were not finally completed until the 'fifties.

---

[78] As the war wore on the volume of currency issued aggregated £T 160 million although no additional gold was deposited as cover.

[79] *Compte-Rendu 1919-20*, p. vii, and *1920-21*, p. vii.

[80] Thus, for example, Greece was to pay 11% of the total £ 130 million, Syria and Lebanon 8% and Iraq 5½%.

[81] See the "Türkische Post" of November 1st and December 31st, 1932. This settlement actually meant that the consequences of any devaluation of the Turkish pound would be borne by the creditors. For information about the fluctuations of Turkey's currency during and immediately after the First World War, see Captain C. H. Courthope-Munroe, *General Report on the Trade and Economic Condition of Turkey for the Year 1919*, Dept. of Overseas Trade, London; & in the 1920's, *La Turquie Contemporaine*, pp. 192-193.

3. THE PATTERNS OF PRODUCTION AND SERVICES IN THE OTTOMAN ECONOMY IN THE 19TH AND EARLY 20TH CENTURIES

Taxes, rent and the barest subsistence consumed the entire income of the peasant in the Ottoman Empire—and more: he stood in desperate need of credit not only for his farm but for his own minimal living expenses, particularly in years of low prices or poor crops. The only credit of which he could avail himself was provided at usurious terms, for with minor exceptions any assistance granted by the government or by public financial institutions was in practice at the disposal of the wealthy and the influential alone. This deprived the peasant completely of any investment capital, and inadequate investment was among the main reasons for the depressed condition of agriculture in the Ottoman Empire.

But it was not the only one. There were other obstacles to development, such as deficient transportation system, the lack of security in the villages and in the country as a whole, and manpower shortage—particularly in areas populated by Muslims, who were liable to conscription and whose farming skills were limited.[82] Further, heavy taxation and the lack of any legal protection against his oppressors effectively deprived the peasant of any economic incentive. The activities undertaken towards the end of the prewar period by the Anatolian Railway Company and the Administration of the Public Debt, designed though they were to draw greater benefit from the land through mechanisation, seed selection, the planting of orchards, etc., were too limited in scope to solve the problem of Ottoman agriculture as a whole.[83] Cultivation methods—ploughing, sowing, planting, irrigation and harvesting—remained primitive. The work was done by hand or by animal power—camels, water buffaloes and donkeys—except in European districts or in areas farmed by Greeks, where mechanisation was beginning to spread.

The excessive number of small holdings was another obstacle to agricultural development. In the Asian provinces of the Empire, on the eve of the First World War, the size of the farm units ranged from 0.1 to 8 hectares, the larges frequency concentration being around 2.5 hectares, or about six acres. Under dry-farming a unit of such size could never support a family, and the overparcellation of the holdings prevented efficient planning, proper rotation and the use of modern equipment.

Yet the Empire occupied an important place in agricultural production, and was even a respectable exporter of produce, owing mainly to favourable natural conditions, and particularly to the region's climatic advantages, which told even under the backward social and economic system. One must bear in mind that since there was no irrigation system to speak of, the Empire's agriculture was all dry-

---

[82] A small number of agricultural schools were set up in the second half of the 19th century, such as the one at Büyük Halkalı near Istanbul or the veterinarian school that was attached to the military academy, but these were negligible in view of the colossal needs. A report published in 1850 in the "Journal de Constantinople" by an expert of Moldavian origin named M. Jonescu blamed inadequate skills, shortages of labour and working capital, and poor transportation for the low state of Ottoman agriculture.

[83] Ch. Morawitz, *op. cit.*, pp. 204-212.

farming except in Mesopotamia richly endowed in water surface and underground reserves, though inadequately exploited,[84] as a result of which there was only one crop year, and this generally on only one-third of the cultivated area, the rest being fallowed.

There were, of course, considerable differences in the character of farm production as well as in yields between the various parts of the Empire, with its sharp variations in climate and soil types from the fertile soil of Moldavia to the desert sands of Arabia.[85] As a result agricultural production was quite varied, the specialities being wheat, barley, tobacco, grapes, maize, rice, dates, olives, almonds, citrus, silk, flax and livestock, particularly goats and sheep. Wheat and barley together accounted for an average of 80% of the cultivated area, yielding some 6 million tons of grain. Yet although Turkey exported wheat grain she was forced to import wheat flour, mainly because of transportation difficulties between the producer villages and the consumer city, which often found it easier to get the grain by sea, from abroad, but also because the local produce was of poor quality.[86]

Cotton, which was to regain an important place in the mid-20th century in the agriculture of several Middle Eastern countries besides Egypt, had been grown on wide tracts in Anatolia, Syria and Macedonia and even supplied an appreciable part of Britain's demand until 1780. But later this crop was hit by the economic depression that swept the whole Empire. It was not until the 1860's that the Turkish government earnestly began to encourage it again, an Imperial Cotton Commission being set up in Smyrna; but as the 19th century drew to its end Turkey had not yet become a cotton exporter again.[87]

Silk, which had furnished the basis for one of the industries with the finest tradition in the Middle East, also suffered from the crisis of the first half of the 19th century and was again given more attention by the government in the second half. The measures taken to strengthen it included the introduction of new silkworm egg selection methods in 1885 and, three years later, the establishment at Brusa of a central Silk Institute where growers from the whole Empire received their training. Between 1890 and 1910 about 60 million mulberry trees were planted on an area of 130,000 acres, and in 1913 the Ottoman Empire occupied fourth place among the world's silk producers after Japan, China and Italy. But silk growing was hit hard by the First World War and required extensive rehabilitation in the 1920's.[88]

In the second half of the 19the century the Empire's main farm export products were tobacco, which accounted for 25% of the total; and raisins, wheat and barley, which together brought in another 25% in good seasons. These four crops, therefore, accounted for one-half of all agricultural exports, and sometimes more.

---

[84] Cf. Adriano Lanzoni, "La Mesopotania economica", 1910, reproduced in Ch. Issawi (ed.), *The Economic History of the Middle East 1800-1914*, Ch. 6.

[85] M. A. Ubicini, *op. cit.*, I, pp. 313.

[86] E. G. Mears, ed., *op. cit.*, pp. 284-293.

[87] The government's attempts at reviving cotton growing were not kept up very long and did not bear lasting fruit, both because of the population's indifference and because of the government's preoccupation with other problems. Cf. W. O. Henderson, *The Lancashire Cotton Famine, 1861-1865*, 1934, p. 46; *Parliamentary Papers*, 1865, LVII, pp. 787-827.

[88] *Le Commerce du Levant*, August 20th, 1935; D. C. Blaisdell, *op. cit.*, p. 111.

One of the greatest obstacles to the development of Turkey's agriculture, the difficulties of transport, tended to favour subsistence farming and to discourage the growing of crops that would have qualified for the outside market but were not in demand at home.[89] On the eve of World War I, major attempts were made to improve this state of affairs, mainly through a more advanced rail network; and in fact contemporary reports by foreign consuls, and particularly the British, give evidence of a rise in the production as well as in the export of agricultural commodities at that time.[90] Unfortunately the process was interrupted by the political complications that supervened, culminating in the war.

The reforms and the nationalist movements of the second half of the 19th century prompted more interest in industrial development. This was being severely handicapped by rigid and absolete production methods, by the low quality and high prices of the products with which the Middle East sought to emulate the West, and by the penetration of Western goods, rendered easier under the prevailing Capitulatory system. At the same time, the Western products were also sweeping the ground from under the traditional crafts and other industries which had been famous in the past, such as copper work, china, the food industries—especially oil—silk textiles, and rugs and carpets. As late as the second half of the 18th century Ottoman manufactures were still fulfilling an important role not only locally but also in other countries. This applied mainly to cotton, woollen and silk textiles. While products made in village homes and in the smaller provincial towns served only local consumption, the manufactures of Istanbul, Cairo, Aleppo and Damascus were also produced for export, both to other provinces of the Empire and to foreign countries. As a matter of fact, the industrial centres and sectors most affected by foreign competition and capitulatory restrictions were those with widest contacts with foreign markets; while domestic handicrafts deep inside the country as well as goods with indigenous aesthetic value, still enjoying comparative advantage, suffered relatively less.[91]

The Ottoman Empire at the close of the 18th century and Mehmed Ali's Egypt at the beginning of the 19th attempted to protect themselves against increasing European competition, and to encourage local industry, by setting up monopolies, but the European Powers' insistence on the implementation of the Capitulations and commercial treaties made the protection of home products difficult if not impossible, particularly after 1838. In the relatively short period between 1812 and 1841 the number of silk looms in Scutari and Tirnovo declined from 2000 to 200; the output of all types of silk products in Anatolia in the first half of the 19th century was one-tenth of what it had been in the second half of the 18th; and in the same period of time the value of Aleppo's output of cotton and silk cloth fell from 100 million to 7 or 8 million piastres.[92] Wars devastated the countryside and impoverished the country; the India trade was diverted around the Cape of Good

---

[89] M. A. Ubicini, *op. cit.,* I, p. 317.
[90] E. M. Earle, *op. cit.,* pp. 230-231.
[91] Cf. Ö. C. Sarç, "The Tanzimat and Our Industry", reproduced in Ch. Issawi (ed.), *The Economic History of the Middle East 1800-1914,* pp. 48-59.
[92] M. A. Ubicini, *op. cit.,* I, p. 339-341.

Hope; the structure and the organisation of production and the crafts militated against the spread of occupational skills; and the government's indifference to industrial development, accompanied by heavy taxation and autocratic administration, completed the work of destruction.

The establishment in the 19th century of extensive public utilities by foreign capital, or with its assistance, did a good deal to aid the development of mining on the shores of the Bosphorus and of certain industrial enterprises. On the other hand the attempt to develop iron and steel production as the basis of modern industry on the European model was on the whole unsuccessful. The reasons were partly technical, as in the projected works at Bashiktash and Istanbul that were never completed, and partly economic, as at the mill on the Bosphorus that produced cast iron at 50 piastres per 100 kilogrammes when imported cast iron was being marketed locally at 42 piastres after customs.[93]

The Ottoman conquerors had been interested in the exploitation of mines, both because they yielded them tithes and other revenue and because precious metals, mainly silver, were a raw material in minting coins. However, the foreign capital invested in the mines abandoned them gradually after the Ottoman conquest, following restrictive measures by the authorities, including a ban on taking silver and lead out of the Empire. The funds of local mining operators, on the other hand, were too limited to allow them to perfect production methods. While a new class of entrepreneurs, consisting of *multazimin* and high officials who had enriched themselves in various ways, did begin to emerge in this field,[94] and while in the 19th century foreign concessionaires began to display a definite interest in the exploitation of mining riches, on the whole it may be said that this sector was largely neglected until the First World War.

Coal production, carried on mainly by the Société Minière d'Héraclée, rose in the Empire from 61,000 tons in 1865, first year of production at that company's mines, to 827,000 tons in 1913. Output fell during the war but began to pick up again in the 'twenties.[95] The Turks blamed the company for the relatively low output at the mines, which were nationalised in the late 1930's. Copper production, neglected in the 19th century (the number of operating mines had fallen during the course of the century from 84 to 14), picked up after incentive measures were applied in 1892 and had risen by 1916 to 92,000 tons of ore or 19,000 tons of copper cement.[96]

Chrome was discovered in the Empire in 1848, and although some of the reserves were later lost to Serbia and Greece the Anatolian fields were so rich that this metal soon became one of Turkey's chief mineral resources, the country taking its place among the world's leading chrome producers. Under the Republic, the German, French and Swedish interests in the exploitation of chrome were progressively liquidated.[97]

---

[93] *Ibid.*, pp. 342-343.
[94] R. Anhegger, *op. cit.*, I, pp. 111-112, 127.
[95] *L'Industrie Minière de la Turquie,* Publié par le "Türkofis", Istanbul, 1935.
[96] *Türkische Post,* January 7th, 1933.
[97] *Idem,* March 15th, 1933.

The value of the production of the Empire's mines aggregated in 1913 about £T. 2 million, or roughly $ 10 million.[98] This represented one-fourth of the country's industrial production (including mining).

Out of the 1,587 "factories" listed in the Turkish Trade Annual for 1900, only some 600 could qualify, according to Morawitz,[99] for the name of industrial enterprises, the others being small shops supplying local demand. Both categories of enterprises, however, suffered from the competition of foreign products. Another source lists the number of industrial enterprises in the country at 269, employing as a criterion a capital of over £T. 1,000, an annual payroll of at least 750 day's wages and a minimum total power rating of 5 H.P.—supplied generally by steam. Of these 269 plants, 219 were owned by individuals, 28 by companies and 22 by the State. The industrial census of 1913 lists only 200 industrial enterprises, all the rest being described as small workshops. Of these 200 plants, which employed 17,000 workers (i.e., an average of 85 per enterprises), 68% produced food—this includes a large number of flour mills—and 14% were spinning and weaving mills. The rest, spread across the country, turned out bricks, glass, leather, arms and ammunition, and rugs and carpets. In the provincial areas of Iraq, Syria and Lebanon handicraft and village industry constituted the bulk of the manufacturing sector, but both the traditional and the emerging modern industries were adversely affected by competing imported European goods. Under conditions of inadequate protection, of limited domestic effective demand and of non-competitive technology and productivity, modern industrial development had small chances only. Consequently, well-established and exportable handicraft enjoyed greater comparative advantage and even, intermittently, a certain upsurge, in particular in Lebanon and Syria.[100] The aggregate value of industrial production on the eve of the First World War was 6.5 million gold Turkish pounds, or over $ 30 million,[101] not including mining; but the World War and the subsequent war with Greece destroyed many of these plants and weakened even further the country's precarious industrial structure.

Three industries in particular were severely affected by the war. The first, as we have noted earlier, was silk. Next came the rug industry, whose output in 1913 was still worth 663,000 gold Turkish pounds or over $ 3 million —10% of the Empire's total industrial production. After the war this industry lost its importance both as a producer and as an exporter. The third industry that was similarly affected was tobacco, although after the war it recovered more quickly. In 1913 the Empire produced 75,000 tons of tobacco, of which 46,400 were exported,[102] yielding over 3 million gold Turkish pounds (including cigarettes). The war combined with the decline in demand for Oriental tobaccos to cut Turkey's production by half, but by the 1930's it climbed back to its former level. A certain success was registered by the paper works at Smyrna and the tarboosh (fez) factory at Eyub.

---

[98] E. G. Mears, *op. cit.,* p. 313.
[99] Ch. Morawitz, *op. cit.,* p. 180.
[100] Cf. Ch. 6 (on Iraq), pp. 179 ff., and Ch. 3 (on Syria), pp. 226 ff., in Ch. Issawi (ed.), *op. cit.*
[101] *La Turquie Contemporaine,* p. 140.
[102] Included in *agricultural* exports.

Adequate transportation facilities are of utmost importance in particular in extensive areas, such as the Ottoman Empire, for the sake of efficient administration, security, tax collection and economic activities. Severe shortages in this field exposed and amplified difficulties and failures in economic performance.

The first to develop modern transport in the Ottoman Empire were the British. As early as the beginning of the 1830's Colonel Chesney[103] proposed to William IV to connect the Mediterranean with the Persian Gulf and India by rail, river and sea, and a Parliamentary Commission approved the required allocation for the project.[104] Twenty years went by, however, without any action being taken, and meantime ambitious railway schemes were conceived by British and other companies.[105] While the planners stressed the benefit that these schemes would bring to Turkey—by enabling her to develop mining, for instance, and by speeding the traffic of passengers and goods—it was clear that uppermost in the mind of the British planners was a quick and safe way to India.[106]

In the thirty years between 1856 and 1886 railways were laid between Izmir and Aydın, between Izmir and Kasaba, and between Mersin, Tarsus and Adana (in Anatolia), and between Çernavoda and Constanza, and Rusçuk and Varna (in the Balkans). Istanbul was finally connected by rail with Vienna on August 12th, 1888, under the concession granted to Baron Hirsch back in 1869. The Hedjaz railway, construction of which was begun by the State itself in 1900, was completed in 1908, though not to the point that had been originally envisaged as the terminal. The declared purpose of the line was to serve pilgrims to the Holy Cities of Mecca and Medina, although it was evidently also designed to give the government easier access to this remote region. Construction was financed by 20 million francs contributed by the Muslims of the Empire in response to an appeal by Sultan Abdul Hamid II; by a series of special levies on stamps, passports and various commercial transactions; and by a deduction of 10% from the government officials' salaries.[107]

Investments in transportation, particularly in railroads, were given a special fillip under the Administration of the Ottoman Public Debt, which attempted to bring in line the safeguarding of the interests of the bondholders, the stabilisation of the

---

[103] Cf. F. R. Chesney, *Narrative of the Euphrates Expedition carried on by order of the British Government,* London, 1868, pp. v-vi.

[104] F. R. Chesney, *op. cit.,* pp. 148-149; also *Reports on the Navigation of the Euphrates,* submitted to the Government by Captain Chesney, 1833, p. 1; *The Expedition for the Survey of the Rivers Euphrates and Tigris,* London, 1850, Vol. I, pp. x-xiii.

[105] Cf. *The Proposed Imperial (Medjidieh) Ottoman Railway,* 1857, pp. 3 ff.; Wilhelm von Pressel, *op. cit.,* pp. 52-53; F. R. Chesney, *Narrative of the Euphrates Expedition,* London, 1868.

[106] "... the Imperial (Medjidieh) Ottoman Railway will be the shortest and most direct route to India under every possible circumstance, and whatever may be the changes which time may bring about in the European systems of railway communication". (*The Proposed Imperial Ottoman Railway,* 1857, p. 13)—It appears that at that time the British considered a trans-Turkish railway a better investment as a road to India than the Suez Canal (See Chapter on the Suez Canal, below).

[107] *Archiv für Eisenbahnwesen,* Berlin, 1914, pp. 1063-1064. In 1909, when part of the railway had been left uncompleted, it was whispered that it would never be finished since it provided the government with such a good excuse for raising contributions (M. Hartmann, *Der Islamische Orient,* II, Leipzig, 1909, p. 534).

economy, i.a., through improved infrastructure. Also the predilection of the sultans for railroads accorded to them high priority.[108]

The main development in the field of railways took place in 1888, when Dr. Alfred Kaulla in the name of the Deutsche Bank was granted, as we have seen, a concession to build a railway line from Haydar Pasha to Ankara. The same agreement awarded to the Germans the operation of the Istanbul-Izmir line for 99 years. As already indicated above, the Anatolian Company which was formed to exploit this concession also later launched the Baghdad Railway Company with the object of building a line that would cross the whole length of Anatolia and connect Europe with the Persian Gulf. The original scheme envisaged a 4,500-kilometre line consisting of a trunk line of 2,700 kilometres and branch lines adding up to 1,800 kilometres.[109] By the time the First World War intervened, the line had been laid to Jarablus on the Euphrates, and another section had been completed between Samarra and Baghdad. The whole scheme was not fully implemented until 1940, when Baghdad was finally connected with Mosul.[110]

Until 1910 the financial position of the railways could not be described as satisfactory, but by then the main investments had been completed, and efficient management set up for smooth operation and increased revenues. By 1914 the return was sufficient to do away with all government payments under the kilometric guarantees.

The promise of more roads and communication canals had appeared in the Hatti Hümayun of 1856. The Empire did have 6,500 kilometres of roads, but half of them were in urgent need of repair and much of the rest in poor condition; many of these roads were completely impassable in the winter months. During the second half of the 19th century several regulations were issued with the object of improving roads, but even when there were enough funds to begin work it had to be abandoned sooner or later for lack of allocations, so that the highway network remained as inadequate as before. There were a few exceptions: the roads used by the Sultan and his retinue, those serving rail junctions, a few post roads such as the one from Alexandria to Aleppo or the one from Beirut to Damascus, and a few strategic highways such as the one connecting Trabzon with Erzurum and Bayazıt. So long as the main transport was on camel back or by means of draught animals, the primitive roads more or less served their purpose; but as the automobile moved in and markets expanded they became a serious handicap. The government, which was trying to save money on roads, could have recouped the expense with increased tax collections if the roads had been built, leading to the development of market crops and expanded production.[111]

The harbours of Istanbul, Izmir, Salonika and Beirut were operated by concession-holding companies, and in 1909 the Anatolian Railway Company and its subsidiary were awarded concessions for Haydar Pasha, Istanbul's port on the Asian side of the Bosphorus. As a result of the various improvements carried out in

---

[108] Cf. our Chapters on the Foreign Concessions and the Public Debt.
[109] Wilhelm von Pressel, *op. cit.*, p. 6. Cf. also Leon Dominian, *op. cit.*, pp. 257-263.
[110] I.B.R.D., *The Economic Development of Iraq*, Baltimore, 1952, p. 314.
[111] Ch. Morawitz, *op. cit.*, pp. 186-188.

the port of Istanbul it was able to handle 17.4 million tons of cargo in 1913 as against 4.9 million tons in 1875/6 and 7.5 million in 1905. Turkey's fleet added up in 1914 to 195 steam vessels—of which 76 were subsequently lost in the war—with an aggregate displacement of 110,000 tons. There were also a number of sailing vessels. After the war the steam tonnage stood at 15,000 tons, and the sail tonnage at 4,000. The rehabilitation of the fleet got under way in 1924.[112]

The government devoted some attention to the mails, which were first organised at the beginning of the 18th century, and to telegraph services.[113] A central post-office department was established in 1840, and a general administration of posts and telegraphs in 1870, under the ministry of the Interior; but until the First World War the postal services were backward and the total number of letters sent out annually averaged one *per capita*. One of the reasons for the slowness of the mails was that postage fees for different destinations within the Empire were not uniform; at the same time, many letters went through the mails unstamped. The local post-office service in Istanbul was suspended for a time owing to a flood of anonymous letters to the Sultan's palace, but the inhabitants could avail themselves of the services of the French, British, Russian, German and Austrian post-offices, each of which was licensed to operate in the Turkish capital and had offices and stamps of its own. In 1874 Turkey appealed to the Universal Postal Congress at Berne that these offices be closed but in vain. Measures taken against them inside the country were equally unsuccessful, owing to the strenuous opposition of the Powers, which considered them their privilege under the Capitulations.

The condition of the telegraphs, operated efficiently by the Eastern Telegraph Company, was more statisfactory. There were 36,640 kilometres of lines in 1912. Both the post-office and the telegraph were subject to censorship, which interfered with the speed of their operation and hence with the country's internal and external economic activity,[114] not to mention civil rights. The censorship also bedevilled the authorities' relations with foreign residents, to whom the same restrictions applied unless they were diplomats.

It is interesting to trace the beneficial influence of the establishment of these public services on the State revenue and general economic activity. They enabled both the government and the Administration of the Public Debt to function more smoothly, since tax and excise collections mounted as merchants and producers found their turnovers and incomes rising amidst the sellers' market which began to develop with better transport and communications, particularly by rail. Thus while before 1890 the government's annual collections from Smyrna Province averaged £T 160,000, when Smyrna was connected by rail with Aydın and Kasaba the revenue for 1890 rose to £T 2 million. The main items making up the latter figure were the tithe (£T 600,000), the Debt Administration's revenue from tobacco and from other taxes (£T 530,000) and land taxes (£T 237,000). Further substantial rise in tax

---

[112] *Türkische Post,* January 16th, 1936; *La Turquie Contemporaine,* p. 173; E. G. Mears, *op. cit.,* p. 214. Mears gives a higher figure for the total postwar displacement, which refers to 1922/3.

[113] Telegraph service between Britain, Turkey & India was established under an agreement signed with Britain on September 3rd, 1864. *Parliamentary Papers,* 1865, Vol. LVII, pp. 489-494.

[114] Ch. Morawitz, *op. cit.,* pp. 150-155.

proceeds, particularly from the tithe, was registered in the province after 1897, when the rail network was expanded further. Another example is afforded by the port of Samsun on the Black Sea: improvements in the harbour and in its transport connections raised the value of the goods exported from it, from half a million Turkish pounds in 1884 to a million in 1890.[115]

The Empire's balance of trade kept deteriorating, owing to the handicaps with which local industrial production was faced, to the decline of the traditional export manufactures and to the difficulties imposed on the export of farm produce, either by poor crops at home or by low demand and prices abroad. While in 1878-1900 Turkey's annual trade deficit averaged 10 million gold Turkish pounds (i.e. $ 50 million), in the years that preceded the World War it had risen to double that figure:[116]

TABLE IV

The Ottoman Empire's Foreign Trade, 1880-1913 [117]
(Goods only; in 000's of gold Turkish pounds)

Year	Imports	Exports	Deficit
1880	17,840	8,490	9,350
1890	22,914	12,836	10,078
1900	23,842	14,905	8,937
1910	42,556	22,080	20,476
1911	45,063	24,909	20,154
1912	43,550	23,920	19,630
1913	41,842	21,690	20,242

Although exports rose after the turn of the century and particularly after the Young Turk revolution, the gap was not closed; quite the contrary, it grew wider owing to the simultaneous steep rise in imports that may partly be ascribed to the needs of the Balkan Wars. By 1914 exports stood at $ 5.10 and imports at $ 9.37 *per capita*. By modern standards both figures were low: this was due not only to low production but also to the low level of commercial activity within the country, which in turn stemmed from the subsistence farming character of Ottoman agriculture and from the Muslim Turk's lack of interest in business.[118]

The breakdown of Turkey's foreign trade by destination changed in the prewar years, particularly after Germany's entry upon the scene. In 1900 Britain still accounted for 35% of the Ottoman Empire's imports, but by the eve of the First World War her share had gradually fallen to 20%-22%, while Germany's share had

---

[115] Derived from Wilhelm von Pressel, *op. cit.*, p. 21.

[116] Ottoman foreign trade statistics may be considered more reliable after 1910, when they began to be based on the customhouse declarations of exporters and importers. See Direction Générale des Contributions Indirectes, *Statistique du Commerce Extérieur de l'Empire Ottoman pendant l'année* 1326 (1910/11), Constantinople 1328, p. 1; *La Turquie en Chiffres*, Ankara, 1937, p. 63.

[117] Direction Générale de la Presse, *La Turquie Contemporaine*, pp. 23-24; General Directory of Statistics, *Small Statistical Abstract of Turkey*, Ankara, 1947, p. 289; Ch. Morawitz, *op. cit.*, p. 86.

[118] E. G. Mears, *op. cit.*, p. 330.

risen in the same period from 2¹/₂% to 11%-13%. The role of France and Britain as purchasers of Turkey's products declined both absolutely and relatively to the Empire's total exports, of which they took 75% in 1900 but only 60% in 1912. Germany, Italy and Austria-Hungary, on the other hand, which together had taken 13% of the exports in 1900, now accounted for 33%.[119]

The foreign trade structure was that of a typical primary producer, since 85% of the exports were of this nature. What is interesting is that Turkey still stood in need of a relatively high proportion of agricultural imports.

TABLE V

Structure of Turkey's Foreign Trade in 1914 (in %) [120]

Commodities	Exports	Imports
Industrial Products	13	59.4
Raw materials (including tobacco)	38.4	7
Grain	45	25
Miscellaneous	3.6	8.6
Total	100.0	100.0

It must be remembered that by 1914 the Empire had lost many territories in Europe and Africa, and that Egypt too is excluded from the above trade figures. The remaining parts of the Empire, however, still constituted a single trade unit, unaffected by the frontiers, tariff walls and other restrictions that were to arise between them after the destruction of the Empire in the war; and this free internal flow of commodities was of great importance to Turkey and to her dependent territories alike.[121]

---

[119] E. M. Earle, *op. cit.*, pp. 104-107; E. G. Mears, *op. cit.*, p. 349.

[120] E. G. Mears, *op. cit.*, p. 336.

[121] In the mid-19th century the Ottoman Empire's foreign trade—exports and imports combined—was estimated at some £ 11 million, and the trade of Turkey proper with the provinces of Wallachia, Moldavia, Serbia and Egypt at £ 2 million. The latter figure does not include the trade of these dependent territories with each other. M. A. Ubicini, *op. cit.*, I, pp. 351-352.

PART FOUR

THE ECONOMIC DEVELOPMENT OF EGYPT IN THE NINETEENTH CENTURY

1. THE RISE OF MEHMED ALI AND HIS AGRARIAN POLICY: TRANSITION TO CASH CROPS

The rule of the Mamluks in Egypt, who seized control of the country as early as the 13th century (1250), lasted till the end of the 18th century. Their economic regime until the Turkish conquest at the beginning of the 16th century (1517) proved quite efficient, though exercised with a great deal of cruelty towards the population, mainly through an extensive network of tax-farmers and fief-holders. Under Ottoman sovereignty, the regime became not only more oppressive from a social point of view, but also increasingly inefficient both economically and administratively, with disastrous effects on Egypt's future development. Despite being defeated by the Turkish Sultan, and forced to abandon Syria in 1516 and to accept the sovereignty of the Sublime Porte, the Mamluks succeeded in maintaining effective control over Egypt. In the course of the 17th and 18th centuries they even managed increasingly to rid themselves of central imperial domination.[1] However, the country reached a social and economic low which, in addition to internal factors (see below), was to a decisive degree determined by the fact that new routes had been found from Europe to the Far East, by-passing Egypt and its port Alexandria. Another important reason causing international trade to make a detour round Egypt was the embargo laid by the Turkish Sultans on European, and in particular British, vessels in the Red Sea,[2] particularly until 1774 (the year of Küçük Kaynàrca).

In the 16th century the Ottoman conquest led to the abolition of the Mamluk military fiefs. Lands which in the past had in many cases been converted into *mulk*, though originally *kharadj*, were confiscated by the Turks and, as conquered areas, redistributed by the State in the form of fiefs. These fiefs were based on tax levies and not on the maintenance of feudal armies.[3] Since, however, *iltizam* in Egypt could be passed on by inheritance, sale, lease and lien, a new class of feudal rulers sprang up, virtually cancelling out all previous attempts at reform. The Mamluk beys, as *multazimin* and fief-holders by virtue of the ruler's grants, also under Ottoman conquest, completely ruined the Egyptian rural population, turning the

---

[1] The total number of Mamluks in Egypt was estimated in 1800 at not more than 9,000. Cf. *Description de l'Egypte,* XII, p. 374. The most profound study of the Mamluk society has been carried out by Professor David Ayalon in his numerous works, i.a., *L'Esclavage du Mamelouk,* 1951, and *Gunpowder and Firearms in the Mamluk Kingdom,* 1956, as well as in his later publications.

[2] *Description de l'Egypte,* X, p. 109; Cf. also H. Dodwell, *The Founder of Modern Egypt,* Cambridge, 1931, p. 5.

[3] A. N. Poliak, *Feudalism in Egypt, Syria, Palestine and the Lebanon,* pp. 39-61.

fellah into a serf, both to their own advantage and that of the central treasury. These feudal, largely absentee landlords gradually turned substantial areas into agricultural *waqf*, called in Egypt *rizak ahbasiyah,* to secure their usage for the preferred predetermined purposes.[4]

With respect to taxation, the usual procedure was for the *multazimin* to make an annual advance payment to the Mamluk governor, and then to collect from the fellahin both *kharadj* and other taxes. In Lower Egypt payment was made mainly in cash, in Upper Egypt mainly in kind. The taxes payable to the Ottoman Sultan were likewise transferred to Constantinople by the governors of Egypt in annual instalments. Examples of two Egyptian villages cited in the report of the French scientific mission show that out of the taxes collected from a village in Lower Egypt, some 15% were allotted to the Sultan, 12.5% to the governor, 72.5% to the *multazim*. In Upper Egypt, 25% went to the Sultan, 17% to the governor and 58% to the *multazim*. The overtaxed fellah groaned and succumbed under the burden of debts on which he paid exorbitant rates of interest (18-45%), and frequently lost his land to the *multazim*. The landless agricultural labourer, according to the evidence of the French expedition, earned 22-35 centimes per day. On the unrealistic assumption that he worked every day of the year he would have had an income of about 100 francs per year. According to the same estimate, minimal living requirements (a diet consisting of durra, some milk and vegetables) amounted to 120 francs per year. As a matter of fact labourers worked only part of the year, and sometimes had dependents to support as well.[5] The gradually dwindling population, reduced by disease and starvation, numbered some 2-2.5 million in 1800 (as against 6-7 millions in the distant past). They showed no capacity for resistance to their miserable living conditions.[6]

Following Napoleon's attack on Egypt in 1798, the hold of the Mamluks over the country was weakened. A stop was called to Napoleon's advance to the north of the country (following his failure to capture Acre) and in 1799 he left Egypt. During the second half of 1801 the last of Frenchmen left Egyptian soil (though the agreement with the Ottoman Sultan on the evacuation of Egypt had been signed by General Kléber in the previous year).[7] The short period of the British conquest from then until 1803 (when the British left Egypt and restored it to the Sultan under the agreement of Amiens) to some extent strengthened the rule of the Mamluks, who held out until their final destruction by Mehmed Ali in 1811.

---

[4] A. E. Crouchley, *The Economic Development of Modern Egypt,* 1938, pp. 13-18; G. Baer, *A History of Landownership in Modern Egypt, 1800-1950,* Oxford University Press, London, 1962, pp. 2 ff.

[5] *Description de l'Egypte,* XI, p. 689.

[6] According to the calculations of E. Jomard, *Description de l'Egypte,* II, 1818, pp. 95-100, the Egyptian population at the end of the 18th century numbered close to 2.5 million, of whom 264,000 lived in Cairo, about 148,000 in the remaining cities and 2.08 million were fellahin and nomads. Hitti, basing himself on Ibn-Tahri-Birdi, estimates that the population of Syria and Egypt diminished by one-third during Mamluk rule. P. K. Hitti, *History of the Arabs,* 5th, ed., London, 1951, p. 696. A similar estimate is given by Crouchley, *op. cit.,* pp. 13-18.

[7] El Djabarti, *Merveilles Biographiques et Historiques,* VI, pp. 161 ff.

Mehmed Ali,[8] a Turkish officer of Albanian origin (born in the small port city of Kavalla) arrived in Egypt in 1801 with a group of reinforcements for the Turkish army engaged in fighting the French. At first he co-operated with the Mamluks, but in 1805 he succeeded, with the active support of the population of Cairo and the fellahin, in seizing power for himself[9] while recognising the suzerainty of the Turkish Sultan.[10]

The rule of the Mamluks was thus undermined by two main stages—the Battle of the Pyramids in 1798 (when they were defeated by Napoleon) and the rise of Mehmed Ali in 1805. The slaughter of the Mamluks in 1811 merely served as the culminating point of this process.

Mehmed Ali's long reign—from 1805 until 1849—constitutes one of the most important chapters in Egypt's history and the history of the Middle East as a whole. Even though many of Mehmed Ali's reforms and methods did not outlast his reign and sometimes failed even in his own days, he nonetheless succeeded in laying valuable foundations for the future development of the country. His main goal was to create a military force and consolidate his personal status at the expense of the landlords on the one hand, and foreign interests on the other. The methods he adopted to achieve these goals reflect the efforts of a centralised regime in a backward agrarian country to achieve rapid industrialisation, with scarce capital and little competitive power as compared with the dynamic industrial development of Europe.[11] In line with his general endeavour to restrict the influence of foreigners and in order to counterbalance British influence in an area forming a passageway to India, Mehmed Ali preferred to rely on French assistance, particularly in the organisation and training of his army, although it was with the British that he concluded particularly successful deals in 1811-1812.[12]

Half of the State revenue was allotted to the maintenance of the army, the erection of fortifications and arms production (see Table VII, Egypt's income and expenditure budget for the year 1833, given below). The still limited labour force in the country was to a decisive extent diverted from agriculture to army service or industrial enterprises, which in turn were largely of a military nature. Despite this interference with agricultural development, Mehmed Ali attempted to introduce far-

---

[8] Owing to the non-Arab origin and background of the viceroy, we preferred the Turkish spelling of his name (though not in its modernised form ending with *t*).

[9] For the stages of Mehmed Ali's rise to power in Egypt, see J. Deny, *Sommaire des Archives Turques de Caire,* Société Royale de Géographie d'Egypte, 1930, pp. 78-90. Also, G. Douin, *L'Egypte de 1802 à 1804,* 1925; and *L'Egypte de 1805-1807,* 1926 (in particular Ruffin's letter to Talleyrand, pp. 60-1). For the titles of Mehmed Ali and his heirs until the conferment of the title Khedive on Ismail, cf. *Recueil des Firmans Impériaux Ottomans, loc. cit.,* pp. XXV-XXVII.

[10] Mehmed Ali rendered a particularly important service to the Sultan in the years 1811-1818 by subduing the Wahabis, who *inter alia* undermined the Sultan's authority as Khalif, and again in the 'twenties when he was called upon by the Sultan to subdue the Greeks. This second undertaking had only a short-lived success owing to the Turkish-Egyptian defeat at Navarino. Cf. Valentine Chirol, *The Egyptian Problem,* Macmillan & Co., London, 1920, pp. 5-7; *Recueil des Firmans Impériaux Ottomans, loc. cit.,* pp. XLII-XLIII, 61, 65, 74-5, 114, 133 and *passim.*

[11] See, *inter alia,* A. E. Crouchley, *op. cit.,* Chapter 2.

[12] H. Dodwell, *op. cit.,* pp. 30-31.

reaching reforms as regards land tenure as well as actual agricultural production, methods of irrigation, crop rotation and marketing methods.

In the years 1808-1814, Mehmed Ali restored to the State the tax collection rights granted the *multazimin*. Furthermore, he confiscated their fiefs, with or without payment of compensation. The former tax-farmers were granted lifetime pensions. The State (officially—the Sultan; in actual fact—Mehmed Ali himself) now became the owner of this land, called *al-madbut*, which was leased out to the cultivators.[13] Following a land survey (1813-1820)[14], each fellah was given an average of 3-5 feddan *(≈ acres)*, registered in the Land Registry Books as a permanent inheritable leasehold. In return, the fellahin had to effect their payments directly to the State treasury through the viceroy's agents, as well as to resume the cultivation of fallow lands. The State obtained a monopoly for the sale of agricultural produce, for which it laid down mandatorily the extent and variety of cash crops and prices. This rendered possible the introduction of new crops, while part of the land in excess of the mandatory cultivation was left to the fellah's free choice of varieties.[15]

In the course of time a change occurred in Mehmed Ali's attitude to land tenure—and to an even greater extent in that of his heirs. Various factors were responsible for this, such as pressure exercised by the feudal lords and foreigners, and considerations of greater agricultural development. In 1829 Mehmed Ali started handing over wastelands *(ibʿadiyat)* to wealthy people and notables, to encourage their cultivation, first as usufruct *(tasarruf)* and since 1836 as nearly full ownership, and granted them tax exemptions for a period of 10 years. Farmers were permitted to sell their produce both to private purchasers and to the government stores, or use them in any other way they saw fit. In 1846, moreover, they received permission to mortgage their land to creditors or even transfer it to others by way of writ *(hudja)*. As from the 1830s, Mehmed Ali used to transfer estates and whole villages to notables and army officers, under the name of *ʾuhdas*, with the main purpose of making tax collection for the central government more efficient. Thus a new process of large landownership was set into motion. The Viceroy's attempts at the nationalisation of *waqf* lands met with partial success only due to the strong opposition of religious leaders and other vested interests, which in most cases finally prevailed, already under Mehmed Ali and still more under his successors. In addition, Mehmed Ali granted extensive areas, called *jiflik* or *shiflik*, exempt from taxation, to his family members, and since 1842, both *ibʿadiya* and *shiflik* became the grantee's freely disposable *quasi*-property.[16]

After the reintroduction of private land ownership and permission to deal freely in land—particularly during the reign of Said in the 'fifties—social differentiation

---

[13] Cf. Mustafa Sabry, *L'Empire Egyptien sous Mohamed-Ali*, 1930, p. 83.

[14] A. E. Crouchley, "A Century of Economic Development, 1837-1937", *L'Egypte Contemporaine*, Le Caire, 1939, p. 144.

[15] Ahmad Ahmad al-Hitta, *The Economic History of Egypt in the 19th Century* (Arabic), Cairo, 1957, pp. 38-42; see also in Ch. Issawi (ed.) *op cit.*, pp. 357-405.

[16] The *ibʿadiyat*, although surveyed, had been excluded from the land cadaster. - For a more extensive discussion of land tenure in that period, see, Muhammad Fahmi Lahitah, *The Economic History of Egypt in Modern Times* (Arabic), Cairo, 1944, p. 115; and, G. Baer, *A History of Landownership in Modern Egypt, 1800-1950, passim.*

became more pronounced. On the one hand extended properties fell into the hands of a few, and on the other the number of small lots, insufficient to support their owners, increased. One of the main factors instrumental in bringing about this state of affairs was the transition to commercial crops, especially cotton. The fluctuations on the market forced the fellahin to obtain loans at exorbitant interests from the merchants. As a result crops were frequently mortgaged, and subsequently the land as well. Members of the reigning family or other wealthy people who had received lands on lease for purpose of improvement finally converted them into their private property, especially through the Mukabele law of 1871 (see below, Chapter 5).

Mehmed Ali's reform in irrigation and cultivation methods were of longer duration than his land reforms. The basin method in general use till then had meant flooding certain plots of land with Nile water during August-October, creating a kind of artificial pools. Afterwards the crops were sown. Thus only one harvest could be reaped per year. The main stress in Egyptian agriculture was laid on winter crops, namely grain (wheat and barley) and pulses (beans and lentils). Any expansion of the few crops grown during the summer months—sugar cane, cotton, durra, rice and maize—was barred. The population was almost utterly dependent on the Nile in a number of respects: the farming season was limited mainly to the period after the flood, namely the end of summer and beginning of autumn; in years when the Nile was low, the moisture retained in the soil was insufficient for summer crops; in years of exceptional floods, on the other hand, harvests were ruined, livestock and houses destroyed, and roads damaged.[17] Mehmed Ali aimed at restricting this dependence on the Nile's caprices and at extending the irrigated and cultivated areas. An essential prerequisite for his programme was an extensive network of irrigation canals and the erection of barrages on the Nile to regulate its flow, so that its waters could be used at all times and not only during the high-water season in the late summer months. In 1820 the construction of canals in the Nile delta was commenced, and all-the-year-round irrigation works with the aid of such canals and sluices started.

The barrages at the juncture of the Rosetta and Damietta branches, whose construction was commenced in 1832, were abandoned until 1842 and their completion was twice delayed,[18] until 1861. Even though about £4 million had been invested in that enterprise its actual utilisation did not start before the 'eighties. Many canals of the required depth to carry Nile water in the summer season were,

---

[17] Cf. El Djabarti, *Merveilles Biographiques et Historiques*, VI, p. 307.
[18] Mehmed Ali himself proposed to dry the Rosetta branch of the delta, divert its waters to Damietta and erect water-regulation works on the latter. Engineer Linant de Bellefonds rejected this plan, proposing instead the construction of dams on two arms of the delta, with all the required installations. The following is Linant's story, as recounted by Senior in his Memoirs: "He (Mehmed Ali) accepted my plan, and a couple of days after, to my horror, I found 12,000 workmen assembled at the apex of the Delta and put under my command. No depots of provisions had been made for them, they had no habitations, they had not even tools." N. W. Senior, *Conversations and Journals in Egypt and Malta*, London, 1882, Vol. I, p. 54. Shortly thereafter the Syrian war broke out in addition to an epidemic. Half of the labourers died, and half were called up. Work on the dam was temporarily stopped.

however, constructed in the delta region, in particular in the period 1835-42.[19] Egyptian forays to the Sudan, their subsequent entrenchment at the juncture of the White and Blue Nile in 1822, the expeditions under Linant de Bellefonds sent out to discover the sources of the Nile in the 'fifties and 'sixties, all had their primary origin in Egypt's growing concern to ensure control over the Nile, particularly following the revolutionised irrigation methods.[20]

The number of traditional pumps, like the *sakiye* and the *shaduf*, was insufficient and their handling required an excess of manpower; new locks and sluices were built in order to raise the water level. In addition to considerably increasing the number of *sakiyes*, steam pumps were installed to pump the water into the drainage canals during the low-water periods, so as to permit irrigation of summer crops. Thus it became possible to reap no less than two harvests a year, while certain crops, such as rice and flax, and above all cotton, could be extended. From 1813 onwards, olive trees were also planted, mainly in the Fayum region, as well as mulberry trees for the breeding of silk-worms. This was done with the assistance of Syrians and Lebanese, brought to Egypt expecially for this purpose.[21] Although at the beginning of the century sugar cane and rice brought in higher profits per unit of land than cotton, and much more than grains,[22] the required input was likewise high and exceeded the fellahin's capacities. They therefore concentrated on growing wheat and durra, which took up 70% of the cultivated area in Upper Egypt and over 30% in Lower Egypt.[23]

The total cultivated area rose by 25% during the years 1824-1840, amounting to 3,756,000 feddan (out of 7 million feddan considered fit for cultivation).[24] The crop area grew even faster, following the transition to perennial irrigation. After improvements in irrigation had facilitated the cultivation of the summer crops—cotton, rice and flax—priority was given to cotton, for which there was a fast-growing demand on the world market.

Until 1820 cotton was cultivated on a small scale only. Thereafter efforts were made not only to expand its cultivation as such, but especially to introduce new

---

[19] W. Willcocks and J. I. Craig, *Egyptian Irrigation*, Third Ed., 1913, Vol. II, pp. 630-4.

[20] See Gabriel Hanotaux, *Histoire de la Nation Egyptienne*, Tome I, Paris, 1931, pp. 382-390; Jean Mazuel, *L'Oeuvre Géographique de Linant de Bellefonds*, Le Caire, 1937, pp. 5-9, and *passim*.

[21] M. Sabry, *op. cit.,* p. 84.

[22] Bowring's report shows that sugar cane cultivation was in one way or another linked up with the process of sugar refining. While very large investments and input were required, the profits were high but the penniless fellah had to confine himself to grain growing. In the 'thirties the value of sugar derived from one feddan was estimated at 5,429 piastres. After deduction of 2,202 piastres expenses, a net profit of 3,226 piastres or 32 Egyptian pounds remained. On the other hand, a feddan of wheat yielded on the average 4 ardebs at 50 piastres. After deduction of 173 piastres expenses (including taxes) the fellah had only 26 piastres left over from each feddan. These figures again confirm the fact that despite the considerable increase in general output, the fellahin's condition was rendered unbearable by the prevailing price and taxation policy, the lack of capital among the fellahin and the increasing transfer of landed property into the hands of the royal family and the wealthy classes. Cf. J. Bowring, *loc. cit.*, p. 22-3.

[23] *Description de l'Egypte*, II, pp. 103-104. This source is full of admiration for the fertility of Egyptian soil. According to the author, durra with yields as high as 3,000 kg per feddan gave a 240-fold return.

[24] Clot Bey, *Aperçu Général sur l'Egypte*, 1840, II, pp. 264-5.

improved strains. In 1821 the yields of the Jumel cotton strain (called after the French engineer Français Jumel, a textile expert brought to Egypt by Mehmed Ali who was also the manager of the large textile mills at Bulak)[25] amounted to no more than 650 lbs. By 1823 they had already soared to 18,000,000 lbs. The total exports of cotton rose from the negligible quantity of 944 kantar[26] in 1821 to 228,000 in 1824. In a short while this sector became the very basis of Egyptian agriculture and its economy as a whole, with all the advantages and risks inherent in a monoculture almost exclusive dependent on foreign markets.[27]

It transpired after some time that the new cultivation methods were fraught with considerable difficulties. Irrigation canals which had not been properly cleaned became a source of disease, especially bilharzia. The problem of drainage, both of the canals and of the ground water which endangered the cotton harvest, became particularly acute. Following the changes in irrigation methods most of the banks of the old basins were destroyed and ploughed, and thus the advantage of utilising the basins during flood seasons was lost.[28] Furthermore, the rich clay which previously reached the fields together with the flood waters was partly retained in barrages and canals. The use of chemical fertilisers thus had to be increased, so as to restore the fertility of the soil. As a result, Egypt became the largest user of fertilisers among Middle Eastern countries.

The government tried to help the farmers in other ways also. It supplied seeds, granted loans, fixed the rotation of crops and the extent of cultivation, and took various measures to control production. These measures, however, were intended to serve the fiscal goals and the industrialisation policy of Mehmed Ali, rather than the purposes of the fellahin. The State monopoly and price policy, while generally ensuring the marketing of the produce, led to a low rate of income for the fellahin and high profits for the government as the intermediary between the fellahin and the market. During the years 1820-34, for instance, the government purchased cotton from cultivators at a price of 5 riyals (or about 12 piastres) per kantar, while selling it for export at 25 *riyals* (or about 60 piastres) per kantar.[29] Over and above the government price policy, the farmer bore the brunt of the heavy taxes imposed mainly on marketed produce, as a rule in addition to the land taxes proper[30], the

---

[25] *Ibid.*, p. 278.

[26] 1 kantar = 44.928 kg.

[27] According to Bowring, after the steep rise from 541 bales of cotton exported in 1822 to 148,276 bales in 1824, considerable fluctuations occurred in the export quotas of the subsequent years, reaching a low of 33,000 bales in 1834 and a peak of 136,697 bales in 1837 (i.e. less than in 1824). J. Bowring, *op. cit.*, p. 66. For a detailed survey and analysis of the cotton sector in Egypt, see E. R. J. Owen, *Cotton and the Egyptian Economy 1820-1914*, Oxford, 1969.

[28] W. Willcocks and J. I. Graig, *Egyptian Irrigation*, Third Edition, 1913, Vol. I, p. 368.

[29] A. E. Crouchley, *op. cit.*, p. 145 (conversion of *riyals* into piastres according to J. Bowring, *op. cit.*, pp. 22-3). Further particulars on Mehmed Ali's price policies can be found in the Correspondance des Consuls de France en Egypte, recueillie et publiée par Georges Douin, *L'Egypte de 1828 à 1830*, Rome, 1935, pp. 400 ff.

[30] For instance, on an ardeb (about 150 kg) of wheat for which the producer received 50 piastres, a tax of 18 piastres—i.e. 35%—was payable. Land taxes on *miri* lands, payable to the Government after Mehmed Ali's reform, varied between 15-28 riyals (or 35-63 piastres) while for certain lands (e.g. sugar cane plantations) they went up as high as 106 piastres. J. Bowring, *ibid.*

military service and the numerous corvée works. This price policy, in conjunction with the heavy taxation, extensive recruitment into the army[31] and corvée work, severely hampered the productive capacity of the fellahin, who in order to escape the corvée abandoned their fields and took to stealing whatever came their way.[32] Even when Mehmed Ali himself, in addition to defreezing the monopoly and the rigid price-fixing system, took steps to curb the arbitrary rule of the land-owners and tax-farmers, he was no longer able to do so. The acquisitiveness and greed, the tyranny and exploitation let loose by his own hands had by then spread throughout Egypt, where it had found a fertile breeding ground.

At the same time the efforts at agricultural development were crowned with a number of major and lasting successes. The actual cultivated area grew from 3.2 million feddan in 1800, to 4.15 million in 1852.[33] On the other hand the population during that period grew from 2.5 million to 4.5 million.[34] It should, however, be taken into account that in addition to the increase in the cultivated area, the cropped area and the yields per unit also increased considerably following the changes in irrigation methods and agrotechnical improvements. Cotton, as the main article of the evolving market economy, introduced a strong capitalist element into Egypt, which enhanced the role of agriculture and for a certain time, particularly from the middle of the 19th century, served to attract European investors who took an active interest in the Egyptian economy.

One of the major handicaps to agricultural development lay in Mehmed Ali's predilection for rapid industrialisation, which required considerable financial means and manpower. Within the short period when the industrialisation policy was put to the test (which it failed), the centralised industry, largely directed towards military and heavy industries, became the competitor of agriculture for the limited resources available, rather than its natural complement.

2. MEHMED ALI'S INDUSTRIALISATION DRIVE—THE SYSTEM OF MONOPOLIES

Egyptian industry, down to the days of Mehmed Ali, was represented by inconsiderable and low-standard handicrafts. The continuous social and economic depression which had hit Egypt during the last few centuries of Mamluk rule had left its marks also on the local industry, which hardly satisfied even the most

---

[31] During the peak mobilisation period, 127,000 men were taken to the army and 42,000 to the reserves, out of a population of about 3.5 million. Senior, on the basis of evidence received by him, reports that Mehmed Ali maintained an army of 280,000 men (date not given) and a further 120,000 men to supply the army with arms and equipment. These latter worked in his palaces and rendered other similar services as well. (Vol. I, p. 127.)

[32] Cf. David S. Landes, *Bankers and Pashas* (International Finance and Economic Imperialism in Egypt), Heinemann, London, 1958, p. 77.

[33] These figures should be regarded with a certain degree of caution, because, according to El Djabarti, Mehmed Ali gradually decreased the size of the feddan from 5,929 sq.m. to 4,200 sq.m. It is not clear to what extent these changes are reflected in the figures quoted. Cf. also *Description de l'Egypte*, II, p. 91.

[34] See below pp. 115-116, notes on changes in population.

primary needs of the population with respect to textiles, oils and simple building materials. Most of these primitive crafts were centred in the agricultural settlements. The number of industrial wage earners in the cites was very small. Their production methods too were traditional, and as customary in the guilds, each craft was located in a certain quarter or street. The artisans' organisations were similar to the European guilds and the Ottoman corporations. An important reason why the government lent its support to these organisations was that they offered a convenient means for collecting taxes from their members.[35]

It was only the French expedition at the end of the 18th century which, within the scope of its construction activities in the main cities, such as Cairo, Alexandria, Rosetta and Damietta, as well as in Upper Egypt,[36] created isolated instances of modern industrial enterprises, especially in Cairo. These took the form of factories for the production of woollen goods, leather, flour, and especially military supplies, including the arsenal of Gizeh.[37]

The period of military and administrative reorganisation between 1805 and 1815 was not yet ripe for extensive industrialisation. But Mehmed Ali's ambition to set up a modern army, on the one hand, and secure the local processing of agricultural raw materials, on the other, prompted him to take energetic steps towards industrial development.

In 1816, almost simultaneously with the agricultural reforms, Mehmed Ali declared a government monopoly in the field of industry. Although the government did not generally interfere with production methods of private manufacturers, it fulfilled the function of a monopolist by supplying the raw materials, and of a monopsonist by buying up the products. In particular the government was interested in fixing the prices of agricultural raw materials, from which it derived two-fold profits: once on delivery to the industrialist or artisan (where it did not itself act as the industrialist) and again on fixing the price of the industrial produce it obtained as a monopsonist from the producers and sold to the consumers, with profits reaching as much as 200-300%.[38] This industrial policy was influenced by pre-industrial European methods of manufacture combined with State capitalism (based on what was called "Verlagssystem" in Germany, or "putting-out system" in England, but with the State acting both as entrepreneur and trader).

The government also put into operation an industrial State sector. Among the first enterprises set up by the State were two factories for woollen goods in Cairo, sugar refineries (for raw sugar only), glass factories in Alexandria, foundries in Bulak (a town situated near Cairo, afterwards merged with it as one of its quarters), ammunition works, especially in Cairo (the arms factories of the Citadel and of Bulak) and in Alexandria, and a large shipyard in Alexandria, where a new navy was built during the years 1829-1840, after the destruction of the previous one at

---

[35] A. E. Crouchley, *op. cit.,* pp. 24-26; Cf. also Clot Bey, *op. cit.,* II, pp. 300-303.
[36] El Djabarti, *op. cit.,* VI, pp. 301-304.
[37] *Description de l'Egypte,* XI, Mémoire sur l'agriculture, l'industrie et le commerce de l'Egypte, par M. P. S. Girard, p. 590; M. Fahmy, *La Révolution de l'Industrie en Egypte et ses Conséquences Sociales au 19e Siècle (1800-1850),* E. J. Brill, Leiden, 1954, p. 4.
[38] G. Douin, *L'Egypte de 1828 à 1830,* p. 406.

Navarino (October 20th, 1827). Thanks to the excellent standard of the foreign engineers and technicians—mainly Frenchmen—at the ammunition works, the quality of the products was high and close to the European level.[39] Twenty-nine cotton mills were also set up in Lower and Upper Egypt, as well as additional service and export enterprises. In order to facilitate exports, the port of Alexandria was expanded and landing installations were constructed. An average of 30,000 workers were employed in these industrial enterprises during the years 1830-1840, while an additional 40,000 men were engaged in further construction.[40] As long as the monopolistic status of the government was maintained, it derived perhaps even larger profits by the State system than by the mixed home-State system, to the tune of 100% of the price at which it obtained the goods from the enterprises.[41]

During the peak period of industrial production, in the middle 'thirties, the annual output of various products was as follows: sugar (raw)—2,100 tons; cotton yarn—5,000 tons; silk cloth—60,000 okes (= 74,880 kg); cast iron (only for Bulak)—1,800 tons; gun powder—15,000 tons.[42]

M. Fahmy stresses the rise of a wage-earning labourers' class within the framework of the capitalist industry. He arrives at an estimate that about 430,000 men went over to industry during the years 1816-1850.[43] Yet both the number given and its analysis give rise to serious doubts. Contemporaries like Bowring or later writers like Crouchley adopted much lower figures, and a comprehensive analysis of Egyptian society and the Egyptian economy during the period of Mehmed Ali and afterwards yields quite a different picture of the country's economic and social structure. If Fahmy's data concerning the population and industrial wage earners

---

[39] Much material on this subject may be found in Clot Bey, *op. cit.*, Vol. II, Ch. IX, p. 263-329. A detailed Table of 'Industries under Mohammed Ali' can be found in D. Mabro and S. Radwan, *The Industrialization of Egypt 1939-1973*, pp. 14-15.

[40] John Bowring, *Report on Egypt and Candia, Parliamentary Papers*, Vol. XXI, 1840, p. 35.

[41] Cf. Colonel Duhamel (Consul Général de Russie en Egypte), *Tableau Statistique d'Egypte en 1837*. According to French sources, quoted by G. Douin (above), the opposite was true, i.e., the profits made on home produce were higher.

[42] M. Fahmy, *op. cit.*, pp. 21-48 (according to documents at the Abdin Palace).

[43] M. Fahmy, *op. cit.*, pp. 82-85. Fahmy also adopts a peculiar method of comparison between the Egyptian and the British labourer of the period. He points to a certain fluctuation in the real wages of the British worker as against the greater wage stability of the Egyptian worker. With respect to the level of wages as such he confines himself to the remark that a comparison is difficult owing to the differences in the price scale. It might be added that it is difficult also because of the large difference in consumption habits. But even though Fahmy is right in stating that "sweatshop methods" were customary also in England at that time, he fails to note or analyse the enormous gap between the average wage levels. The respective wages were 8-10 times higher in England than in Egypt, where they varied between 1-3 piastres per day or 25-27 piastres per month (while a factory manager received a salary of £E. 25 per month)—*ibid*, p. 69. For comparison, prices of several items as quoted by Lane (*op. cit.*, p. 312) for 1835 are given: 1 litre rice—1.3 piastres; 1 ratl (15$^{3}/_{4}$ oz.) mutton—1 piastre; 1 fowl—1.15 piastres; 3 eggs—$^{1}/_{2}$ piastre; 1 ratl coffee—6.7 piastres; 1 ratl sugar—2 piastres. Bowring gives the price of a fez as 17 piastres. Even in most favoured enterprises like the arsenal in Alexandria the wages of even qualified local workers were only 5 piastres per day or 120-150 per month, while European workers in the same occupations received 15 piastres per day and experts, like doctors or Copt secretaries, received 500 piastres per month and the Bey 9,000 piastres per month as well as food rations and clothing. J. Bowring, *op. cit.*, pp. 42, 59.

are accepted, the absurd conclusion might be reached that about 50% of the labour force was employed in industry, in a country where actually the decisive majority was still living on the land and deriving its livelihood from farming, and a large part was employed in non-industrial corvée works and in the army. At most one might agree with Fahmy that the relaxation of employment restrictions of the corporative system and the industrialisation experiments laid the foundations for the formation of a city proletariat. The failure of the audacious projects, however, caused part of this proletariat to return to the countryside and reduced another part to the status of a lumpen—proletariat in the slum quarters of Cairo and Alexandria.

In industry, as in agriculture, many obstacles were encountered during the first stages of industrialisation, and these increased continually. Clot Bey, who wrote still during the period of comparative security experienced by this industry (1840, just before Mehmed Ali yielded to the demand for the abolition of the monopoly) pointed out a whole series of disturbing factors: Egypt was dependent on Europe for the supply of the required machinery; lack of necessary profit incentive was among the major factors of inefficiency in the management of State enterprises; there were many cases of economic miscalculations;[44] the workers lacked vocational training; there was a shortage of engineers and foremen; there was little experience in modern production methods; difficulties were encountered in the supply of spare parts for machinery, which went out of use prematurely. While exclusively or mainly local raw materials were sufficient for the cotton, wool and silk industries, raw materials had to be imported from abroad—in addition to machinery, experts and technicians—for the foundry and ammunition works—all at a high cost. A further difficulty was caused by the absence or poor exploitation of power resources. In absence of local coal, the use of steam was restricted, and it started to come into general use only at the end of the 'thirties and 'forties. "White coal", the Nile, had not yet been harnessed to drive engines, and draught animals were still widely used for this purpose.[45]

The indifference shown by the workers, who mostly worked under compulsion, increased losses and wear and tear. Moreover, the workmen's hostility to modern production methods and to their exponents—generally shown by lack of interest and truancy from the factories[46]—sometimes took the more active form of destruction of or intentional damage to machinery.

These difficulties were augmented by the competition of cheap imported goods from Europe. The Egyptian products were on the average 20-30% dearer than those brought from Europe. Mehmed Ali attempted to protect domestic industry, *inter alia*, by appealing to his own ministers and officials to buy Egyptian products despite their higher prices and lower quality than imported goods.[47] The

---

[44] The sometimes apparently high profits turned out to be fictitious if in addition to the work and raw materials calculated in the price, other expenditures were also taken into account, such as rental, interest, amortisation, and miscellaneous general expenditures not included in the accounts of most enterprises. Cf. A. E. Crouchley, *op. cit.*, p. 73.

[45] See Clot Bey, *op. cit.*, II, pp. 296-9.

[46] M. Fahmy, *op. cit.*, p. 31.

[47] A. el-Gritly, *History of Industry in Egypt* (Arabic), Cairo, 1952, pp. 43 ff.

government as a monopolist also tried to prevent the influx of competitive foreign goods, but without lasting success, owing to the intervention of the Powers with the Sultan's support.[48] Because of the high production costs the deficits of the enterprises grew, exerting a severe pressure on the State. It was necessary gradually to close down enterprises which ran serious deficits. Thus internal developments also helped to prepare the ground for the failure of the industrialisation experiment.

These difficulties and failures did not escape Mehmed Ali's notice. But his argument was that industrialisation in Egypt did not aim at profits, but first and foremost at familiarising Egyptians with industrial processes.[49] Strong and energetic foreign intervention caused the death blow to be dealt to this experiment. Mehmed Ali still tried to save his pet project by ignoring the agreement of 1838, which stipulated the abolition of the monopoly, but he was forced to close down a large part of the enterprises in 1840 owing to their inefficiency and constant deficits. Thus the entire undertaking was brought to a still speedier end once Mehmed Ali gave his consent to the abolition of the monopolies in 1842.

Crouchley[50] rightly points to the cruel inherent logic of the closing down of Egyptian industry. The effects of modern industry and its relocation, of Mehmed Ali's monopoly, and of removal of the guilds' employment restrictions led to the weakening of the guilds, the official, though not yet effective, abolition of their monopoly by Said in 1854-6, and their final, albeit gradual dissolution since the 1880s.[51] The industry which came in their stead was destroyed owing to its own inefficiency and to foreign influence. Thus neither the traditional industrial structure nor the nucleus of modern industry had survived, and many years passed until new foundations were again laid for a modern industry.

The generally hostile attitude of Great Britain to Mehmed Ali's general and economic policy lasted for most of his reign. A relatively strong Turkey was more favourable to England's policy in the Middle East.[52] Great Britain aroused a wave of protests against interference with the business of English and other traders from 1835 onwards. The French, Austrians, Russians and others followed in England's footsteps by protesting against Mehmed Ali's monopoly as contradicting the capitulations and the special agreement signed with the Sultan in 1838, which promised foreign nationals freedom of trade and navigation, and abolition of the

---

[48] In Alexandria alone there were over 70 foreign commercial firms in 1837, representing Greek, French, British, Austrian, Italian and other interests. The waves of foreigners which flooded Egypt waxed particularly numerous during later periods, between 1857 and 1861, when an average of 30,000 foreigners entered the country every year. Cf. pp. 102-103 below and J. Bowring, *loc. cit.*

[49] J. Bowring, *loc. cit.*, p. 30.

[50] A. E. Crouchley, *op. cit.*, p. 76.

[51] Actually Mehmed Ali went further than any other monopolist. By virtue of an official decree he forbade in 1823 the production of yarns and cloths traditionally manufactured in the villages. Punishments for transgressors of this decree consisted of flogging, compulsory labour at Bulak, or execution. Cf. M. Fahmy, *op. cit.*, pp. 16-17, 82 and *passim*. For the decline of guilds, see G. Baer, *Egyptian Guilds in Modern Times*, The Israel Oriental Society, Jerusalem, 1964, Ch. V.

[52] In this respect cf. Viscount Stratford de Redcliffe, *Turkey*, in *Current Discussion*, Vol. I, p. 59; Cf. also H. Dodwell, *op. cit.*, pp. 133-153, and H. von Moltke, *Der russisch-türkische Feldzug in der europäischen Türkei 1828 und 1829*, Berlin, 1845, p. 8.

monopoly throughout the Ottoman Empire.⁵³ The British were interested in Egyptian cotton which they wanted for their own cotton industry, while Mehmed Ali's monopolistic system endangered both the free approach to their raw materials as well as the market for their produce. Moreover, England acted on commercial and strategic considerations which found their renewed expression afterwards during the digging of the Suez Canal.

This state of affairs required strict control over communication and transportation routes, and prevention of foreign domination over this vital region. The problem of communications became closely linked with outside political and economic influences. Mehmed Ali tried to a certain extent to lean on the French both in the military and economic sphere,⁵⁴ as in the construction of canals and sluices, or the extension of the navy, and to interfere with British attempts to establish and improve communication lines through Egypt of India.⁵⁵ Yet the British had the upper hand in this region. Following the defeat of his son Ibrahim by the combined forces of Britain and the Sultan, Mehmed Ali had to waive his claim to the Levant, and his rule became restricted as from 1841 to Egypt alone.⁵⁶ The pressure exercised by Britain following the agreement of 1838 bore fruit. The monopolies were abolished both in Turkey and in Egypt, and thenceforth improved communications were able to serve with enhanced efficiency not only the internal trade, but international commercial ties as well. The relations between England and Egypt improved and co-operation between them increased, especially in the field of communications and commerce. In 1849, the year of Mehmed Ali's death, Britain received 49% of Egypt's exports, and supplied 41% of its imports.⁵⁷

In the field of transport and communications Mehmed Ali laid important foundations for future development. Despite the numerous disputes between him and Great Britain, quite a number of British experts were employed, *inter alia*, in the development of the communications network. The authorities provided improvements in both the land and sea routes between Alexandria and Cairo as well as between Cairo and Suez. For this purpose roadside stations were set up. A regular coach service was organised as well as a camel service for the transportation of goods from Alexandria te Cairo, and in particular of coal from Alexandria to Suez.⁵⁸ In 1819 the Mahmudia canal was dug from Alexandria to Atf on the Rosetta

---

⁵³ Recueil des Firmans Impériaux Ottomans, *loc. cit.*, pp. 191-212 & ff.
⁵⁴ Cf. V. Chirol, *The Egyptian Problem*, p. 17.
⁵⁵ F. R. Chesney, *Narrative of the Euphrates Expedition*, 1868, p. 2 & *passim*.
⁵⁶ The agreement and appendix signed in London on July 15th, 1840, between the Sublime Porte of the one part and Austria, Britain, Prussia and Russia of the other, promised the assistance of the Powers to the Sultan in restraining Mehmed Ali, but on the other hand obliged the Sultan to grant Egypt to Mehmed Ali on terms of hereditary rule (in addition to Governorship over the Pashalik of Acre, south of Ras-el-Nakura, for the rest of his lifetime). But additional pressure had to be brought to bear by the Powers to obtain due performance of the agreement by the Sultan. According to the Firman of 1841 the Sultan left Egypt full control over the tax revenue: *jizya*, customs and '*ushr*—in consideration of which Mehmed Ali undertook to raise an annual tax for the Sultan to the amount of 40 million piastres (400,000 Egyptian pounds). Recueil des Firmans Impériaux Ottomans, *loc. cit.*, p. xl.
⁵⁷ Cf. M. Sabry, *op. cit.*, pp. 571 ff.
⁵⁸ Clot Bey, *op. cit.*, II, pp. 327-8.

branch of the delta. Subsequently internal communications were improved and Alexandria received an assured supply of fresh water. All these improvements resulted in significant cuts in the costs of communications and transportation.

As steamships came to be regularly used, the travelling time from Europe to India decreased considerably, but not by the Cape route, since steamships were not yet fit for navigation on the stormy ocean. The quickest route consisted of a combination of sea and land routes—by sea to Alexandria or the Levant, from there by land to Suez or the Persian Gulf, and then again by steamship to India. This route took about 40 days, as against 5 months round the Cape.[59] The first steamship voyage from Suez to India was carried out in 1830, and during the subsequent years permanent communications were maintained between London and Alexandria[60] and between Alexandria and Suez.[61] As a matter of fact, even prior to the digging of the Suez Canal the transportation of goods from Europe to the East was thus again effected via Egypt, after the long centuries during which this area had been by-passed.

3. A RETROSPECT OF THE FIRST HALF OF THE 19TH CENTURY

Most of Mehmed Ali's experiments in the field of social reforms and economic development were eventually doomed to failure. Some of the reasons for this failure, especially in industry, have already been discussed. The attempt to graft a modern industry on to the primitive trunk of fellahin masses, plunged as they were in an economic and cultural morass, was bound to fail. Active participation in reform and development could be expected only after serious preparation, if not of the entire population, then at least of certain cadres in town and country, and their absence has defeated both past and contemporary development experiments in different parts of the world.

The modest projects launched by Mehmed Ali in the field of general and vocational education were insufficient to meet the needs of the country and its future development. At the end of the 'thirties the number of pupils attending the elementary schools set up at the beginning of the century was no more than 5,500, There were in addition 2,300 pupils in preparatory classes, while all vocational and higher schools together comprised only about 2,400. This meant a total of 11,000 students (including 1,200 special-school pupils) out of 500-600,000 school-age youth.[62]

---

[59] According to the calculations of Chesney in 1830, the journey from Bombay through Egypt to Alexandria took 20 days, and to Iskenderun through Iraq and the Persian Gulf 29$^1/_2$ days, but the travelling time in the opposite direction was almost the same (because the journey through Iraq was alternately downstream and upstream the Euphrates). This state of affairs prompted the "Euphrates Projects". F. R. Chesney, *Report*, 1833, p. 25.

[60] J. Bowring recounts in *Report on Egypt and Candia*, p. 70, that in 1837 6 steamships per month plied the route from Alexandria to Europe (3 to Marseille, 2 to Trieste and 1 to England).

[61] The railway between Cairo and Suez was planned as early as 1834, and in 1836 the first shipment of railway tracks arrived, but the plan was abandoned and the line constructed only in 1854-56.

[62] Clot Bey, *op. cit.*, Vol. II, p. 338; M. Fahmy, *op. cit.*, pp. 77-8.

The low technical qualifications of the workers made it impossible to exploit the machinery efficiently. This frequently became an object of acute hostility and hatred on the part of workers mobilised for corvée work or living on low wages and cut off from their villages.[63] Many cases of desertion from corvée and from industry occurred. It is typical that in 1824 about 350,000 men were engaged on corvée works, digging canals for a period of 4 months, at a time when Egypt's total labour force was estimated at less than a million. Actually such mass mobilisation for corvée labour was nothing exceptional in Egypt, where the life and economic fate of the population were directly dependent on the Nile and its control through mass-mobilisation by the central government. However, particularly since the beginning of the 'thirties, the intense competition for the limited labour force between industry, agriculture and the northern military front created unbearable economic and social conditions in a regime characterised by monopolies and arbitrary price and wage scales, where compulsion and tyranny were rampant. Had the available labour force been free at least to some extent, such competition would necessarily have caused a rise in wages and prices. But under the circumstances the wages were kept low while the government reaped the benefit of the rising prices in the monopolistic sector. Many of the fellahin, weary of the slavery and hopelessness prevailing in Egypt, escaped to the North towards Syria. It is typical that one of these mass escapes of 6,000 men to the Acre region served in 1831 as an excuse for Mehmed Ali to conquer Acre and Syria, with the Sultan lending his support to the Governor of Acre.[64]

The low prices paid by the government monopoly for agricultural produce led to increasing apathy. Even on the domestic market prices were twice and more higher than those paid to the producer, and some of the produce marketed abroad—three times as much. For instance, one ardeb of wheat cost the government monopoly 27 kurush, while its domestic market price fetched 56 kurush, and export price 90 kurush. Similarly, prices for one ardeb of beans were, 18, 32, 56 kurush, for rice—90, 140, 270 kurush, and for maize—26, 27 and 61 kurush, respectively.[65] Eventually the productivity and taxability of the villages were adversely affected, concomitantly reducing the State revenue[66] (an effect which became apparent only during the time of Mehmed Ali's heirs), especially since most of the reforms aimed at the protection of the landless or the smallholders were soon discarded.

Conditions in a country which was so backward in all respects were not yet ripe for fundamental changes in the life of the population. To a considerable extent, however, the responsibility also lies with Mehmed Ali, owing to his imperious ambition to consolidate his personal position and that of his descendants and because his social and political conception lagged behind his great economic goals. The failure of the industrialisation experiment is particularly serious in view of the

---

[63] N. W. Senior, *op. cit.*, Vol. I, pp. 38-9.
[64] Cf. M. Sabry, *op. cit.*, p. 191.
[65] Muhammad Fahmi Lahitah, *op. cit.*, p. 118.
[66] Cf. John Bowring, *Report on Egypt and Candia*, pp. 14-15. - For the interaction of various factors which together led to the collapse of the industrialisation experiment of Mehmed Ali, see Mabro & Radwan, *op. cit.*, pp. 16-18.

fact that at least as regards cotton Egypt had a great natural advantage over many industrial countries, who had to import this raw material from a distance.[67]

Despite its sorry end, it cannot be denied that the example set by Mehmed Ali's reign was of great importance to the later development of Egypt[68], and had a considerable impact on other Middle Eastern countries. Thanks to him, not only was the idea of economic development together with the idea of reform and liberation from foreign rule implanted in Eastern soil, but in addition lasting values were created, such as the more efficient use of the Nile waters, the increase of agricultural yields, and in particular the expansion of cotton cultivation and encouragement of town development.[69]

The value of exports during Mehmed Ali's reign rose from £ 200,000 to £ 2 million per year. Imports also increased at the same rate to about £ 1.5 million, with a surplus of £ 500,000 in the trade balance for 1849/50. The composition of imports showed a notable change in the course of the industrialisation campaign. Mainly capital and production goods were imported, as well as men-of-war, the local production of which did not meet requirements. Gradually the import of industrial consumer goods was reduced. In the 'forties, however, with the cancellation of the monopolies and the industry falling apart, the emphasis was again transposed from the import of producer to consumer goods, especially textiles and tobacco.

Mehmed Ali left the country free of debts. This was due to the fact that his development enterprises were based exclusively on the recruitment of internal capital resources,[70] although his taxation methods and price policy put the brunt of the burden on the fellahin. Also his monetary policies were, *inter alia*, designed to provide additional funds for the treasury. The French had left Egypt in a state of a monetary anarchy. Not only foreign, Turkish, and different local currencies, but even metallic buttons of the French army uniforms circulated among the illiterate masses. Only as late as 1834 was Mehmed Ali able to introduce a major monetary reform, based on a bi-metallic currency, the gold and silver talari, or *masriyeh*, worth 20 piastres, i.e. one-fifth of a pound (called also *yuzluk*). Since the nominal value of the pound sterling ($\approx$ 97 piastres) exceeded its intrinsic value, Gresham's law went into effect, with the sterling in, and other currencies—including the Egyptian pound—out of circulation, the latter having been largely exported. Soon, however, Mehmed Ali himself started making profits by decreasing the gold content of the pound, and by minting coins of small denominations with intrinsic values

---

[67] For a description of the defective structure of Egyptian industry and the effects of forced labour in industry and agriculture during the 'thirties, see the letters of Richard Cobden in John Morley, *The Life of Richard Cobden,* London, 1905, in part. pp. 66-68.

[68] Cf. Lord Cromer's statement in *Reports of His Majesty's Agent and Consul-General on the Finances, Administration and Condition of Egypt and the Sudan in 1905,* London, H. M. Stationery Office, 1906, pp. 19-20.

[69] The population of Alexandria grew from 15,000 in 1800 to 143,000 in 1848. A. E. Crouchley, *op. cit.,* p. 60.

[70] In fact, Mehmed Ali did contract foreign loans occasionally, but he usually mortgaged the immediate cotton crops and succeeded in paying off his debts in the short run. If bad seasons, however, occurred, the payments had to be temporarily deferred. Cf. G. Douin, *L'Egypte de 1828 à 1830,* pp. 400-1, and *passim*.

much below their nominal ones.[71] The gradual depreciation of money faced, later on, Mehmed Ali's successors with the necessity of further reforms.

Authoritative data on the Egyptian budget at that time are few. However, in view of the structure of the Egyptian economy in Mehmed Ali's time, the Egyptian budget should reflect not only the ordinary government activities in the sphere of civil and military administration, but should give an insight into the economic affairs of the country as a whole, and the development enterprises in particular. In Bowring's report of 1840[72] data are found which render possible, at least partly, to reconstruct the situation. The overall budgetary changes during that period were as follows:

TABLE VI
Egypt's Budgets for the Years 1821-1840

Year	Income		Expenditure	
	In purses	in £st. (millions)	In purses	in £st. (millions)
1821	239,940	1.2	189,400	0.95
1829/30	493,794	2.47	444,872	2.23
1833	505,135	2.53	415,513	2.08
1840	900,000	4.5	no data available	

The earliest data Bowring was able to obtain regarding the detailed budget relate to the year 1833. The budget for that year (adapted by us according to our calculations in pounds sterling and in round figures) is as follows: (on p. 98)

This presentation of the budget, however rudimentary, clearly shows that: a) the government (Mehmed Ali) appears both as administrator and entrepreneur in the widest sense of the term; b) every finance minister nowadays may well envy Mehmed Ali's inventiveness in discovering sources of revenue in order to balance his budget and accumulate surpluses. With respect to the expenditure it transpires that more than half of it was allotted for military purposes, including war supplies (it should be borne in mind that at that time Egypt was expanding both northwards and in the Sudan). In later sources than Bowring, the State revenue towards the end of Mehmed Ali's life was estimated at 4-4.5 million pounds sterling per year: about 2.5 million and more from land taxes, and the rest from customs duties and taxes on dates, bread (or grain), vegetables, fish and meat and other consumer goods.[73]

---

[71] G. Vaucher, "La livre Egyptienne de sa création par Mohamed Ali à ses récentes modifications", *L'Egypte Contemporaine,* Tome XLIe, 1950, pp. 115-145.

[72] J. Bowring, *loc. cit.,* pp. 44-45. Cf. also, *Report by Mr. Cave, etc., Parl. Papers,* 1876, LXXXIII, p. 105.

[73] N. W. Senior, *Conversations and Journals in Egypt,* Vol. I, pp. 182-3; A. E. Crouchley, *op. cit.,* pp. 110 and 275. Until the end of the 'thirties Egypt largely succeeded in evading various restrictions imposed by the Capitulations, e.g. on customs tariffs, or on imports policies in general. This evasion took the form of the setting-up of monopolies, raising of tariffs high above the limit set by Capitulations, imposing of substantial transit duties on European and African goods, etc. Thus the reinstitution of the

TABLE VII

Egypt's Income and Expenditure Budget for the Year 1833

Revenues	Purses	Million £	Expenses	Purses	Million £
Miri, or land tax	225,000	1.12	Army expenses	120,000	0.60
Ferdeh, or capitation tax	70,000	0.35	Principal functionaries	39,000	0.20
Profit on cotton, indigo, flax, opium, sugar, rice, honey, wax, rose water, linseed, lettuces and saffron	90,000	0.45	Coptic secretaries and other employees	20,000	0.10
Profit on cotton goods	12,000	0.06	Pensions to the old Moultezims	3,500	0.02
Profit on stuffs and silk goods	9,500	0.05	Expenses of the caravan of pilgrims	2,200	0.01
Customs at Alexandria and municipal duties	6,000 } 7,353 }	0.08	Cost of the manufactures and wages of workmen, etc.	21,600	0.11
Customs at Damietta and Boulaq	1,601 }		Expenses for the construction of many factories, dykes, bridges, etc.	18,000	0.09
Customs at Fostat	2,750	0.01	Remittance to Constantinople	12,000	0.06
Fisheries at Menzeleh	36,000	0.18	Budget of the Navy	60,000	0.30
Corn tax at Cairo	3,500	0.02	Expenses of the viceroy's court	10,000	0.05
Salt, roots and fish	2,771	0.01	Rations to public functionaries	5,000	0.02
Appalte* of liquors	7,000	0.04	Pay of the irregular Turkish cavalry	6,500	0.03
Profits on hives	200	—	Pay of the Bedouin Arabs	5,000	0.02
Land customs from Syria	4,400	0.02	Pensions to harems	6,000	0.03
Lime, plaster, bay-salt and stones	6,000	0.03	Articles brought from Europe	15,000	0.08
Customs at Suez and Cosseir	3,300	0.02	Boat building at Boulaq	3,500	0.02
Municipal duties of Upper and Lower Egypt	900	—	Military School	1,500	0.01
Taxes on dancing women, musicians and public singers	2,000	0.01	Printing establishments	350	—
Municipal duty on cattle	290	—	Ship building	15,505	0.08
Appalte¹ on senna	3,000	0.01	Household expenses of the viceroy	4,000	0.02
Mint	4,000	0.02	Material of war	14,000	0.07
Duty on date palm trees	800 } 600 }	0.01	Forage for camels and beasts of burden	4,000	0.02
Profits on sale of mats	300 } 270 }		Secret expenses, missions, presents at Constantinople, etc.	16,000	0.08
Profits on sale of natron	400 } 490 }	0.01	Purchases of horses, camels, etc.	3,000	0.02
Customs at Daronay		0.01	Purchases of cashmeres, cloths, silk, jewels, etc.	14,000	0.07
Sal ammoniac	400	0.01			
Silver-melting and jewellery	1,200	0.01			
Sugar manufactures	400 } 640 }	0.01			
Okels and bazaars of Upper Egypt					
Kharadj duty	581	0.01			
Duties of the Feyoum and fishery of Lake Moeris	2,400	0.01			
Boats on the Nile					
	505,145	2.53		420,505	2.11

*Exclusive right to sell.

There are slight differences in the total of income and expenditure over the previous table. Also slight mistakes in summing up the figures have remained as in the original.

Following the disintegration of the monopoly system, the revenues from monopolies gradually fell towards the end of the 30s and in the 40s.[74] One of the more valuable fiscal innovations introduced in Mehmed Ali's time was the more regular taxation of the town populace, who had in the past opposed any such attempts.

With the aid of the French economist, M. Rousset, invited to Egypt in 1844, the treasury was reorganised, and in 1846 the first income and expenditure budget along European lines was passed. In the same way that Mehmed Ali managed to avoid external debts by draining to the full the local agricultural and other sources and thus left the State free of debts to his heirs,[75] he also succeeded in avoiding the grant of concessions of foreigners. To the extent that he needed experts in industry, he hired them as officials or technicians directly subordinated to him.

4. PROSPERITY AND DEPRESSION ON THE COTTON MARKET AND PENETRATION OF FOREIGN CAPITAL

The formation of the Egyptian National Debt characterised the second half of the 19th century. Mehmed Ali's heirs plunged into debt owing to their profligacy and their attempts at copying and outdoing the head of their line in showcase development projects. The State budgets during most of this period show steadily growing deficits. This was the case especially in Ismail's reign, in the 'sixties and 'seventies. A peak deficit was reached in 1868, with a revenue of 5 million pounds sterling and an expenditure of 16.6 million pounds sterling.[76] The increasing indebtedness to European creditors finally brought about the active intervention of foreigners not only in the economic sphere but also in the country's other internal affairs. To a certain extent the control by foreign interests over Egyptian finances was due to the Muslim law which did not permit the lending of money against interest, a law which caused difficulties throughout the Ottoman Empire. Partly it may also be due to the preference shown by certain Egyptian circles for foreign domination over the control of the viceroy.[77]

Capitulations after the Balta-Liman Convention must have undermined most seriously the very basis of Mehmed Ali's economic concept.

[74] Cf. Muhammad Fahmi Lahitah, *op. cit.,* pp. 164-5.

[75] J. Bowring, *Report on Egypt and Candia, loc. cit.,* p. 47. Certain small loans from foreign creditors made in the years 1804-1812 did not cause any financial complications. *Recueil des Firmans Impériaux Ottomans, loc. cit.,* p. XLV. From records published by G. Douin (*L'Egypte de 1828 à 1830*, pp. 400-1, & *passim*), a somewhat different development seems to have taken place. The French consuls in Egypt in particular pressed the point that Mehmed Ali exceeded all economically permissible limits by channelling into the treasury 45 million French francs out of some 100 million francs of total national revenue in 1830 (Douin, p. 415). While the first figure is more or less corroborated by other sources, there is no adequate supporting evidence of the latter figure for national income.

[76] A. E. Crouchley, *The Economic Development of Modern Egypt,* 1938, pp. 274-6.

[77] Hekekyan, one of the major figures in the government, who was deposed by the Pasha, stated as follows (quoted by N. W. Senior, Vol. II, p. 104-5): "The calamity of Egypt, as of every barbarous despotism, is insecurity. Nothing that I or any other Egyptian possesses is really mine. I have a house; the Pasha can take it from me. I have a village—its taxes now amount to 50,000 piastres a year; he may raise

During the period of Abbas (1849-54) a considerable rise occurred in cotton crops, from 120,000 kantar in 1848 to 670,000 in 1852. But Abbas himself, who at the beginning of his reign was anxious to economise and avoid debts—giving rise to the accusation that he was thus abolishing Mehmed Ali's reforms[78] (a fundamentally false accusation since these reforms had already faltered prior to his accession)—in course of time involved himself in considerable expenses. Most of the funds were spent on luxuries, such as gardens and parks, the embellishment and rebuilding of palaces and pleasure trips. On his death he consequently bequeathed a considerable debt to his heirs. In the meantime he provided for greater freedom in the marketing of agricultural produce by allowing direct trading in local produce with foreigners, without the mediation of the government monopolies which had already been annulled at the end of Mehmed Ali's reign.

Said (1854-63) further encouraged the cultivation of cotton by decreasing export dues from 10% to 1%, by subsidising the expansion of the cultivated areas and permitting a free choice of crop rotation, and by strengthening the direct ties between the market and the fellahin-producers, in line with Abbas's economic policy. The distribution of lands by Said to the village and tribal chiefs, although on the one hand promoting agricultural development, on the other hand perpetuated and enhanced the process of polarisation of ownership which had begun in Mehmed Ali's time.[79] The despotism which was Mehmed Ali's heritage continued to prevail in all walks of life, and again the main sufferer was the fellah, the weakest member of society.[80]

Following cuts in the size of the army, the navy and the schools as well as in irrigation works, made during the period of Abbas and at the beginning of Said's reign, the main stress was again laid by Said on public works and efforts at Westernisation. As a result of increased construction and infrastructure investments (railways, canals, telegraphs, in addition to the commencement of the Suez Canal), the public debt and the private debts of the royal house started rising. Loans were contracted both with local financial institutions (in which foreigners as a rule participated)[81] and particularly with foreign financiers.

---

them to 80,000 or to 100,000; he may require it to furnish him with camels, oxen or corn; he may take all its able-bodied men as recruits; he may take all its inhabitants—men, women and children—and send them to dig a canal in the desert; when he has rendered it incapable of paying its taxes he may seize it for arrears, and grant it to one of his friends. No property, no rank, no institution is stable, except the few that enjoy European protection."

[78] M. Sabry, *L'Empire Egyptien sous Ismail,* Paris, 1933, pp. 14-15.

[79] J. F. Nahas, *Situation Economique et Sociale du Fellah Egyptien,* Paris, 1901, p. 43; V. Chirol, *The Egyptian Problem,* p. 22.

[80] The following story of N. W. Senior testifies to the low status of the fellahin, especially those in personal service in the cities, referring to the period of Said: "By his (the viceroy's) side ran a groom, on whose head he rested his hand. The powers of running possessed by the fellah are wonderful; one seemed to be attached to each superior officer, and ran by his side whatever were the pace of his horse. When we drive out, one runs at each side of our carriage and keeps up with it though drawn by four horses moving as quickly as the roughness of the roads will permit." N. W. Senior, *Conversations and Journals in Egypt and Malta,* 1882, Vol. I, pp. 38-9.

[81] The first Egyptian bank, the Bank of Egypt, was set up as a limited company according to the viceroy's firman of 1856. The registered capital of the bank was half a million pounds sterling and the

Already in 1863, the year of Said's death, the debt amounted to 10-12 (according to some sources, 15) million pounds sterling.[82] The situation deteriorated considerably in the days of Ismail, who in the well-hallowed tradition had at the beginning of his career led the clamour for savings and orderly management of financial affairs, but afterwards changed his ways.[83] As early as 1864 he himself estimated the Egyptian debt at 24 million pounds sterling, i.e. double its size only a year and a half before.

The great yet short-lived success achieved in marketing Egyptian cotton during the first half of the 'sixties, when the American Civil War caused the disruption of American cotton exports, aroused sky-rocketing hopes as to the capacity of the Egyptian economy. In 1860, the U.S.A. had supplied five-sixths of the European and 80% of the British demand.[84] This dependence on practically one single source of suppply led to numerous difficulties and crises in the British textile industry, and prompted it to look for alternative sources of supply. The increasing importance of Egyptian cotton for the British market, where it rose from the 15th place in 1854 to the 6th in 1861 and the 3rd in 1865, largely determined not only the economic[85] but also the political relations between the two countries (see below, Chapter 7).

The brilliant prospects for cotton cultivation gave an impetus to Westernisation and development experiments. The implementation of daring town development projects was commenced: sumptuous buildings were erected; the network of canals, irrigation works and communication lines was expanded; the use of steam in pumping installations and cotton gins became widespread. The *Mejidiyeh*—an Egyptian steamship company set up by Said but in fact dissolved in the meantime—was revived under the name of *Aziziyeh el-Misriyeh* during Ismail's reign (1864)[86] as a monopolist company with the participation of foreign capital. Most of the capital was Egyptian, half the shares being held by Ismail himself.

As a result of its constant losses and growing administrative expenses the company went bankrupt. On its ruins the Khedivial Company was set up in 1873,

---

paid-up capital, held by businessmen in London, 250,000 pounds sterling. Most of the business of this bank and of the other banking institutions established subsequently was until 1875 conducted with the viceroy and the Egyptian government. Cf. A. E. Crouchley, *The Investment of Foreign Capital in Egyptian Companies and the Public Debt,* Egypt, Ministry of Finance, Technical Paper No. 12, Cairo, 1936, pp. 27-29.

[82] Pierre Crabités, *Ismail, the Maligned Khedive,* G. Routledge and Sons, London, 1933, pp. 20-25; M. Sabry, *op. cit.,* p. 106. The differences in estimates as to the size of the debt stem mainly from the non-inclusion of the current debt in the lower estimates.

[83] In his speech to the diplomatic corps which had come to greet him upon his accession to the throne, Ismail outlined, *inter alia,* his future economic policies of development, avoidance of extravagance in public expenditure, cutting his private expenditures within the framework of an approved budget and Civil List, and promised to abolish the corvée. Cf. his speech in G. Douin, *Histoire du Règne du Khédive Ismail,* I, 1933, pp. 1-2.

[84] Cf. W. O. Henderson, *op. cit.,* p. 35.

[85] According to Henderson (pp. 45-6), 400 British ships unloaded in Alexandria in 1860 and 932 in 1865. Ships which brought coal for the railways and steam engines loaded cotton as their return cargo; British engineers arrived in Egypt to give instruction in the use of machines; the two countries exchanged commercial and other representatives; the value of Egypt as a brigde between Britain and India grew following the developments in the communications network.

[86] *Recueil des Firmans Impériaux Ottomans, loc. cit.,* pp. 280-1.

the Egyptian treasury taking over the debts of the defunct company. In addition, the liabilities incurred through the construction of the Suez Canal (dealt with in a separate chapter below) grew constantly. The implementation of all the various projects required considerable funds for which Ismail relied on the boom in the cotton market where prices rose staggeringly from $7^1/_2$d. per pound (in Liverpool) in the first half of 1861, to 12d. in October that year, $26^1/_2$d. in August 1862 and $30^3/_4$d. in August 1864.[87] But even during the peak prosperity on the cotton market, the government did not have the necessary means available and had to borrow abroad. The situation obviously deteriorated greatly upon the collapse of the cotton business and the termination of credits at the conclusion of the American Civil War, when the prosperity came to an end.

As stated, even at the peak of the cotton boom losses were inflicted both on the general economy and on the viceroy's private affairs by various obstacles and mishaps. In June 1863 a livestock epidemic broke out which killed, according to balanced estimates, up to three hundred thousand head of livestock.[88] In the same year the Nile floods destroyed large quantities of cotton and wheat, and severely damaged communications. Two years later, in 1865, the people of Egypt, in particular of Alexandria, were directly hit by cholera epidemics with about 60,000 fatal cases.[89] Additional financial means were required to repair the damage, organise supplies to the outlying districts and prevent repetition of the disasters. The economy, carried on the waves of the inflation due to the cotton prosperity, continued to clamour for funds for investments and current expenses, both on the strength of existing obligations and of Ismail's policy, which required a constant flow of investments and considerable operating expenses.

The end of the Civil War in the U.S.A. caused Egyptian cotton prices to fall rapidly. In August 1864 the price of a pound of cotton was still $30^3/_4$d.; by October that year it had gone down to 21d. Considerable price fluctuations took place in 1865-6, round an average of 19d. The steepest decline came in 1867, with an annual average of 13d., falling to only $7^3/_4$d. per pound in December that year.[90] The crisis which reached its fullest extent in 1866/7 deterred prospective suppliers of credit—but not Ismail, who under the new circumstances had to agree to less favourable credit terms.

At this period the country was flooded by foreign concessionaires, mainly as a combined result of the cotton prosperity and the construction of the Suez Canal under a capitulation regime. Following the political and economic failures of Mehmed Ali towards the end of his reign, Egypt's dependence on the Sultan on the one hand and on the European Powers on the other grew. The capitulations in their legal and economic sense assumed a more severe form, and foreign intervention became more far-reaching than in Turkey.[91]

---

[87] Henderson, *op. cit.*, pp. 112-3.
[88] *Times* of 28.9.1863, quoted by W. O. Henderson, *op. cit.*, p. 45; G. Douin, *op. cit.*, p. 234.
[89] Many richer people escaped the danger by flying from Alexandria and the country. Among the first of them was Ismail. Cf. G. Douin, *op. cit.*, I, p. 239.
[90] W. O. Henderson, *op. cit.*, pp. 122-3.
[91] G. Pélissié du Rausas, *op. cit.*, II, pp. 177-8 and ff.; Viscount Milner, *England in Egypt*, p. 39.

During the reign of Abbas the Sultan's firmans, as for instance that granting the Pasha of Egypt the right to construct railways, were still accompanied by various stipulations, such as the prohibition to raise special taxes for the purpose, to set up a foreign company and to take on a foreign loan for the financing of the project.[92] Yet shortly afterwards, in 1856, the Sultan approved a concession for the construction of a telegraph network by an English company. During the 'sixties and 'seventies a further series of concessions and loans signed by the Khedive were approved, and in 1873 a special firman was published which considerably enlarged the Khedive's authority, in particular in the economic and financial sphere.[93] This threw the country wide open to foreign capital and various interested parties. Following the evasion and then the gradual abolition of the ban on land acquisition by foreigners, large tracts became concentrated in their hands, either privately or through companies. The number of these foreign landowners reached 8,220 in 1914, or about 0.5% of the total landowners, while the land held by them amounted to close to 700,000 feddan, or about 13% of the total cultivated area at that time.[94]

The numerous conflicting interests prevented co-operation between the various factors instrumental in the economic life of the country. Dervieu competed with Oppenheim (see below), the French with the British, and Egypt was engaged in its struggle against Europe. The Europeans exploited the absence of local entrepreneurship and tended to expand their investments. However, in their desire for assured profits, they tried to shift all risks on to the Egyptians, either by obtaining guarantees from the Khedive or by high rates of interest, discounts and expenses which reduced their capital risk to the minimum. Egypt groaned under the burden of various claims, especially those advanced by foreign money-lenders who based themselves on their capitulatory rights. When the depression came, both parties vied in shifting the responsibility and the burden on to the other.[95]

In the meantime, the extent of foreign investments grew. Apart from investments in the Egyptian National Debt, they reached 6.3 million pounds sterling in 1883, with another 15.6 million in the Suez Canal; 24.6 million by 1902,[96] with an additional 18.4 million in the Canal; and 81.3 million plus 20.9 million in the Canal, by 1933. The main investors were the French (in 1902 there were 6 companies with

---

[92] This was the result of a certain compromise achieved between the Sultan and Abbas concerning the implementation of the Tanzimat regulations in Egypt. M. Sabry is mistaken in making Abbas solely responsible for this policy (both regarding its advantages and disadvantages). The sources do not confirm this view. Cf. M. Sabry, *L'Empire Egyptien sous Ismail,* pp. 22 ff., and also the source in our following footnote.

[93] Recueil des Firmans Impériaux Ottomans, *loc. cit.,* pp. 225-342.

[94] *Annuaire Statistique de l'Egypte,* 1916, pp. 106-7.

[95] Some historians of the period arrived at the conclusion that many applied for concessions without being able to keep their terms, or perhaps in the knowledge that they would not be able to do so and that if the contract was cancelled for whatever reason, the concessionaire was sure to receive damages. See D. S. Landes, *op. cit.,* p. 100.

[96] The foreign investments were effected through banks and companies established *ad hoc,* whose scope in 1902, as compared to local capital investments, is seen from the following data:

£st. 11,548,000); after them came the British (26 companies with £st. 9,977,000).[97] The French were active mainly in the Crédit Foncier and the sugar industry, and the British in banking, transportation and industry.

5. THE GROWTH OF THE NATIONAL DEBT, "CAISSE DE LA DETTE PUBLIQUE" AND "DUAL CONTROL"

The French banker, Edouard Dervieu, who had chosen Egypt as his residence, held a key position in the management of the private and governmental financial affairs of Ismail during the first part of his reign. Dervieu had previously served as agent and banker to Said[98] in some of his financial transactions; but with the expansion of business and the growing credit requirements of the government and the Khedive, a much larger supply of capital was needed than he could raise even with the aid of his friend the French banker, André, who, by the way, took a more cautious attitude as to Egypt's ability to meet its obligations. Dervieu's funds were too restricted to meet the limitless needs of Ismail, nor could he withstand the competition between foreign firms for the Egyptian money market, which at that time was a real godsend to them. Actually most European banking firms were in one way or another involved in the Khedive's financial operations.

In 1864, a loan of 5.7 million pounds sterling was obtained from the British banker Goschen, and in 1866 Oppenheim's bank granted a loan of a further 3 million pounds sterling for the rehabilitation of livestock (in particular cattle) and for railway development.

TABLE VIII

Foreign and Local Capital Investments in Egypt in 1902
(in thousands £st.)

Companies	Foreign Capital	Local Capital	Total
Mortgage companies	10,525	—	10,525
Banks and financial institutions	2,174	118	2,292
Immovables (rural and municipal)	2,395	1,242	3,637
Transportation	3,645	325	3,970
Trade and industry	5,903	616	6,510
TOTAL	24,642	2,301	26,943

Local capital was mainly invested by merchants, especially in immovables, construction and export industries based on local raw materials (particularly, cotton carding and cleaning). See A. E. Crouchley, *The Investment of Foreign Capital in Egyptian Companies and the Public Debt*, p. 45.

[97] *Ibid.*, p. 46.

[98] It is typical of Egypt at that time that personal relations frequently determined decisive affairs of the State. Thus de Lessep's connections influenced the grant of the Suez Canal concession. Similarly, the ties of friendship created between Dervieu and Ismail, while the latter was still only Crown Prince, led to closer business relations later on. Dervieu, who was the moving spirit in Ismail's financial affairs, was forced, owing to his failure in business—especially in the 'eighties—to confine his activities to France and Italy. He died in 1905.

Many firms came near to closing down as a result of the depression in the cotton business. The mortgaged land of the fellahin who were unable to meet their payments found no purchasers when offered for sale. Ismail, who had embroiled himself in the affairs of his private estates, the *Daira*, was forced to extend assistance to the foreign firms as well as to the fellahin. His support to the fellahin was given in a rather doubtful manner. He paid their creditors with treasury bonds, bearing interst at the rate of 7%, with the intention of collecting the debt from the fellahin over a period of 7 years with an additional interest of 12%.

The large budgetary deficit incurred by paying up debt arrears, by payment of compensation to foreign firms and by heavy expenditures on army and public works, in addition to the pressure exerted by various consuls for the payment of Egypt's previous financial obligations, prompted Ismail in 1867—the year of the greatest depression in the cotton business—to ask for another British loan of 11.9 million pounds sterling, of which actually only 7.2 million were received.

These loans, like those granted to the Ottoman Empire, were mainly mobilised through debentures issued to the public, for which the creditors paid much below (by as much as 65%) their nominal value. Therefore the effective value of the loans was considerably smaller than their nominal issues, while the debtors—i.e. the treasury and the viceroy—undertook to pay interest and expenses, these being deducted in advance, at the face value of the loan. (Crouchley, on the basis of reliable sources, estimates that of the nominal value of the loans of 65 million pounds sterling up to 1873, Egypt actually received only 45 million pounds sterling.)[99]

The steep decline in cotton prices, especially in 1867, as well as the, at least temporary, failure of the sugar refining industry—with a fall in output from a yearly average of 25,000 kantar in the period 1853-9 to 13,200 in 1862, 7,700 in 1863, and to 1,100 in 1866[100]—adversely affected all strata of the population: the fellah, the merchant, the financier, and obviously also Ismail and the government—either as recipients of taxes or as parties to various transactions. Egypt was constrained to ask for an additional loan of 7 million pounds sterling, of which actually only 5 million were cashed in. Ismail tried to overcome some of his financial difficulties by raising funds within the country. Thus the *Mukable* (= compensation) loan, or rather tax, imposed in 1871, brought in an amount of 12-15 million pounds sterling by 1880, but this was done at the expense of the future State revenue. This loan was converted into a compulsory loan in 1864. Accordingly all land owners (including *miri* lands) had to pay surtax at the rate of 50% of the land taxes (in addition to the ordinary land taxes) in equal instalments over a period of 12 years. In return the government undertook not to levy further increases in land taxes and to grant full official property rights to all those who paid the tax 6 years in

---

[99] A. E. Crouchley, *The Investment of Foreign Capital in Egyptian Companies and the Public Debt*, p. 18.

[100] Until 1881 raw sugar only was extracted from sugar cane. In 1881 the first and in 1892 the second refinery for finished products was set up. In 1897 the two companies were merged in the Société Générale de Sucreries et de la Raffinerie d'Egypte. For Ismail's period cf. Milner, *op. cit.*, p. 176; P. Crabités, *op. cit.*, pp. 138-147; G. Douin, *op. cit.*, I. p. 263.

advance. Consequently, the status of *kharadj* lands was nearly equated with that of the private (*'ushri*) land, except for the still prohibited transformation of the former into *waqf*. In result, a significant reduction took place in land taxes, since until that time the taxes for *'ushri* land were about a quarter of those imposed on *kharadj* lands.[101] According to Sabry, the total income from the Mukabele during the years 1871-1878 amounted to 15.7 million pounds sterling.

Another loan, known as the *Ruzname*, was imposed by Ismail in 1874 on the high-income classes. The revenue from this loan amounted to 1,878,000 pounds sterling (according to certain sources, twice that amount).[102]

The large liabilities incurred by the expansion plans in the Sudan, in addition to the expenses for various modernisation experiments, luxuries, the army and gifts for the Sultan[103] caused the accumulation of short-term debts of 23 million pounds sterling in 1873, side by side with the long-term obligations.

Facing the risk of bankruptcy, Egypt made a further effort to pay its current debts or, at least, to consolidate them, and in that year (1873) obtained a new loan through Oppenheim for the amount of 32 million pounds, mainly to ease the pressure of the current debt. Of this loan, too, only 20 million pounds sterling were received in cash, and in the end result Egypt's consolidated debt to foreign creditors in 1873 amounted to 40 million pounds sterling.[104] (The total indebtedness for that year, as suggested by Crouchley above, also includes Egypt's current debt.)

During the next two years Egypt's foreign debt grew considerably. It reached 91 million pounds sterling in 1875, including Ismail's private debt, estimated at 11 million pounds sterling.[105] Under these circumstances, not only were there no prospects whatsoever for the refund of the capital, but the Egyptian treasury was unable even to meet the interest charges. The 4 million pounds sterling it was short for this purpose were obtained by the sale to Britain of Ismail's shares in the Suez

---

[101] At first sight it seems natural that the Mukabele, like any other loan, should be collected at the expense of future revenues. However, both the loan as such and the mortgaging of future income resulting from it bore an exceptional character; cf. pp. 108 and 110, below. M. Sabry, *L'Empire Egyptien sous Ismail*, p. 351, n. Cf. also *Mr. Cave's Report*, in J. C. McCoan, *Egypt As It Is*, p. 390.

[102] J. C. McCoan, *Egypt Under Ismail*, p. 169.

[103] Said, Ismail's predecessor, had actually pointed the way towards the wasting of State funds on luxuries. Amongst other things, he spent an amount of some 20 million francs (about 2 million dollars) on the renovation of his palace in Abdin. Ismail started the tradition of monetary and other gifts to the Sultan immediately after he came to power, during the mutual visits of the two rulers in each other's countries. The presents amounted to thousands of pounds sterling. In 1867 Ismail purchased from the Sultan the title of "Khedive" (from the Persian word meaning "Lord"), to be passed on by primogeniture while part of the limitations imposed on Mehmed Ali were cancelled. Ismail also raised the annual payment to the Sultan to £st. 682,000, twice the amount paid by Mehmed Ali in 1841 (£st.337,000). (According to the Firman of May 1866, the annual payment was fixed at £ 750,000.) Cf. *Code Administratif Egyptien*, loc. cit., pp. 300-304; Recueil des Firmans Impériaux Ottomans, *loc. cit.*, pp. xxxvi, 296/7; J. McCoan, *Egypt under Ismail*, London, 1889, pp. 23-25, 36, 41. For detailed explanations of the titles borne by Ismail's predecessors until his accession to the title of Khedive or Viceroy, see J. Deny, *Sommaire des Archives Turques du Caire*, Socièté Royale de Géographie d'Egypte, 1930, p. 35 ff.

[104] *Report by Mr. Cave on the Financial Condition of Egypt*, Parl. Papers, 1876, Vol. LXXXIII, p. 107.

[105] Edward Dicey, *England and Egypt*, London, 1881, pp. 4-5; Report by Mr. Cave, *loc. cit.*, p. 107.

Canal Company (constituting about 44% of the company's total share capital). Britain's Prime Minister, Disraeli, carried out the purchase despite past British opposition to the Suez Canal project as such, and to any financial participation therein, until its completion (see chapter on the Suez Canal below). Even this transaction no longer helped Egypt in its desperate situation. All new sources of credit had dried up and the creditors clamoured for their due. The main sources of Egyptian revenue, such as customs, salt, railways and a whole series of taxes and duties, were already mortgaged to the creditors, who were mainly Europeans. Now the government adopted the course of disinvestment, as reflected in the sale of the Suez Canal shares.[106] This step, however, was no longer sufficient to solve the overall budgetary and financial problems of the country.

The Egyptian budget estimates for this period, which are difficult to glean from official sources, have been preserved in the report of the Cave commission. This commission estimated the growth of revenues since the beginning of the century as follows: 1804—£st. 55,000; 1830—3,300,000; 1864—4,937,405; and 1871—7,377,912.

For the fateful year of 1876, Cave estimated the revenue at £st. 10,689,070 (or elsewhere, in round figures, at £st. 10,900,000). This, however, includes £st. 1,531,118 yearly income from the Mukabele. The expenditure was estimated at £st. 9,080,681 (subsequently rounded off to 9,100,000), including payment of interest and allocation for the sinking fund of £st. 5,036,675 (later rounded off to 5,050,000). The budget surplus was intended for repayment of part of the current debt (completely excluded from the previous item).[107]

TABLE IX

The Budget of Egypt, 1876 (in Pounds Sterling)

Receipts		Expenditures	
Land tax (kharadj and 'ushuri)	4,700,000	Tribute to Constantinople	680,000
Date trees	160,000	Civil List of Khedive	300,000
Patents (licences)	420,000	Allowances to Princes	90,000
Duties on sheep, etc.	500,000	Ministries and administration	430,000
Mukabele	1,570,000	Pensions and allowances	270,000
Railways-net	900,000	Appointments and expenses of provinces of Upper and Lower Egypt	180,000
Municipalities, etc.	700,000		
Salt revenues	250,000	Appointments and expenses of Government Prefects, Public Ways, Hospitals	400,000
Mahmudieh Canal, ports, bridges	150,000	Ministry of War and Marines	850,000
Salt fish, various duties	550,000	Public Works, Institutions, pensions, charity	250,000
Revenues from Sudan	150,000		
Tobacco duties	250,000	Works contracted in Sudan Railway, Canal of Ismailia	200,000
Miscellaneous	600,000	Miscellaneous	400,000
	10,900,000	Annuities and interests	5,050,000
			9,100,000

---

[106] C. Lesage, *L'achat des actions de Suez,* Paris, 1906, pp. 20-21.

[107] *Report by Mr. Cave on the Financial Condition of Egypt, Parliamentary Papers,* 1876, Vol. LXXXIII, p. 113. The figures have been re-calculated here in pounds sterling.

Most of Ismail's investments are not included in this budget, which is called the ordinary budget. These may be assessed from the data given below (i.a., in Tables X & XI, on his investments and financing methods. This budget is similar to that of Mehmed Ali in that here, too, the land taxes account for about 50% of the total revenue. Actually they amount to much more if the Mukabele is included in the first item. As pointed out by Cave, the Mukabele threatened to come to an end, while a decreased income from land taxes was also to be expected if the undertakings of the Mukabele were kept and the land became private property, yielding lower taxes than *miri* land.

As against this, the "entrepreneur" items which were so prominent in Mehmed Ali's budget are missing. To the extent that Ismail intervened in business affairs—which was quite frequently—his transactions were carried out through the *Daira*, the private fund (though the treasury assumed part of its liabilities). Likewise the share of customs duties (which appear under "tobacco and miscellaneous") is reduced, since these, like the income from the Suez Canal, were mortgaged directly to the creditors to be collected by them.

Egypt's bankruptcy in the critical year of 1876 became a *fait accompli*. In order to settle the debts and assure their collection Ismail, on May 2nd of that year, announced the establishment of the Caisse de la Dette Publique (Public Debt Fund) whose management was handed over to the creditors' representatives: one British, one French, one Italian and one Austrian. The total debt, which stood at £st. 91 million in 1876, varied between £st. 96.5 and 98.7 million during the years 1880-83. The annual interest and principal charges amounted to £st. 4,268,000 in 1883.[108] It was intended that the Caisse should receive from the Egyptian treasury the sole administration of certain revenue sources and provide for the distribution of payments among the creditors, both in respect of the current debt and the bonds and debentures. But the bondholders were unwilling to accept Ismail's plan, which put them on the same footing as the current creditors, and they demanded special securities and priority.

Towards the end of 1876 an Investigation Committee visited Egypt, headed by the Frenchman Joubert and the Englishman Goschen,[109] on behalf of the bondholders (as distinct from the current creditors). According to the new arrangement subsequently ratified by laws issued by Tewfiq on April 5th and 17th, 1880,[110] two Comptrollers, one British and one French, were appointed to raise the revenue and distribute it among the bondholders. From then on until the period of exclusive British rule in 1883, this system, known as "Dual Control" remained in force in slightly modified form. Accordingly Egyptian economic affairs were conducted by the British and French representatives, who imposed their "counsel" on the Egyptian government.

---

[108] See *Reports, etc., loc. cit.,* pp. 37-8; Cromer, *Modern Egypt,* London, 1908, Vol. II, p. 449; Milner, *op. cit.,* p. 181. See the text of Ismail's decree in our Appendix 16.

[109] Cf. J. Marlowe, *Anglo-Egyptian Relations, 1800-1953,* London, 1954, pp. 93-96.

[110] Ali Bey Ismail, *Les Conséquences Financières de l'occupation de l'Egypte par l'Angleterre,* Discours prononcé le 24 septembre 1910 devant le Congrès National Egyptien tenu à Bruxelles.

The debts were sub-divided into four major categories: Privileged Debt, the Daira Debt, the State Property Debt, and the Unified Debt. Accordingly, the revenue from the railways, telegraph and Alexandria port were apportioned to the service of the Privileged Debt debentures amounting to £ 23 million, and their management was handed over to an International Council. The revenue from half a million feddan of Ismail's estates was allocated to the service of £ 9.5 million which constituted a part of the Daira Debt.[111] These estates were put under the management of a Board of Directors, headed by an Egyptian manager and two Comptrollers, one British and one French. (Until 1891 there was a deficit under this item. Afterwards the situation improved, and in 1898 the estates were sold to a private company which in due course sold them in small lots.)

Four hundred and twenty thousand feddan of State property were likewise put under the control of a Commission to secure repayment of the State Property Loan of £st. 8.5 million to the House of Rothschild. Here, too, there was an initial deficit. Land sales commenced only in 1899, when the debt started to be repaid.[112] In this way about a million feddan[113] of the best land over which the Khedive had gradually obtained control since Mehmed Ali's days, as well as of the State lands, were put on sale. However, the process of polarisation of ownership as a result of extremely unequal distribution of the purchasing power (with respect to the acquistition of the lands offered for sale) and the absence of land reform in the modern sense prevented the majority of Egyptian fellahin from availing themselves of the opportunity.

The payments for the Unified Debt, which amounted to some £st. 58 million, were to be effected out of the general revenue (taxes, customs, income from the monopolies).

The difficulties in carrying out this programme were due to the non-inclusion of the current debt in the general settlement and the scarcity of the available resources, which were insufficient to cover all obligations. Under the pressure of the Caisse de la Dette Publique the Khedive, in 1878, appointed a committee composed of the four representatives constituting the management of the Caisse and an Egyptian, Riaz Pasha, presided over by de Lesseps and Rivers Wilson. As a result of the recommendations of this committee an "international" government was appointed by Ismail, who endeavoured to shift the direct responsibility for the desperate financial situation on to the foreigners and the Powers behind them. The international government appointed at the end of August 1878 was headed by Nubar Pasha, with Sir Rivers Wilson as Minister of Finance and M. de Blignières as Minister of Public Works. It succeded in obtaining a new loan from the House of

---

[111] This debt, created mainly by three loans contracted by Ismail who mortgaged the revenues from his and his family's property, originated, in particular, in two, out of seven, kinds of *daira*, viz. the *daira khasa* (the civil list), and the *daira saniyeh* (Ismail's private estates). Cf. J. C. McCoan, *Egypt under Ismail*, London, 1889, p. 49, n. 1.

[112] Cromer, *op. cit.,* pp. 313-315. This loan of £st. 8.5 million was actually obtained only in 1878, when Rivers Wilson was already responsible for Egypt's financial affairs. This debt should therefore be regarded as a later supplement to the three classes of debts laid down in 1876. The lands whose income was mortgaged to the payment of this debt had also belonged to Ismail in the past, and on receipt of the new loan became State property.

[113] J. C. McCoan, *op. cit.,* p. 116.

Rothschild under international guarantee[114] and tried to reorganise the treasury on sound economic principles, introducing a more efficient method of revenue collection so as to prevent tax evasions by the wealthy and by foreigners. The latter step provoked the opposition of the consuls. The Khedive exploited the dissatisfaction among the taxpayers and the corrupt officialdom which was under threat of dismissal, in order to get rid of the government which had been foisted on him by circumstances. Further political complications in the financial sphere were caused by the foreign creditors. All this brought about the dismissal of the "international" government by Ismail in April 1879, and the intervention of Bismarck under the influence of the House of Rothschild and the German creditors of the current debt, and finally led to the dismissal of Ismail by the Sultan (26.6.1879).[115]

When Tewfiq came to power during the period of the Dual Control certain changes were introduced at the suggestion of the International Liquidation Committee in the method of payments made on account of the debts. In the meantime these had grown considerably and by 1890 new liabilities of £st. 18.2 million (for financing of public works, payment of pensions and allowances, and conversion transactions) had been added. According to the "Liquidation Law" (see p. 125) an amount of £st. 150,000 per year was *inter alia* allotted for a period of 50 years (i.e. about 1.5% per year on the entire debt of about £st. 9 million, as assessed by the Liquidation Committee) to the holders of Mukabele, in compensation for the cancellation of the "loan" collected from them as of 1871.[116] It was further provided that any amount which would remain of the revenue after deduction of the standard expenditures would be transferred to the Sinking Fund. As a result of the settlement reached regarding the debt, the payments on account of the debt and the yearly tribute to the Ottoman Empire amounted in 1881 to 52%, and in 1904 to 41% of the total public expenditure.[117] The administration, acting under British tutelage, bore the main responsibility for the execution of the Liquidation Law and the other arrangements connected with the Egyptian debt and the retrieval of the country's finances, from the 'eighties until the First World War. This problem will therefore be discussed again in the chapter on Economic and Political Control by the British.

6. THE ECONOMIC CONSEQUENCES OF ISMAIL'S RULE

Some of the economic achievements of the 'sixties and 'seventies, especially until 1875, like some of Mehmed Ali's experiments, became lasting assets of the country's

---

[114] Edward Dicey, *England and Egypt,* 1881, pp. 18-21, 131-177; Cromer, *op. cit.,* I, p. 62, II, p. 370; T. Rothstein, *Egypt's Ruin,* 1910, p. 259.

[115] Ismail was allowed to move to his palace on the Bosphorus where he died in 1895. His situation towards the end of his days is summed up by D. S. Landes, *op. cit.,* p. 315: "Of all the actors in our drama the one who came off worst (excepting the people of Egypt, of course) was Ismail." It is doubtful whether this evaluation of Ismail is correct if we consider that prior to his leaving Egypt he robbed the palaces of all movable property and enjoyed a lifetime pension from the treasury. Cf. J. C. McCoan, *Egypt under Ismail,* pp. 268-9, 274-5.

[116] T. Rothstein, *op. cit.,* p. 111; E. Dicey, *England and Egypt,* p. 244.

[117] *Reports,* etc., *loc. cit.,* p. 19.

economy, aiding its future development. In the years 1854-56 Egypt's first railway line was completed. During Ismail's time the railway network was expanded from 400 km at the beginning of his reign to 1,900 km at the end of it. In 1854 telegraph communications were established internally and in 1862 also between Africa and Europe. The total telegraph network established covered 8,000 km. The use of steam engines became adopted not only on ships, but also in irrigation works and even in ploughing. The system of irrigation canals was expanded by 13,000 km and further investments were made on port improvements and bridge building.

TABLE X

Investments in Public Works during Ismail's Reign [118]

Suez Canal (after deduction of shares sold)	£st. 6,770,000
Nile (irrigation) canals (13,000 km)	12,600,000
Bridges (430)	2,150,000
Sugar mills (64)	6,100,000
Alexandria port	2,542,000
Suez port installations	1,400,000
Alexandria water works	300,000
Railways (1,500 km)	13,361,000
Telegraph lines (8,000 km)	853,000
Lighthouses (15)	188,000
Total	£st. 46,264,000

These improvements brought about an expansion of agriculture, which in turn caused a considerable rise in exports, which increased steeply from £ 3.4 million in 1860/61 to £ 14.4 million in 1863/4. Although they decreased at times of depression, they still remained at a higher level than before the peak period (£ 13.8 million in 1879). [119] Despite the considerable surplus in the trade balance, there was a deficit on current account owing to the heavy burden of the services, interest charges and expenses payable to creditors abroad. This deficit was balanced by the influx of additional capital, although in much smaller quantities towards the end of Ismail's reign than before. Because of the size and composition of the public debt, the imported capital and about half of the revenue from exports were inevitably used up to cover the service charge of this debt and not for further imports.

---

[118] The above breakdown of public works (including one industrial item) carried out during Ismail's reign is given by Pierre Crabités, *Ismail, The Maligned Khedive*, p. 130, based on M. G. Mulhall, "Egyptian Finance" in *The Contemporary Review,* London, Oct. 1882. Crabités states that he did not check the reliability of his source, but by examining the findings of the Cave Commission he proves that the investment of over £st. 16 million in the Suez Canal credited to the Khedive (which, after deduction of the shares acquired by the British, is also quoted by Crouchley in his book on Egypt, p. 117) is mostly fictitious and that Mulhall's figures are closer to the truth. Since Said's chief investment in the Suez Canal were his shares, and these have been deducted both from the Table above and by Crouchley, Ismail may be credited with all the rest of investment up to 1879.

[119] T. Rothstein, *Egypt's Ruin,* London, 1910, pp. 34-35; J. C. McCoan, *Egypt under Ismail,* London, 1889, p. 30.

The campaign conducted in Ismail's time, during the 'seventies, under the leadership of Samuel Baker, against the slave trade in the Sudan deserves mentioning here. This campaign was intended, *inter alia*, to open up better prospects for general trade by abolishing the interference of the armed slave-traders. But Ismail's main goal was to expand his dominion and to secure the approach to additional regions in the south, especially in the Nile valley. Achievements in both directions were in fact negligible. (In the not unfounded opinion of Egyptian historians of the period, Baker's campaign ultimately opened up central Africa mainly to British influence.)[120]

A breakdown of the public works (as given in Table X) and the changes which occurred both in infrastructure[121] and in production, show that the negative evaluations of Milner and Cromer as to the quality of investments and expenditures made by Ismail are exaggerated.[122] At the same time the data indicate that at least half of the debt increase in Ismail's time was used for current expenditures (mainly luxuries) and that part of the investments was inefficient, wasting resources and leaving a gap between their nominal and actual value.

On a long-range view the achievements expressed by the statistical data are of greater value than on a short-term basis, where the inflation accompanied by inefficiency and under-utilisation of capacity played its role. After the disturbances and violent fluctuations had passed, most of the achievements became an important new structural basis for future development. Hence a summary of some of the data for this period may be instructive: (see p. 113)

It is clear from the above and the preceding remarks on the cost of investments, that almost all investments were made from refundable foreign sources (in addition to the fact that part of the credit was used for non-productive purposes). Future generations were left with not inconsiderable investments on the asset side, and a burdensome national debt (particularly owing to the interest charges and the pressure of the current debt) on the debit side.

Despite the achievements noted, Egypt's social and economic situation towards the end of Ismail's reign was gloomy. The ambition of Egypt's rulers to achieve Westernisation at any price, the lack of differentiation between their private and

---

[120] G. Douin, *Histoire du Règne du Khédive Ismail*, III, 1936, pp. 456-7; P. Crabités, *op. cit.*, pp. 70-100; M. Sabry, *L'Empire Egyptien sous Ismail*, Ch. XIII; J. C. McCoan, *Egypt under Ismail*, 1889, pp. 91-92.

[121] The efforts to promote the educational system had a certain degree of success; 4,500 new schools were opened, and the consular reports of the period as well as Cave's report speak with appreciation of the progress in education. See *Report by Mr. Cave, etc., Parl. Papers, loc. cit.,* p. 106. On the other hand, while the number of pupils in public schools rose from about 3,000 in Mehmed Ali's time to 60,000 and more in Ismail's time, the last figure, even if reliable, does not constitute more than 3-5% of the total population of school age, or 6-10% of all the male children of that age.

[122] Milner claimed that apart from the Suez Canal only about 10% of the investments were of long—range value. Cromer goes still further and rules out the value of all investments apart from the Canal. *England in Egypt*, by Viscount Milner, London, 1904, pp. 176 ff; Cromer, *op. cit.*, Vol. I, p. 5. Cave's report is not at all detailed on this point, but it mentions large investments and expenditures of doubtful value. *Report by Mr. Cave, etc., Parl. Papers, loc. cit.,* in part. pp. 101-104.

TABLE XI

Changes in Economic Values during Ismail's Reign [123]

	1862 Year preceding Ismail's accession	1879 Last year of Ismail's reign
Population	4,833,000	5,518,000
Feddan cultivated	4,052,000	5,425,000
Value of imports, £	1,991,000	5,410,000
Value of exports, £	4,454,000	13,810,000
Treasury revenue, £	4,930,000	8,562,000
Public debt, £	3,300,000	98,540,000
Number of schools	185	4,817
Railways (in miles)	275	1,185
Canals (in miles)	44,000	52,400
Telegraph lines (in miles)	530	5,820

State funds,[124] their lavish expenditures which exceeded the economic capacities of any country, all these not only resulted in financial distress during the 'seventies but also helped to bring about the intervention of foreigners in the internal affairs of the country.

Egyptian economic policy of the 'sixties and 'seventies was a combination of profit-hunting by foreign capital with Ismail's hankering after extravagance and the external trappings of Westernisation, and his desire to secure his private enterprises, being himself the largest wholesale and retail businessman in Egypt—rather than the result of any serious care for the advancement of the country's economy and its population. One-fifth of the cultivated land of Egypt served as a source of profits for the Khedive. The railway lines laid mainly served Ismail's estates. The attempt of the head of the Société Agricole, Lucovich, (who was also one of the suppliers of the Suez Canal, backed by Dervieu and Oppenheim)[125] to organise an extensive supply of modern irrigation equipment to agriculture and to assure a regular supply of water failed because Ismail wanted, as far as possible, to maintain sole control over this vital field. Moreover, certain private contractors objected to Lucovich's monopoly in the same way as to Ismail's. Finally the Khedive had to compensate the shareholders of the Société, and the contractors whose work had been interrupted.[126] This was another reason for increasing the debt on the one hand and taxation on the other.

---

[123] The article of Mulhall in *Contemporary Review,* Oct. 1882, quoted in P. Crabités, *op. cit.,* p. 154; also in J. C. McCoan, *op. cit.,* p. 282, with certain alterations.

[124] The Khedives ignored the express provisions of the Hatti Hümayun, which applied also to Egypt and explicitly required the publication of the revenue and expenditure, thus showing the ruler's Civil List. In this respect, as a matter of fact, they did not lag behind the Ottoman government itself.

[125] Cf. M. Antoine Lucovich, *Episode de l'Histoire contemporaine, La Société Agricole et Industrielle d'Egypte,* Paris, 1865.

[126] G. Douin, *Histoire du Règne du Khédive Ismail,* I, pp. 242-7.

For the population the regime meant above all an unbearable burden of taxes and corvée works. Immediately after a temporary revival of the cotton market took place in 1866, the farmer's taxes were doubled. Despite Ismail's solemn declarations at the beginning of his reign that an end had to be put to the corvée, he extended it even further, especially owing to the enormous accumulation of landed property (one million feddan) owned by him and his family.

While at the Suez Canal works the labourers, or at least part of them, received wages—even though very low ones—in Ismail's corvée work they toiled for nothing except poor food. This situation ruined their capacity for work, while at the same time it damaged the fellahin's own neglected farms.[127] Any value at all can be attributed to the output of corvée inefficient labour only if its cost is considered practically nil, although its social cost in terms of adequate social accounting might have been extremely high.[128]

It is difficult to estimate the actual income of the fellah from his land, but from de Lesseps' data it transpires that a labourer employed at the Canal—despite corvée conditions—received the relatively high wage of 1 franc per day, and in contract works could even obtain as much as 1.5-2 francs. This was in the 'sixties when 1 kg bread cost 0.50 francs, 1 kg of meat 0.99 francs, and 1 kg mutton 1.6 francs. Yet such workmen usually supported, at least partially, numerous members of their family as well.[129]

J. C. McCoan in the appendix to his book *Egypt As It Is*, written in 1877, gives (pp. 382-3) an interesting list of the average prices of various products of Cairo and Alexandria. These prices are significant mainly with respect to that part of the Egyptian population which was dependent on these markets (which in turn were affected by the presence of a non-Egyptian high-income population), but they may also serve as at least an approximate basis for the evaluation of the purchasing power of Egyptian wages in other regions as well. Below, only some of the items mentioned in the original are given.

To allow comparison with the data expressed in francs, a rate of 1 franc = 5 piastres should be employed. During the 'seventies the Egyptian wage labourers did not earn more than in the 'sixties, i.e. 5-10 piastres per day, and accordingly the purchasing power may be calculated approximatively. According to McCoan himself (pp. 300-2) a worker in a fez factory in 1875 earned 8d. per day on the average, and in government leather factories 10d.-1s., data which confirm our previous remark.

---

[127] E. Dicey, *England and Egypt,* pp. 110-120.

[128] W. Willcocks given the following account of corvée work he attended as late as 1883: "The first time I saw the Corvée working I had before me a deep trench some 80 feet wide and 50 feet deep to the tops of spoil banks, out of which 10 feet in depth of slush and mud were being removed by a gang of 3500 naked labourers. Some were standing knee-deep in the slush, out of which they were grubbing up handfuls of the stuff, which they were throwing into the outstretched hands of men just above them on the slope. These men were handing it on to others higher up, until what remained of the slime reached the man on the top of the bank, who flapped his fingers and deposited over the reverse slope about one-tenth of the material which had started." The supervisors' contribution to work going on was flogging the backs of the labourers with canes. W. Willcocks, *Sixty Years in the East,* 1935, pp. 89-90.

[129] F. de Lesseps, *op. cit.,* III, p. 397; IV, p. 131.

TABLE XII

Cost of Living in Cairo and Alexandria in 1877

Item	In piastres (£1 = 195 p.)	In English currency s. d.
beef, lb	7.28	0. 9½
mutton, lb	6.36	0. 8½
fowl, unit	8.38	0. 11
fish, lb	9.30	1. 0
eggs, dozen	5.27	0. 7
bread, loaf	9.30	1. 0
milk, pint	4.35	0. 4
tea, lb	39.00	4. 0
coffee, lb	8.38	0. 11
potatoes, lb	1.08	0. 1½
cabbage, head	1.24	0. 2
rice, lb	2.17	0. 3
figs, lb	0.32	0. 1
grapes, lb	1.24	0. 2
melons, lb	6.0	0. 7

In the course of time an acute turn took place in the demographic condition of Egypt. The Egyptian population, which at the beginning of the 19th century was still relatively small and whose labour force was seriously curtailed by recruitment, corvée works and recurring epidemics, grew considerably and by the end of the 19th century reached 10-11 million.[130] This increase created severe problems of employment, which could not be solved owing to the financial difficulties of the State and the shortage of job opportunities which would answer the needs of this growing population.[131]

---

[130] Cf. J. M. McCarthy, "Nineteenth-Century Egyptian Population", *Middle Eastern Studies*, Oct. 1976, pp. 1-39.—Today it sounds paradoxical, that as late as the beginning of the 19th century there existed plans in Egypt for the settlement of negroes and of immigrants from China in order to increase the population and the labour force. A considerable growth in the size of the population took place as from 1840. However, the shortage of manpower was still making itself felt in the 'fifties. For instance, when the fresh water canal from the Nile to the Red Sea was to be dug in conjunction with the Suez Canal, and a more efficient exploitation of the Fayum region for agricultural purposes was planned, the importation of immigrants from Syria and even Germany was envisaged. A. E. Crouchley, "A Century of Economic Development, 1837-1937", *L'Egypte Contemporaine*, Le Caire, 1939, pp. 136-7; N. W. Senior, *Conversations and Journals in Egypt*, Vol. II, pp. 127-8.

[131] In N. W. Senior, *op. cit.*, Vol. I, p. 32, describing his voyages in Egypt at the beginning of the 'fifties of the last century, we find an estimate of 6 million inhabitants in 1854. This figure, if close to the truth, explains the considerable rise in the population at the end of the century, at the same time cutting down its *rate* of increase. But other estimates fluctuate between 3 and 6 million for that period. Cf. J. C. McCoan, in *Egypt As It Is*, p. 23. and J. M. McCarthy, *loc. cit., passim*.

An inexact census (conducted during the period of uprisings against the government and of general unrest in 1882) estimated the Egyptian population at 6.8 million. Another more reliable census of 1897 gives the figure of 9.7 million (including close to half a million nomads and about 150 thousand Ottoman citizens outside Egypt and Europeans). The estimate for 1907 gives a figure of 11.2 million. Cromer, *op.*

During this period the capitulatory regime underwent important changes which also affected economic affairs. The method of consular jurisdiction, which officially applied to nationals of capitulatory countries only, in fact intervened also in local judicial matters, both civil and criminal, and disputes between foreigners and local inhabitants. Since in these cases it was difficult to find an umpire acceptable to both parties, the arbitrary intervention of the foreign agents grew, and frequently a state of complete chaos prevailed. Said was prepared to apply the provisions of the Hatti Hümayun of the Sultan, dated 1856, to Egypt as well, but met with opposition on the part of the foreign consular representatives. Especially in the field of business and finance they preferred to use their personal influence or the pressure of the Powers behind them in cases concerning claims for compensation on the part of companies or contractors, or decisions concerning debts due from the Khedive—rather than to apply to mixed courts whose judgment would be binding. This grave problem was eventually settled according to the proposals of Nubar Pasha, one of Ismail's chief ministers. After protracted negotiations it was agreed at the Istanbul conference of 1873 to set up mixed courts of Egyptians and foreigners, with a majority to the foreign representatives in all instances of jurisdiction.[132] The announcement concerning the establishment of mixed courts was delayed until June 28th, 1875, and they started functioning only on February 1st, 1876.[133]

According to a special "Mixed Law", these courts had jurisdiction in disputes between Egyptians and foreigners, between foreigners from different countries, and between the government and the royal house and foreigners. The number of foreign nationals in Egypt at that time was about 80,000 (including 35,000 Greeks, 17,000 Frenchmen and 19,000 Italians).[134] The mixed courts, with various modifications, lasted until 1949, despite the many differences of opinion that arose between them and the Egyptian government. By their establishment, neither the principle of capitulations as such nor the consular courts were abolished.[135] In 1905, when the British were already firmly entrenched in Egypt, the Consul-General still complained that "it is impossible to change any law concerning Europeans without the consent, without exception, of almost all European powers and the United States of America" and that this consent could only rarely be obtained.[136] This situation persisted in fact until the First World War, when an official British protectorate was declared in Egypt.

---

cit., Vol. II, p. 129. According to various sources (but mainly general censuses) published by W. Cleland, *The Population Problem in Egypt*, 1936, pp. 6-7; and L'Egypte, *Memento Economique*, Paris, 1950, p. 39, the size of the population was as follows: 1800—2.46 million; 1821—2.54; 1846—4.48; 1873—5.25; 1882—6.80; 1897—9.71; 1907—11.29; 1917—12.75; 1927—14.22; 1937—15.93; 1947—19.25 million. (These figures are based on the Statistical Yearbook of the Egyptian Treasury, and the authors tend to give a lower estimate for 1947. Cf. Ministère des Finances, *Annuaire Statistique de l'Egypte*, Le Caire, 1916, 1918, 1919, 1921/2.)

[132] For the various stages of the negotiations see J. C. McCoan, *Egypt under Ismail,* 1889, pp. 119 ff.

[133] *Les Juridictions Mixtes d'Egypte, 1876-1926,* par le Journal des Tribunaux Mixtes, Alexandrie, février 1926, pp. 21-2, 65, 473 ff.

[134] *Ibid.,* p. 66.

[135] Side by side with the Mixed Courts Egypt had: Civil Courts (administering the Ottoman Civil Law), Shari'a Courts, religious Courts of non-Muslims, and Consular Courts.

[136] *Reports of His Majesty's Agent and Consul-General, etc.* London, H.M.S.O., 1906, p. 2.

As stated, the intervention of the Sublime Porte had led to the removal of Ismail and his replacement by Tewfiq (June 25th, 1879).[137] In the meantime, however, the political situation inside the country had become worse. Bloody riots broke out under democratic and nationalist slogans, directed against the Khedive and the "Dual Control", which was the actual ruler. They were fed by the bitterness of the officers and soldiers over the reduction of the armed forces. The nationalist government, imposed by the Arabi Pasha's group of army officers upon Tewfiq, paralysed the Dual Control (Sept. 1881-Sept. 1882). The French demanded that Britain should join them in measures to control the situation, but Britain preferred Turkish or international intervention, until the anti-foreign riots started in Alexandria. This time the British acted with unwonted energy, despite the fact that Arabi himself had succeeded in suppressing the riots and prevented them from spreading. Those who claimed that British rule in Egypt was vital for British as well as Egyptian interests won the upper hand.[138] It is a well-known historical paradox that the conquest was carried out during the premiership of Gladstone, the chief opponent of the occupation of Egypt in the past.

Since the Egyptians did not obey the British ultimatum requiring stoppage of fortification works at Alexandria, and this time the French refused to act, the British shelled Alexandria in July 1882. Arabi had to retreat from the burning city. The Alexandrian affair marked the beginning of exclusive British control over Egypt, which followed Arabi's defeat in the decisive battle near Tel-el-Kebir on September 13th, 1882.[139]

7. ECONOMIC AND POLITICAL CONTROL BY THE BRITISH

The "Dual Control" was abolished in 1883 by the Khedive of Egypt, and actual control passed into the hands of the British Agent, Evelyn Baring (afterwards Lord Cromer). Baring had previously been, since 1877, a member of the Board of the Caisse, and from 1879 he had served as one of the Comptrollers on behalf of Britain and France. In 1880, he left for India for a period of two years and was called back to Egypt upon the uprising of Arabi Pasha to replace the former Consul-General Malet. Now the actual management of the affairs of state passed into his hands in

---

[137] The official Firman dealing with the appointment of Tewfiq is dated 7.8.1879. Cf. *Code Administratif Egyptien, loc. cit.,* pp. 306-308.

[138] Cf. Viscount Milner, *England in Egypt,* Ch. II, (pp. 12-35); E. Dicey, "The Future of Egypt" in *Current Discussion,* Vol. I, 1878, pp. 225-245.

[139] Turkey, for the time being, was content with a declaration signed at Constantinople in July 1882 by the representatives of Great Britain, Germany, France, Austria-Hungary, Italy and Russia, by which these Powers undertook to refrain from seeking territorial, commercial or other advantages as a result of the situation created in Egypt. See G. Noradounghian, *op. cit.,* IV, p. 304. The special agreement with Britain concerning Egypt was signed by Turkey only in 1887. Accordingly, the *status quo* was confirmed for 3 years, but the provisions under which the British, subject to certain conditions, were to be allowed to maintain their forces in Egypt served as a sufficient excuse to hold on until the First World War. Cf. *ibid.,* pp. 426-429.

his official capacity of British Agent and Consul-General. He served in this post from September 1883 until 1907.

British rule in Egypt was indirect. The Khedive continued to appoint a government which consisted of Egyptians; but Cromer was represented in every department by a British adviser whose "advice" decided every disputed issue and determined policies according to principles laid down by Cromer.

With the accession to the throne of Abbas II, in 1892, British influence increased still further, after the Khedive's attempt at restricting it had failed.[140] The first stage of British rule was marked by friction with France, mutual accusations, conflicts over the Sudan (the Fashoda incident) and great doubts on the part of Britain as to the advisability of proceeding with the occupation of Egypt. On the other hand, the subjection of the country by the West led to the formation of revolutionary movements against the foreigners, who had penetrated key positions in the wake of the British-French control, and there was a growing wave of xenophobia.

Among the major personalities of the national revival movement was Jemal el-Din el-Afghani, who after being expelled from Istanbul went to Cairo where he lived from 1871 till 1879. There he preached liberation from the yoke of the exploiters and the influence of the West, and preservation of the fundamental values of Islam while utilising certain elements of Western progress. This last feature was particularly pronounced in the line of action taken by Muhammad Abdu, who emerged as the leader of the new Islamic Movement, especially when he became the Mufti of Egypt and the leading reformer of the University of El-Azhar. Of fundamental importance was the action taken by Muhammad Abdu at the initiative of the Egyptian Government in 1903 with the publication of the *fetwa*, which interpreted Muslim law so as to distinguish between the legitimate, and therefore permitted, benefit derived from loans and exorbitant interests, i.e., usury, forbidden by the Faith. The Mufti included bank interest among permissible benefits and thus opened up possibilities for legitimate financial transactions, instead of the prevailing confusions and evasion of the law.[141]

In 1895 the National Party (*el-Hizb el-Watani*) was founded, borne on the waves of hatred against the British, who were accused of acts of cruelty against the Egyptians. This party was headed by Mustafa Kamel, who adopted the slogan "Egypt for the Egyptians".[142] Cromer endeavoured to rely on the more moderate movements, such as *Hizb el-Umma* (and especially one of its central leaders, Saad Zaglul, who afterwards left and joined the extremist party). He tried to appease Egypt's economic-national aspirations with the foreign interests in the country, in view of the fact that 78% of the Egyptian debt and the investments were held by foreigners.[143] This fact also to a considerable extent dictated the economic policy of Egypt during Cromer's time until the First World War, with the financial equilibrium of the country as its focal target.

---

[140] In January 1893 an attempt at something like an anti-British *coup-d'état* with the support of the Khedive was foiled by Cromer. See Cromer, *Abbas II,* pp. 7-27.

[141] Cf. S. B. Himadeh, *Monetary and Banking System of Syria,* Beirut, 1935, pp. 190, 287.

[142] Moustafa Kamel, *Egyptiens et Anglais,* Paris, Perrin, 1906.

[143] G. Kirk, *A Short History of the Middle East,* London, 1955, pp. 115-117.

Cromer took several measures to improve the state of agriculture. He abolished the corvée,[144] thus making possible an increased input of labour in Egyptian agriculture. He encouraged the expansion of cultivated areas, especially by subsidies for the erection of barrages and dams on the delta (completion of the Delta Barrage in 1890) and near Aswan (beginning of the works in 1898; dam put in operation in 1904). Following improvements in irrigation which enhanced the fertility of the soil, a steep rise took place in land prices. Along the Ismailia canal, for instance, prices rose from 3.68 Egyptian pounds per feddan in 1902 to 7.27 Egyptian pounds in 1905. Consequently, real estate business flourished, and of the 160 new companies set up between 1900 and 1907, 51% were engaged in the acquisition, preparation, cultivation and transfer of lands. The profiteering and speculation in this field came to a temporary halt in 1907 with the stoppage of credits from Europe. An extensive land survey, including determination of ownership and re-evaluation of land for the purpose of taxation, was carried out during the years 1896-1905 under Sir William Willcocks. It comprised 3,385 villages and 1,100,000 landowners and ensured more regular income to the treasury on the one hand, while giving the fellahin a feeling of greater security in their possessions and leading to a more just distribution of taxes, on the other.[145]

In principle Cromer recognised the importance of education for a backward country like Egypt, but more was left undone in this field than was done.[146] The criticism levelled on this account against the British administration came not only from Egyptian circles[147] but also from the British themselves, such as the Milner Commission. Only 1½% of the State expenditure was earmarked for education in the years 1882 until 1901.[148] Despite a certain increase during the first decade of the present century, up to 3%, the proportion went down again to 1.7% in 1920/21.[149] Cromer, who adhered to conservative administrative methods, was interested in training the Egyptians to carry their share of responsibility (especially in the

---

[144] The corvée had in the past been essential mainly in order to maintain the irrigation canal system. Even during the 'eighties of the 19th century its abolition could be achieved only gradually, with the increase in government revenue and the possibility of paying in cash for work done. The abolition of the corvée was bound up with proposals for reduction of land taxes, contrary to Nubar Pasha's view who thought that they should remain in force so as to permit the abolition of the corvée. Nubar succeeded in getting the consent of Cromer and of Lord Salisbury, to whom the matter had been referred for final decision, to the allocation of £ 250,000 out of the general revenues of the treasury for paying off expenses resulting from the abolition of the corvée. European bondholders opposed this measure as affecting, allegedly, the redemption of their coupons.
Differences of opinion between Britian (which took Nubar's side) and the rest of the Powers (which supported their citizens-creditors) delayed the final abolition of the corvée until 1892; the corvée in canal works was, however, cancelled in 1889. Décret du 28 Janv. 1892, supprimant la corvée, *Code Administratif Egyptien*, p. 233; W. Willcocks, *Sixty Years in the East*, 1935, pp. 97-8.

[145] V. Chirol, *The Egyptian Problem*, pp. 73-4.

[146] *Ibid.*, p. 77.

[147] The Egyptian critics, *inter alia*, made much of Cromer's reasons against the overspeedy development of the educational system, as expressed in his reports, namely, the dangers involved in the spreading of over-progressive ideas. Cf. M. Sabry, *La Révolution Egyptienne*, 1919, p. 124.

[148] Cf. Appendix I, in Viscount Milner, *England in Egypt*, 1904, p. 367.

[149] Cf. Nejla Izeddin, *The Arab World, Past, Present and Future*, Chicago, 1953, pp. 124-125.

financial sphere since the redress of finances seemed to him to be first in the line of priorities). He abolished free education (announced by Mehmed Ali, abolished by Abbas, reintroduced by Ismail but actually given free of charge only to the privileged classes), started collecting school fees to an increasing extent and tried to build up a method of payment of fees accompanied by subsidies for those unable to pay. Under the then prevailing conditions in Egypt the achievements obtained were very poor.[150] In particular, primary education was being neglected. Milner pointed to the "inverted pyramid" of the Egyptian educational system, with a number of high schools for the élite, enjoying government support, on the relatively wide top, and poor, neglected primary education at the narrow basis.[151]

Cromer had to deal in the first line with the complicated financial situation which became still more acute during the change in government, because of the expenses involved in maintaining an occupation army and the compensation payable in respect of the Alexandria riots. The "Dual Control" was annulled, but the "Caisse" continued to exist and to demand its share of Egyptian revenue. England, which was now practically responsible for the management of Egypt's affairs and whose financial adviser took part in cabinet meetings[152], had to oppose the claims of the creditors so as to prevent a new State bankruptcy. After much friction[153] an agreement was signed in London in March 1885 by which the questions in dispute were settled. A new loan, under international guarantee, for an amount of over £ 9 million, facilitated urgent payments, including Alexandria compensations. The foreigners in Egypt had to pay residence taxes, stamps and licence fees. Egypt was given two years' grace in which to pay the interest due on the "privileged" and the "unified" debt. A whole additional line of clauses settled the relations between the Caisse and Egypt, granting considerable facilities to the Egyptian treasury. But it was provided that all the surplus of the current budget should be equally distributed between the Caisse and the Egyptian treasury, i.e. that over and above the approved administrative expenditure Egypt would be free to spend only half of the additional revenue. This to a considerable extent blocked Egyptian government action in the field of development and social expenditure. Only at a later stage did the British financial adviser make provision for the creation of a reserve fund out of the

---

[150] T. Rothstein, *op. cit.,* pp. 315-324; *Reports,* etc., pp. 82-3.

[151] "Education in Egypt resembles an inverted pyramid. High-class schools were created by the fiat of Mehemet Ali in order to turn out Government employés. The Ministry of Public Instruction has confined its attention to these higher schools ever since; the basis on which they should rest had been neglected. While the Government in 1897 spent more than £E. 93,000, drawn from the pockets of the general mass of the taxpayers, on educating some 11,000 pupils, mostly of the well-to-do classes, and mainly for the careers of civil employés or lawyers, over 180,000 children found shelter in the village or mosque schools entirely supported by the voluntary efforts of the people. In these indigenous schools, which are not unlike the old dame schools of England, instruction is given—in theory, at least—in the Koran, and in reading, writing, and simple arithmetic. In practice, owing to the ignorance of the teachers, instruction is usually confined to learning the Koran by rote. As a result of this neglect of primary education, over 91 per cent. of the population are unable to read or write." Viscount Milner, *England in Egypt,* XI ed., 1904, pp. 391-2.

[152] See Cromer, *op. cit.,* p. 286.

[153] *Ibid.,* pp. 306-310.

surpluses for purposes of investments and special expenditures, under the approval of the "Debt Administration".

In the course of time the financial situation improved considerably. Upon signature of the agreement of 1904 with France, which co-ordinated British and French interests in Africa, the position of the British in Egypt was made easier. From then on efforts were made at achieving greater administrative efficiency, and further inprovements were introduced in the management of financial affairs. The tasks of the Caisse were confined to receiving revenue on behalf of the bondholders. It had no administrative authority with respect to Egypt and the balances were transferred to the Egyptian government. As Cromer himself testifies in *Modern Egypt*, he aimed at easing the load of taxes weighting down on the population rather than at carrying out extensive development plans. According to supplementary data found in *Reports*, etc., p. 19, the rate of taxes per head decreased from £ 1.1.1^1/$_2$d. in 1882 to 15s. 2d. in 1902 and still lower in 1905.[154] Some doubts might be raised whether this *average* decrease was justified from the point of view of the country's development and whether, perhaps, a different tax distribution would not have been preferable. At the same time considerable public investments of nearly £E. 20 million were made in Cromer's days—mainly in railways,[155] dams and canals. Despite new credits opened for purposes of conversion, public works, etc., he succeeded in reducing the Debt fund as a whole from 96.5 million Egyptian pounds in 1883 to 87.4 million Egyptian pounds in 1906, i.e. by 9 million Egyptian pounds.[156] Also in the annual payment of interests there was a decrease by £E. 900,000 to £E. 3,368,000 per year. This was made possible by the surpluses of the Egyptian treasury which in the years 1886-1906 accumulated to an amount of £E. 27.5 million. The ordinary annual budget, which in 1883 stood at £E. 8.6 million expenses and £E. 8.9 revenue, rose in 1906 to £E. 12.4 million expenditures and 15.3 million revenue.[157] The increased revenues came as a result of improved collection methods and discovery of new sources of income.[158] The budget surpluses were also maintained during the time of Cromer's successors, Gorst and Kitchener. Thus a reserve could be set aside and the regular financing of expenditures achieved. In

---

[154] *The Statistical Yearbook of Egypt* of 1916 (p. 281) states that the annual average per person in 1905 was 0.969 Egyptian pounds and in 1913—0.935 Egyptian pounds.

[155] The State railways (there were also private railways—"the agricultural railways") which in 1890 transported 4.7 million passengers and 1.7 million tons of goods, transported in 1906 22.5 million passengers and 20 million tons of goods.

[156] It should be taken into account that until 1891 the debt rose to £E. 106.8 million, so that the decrease between 1891 to 1906 was very steep indeed, namely by £E. 19.4 million.

[157] Cromer, *op. cit.,* pp. 444-450.

[158] In 1890 the cultivation of tobacco was prohibited so as to safeguard government revenue from customs duties. Décret du 25 juin 1890, *Code Administratif Egyptien,* p. 556. Ali Bey Kamel, vice-president of the National Egyptian Party, vehemently attacked the British Administration for failing to bring up the tax collection methods to an adequate standard of efficieny. He showed that between 1882 and 1908 the income from land and harvest taxed did not increase at all. But even his figures prove that in that time the revenue from customs duties rose six-fold, from railways, telegraph and posts three-fold and from the courts six-fold. Under the impoverished conditions of the Egyptian rural population, these data may be regarded as evidence of a more correct fiscal policy than had been adopted in the past. Cf. Ali Bey Kamel, *op. cit.,* p. 23. See also our comments in the text on pp. 122, 128, 129.

1913 the debt, after deduction of the State reserve fund, amounted to £E. 89 million, i.e. only slightly over the level of 1906[159] and £E. 18 million less than in 1891. The burden on the government budget and the balance of payments of annual interest charges and their gradual decrease are reflected in the following Table which, *inter alia*, shows the interest as a percentage of the value of exports (taking into consideration the transfer of interest payments to creditors abroad).[160]

TABLE XIII

Burden of Interest on the Egyptian Economy During the Years 1880-1929

Period	Average Annual Interest (in thousands £E.)	Average Annual Government Revenue (in thousands £E.)	Average Yearly Exports (in thousands £E.)	Annual Interest as a percentage of	
				Govern. Revenue	Exports
1880-89	4,137	11,488	11,871	36	35
1890-99	3,920	11,228	12,573	35	31
1900-09	3,673	14,909	15,769	25	23
1910-19	3,455	20,666	32,908	17	11
1920-29	3,444	37,317	59,951	9	6

This undoubtedly indicates considerable progress in the financial development of the country. As a result, an absolute though only gradual decrease in interest charges took place, constituting a very marked relative reduction as compared to the State revenue and the country's exports.

Cromer's cautious policy took the sting out of the nationalist movement. However, the situation deteriorated during the time of Gorst, who succeeded Cromer in 1907. In England a Liberal Government was at the helm, which at Gorst's recommendation issued instructions for a number of reforms in favour of Egyptian self-government. Yet the British officials and businessmen then living in Egypt objected to the concessions and Gorst did not carry out the reform proposals. In the meantime, events in Ottoman Turkey, where the Young Turks had risen to power, did not fail to have their effect on Egypt. In February 1910 the Egyptian Prime Minister Butros-Pasha Ghali, of Copt origin, was assassinated, having been accused by the nationalists of following a pro-British policy (an accusation levelled against the entire Copt community) and for concluding a new Suez Canal agreement to Egypt's disadvantage.[161] In July 1911 Gorst died, and was succeeded by Lord Kitchener.

---

[159] *Report by H. M. Agent and Consul-General on the Finances, Administration and Condition of Egypt and the Soudan in 1913*, p. 24.
[160] Source: A. E. Crouchley, *The Investment*, etc., p. 21.
[161] *Reports By His Majesty's Agent and Consul-General on the Finances, Administration and Condition of Egypt and the Soudan in 1910; Parliamentary Papers, 1911*, Cd. 5633, Vol. CIII, pp. 250-251.

The government in London and its Agent in Egypt gave two main reasons for the continued British occupation: a) that the Suez Canal may serve as a means for the spreading of German influence in the entire area (cf. p. 131, below); b) the need to protect the large British investments in Egypt.[162] Kitchener adopted a strong-handed policy, but at the same time tried to carry out a number of reforms in the policital and economic sphere. During his time, Egypt received a new "organic law" (in 1913) which implied the extension of civil rights and self-rule, especially through the establishment of a legislative assembly—this time composed of a majority of elected representatives (66) against a minority of representatives appointed by the government (17) and having wider powers than the previous institutions of its kind.[163] Even if the new legislative assembly lacked any far-reaching binding influence on the executive organs, its public deliberations and the weight of its representation fulfilled an important function in the life of Egypt at that time.

Considerable attention was given to problems of irrigation and agriculture. A special Ministry of Agriculture was set up in 1911.

The Aswan dam was raised and its storage capacity increased from 1 billion cub.m. (1904) to 2.3 billion cub.m. (1912). The cultivated area was increased to 5.5 million feddan, and the cropped area to 7.7 million feddan in 1913.[164] On December 4th, 1912, the amendment known as "the Five Feddan Law"[165] was published, along the lines of the Indian law known as the "Punjab Land Aliénation Act", which was intended to prevent the forfeiture of small farm untis (five feddan and below) owing to the lands being mortgaged on account of loans.[166] The experience of the past proved that many of the farmers had lost their mortgaged lands through their inability to meet heavy liabilities towards the creditors. The almost continuous decline in the prices of agricultural produce in the 'eighties and 'nineties played an important role in aggravating the lot of the farmer, and especially the fall in the price of cotton, followed by sugar, wheat, barley and pulses.[167] The service rendered by the Agricultural Bank, established in 1902, to the fellahin was limited. This fact, *inter alia*, led to the failure of the law. During the same year when the law was issued, the Agricultural Bank granted loans to 23,000 farmers, a total sum of £E. 1 million, i.e. an average of £E. 43 each. The average to most borrowers was much

---

[162] The British investments in Egypt amounted to £ 30 million in 1914. On the other hand, French sensitivity to British policy in Egypt will be readily understood on considering that French investments in that country amounted to £ 46 million.

[163] As far back as Ismail's reign, in 1867, a Representative Assembly, composed of shaykhs, was set up in order to conciliate the taxpayers and their authorised representatives. In 1883 (May 1st) an organic law had been issued calling for the establishment of regional councils, a Legislative Council, a General Assembly and a Government Council. The electoral procedure was expressly directed at a representation of notables, but the law was anyhow not implemented, and the provision with respect to the Government Council was officially annulled in 1884. Code Administratif Egyptien, *loc. cit.*, pp. 309-334.

[164] A. E. Crouchley, *op. cit.*, pp. 152-3.

[165] See Appendix 18 for main sections of the text.

[166] *Parliamentary Papers,* Cf. 6682, 1913, Vol. LXXXI, pp. 259-260; V. Chirol, *The Egyptian Problem,* p. 103.

[167] J. F. Nahas, *op. cit.*, p. 103. Europe too suffered from an economic depression at that time (this being the main cause for the decline in the price of Egyptian cotton) but the damage inflicted on Egypt, which had already become decisively dependent on cotton, was particularly severe.

lower since part of the loan "seeped through" to the estate-holders. Moreover, the total number of borrowers constituted only 1-2 per cent of the farmers. Some of the farmers who did not have the necessary means for the payment of debts and for operating capital had to become hired labour in agriculture or to move to town. Another part who clung to their land, became increasingly indebted to money lenders who inflated the already exorbitant rate of interest, following the new law. Thus the law failed in its objective. Kitchener was somewhat more successful in restricting the Khedive's direct personal supervision over *waqf* funds and handing over their control in 1913 to a special Ministry. However, since the Minister was appointed by the Khedive's special authorisation and the *waqf* administration retained budgetary autonomy, the ruler's indirect interference could not be prevented. Still, in the budget year 1915/16 the first positive results of this new arrangement made themselves felt. Instead of the traditional deficits, this sector began to show surpluses.

In the political field the hatred against the foreigners increased. To the local population, the foreigners appeared to be the source of all their disasters and misfortunes. The nationalist leaders blamed the army of British and other foreign officials who controlled all the key positions in the country. The number of British officials alone rose from about 100 at the beginning of the occupation up to 1,000 and more in the 'nineties. The internal tensions in Egypt and the fact that the Turkish Sultan joined the German camp on the outbreak of the First World War prompted the British to impose military rule in Egypt and to declare it a British Protectorate on December 18th, 1914. Abbas II was deposed and Hussayn, the son of Ismail, appointed in his stead with the title of Sultan.[168]

8. THE EGYPTIAN ECONOMY ON THE EVE OF THE FIRST WORLD WAR

During the eventful period discussed so far, considerable changes took place in several areas of the Egyptian economy. The end of the period under review is characterised in particular by the developments in currency and central banking.

The bi-metallic monetary system, originated by Mehmed Ali's reform in 1834 (cf. p. 96, above), started disintegrating rapidly with the at first gradual fall in the price of silver after 1860 and then a catastrophic one, after 1873, when its gold ratio reached a low of 35: 1 instead of 15: 1. Speculation flourished in trade with metals and specie, enhanced by the seasonal changes of the cotton market resulting in the flow of gold into and out of the country. Hoarding of gold and coins became common and foreign money again inflated the market. It was necessary that these fluctuations be checked and a central direction and control given to the flow of money. But the matter had to wait until 1885, when a new monetary reform established a mono-metallic gold basis of the Egyptian pound, limiting at the same time the silver coins in circulation to a maximum of 40 piastres, and the nickel and bronze coins to 8 piastres per capita. Also foreign exchange acceptable by the treasury was restricted to few currencies only.[169]

[168] V. Chirol, *op. cit.,* p. 123; G. Douin, *L'attaque du Canal de Suez (3 Février 1915),* Paris 1922.
[169] G. Vaucher, *loc. cit.,* pp. 126-9.

A further measure taken was in the direction of central banking arrangements. The Egyptian National Bank, set up in 1898 as a commercial bank, received on June 25th that year the exclusive right to issue banknotes of legal tender in Egypt and the Sudan. A separate issue department was established, distinct from the commercial sector of the bank. The idea of using paper currency had cropped up as early as Ismail's time, but he objected to it on the grounds that the fellah was still unable to grasp the idea. The National Bank's paper notes were introduced with the beginning of the present century and gradually acquired confidence in business circles.[170] Provincial branches of some banks still tried to obtain a discount on payment by these notes, but this also ceased rapidly upon the intervention of the National Bank. Until 1914 the banknotes were convertible to gold. However, the rise in cotton prices and local expenditure of the armed forces during the war inflated the amount of banknotes, while part of the gold reserves was used, upon British request, to finance the Arab revolt headed by Hussayn, the Sheriff of Mecca.[171] In 1916 new principles of coverage were laid down according to which 50% of the banknotes had to be covered by gold and British and Egyptian treasury bonds, while the remaining 50% required coverage by securities held by the bank with government approval.[172]

In 1904 an average of £E. 454,000 in banknotes were in circulation; at the end of 1914 the amount of banknotes reached £E. 8,250,000 and after the end of the war, in 1919, £E. 67,000,000. New measures had to be taken to restore the monetary balance. (Cf. the developments during the inter-war period, below.)

Let us now turn to a summary of changes in agriculture. During the years 1858-1871 part of the leased lands were converted to fully owned lands. This by itself gave an impetus to more intensive cultivation methods. The *Mukabele* loan promised, as already mentioned, full ownership to all those who paid the tax for six years in advance. While the law as such was cancelled within the framework of the Liquidation Law of 1880,[173] the additional land law amendments of the years 1891-1896 and 1899 abolished the distinction between *'ushri* and *kharadj* lands and introduced a uniform basis for taxation (28% of the rental).

The sharp increase of the number of smallholders (5 feddan and less) between 1895 and 1913 (from 611,000 to nearly 1,500,000) unaccompanied by a similar rise in the cultivated area or by a decrease in the number of large landowners and their share in the landed property (which kept rising until 1906), caused the land to become split up in small units. Thus the average unit held by the smallholders went down from 1.5 to 1 feddan.[174]

---

[170] Reports, *loc. cit.*, p. 31.

[171] G. Vaucher, *loc. cit.*, p. 130.

[172] *Annuaire Statistique de l'Egypte,* 1921-2, pp. 286, 296, 319.

[173] Loi de liquidation (17 juill. 1880), *Code Administratif Egyptien,* pp. 251-2; Cf. also, E. Dicey, *England and Egypt,* pp. 223-5.

[174] A. E. Crouchley, *op. cit.*, p. 292. The Egyptian Statistical Yearbook attributes the changes mainly to two phenomena: a) the growth of the rural population and the prevailing inheritance laws, which together brought about a decrease in the average size of units under five feddans; b) putting new land under cultivation, chiefly enjoyed by big landlords, thus increasing the average holding of landowners of more than 50 feddan, while the average of medium-size units decreased. *Annuaire Statistique,* 1916, pp. XXII-XXIII, 106-107. Cf. also C. Issawi, *Egypt, An Economic and Social Analysis,* pp. 73, 125 & *passim.*

The following Table shows the changes in land distribution and the conditions of ownership in Egyptian agriculture during the years 1896-1916 (according to official sources). Despite the doubtful accuracy of the data, they nonetheless indicate a clear trend, also confirmed by private investigations.

TABLE XIV
The Changes in the Distribution of Landed Property in Egypt, 1896-1916

Size of Unit	1896		1906		1916	
	Landed Property Area	No. of Owners	Landed Property Area	No. of Owners	Landed Property Area	No. of Owners
1 feddan and less[175]	—	—	—	—	429,532	1,006,866
1.1- 5 feddan	993,843	611,074	1,292,786	1,084,001	1,020,928	473,688
5.1-10 feddan	565,810	80,810	538,111	76,935	528,560	76,641
10.1-20 feddan	574,084	41,276	512,199	36,951	509,991	36,982
20.1-49.9 feddan	675,639	22,225	611,669	20,029	607,002	19,852
50 feddan and over	2,191,625	11,875	2,476,007	12,665	2,356,453	12,297
Total	5,001,001	767,260	5,430,772	1,230,581	5,452,466	1,626,326

(Sources: *Annuaire Egyptien*, 1948; *Statistical Handbook of Middle East Countries*, Jerusalem, 1945).

The financial predicaments of the rulers and the lack of progressive agrarian reform led to renewed domination by the large landowners which the limited reforms introduced on the eve of the First World War were unable to halt. The backbone of the smallholder farmers was broken by the taxes squeezed out of them in order to cover the new expenditures and loans. The fellahin cultivated *kharadj* lands, either as State lessees or as peasants in the service of the large landlords. These were the lands which brought in the bulk of agricultural taxes while the large landowners succeeded in shifting their payment on to the fellahin. According to the investigations of the International Commission for the examination of Egypt's finances the *kharadj* lands in 1878 amounted to 3,487,000 feddan, yielding £ 3,143,000 in taxes, while only £ 333,000 was collected from the *'ushri* lands, which comprised 1,323,000 feddan. This means that at a ratio of 1 :2.5 between the two categories of land, the ratio of taxes was about 1 :10 (the average tax on *kharadj* (or *miri*) land being at that time 18-22 shillings per feddan, and on *'ushri* land only 7 shillings).[176] Despite the pressure exerted by the creditors and their representatives in the Caisse, the burden of taxes imposed on the fellahin was somewhat eased during the British Administration (see preceding chapter). However, as late as 1902, Willcocks found it opportune to quote the fellahin saying: "however much you may shake an empty bag of flour, you can always knock some more flour out of it by striking it with a stick."[177]

[175] For 1896 and 1906, this category was included in that of 1.1-5 feddan.
[176] Cf. J. C. McCoan, *Egypt under Ismail*, 1889, p. 147.
[177] W. Willcocks, *Egypt Fifty Years Hence,* Cairo, 1902, p. 14.

Thanks to developments in irrigation and irrigation methods, the cultivated area during British rule grew by a million feddan. The cotton sector in particular was expanded, and its yields grew from 2.25 million kantar in 1880 to 6-6.5 million in 1905,[178] and 7.3 million prior to the outbreak of the First World War.[179] Yet the monoculture type of economy which cotton imparted to Egypt involved considerable economic difficulties, either due to plant diseases or, in particular, as a result of price fluctuations.

The new irrigation methods also had unfavourable side-effects, such as salination, impoverishment of the land by over-exploitation through one harvest after another, or diseases like bilharzia and malaria. At the beginning of the 20th century the average yields, especially those of cotton, decreased as compared to the 'nineties of the preceding century. The need for intensifying the measures for fighting diseases and for soil fertilisation grew.

Nevertheless the general trend towards growing income from cotton was of considerable benefit to other sectors of the economy. It enhanced the purchasing power and expanded the market for the products of these sectors. While the value of cotton export at the end of the 'eighties was about £ 9 million per year, the average rose in 1910-1914, after the price crisis had passed, to about 29 million pounds, with fluctuations in the price level which were balanced off by increased production. Even in grain cultivation a rise took place following the general expansion of cultivated areas. As the proportion of grains in the total agricultural output (and area) went down, they disappeared from the list of export items, both because of the preference given to cotton and the strong competition on the grain market.[180]

The prosperity of the sugar market brought about increased cultivation of sugar cane and encouraged experiments in sugar milling and refining. This sector, too, was able to develop following the changes which had occurred in irrigation methods. On the other hand the production of sugar encountered serious obstacles. The refineries had been set up at too large a distance from the railway lines; the organisation of the enterprises was defective; corruption was rampant among most of their managements. Furthermore, sugar failed to enjoy stability on the world market, and also Egypt was affected by the strong fluctuations in demand and in price.

The performance fo the Egyptian industry on the eve of the First World War was hardly encouraging, especially if one compares it with the stupendous plans and daring experiments of Mehmed Ali. Official sources estimated the proportion of wage-earners in industry (including crafts, home industries and mines) at 4-5% (about 60-80,000) of the total wage earners in 1875[181] and at 13% before the War, but it is doubtful whether this latter percentage was actually reached.[182] In mining,

---

[178] Reports, *loc. cit.*, pp. 20-21.
[179] *Annuaire Egyptien*, 1948.
[180] A. E. Crouchley, *The Economic Development of Modern Egypt*, p. 164.
[181] J. C. McCoan, *Egypt As It Is*, 1877, p. 298.
[182] Even these sources themselves give entirely different figures elsewhere. Thus it was stated that according to the 1907 census, only 380,000 out of 9.5 million inhabitants (of 5 years old and above), i.e. 4 per cent, derived their livelihood from industry. The census of 1917 adopted the figure of about 11

only phosphates showed a notable increase in production. The phosphates rock output reached a yearly average of 100,000 tons in the years preceding the outbreak of the War. The country's industry was mainly based on agricultural raw materials such as cotton, oil crops and sugar cane. But even these industries, and all the more so those deprived of comparative advantages (such as tannery, procelain manufacture and woodwork), suffered severely from the competition of foreign products. The production of cigarettes based on imported tobacco grew considerably, but it was adversely affected by protectionist measures adopted by some importing countries. Particularly following the depression of 1873, foreign purchasers limited or even cancelled altogether the importation of cigarettes, which played an important role in Egyptian exports. The damage thus caused to Egypt's exports limited its import capacity with respect to raw materials, fertilisers, machinery and spare parts. Consequently, domestic production was impaired, especially in fields other than agriculture, such as the modern industries which Egypt was interested in developing.[183]

In the field of communications and transportation, where important foundations were laid during Ismail's time, progress continued until the eve of the First World War. This was inevitable under conditions of intensive transition to commercial agriculture and extensive cotton transactions. From the end of the 'seventies until 1914 the railway network was expanded from about 2,000 km to about 4,600 km. The telegraph network grew from 9,300 km to approximately 11,000 km. At the same time the use of means of communication grew and a rather high profitability level was maintained. A considerable contribution was thus made to the budget, especially by the railways, which were mainly State-owned. On the outbreak of war, however, steamship traffic, including both passengers and goods, suffered a setback.

It is typical that at a time when imports were considerably restricted, partly owing to prevailing war conditions in the exporting countries and partly because of the production of substitutes and the using-up of existing stocks, there was a relatively much slower decline in exports thanks to the large demand for Egyptian export goods, so that a further improvement took place in the country's payments balance.[184]

Egypt's commodity balance showed surpluses throughout the British period until the First World War; the value of average yearly exports in 1910-1914 was about £E. 32 million and of imports about £E. 25 million. Most of the surpluses were spent on the consolidated foreign debt annuities. Whereas the Egyptian nationalist leaders of

---

million inhabitants (as above), of which 443,000, i.e. again about 4%, were occupied in industry. *Annuaire Statistique de l'Egypte,* pp. 20-1. It transpires from this that both the ratio of industrial wage-earners to total wage-earners and the proportion of inhabitants deriving their livelihood from industry to the total number of inhabitants was between 4-5% throughout the entire period between 1875 and the First World War (if the official figure of 13% on the outbreak of War is ignored).

[183] *Annuaire Statistique de l'Egypte,* 1916, pp. 7-8.

[184] *Annuaire Statistique de l'Egypte,* 1916, pp. xxviii-xxx. For a short but useful summary of major economic trends in Egypt during the 19th century and first half of the 20th century, including imbalances in foreign accounts, see R. Mabro, *The Egyptian Economy 1952-1972,* pp. 1-24.

that period were right in claiming that in the years before the World War Egypt was in a state of severe economic backwardness, their attempt to put Mehmed Ali's and Ismail's actions in a favourable light and class them as achievements and those of the British as attempts at destroying these achievements is a major distortion of facts.[185] At most it may be said that, except in the financial and fiscal sphere, British imperialist rule with an eye to its selfish interests did not seriously try to repair the damage inflicted on the country by its own rulers, including Mehmed Ali[186], nor to given Egypt the "big push" towards a modern industrial take-off.

9. THE SUEZ CANAL[187]

Three events which occurred in Egypt in the 'sixties and 'seventies of the 19th century may count among the decisive factors affecting the country's economic and political development. These were the creation of Egypt's debt and the "Caisse"; the establishment of the Mixed Courts; and the construction of the Suez Canal.[188] Owing to the importance of the last of these factors it is discussed more extensively here.

The idea of connecting the Mediterranean with the Red Sea and thus with the Indian Ocean was not new. Herodotus[189] already tells of the unsuccessful attempt of Necho, King of Egypt, to build a canal at this place, and of Darius, King of Persia, successfully linking the Red Sea with the eastern branch of the Nile and through it with the Mediterranean. Diodorus of Sicily mentions Darius's view that differences in the levels of the Mediterranean and the Red Sea were thought to exist and that a direct connection between the two seas was feared to cause the flooding of Egypt by the Red Sea, whose level was supposed to be higher. Nevertheless both Diodorus and Strabo after him claim that Ptolemy the Second dug such a canal and avoided the risk of flooding by erecting a gate within the canal which was opened only at short intervals. According to this and further sources the construction of the canal led to an immense flourishing of trade, large ship traffic and the development of the city of Alexandria. There is again information to the effect that during the days of Khalif Omar a new canal was built between the Nile and the Red Sea to assure supplies from Egypt to the southern Arabian peninsula. It is not clear when this

---

[185] Cf. Ali Bey Kamel, *op. cit.*, pp. 28-29.

[186] For this more balanced attitude, see an otherwise severe critic of the British administration, T. Rothstein, *Egypt's Ruin, A Financial and Administrative Record,* London, 1910, p. 290.

[187] In the first edition of this book (1964), the story of the Canal was told until the end of the 1950's, to make it complete. Since then, however, some 15 years have passed fraught with events, wars and repeated closing, and re-opening of the Canal. In the meantime, also my book on *The Economic Structure of the Middle East* (1975) was published, including the more recent economic impact of the Suez Canal. Consequently, in this second edition, the uniform World War II deadline has been also adopted for the Canal.

[188] *Les Juridictions Mixtes,* etc., *loc. cit.,* p. 432; Rifaat Bey, *The Awakening of Modern Egypt,* p. 125.

[189] Quotations from Herodotus, Diodorus, Strabo, Plinius and later authors, Arab and others, are given in *Descriptions de l'Egypte,* X, pp. 177-185.

canal went out of use. At any rate the idea was brought up again several times between the 16th and 18th century and was also conceived by Napoleon, who even ordered his engineers to prepare plans for such a canal. A survey and detailed plan of the canal were indeed drawn up, including all the installations along the route from the Mediterranean through the Nile to Lake Timsah and the Red Sea, and the cost of its construction was estimated at 30 million francs. Owing to Napoleon's defeat in the Middle East and the ensuing conflicts between the Powers the plan was not carried into effect.[190]

In the 19th century misgivings with respect to differences in the level of the Red Sea and the Mediterranean were again voiced. These were proved to be groundless by Chesney, one of the first modern protagonists of the idea of digging the Suez Canal who personally explored the area (contradicting the view of the French expedition to Egypt).[191] Linant, who investigated this question towards the end of the 'thirties and beginning of the 'forties, arrived at the conclusion that there was indeed a difference in the level of the two seas, but that it was nevertheless possible and even necessary to implement the direct canal project and that the levels would become equilibrated in the course of time if suitable precautions were taken.[192]

When the Canal project sprung up anew during the first half of the 19th century it had two strong opponents who delayed its execution for some time: Mehmed Ali and Great Britain.

Mehmed Ali was afraid of two things in particular: a) that the Canal might cause trade and communication routes to avoid Alexandria and would thus undermine the position of this growing port;[193] b) that the Canal would give rise to political problems similar to those of the Dardanelles and the Bosphorus, which had become a constant point of dispute between the Great Powers. This would increase the danger of foreign intervention and even occupation of Egypt.[194] Accordingly Mehmed Ali refused in 1834 to grant the Frenchman, Fournel, a concession for digging the Canal, and persisted in his refusal until his death.[195]

---

[190] C. F. Wurm, "Der Projectierte Canal Von Suez", *Deutsche Vierteljahrsschrift,* Stuttgart und Tuebingen, 1844, pp. 274-319. In *Description de l'Egypte* there is a French engineering plan of 1838 suggesting a canal between the Red Sea and the Nile Delta, but also envisaging an adequate possibility of linking the Red Sea directly with the Mediterranean, at any rate according to the recommendations of the chief engineer of the French Expedition of December 6th, 1800 to the First Consul (Napoleon) where it is stated that: "Regarding the communication between the two seas by means of the Nile, before as yet having ascertained the most appropriate direction for establishing active communications between the different commercial sites in Egypt, we think that it would be best to adopt its original direction, that of the Kings' Canal, leaving the Nile near Bubaste." An interesting point here is the care shown for the internal trade routes of Egypt. *Description de l'Egypte,* X, p. 79; cf. also pp. 142-146.

[191] *The Life of the late General F. R. Chesney,* by His Wife and Daughter, London, 1885, pp. 466-7.

[192] Extracts from the Linant Report in A. Anderson, *Observations on... a Communication between the Red Sea and the Mediterranean,* London, 1843, pp. 9-15. For a comprehensive account of the whole Suez Canal story see A. Linant de Bellefonds, *Principaux travaux,* etc., Le Caire, 1872-3; Jean Mazuel, *L'Oeuvre Géographique de Linant de Bellefonds,* Le Caire, 1937, pp. 236-388.

[193] Even in Ismail's time during the middle of the 'sixties, commercial circles in Alexandria still objected to the opening of the Canal for fear of competition by Port Said. See J. C. Roux, *L'Isthme et le Canal de Suez,* Paris, 1901, Vol. I, p. 356.

[194] F. R. Chesney, *Reports on the Navigation of the Euphrates,* Appendix I, p. 371.

[195] M. Sabry, *L'Empire Egyptien sous Mohamed-Ali,* 1930, pp. 564-5. Some sources relate that

In the course of the 'thirties and 'forties of the 19th century it became clear to Britain that she would have no chance of exclusive control over the Canal, once it were constructed. There was growing interest in the Canal on the part of the French as well as the Germans, which caused the British to take a disfavourable view towards the Canal project. England persisted in its opposition to the project until the middle of the 'seventies, suspecting the intentions of the French who had not yet given up their ambition to retrieve their position in the area after the failure of Napoleon's campaign. Palmerston, the British Prime Minister of the 'fifties, feared the secession of Egypt from Turkey and interference with the traffic to India, following the upsurge of new parties who would have a stake in the area. (These apprehensions re-emerged on the eve of the First World War when the Germans appeared on the horizon.) Palmerston did not hide his desire to prevent the digging of the Canal or at least British participation in the acquisition of shares in the company to be formed (perhaps in the hope that thus the enterprise would fail to be carried out). The open arguments advanced by the British[196] centred mainly round their opposition to the compulsory labour customary in the Canal works[197] (even though the very idea of using such labour to the extent of 500,000 men[!] was put forward in a letter by Chesney, the head of an official British exploring mission, written as early as 1830, *loc. cit.,* p. 373), and to the grant of a concession to the company for the areas adjacent to the Canal. At the same time Palmerston made no secret of his various political objections. England, which was not convinced by de Lesseps'[198] arguments that British interests would in no way be jeopardised and that the economic success of the enterprise was assured, exerted pressure on the Sultan[199] to delay his approval of the concession until 1866 (see below). But Said's commitments, the relentless zeal and excellent connections of de Lesseps, who even managed to win over the British Chambers of Commerce in favour of his plans and in 1857 travelled across England to conduct his propaganda campaign (received in good humour by Palmerston himself)[200], and the attitude adopted by France, which at first was hesitant in giving its whole-hearted support to the French engineer, all these in the end helped to pave the way towards the construction of the Canal.

The concession for the digging of the Canal was granted by Said to Ferdinand de Lesseps on November 30th, 1854. It was officially published in 1855 and was

---

Mehmed Ali's refusal to grant the concession stemmed from his preference for an impressive project of a Nile dam as against Fournel's Canal project which, in his eyes, would have to compete with the former for scarce resources. Cf., *Le Percement de L'Isthme de Suez, Enfantin (1833-1855), M. de Lesseps (1855-1869),* Paris, 1869, pp. 10, 14.

[196] Cf. P. Fitzgerald, *The Great Canal at Suez,* Ch. IV, pp. 52-70. An interesting chapter on the less openly-advanced British claims is found in N. W. Senior, *Conversations and Journals in Egypt and Malta,* 1882, Vol. II, pp. 97-103.

[197] While in agriculture at that time there was a shortage of manpower, an average of 30,000 men were employed on the Canal works.

[198] F. de Lesseps, *Lettres, Journal et Documents,* I, pp. 45-6, 127-8, 134-8, 199-203, 211-227, 238-241 and 385-9. Most of the second volume of de Lesseps' writings is devoted to the British opposition and the attempts made at overcoming it.

[199] A lively and interesting description of the Canal project and the circumstances under which the concession was granted may be found in N. W. Senior, *op. cit.,* Vol. II, *passim.*

[200] De Lesseps, *op. cit.,* II, pp. 69-97.

redrafted on January 5th, 1856. As early as 1846 de Lesseps had held a share in a company formed by another Frenchman, Enfantin,[201] in order to investigate the construction of the Canal, which, however, failed to receive the required concession. During the 'fifties de Lesseps' father had been French Consul-General in Egypt, and between his son Ferdinand (who also belonged to the consular service and for several years served as French Consul-General in Egypt) and Said ties of friendship were knitted which contributed to the grant of the concession upon Said's accession in 1854. In 1855, an international commission was set up by de Lesseps which on 2.1.1856 expressed its favourable opinion on the digging of a canal between the Mediterranean and the Red Sea, estimating the required expenditure at not more than 200 million francs (or about 8 million pounds sterling). From then on the plan became more realistic.[202] On the basis of the new concession of 1856[203] which in turn was also amended in course of time, the Suez Canal Company (*Compagnie Universelle du Canal Maritime du Suez*) was founded in 1858, with de Lesseps as Chairman of the Board of Directors.[204]

The registered capital of the company was 200 million French francs (8 million pounds sterling) divided into 400,000 shares. Since the British, the Russians, the Austrians and Americans refused to take up the shares allotted to them, and the French (25,000 shareholders) acquired only half (207,111 shares), Said was compelled, in course of time, to acquire most of the remaining shares as well, in addition to his allotment of 64,000 shares, so that his total shareholding amounted to 177,642 shares.[205] By a secret agreement Said also undertook to supply about 20,000 regular labourers[206] for the construction works (by requiring every Egyptian village to supply 3-5 workers for the Canal) on corvée terms. In his official decree concerning the employment of Egyptians on the canal works it was merely stated that he would provide for the supply of manpower. The decree further laid down terms of employment and wages which at first sight seem reasonable (obviously

---

[201] Barthélemy-Prosper Enfantin, (1796-1864), one of the founders of the Saint-Simon Movement in France, stayed in Egypt for two years with some of the members of the Movement. Within the scope of the Saint-Simonian ideals according to which a world-wide network of railways and canals would advance social and economic progress (at first within the "Mediterranean System"), they became interested in the project of the canal to link the Mediterranean with the Red Sea. They even set up a Société d'Etudes pour le Canal de Suez, with the intention of interesting European investors not merely in the canal as such but in the development of Egypt as a whole. But the plan failed until de Lesseps and his new company appeared on the scene. Cf. H. R. d'Allemagne, *Les Saint-Simoniens, 1827-1837*, Paris, 1930, in particular Ch. XII. For a detailed account of Fournel's and Enfantin's initiative, and the foundation of the Société d'Etude, cf. *Le Percement de L'Isthme de Suez*, 1869, mentioned above.

[202] In his diary of January 1855 de Lesseps (I, 79, ff.), on entering the Land of Goshen, used material from the Bible on the exodus from Egypt as a basis for his findings on the feasibility of constructing the canal. *Report of the International Commission*, in de Lesseps, *ibid.*, I, pp. 320-4, and 434-51.

[203] See text of the concession in Appendix 15.

[204] Cf. F. de Lesseps, *op. cit.*, II, pp. 405-412.

[205] *Ibid.*, III, pp. 2-3 and 381-391.

[206] According to some estimates the construction of the Canal actually caused the shifting over of 60,000 workers from other employment; in addition to the 20,000 workers employed on the Canal there were 20,000 on their way to work and another 20,000 on their way back to their villages. P. Crabités, *op. cit.*, p. 48.

under the labour conditions and wage scales prevailing in Egypt at that time).[207] But from de Lesseps' memoirs it transpires beyond all doubt that a lot of corvée labour was actually employed on the Canal, to an even greater extent than promised, while it was attempted to keep this fact secret. The Company was allotted an area of 2 km on either side of the Canal and round each harbour, as well as a concession for digging a canal for conveying fresh water from the Nile to the shores of the main Canal. The hitherto uncultivated area along the fresh water canal—63,000 hectares—was put at the disposal of the Company, which had the right to cultivate it. The farmers had to pay the Company for the use of water. The Company was further entitled to collect tolls in respect of the fresh water canal, which was also intended to serve as a communication channel. The Company was exempted from paying taxes for a period of 10 years for the area cultivated by it, and was totally exempt from taxes for the land required for the construction of the Canal itself (70,000 hectares), i.e., a total area of 133,000 hectares. It was agreed that Egypt, in consideration of the concession, would receive preference shares, entitling it to 15% of the net profits of the Company. Ten per cent of the profits were allocated to the holders of the founders' shares (whose title was not at all clear) and the remaining 75% to the holders of the ordinary shares.

During the subsequent reign of Ismail certain changes were made in the terms of the concession. In 1863 he exploited the hesitant attitude of the Sultan in order to obtain concessions from the Company, and in particular the return of the fresh water canal concession and the right to cultivate the lands.[208] It was provisionally agreed to decrease the number of permanent laboures which Egypt had undertaken to supply under corvée terms. These terms were held by the British to constitute effective slavery and they succeeded in stopping corvée work, especially in 1859 and 1863, thus temporarily paralysing the construction work.[209]

The differences of opinion between the Khedive and the Company continued to exist.[210] According to an agreement between Nubar Pasha and de Lesseps that Napoleon III would act as arbitrator in case of dispute between the parties, they applied to him at the beginning of 1864.[211] At that time Napoleon III was no longer hesitant about giving his support to the Company, in which French interests were represented to a very marked extent. On July 6th, 1864, he gave his award based on the recommendations of the commission appointed by him on 3.3.1864 to the effect that Egypt had to compensate the Company for the loss of corvée labour, the areas under the concession along the canal which were returned to Egypt, the fresh water concession returned to Egypt, as well as for a whole series of rights deriving from

---

[207] Cf. *Decree as to the Native Workmen* (1856), in P. Fitzgerald, *The Great Canal at Suez,* Vol. I, pp. 307-310.

[208] *Ibid.,* IV, pp. 349 ff.

[209] As quoted by de Lesseps (Vol. IV, p. 325), *The Spectator* in 1863 wrote "compulsory labour must cease, and this means the prohibition of the Canal".

[210] Ismail tried to make a stand against the Company and de Lesseps by means of manipulations on the stock exchange and by affecting the quotations of the Canal shares. Possibly he also intended to concentrate the majority of shares in his own hands but unsuccessfully, and was finally bound to accept Napoleon III's arbitration. D. S. Landes, *op. cit.,* p. 187.

[211] P. Crabités, *op. cit.,* p. 53.

this concession, such as irrigation, operation of machinery, communications, etc., which the Company had yielded up. The amount of the compensation was set at 84 million French francs (about 3.5 million pounds sterling) in gradually decreasing annual instalments payable until the end of 1879.[212]

It was subsequently agreed to mortgage until 1895 the dividends of the ordinary shares held by Egypt in the Suez Canal Company for the payment of compensation.[213]

Once the arbitrator had given his award the sublime Porte finally approved the concession granted by Said to de Lesseps on March 19th, 1866.[214] The arbitrator's verdict aroused much bitterness in Egypt. One of its results was an increasing trend on the part of the Egyptians to turn for credits and orders to the British instead of the French. Despite all difficulties, the Canal was finally completed. The fresh water canal which served both as a source of fresh water supply and as a communication channel was completed from the Nile as far as Lake Timsah in the centre of the Suez Canal on February 2nd, 1862,[215] and as far as Suez in 1865 (a total of 220 km). The economic significance of the fresh water canal for this part of the country, although it can hardly be assessed in exact figures, was very great. From the point of view of Egypt its importance was perhaps no less than that of the Suez Canal proper (at least until it was nationalised). The Suez Canal itself was ceremonially opened on November 17th, 1869, in the presence of Heads of States and representatives from all parts of Europe, and with unusual pomp and circumstance which cost a great deal of money.[216]

The first ships which passed through the Canal reached the Red Sea on November 20th after a voyage of 16 hours. Since the concession was granted to the Company for a period of 99 years from the date of the opening of the Canal it would have officially lapsed on November 16th, 1968. At that date the ownership of the Canal should have passed to Egypt, which would have had to pay the Company solely for installations and materials at that time situated in the Canal zone according to a mutually agreed evaluation, or the decision of a board of arbitrators in case no agreement were reached.

---

[212] See for data on the Company's proposals and the "Sentence Arbitrale" of Napoleon, F. de Lesseps, *op. cit.*, IV, pp. 379-385, 476-493. The compensation was calcutated as follows: 38 million francs for the Company's surrender of original terms of supply of Egyptian labour; 3 million francs for the return of the lands; 6 million francs for the rights deriving from the fresh water canal; and 10 million francs for its construction expenses (until it was handed over to Egypt).

As a result of direct negotiations between Ismail and the Company following the arbitration, an agreement was signed on February 22nd, 1866, by one of whose clauses permission was granted to Egypt to entrench itself at strategic and administrative points along the Canal. This had previously been prevented by means of the original concession. *Ibid.*, V. pp. 227-230.

[213] C. Lesage, *op. cit.*, p. 29.

[214] F. de Lesseps, *op. cit.*, V, pp. 197-8, and 265. *Recueil des Firmans Impériaux Ottomans*, loc. cit., pp. 288-295.

[215] F. de Lesseps, *op. cit.*, IV, p. 160. The point of juncture was, at de Lesseps' suggestion, called Ismailia.

[216] The expenses connected with the opening celebrations were estimated at 1 million pounds sterling and constituted a further Egyptian 'investment' in the Canal. *Ibid.*, V, pp. 318 ff. (J. C. McCoan estimates the expenditure at 1.3 million pounds sterling, p. 107).

The investments in the Canal at its opening in 1869 amounted to 16-18 million pounds sterling. Egypt claimed that until that time it had invested about 8 million pounds. According to a higher estimate, Egypt's share was 11.5 million pounds sterling, including the Egyptian expenses for digging the fresh water canal (cf. the data in Table X). Owing to their numerous liabilities, the Egyptians, who had borrowed at an official interest rate of 10%[217] the entire sum invested as their share in the capital of the Canal Company (about 4 million pounds sterling), in addition to providing the labour force, were gradually forced to give up many of the rights attached to their share in the Company. First of all they had to mortgage the income from the ordinary shares until 1895 for payment of compensation due to the Company according to the arbitration award of Napoleon III. Secondly, they had to sell these shares to the amount of 4 million pounds sterling (100 million francs) on November 25th, 1875, in order to raise the necessary funds to pay the interest on the debts due for that year.[218] Thirdly, in 1879 they assigned their preference shares carrying 15% of the net profits of the Company in favour of the Caisse which subsequently sold them to the Crédit Foncier de France for 880,000 pounds sterling.[219]

Differences of opinion exist as to the advantages of the deal concluded by Disraeli of acquiring the Egyptian shares through the Rothschild Bank (the actual instructions for the purchase of the shares were given by the Foreign Secretary, Lord Derby).[220] Critics claim that Disraeli paid more than their current market price and that at the time of their acquistition he was unaware of the fact that the dividends would until 1895 be mortgaged for payment of the compensation, so that their holder would be deprived until then not only of the dividends but also of their voting rights which anyhow were restricted to a maximum of 10 votes per

---

[217] *Ibid.*, III, p. 381-2, and IV, pp. 133-138.

[218] For the text of the agreement concerning the acquisition of the shares see P. Fitzgerald, *op. cit.*, Vol. II, pp. 323-314. For the deal made by Disraeli, see Charles Lesage, *L'achat des actions de Suez*, Paris, 1906. Upon signature of the purchase agreement it transpired that the number of shares held by Ismail was no longer 177,642 but 176,602, and the payment to Ismail was fixed at £ 3,976,582. *Ibid.*, p. 154.

It should be pointed that the French, headed by Derviéu, also conducted negotiations with Ismail in connection with the shares. Derviéu even signed an agreement with Ismail, several hours before the final instructions came from Britain that the shares be acquired on its behalf. According to this agreement Ismail would have received a loan of 85 million francs for 3 months at an annual interest of 18%, with a mortgage on Egypt's shares in the Canal Company, and on 15% of Egypt's income from the Canal. In case of non-payment at the date stipulated the shares and the percentages would go to the creditors. But the vacillations of the French financial circles (by whom the agreement still had to be ratified) and politicians in the meantime enabled the British to conclude the deal. Evidence is also available as to the fact that on November 20th the French officially applied to Britain regarding the attitude it would take to the acquisition of the shares by French capital, and that the British objected to almost all the shares being concentrated in the hands of one national group. Lesage, *ibid.*, p. 33-80.

[219] P. Crabités' description of this affair (pp. 57-59) is influenced by his favourable opinion of Ismail and is inaccurate both in dates and in facts.

[220] C. Lesage, *op. cit.*, pp. 1-15. According to this source a decisive role in the supply of information to the British on French-Egyptian negotiations (prior to the official French Note) was played by the London banker Henry Oppenheim and the Editor of the Pall Mall Gazette, F. Greenwood, who helped to explain the matter to the British Foreign Office. *Ibid.*, pp. 83-99.

shareholder. But it should be pointed out that England at that time regarded the deal mainly as a political and not as an economic venture. Likewise it is manifest from the text of the agreement that the British were aware of the lien since it contained a clause according to which Egypt undertook to pay to England 5% per year of the purchase price (i.e. 5 million francs) until 1894, as compensation for the loss of dividends until then.[221] The annual distributable dividends during the years preceding the First World War stood at 2.5-3 million pounds sterling[222] and after some time the value of the shares held by Britain rose considerably. In 1939 it was estimated at about 30 million pounds sterling (as against the purchase price of 4 million pounds sterling), a very considerable rise in price even if the depreciation of the pound is taken into account. Furthermore, following negotiations with de Lesseps, the British retrieved 10 votes and were promised 3 out of the 24 seats on the Board of Directors of the Company (in 1882 they received another 7 representatives, so that their total number was 10 out of 32). The protection of the Canal and its investments afterwards served as the main grounds for Britain's occupation of the area. Those who objected to Disraeli's initiative lay the main stress on the obligations thereby imposed on Britain, while his supporters point to economic and political advantages won henceforth.

In 1888 the Constantinople Convention was signed between all the major European powers (Britain, Austria-Hungary, France, Germany, Italy, Spain, Holland, Russia and Turkey). This convention *inter alia* declared the Canal neutral and open to all vessels, without distinction of flag, in times of peace as in times of war.[223] The validity of the convention (which should actually have come into force after the end of the British occupation, but by mutual consent was already applied in 1904) has not lapsed to this day, even though its provisions were evaded in the First World War during the clash between the British and the Turks[224], and again in the Second World War. According to the convention signed between Britain and the Egyptian Government in 1922 on the grant of independence to Egypt, Britain was made responsible for the defence of the Canal.[225] By the Anglo-Egyptian treaty of 1936, Egypt agreed that Britain should maintain forces to protect the Canal until Egypt alone should be able to assure its safety and guarantee freedom of navigation.[226] Egypt in *its* interpretations of the Constantinople Convention and the 1936 treaty has tried to justify its attempts to break the express provision of the Constantinople Convention not to make any distinctions between nations with respect to their right of passage through the Canal.[227]

---

[221] *Ibid.*, p. 160; text of the agreement, *ibid.*, pp. 273-5.

[222] Owing to the limitations of the original concession and the subsequent amendments the toll-fee per net ton transported across the Canal varied from 6 to 10 francs, of which 2/3 were charged on each ton of the loading capacity of empty vessels. A toll of 10 francs was also imposed on every adult passenger. *Annuaire Statistique de l'Egypte*, 1916, pp. 254-5.

[223] See Appendix 17.

[224] G. Douin, *L'attaque du Canal de Suez*, Paris, 1922, pp. 33-5.

[225] Text, Hurewitz, *ibid.*, Vol. II, pp. 102-3.

[226] Text, *ibid.*, Vol. II, pp. 203-211 and especially Clause 8 and the appendix to this clause.

[227] The clauses of the Constantinople Convention which allow special measures to be taken for the protection of Egypt in case of need, expressly forbid the breach of the clause granting the right of free passage through the Canal; see Clause 11 of the Convention.

After the Second World War the growing Egyptian influence over the affairs of the Canal made itself felt. Until 1948 the composition of the Board of Directors of the Company was as follows: 19 Frenchmen, 10 British, 2 Egyptians, 1 Dutchman, 1 American—total 33 members. According to the new agreement signed that year between the Company and Egypt it was stipulated that by 1956 five further Egyptian directors should be added to the Board, so that the number of Egyptians sitting on the Board should be increased to 7. It was provided that the proportion of Egyptian workers employed would be increased and that 7% of the Company's income be paid as taxes to the Egyptian treasury; further, that the navigation of Egyptian vessels between Canal ports should be free of any charges.[228]

The volume of goods which crossed the Canal in both directions, amounting to 437 thousand tons in 1870, reached 55 million tons by 1948. The number of transit passengers increased from 26.5 thousand to 454.8 thousand, respectively.

In the course of time, the bulk of cargo (some 80%) was conveyed from the south to the north, chiefly oil, on the heels of the growing demand of Europe for Middle Eastern oil.

TABLE XV

Suez Canal Traffic and Receipts, 1870-1948

Year	No. of passengers	Cargo (in '000 tons)	Receipts (in '000 francs)[229]
1870	26,758	437	4,600
1880	101,551	3,057	37,500
1890	161,353	6,890	67,000
1900	282,511	9,738	90,000
1910	234,320	16,581	129,500
1920	500,147	17,574	150,000
1930	305,202	31,668	1,047,000
1938	479,802	34,418	1,649,000
1948	454,864	55,081	16,545,000

Annuare Statistique de l'Egypte, 1916, Chapitre XVIII, Le Canal Maritime de Suez, pp. 253-257; F. de Lesseps, *op. cit.*, V, p. 394; *L'Egypte, Memento Economique*, Paris, 1950, pp. 123-4; Compagnie Universelle du canal maritime de Suez, *Le Canal de Suez, Documents Statistiques*, Paris, 1950, pp. 8-9, 12-13; National Bank of Egypt, *Economic Bulletin*, Vol. XV, No. 1, 1962, Table 30; U.N., *Monthly Bulletin of Statistics*, January 1962.

The study carried out at the instigation of de Lesseps in 1854 by the geologist, Prof. M. Cordier, already pointed out the great advantages of the Canal for international trade and the large saving achieved by shortening the route to India and the Far East. According to the data summed up in this study the alternative

---

[228] In the Canal itself many improvements and repairs have been made since its construction. Also its present condition is not satisfactory and further expansion plans exist. The length of the Canal is 173 km; its width at the bottom 60-75 metres and at the top 120-150 metres. At first the depth of the Canal was 8-8.5 metres, reaching 10.5 metres prior to the First World War. The expansion plans envisaged a further deepening of the Canal and the addition of an auxiliary Canal to enable traffic of vessels simultaneously in both directions.

[229] At current prices.

distances from western ports to Bombay, India, would be as follows:[230]

TABLE XVI

Shortening of Communication Lines by the Suez Canal (Distance to Bombay)

Port	Through Suez Canal (in leagues)	Through Atlantic Ocean (in leagues)	Difference
Constantinople	1,800	6,100	4,300
Malta	2,062	5,800	3,778
Trieste	2,340	5,980	3,620
Marseille	2,374	5,650	3,276
Cadiz	2,224	5,200	2,976
Lisbon	2,500	5,350	2,850
Bordeaux	2,800	6,650	2,850
Le Hâvre	2,824	5,800	2,976
London	3,100	5,950	2,850
Liverpool	3,050	5,900	2,850
Amsterdam	3,100	5,950	2,850
Petersburg	3,700	6,550	2,850
New York	3,761	6,200	2,439
New Orleans	3,724	6,450	2,726

Calculations show that the transportation of the cargo shipped through the Suez Canal in 1955 round the Cape of Good Hope would have cost 600 million dollars more.

The installation of pipelines from the oilfields in the Persian Gulf to the Mediterranean interfered somewhat with the business of the Canal. The Board of the Suez Canal Company decided to introduce certain reductions in the transit tolls (however only until the nationalisation of the Canal, upon which charges were increased). On the whole, the gap created by the direct flow of oil through the pipelines was filled by the increase in the general oil production in the area, as well as by other supplementary cargoes.[231]

A short-range view does not fully reflect the true value accruing to Egypt from the Canal (ignoring for the moment the international complications) especially since Egypt was compelled to abandon a number of its direct advantages owing to the mortgage of the ordinary shares, and their subsequent sale, and the surrender of the preference shares.

But on a longer view, the Canal brought about important changes in the status and economy of Egypt. The main Canal ports, Port Said and Suez, received a new impetus towards development and the many auxiliary services brought in considerable sums to Egypt over and above its share in the Company's income according to the new arrangments of the 'forties and 'fifties of the present century.

---

[230] From the memorandum (dated 15.11.1854) of de Lesseps to Said, the Viceroy of Egypt.

[231] On the eve of the nationalisation of the Canal, in 1955, the Company's income from transit tolls amounted to approximately £ 32 million per year. U.N., *Economic Developments in the Middle East, 1959-1961*, N.Y., 1962, p. 169.

Although employment on the construction of the Canal came to an end (and under the then prevailing conditions it hardly brought much benefit), the proportion of Egyptians among the regular employees gradually rose in the meantime, and the improvements of the Canal also brought employment at improved conditions. The entire agricultural area along the Main and the Ismailia Canals[232] was given a strong incentive by the development of the new lines of communication, the more intensive cultivation of additional areas, based on irrigation canals, and the increased purchasing power of the local population.

The overall direct addition to the Egyptian national income (share in the transit tolls and other expenses of the Company and the ships crossing the Canal) amounted to about 1.5 per cent of the national income after World War II. This calculation does not include wages and salaries paid to the Egyptian workers of the Company, who constituted the majority of its 5,000 employees, nor the expansion of economic activity mentioned above, which is difficult to assess. This state of affairs lasted until the nationalisation of the Canal on July 26th, 1956.[233]

---

[232] Regarding the changes which the Ismailia Canal, upon its completion, wrought in the area, see P. Fitzgerald, *op. cit.,* Vol. I, pp. 180-185.

[233] For the nationalisation of the Canal, see Republic of Egypt, *White Paper on the Nationalisation of the Suez Maritime Canal Company,* Gov. Press, Cairo, 1956; for the compensation arrangements, see Compagnie Financière de Suez, *Bulletin d'Information,* No. 3, Paris, oct. 1959, p. 37.

PART FIVE

PERSIA AND ITS ECONOMIC PROBLEMS IN THE 19TH AND 20TH CENTURY
(until World War 1)

1. THE DECLINE OF PERSIA'S ECONOMIC RESOURCES AND PUBLIC FINANCES

From one point of view, at least, the fate of Persia was similar to that of Egypt, Iraq and other parts of the Ottoman Empire: Under the impact of the migration of peoples, the changing of regimes and the conquests which led to the destruction of an ancient civilisation, the population and its economic resources had severely dwindled. The self-same resources which in the times of Darius had maintained a population of about 50 million inhabitants in Persia, and at the zenith of Safawid rule (at the end of the 16th and beginning of the 17th centuries) had sufficed for some 40 million inhabitants,[1] were hardly enough to keep alive a population of some 6 million people at the beginning of the 19th century and of 9-12 million at the end of the century.[2] The population had suffered directly mainly through wars and epidemics, which frequently went hand in hand. The ruin of economic assets by infliction of direct damage or through neglect brought about a shortage of food and poor health conditions. Despite the decrease in the population, famine became a dominant feature in the Persia of the 19th century.

Much Persian blood was shed in the wars of conquest conducted by Nadir Shah in the middle of the 18th century in India and the Ottoman Empire, even though the booty was considerable. Upon the assassination of Nadir (in 1747) the situation of the people was revealed in all its calamity. They were grossly overtaxed, weary of military service and compulsory labour. Most investment plans, for instance in construction and communications, were arrested in the first stages of execution and failed.[3] The entire subsequent period—perhaps excepting that of Karim Khan—merely constitutes the continuation of the social and economic decline which had revealed itself in all its nakedness on the removal of Nadir Shah.

The attempts of a despotic regime to provide in the first instance for the filling of its constantly empty coffers—and in the absence of foreign resources the entire pressure was now directed inwards—completely impoverished the large class of taxpayers, the fellahin. Again, as in the case of the economy of the Ottoman Empire in the 18th and 19th centuries, the plundering of static resources in the absence of

---

[1] J. Chardin, *A New and Accurate Description of Persia,* 1724, II, *passim.*
[2] Moustafa Khan Fateh, *The Economic Position of Persia,* London, 1926, p. 2; Cf. also John Malcolm, *History of Persia,* 1888, p. 17. An interesting discussion of the demographic trends can be found in G. G. Gilbar, "Demographic developments in late Qajar Persia, 1870-1906", reprint from *Asian and African Studies,* Vol. 11, No. 2 - 1976, Jerusalem Academic Press.
[3] Moustafa Khan Fateh, *op. cit.,* p. 36.

new investments in manpower and equipment undermined the country's productive capacity and taxability, rendering the country's economy and independence highly susceptible to foreign influence. This feature was basically common to the entire region, as were two further factors: the rerouting of the major communication lines and the impoverishment of the soil,[4] conjointly leading to economic decline and political disintegration.

The deterioration of the economic situation was to a considerable extent the result of the absence of an adequate economic and financial apparatus (despite the official existence of a Finance Ministry). The ministers, who changed frequently, were not familiar with the matters in their charge; the customs service was run by foreigners (since the end of the 19th century—by Belgians) without real public or even governmental supervision; and although the Belgian directors achieved a more efficient collection and managed to increase the customs revenue, owing to the lack of control a substantial part of the revenue leaked out and did not enter the State treasury. The officials in charge of tax collection were given their posts on the basis of family or personal connections, under a system of bribery, rather than according to qualifications and suitability.

The customary method of taxation which had obtained in Persia for generations also reflected the backwardness of the socio-economic structure, while at the same time forming a decisive factor in preventing the State from organising its economic life on modern lines. For purposes of taxation and tax collection the country was divided into 18 provinces, in turn sub-divided into sub-provinces at the head of which stood tax collectors and deputy tax collectors, while the village heads were responsible for local collections. Part of the taxes were paid in cash, but a large share was collected in kind (by the 19th century it had become customary to pay half the agrarian taxes in cash and half in kind)[5]. This led to transportation and storage difficulties, and in fact prevented the keeping of proper accounts. As a rule the central government was ignorant of the state of assessments and collections and had to rely on the local and district collectors who generally owed certain fixed quotas to the government. To the extent that accounts were kept, in little books called *katabtche*, these were in charge of the *mustawfi*, the central or local bookkeeper, who in course of time turned into a special class on whom both the taxpayers and the government became dependent.[6] W. M. Shuster (whose economic activities in Persia will be discussed later in Chapter 5: "Attempts at Reform") mentions the lack of any real budget and any real account of State debts. Shuster's request as chief treasurer that all bank and cash balances be transferred to him was indeed fulfilled, but in actual fact it meant that all the government could show was a deficit covered by an overdraft in the government's account with the Imperial Bank,[7] even this without reflecting the actual total liabilities of the government. The low salaries of the government tax officers (to the extent that the collectors were not tax-farmers

---

[4] Jules de Hagemeister, *Essai sur les Ressources Territoriales et Commerciales de l'Asie Occidentale*, St. Petersbourg, 1839, p. 287.

[5] J. Malcolm, *op. cit.*, 1888, p. 177.

[6] W. M. Shuster, *The Strangling of Peria*, New York, 1912, pp. 277-282.

[7] *Ibid.*, pp. 28-44.

who had undertaken to pay a fixed sum to the government) caused a considerable part of the taxes collected to flow into their pockets. In particular, the government incurred immense losses by the disappearance of taxes paid in kind on their way to the government stores.[8] This matter was actually of much greater than merely fiscal significance.

The bread supply in Persia had for generations constituted a difficult problem and bread riots, especially in the larger centres of population, were quite frequent. Even in years when the harvest was good or had succeeded in at least certain parts of the country which under good transportation conditions might have supplied the rest, starvation nevertheless prevailed in other regions owing to the defective communications between the sources of production and centres of demand.[9] One of the purposes of central grain storage was to assure a regular supply at adequate prices of this important commodity in the cities and to make good the shortages due to drought or speculation (i.e. concealment of the goods). Had the government machinery worked efficiently, this system would have provided an important means towards correcting economic and social abuses in a backward country. But frequently serious administrative defects or official corruption intervened, involving the members of the government and the provincial governors,[10] not to mention the exploitation of shortages by the landowners for purpose of speculation.

As stated, the agrarian taxes were not collected according to a uniform method. Sometimes they were paid by the landlord and sometimes by the cultivator, sometimes in cash and sometimes in kind, or according to a mixed system. The *waqf* lands and part of the lands held under special terms as trusts received from the Shah were exempt from land taxes.[11]

Not only the state of collection but the fiscal structure as such brought the average annual deficit of the Persian government to an estimated amount of over 5 million dollars between the end of the 19th and the beginning of the 20th century, even assuming a more or less regular collection of the internal taxes (i.e. excluding customs). The customs revenue was very low in view of the tariffs in force by virtue of the capitulations (e.g. in 1909/10 the duty on sugar was 3% and on refined petrol $1/2$%). The taxes on goods exported and imported constituted 4-5% of the total value of exports and imports. In contrast to Shuster, Chirol mentions major achievements made by the Customs Management set up by the Belgian Nauss at the beginning of the present century. The system of farming out customs was abolished and a uniform rate of 5% on all imports and exports at all customs stations was imposed. In a short time the customs revenue increased by 60-70%.[12] From the end

---

[8] Shuster tells of cases where the government lost up to $ 100,000 on a single day as a result of such deals. *Ibid.*, p. 288; cf. also E. Aubin, *La Perse d'aujourd'hui*, 1908, pp. 178-9.
[9] V. Chirol, *The Middle Eastern Question or Some Political Problems of Indian Defence*, London, 1903, pp. 97.
[10] See Shuster, *op. cit.*, Chapter on Bread Riots (VII), pp. 169 ff.
[11] Cf. Ann K. S. Lambton, *Landlord and Peasant in Persia*, 1953, pp. 118 ff.
[12] V. Chirol, *The M. E. Question,* p. 69. According to Curzon's data it transpires that in the pre-Belgian period, e.g. during the decade 1879-1889, the almost stagnant annual income from customs in real terms was about £ 236,000. G. N. Curzon, *Persia and the Persian Question,* London, 1892, Vol. II, p. 476. Chirol, however, remarks on the decisive influence exercised by the Russians over the Belgian

of the 19th century onwards the customs revenues were mortgaged to the payment of debts under foreign State loans.

The customs constituted only one out of four categories of revenue which were considered to be "fixed" revenues. There were also fixed revenues from regular taxes on land, cattle, trade and industry; the income of the crown lands; and the rental for the leasehold of State lands. In addition there were irregular sources of revenue—gifts, fines, confiscations, bribes, etc. One of the most burdensome among the irregular taxes was *sadir*, a levy imposed on a certain area or even on the whole State to cover some special expenditure, such as the expenses of carrying on a war, the construction of a palace, a reception for foreign ambassadors, etc. The governor of the province was responsible for collecting such taxes in any way he saw fit. The absence of central control over the taxes generally; the fact that any changes in the ability of the landowners and villages in the various regions to raise the required amounts were ignored as well as the corrupt method of collection—all led to abuses and showed the utter lack of a guiding tax policy.[13]

Owing to the constantly increasing expenditures the deficits were in danger of incessant growth.[14] Shuster temporarily succeeded in 1911 in remedying the situation by increasing the revenue and severely curtailing the expenditure of government offices, but this was no more than a temporary respite. The structure of the expenditures of the government budget—to the extent that one may speak of a budget prior to Shuster's arrival—was a clear expression of the backwardness of the country and the nature of its government. Two-fifths of the budget were spent on the army (whose fighting capacity by the way was very low), one-fifth was allotted to payment of pensions (a kind of organised system of bribery for the higher officials and the nobility) and one-fifth was used by the Shah's court and his tribal relatives (the Kajar tribe). Only the last fifth, and usually less, was allotted to all the other economic, social and administrative functions of the State.[15]

The deficits which had accumulated by the end of the 19th and beginning of the 20th century (without any increase in the national product being achieved by the increased expenditures) in conjunction with the deficits on current account in the balance of payments, and the general decline in the price of silver metal brought about a constant depreciatation of the silver *kran*, after the gold *tuman*[16] had

---

management and in this respect is not far removed from Shuster's evaluation. The Russian influence was *inter alia* reflected in the Russian-Persian trade agreement of 1901 (which in respect of customs remained in force until 1903) according to which the *ad valorem* system was replaced by a weight system and specific tarrifs. It turned out in fact that a particular increase took place in the duties on import and export commodities to and from Britain while duties relating to the Russian market were raised only slightly or were cancelled altogether. Although the agreement signed between Persia and Britain in 1903 provided for the same customs rates as the agreement with Russia, as stated, the *structure* of the tariff favoured the Russian trade. Chirol, *ibid.*, pp. 77-88.

[13] J. Malcolm, *op. cit.*, p. 179; G. N. Curzon, *op. cit.*, pp. 470-8.
[14] W. M. Shuster, *op. cit.*, p. 303.
[15] V. Chirol, *op. cit.*, p. 91.
[16] The *tuman*, a term introduced by the Mongols in the 13th century, had several monetary meanings; but chiefly it indicated the value of 10,000 *dinars*, or 10 *krans* at the beginning of the 19th century, and 100 *krans* on the eve of the monetary reform of 1930-2. Following this reform the *tuman* was replaced by

disappeared from the market. It fell rapidly from 10 *kran* per £ 1 at the beginning of the 19th century to 21 *kran* in 1836, 25 *kran* in 1875, 35 *kran* in 1890, and 61 *kran* per £ 1 in 1914/15.[17] During the war years, the state of the *kran* in relation to the currency of the belligerent nations (accompanied also by a rise in the price of silver metal) relatively improved while a new decline set in only as from 1920/21.[18] Whenever the budget showed any surpluses, these were largely channelled into the private coffers of the Shah, rather than applied for investments or the consolidation of the shaky financial and monetary situation of the country. Even in such years, the general State treasury thus had no relief from the unbearable pressure of expenditures bearing down on its limited resources.[19]

2. SOME PROBLEMS OF MAJOR ECONOMIC SECTORS

The difficulties of Persian agriculture stemmed mainly from the low level of investments and the backward methods of farming, ownership and taxation. The fact that the mountain ranges both in the north and in the south prevent precipitates and moisture from reaching the inside of the country vitally affected Persian agriculture. Hence, apart from narrow strips along the shores of the Caspian Sea, agriculture had to rely on artificial irrigation. On the other hand, students of the area are sometimes too hasty in attributing the economic backwardness of the Middle Eastern area to the soil and the climate on the one hand and the farmers' unwillingness to engage in hard physical labour on the other. The validity of such generalisations is doubtful, at any rate as regards Persia. With greater and more efficient input of water most of Persia's soil may be rendered fertile,[20] while water, though mostly unexploited, is present in not inconsiderable quantities. Moreover, the Persian farmer has excelled in past generations in diligence and strenuous efforts to utilise the soil to the maximum with the aid of the most primitive tools and canals—partly subterranean (*qanats*)—which were most difficult to construct and

---

the *pahlevi*, and the *kran* by the *riyal*. Their value, however, has changed in terms of foreign exchange. Cf. discussion of Persia's finances in the period between wars, below. Also, H. L. Rabino di Borgomale, *Coins, Medals, and Seals of the Shâks of Iran (1500-1941)*, 1945, p. 12.

[17] John Malcolm, *Sketches of Persia*, I, 1829, p. 43; Moustafa Khan Fateh, *op. cit.*, pp. 71-2; G. D. Turner, *Lecture on main events, Oct. 1912-Oct. 1913*, to Persia Society, London, Oct. 17, 1913; A. T. Wilson, *Persia*, London, 1932, p. 254.

It the sporadic and short-term experiments between the 13th and 19th century are ignored, the extensive use of paper notes started only after a concession for the issue of such notes had been granted to the Imperial Bank of Persia, founded by the British (cf. below).

[18] *Bulletin de la Banque Nationale de Perse*, Janvier 1934, p. 3.

[19] G. N. Curzon, *op. cit.*, II, 479-483. On the efforts to improve the State finance system prior to the First World War, see below in the Chapter "Attempts at Reform".

[20] It is true that large and even fertile parts of Persia have turned into swamplands and become salinated. This however can be remedied relatively easily by capital investment and employment of modern cultivation methods. Cf., The Persia Society, a Lecture by H. F. B. Lynch, *The Importance of Persia*, June 14, 1912, London.

With regard to the special nature of Persian agriculture, cf. also J. Chardin, *op. cit.*, London, 1724, II, pp. 8 ff.

maintain, especially in the absence of adequate equipment. Although under conditions of primitive, non-mechanised technology the *qanats,* relying on gravitation, have performed a first-rate task, their drawbacks, reflected in loss of water and topographical limitations, were significant.[21] The secret of Persia's prosperity in the past lies to a great extent in the achievements of agriculture. Neither water and soil resources nor the working capacity[22] were to blame. The ruin was caused directly by warring armies which from time to time ravaged the country or indirectly by a regime which prevented the limited resources available from being channelled towards the maintenance of the existing and construction of a modern system of irrigation, while contributing to and encouraging the ruinous exploitation of the water system by the large landlords at the expense of the smallholders.[23]

Under the prevailing topographical and hydrological conditions and the poor income level of the farmers, water works in Persia had of necessity to be carried out by a public body, as, according to the available sources (Nearchus, Strabo)[24], had indeed been done in ancient times. But for generations both the government and the landlords merely squeezed out all possible revenue from the peasant without putting into effect any serious long-term irrigation plans (see also chapter 4. on Social Structure below). Various attempts during the first half of the 19th century to build dams and a network of canals failed, largely owing to faulty planning. In 1903-6 plans for major irrigation works, mainly on the Karun river, were put forward by Belgian, Dutch and British advisers, this time according to a comprehensive plan fully approved by Willcocks in 1909. However, the political and economic conditions in Persia at that time prevented its implementation.

As in other countries in the region, the conditions of land tenure (including absenteeism) and methods of cultivation in Persian agriculture retarded and even reversed the development of agricultural produce which in the past had been known for its high standard, such as silk or sugar cane. In the main branches of agricultural production—grains—the yields were likewise low, because of poor equipment, non-cultivation of large tracts of arable land and non-execution of irrigation plans.[25] Most of the produce, especially wheat, barley, maize and rice, was consumed within the country. Although from time to time certain quantities were left over for exports—especially of rice, which prior to the First World War was exported to Russia at the rate of half a million pounds sterling—there was generally a shortage of grains. Prices rocketed in urban centres as well as in seasonally affected rural areas with landlords and speculators reaping the fruits of the sellers' market.

---

[21] Cf. Henri Goblot, "Le probléme de l'eau en Iran", *Orient,* 1962, reproduced in Ch. Issawi (ed.), *The Economic History of Iran 1800-1914,* pp. 214-219.

[22] With the primitive equipment available, the amount of labour invested was, and still is, insufficient to utilise the country's entire possibilities to the full. The diligence of the Persian fellah is stressed not only by Chirol but also by Paul Rohrbach, *Die Wirtschaftliche Bedeutung Westasiens,* Frankfurt a. M., Zweite Auflage, 1908, pp. 31-2.

[23] Examples of the landlords' misuse and of the efforts made by the farmers without any major investments may be found in V. Chirol, *The Middle Eastern Question,* pp. 129-132.

[24] Cf. W. Willcocks, *The Irrigation of Mesopotamia,* 1911, *passim.*

[25] A. T. Wilson, *op. cit.,* pp. 200-212. - For useful information on Persian agriculture based on contemporary sources, see Ch. Issawi (ed.), *The Economic History of Iran 1800-1914,* pp. 206-257.

Persian cotton, like Egyptian cotton, enjoyed a temporary prosperity during the American Civil War. It even succeeded in penetrating several foreign markets, but its short fibres and the lack of adequate government support prevented its serious development. Only tobacco and opium, which received considerable encouragement and organised supervision—either by foreign concession-holders or by the local government—became major profitable branches of agricultural production, especially among export items. Opium growing, for which conditions are excellent in Persia, received a special impetus when its demand on the world market rose in the 'fifties and as a reaction to the blow inflicted by a silkworm disease on the production of Persian silk in the 'sixties of the 19th century. On the other hand opium, which became a central export item, mainly to China, and an important source of government revenue, had a devastating effect on the health of the Persian population, most of whom became addicted to this drug.[26]

Sericulture, which constituted one of Persia's outstanding economic sectors until the middle of the 18th century, suffered major setbacks later on due both to natural causes and to neglect and lack of the special care which is indispensable for this particular branch. In effect, the output of silk fell steeply from 1,900 metric tons in 1669 to only 200 tons in 1750. The rise in silk consumption and prices in Europe in the 19th century also stimulated sericulture in Persia, and silk output grew again in 1850 to above 1,000 tons, of which 610 tons went for exports. But soon this sector became affected by the *Pébrine* disease, which resulted in a heavy fall in output to 100 tons only in 1860. It was not before the beginning of the 20th century that renewed attempts were made at the rehabilitation of sericulture and the silk industry, effecting a gradual rise in production up to 500 tons in 1909.[27]

Persia had a rich tradition in livestock breeding and enjoyed many natural advantages, especially for the breeding of camels, mules, goats, sheep and fish. These also formed the basis for associated industries, such as the leather industry, wool of various kinds, and caviar. Some of these industries, however, for instance caviar, were farmed out as a concession, first to Persian but then mainly to Russian subjects,[28] while another part laboured under the same difficulties which beset the whole of private industry.

While stagnation characterised the Persian countryside, a severe deterioration took place in the economic status of the cities. At the beginning of the 19th century only the two holy cities of Persia (Kum and Meshed)[29] still enjoyed some income from Shi'ite pilgrims and to some extent managed to maintain their economic activity and exterior aspect, but even there the glory of the rich quarters had passed.[30] In most of the other cities the economic depression manifested itself both in the reduction of the population and by whole quarters being reduced to ruins. An

---

[26] Elgin Groseclose, *Introduction to Iran*, New York, 1947, pp. 106-109, 207-216.
[27] F. Lafont et H.-L. Rabino, *L'Industrie Séricicole en Perse*, 1910, pp. 12-14.
[28] Cf. Ch. Issawi (ed.), *op. cit.*, pp. 255-7.
[29] G. N. Curzon, *op. cit.*, Vol. II, pp. 8-12.
[30] John Malcolm, *Sketches of Persia*, 1828, II, p. 33. Elsewhere Malcolm states that even Meshed, which in Nadir Shah's time still had a population of 60,000, had only 20,000 inhabitants at the end of the 18th century. J. Malcolm, *History of Persia*, 1888, p. 76.

example of this is the city of Kashan, known in the past for its industry—silk, carpets, copper and clay vessels—which was in a state of deepest depression at the end of the 19th century.[31] Isfahan met with a similar fate, especially after Teheran became the political capital.[32] In the course of the 19th century many of the traditional industries of Persia were destroyed.

Commerce and industry suffered not only through the influx of foreign products but also as a result of the general depression prevailing in the country, the decrease in the value of the *kran* (see Ch. 1, above), political unrest (especially in the capital Teheran) and the lack of adequate means of transportation and communication.[33] The existing industry was largely in the hands of minorities and foreigners. One of the main branches—the wine industry—may serve as a major example. The production of wine was forbidden to Persians (apart from some rich families) and was in the hands of Armenians, Jews and Europeans[34], although considerable local production and consumption of wine and spirits also went on in the face of religious prohibitions.

Already in previous centuries, and especially since the beginning of the 19th century, the Persians had tried to exploit their mineral resources, sometimes by encouraging foreign and particularly British initiative. Frequently both they and the foreigners exaggerated the country's potentialities. Among the minerals, copper and iron took up an important place, and military industries were set up for the production of guns and ammunition (in Tabriz) from local raw materials.[35] In 1890 a subsidiary company of the Imperial Bank, called The Persian Bank Mining Rights Corporation, with a capital of about one million pounds sterling, was set up, and received a 60-year concession from the government (with monopoly rights) over all the mines (excepting precious metals) not yet handed over to other bodies or persons. Mining, however, did not give satisfactory results except with regard to oil (dealt with, *i.a.*, in the following chapter).

The carpet industry, despite the decline felt in this branch as well, and the downgrading of the quality—not least through Western influence—still constituted an important source of income for many thousands of the inhabitants and for the country's economy as a whole, both by complementing agriculture and by contributing substantially to exports.[36] Persia's most serious competitor in this field was Turkey, which in 1909, for instance, produced 668,000 sq. yards as against 55,000 sq. yards produced by Persia; but prior to and during the World War Persia considerably surpassed Turkey, with a record of 435,000 sq. yards in 1913, while Turkish production decreased sharply. New records were set again in the 'twenties,

---

[31] G. N. Curzon, *op. cit.*, II, pp. 12-15; V. Chirol, *op. cit.*, pp. 133-4.

[32] F. R. Chesney, *op. cit.*, pp. 109-110.

[33] F. R. Chesney, *The Expedition for the Survey of the Rivers Euphrates and Tigris*, Vol. I, 1850, Ch. XI, pp. 236-7; A. T. Wilson, *op. cit.*, pp. 104-112.

[34] Mainly through the Société Générale du Commerce et de l'Industrie which had its main office in Brussels, Belgium.

[35] G. N. Curzon, *op. cit.*, II, p. 512.

[36] Although within the scope of the general exports the value of carpets went down, e.g. in 1889 to just over 5% of the total value of exports, their share in exports rose again, taking second place at the beginning of the 20th century and even first place during the war.

but by then the Turkish, and also in particular the Chinese and Indian competition had grown.[37] Some other textile products, too—such as cloth and shawls made of camel hair, or silk and brocades—maintained their position and continued to attract Western customers. On the other hand the traditional metal and pottery industries underwent a serious crisis.

Attempts at setting up modern large-scale industries in the second half of the 19th and early 20th century, in cooperation with foreign entrepreneurs, were hardly successful. Apart from the already mentioned oil sector, only a few modern plants, mainly in textiles, sugar, fish processing, glass, paper and bricks, were able to survive and employed a negligible number of less than 2,000 workers.[38] Another major industrial drive had to wait until the post-War I modernisation efforts.

Three branches contributed 55% of the entire value of exports, namely opium, raw silk (with particularly strong fluctuations) and rice. The other items, too, were mainly agricultural, including tobacco, raw cotton, fruit, grains, the only industrial products exported being carpets, shawls, skins and some cotton and woolen goods.

In view of the poor state of its own industry, Persia required considerable imports despite the low living standards of most of the population. These imports supplied the demand of the wealthy classes for luxuries as well as the general demand for cheap industrial products not manufactured in the country.

Persia, which was in any case a country of primary exports, needed even imports of those industrial products which in the past had been supplied by local industry and crafts but had not been able to hold out against the influx of cheap European goods to the Persian market. Finished cotton, wool and silk products constituted 80% of total imports, the other commodities imported being mainly glass, porcelain ware, sugar and spices.

Imports amounted to twice as much as exports. In 1889 the imports were £st. 4 million while exports amounted to slightly more than £st. 2 million. They consisted principally of products most of which, under a different regime and different programme of investments, could undoubtedly have been produced locally. In the course of time the deficit in the trade balance (in absolute figures) grew still worse. In 1901, when particulars of Persian foreign trade were first given, the exports totalled £st. 2.75 million and the imports £st. 5.5 million. In 1907, however, the deficit went down to £st. 1.5 million with exports of 6.5 million and imports of £st. 8 million.[39] The deficits were balanced by foreign loans which were on the increase at that time (see below).

Simultaneously, an important change took place in the destination of foreign trade. In 1897 the shares of Russia and Britain in the total exports and imports had been almost equal. In 1907 Russia took up practically 60% of the total Persian trade, or about 3 times as much as Britain's share. The deficits in the trade balance persisted despite the total reduction in commerce during the war years to 2/3-4/5 of

---

[37] *Eighteenth Report... of Finance in Persia,* 1927, p. 31.
[38] Cf. writings of Z. Z. Abdullaev, M. A. Jamalzadeh and E. Lorini, excerpts of which are quoted in Ch. Issawi (ed.), *op. cit.,* pp. 297-310.
[39] A. T. Wilson, *op. cit.,* p. 79.

its previous level. Immediately after the war the deficit grew still more owing to increased imports (and only a negligible rise in exports). A major change took place only in 1922/3 when the value of exports exceeded that of imports, even without taking into account the exportation of oil.[40] The emerging oil sector, despite the relatively low royalties at that time, became a potentially important instrument of balancing deficits and of capital accumulation for investments, provided that political, administrative and economic decision-making and efficiency would meet the requirements (see Part Eight, below).

3. Exogenous causes of Persia's economic difficulties—the competition between the Powers

The economic position of Persia in the 19th century deteriorated as a result of two principal factors:
 a. The competition of the Powers for influence over Persia;
 b. Persia's social structure and the weakness and corruption of the central government.
This chapter deals with the first, exogenous factor.

The backwardness of Persian agriculture, due mainly to the neglect of the irrigation network, the disintegration of local crafts and the severity of taxes whose obsolete and inefficient levying and collection impoverished the population without such revenue being properly utilised—weakened the State and rendered easier its growing dependence on foreigners. The pressure exerted by the European Powers on Persia, especially since the middle of the 19th century, was sometimes even stronger than that exercised on the Ottoman Empire, and adversely affected the economic structure and development of the country. The capitulations regime applied to Persia as well as to Turkey and Egypt. Accordingly customs tariffs could not be raised nor could a purchase tax on foreign produce be imposed inside the country without the consent of the Powers, which restricted the competitiveness of local produce.[41] Concessions for most of the major branches of the economy were handed out to foreigners, involving a constant economic and political struggle between Persia and the holders of the concessions and credit funds, and between the latter parties *inter se.*

At the beginning of the 19th century three Powers competed for domination over Persia: Britain, France and Russia. Already towards the end of the first decade, however, France ceased to constitute an influential factor in Persia, and throughout the 19th century until the beginning of the 20th century the competition was limited

---

[40] A. C. Millspaugh, *The Financial and Economic Situation of Persia,* 1926, pp. 21-22.

[41] Salt may serve as a typical example. Before the arrival of Morgan Shuster (1911) the tax on salt produced locally was 5.70 dollars (64 *krans*) per 500 lbs. while the duty on imported salt was only 0.9 dollars free of any further taxes. It is worth adding that the net yearly income from taxes on local salt reached $ 180,000 but after deduction of collection expenses only $ 37,000 were left to the government. The existing regulations were annulled by the Majlis only after Shuster's intervention. W. Morgan Shuster, *op. cit.,* pp. 33-4.

to an open or hidden struggle between Britain and Russia. Then the Germans had also succeeded in gaining an economic foothold in Persia. Later on they even received the support of the Democratic Persian Party so that they might counterbalance the British-Russian influence. But at the end of the First World War the Germans again temporarily ceased to play a part in the economic and political life of Persia, returning only with the rise of the Nazis in the 'thirties.[42]

After the French invasion of the Middle East in 1798, Britain increased her interest in Persia, in fear of the French threat to India. Simultaneously Russia showed an increased interest in securing an exit to the southern seas and a growing desire to conquer large territories in northern Persia and Central Asia. With the Napoleonic invasion of the Middle East Persia was thus for the first time turned into a pawn in the play between the Powers.

Immediately after Napoleon's invasion of Egypt and Syria in January 1801, Sir John Malcolm signed a friendship treaty on behalf of England with Fath Ali Shah, containing a clause which promised British aid to Persia against a potential French threat. In a supplementary commercial agreement, the British were accorded a number of trade and tax facilities and assurances for the security of their lives and property, jurisdiction and freedom of movement.[43] The treaty soon became useless, especially when the British wanted the Russians—the enemies of the Persians—to participate in the defence against France. The Persians reacted by signing the Finkenstein agreement with France in 1807, under which a French military mission came to Persia.[44] Hardly two months had passed from the signature of this treaty before the Persians put it in cold storage, owing to France's rapprochement with Russia under the Treaty of Tilsit, which again exposed Persia to Russian danger. The Shah went so far as to expell the French missions, and was instead prepared to receive a similar mission from Britain, which only too readily responded to the invitation. The agreement accordingly signed between the parties provided for financial support and supply of arms, ammunition and military instructors to Persia.

At the same time the Russians intensified their attacks on northern Persia. In 1813 Persia was forced to sign the Gulistan Agreement by which it gave up considerable parts of Trans-Caucasia.[45] In the years 1825-1827 the Russians conquered further areas in the same region, as well as Tabriz, and Persia was bound to sign the Turkman-Chai agreement in February 1828, which defined the Persian-Russian border south of the Caucasus along the Aras, to this day (the north-eastern border, along the Atrek river, was fixed only in 1869, and again moved northwards by the agreement of 1881). Persia moreover had to pay war damages to Russia.

In addition, Russia obtained extensive commercial and legal capitulations from

---

[42] The constant strain in the relations between Persia and the Ottoman Empire was dispelled mainly as a result of political and economic treaties concluded between them in 1875/6. Cf. C. U. Aitchison, *A Collection of Treaties,* etc. Vol. XII, 1909, pp. 21-22, and *passim.*

[43] See text in Appendix 20.

[44] Hurewitz, *op. cit.,* I, pp. 77-8.

[45] C. U. Aitchison, *A Collection of Treaties,* etc.,XII, pp. xi-xiv.

Persia through special supplements to the Turkman-Chai Treaty.[46] The important chapter of the capitulations in Persia as a whole deserves some amplification.

A liberal interpretation of the term "capitulations" had led several scholars to seek their first beginnings in Persia in the sixth century B.C., when Cyrus in 538 B.C. allowed the Jews to return to Palestine with certain duties and rights greatly reminiscent of modern capitulations.[47] The centuries-old tradition of tolerance was not broken by the conquest of Persia by Arab Islam in the 7th century A.D.

In the 13th century important trading rights were granted to Christians. These first beginnings of modern capitulations were expanded further in the 17th century, when the rights previously granted became applicable to additional areas, such as civil and religious protection, official recognition of representatives and independent jurisdiction.[48]

The capitulations of the 19th century mainly served to define more clearly the rights granted to foreigners in the past and extend them to most European countries. The capitulations obtained by Russia in 1828 granted the official Russian representatives the right of extraterritorial jurisdiction over Russian nationals in this country. The Russians enjoyed lower rates of taxes and customs tariffs, of 5% and less, on an *ad valorem* basis, as well as a series of additional commercial advantages.[49] Shortly afterwards, in 1836 and 1841, the same rights were promised to the British as well by the Firman of the Shah and by a commercial treaty.[50] The capitulation treaties which were signed with most of the Powers in the 19th century are strikingly similar to each other and hence one example will suffice. In the Appendices, the Treaty of 1856 with the U.S.A. is reproduced in order to give an idea of the nature of arrangements made.[51]

The economic and political developments until the outbreak of the First World War confirm Wilson's view that the capitulations in Persia did not have the same force as, for instance, in the Ottoman Empire. But in times of crisis the Powers brought pressure to bear on Persia, based *inter alia* on the capitulations.[52] While the Persian capitulations did not provide for the establishment of mixed courts with jurisdiction between Persians and foreigners, in the 19th century Persia was nevertheless forced under the pressure of circumstances to establish mixed courts and to finance their activities. These courts were abolished only in 1927.[53]

In effect the chapter on the concessions opens in 1865, when a British company

---

[46] Cf. C. U. Aitchison, *op. cit.*, Vol. XII, pp. xv-xxxv; A. C. Millspaugh, *Americans in Persia*, 1946, p. 13.

[47] Cf. Abdollah Moazzami, *Essai sur la Condition des Etrangers en Iran*, 1937, pp. 16-17, who quotes the jurist Holtzendorff and others in order to demonstrate the method prevailing in Persia at that time, based on a combination of the principles of *millets* and capitulations.

[48] See Appendix 19, The Capitulations of Shah Sefi.

[49] Text of the agreement is given in Hurewitz, I, pp. 96-102; Cf. also G. N. Curzon, *op. cit.*, II, p. 553.

[50] C. U. Aitchison, *op. cit.*, Vol. XII, 1909, pp. 60-62.

[51] See Appendix 21.

[52] A. T. Wilson, *op. cit.*, pp. 224-5. A good though incomplete survey of Persian treaties and capitulations, especially during the 19th century, is given by E. Hertslet, *Treaties concluded between Great Britain and Persia*, London, 1891.

[53] A. Moazzami, *op. cit.*, p. 62.

was granted a concession to set up a telegraph line between Baghdad and Bushir through Kermanshah and Hamdan, as an extension of the Khanaqin-Bushir line (constructed according to a concession of 1863)[54]. In 1872 Baron Julius de-Reuter, an Englishman, obtained a comprehensive concession for 70 years to lay railway lines between the Caspian Sea and the Persian Gulf, construct telegraph lines, regulate the navigation on the rivers, exploit all mines other than of gold, silver and precious stones, and to found a bank. In view of Russian opposition, however, Nasr el-Din Shah (1848-96) had to rescind this concession a year after it had been granted. De-Reuter did not give in and in 1889 succeeded in obtaining a concession for the establishment of the Imperial Bank of Persia with the right of issuing notes (the agreement according to which this right was transferred to the National ((Melli) Bank of Persia was reached only in 1930). Simultaneously restricted issuing rights were given to the Russian bank. In the course of time competition developed between the two banks for the acquisition of each other's notes and their conversion into metal currency, in order to cause difficulties to the competing issuing bank.[55] In 1890 a further concession was granted to the British for the acquisition, manufacture and marketing of Persian tobacco.[56]

In compensation for the concessions granted to the British during the 'sixties and 'seventies, the Shah granted the Russians a concession in 1874 for the establishment of a Bank (Banque d'Escompte de Perse) and the construction of railway lines to connect Tabriz with the Trans-Caucasian network.[57] Two years afterwards, in 1876, Russia obtained an exclusive concession over the fishing on the southern shore of the Caspian Sea and in 1881 for the construction of a road in Azerbaijan. In the 'nineties many concessions were granted to lay railway lines and pave roads, especially west and south of Teheran. The British and the Russian continued to compete for these concessions, followed at a considerable distance by the Belgians and the French. The Russian Transport and Insurance Company established in 1890 by Lazar Poliakov was of particular importance. Its business extended from the paving of roads to the construction of piers and hotels and prospecting for oil and coal in the Azerbaijan region. At the same time, Russia brought pressure to bear on the Persian authorities[58] to cancel the tobacco monopoly granted to the British. Since the 'ulema (religious leaders) likewise objected to this monopoly and organised the closing of the tobacco shops and a "smokers' strike" throughout the country, the government of Persia was forced to cancel the monopoly in 1891 and to compensate its holders with half a million pounds sterling. Owing to lack of cash the

---

[54] C. U. Aitchison, *op. cit.*, XII, pp. 83-89. Britain, through agreements with the Arab rulers on the Persian Gulf, from 1864 onwards assured the regular operation of the telegraph lines passing through adjacent territories. *Ibid.*, p. 182.

[55] Cf. *note* 4 on p. 159, in E. Groseclose, *op. cit.*

[56] See text in Appendix 22.

[57] For the railway treaty, see Hurewitz, *op. cit.*, I, p. 207.

[58] It should be borne in mind that at that time there existed in Persia the Cossack battalion formed in the times of Nasr el-Din in 1882, under the command of Russian officers. Of course, this unit was maintained at the expense of the Persian government, but at various periods it served not merely to protect the Shah's throne but also to defend the interests of Russia. W. M. Shuster, *op. cit.*, pp. 291-3.

compensation remained in the nature of a loan made by the company to the Shah at an interest of 6%.[59]

As a result of the prodigality of the Persian rulers the coffers of the treasury were empty. In 1900, Shah Muzafer el-Din, in addition to the debt he had inherited from his father, had to take on a loan of 22.5 million rubles (i.e., £ 2.4 million) from Russia at an interest of 5%. A further loan of 10 million rubles (£ 1.07 million) was received from Russia in 1902 and another of 6 million rubles in 1910.[60]

Russia prevented Persia from receiving any further loans elsewhere without its consent until the repayment of its loans for which the Persian customs revenues served as securities. Without Russian consent, the Persians were forbidden to grant concessions to foreigners for the construction of railway lines. Furthermore, the Russians received concessions for prospecting for oil and coal. By an initially clandestine agreement they secured for themselves low customs tariffs on goods Persia purchased from Russia (mainly sugar and oil) while the customs tariff on tea, for instance, which was purchased from Britain, was considerably increased. An agreement to remedy this situation was signed by Britain only after the lapse of several years.

In 1904 and 1905 Persia received two additional British loans with the approval of Russia, to the amount of £ 190,000 and £100,000 respectively.[61]

The general trend in Persia's foreign economic relations during the period between 1890 and 1903[62] showed an increase in trade with Russia (by 80%) and a reduction in trade with Britain (by 15%). Nevertheless Britain just at that time managed to get a foothold in one of Persia's main economic sectors, namely oil. In 1901 William Knox D'Arcy[63] obtained an oil drilling concession, which applied to all Persian territories except for the five northern provinces. A concession for prospecting for oil in these provinces had previously been granted to Russia, whose stake in oil output and exports, even successfully competing with the United States, was then significant. However, Russian attempts to outbid or eventually to foil western oil ventures in Persia ended in complete failure.[64] D'Arcy, and Australian engineer of British origin, based his surveys and prospecting in the concession area on previous geological findings, especially those made by the French under Prof. M. de Morgan at the beginning of the 'nineties. A general tax exemption was among the various facilities granted by the government to the company. As against that the

---

[59] V. Chirol, *The M. E. Question,* pp. 51-2; W. M. Shuster, *op. cit.,* p. xvii.

[60] Percy Sykes, *History of Persia,* 1951 ed., II, p. 376; A. T. Wilson, *op. cit.,* p. 287.

[61] *Behind the Veil of Persia,* pp. 11-12 (see note 68 below).

[62] V. Chirol, *op. cit.,* pp. 65-6. It should be added that the Russian production and transportation expenses were higher than those of most Western countries which traded with Persia. In order to withstand the competition, Russia was aided by the twofold measures of export premiums and Persian customs tariffs which were particularly favourable to Russian goods. Cf. P. Rohrbach, *op. cit.,* p. 35.

[63] D'Arcy's concession was preceded by a concession granted in 1884 to a Dutchman named Hotz, who started prospecting and drilled a number of oil wells near Bender Rig, but soon despaired of finding oil. Cf. N. S. Fatemi, *Oil Diplomacy,* New York, 1954, p. xix.

[64] Cf. below, section on oil in Book Two. For the text of d'Arcy's concession, see Appendix 23. Also, B. V. Ananich, "Russia and the d'Arcy Concession" (in Russian), reproduced in Ch. Issawi (ed.), *op. cit.,* pp. 327-334.

government received shares to the value of £ 20,000 in the company and was assured 16% of its net profits. The company got out of the red only when rich oil deposits were found in Maidan-i-Naftun in 1908. In the following year (1909) the successor of the D'Arcy Company, the Anglo-Persian Oil Company was formed. This company was founded jointly by the British Government and the Burmah Oil Company, and many wondrous tales were told as to how the original concession was wrested from D'Arcy.[65] Most of the activities of the company and the role played by Persia in the field of oil belong to a later period.

Foreign and especially Russian influence in Persia was not confined to the economic sphere but had a decisive political effect. In 1857, by the Treaty of Paris, the British forced Nasr el-Din Shah to give up Herat, the capital of Afghanistan,[66] which had been conquered by Persia a year before. The Russians were able to make the Persians cancel the concession to De-Reuter in 1873. In the first decade of the 20th century the subjection of Persia to these two Powers increased, especially after August 31st, 1907, when an Anglo-Russian treaty was signed according to which Persia was divided into three spheres of influence: the northern and central part (from Kermanshah to Yezd and from there to the eastern border, south of Meshed), under Russian influence; the south-eastern part (from Bender Abbas through Kerman to east of Birjand) under British influence; and the south-western part as a neutral zone having a border in the east and separating the Russian and British zones. Officially the two Powers recognised Persia's independence.[67] To what extent this independence was fictitious may be seen from the fact that in 1911 the Russians forced the Persian authorities to dismiss their American financial adviser, Morgan Shuster, after no more than half a year's work at trying to improve the financial situation. They even went so far as to suppress by force demonstrations held in Tabriz against the removal of Shuster. Two years previously the Russians had offered refuge to the Persian Shah who had had to escape from the capital under the pressure of the Persian parliament. Moreover, in 1911 the Russians tried to help the same ruler, Mehmed Ali Shah, to conquer back his throne by force, an attempt which failed in view of the strong opposition of the British.

The two Powers also intervened in other internal affairs of Persia. The Russians objected to the Persian constitution and supported the Shah against his parliament and ministers, while the British supported the democrats who had forced the Shah to grant a constitution and parliament. However, after signature of the Anglo-Russian Agreement on spheres of influence in 1907, even the democrats despaired of the British and started encouraging German influence. Yet the absolute rule of the Russians and British in Persia foiled any attempt at serious German penetration into this country.[68] In 1910 Russia and Britain jointly exerted pressure on Persia to

---

[65] See in this respect N. S. Fatemi, *op. cit.,* Ch. I, II, and, Laurence Lockhart, "The Emergence of the Anglo-Persian Oil Company, 1901-14", in Ch. Issawi (ed.), *op. cit.,* pp. 316-322.

[66] C. U. Aitchison, *op. cit.,* XII, pp. 76-81.

[67] For the text of the agreement, as regards Persia, see Appendix 24.

[68] A most interesting document on the activities of the British in Persia, especially after 1907 until 1917, was published in 1917 simultaneously in Berlin and Amsterdam on German initiative. The German publisher was Verlag Der Neue Orient and the name of the book *Englische Dokumente zur Erdrosselung*

abstain from granting railway concessions without prior consultation with them (mainly German concessions were meant). In the Shuster affair at the end of 1911 Britain supported the Russian ultimatum and their demand for the dismissal of the Director of Finances.

At the end of the 19th century, the Belgians fulfilled quite an important function in the economic life of Persia, both as economic consultants and organisers (see below, especially the organisation of the customs system) and as concessionaires. It is typical that the Belgians were active in the field of industry, while other foreign concessionaires in Persia and Turkey concentrated on services and finances. Three Belgian companies were set up in the years 1891-5: Compagnie Générale pour l'Eclairage et le Chauffage en Perse, following the purchase of a gasworks from its Persian owner; Société Anonyme des Verreries Nationales de Perse which ran a glass works in Teheran; and Société Anonyme pour la Fabrication du Sucre en Perse. All three companies had to close down at the end of the 'nineties, for technical reasons, because of difficulties in obtaining raw materials or owing to competition, particularly by the Russians who in the field of sugar were aided by preferential customs tariffs.[69]

4. ENDOGENOUS CAUSES OF PERSIA'S ECONOMIC DIFFICULTIES—THE SOCIAL STRUCTURE AND THE WEAKNESS OF THE CENTRAL GOVERNMENT

The Persian people were not all of one piece. About a quarter to a third were tribesmen, each tribe constituting an autonomous group, with plunder and war and inter-tribal hostility stamped deep in their blood.[70] The central government headed by the Shah not only exploited existing inter-tribal conflicts but frequently poured oil on the flames.[71] Sometimes the tribes exercised a decisive influence over the internal affairs of the State. In 1907, for instance, the Bakhtiari tribe took part in an uprising, as a result of which the Shah had to flee to the Russian Embassy. Later on this tribe caused the dismissal of the Persian minister of war, who tried to suppress the democratic party, the ally of the Bakhtiaris. Gradually, however, the position of the Beduin tribes became less strong, either for economic reasons such as drought, hunger and the dwindling of the population, or as a result of technical changes and Western political influences, mainly during the second half of the 19th century.[72]

The social stratification of the Persian, overwhelmingly rural population, in addition to the tribal division, was the same as in all Middle Eastern countries: the landlords and the fellahin (smallholders and a majority of tenants). The owners of the large estates lived a life of luxury in the cities, especially the capital, having the

---

Persiens. The Dutch (Amsterdam) publisher was C. L. van Langehuysen and the name of the book is *Behind the Veil in Persia, English Documents*. We shall quote this source as *Behind the Veil in Persia*.

[69] Moustafa Khan Fateh, *op. cit.*, p. 48.

[70] Cf. G. N. Curzon, *op. cit.*, pp. 112-114, and *passim*. The warlike nature of certain tribes finds apt expression in the common saying that "No real Bakhtiari dies in his bed."

[71] *Ibid.*, p. 272.

[72] C. N. Curzon, *op. cit.*, II, pp. 113-114.

authorities on their side in the oppression and exploitation of the fellahin, who lived a life of indescribable poverty in the villages. Especially during the 19th century four classes of land ownership had become well established and consolidated in Persia: 1) crown lands (*khalissa* or *diwani*); 2) feudal estates, mainly held by tribal chiefs who, in return, undertook to furnish soldiers and sometimes also to levy taxes; 3) *waqf* lands; 4) privately owned land (*arbabi*) which belonged mostly to rich individuals (the majority of whom lived in the cities) but was actually cultivated by peasants. In the course of time the Shah's lands increased; in addition to the tracts confiscated in past military campaigns, these comprised lands confiscated from individuals who had lost favour in the Shah's eyes.[73] As a result the "system of fifths" emerged, according to which the income was divided between the main owners of the production factors, namely land, water, seeds, work animals and human labour. Usually the landlord had two- to three-fifths.[74]

Another cross-section of the Persian population reflects its numerous minorities and nationalities which constituted a disturbing factor in the internal consolidation of the State. In Persia there are Turks (Azerbaijani, Turkmen, Kashkai), Arabs, Kurds, Lurs, Bakhtiaris, and Baluchis. Many conflicts existed among the various minorities which the authorities did not succeed (and frequently did not want) to quash. Far from seeking to impose unity, they tried from time to time to utilise the existing differences for their own purposes. The religious leaders and the intellectuals wielded a great influence over the political and economic life of Persia. The Shi'ite priesthood, at all levels of the hierarchy (*mujtahid, shaykh-ul-Islam, kazwi* and *mufti*) had an enormous influence over the masses in town and country, who in their ignorance practically all needed the help of the '*ulema* in order to know what was written in the Koran, not to mention the accepted exegesis.[75] A single *fetwa* (religious judgment) might upset the stability of the entire regime and cause riots throughout Persia, since the '*ulema* were held in great esteem and profound reverence. The *fetwa* of the great *mujtahid* (the greatest religious authority of Persia) by which the use of British-made tobacco was forbidden, whitin a short time brought about the cancellation of the concession granted to the British company. In Persia, as in other Islamic countries, the ban on the taking of interest (officially—usury) prevented investments in financial institutions and companies, and was one of the causes for the accumulation of funds in the hands of individuals, to be used for the acquisition of houses or other properties, or hoarded for the purchase of women and slaves, etc.[76] Another aspect of the deficient local credit facilities were the exorbitant rates of interest paid by the fellahin under conditions of scarcity of credit and evasion of the law. Evidence from the beginning of the 20th century reports prevailing rates of interest of 30-40 per cent, at least.[77]

The admiration for the religious leaders came to a climax in the 'forties of the 19th century. A young man of about twenty, Mirza Ali Muhammad, declared

---

[73] *Ibid.*, II, pp. 488-491.
[74] *Ibid.*, p. 490.
[75] E. Aubin, *op. cit.*, pp. 179 ff.
[76] J. Chardin, *op. cit.*, II, p. 143.
[77] F. Lafont et H.-L. Rabino, *op. cit.*, p. 64.

himself to be "The Gate of Knowledge" (*Bab*) through which the believers would contact the presumed hidden Chief (*Imam*) claimed by the Shi'ite Islam,[78] and acquired a numerous following. They continued to believe in him even after he declared himself to be the "mirror" through which the believers might see Allah himself. His main preaching was directed against the corruption of the rulers, especially the religious leaders, though in course of time his interpretations of the Koran started to diverge widely from Muslim tradition. Thus the Babic movement arose which already by 1848 had exerted a decisive influence in Persia to such an extent that Nasr el-Din Shah found it necessary to suppress it by force. The execution of the *Bab* in 1850 still further enhanced his greatness in the eyes of his followers, who were particularly numerous among women, whom the *Bab* in his teaching had raised from their lowly position and put on an equal footing with men. As a first step towards equality he demanded the abolition of the veil.[79] As a result of the dissatisfaction among his believers a prime minister was deposed and an attempt made to assassinate the Shah himself. A hard war had to be fought until most of the believers of this sect fled to Iraq, from where they were transferred by the Ottoman authorities to Istanbul. The sect subsequently divided in two, one section following Baha Allah (the glory of Allah) who pronounced himself the messianic prophet heralded by the *Bab* and greater than the latter. Baha Allah laid the foundations for a universal religion with new ceremonies and hierarchy—the religion of the Bahais.[80]

The intellectuals, despite their small number, enjoyed great influence, especially in the cities. This class was composed of officials, army officers, merchants and crafsmen. From among its ranks came the organisers of the sit-down strike (*bast*) against the despotism of the Shah in 1906, which led to the weakening of the Shah's arbitrary rule.

Most of the Persian rulers of the Kajar-Turkish dynasty which assumed power at the end of the 18th century imposed a regime of despotism and exploitation on Persia, and more than one of them was assassinated by his citizens. Such was the fate of the first ruler of this dynasty, Aga Muhammad, who distinguished himself by his cruelty and greed and was murdered in 1797. During his reign Teheran became the capital and embarked since then upon rapid development. However, largely owing to this fact other cities known for their glorious past, such as Shiraz, Isfahan and Kerman, suffered serverely.[81] His nephew, Fatah Ali Shah, who succeeded him to the throne (1797-1834) was no better. He ruled over Persia like a foreign conqueror, and in order to maintain his harem confiscated property and

---

[78] With respect to the affair of the *Bab* and his heirs, see Napier Malcolm, *Five Years in a Persian Town*, London, 1905, Chapter III (pp. 60-114).
[79] Sixty years afterwards Persian women took a most active part in the Persian national movement, taking a firm stand against the Russian ultimatum and threat of conquest and going so far as to intimidate the Majlis into not daring to submit to the demands. Possibly there is some exaggeration and subjectivity in the description of this affair by Shuster but the central facts are correct. See W. M. Shuster, *op. cit.*, pp. 191-199.
[80] V. Chirol, *op. cit.*, pp. 117-128.
[81] J. Malcolm, *History of Persia*, p. 72 and pp. 106-7.

imposed fines on his citizens. The provincial governors behaved similarly in order to maintain their army and administration, since they had to shift for themselves. Fath Ali's successor, Muhammad Shah, handed over the provinces to whoever paid the highest price. For such governors, who did not know when they in turn would be removed by the Shah, no means were too low to collect the taxes required to cover the amount they had pledged to pay for their post and to hoard money for a rainy day. In 1896, for instance, the governor of Kermanshah confiscated all the sheep within his province and exported them, despite the famine which frequently visited the region.

Shah Nasr el-Din, the son of Shah Muhammad, who managed to keep his throne for 48 years, also inflicted economic disasters on his country, especially after he discovered the "new world"—Europe—as a pleasant place to visit. His first visit took place in 1873, followed by visits in 1887 and 1889. These trips cost the treasury a great deal of money since no distinction was made between State funds and the Shah's private funds. The State budget had to carry the burden of the Shah's expenditures whereas surpluses accumulated in good years were transferred to the Shah's private coffers.[82] The constant lack of cash forced him to sell concessions to whoever offered most. The Persian people, both intellectuals and simple folk, were loath to see the treasures of their native land being sold to foreigners for the private amusement of the Shah, and in 1896 he was assassinated (although the direct causes of his assassination are not clear).[83]

His son, Muzafar Shah, differed little from his father in his love of Europe pleasure trips, and consequent need for funds. Repulsed by Great Britain, he approached the Russians who, as mentioned above, granted him two loans, in 1900 and 1902, of 32 million rubles. Again the Persian people grumbled and expressed their discontent by the usual sit-down strike (*bast*) held in the square of the British embassy by students, intellectuals, merchants and others in the spring of 1906. The strike led to the dismissal of the prime minister, the grant of a constitution and establishment of a parliament, all at the end of the same year, shortly before the Shah's death.[84]

5. ATTEMPTS AT REFORM

The first to preach social reform in Persia in the 19th century was the *Bab*, who called for the abolition of class differences, general peace, a less extremist interpretation of religious commands, and reforms in the educational system. The *Bab*, as mentioned, was executed in 1850, some of his followers were killed and others had to flee Persia.

Nasr el-Din Shah, who was responsible for the *Bab*'s death, himself took certain steps towards remedying the economic situation, especially in order to increase his

---

[82] C. N. Curzon, *op. cit.*, II, p. 484.
[83] Morgan Shuster, *op. cit.*, p. xvii.
[84] For events leading to the 1906 upheaval, see G. G. Gilbar, "The big merchants (tujjār) and the Persian constitutional revolution of 1906", *Asian and African Studies,* Vol. II, No. 3, Jerusalem, 1977.

income and from time to time pacify the periodical uprisings among the population. He invited Jemal el-Din- el-Afghani to visit Persia in 1886 (cf. remarks on el-Afghani in chapters on Turkey and Egypt) and again in 1889, after a visit to Munich, where Afghani had been staying at that time. Soon, however, the Shah realised the latent danger this man represented for the foundations of his throne and forced him to leave Persia in 1891. In the economic sphere the Shah concentrated on communications and granted concessions for the laying of telegraph lines to connect Persia with Iraq and with Russia and Great Britian, and the provincial cities of Persia with the capital.

In 1891 the demand for national representation was put forward. This demand had first been presented in the journal "Kanūn" (the Law) which started appearing in London under Armenian editorship in 1890. The demand was fulfilled only after the *bast* (strike) held in Persia in 1906. At the same time the discontent in Persia itself and among the groups of Persian expatriates in Europe grew, owing largely to the effect of revolutionary ideas originating from Russia, India, Turkey and Egypt. The Russo-Japanese war and the first Russian revolution of 1905 increased the restlessness and discontent in a country whose political, economic and cultural ties with Europe at that time were quite strong. From the north there was an influx of Russian Muslims who encouraged revolutionary ideas. Even among religious cricles reformational trends were spreading. All were agreed in their desire to change the present situation, to restrict despotism and to prepare the road for a more modern way of thought. But fundamentally, the movement was split into numerous groups with varying or ill-defined objectives.[85] Under the pressure of the revolutionary movement the Shah, on December 30th, 1906, granted a constitution[86] under which the Majlis (House of Representatives) was elected—which in actual fact constituted a kind of municipal council of Teheran. The Upper House (Senate) consisted of members of the royal house, notables, merchants and landlords (half of them appointed directly by the Shah). On October 7th, 1907, Shah Muhammad Ali approved supplementary fundamental legislation, which *inter alia* extended civil rights and laid down more explicit budgetary regulations (clauses 94-103)[87]. Great hopes were entertained both inside and outside Persia with regard to the revolution in progress.[88]

Yet the path of the Persian revolution was not all smooth going. The new Shah, Muhammad Ali Mirza, who acceded to the throne in 1907, in turn required funds which he tried to obtain by a new loan. In view of the opposition of the parliament he decided to dismiss it and to cancel the constitution. In December 1907 he took the first unsuccessful steps in this direction and was forced to seek refuge at the Russian Embassy. From there he ordered the Cossack brigade led by the Russian officer Liakhov to attack the Majlis. Finally, however, in the face of an open uprising in the northern part of the country which spread until the city of Teheran was taken over

---

[85] E. Aubin, *op. cit.*, pp. 193-7.
[86] For the text of the constitution, see L. P. Elwell-Sutton, *Modern Iran,* London, 1941, Appendix I.
[87] *Ibid.*, Appendix II. At that time, between 1907 and 1914, the system of civil legislation and civil courts became consolidated and the scope of their authority grew at the expense of the *shari'a* courts.
[88] E. Aubin, *op. cit.*, 1908, pp. vii-viii.

by the insurgents, the Shah abdicated on July 16th, 1909.[89] He was formally succeeded by his son Ahmed, but owing to the latter's tender age a regent was appointed by the Majlis. Owing to the growing Russian-British influence, on the one hand, and the strengthening of the Majlis—which reconvened on November 15th, 1909, following new elections—on the other, his position was far from strong. In the middle of 1911 the previous Shah, Muhammad Ali, tried to reconquer Persia by force and recover his throne, receiving at least the passive support of the Russians, but his attempt proved unsuccessful. The short period between 1906 and the outbreak of the First World War was full of inter-Power conflicts and friction between the Shah and the reform movement. The failure of Morgan Shuster's economic mission symbolised and underlined the extent and severity of these struggles.

A group of democrats formed in the Majlis who regarded the improvement of the economic situation as one of their main goals. Under the influence of this group the Persian foreign minister asked the government of the United States for a financial adviser to assist the Persian Government. Upon the prior approval of the Majlis, W. Morgan Shuster arrived in Persia at the beginning of May 1911, accompanied by three assistants, and was appointed Director General of Finances for a period of three years.[90]

In order to obtain control over financial matters and particularly to cope with the collection of taxes, the various ministers had to be deprived of the autonomy they had enjoyed hitherto in the collection of revenues and in their spending, and all such authority had to be vested solely in the hands of the Director General of the Treasury, so as to enable him to draw up a budget and stand by his commitments. The parliament acceded to Shuster's request to grant him wide powers with respect to the organisation of revenue and expenditure (on June 13th, 1911) and afterwards put at his disposal a special Gendarmerie (police force) to assist in the collection of the taxes together with the civilian collectors. Shuster had ample success in cutting down expenditure, introducing a fairer distribution of taxes and a more thoroughgoing collection method and establishing a sounder financial foundation for administration.[91] However, owing to Russian opposition to Shuster's activities, the Persian government was compelled to demand from the parliament his dismissal. When the latter refused to accept the Russian ultimatum the members of the House were chased out of the Majlis building by government forces on December 24th and the next day Shuster received a notice of dismissal from the government.[92] His place

[89] W. M. Shuster, *op. cit.*, p. xlix.

[90] *Ibid.*, pp. 3 ff.

[91] A description of the obstacles put in Shuster's way both by the foreign representatives in Persia —especially Russia and Belgium—and certain members of the Persian government would sound quite grotesque, were it not for the ruined economy, corrupt administration and grievously oppressed population masked by this play. See *ibid.*, pp. 47-67.

[92] *Behind the Veil in Persia* claims (p. 29) that actually the British were the first to suggest Shuster's dismissal, according to the exchange of telegrams between Sir Edward Grey and Sir G. Buchanan. At any rate it is admitted that the dismissal was formally requested by a Russian ultimatum to Persia of November 29th, 1911. Shuster himself tells in great detail of the constant interference on the part of the Russians and of the British support they mobilised from time to time, sometimes under the threat of military action. Shuster, *op. cit.*, esp. pp. 165-221.

was taken by a Belgian, Mornard, who had until then served as director general of customs (and continued to keep his former post as well).[93]

At the end of the First World War, the Belgians were removed and a local directorate put in their stead until a British economic mission, followed by an American one, headed by Millspaugh,[94] were called in.

With the aid of an American-European staff Shuster, despite countless obstacles, succeeded at least temporarily in obtaining control over the *mustawfi* class which zealously guarded its rights and privileges, and over the funds accumulated by them. The receipts of the tax collectors and the various government departments which until then had only partially and irregularly entered the central treasury, started being paid into the Imperial Bank, acting as the financial agent of the government. (Shuster recounts, however, that throughout the period he served as general treasurer he never received a single penny from the Azerbaijan province over which it was impossible to gain control in view of the almost constant presence of Russian forces in the area.[95]) Moreover, the tax collectors started receiving better salaries and thus their natural tendency towards bribery and corruption was at least partially curbed.

Shuster proposed to the government a series of new taxes on opium and the slaughter of animals for meat; changes in the taxes on tobacco and stamp duty on documents, in customs, and in the imposition of internal taxes on commodities in co-ordination with the Powers; amendments in the payment of pensions; and the taking up of consolidation loans of 4 million pounds sterling. He intended to use part of the new revenue and the balance of the loan for land registration, a national census, a forestry and mining survey, and communications and irrigation plans.[96] Although the Persian government approved these plans in 1911, the Russian ultimatum and the removal of Shuster intervened, and the plans were buried forever. Shortly after Shuster's removal, the rest of the American staff also left Persia.[97]

Thus ended the pre-World War I attempts at social and economic reforms in Persia. Their scope was infinitely smaller than that of the reforms carried out in the Ottoman Empire in the 19th century. Even the attempts to restrict the scope of the

---

[93] Shuster in his books described Mornard (a Belgian, like his patron Nauss) in a distinctly unfavourable light in view of his financial corruption which led to his rapid enrichment at the expense of the Persians and because of his disguised services to the Russians. W. M. Shuster, *op. cit.*, pp. 23-25. Other testimonies by more impartial parties give a different and more favourable picture of the Belgian director and at any rate of Nauss. Cf. V. Chirol, *The M. E. Question*, pp. 67-69.

[94] A. C. Millspaugh, *The Financial and Economic Situation of Persia*, 1926, p. 26.

[95] W. M. Shuster, *op. cit.*, p. 287.

[96] *Ibid.*, pp. 305-307.

[97] The personality and activity of Shuster gave rise to many differences of opinion among his contemporaries and later scholars. His critics were more or less divided along geographic-political lines. The Russians of course severely criticised and found fault with his activities; the Germans praised him to a large extent; the British were divided in their opinions, but even severe personal critics like P. Sykes lay the main responsibility on political and social conditions. British official representatives tended to criticise more severely than independent British observers, but even the official Blue Books confirm that the state of affairs at the beginning of the 20th century was essentially as described by Shuster in his book. See Sir Percy Sykes, *op. cit.*, II, pp. 424-6; *Blue Books, Persia*, No. 1, 1909.

capitulations during the years 1906-1912 were in vain owing to the immediate failure of the relevant legal and legislative amendments.[98] On the other hand, even though during the war Persia had been the scene of military operations and the brigands jeopardised the communication lines, Persia's relatively small indebtedness[99], her official neutrality in the first World War[100] and the first oil receipts saved the country from the fate which overcame the Ottoman Empire.

---

[98] A. Moazzami, *op. cit.*, pp. 64-70.

[99] Estimated, on the eve of World War I, at £ 6.8 million consolidated debt and less than £ 1 million floating debt. Cf. M. A. Jamalgadah and F. Mochaver, quoted in Ch. Issawi (ed.), *op. cit.*, p. 371.

[100] To a certain extent the very agreements which were directed against Persia's independence (like the Anglo-Russian Treaty of 1907 which laid down the respective spheres of influence of these two states and the Potsdam Treaty of 1910 between Russia and Germany which secured the new German economic interests in Persia while preserving the status and interests of Russia) actually helped Persia to keep its neutrality. In order to declare this neutrality the Shah specially convened the national assembly for the first time since it was dispersed by force in 1911. Cf. W. M. Shuster, *op. cit.*, pp. 253-276; P. Sykes, *op. cit.*, II, p. 433.

BOOK TWO

THE ECONOMIC AND SOCIAL CHANGES IN THE INTER-WAR PERIOD

PART SIX

THE MIDDLE EAST AT THE END OF THE FIRST WORLD WAR

GENERAL REVIEW

A. The Renewed Meeting between East and West

The First World War again brought Eastern society into direct contact with the Western world. The first impact came in the form of a military clash, with the slogan of *jihad*—the war against the unbelievers—being used as a weapon alternately by the Turks in their *anti* French and British propaganda, and by Hussayn, the Sherif of Mecca, in his appeal for mutiny on behalf of the Allies against the Turks, who enjoyed the support of Germany and Austria-Hungary. Towards the end of the War and after it the contact between East and West took on a new character: the political and economic domination of the West over a major part of the region on the one hand, and the influx of Western ideas and attempts at social and economic reforms based on such ideas, on the other. The meeting with the soldiers of the West, with more modern forms of warfare, modern methods of civil and military administration, and different elements of Western culture borne on the waves of military conquest left its imprint on the soldiers of the Ottoman Empire who had been conscripted to the front from all its various parts. Some of the Turkish officers were influenced by this contact not alone in the military sphere, but also in political and social matters. The strong impact of this ideological and practical influence manifested itself later on in the reforms of the 'twenties and 'thirties.

The roots of the ideological revolution in the East lie buried in the 19th century, especially the second half. The movement as a whole represented by el-Afghani and Abdu in Egypt, and Ziya Gökalp, at the beginning of the present century, in Turkey, generally favoured the utilisation of the most desirable elements of Western civilisation while preserving the traditional cultural and national framework. The focal point was the clash between the traditional immobility of the social and economic institutions (the village and land ownership system, the municipal corporations, the government machinery, the structure of the State budget) and modern conceptions of economic administration and social structure. Those who strove for change saw no choice but to destroy obsolete and rigid social forms and to overcome the psychological obstacles which hampered modern development. A new form of fanaticism sprung up: the fanaticism of modernisation, of territorial nationalism, even at the expense of dreams of greater unities of the kind of the Pan-Islamic, Pan-Arabic or Pan-Turanic movements;[1] of social reforms according to the

---

[1] It would be interesting to conduct a comparative historiosophical study between this conception which was the result of the First World War and Abdul Nasser's conception of the three circles (and perhaps also that of other African leaders, in somewhat altered form) which expressed an opposite trend of going out from a small national to a comprehensive unit. Has this latter trend been merely an expression of a general tendency which emerged after the Second World War, towards the formation of major

European example; of economic enterprises based on the technical, organisational and financial experience of the West.

These ideas, which had not yet become the property of oriental society at large but were conceived only by a thin veneer of the intelligentsia and a small group of leaders of varying stature, appeared on the background of a new reality moulded by the War. Even the leaders themselves failed to realise that while in the past the neglect of the needs of the countries and peoples of the area by domestic rulers and foreign interests had been the major cause of regression, new factors had sprung up which necessitated a far-reaching economic and social revolution. These factors were: the increase of the population and the pressure it exerted on the sources of livelihood, the increase of the city proletariat, the transition to a market economy in agriculture, Western methods in economics, technology, administration and social institutions. In addition to a misapprehension of the real needs of the population, objective factors prevented a sweeping advance towards progress. These latter included shortage of capital and entrepreneurship (even the "traditional" European investors refrained from serious investments and credits after World-War I); the economic slump all over the world; and the foreign domination of part of the area along colonial lines. In the mandated countries the conflicting interests of the mandatory government and the wishes of the population became evident. Here stress was laid on improving public administration and settling problems of land ownership as a prerequisite for gradual economic development. Regarding land tenure, however, considerable difficulties were encountered since the main support of the government came from the effendis.

Nevertheless, the meeting of East and West on the one hand and the distress suffered during the war on the other, both helped to promote an ideology of political independence linked up with development plans generally and industrialisation in particular. At least in part of the region, nationalist slogans and the demand for industrialisation have ever since been going hand in hand. In the absence of capital and a strong middle class, industrialisation meant government initiative and encouragement mainly in the form of industrial legislation, tax allowances for investors and entrepreneurs, and protective tariffs. State initiative took the form of actual industrial entrepreneurship only in Persia and Turkey. In the 'twenties and especially in the 'thirties of the twentieth century, these two countries as well as Palestine constituted the three main foci of progress within the area. The problems of Persia and Turkey (as well as of the principal Arab states) will be discussed below.

Palestine had been, somewhat arbitrarily, excluded from our present discussion.[2]

---

economic and political blocs or was it a special trend typical of a region in the process of emancipation? Does it foretell a higher socio-political phase of a kind of indigenous breed of imperialism? And, finally, has not the recent decade offered examples of a turn to new, ideologically coloured, ethnocentric formations, rather defying the concept of integrative blocs and closer perhaps to post-War I ideals?

[2] Some reviewers of the first edition of this book have disagreed with this exclusion by an author who has resided in Palestine (and now in Israel) and could follow events from close quarters and first-hand sources. Although I partly responded by including *Israel* in my *Economic Structure of the Middle East* (1975), I still preferred to leave Palestine out from *this* edition, due to its specific dual character and

Some of its influences, however, should at least be noted in view of their great significance for the entire region and the progress of developing countries at large. The Zionist territorialist concept, the transplantation of human beings to a new soil with all their ideas, their way of life and material resources (either their own or those of the nation) and the vast undertaking of their resettlement in all its social and economic aspects served not only to alter the face of one little niche of the Middle East, but aroused a great deal of attention throughout the area. The reaction to the appearance of this new factor alternated between extreme opposition and imitation.

The Jewish national idea served as an important example to the other peoples of the region in strengthening both their national claims and their desire for a greater degree of internal national consolidation. On the other hand, the fear of the revived Jewish nation, equipped as it was with modern organisational tools and means for propaganda and action, was great. It grew under the influence of Arab feudal and conservative elements which regarded the new factor as a threat to the very existence of traditional social and economic institutions, the supremacy of religion over social and legal matters, the existing authoritarian hierarchy and the prevailing system of land tenure.[3] There were also many outside factors which enhanced this fear. But both the Jewish experiment and the definite changes which gradually occurred in the life of the Palestinian Arabs became an undeniable far-reaching factor in the life of the area, altering social customs and increasing social demands. It also affected the economic order, especially in agriculture—in methods of fertilisation, crop rotation, mechanisation and irrigation—and showed itself in an increased striving for industrialisation and wider propagation of the idea of development with a view to raising the general level of production and consumption. A considerable improvement in sanitary conditions also came about largely owing to the example set by the Jews of Palestine.

B. *The New Political Structure and Its Economic Effects*

The political disunity of the area, which had already started before the war, increased considerably after it was over. State boundaries were laid down and problems of trading arose. Tariff barriers were erected between the various successor states of the Ottoman Empire which until the war had formed one political and economic framework. Existing economic and strategic power interests assumed a new direction while completely new interests gradually sprung up, such as the special significance attached to Middle Eastern oil. The big Powers sought ways and means of finding a compromise between one of the declared objectives of the war—the right of peoples to self-determination—and their own political and

---

history and the relatively abundant monographs on the subject by Bonné, Horowitz, Nathan, Gass and Creamer, and others.

[3] The fact that several of these feudalists were ready to sell land to the Jewish settlers at good prices does not invalidate the above explanation. Political differences grew more profound and the anti-Jewish front served to form an alliance between feudal rulers, nationalist dictators and communist movements, whose fear of the economic and social Jewish challenge stemmed from widely different sources.

economic interests. A solution was found which, while losing its validity towards the end of the Second World War, nevertheless answered a number of burning problems during the in-between period, i.e. mandatory rule, proposed in 1918 by General Smuts as part of his plan to establish a League of Nations.[4] The Powers intended to settle a number of problems at one single stroke and sometimes deliberately ignored essential contradictions such as between national aspirations for independence and foreign rule. In their desire for a settlement, the Powers not infrequently mixed up utterly selfish aspirations with noble and well-intentioned goals, or at least the observance of certain obligations.

The factors which determined the often mutually conflicting selfish interests of the major Powers included: the first discoveries of oil in the area; Western investments and the vested interests of the creditors; the existence of raw materials; the need for marketing outlets; prestige factors; and perhaps above all strategic considerations with respect to a vital area which included the Dardanelles, the Suez Canal and the most convenient passage to Southern Asia which, from the point of view of Britain, France and the U.S.A., was constantly jeopardised by the Germans or the Russians.

On the other hand the Powers were unable to ignore the regional national aspirations enhanced by the slogans used during the war and by express promises given to encourage friendly sectors and pacify enemies. The lack of clarity or equivocal nature of these promises, as to their political and moral implications, sometimes gave rise to arguments which have not ceased to this day.

In all events, the at least partial fulfilment of the promises given to the Arabs and the Jews created a new situation in the Middle East and constituted one of the causes of friction within the mandatory system. The political tension and lack of security caused distortions in the use of the limited economic resources and hampered the process of development.

In addition, the West strove to secure the interests of the Christian minorities which at various times during the existence of the Ottoman Empire had been the victims of cruel persecutions. The unilateral cancellation of the capitulations by Ottoman Turkey during the First World War and the gradual international recognition

---

[4] Cf. General Smuts, *The League of Nations, a Practical Suggestion,* London, 1918; *La Société des Nations et les Mandats,* p. 5. The most honest approach to the mandatory system was no doubt formulated by Rappard: "The Arab population was deemed to have reached a standard of civilisation which was sufficiently high for them to be recognised as independent nations, provided that their administrations be guided by a mandatory power until such time as they could rule themselves." League of Nations, *Permanent Mandates Commission,* 1st Sess., p. 4. This approach, however, contradicts a view which perhaps better reflects the reality of that period, such as that of Lord Curzon, the British Foreign Secretary, who on June 1920 said: "It is quite a mistake to suppose that under the Covenant of the League or any other instrument the gift of a mandate rests with the League of Nations. It rests with the Powers who have conquered the territories, which it then falls to them to distribute." Lord Balfour, on the other hand, expressed a more moderate opinion on the subject when he said to the Council of the League of Nations on May 17th, 1922, that the mandate is a "self-imposed limitation by the conquerors on the sovereignty which they obtained over conquered nations." See G. Kirk, *A Short History of the Middle East,* p. 130; League of Nations, *The Mandates System, Origin-Principles-Application,* Geneva, April 1945; E. G. Mears, *op. cit.,* p. 545.

of their abolition after the War further necessitated an arrangement to safeguard the interests of foreign nationals and investors and prevent their being discriminated against in matters of customs and trade. Under Clause 9 of the Treaty between Britain and Iraq of October 10th, 1922 (Iraq was the first among the mandatory countries to receive formal independence and to be admitted into the League of Nations) the King of Iraq undertook "to accept and give effect to such reasonable provisions as His Britannic Majesty may consider necessary in judicial matters to safeguard the interests of foreigners in consequence of the non-application of the immunities and privileges enjoyed by them under capitulation or usage. These provisions shall be embodied in a separate agreement, which shall be communicated to the Council of the League of Nations." Pursuant to this agreement the famous Clause 11 of the Iraqi mandate was passed, similar to Clause 18 of the Palestinian Mandate and Clause 5 of the Syrian-Lebanese Mandate, which assured non-discrimination in matters of taxation, trade, communications and any economic activity whatsoever between members of the League of Nations, including non-members allied by treaties to Britain.[5] Thus the partial continuation of the capitulations in the mandated countries (as well as in Persia and Egypt until their final abolition in 1928 and 1937, respectively) was assured for some time.

Four forms of government arose during this period on the ruins or at the fringes of the extinct Ottoman Empire: a) theoretically free States with a varying degree of actual independence, namely Persia, Turkey, Egypt, Yemen and Saudi Arabia; b) the principalities of the Arabian peninsula, most of which were linked by treaties to Britain; c) the British colonies in Cyprus and Aden; d) mandated territories of category A[6] whose Mandatories undertook to prepare them for self-government within a relatively short time,[7] namely Palestine, Transjordan and Iraq[8] under a British Mandate; and Syria and the Lebanon, under a French Mandate.

This new political structure and the lack of interest shown by the Powers—in the period between the two World Wars—in any serious attempt at development in the backward and apathetic region of the Middle East brought about a considerable retardation in the economic and social advancement of the independent countries (excepting Palestine and to some extent the Lebanon), while more daring development plans were carried out in Turkey and Persia where the State stood in the forefront of economic initiative and social reform.

At the prevailing economic and administrative level of the mandated countries it was difficult to find financial resources even for current expenditures, not to men-

---

[5] For texts of Clause 11 of the Iraqi Mandate, 18 of the Palestinian Mandate and 5 of the Syrian-Lebanese Mandate, see Appendices.

It should be stressed that these restrictions did not preclude general increases in customs tariffs, but merely forbade discrimination between the different countries (apart from special agreements between neighbouring countries, which were permitted).

[6] For texts of the Mandates see U.N., *Terms of League of Nations Mandates,* New York, Oct. 1946.

[7] Cf. Clause 22 of the *Covenant of the League of Nations* as well as *La S.D.N. et les Mandats,* p. 38.

[8] The Iraqi Mandate was formulated as an agreement between the Kings of Great Britain and of Iraq, signed on October 10th, 1922 and subsequently ratified, together with supplementary documents, by the League of Nations. This Mandate terminated in 1932. Cf. L. of N., *The Mandates System,* Geneva, 1945, p. 21.

tion the means for development plans. The Mandates Commission of the League of Nations frequently examined this question. Although the Mandatory Powers excused their failure by blaming objective circumstances and lack of capital and of initiative in the dependent countries themselves, the large factual material which accumulated during this period shows that the responsibility is at least divided between objective difficulties and the faulty understanding of the Powers of their task as trustees on behalf of the League of Nations. In the deliberations of the Mandates Commission it was further pointed out that private financial circles were deterred from investing in these countries through fear that the Mandate might be transferred to some other Power or cancelled altogether, when their investment would be left unprotected. This consideration, by the way, also acted on the Mandatory Powers themselves.[9] In League of Nations circles it was thought and even laid down as a principle that appropriate guarantees should be given in this connection. Since, however, the question of the Mandates was basically a political one, the guarantees proposed by the Commission were hardly of any great value.[10]

C. Derangement of the Village and Town Structure

An important role was played in the traditional society of the Middle East by the nomadic tribes which left the imprint of their customs, legal conceptions and economic way of life on the entire region. As early as the 19th century this social group started disintegrating owing to the impact of the West and the consequent local changes—new methods of land registration, irrigation networks which required more regular cultivation, and the gradual yielding of the camel as a means of transportation to the railway, navigation and motorcars which infiltrated the area. From this point of view the World War gave a considerable impetus to social and economic development on the one hand, and to undermining the position of the nomadic tribes on the other. Thanks to improved communications the security of the town dweller and the fellah grew, and encouragement was given to a market economy. Similarly, the rule of the Beduin was greatly limited, and robbery as a means of livelihood became well-nigh impossible; thus the traditional life of centuries was upset. The new political realignment in the Middle East as a result of the First World War, by which boundaries were created between the various States in the area, further limited the freedom of movement of the nomads, who previously had been free to roam over the entire Ottoman Empire. Measures were taken already before the war to check this movement and to control the tribes but with little success. The process of their settlement on the land was now speeded up.

This process increased the uniformity of the oriental village, but at the same time, owing to the lack of serious agrarian reform, the polarisation in ownership conditions became more acute: generally the shaykh received from his settled tribesmen part of their harvest, like an absentee landlord; frequently a considerable

---

[9] Cf. below, Chapter on economic policies.
[10] In this respect see League of Nations, *Permanent Mandates Commission,* 2nd Session, pp. 197-198.

share of these lands was registered in his name and thus the great estates became consolidated.[11] The nomads who had in the past been free gradually became peasants, ofter under conditions of serfdom, so that the advantage they derived from settlement was doubtful. In Turkey attempts were made at settling the nomads of East Anatolia in western districts, but only on a small scale.[12] In Syria and the Lebanon the semi-nomads penetrated the towns where they competed for local work and caused an increase of unemployment and a decrease in the already low wages.[13]

In the oriental towns, too, transformations which had already started in the previous century continued to take place. The influx of Western commodities and Western technology—to the extent that modern industries started developing within the area—destroyed the old structure of the towns, the remnants of the guilds and the artisan class. Many of the artisans remained without livelihood, while not yet being absorbed in industry. Under conditions of social, technical and economic backwardness, the new intellectual class did not succeed either in forming itself into a social unit. Both these rootless elements in addition to the labour force driven out from the villages have constituted to this day the great problem of the numerically fast growing Eastern towns where the increase in sources of livelihood lay far behind. This urban labour reserve gave much concern to both politicians and economists, and its influence on the shaping of political tenets grew constantly. The city, more than the village, reflected the clash between Western technology and ideas and the disintegrating social structure. The process of new social integration met with many obstacles.

---

[11] *The Special Report of the British Government of 1931,* according to *The Baghdad Times,* 26. and 27. VI. 1931.
[12] *Türkische Post,* 8.11.1931.
[13] *L'Orient,* Beyrout, 24.11.1933.

PART SEVEN

THE ECONOMIC DEVELOPMENT OF REPUBLICAN TURKEY*

1. FROM SÈVRES TO LAUSANNE—A NEW PAGE IN TURKISH HISTORY

The Republic of Turkey was one of the first of the less developed countries to adopt dynamic measures with a view to economic and social advancement. It served as a leading example to all who had the development of the Orient at heart, although more than once opinions of both local and foreign economists and politicians were divided as to its economic policy. Great differences of opinion were aroused by the adoption of the étatist system, typical of the 'thirties and 'forties of the 20th century, despite the fact that it included already known elements of European mercantilism also found in the Middle East in the economic policy of Mehmed Ali and of Riza Shah. The social and economic reforms in Turkey were largely inspired by the theories of Ziya Gökalp, one of the outstanding spiritual leaders of the country towards the end of the Empire and the beginning of the Republic. Gökalp insisted that the economic and social standing of the fellah must be raised, that he be freed from the yoke of moneylenders and tax collectors. He further demanded the abolition of the 'ushr, the education of the people in the light of Western cultural attainments, and the establishment of economic and financial institutions for the encouragement of agricultural and industrial progress.[1] In preaching a "national economy" after the fashion of Friedrich List, Gökalp called for inter-class solidarity and a co-operative social structure. His views were instrumental in bringing about the adoption of the étatist system in the 'thirties.

The First World War and the events of the beginning of the 'twenties put an end to the Ottoman Empire and to the hope still nestling in the hearts of its rulers that at least part of the inheritance and tradition of an Ottoman and Muslim centre might be maintained. Ideas of Ottomanisation were fostered by the leaders of the Young Turks, while the court of the Sultan and the Khalif during the beginning of the 'twenties toyed with the illusion that the dynasty might be continued. Perhaps the greatest achievement of Atatürk was that he dared see things as they were, and invested all his force and energy in putting an end to illusions and burying the vestiges of the past.[2] His position was far from easy. As soon as the First World War was over, in 1919 the Greeks invaded Turkey with the intention of splitting up the country. In this they received the active support of the Western Powers,[3] who were no longer interested in the protection of Turkey's independence. The attempt to set up a young State aspiring to independence on the ruins of the Empire, aiming at freedom from foreigners, cancellation of the capitulations and a revision of the

---

* For a more extensive study of this subject, see the author's *Turkey, An Economy in Transition,* Van Keulen, 1959, and, *Turkey, The Challenge of Growth,* Brill, 1968.
[1] Ziya Gökalp, *Türkçülüğün Esasları,* Istanbul, ed. 1939, pp. 37-52; 137-9.
[2] Cf. *The Encyclopedia of Islam,* Leyden, London, 1913-1934, Vol. IV, p. 970.
[3] Gazi Mustafa Kemal, *Nutuk,* Devlet Basımevi, Istanbul, 1938, p. 1. and *passim.*

status of foreign investments and the liquidation of the Ottoman debt on terms unfavourable to the creditors—all these appeared as formidable threats to the vested interests of the Powers.

The Sultan-Khalif and his staff were in fact captives of the Western Powers whose armies occupied the country, and while the war with the Greek invaders was still in progress the representatives of the Sultan in August 1920 signed the Treaty of Sèvres to settle the problems of the former Turkish dependencies and of Turkey itself.[4] By this treaty the independent part of Turkey was limited to Ankara and its environment. The Straits and the Dardanelles were internationalised. Izmir and its surroundings were handed over to the Greeks and the shore of the Mediterranean was divided among the French and Italian conquerors. The establishment of an Armenian State in East Anatolia, under the protectorate of Britain and the U.S.A., was declared. The capitulations and concessions remained in force. A financial commission of the Powers (France, Britain and Italy) was set up, nominally to supervise the currency and the budget, but actually, in view of its wide authorities, to run the economic affairs of the State. The capacity of the Turkish commissioner sitting on this commission was merely consultative.

However, the treaty was signed on behalf to Turkey by men who no longer represented its people. The actual reins of government, since the first half of 1919, were beginning to be held by Mustafa Kemal—later called Atatürk. He had been sent on a military mission to Anatolia, where he acquired the sympathies of the masses and gathered round him a group of faithful officers.[5] While leading the military front against the Greek invader and the political struggle against the government in Istanbul, Kemal simultaneously prepared political and economic plans for the future State to spring up on the ruins of the defunct Empire.[6]

The Turks succeeded in repulsing the Greek invasion both by their victories in the field and thanks to the change which occurred in the attitude of the Western Powers. Communist Russia recognised and supported the new Turkish regime.[7] France and Italy withdrew their support for the invaders. For a while Britain tried to continue its support, but met with increasing internal criticism. Indeed the failure of the Greek front was one of the important factors leading to the downfall of the British government.[8] The armistice of Mudania in October 1922 put an end to the Greek adventure and prepared the ground for a new peace treaty to be concluded at Lausanne.

Turkey proper suffered more from the Greek invasion than as a result of the World War. Serious economic problems arose: devastated cities and villages had to be rebuilt; the local population had to be rehabilitated as had the Turks returning

---

[4] The Treaty of Sèvres, Select Documents, No. 22, in E. G. Mears (ed.), *Modern Turkey*, pp. 634-7.
[5] Gesellschaft zur Erforschung der Türkischen Geschichte, *Geschichte der Türkischen Republik*, Istanbul, 1935, pp. 81, 135-136; Halidé Edib, *The Turkish Ordeal*, 1928, pp. 41-47.
[6] *Nutuk*, p. 1.
[7] *Treaty of Friendship between Russia and Turkey*, Moscow, March 16th, 1921, in *British and Foreign State Papers*, 1923, part II, Vol. 118, pp. 990-4. Cf. Appendix 26, below.
[8] Sir E. D. Ross, "The Making of Modern Turkey", *Journal of Royal Central Asian Society*, April 1937, p. 229.

from Greece and the Greeks expelled or transferred to Greece. The severe inflationary trend of the war years which was reflected in the rise of the currency circulation from 6.5 million Turkish pounds in 1915 to 161 million Turkish pounds in 1919[9] undermined the stability of the currency and the entire economy, further enhancing the difficulties due to the material damage caused by the Greek War.

This deterioration of the economic situation and the sad heritage of the Empire in the field of economics and finance from the first showed the decisive need for a stronghanded and well-directed economic policy. Already in 1919, during the two congresses of the national party at Erzurum and Sivas, at which the national aspirations of Turkey were first formulated, the economic goals of ensuring economic independence were stressed. It was declared that foreign aid would be acceptable provided the country's political and economic independence would remain untrammelled. This objective also formed the basis of the "National Pact" of January 1920[10] subsequently ratified by the National Assembly at Istanbul, and of the Organic Law passed on January 20th, 1921.[11] In the interval between the meetings of the Lausanne Conference in 1923, a special economic congress met at Izmir in February 1923 and laid down the principles of Turkey's economic policy. In the conclusions of the congress the presence in Turkey of the required natural resources and facilities for economic development was stressed, as was the need to utilise progressive and scientific ideas for the development of its primitive economy and the local production of the goods in demand. Turkey declared its readiness to permit the operation of foreign capital provided it did not run counter to Turkey's aspirations towards economic and political independence and infringe the laws of the country. It was recognised that the economic life of the country had to be organised on a basis of free enterprise, rejecting all monopolistic methods.

Some of the conclusions of the Izmir congress were again reflected in later plans and in the practical policy adopted by the government, especially during the 'thirties. On the other hand, a far-reaching change took place in the 'thirties in the attitude to free enterprise and the role to be played by the State in the economic sphere.

In the meantime the Lausanne Conference reached a successful conclusion, despite the innumerable stumbling blocks it had to overcome. The Treaty was duly signed on July 24th, 1923, by Turkey of the one part and Britain, France, Italy, Japan, Rumania and Yugoslavia of the other part (the U.S.A. was reprensented at the convention by an observer). A separate treaty was signed with Greece. The various financial and economic matters were settled by special Appendices. The

---

[9] Capitain C. H. Courthope-Munroe, *General Report on the Trade and Economic Conditions of Turkey for the Year 1919,* Dept. of Overseas Trade, London, 1920.
[10] See Turkish National Pact, 28.1.1920, in Select Documents No. 18, and Declaration of the Congress of Sivas, Select Documents, No. 16, in E. G. Mears, *op. cit.*
[11] *La Législation Turque,* Edition Rizzo & Son, Galata, Constantinople, Tome I. This House of Representatives was still elected according to the law by which the vote was given to all men above the age of 20 without the right of eligibility being expressly limited to men. The Law was changed only by the new constitution of 1924 which extended the right of vote to women. Cf. Halidé Edib, *The Turkish Ordeal,* p. 48.

chief representative of Turkey at Lausanne was Ismet Pasha (afterwards known as Ismet Inönü), the closest assistant of Mustafa Kemal, and the future Prime Minister and President of Turkey.

The Treaty of Lausanne[12] which granted political independence to Turkey, also dealt with a series of economic problems, some of which were settled on the spot and some left open for solution at a later date. It is the accepted opinion that the Lausanne Treaty constituted a victory for Republican Turkey.[13] This is largely true, especially considering that here there stood up against the array of the major Powers a country which together with Germany had been defeated in the First World War. On the other hand it should be remembered that Turkey had emerged victorious from its struggle with the Greeks, while it was nevertheless forced to make important concessions, especially over a certain period. In addition, some of the achievements of the Treaty—as in the matter of capitulations—had rather deleterious effects at least in the short run.

The Treaty finally abolished the capitulations since the Powers realised that it would no longer be possible to impose them on the new State. On the other hand several problems, directly or indirectly connected with the capitulations, remained extant for several years to come. Thus, for instance, a special commercial agreement provided that for five years from the date it came into force (1924) Turkey would be unable to change the customs tariffs as laid down on September 1st, 1916 and might forbid imports or exports solely under the special circumstances specified therein.[14] Most of the foreign concessions remained in force and their gradual nationalisation took 15 years, until the end of the 'thirties.[15] The foreign concessions for navigation rights along the shore (*cabotage*) were extended for an additional 2 years.[16]

The liquidation of the capitulations and the administrative difficulties put in the way of the concessionnaires reduced the willingness of foreign capitalists to participate in the economic life of Turkey on its terms. This unwillingness became especially marked after the French (largely owing to British intervention) failed to obtain extensive communications, oil and mines concessions and following the unsuccessful attempt, on the part of the American Company of Admiral Chester at the beginning of the 'twenties, to operate his concession.[17] The hopes that American

---

[12] *Treaty of Peace with Turkey and other instruments,* Treaty Series No. 16 (1923), London.

[13] Cf. P. P. Graves, *Briton and Turk,* p. 209; *Nutuk,* pp. 538-551, 619-620. W. W. Cumberland, "The Public Treasury", in E. G. Mears, *op. cit.,* p. 385.

[14] *Treaty of Lausanne, Commercial Convention,* Article 3.

[15] The Turks were permitted to cancel their agreements with Armstrong and Vickers, and Régie Générale des Chemins de fer, against payment of compensation. (These concessions had not been implemented prior to the Peace Treaty.)

[16] *Geschichte der Türkischen Republik,* pp. 161-2.

[17] This American company (Ottoman American Development Company) tried twice to implement its plans for obtaining and operating concessions in Turkey, once in 1909-11 and again in 1923 (the concession area approved in that year was three times as large as Chester's original concession). It intended to set up a ramified network of railways in Central and Eastern Anatolia as well as to construct and manage ports, mining enterprises, forests and agricultural undertakings—on financial and fiscal terms similar to those of the Baghdad railway. The concession was finally cancelled by Turkey, in December 1923, after having four months previously been transferred to a group of Canadian capitalists. Cf. p. 53, above, as well as E. M. Earle, *op. cit.,* pp. 332 ff. and *passim*; Henry Woodhouse, "The

capital, free of imperialist stigma, might be recruited for extensive investments in Turkey instead of the traditional capital ended in frustration. At least until the 'thirties the Turks failed to achieve a satisfactory mode of co-ordinating the goals of political and economic independence with participation of foreign capital on terms desirable to the State.

Developments concerning the Ottoman Debt further served to undermine the confidence of foreign investors. In this matter the Lausanne Conference had failed to reach a final agreement. The total amount of the debt was fixed at 130 million Turkish gold pounds (equivalent to approximately £ 130 million). Turkey's share in this debt was 84.6 million pounds, the rest being divided among the various successor States of the Ottoman Empire. (The particulars of the settlement and of how Turkey managed to reduce the debt and the amount of annual payments have been dealt with on pp. 69-70, above). Although Turkey succeeded in considerably reducing its payments, under the prevailing economic conditions even the agreed annuities of 7 million Turkish pounds constituted a heavy burden on the annual budget, which in the first years of the 'twenties amounted to about 100 million Turkish pounds.[18] Since the payments actually started only in 1929, they amounted to as much as 13-18% of the budget in the 'thirties, a proportion gradually reduced to 5%. As compared with the previous period, even such high rates as 18% obviously meant a considerable achievement for the Turkish economy, which in 1914/15 still had to set aside more than one-third of its budget for payments to foreign creditors.[19]

The whole chapter of compensation claims ended in a draw. The Powers, especially Britain, demanded that Turkey, as a defeated nation in the World War, pay compensation while the Turks on their part claimed compensation from the Greeks for their invasion of Turkey and the damage they had inflicted. Finally both parties waived their claims. In its treaty with Turkey, Greece agreed in principle to acknowledge its duty to pay compensation while the Turks expressed their consent to relinquish such payment.[20]

A problem which was discussed, but not solved at the Conference or by the Treaty was the future of the Mosul area. The actual control of this area was in the hands of the British, who demanded its transfer to Iraq (a British Mandate) while the Turks claimed it for themselves. The argument, and even the danger of armed conflict,[21] continued until 1926 and both France and the U.S.A. played an active part in staying the decision until their own interests in the area were secured.[22] Finally,

---

Chester Concession as an Aid to New Turkey", *The Current History Magazine,* New York, 1923, xviii, pp. 393-400. For the full text of the Chester Concession see *ibid.,* pp. 485-489; for its main clauses see our Appendix 31.

[18] Cf. Z. Y. Hershlag, *Turkey, An Economy in Transition,* p. 50.
[19] Ayni, H. T., *Borsa Rehberi,* Istanbul, 1928, p. 297.
[20] *Treaty of* Lausanne, Section II, Articles 58, 59, pp. 49-51.
[21] League of Nations, *Question of Frontier between Turkey and Iraq,* Geneva, Sept. 27, 1924.
[22] The fact that the U.S.A. supported Admiral Chester's concession in the course of 1923 and that this concession included the Mosul area (despite territorial and legal counter-claims by the British regarding the concession of the Turkish Petroleum Company—either on behalf of Iraq or in their own behalf) indicates the vacillating attitude adopted by the U.S.A. in this matter and highlights the role which the

when the differences between the Powers had been settled and the League of Nations had decided in favour of England and Iraq the Turks were forced to give in on condition that the Iraqi government would, for a period of 25 years, pay Turkey 10% of the royalties received from the Turkish (afterwards—Iraq) Petroleum Company or any of its subsidiary companies for oil produced in the Mosul area.[23] This condition was laid down in Clause 14 of the agreement signed on June 1926 between Britain and Iraq of the one part and Turkey of the other part, which defined the respective frontiers according to the recommendations of the League of Nations.[24]

The last problem of major economic significance connected with the Turkish-Greek conflict and the Lausanne Treaty was the exchange of population between Greece and Turkey. Prior to the war there were about two million Greeks living in Turkey (Anatolia and Eastern Thrace) and some half a million Turks in Greece. The problem of these minorities became particularly acute during the Turkish-Greek war. When the Greek armies started their retreat in 1922, the Greek inhabitants of Anatolia fled for fear of annihilation by the advancing Turks. Villages and towns were destroyed, and in Izmir the Turkish and Greek quarters were burnt down by the retreating and the victorious parties, repectively. At the suggestion of F. Nansen (the Norwegian scientist and diplomat)[25]—approved in principle by the Lausanne Convention—and with the mediation of the League of Nations, the two countries arrived at an agreement concerning an exchange of populations through the Commission for the Settlement of Greek Refugees. During the 'twenties, 1,400,000 Greeks (one million prior to the signature of the Lausanne agreement) left Turkey and 400,000 Turks returned to Turkey from Greece.[26] Exempted from the transfer were the Muslims of western Thrace and Greeks who had lived in Constantinople before October 30th, 1918.

Side by side with the problem of the Greek refugees there was that of the 220,000 Bulgarian refugees.[27] Despite their considerably smaller number, it was difficult to find a solution since no exchange could be contemplated as in the case of the Greeks but refugees from Turkey had to be resettled in Bulgaria. At that time, however, this matter concerned Bulgaria (and the League of Nations) in the first line while the problem of Turks returning from Bulgaria became acute only after the passage of years.

The Turkish-Greek exchange had several positive aspects even though it involved much suffering for the refugees. Famine and epidemics broke out and people were

---

question of oil played in the final decision to recognise the Mosul area as part of Iraq. Cf. *Current History*, N.Y., xviii, 1923, pp. 393-400; Also see Raymond Leslie Buell, "Oil Interests in the Fight for Mosul", *Current History*, xvii, No. 6, March 1923, pp. 931-938.

[23] *Question of the Frontier between Turkey and Iraq* (Report submitted to the Council of the League of Nations by the Commission instituted by the Council Resolution of Sept. 30th, 1924), 1925.

[24] *Treaty between the United Kingdom and Iraq and Turkey,* Angora, June 5th, 1926, *H.M.S.O.,* London, 1927.

[25] Cf. Fridtjof Nansen, *Report on the Work of the High Commission for Refugees,* Geneva, 1923.

[26] League of Nations, *Greek Refugees Settlement,* p. 3 ff.

[27] League of Nations, *Settlement of Bulgarian Refugees,* Rapporteur: Commander Hilton Young, Geneva, Sept. 21st, 1926.

uprooted from the land where they and their forefathers had been living for generations. Frequently the regulations were evaded, causing constant tension. On the other hand both countries at one stroke solved the problem caused by large minorities which particularly in Turkey had brought about constant friction and led to frequent calamities for the minorities themselves. The exchange proved that even where the fate of 2 million people was concerned a satisfactory settlement might be reached. With the exit of the Greeks additional means of livelihood became available to the Turkish population in those occupations which previously had been exercised mainly by foreigners.[28] The Commission had only partial success in dealing with the resettlement of the returning refugees. Especially in Greece resettlement was aided by the allocation of land by the Greek government under conditions as similar as possible to those prevailing in the Turkish provinces which the refugees had left.

In the short term, however, the negative side prevailed over any possible economic advantages. On the whole Turkey hardly suffered from a surplus of manpower, while the development of its economic resources required a considerable input of labour. When the Greeks left the loss was not merely quantitative but mainly qualitative. They had largely been economically active and enterprising and taken up important positions in commerce, the civil service, banking and craftsmanship while the Turks who came back from Greece were peasants of a low cultural and professional standard. It was not easy within a short space of time to fill the place of those who had left, so that the national element was strengthened at the expense of the economic advantage and occupational structure of the population.[29] The land left by the Greeks was moreover neglected owing to the ravages of the war so that extensive rehabilitation was required. The Turkish peasants were unable to take great advantage of the agrarian reform of the 'twenties since this was intended mainly to secure lands for the refugees from Greece.

On June 10th, 1930, an agreement was signed in Ankara which restated the problems of resettlement of populations resulting from the previous agreement. This time, however, the execution of the decisions was easier since in most cases the principle of *fait accompli* was recognised.[30]

Despite the many drawbacks of the Lausanne Treaties, especially in the short run, they freed Turkey of most of the legal, financial and economic shackles left by the heritage of the Empire so that the road for independent action in the field of economic development now lay open.

---

[28] Both sides promised that the exchange would not prejudice the rights of the exchanged persons with respect to immovable and cash property. A system was worked out whereby the Commission supervised the restitution of property to the transferees in their new country of settlement by acting as intermediary between the respective government concerning the mutual settlement of accounts. This system, however, was implemented only partially.
[29] Cf. Celal Nuri in *Milliyet,* 24.9.1929.
[30] S. P. Ladas, *The Exchange of Minorities: Bulgaria, Greece & Turkey,* New York, 1932.

2. THE ECONOMIC DEVELOPMENT OF THE TWENTIES AND ITS LIMITATIONS

The economic development of Turkey between the two World Wars falls into two main periods: the period of rehabilitation from the ravages of the wars, based on private initiative and limited government intervention—mainly by administrative and legislative means; and the period of étatism, from about the year 1929/30, i.e., energetic government action in the economic sphere especially in the establishment of industries and financial institutions.

The relatively slight intervention of the government in the economic life of the country during the 'twenties was due to several causes. The Lausanne Treaty imposed certain limitations on the government, especially as regards customs and concessions; the exchange of population had given rise to complicated problems of resettlement and finance, which occupied its attention; the new administration was still in the formative stage, while internal riots against a national and socio-political background attracted the attention of the ruling coterie.[31] The government had not yet found the means for recruiting the required capital for public investments in development projects. Even the tobacco, alcohol and salt monopolies, previously held by the Ottoman Debt Administration, passed over to the government only in 1927, with an annual revenue of about 40 million Turkish pounds. On the other hand the fact that the republican government ignored a number of restrictions imposed upon it by the Treaty of Lausanne with respect to customs and concessions, and the high-handed manner in which it treated foreign companies deterred foreign capitalists. Government and international capital in the more developed parts of the world had not yet been mobilised for the development of backward countries (this occurred mainly after the Second World War) while private capital was still faithful to colonialist principles, i.e., the primary exploitation of the resources of backward countries and the flooding of their markets with one's own industrial products. Only oil had started to attract major investments to the Middle East, but Turkey within its new boundaries was deprived of this treasure.

To the extent that the government was able to mobilise economic resources and administrative and technical manpower, these were in the first instance directed towards repairing the damage caused by the continuous wars.[32] By 1924 the main vestiges of the old Empire had been liquidated. In November 1922 the Sultanate was abolished as well as the office of Shaykh-ul-Islam.[33] In October 1923 the Republic was declared, in March 1924 the Khalifate was abolished and the Shari'a and Waqf ministry liquidated, and on April 20th, 1924, the Republican constitution was ratified.[34] Now a series of reforms was instituted in the social and economic legislation, which to a certain extent prepared the ground for more practical steps during the 'thirties. Both the constitution and the code of laws were influenced by the French and Swiss models. The Civil Code of 1926 settled and clarified a number

---

[31] See *Geschichte der Türkischen Republik*, pp. 245-6.
[32] Cf. Nermin Menemencioğlu, "The Progress of Turkey", *Progress*, Winter 1950/51, Publ. by Lever Brothers & Unilever Ltd., London.
[33] *Geschichte der Türkischen Republik*, pp. 153-155.
[34] *La Législation Turque*, Tome II, pp. 296-311.

of problems which had remained unclear in the eclectic Mejelle, including *inter alia* the rights of inheritance; possession and transfer of immovable and other property; and in particular the possession, mortgaging, registration and transfer of lands in ownership or under lease.[35] The introduction of the Gregorian calendar, European dress, the removal of the veil and the grant of equal rights to women[36] as well as the introduction of the Latin script all served as an outward expression of Western influence. The abolition of Islam as the State religion in 1928 constituted a revolutionary step by a government which by then had already gained confidence in its political and moral powers.[37] All these measures were taken by a determined ruling junto which relied on the support of one single party, the People's Party, reorganised in 1923 as the Republican People's Party, which maintained its rule until 1950.

The party paid great attention to economic development, as may be seen from the resolutions of the party congresses at Erzurum and Sivas and of the economic congress at Izmir, prior to the establishment of the Republic. During the 'thirties, both the party and the government continued to consolidate their economic policy, this time with a view to increasing direct State entrepreneurship.

Already during the 'twenties, the government had aspired towards industrialisation. However the restrictions on customs tariffs, the scanty financial resources available and the prevailing trend of non-intervention in economic affairs led to more emphasis on agriculture at least until 1927. In 1925 the *'ushr* tax was abolished.[38] The new regime regarded it not merely as too heavy a financial burden on the population, but above all as a symbol of the old feudal order and the exploitation of the fellah by the system of crop assessments.[39] Little success was achieved with alternative methods of taxing the rural population. The "land produce tax" failed because it proved to be too haphazard and arbitrary. It had to be replaced by a land tax based on an *ex-post* estimate of the real income of the farmer (as opposed to the *'ushr* which was based on prior estimates).

Greater uniformity in the system of land tenure, which had taken shape during the 19th century, was achieved by the new Civil Code of 1926. Accordingly, the previous distinctions in the use, transfer and succession of *mulk*, *miri* and part of the *waqf* lands were removed. Agrarian reform aimed at a redistribution of land ownership was started as early as 1923.[40] Abandoned lands, *waqf* lands and part of

---

[35] Code Civil Turc, *La Législation Turque,* Constantinople, 1926, in part. pp. 117-174.

[36] The revolutionary character of the Kemalist movement was reflected *inter alia* in the important role played in the national movement by Halidé Edib, one of the most outstanding personalities of that time in Turkey. Perhaps it is also typical of the political and social strings which still tied down this movement that the participation of Halidé Edib did not outlast the victory of the revolution and that she was forced to leave the country following differences of opinion between her and Kemal Pasha. The background for this development may be found in the books of Halidé Edib, *The Turkish Ordeal; Turkey Faces West.*

[37] *La Législation Turque,* IV, Law No. 1222, p. 125.

[38] *Ibid.,* III, Law No. 552, p. 72.

[39] See M. O. Dikmen, "Entwicklung der türkischen Umsatzsteuer", *Revue de la Faculté des Sciences Economiques de l'Université d'Istanbul,* Oct. 1943, p. 77.

[40] For the agrarian reform carried out during the period of the Republic, see Ö. L. Barkan, "La Loi sur la distribution des terres aux agriculteurs et les problèmes essentiels d'une réforme agraire en

the large estates were considered for redistribution. Two classes were to benefit from this first reform: 1) the farmers who had been repatriated as a result of the exchange of populations between Greece and Turkey; 2) the landless peasant. In the 'twenties the main benefit of the reform accrued to the first category while the numerous smallholders had no share in the distribution. The plots handed out to cultivators, mainly land suited solely for extensive agriculture, varied in size from 17 to 24 *dunams*, i.e. less than was required to maintain a family. The implementation of the law met with many difficulties and the distribution went on staggeringly until the end of the 'forties. During the 12 years between 1923 and 1934 a total of close to 7 million *dunam* (= 700,000 ha.), were distributed, i.e. less than 1% of the area of the country or about 5% of the gross cultivated area. Nonetheless, the achievements of the reform were of importance considering that Turkey's share in the feudal inheritance of the Empire was much smaller than, for instance, that of the Arab countries, with a smaller concentration of large estates. Further measures for the encouragement of agriculture included the establishment of experimental stations, agricultural schools and model farms, the supply of seeds, the sending out of instructors to the villages and the introduction of compulsory agricultural training for soldiers during their period of military service.[41]

A hard-core problem in the Turkish economy as a whole, including agriculture, was the problem of financing. The farmer by himself was unable to generate the required funds for investment in his farm, for mechanisation and other improvements. He had enough to do merely to subsist from one season to the other under constant lack of operating capital and of credit facilities. The few credit institutions existing rendered service mainly to the wealthier classes, especially since until 1924 loans were granted only against mortgages and not against collateral guarantees. The Agricultural Bank grew only slowly and provided a limited amount of loans. In 1924, with the transfer of its central office from Istanbul to Ankara, its functions were extended. The bank was granted many facilities, and according to its new constitution and guiding principles its primary concern should become the welfare of the peasants rather than the seeking of profits.[42] The extent of the loans granted rose considerably. The registered capital of the bank was raised to 30 million Turkish pounds. While previously aggregate loans were given up to 30% of the paid-up capital, they now amounted to 100% and more, making use of deposits and other resources.

The form of securities required was altered to include collateral guarantees, apart from mortgage.[43] In pursuance of these changes the credits given by the bank to its customers expanded as follows:

Turquie", *Revue de la Faculté des Sciences Economiques de l'Université d'Istanbul*, Oct. 1944, Jan. 1945.

[41] *Geschichte der Türkischen Republik,* pp. 354-9.

[42] Türkiye Ziraat Bankası, *Nizamnamei Esası,* 1929.

[43] The establishment of agricultural credit societies, started by Midhat Pasha in 1863 according to the German and Danish models, proved less successful. The Law of Agricultural Credit Co-operatives was drafted only in 1929.

TABLE XVII

Increase in the Credit of the Agricultural Bank of Turkey during the Years 1922-1929 [44]

(as at the end of the year)

Year	Turkish Pounds
1922	928,000
1923	4,807,000
1924	16,400,000
1925	15,456,000
1926	16,214,000
1927	17,124,000
1928	29,046,000
1929	25,880,000

The decrease which occurred in the credit balance in 1929 already reflects the beginning of the world depression.

The practical results of these measures in the field of agriculture, though favourable, were still limited in scope. Between 1923 and 1932, the cultivated area increased by about 58% while the population grew by 25-28%. Thus despite the scanty improvements in productivity per unit of land this increase in area accounted for a certain rise in total yields and in the farmers' income. Viewed against the background of the destruction and neglect of the wars—especially the war against the Greeks—this rise in output and income represented rehabilitation rather than development, if compared with the pre-war standards. Actual development started from 1927 onwards[45] and relatively more attention was given to the cultivation of grain. By 1930 Turkey was able to put an end to the importation of wheat, and became a grain exporter for most of the following years. Considerable progress was also made in the cultivation of tobacco, which had been neglected as a result of the war, so that by the beginning of the 'thirties Turkey had returned to its 1913 level. Thanks to the numerous improvements introduced by the government monopoly in both the agricultural and the industrial stages (for industry see below) of tobacco production the output reached 70,000 tons by 1927. Although Turkey's share in the overall world production of tobacco was relatively small, it produced 20-30% of the oriental brand at the end of the 'twenties.[46]

The high prices obtained for agricultural produce in the 'twenties, until the outbreak of the 1929 crisis, were a great help to Turkish agriculture. Thenceforth the depression on the one hand and the intensified industrialisation policy of the government on the other dealt a serious blow to agriculture which in any case lagged behind the standard even of Eastern and Southern Europe.

---

[44] Cf. Z. Y. Hershlag, *op. cit.*, p. 56.

[45] In that year the entire cultivated area of Turkey was no more than 5% of the country's total area and cereals took up 89.5% of this. *La Turquie Contemporaine*, pp. 64-5.

[46] *Türkische Post*, 9.6.1931.

As early as the days of the Young Turks attempts had been made at industrialisation. In 1909 and 1913 two laws for the encouragement of industry were passed, but development plans were not carried out owing to the almost continuous warfare in which the Empire was engaged until the end of the First World War. Immediately upon the establishment of the Republic—in the wake of the Izmir congress—the party and the government expressed their readiness to do their utmost for the acceleration of the process of industrialisation. In the course of the 'twenties several preparatory steps were taken for the promotion of industry, while actual industrial activity was still limited.

In 1924 customs exemptions were introduced for raw materials required for industry. Legal status was given to artisans' corporations—the successors of the guilds—(not to be confused with workers' trade unions) which were subjected to government control. Their duty was to provide for the development of the crafts, to organise mutual aid funds, to settle disputes with members of their trade, etc.[47] A regulation of 1925 made it compulsory for government departments and government-supported institutions to purchase local produce provided its price did not exceed that of similar foreign-made commodities by more than 10%.

The Law for the Encouragement of Industry of May 28th, 1927, forms the focal point of the economic legislation of the 'twenties. Its objective was to support real industrial undertakings (and not small workshops), to whom the following facilities were granted:

1. Grant of land free of charge up to 100 *dunam* and, if necessary, confiscation of land against payment of compensation in favour of such enterprises.
2. Reductions in telegraph or telephone charges.
3. Exemption from a number of taxes, such as property, land, profits and licence tax.
4. Exemption of shares and debentures of industrial firms from stamp duty.
5. Abolition of customs on essential materials and equipment, and facilities regarding their transportation.
6. Availability of government premiums of up to 10% of the value of annual production.
7. Reductions on the price of salt, alcohol and dynamite.
8. An undertaking on the part of government departments and enterprises and government-supported institutions to purchase the produce of the enterprises specified in the law provided its price did not exceed that of foreign-made goods by more than 10%.

The industrial enterprises were divided into four groups according to their mechanical equipment and the number of working-days provided. Only the first group of enterprises with machinery of at least 10 H.P. and 1,500 working days per year enjoyed all the benefits conferred by the law while the remaining groups received only partial facilities. The mines were likewise divided into two categories according to the size of their capital investment and their motor power, and obtained reductions and facilities accordingly.

---

[47] Osman Mukdim, *op. cit.,* pp. 18-19.

The law further stipulated that only Turkish citizens should be employed in the approved enterprises, while certain foreign experts could be hired for a limited period.

The Law for the Encouragement of Industry became one of the major nuclei of planned industrialisaton during the 'thirties.[48]

The difficulties encountered in financing industrial development had a detrimental effect both on private industry and on government planning. The foreigners temporarily drew back from participation in the economic life of the country, including financing operations.[49] The national minorities—the Armenians, the Jews, and in particular the Greeks—were to a far-reaching extent ousted from commercial and financial activities. The government fostered the establishment of new tools for the financing of industrial enterprise. In 1924, largely due to the initiative of Mustafa Kemal, İş Bankası, a private business bank[50] (though subject to considerable government influence) was founded. It acquired a sound reputation abroad and remained one of the important banks even in the 'thirties and 'forties, when the network of State Banks was set up. The varied and manifold functions of the bank—which were expanded in course of time—comprised the grants of loans to industry, mining and commerce; direct participation in a number of enterprises, especially for the production of glass, sugar and coke; insurance business; participation in railway operation; and savings campaigns. By 1929 the nominal capital of the bank, which initially stood at 1 million Turkish pounds, had risen to 4 million while in the same year the savings deposits increased to 44 million Turkish pounds. The İş Bank further shared in the financing of government-sponsored enterprises, and set up branch offices in Alexandria (Egypt) and Amsterdam (Holland) to deal in import and export business. The activities of the special Bank for Industry and Mining, founded in 1925, gathered momentum only during the 'thirties, in particular since it developed into the powerful financing arm of the State, the Sümerbank.

Two principal factors make it difficult to draw up a comparison between the industry of Republican Turkey of the 'twenties, and that of the pre-War Ottoman Empire: a) in the Empire's industrial abstracts (as indicated on p. 75) the industries of Damascus, Beirut, Baghdad, etc. still play an important part; b) Turkey's ramshackle industry was severely shaken up by World War I and the War of Independence. As in agriculture, rehabilitation had to precede development.

---

[48] *Loi sur l'Encouragement de l'Industrie,* Loi No. 1055 de 28 mai 1927, J. A. Rizzo, Stamboul, 1929.

[49] In 1924, after Lausanne, 94 foreign companies with an invested capital of about £ 63 millions were still operating in Turkey. They included 7 railway and 6 mining companies, 23 banks, 11 municipal concessions, 12 industrial firms and 35 commercial firms. Most of the capital was German (45.4%), followed by French (25.0%) and British capital (16.9%). The process of nationalisation of most of the major enterprises, particularly railways, mining, electricity, water, tobacco, and urban transportation lasted until the eve of the Second World War. *La Turquie Contemporaine,* 208-9; E. R. Lingeman, *Turkey, Economic and Commercial Conditions in Turkey,* Sept. 1947, H.M.S.O., London, 1948, pp. 133-4.

[50] *Geschichte der Türkischen Republik,* pp. 381-2; *Türkiye İş Bankasının bu Yılı 1924-34; Türkische Post,* 2.9.1935.

The first results of the encouragement given to industry became noticeable at the end of the 'twenties and the beginning of the 'thirties. In 1932, close to 1,500 approved enterprises, of which about 1,150 were founded between 1923 and 1932, enjoyed the facilities of the Law for the Encouragement of Industry.[51] It is difficult to make a clear distinction between real industrial enterprises and workshops, as is evident also in the analysis of the number of earners. The official Turkish sources give a number of 76,000 industrial earners in 1921, and 257,000 in 1927. The absolute majority however were working in small primitive workshops, while at most some 27,000 men employed in 1927 in the approved enterprises[52] could be considered as industrial labourers, as compared with 17,000 industrial labourers employed in the major enterprises on the eve of the First World War (though the latter figure covered a larger geographical area).

The investment in the enterprises was small, and the entire structure of the industry showed that it was still in the early stages of development. Forty-five per cent of all industrial enterprises were concerned with the production of food and twenty-four per cent with textiles. The estimated value added of the mines, industry and crafts at the end of the 'twenties amounted to about 20 million Turkish gold pounds (at a ratio of 10 : 1 between the gold and paper pounds), i.e., an increase of more than 100% over 1913. If these estimates are more or less correct they would point to a quite considerable progress achieved during the period of rehabilitation.

In several industries the period of rehabilitation, 1924-1927, already marked a notable growth. Further progress was made during the short time between 1927 and 1929, when the Law for the Encouragement of Industry came into force. Thus in the last-mentioned period the output of cotton products rose from 2,500 to 3,800 tons; sugar from 5,000 to 8,000 tons; cement from 41,000 to 73,000 tons. A smaller rise was noted in the field of wool, silk and leather.[53] Considerable fluctuations in yields and prices occurred in the tobacco industry. Until 1927 both rose appreciably and the government took energetic steps to increase the efficiency of the existing enterprises by renewal of equipment and establishment of essential services, while also setting up new enterprises. The 1929 depression reduced the demand on the world market and lowered prices. The tobacco crops were simultaneously reduced by natural disasters;[54] with little effect on the price level on the world market, the fall in output further reduced the cash income of the farmer.

One can hardly speak of a well-co-ordinated, thorough-going development policy during the 'twenties, though certain preparatory steps were taken which helped to pave the way for the more daring experiments of the 'thirties. Between 1925 and 1929 the government tried to promote economic and fiscal targets largely by the formation of industrial government monopolies, such as for tobacco, alcohol, matches and sugar. The full range of measures taken by the State in order to encourage and foster local industry did not come until later.

---

[51] İstatistik Yıllığı, 1942-45.
[52] İstatistik Yıllığı, 1930, pp. 187 ff.
[53] For particulars and sources, see the author's book *Turkey, An Economy in Transition,* pp. 64-69.
[54] İstatistik Yıllığı, 1930 p. 177; *Türkische Post,* 27.4.1933.

In view of the limited development of industrial initiative and the backwardness of agriculture (as reflected in low productivity) the changes in real *per capita* income were still small. Although a certain rise was registered in national income, the data are unreliable so that any accurate assessment can hardly be made. Estimates for the 'twenties indicate a slight average rise, in real terms, of 2-3% in the *per capita* income between 1927 and 1929, and a somewhat greater relative rise in comparison with 1923.[55]

3. THE CAUSES OF THE CHANGES IN ECONOMIC POLICY

Towards the end of the 'twenties the consciousness grew in Turkey that if the economy continued to advance at the then prevailing rate, fifty or even a hundred years would pass before Turkey would be on an equal footing as regards its income level and standard of living even with countries of no more than average development.[56] Private initiative was unable to carry the burden in the absence of the required capital and organisational and economic potential. Shortage of foreign capital made itself felt under the new conditions of the Republic both because of the "sitting on the fence" attitude adopted by foreign investors, and the drastic means taken by the Republic to safeguard its economic and political independence. Government intervention in the economic life of the country—especially by means of laws and regulations—as practised in the 'twenties, was insufficient to lever far-reaching economic progress. New instruments were needed—financial, organisational and managerial—in the planning of development and the thorough exploitation of the country's resources in agriculture, and above all in industry. Various external and internal factors helped to bring about the direct intervention of the State in the economic field, leading to the regime known as étatism.

Among the *external* factors contributing to the rise of the new economic regime two deserve special mention: the effect of the world crisis on Turkey; and the influence of the Soviet Union. The primary producing countries were hit hard even in the early stages of the depression; owing to the falling demand for, and the low elasticity of supply of agricultural (as compared to industrial) produce, and the resulting pressure on prices, on the one hand; and owing to the decreased demand for mineral raw materials and the parallel decline in their price and output, on the other hand. A diagram of world production in that period (on next page) shows the differences in the scope of fluctuations in agricultural, industrial, and raw materials production. In this respect the beginnings of the 'thirties are particularly significant.

Since Turkey was not decisively dependent on its foreign trade (the share of exports in the national income of 1929 was 8-9%) and its international economic relations were not highly developed, it was affected to a much smaller extent than

---

[55] *Turkey, An Economy in Transition*, pp. 71-72.
[56] Cf. *2inci 5yıllık Sanayi Planı*, 1936, pp. xxx-xxxi; *La Turquie Economique*, p. 17.

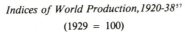

Indices of World Production, 1920-38[57]
(1929 = 100)

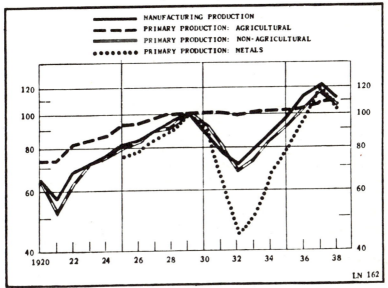

most other countries. However, even the Turkish economy suffered during the period between 1929 and 1934 from the astonishing drop in the prices of raw materials and agricultural produce, which made up 80-90% of exports. The export returns fell from 155 million Turkish pounds in 1929 to 92 million Turkish pounds in 1934.[58] This decline was one of the factors which prompted the government to free the country from its excessive dependence on agriculture.

The world depression had a much stronger effect on the economic *policy* of Turkey than on its economy as such. At first the reaction of Turkey was similar to that of other nations where the governments almost blindly turned to a policy of "sauve qui peut".[59] The consequence was economic retrenchment, with maximum avoidance of imports, and internal thriftiness—two measures which merely aggravated the crisis. The standstill in production, the decline in the standard of living, the world mass unemployment, and the threat to the existing social and economic structure—all prompted the demand for active State intervention in order to revive the economy, increase employment, plan investment and production, and achieve a more rational distribution of the national income.

The writings of Keynes, particularly those of the 'twenties and the beginning of the 'thirties, did much to foster this new approach among both politicians and economists.[60] The Turkish politicians, in their defence of the étatist system during

---

[57] League of Nations, *The Transition from War to Peace Economy,* Part 2, Geneva, 1945, p. 76.
[58] *La Turquie Contemporaine,* p. 201.
[59] League of Nations, *The Transition from War to Peace Economy,* p. 20.
[60] See especially J. M. Keynes, *The End of Laissez Faire,* at the Hogarth Press, 1926.

the middle 'thirties, pointed out with considerable justification that the argument about the role played by the State in the economic life of the country in many places had already been decided in favour of far-reaching State intervention.[61]

The West, however, provided more of a negative example, teaching Turkey that the liberal capitalist economies had lost their way and that a free economy with its traditional instruments was unable to meet the crisis. Despite the fact that in the social and political field Turkey refused to act on the Soviet model both in the inter-war period and even more so after the last war, Soviet influence was considerable in the field of economic planning and development. Turkish sources of the 'thirties confirm that Soviet ideology affected the concept and implementation of economic plans, which were carried out in close co-operation with the Soviet Union.[62]

In 1928, the Soviet Union published its first Five Year Plan, which constituted an important turning point in the history of modern economics, even in countries which did not accept the Soviet regime. Turkey followed the course of events in Russia with mixed sentiments, especially in view of the severe recession in the West. On the one hand the Turks admired the tremendous impetus of the Soviet experiment; on the other hand they distrusted their powerful neighbour in view of the strained relations between the two nations in the past. Moreover, Kemal Atatürk feared the spread of the communist idea in Turkey itself, and took severe measures to prevent the formation of any social and political movement tainted by socialism or communism. While the agreement by which the two States had undertaken to refrain from intervention in each other's internal affairs was in force, increasing State intervention in the economic life of Turkey led to a greater degree of economic co-operation between Turkey and the Soviet Union. Soviet aid received included: a 20-year loan of 8 million gold dollars, without interest, for the partial financing of the first Five Year Plan of 1933/34; the despatch of Soviet experts to Turkey and Turkish students to the Soviet Union; the construction of several Turkish plants by Russian technicians; the establishment of a special institution in Russia, called *Turkstroj*, to conduct commercial affairs between Turkey and the Soviet Union; and various symbolic presents made by the Russians to Turkey, such as a limited number of cars or tanks.[63]

In the West suspicions arose that Turkey was proceeding towards collectivisation[64] but under the prevailing ideology and social and political regime, and in view of the agrarian policy of the government and the absence of comprehensive overall plans so typical of the Soviet method their qualms were unfounded.

The slow pace at which the Turkish economy progressed during the 'twenties was among the main *internal* causes leading to a change in the economic regime. There might be a certain degree of justification in the claim that this short period had been

---

[61] Ismet Inönü's article in *Kadro* of October 1933.

[62] *Geschichte der Türkischen Republik*, p. 74; *Der Nahe Osten*, Istanbul, 15.1.1936.

[63] *Türkische Post*, 15.5.1932; *Milliyet*, 7.5.1932, and also later issues of this journal. Cf. also Max Beloff, *The Foreign Policy of Soviet Russia, 1929-1941*, 1949, Vol. II, p. 41; Gotthard Jäschke, *Die Türkei in den Jahren 1935-41*, Leipzig, 1943, p. 5.

[64] Cf. *Handelsblatt des Berliner Tageblatts*, 28.2.1931.

insufficient for private initiative to unfold its organisational and economic capacities and that any judgment which might be passed on the failure of private initiative was overhasty. In the 'twenties the State had only just started healing the wounds left by the World War and especially the War of Independence against the Greeks. The new regime had to consolidate its position and stamp out any signs of internal opposition still existing among the national and political minorities until about 1927. Any efforts in the economic field were directed towards rehabilitation, i.e., the restoration of the pre-War *status quo* rather than towards an increase of the economic potential and the encouragement of private initiative. With the evacuation of the Greeks, the middle classes who might have provided such initiative were weakened still further.

These circumstances to a certain extent explain but hardly alter the fact that the more liberal economic regime of the 'twenties failed to achieve any appreciable improvements, so that in most areas no significant progress could even be envisaged. Until the end of the 'twenties the trade balance was unfavourable and the influx of capital too slight to enable any considerable expansion of imports. The country's budget was unbalanced and internal loans were required to cover the deficits caused, *inter alia*, by large security, military and police expenditures. Most of the administrative staff had been taken over directly from the ancient regime with all its corruption and inefficiency.[65]

Economic progress was one of the overriding goals of the Turkish government which cavilled at its languishing pace and which it refused to countenance. Thus in the discussion of the Second Five Year Plan in 1936, a Turkish minister said: "If we leave to private enterprises the execution of all the works necessary for the reconstruction of our country we may wait fifty years—and even then private enterprise may not be able to tackle them. Fear, based upon painful experiences of foreign financial exploitation, and the lack of private capital, have made State control necessary."[66]

The *volte-face* in Turkish policy was facilitated by the new Customs Law of 1929. As will be remembered, the Lausanne Treaty stipulated that customs tariffs might not be changed for five years from the date it came into force, i.e., until 1929,[67] when Turkey seized the opportunity to issue a new customs law.[68] It was based on the principle of trade reciprocity as outlined in the declarations of the Turkish leaders and the decision of the Republican People's Party. Turkey was prepared to grant customs reductions and import facilities to countries who accorded her the same privileges; while taking counter-measures against all countries which showed a discriminative attitude. This was a major protective weapon, but a very dangerous

---

[65] J. B. Kingsbury and Tahir Aktan, *The Public Service in Turkey, Organization, Recruitment and Training,* Brussels, 1955.

[66] Cf. P. P. Graves, *Briton and Turk,* p. 218.

[67] While Turkey had used the opportunity of the war in order to change its customs law unilaterally and go over from the *ad valorem* to the specific customs system (by the regulation of 4.9.1916), the Powers were interested in preserving at least the tariffs obtaining at that time.

[68] *Resmi Gazete,* 17.1.1929; *Zolltariffgesetz und Zolltariff der Türkischen Republik,* Konstantinopel, 1929.

one in a period of extensive economic conflicts following the protectionist methods adopted during the world crisis. Chain reactions of discrimination and counter-discrimination set in.

Nonetheless progress was registered in certain fields as a result of the new foreign trade and economic policy generally. The trade balance no longer showed a deficit; secondly, with the introduction of a specific tariff, freer in form than the law of 1916, a distinction could be made between more desirable and less desirable commodities, according to the prevailing economic policy; thirdly, by controlling foreign trade the government was able to protect local production, to import mainly raw materials, machinery and other equipment, and to prevent the free influx of consumer goods or of products which could be substituted domestically.

On this point the provisions of the Customs Law coincided with the Law for the Encouragement of Industry which, as mentioned, made it incumbent upon government departments and government-supported institutions to prefer local to foreign produce, even if somewhat more expensive. The customs policy which in the past had mainly served fiscal ends was now better co-ordinated with the strategy of economic development to serve as one of the major tools of the étatist regime.[69]

4. THE NATURE AND METHODS OF ETATISM

Autocracy was not new to Turkey. The Ottoman Empire had almost throughout been identified with the idea of despotism. The area therefore provided a most fertile soil for the constitution of a centralised regime strictly supervising both the social and economic life of the country. The basic difference lay in the fact that while in the past taxation, land distribution, control of artisans' corporations, and the army had been applied as a means of upholding the corrupt rule of a single despot with his following and harem, the étatist regime now meant to serve the economic development needs of the country and to raise the living standards of the population. The means were similar, but there was an essential difference in ends.

By 1931 the intentions of the new regime were already clearly outlined. Prior to the Congress of the Republican Party Atatürk addressed the nation in a manifesto[70] in which he defined the principles of the regime (as reformulated later in the new constitution of 1937). According to these principles the Party, and with it the State, were to be republican, nationalist, populist, secular, and revolutionary. Consistently with this matrix, the new étatist economic regime was cast. At that time, however, (in 1931) it did not intend to clip the wings of private enterprise, but rather to bring about State intervention "in those fields where private enterprise is unable to assure the well-being and advancement of the State."[71] The Turkish term for étatism (from the French: l'état) is *devletçilik*, which means—statehood, or in a

---

[69] F. Neumark, "Betrachtungen zur Türkischen Aussenhandels und Währungspolitik", *Aussenwirtschaft*, Bern, März 1947, pp. 12-13.

[70] For the text see *Oriente Moderno*, Maggio 1931, pp. 225-6.

[71] C. H. P. *Üçüncü Büyük Kongre Zabıtları*, 10-18 Mayıs 1931, Devlet Matbaası, 1931.

derived sense a policy of State control, whereby the *economic* policy[72] was meant. Atatürk and other Turkish leaders repudiated any attempt to identify étatism with socialism, and stressed the special character of Turkish étatism "which grew out of the principle of the private activity of the individual, but makes the State responsible for the national economy, considering the needs of a great nation and a great country, and regarding many things which have not so far been done".[73] Professor Bernard Lewis defined étatism in Turkey as "the emergence of the State as a pioneer and director of industrial activity, in the interests of national development and national defence, in a country where private enterprise and capital were too weak to do anything effective."[74] This definition epitomises both the economic situation and the emerging policies at the beginning of the 'thirties. It should, however, be added that in certain fields, as in financing or in foreign trade, the actual role played by the State was even more prominent than the definition quoted would indicate.

While the government's economic programme aspired to embrace a wide range of objectives—raising the standard of agriculture, improvement of communications, expansion of services, increase of the national income and raising the general standard of living—in effect, industry was accorded the leading role. By means of industrialisation the government hoped to bring about the economic independence of the country, to strengthen its security position, to improve its trade balance and balance of payments, and approximate the standard of other countries which had long since overcome the first stages of the industrial revolution. The main significance of étatism lay in the fact that the government had assumed the task of financing development, of creating adequate financial tools and of establishing and managing industrial enterprises.[75] With this end in view the government acted in three main directions: 1) legislation; 2) recruitment of capital resources; 3) Five Year Plans.

The government continued and intensified the economic legislation commenced in the 'twenties. In addition to the Customs Law and its numerous amendments, the Law of 1927 for the Encouragement of Industry was supplemented and amended with a view to increasing the utilisation of local raw materials and ensuring the efficiency of the enterprises. By a new settlement regarding the distribution of land, over 2 million *dunam* (i.e. 200,000 ha.) were distributed during the years 1934-1939, over and above the 7 million *dunam* (700,000 ha.) distributed between 1923 and 1934.[76] New financial institutions were formed, such as: the State Office for Industry, established in 1932, with the task of founding and managing the State industries; a separate institution for mining research (M.T.A.) set up in 1933; and various banking institutions.[77] Special laws were passed, in particular during the years 1936 and 1937, to ensure increased government control over private

---

[72] For a more comprehensive discussion of the sources and history of étatism, see *Turkey, An Economy in Transition,* The Hague, 1959, in particular Chapters 8, 15 and 16.
[73] From Atatürk's opening address at the Izmir Fair of 1935, *La Turquie Economique,* p. 17.
[74] Bernard Lewis, *Turkey To-Day,* Hutchinson & Co., p. 49.
[75] Cf. *The Republican People's Party Programme,* May 1935, Ankara, p. 6.
[76] Ö. L. Barkan, *loc. cit.,* p. 51.
[77] *Resmi Gazete,* 10.7.1932; 27.5.1933.

enterprises and regulate the prices of their products and the wages paid to their employees. This control was largely intended to prevent private firms from competing with government undertakings and undoubtedly constituted a policy of government discrimination against private initiative by means which could hardly be expected to lead to greater efficiency.[78]

The State revenue and additional means, such as deposits, savings, loans and participations, raised by the State and private banks served as the main sources of capital. Taxes were heavy. Temporary facilities were granted to agriculture at the beginning of the 'twenties, but the burden was increased again in subsequent years, although this time a greater share was made to fall on the shoulders of the urban taxpayers, especially the civil servants, and during the Second World War also the minorities. The Income Tax, officially approved in 1925, went through various stages of transformation in the 'thirties. Actually it began only in the middle 'thirties, together with the Property Tax, to constitute a factor of any significance in the State revenue. Even then, however, these two taxes together amounted to no more than about 15% of the State budget.[79] The monopolies provided a considerable contribution to the State budget, accounting for 20-25 per cent of the total income.

The remaining revenues—about 60%—derived mainly from turnover and consumption taxes and from customs. Expenditure on security, investments in development plans and payments of the public debt required constantly increasing funds. The expenditure budget, which approximated 200 million Turkish pounds at the beginning of the 'thirties, increased to 300 million Turkish pounds by the end of the 'thirties (and 400 million Turkish pounds in 1939/40).

TABLE XVIII

The Budgets of Turkey during the Years 1930/31-1939/40 [80]
(in million Turkish pounds)

Year	Receipts	Expenditures	Deficit (—) or Surplus (+)
1930/1	196.3	210.1	— 13.8
1931/2	165.2	181.9	— 16.7
1932/3	182.5	174.0	+ 8.5
1933/4	170.2	173.6	— 3.4
1934/5	195.0	202.1	— 7.1
1935/6	218.3	223.7	— 5.4
1936/7	250.8	260.3	— 9.5
1937/8	275.8	303.5	— 27.7
1938/9	266.9	311.1	— 44.2
1939/40	273.4	398.7	— 125.3

---

[78] Ö. C. Sarc, "Economic Policy of the New Turkey", *The M. E. Journal,* October 1948, p. 44.
[79] *Der Nahe Osten,* 15.5.1937; 1.5.1938.
[80] *İstatistik Yıllığı,* 1942-5; A. Erginay, *Le Budget Turc,* Genève, 1948, p. 152.

The receipts lagged behind the expenditures (while not all expenses were shown in the budget, being in part covered up by the accounts of the State enterprises). In addition to a number of external loans and means raised through the State banks for extra-budgetary investments, the government required a constant series of internal loans to cover its deficits. Most frequent were loans to finance the construction of railway lines, although, despite pressure, the issues were not always taken up by the public.

The State banks fulfilled an important function in financing development projects. The Bank for Industry was reorganised and by the law of 3.6.1933 turned into Sümerbank, which became the main industrial bank for the implementation of the Five Year Plans.[81] For the financing of mining and other activities, the Eti Bank was set up.[82] A special bank, Deniz Bankası, served the needs of shipping development. The İş Bank—the only major bank which, at least officially, was not a government institution—also took part in the numerous development activities. The banks derived their resources from government allocations, their own profits and those of their enterprises, external loans, public savings and the discounting of bills, under government guarantee, with the Central Bank founded in 1931 to succeed the Ottoman Bank in matters of issuing currency and of monetary control.

By the end of the 'thirties Turkey had received only two foreign loans: one of 10 million gold dollars from the Swedish-American concern of Ivar Kreuger at a rather high rate of interest (officially 6½%) and against the grant of the matches and briquettes monopoly (this loan was repaid within a short time while the monopoly reverted to Turkey after the well-known bankruptcy of the concern following the world crisis); and the loan from the Soviet Union of 8 million gold dollars, mentioned previously. During the second half of the 'thirties Turkey's debts were augmented by the amounts owed in respect of compensation for the railways taken over by the State. Negotiations with Britain and Germany concerning new loans[83] were entered upon only at the end of the 'thirties, on the eve of the Second World War.

Despite the heavy taxes and the public loans, the large volume of expenditures and investments resulted in an increase in money supply, obtained either through discounts by the State banks with the Central Bank or through direct application by the government to the Central Bank. The currency in circulation increased from 165.5 million Turkish pounds in 1913 to 281.4 million Turkish pounds in 1939. The movement of deposits during that time cannot be followed for lack of reliable data. The Turkish pound, whose value rose in relation to Western currencies after their devaluation in 1931, was again weakened by about 40% towards the end of the 'thirties with an effective rate of exchange of 180-190 piastres per dollar in 1939, as against the official rate of 128 piastres. As a matter of fact, the depreciation rate of

---

[81] *Geschichte der Türkischen Republik,* pp. 373-4; Annual Publications of the *Sümerbank,* Ankara.
[82] Press Department of the Ministry of Interior, *The Development of National Banking in Turkey,* Ankara, 1938, pp. 58-61.
[83] Cemal Kutay, *Celâl Bayar,* IV, 1938, pp. 1537 and 1710; İstatistik Yıllığı, 1932-3; G. Jäschke, *op. cit.,* p. 5.

the Turkish pound (40%) was lower than the increase in currency in circulation (70%), thanks to expanded production, improvement in the balance of payments and increased reserves at the Central Bank.[84]

The Government succeeded in mobilising considerable funds for development purposes (its investments in 1933-39 reached a total of about 450 million Turkish pounds) without causing extraordinary financial and monetary upheavals until the Second World War.

5. THE FIVE YEAR PLANS[85]

Economic legislation as well as mobilisation of capital were mainly designed to implement the Five Year Plans and to establish a Turkish State industry. The new customs law was to aid those industries which in free competition with foreign-made goods might not have sprung up at all or would not have been able to subsist without customs protection, subsidies and the special price policy contrived by the étatist regime. The decisive problem was whether a relatively short protection period would be sufficient to render the newly established industries self-supporting and efficient. While various economic aspects were taken into account, questions of security, propaganda, and general and national progress were not overlooked, as for instance, the need to spread out the population and set up industries in the more outlying and less populous parts of the country.

The first Five Year Plan, drawn up in 1933 and finally approved in January 1934, started being implemented in May 1934. Characteristically, despite its being modelled largely on the Soviet example, an American commission headed by W. D. Hines and E. W. Kemmerer[86], took part in its preparation. The plan formulated the following principles:
a) Utilisation of domestic raw materials by the future industries.
b) The fostering of a widespread textile industry, largely based on local raw materials.
c) Appropriate geographic disperion of industrial centres.
d) Priority to be given to the production of consumer goods while preparing the way for the manufacture of producer goods.

Along these lines the plan envisaged the specific enterprises to be set up within five years or less: *textiles*: cotton mills, wool and flax plants; *minerals*: steel and iron works (in Karabük) and coke (in Zonguldak); *cellulose*: cellulose, paper and rayon; *porcelain*: glass and kaolin works; *chemical industries*: sulphur refinery, sulphuric acid, chlorine and caustic soda plants, and rose essence. The sugar industry was not included in the Five Year Plan and continued to develop side by side with the new industries.[87]

---

[84] Cf. *Turkey, An Economy in Transition,* pp. 109-117.

[85] The particulars of the two Five Year Plans of the 'thirties together with statistics, tables of input and output and diagrams may be found in T.C. İktisat Vekâleti, Sanayi Tetkik Heyeti, *2inci 5yıllık Sanayi Planı,* 1936.

[86] J. K. Birge, *A Guide to Turkish Area Study,* American Council of Learned Societies, Washington, 1949, p. 115.

[87] Cf. Cemal Kutay, *Celâl Bayar,* IV, 1938, p. 1479.

The calculation of the investments required to establish the industries included in the Five Year Plan was altered in the course of time. Instead of the first estimate of 44 million Turkish pounds, about 100 million Turkish pounds were found to be necessary by the end of the five-year period without the plan having been fully carried out. Nevertheless even within three years the grand conception of the planners was seen to bear fruit. Some ten newly set-up plants started producing textiles, rayon, coke, glass, paper, sponges and sulphur. The construction of several additional factories was completed and the final plans for further enterprises were elaborated.[88]

Discussions concerning the second Five Year Plan[89] started at the beginning of 1936, although it was not finally drawn up until September 1938. Once again the main stress was laid on the efficient exploitation of local raw materials (if their export did not prove more profitable). In particular it was suggested to explore the potentials of so far neglected resources like those of the sea, the lakes and the rivers, fruits and livestock. The production of electricity and the engineering industry were to serve as springboards for a sweeping advance into the realm of producer goods. These objectives were to be attained by:

a) Exploitation of the mines and the natural resources of land and sea;
b) Initiating of heavy industry, particularly by developing the Zonguldak-Karabük area, with a view to increasing the output of coal and expanding the steel and iron works, and establishing auxiliary enterprises (e.g. for the production of coke) and better transportation facilities for this industry;
c) Special concern for the development of East Anatolia by setting up various industrial enterprises in Erzurum and Sivas, the improvement of the port of Trabzon, etc.;
d) Extension of the industrial network in the rest of Turkey (in addition to Zonguldak-Ereğli and East Anatolia) with a particular stress on power stations;
e) The development of the merchant marine by the addition of 28 new ships;
f) Increased exports of agricultural produce;
g) Housing schemes, especially near the large industries.

In the Second Plan, as in the First, the planners did not confine themselves to a general outline but proposed a number of specific factories and plants to be erected, including factories for farming equipment, machinery, synthetic oil, aluminium, tinned meat, refrigeration enterprises, jute mills and cement works. In order to facilitate the development of the mines a law was passed in 1935 which authorised the government to confiscate mines left unexploited by their owners or leased for one year only. A special Three Year Plan approved in 1937 and co-ordinated with the overall Five Year Plan was specially designed to promote the more efficient exploitation of the mines. The railway network was still being expanded since the

---

[88] *2inci 5yıllık Sanayi Planı,* p. xviii.

[89] British experts and manufacturers played an important part in the drawing-up and implementation of this Second Plan. Sir Alexander Gibb served as adviser on port development; a British engineering firm acted as consultants for development of the Morgul copper mines and considerable orders were placed with British shipyards and railway engine manufacturers. J. B. Mackie, "Turkish Industrialisation", *R.C.A.J.,* July 1939, pp. 451-2.

'twenties. Though its expansion lagged behind the country's needs and was far removed from the standard of more developed Western countries, it contributed much to mining development and the marketing of produce, while at the same time promoting the political and economic integration of the country.

The Second World War put a spoke in the wheel of Turkish economic policy in general and its Second Five Year Plan[90] in particular. Much greater attention had to be diverted to matters of security than during the inter-war period.

Nevertheless Turkey managed to invest considerable amounts in public works, services, Five Year Plans and other development projects, totalling no less than 450 million Turkish pounds, i.e., about 350 million U.S. dollars at the official rate of exchange of 1.26 Turkish pounds per dollar between 1933 and 1939, or about 300 million dollars at the average effective rate for that period. It is estimated than an approximately similar sum was invested in the Turkish economy at that time by the İş Bank and various private sources[91], so that total investments between 1933 and 1939 came close to one billion Turkish pounds, or 650-700 million dollars.

6. THE RESULTS OF THE ETATIST POLICY

What were the actual results of government initiative in the field of development and of the étatist regime as a whole until the outbreak of the Second World War?

Considerable progress was achieved in various fields of production. In mining, output during the decade between 1930 and 1940 grew considerably. The total index of mineral output, on the basis of 100 in 1930, reached 232 in 1940.[92] The annual output of coal increased from 1.5 million to 3 million tons, lignite from 9,000 tons to 230,000 tons, chrome from 28,000 to 170,000 tons. The output of copper, the mining of which was stopped at the beginning of the 'thirties for purposes of reorganisation and nationalisation, reached 9,000 tons in 1940; iron ores, not mined at all at the beginning of the period, yielded an annual output of 130,000 tons towards its end.

New essential facilities assisted industrial growth of the public sector. State banks, by-laws to supplement the Law for the Encouragement of Industry, the Customs Law, the fiscal system, government monopolies and a stricter control of private industry and discrimination in favour of government industries all served the étatist goal of fostering State industry—to some extent at the expense of private industry. The investment in the approved enterprises benefitting under the Law for the Encouragement of Industry, which in 1935 amounted to 63 million Turkish pounds, increased to 150 million Turkish pounds in 1939. The value of their net output rose from 104 million Turkish pounds in 1933 to 266 million Turkish pounds in 1939, though the rise in value reflected only partly output expansion and partly

---

[90] Cf. Direction Générale de la Prese, *La Turquie Economique*, p. 17.

[91] Cf. *Turkey, An Economy in Transition*, pp. 123-4.

[92] Türkofis, *L'Industrie Minière de la Turquie*, Istanbul, 1935; İstatistik Yıllığı, 1942-45; pp. 292-3; *L'Economiste d'Orient*, Istanbul, 15.12.1950.

price increases.[93] It further transpires that practically all additional investments in the major enterprises were made by the State and its various financial agencies. The number of exployees in those plants which deserve to be called industrial firms rose from approximately 27,000 in 1927 to approximately 90,000 in 1939. New enterprises were set up in the various branches of industry, some on a large scale—perhaps too large in relation to available raw material supplies, managerial ability and marketing conditions.

Although deficient statistics and non-inclusion of important items, such as depreciation or interest, in the balance accounts of the enterprises make it difficult to assess their profitability some of them obviously operated under constant losses. General attention was drawn to the iron and steel foundry of Karabük which was severely censured for its defective location and production structure. This plant however was put in operation only in 1939, i.e., at the beginning of a period which is already outside the scope of our present discussion.

The sugar industry likewise encountered many difficulties.[94] In its reliance on local raw materials (sugar beet) it met, on principle, the prevailing requirements of the economic policy; but, again, its deficient location and the lack of co-ordination in the supply of raw materials and the running of the mills hampered production and reduced efficiency.

During the 'thirties agriculture did not enjoy the same degree of encouragement by the government as did industry. The very nature of étatism was symbolised by a veering towards industrialisation. But in an agrarian country certain basic needs of 70-80% of the working population could not, of course, be ignored, and in effect the legislation passed in this domain as well as several practical measures introduced were far from negligible.

The Turkish refugees from abroad obtained a considerable share—over one-third—of the lands distributed under the agrarian reform continued since 1923 and amplified by supplementary regulations passed in 1934 and 1938. Hence ownership conditions had improved only slightly. Even according to the official sources, about half the agricultural earners had no land of their own. The other half shared the cultivated land on a much more egalitarian basis than for instance in Egypt, but even in Turkey most farms consisted of small units, considering that its agriculture was extensive and that annual crops were reaped only from half or even one-third of the area. The gross size of the units owned by about 65% did not exceed 30 hectares, out of which a high percentage of holdings were untenably small (not specified in the official sources).[95]

The years of crisis inflicted twofold damage on agriculture: Prices, particularly of export goods, fell while a series of natural disasters cut down yields too. Under conditions of depression the fall in supply was unable to effect a consequent rise in prices. Turkey moreover had difficulty in getting rid of tobacco surpluses accumulated as a result of the slack world demand and protectionist measures.

---

[93] Cf. Vedat Eldem in *R.F.S.E.*, Istanbul, oct. 1946-juill. 1947, p. 73.
[94] Ö. C. Sarc, "The Demand for Sugar in Turkey", *R.F.S.E.*, avr.-juill. 1944.
[95] *Law No. 2510*, 14.6.1934; Ö. L. Barkan, *loc. cit.*, p. 51; Turkish Information Office, *Facts on Turkey*, New York.

Agriculture largely recuperated from the crisis through government assistance, both by way of subsidies, and the establishment of credit and marketing co-operatives, especially through the central marketing institution Toprak (*Toprak Mahsulleri Ofisi*—The Central Office for Soil Produce). This new institution, set up in 1938, replaced its predecessor (of 1932) in the implementation of government agricultural policies. Toprak co-operated with the Central and Agricultural Banks in providing advances to producers, discounting bills, offering better credit and interest terms, alleviating the burden of old debts, and storing produce. Despite these major endeavours, the limited funds allotted to agriculture and the relative weakness of the co-operative organisation (as compared with the needs) rendered difficult any serious intensification of agriculture and increase in productivity. Hence the rise in total yields was mainly due to an extension of the cultivated area rather than to more intensive cultivation. The equipment remained primitive (85% of the ploughs were made of wood) and the mechanisation drive started in the 'twenties was deliberately halted by the government during the slump so as to prevent rural unemployment. After the slump was over stress was again laid on mechanisation and other improvements, and in 1937 a Four Year Agricultural Development Plan was worked out. In the meantime agricultural development became integrated in the process of industrialisation, especially as regards the supply of agricultural raw materials to local industry and the efforts made to export agricultural produce in order to utilise the export revenue to import the capital goods required for the development plans.

These efforts were indeed rewarded by success. The annually cropped area increased from 5% of the total area of the country in 1927 to 12% in 1939. Hence—even though the productivity per unit of land did not increase on the whole, apart from certain industrial crops—the total yields had risen considerably by the end of the 'thirties, as did the income from agriculture, especially as compared with the years of depression at the beginning of the 'thirties. Even as compared with 1929, the income from agriculture in real terms grew by 20% until 1939[96] (for conclusions regarding productivity and per capita income, see below).

The rise in the output of mining and industry, and the regeneration of agriculture after the slump, coupled with import restrictions and encouragement of exports, served to improve the country's balance of payments. During this period Turkey adopted a singular trade policy of its own, based on a combination of the barter, clearing and compensation[97] systems, which complicated the working system of Turkey's international trade and in course of time made it dependent on certain particular markets, especially Germany.[98]

---

[96] *İstatistik Yıllığı*, 1942-45, pp. 219-20, 251.

[97] The compensation method was based on linking a certain export shipment to a certain import shipment so that the revenue from the first might serve in payment for the second according to the government regulations and government approval in each case.

[98] An enquiry into clearing agreements carried out by the League of Nations in 1935 showed that Germany and Turkey topped the list of countries linked by clearing agreements, with 19 countries and with 13 countries, respectively; see League of Nations, *Enquiry into Clearing Agreements,* Geneva, 1935, pp. 152-154.

The economic development trends were most notably reflected in the changes which occurred in the structure of imports. Textiles decreased from 44% of total imports at the beginning to 27.5% at the end of the 'thirties; foodstuffs from 17% to 4.3%. On the other hand there was an increase, from 14.5% to 37.2%, in imports of capital and producer goods such as machinery, cars, iron and steel. A special institution called *Türkofis* was set up in 1934 for the planning of imports and exports. The government also tried to plan the foreign currency budgets so as to ensure the balancing of the current account and reduce the debt to foreign creditors. The change in the structure of imports resulted from two main trends in the Turkish economy during the 'thirties: 1) an increasing supply of import-substituting local consumer goods; 2) economic policies which granted preference to the import of capital goods even if domestic supply of consumer goods did not catch up with domestic demand. Obviously this second factor increased, in the short run, the danger of inflationary pressure that could have been checked to a certain extent only by increased taxation, loans from the public and price control.

Thanks to these efforts and the extensive control of the movement of goods and foreign currency, Turkey succeeded in preserving a favourable trade balance throughout the 'thirties—except in 1938—and in reducing its external debt by 19 million Turkish pounds during the years 1934-1939. However, while the reduction of the long—term debt was even more considerable, the current debt grew, placing a substantial burden on the limited potential of the economy.[99]

Along with achievements referred to above, the road of étatism was strewn with obstacles, and certain important targets of restructuring the economy could not be met. The occupational structure was of paramount importance, with 80% employed in agriculture. The purpose of the industrialisation was not merely to increase domestic industrial production and reduce the dependence of the country on foreign goods, but to increase the proportion of industrial workers in total labour force and industry's share in national product. Thus, less reliance on agriculture and securing higher income levels through industrialisation should bring up economic and social standards to those of well-developed industrial economies in other parts of the world. In fact, during the period under review not only an absolute but also a relative rise (as compared with workers in other sectors) occurred in the number of artisans. Consequently, the total rise in crafts and industry was not significant, considering the concurrent increase in population, and by the end of the 'thirties close to 80% of the population[100] still derived its livelihood from agriculture.

The low level of income in agriculture, which did not appreciably improve until the end of the 'thirties, determined the general level of income of the population, by virtue of the size of the agricultural sector. The net yearly output per agricultural labourer in Turkey was around 120 International Units[101], a rate more or less

---

[99] Cf. *Turkey, An Economy in Transition*, pp. 153-157.
[100] Cf. *İstatistik Yıllığı*, 1942-5, p. 296.
[101] The International Unit, according to the definition of Colin Clark, equals the amount of goods and services exchangeable for one U.S. dollar on the average for the years 1925-34. Cf. Colin Clark, *The Conditions of Economic Progress*, Macmillan & Co., London, Second Edition, 1951, p. 19.

equivalent to that of the neighbouring Arab states, but more than five times lower than that of Western European countries.

Whereas in industry the net output per worker amounted to 350 International Units approximately, this again represented only one-third of the net output of a British, or one-fifth of a U.S. labourer.[102] The higher rate of income in industry was hardly able to effect an increase in the average income level since industry still played a negligible role in the total occupational structure, and was moreover subject to numerous setbacks (see above) while several enterprises continued to exist only thanks to government support and an artificial price structure. A more vigorous development of agriculture could provide the key to any serious change in the level of income and standard of living, at a short range anyway, and the reforms introduced during the period of étatism failed to achieve the progress required in this field in a distinctly agrarian country.

Attempts to assess the national income of Turkey were commenced only in 1935, and approximately correct evaluations are available only as from that date, though more general estimates also exist with respect to the foregoing period. In the period under discussion agriculture's share in the national income of Turkey decreased proportionally to the extent that industry and services grew. In 1929, income from agriculture amounted to 50% of the total income, while in 1939 it fetched only 38%. These relative rates of course depended largely on the unstable level of crops achieved under conditions of extensive cultivation and on price changes unfavourable to the agricultural sector following the depression at the beginning of the 'thirties. Therefore the income of the constantly growing industry also failed to record a steady trend in its relative share in national product. In summing up the development of the years 1927 to 1939, the following picture of the national income calculated at constant prices (basis—1938) is obtained:[103]

TABLE XIX

Changes in the National Income of Turkey during the Years 1927-1939

Year	National Income at 1938 Prices (in million Turkish pounds)	Per capita (in Turkish pounds)
1927	1,000	75
1929	1,147	80
1935	1,315	82
1938	1,589	92
1939	1,652	95

The growth of income was not equally distributed over the years. During the world depression only a tiny increase was registered while subsequently, with the implementation of the étatist policies, a considerable rise took place in the relatively

---

[102] *Ibid.*, pp. 266, 269.
[103] Cf. *Turkey, An Economy in Transition,* pp. 165-6; Vedat Eldem, in *Revue de la Faculté des Sciences Economiques de l'Université d'Istanbul,* oct. 1950-jan. 1951, pp. 133-140; Şefik Bilkur, *National Income of Turkey,* Ankara, 1949; *Türk Ekonomisi,* Ankara, Mart 1952, pp. 72-3.

short period between 1935 and 1939. The distribution of national income among the different strata of society is difficult to follow owing to lack of adequate data. The relative decrease in the share of agriculture from 50 to 38% during the 'thirties, in favour of the industrial and service sector,[104] accompanied by only a limited increase in the overall national income, and the protracted polarisation in the distribution of agricultural income account for the poverty of the Turkish farmer at that time, as reflected in the accounts of both Turkish and foreign observers. In this respect there is the overriding evidence of Mahmut Makal, a village teacher in Anatolia. In his book Our Village[105] he vividly illustrated the hardships of Turkish rural life which persisted down to the 'forties, and stressed the absence of any significant progress despite the many official propaganda announcements to the contrary.

In a country where an exact assessment of national income meets with practically insurmountable difficulties it is worth while to pay attention to complementary data which, in a more concrete form, may shed light on the various developments. One of the criteria can be the changes in food consumption during the years when the new policy was in force. The following Table records the situation during the short period between 1936 and 1939, for which national averages are available:

TABLE XX

Changes in the Consumption Level in Turkey during the Thirties [106]

Commodity	Per Capita Consumption in 1936	Per Capita Consumption in 1939
grains (for flour)	183 kg	193 kg
meat and fat	6 kg	16 kg
milk, butter, cheese	47 kg	38 kg
various fats	2 kg	9 kg
eggs	2 kg	3 kg
potatoes	7 kg	6 kg
vegetables	29 kg	58 kg
fruit	46 kg	62 kg
sugar	4 kg	6 kg
no. of calories per day	2,100 calories	2,600 calories

First of all, these data must of course be regarded with caution in a country where no authoritative statistics were available. Secondly, the rise in the consumption of certain foodstuffs should, at least partially, be charged to the account of the growing consumption of the wealthier classes, so that the changes in the consumption of the masses might not be as substantial as the Table would seem to indicate. Thirdly, special caution is required regarding the consumption of calories,

---

[104] After the Second World War the ratio of agriculture increased somewhat, but even then no stable trend could be observed.
[105] Mahmut Makal, *Bizim Köy*, Varlık Yayınevi, Istanbul.
[106] *Foreign Agriculture*, June 1951, p. 123; Colin Clark, *op. cit.*, pp. 372-3.

both because of difficulties of assessment and also because of the wide fluctuations in this field from one month to the other, varying especially with changes in the composition of the diet. Fourthly, a comparison between only two years not far removed from each other engenders a strong element of chance. Despite all these reservations, the Table shows a distinct though far from uniform improvement in the nature and composition of the Turkish diet.

In briefly summing up the period under review, we find that a certain amount of the criticism levelled against the economic policy of the country during the 'thirties (and then also during the 'forties) was justified. Even if we take exception to the exaggerated fault-finding dictated to no small extent by fundamental objections to a State-run economy, the negative results or deficiencies of this policy may be seen in the relative neglect of agriculture and the continuing low standard of living of the rural population, i.e., 80% of the total population; the insignificant improvement of the occupational structure; the difficulties encountered by industry owing to the shortage of qualified personnel, faulty organisation, bureaucracy and erroneous economic calculations in the establishment of certain industries.

On the other hand, a few outstanding positive achievements should be recorded, especially if one regards this as a preparatory phase during which the foundations were laid for the future. Despite a certain neglect of agriculture new areas were put under cultivation, and this—rather than more intensive cultivation—led to an increase in yields and in income in line with and even somewhat surpassing the increase in population. The country succeeded without too many upheavals in absorbing the refugees returned from Greece as a result of the exchange of population, as well as other refugees. Considerable capital was raised locally. While the financial resources of the population were thus strained beyond the ability of many classes, both rural and urban, modern beginnings of industry, transportation and communications could be financed without any loss of economic and political independece. A considerable improvement took place in the balance of trade and of payments. Thus several of the fundamental basic goals of the Republican Party programmes and the government plans were achieved—with the cardinal emphasis on the political and economic independence of the new Republic as opposed to the bondage of the Ottoman period.

PART EIGHT

PERSIA BETWEEN THE TWO WORLD WARS*

1. POLITICAL CHANGES AND SOCIAL REFORMS

After the War, in 1919, the British put pressure to bear on Persia to sign an agreement which would in effect have given them control over its army, finances, communications and administration. The Persian Majlis (parliament), however, rejected the proposed treaty, which met with disapproval in the U.S.A. as well. Britain had to bow to this decision, especially in the light of Persian relations with the Soviet Union. In 1918 the revolutionary Soviet government announced the voluntary abandonment of all its rights in Persia under the agreement of 1907, which it regarded as null and void. A new treaty was signed between the two countries in February 1921.[1] The Soviet Union, in defence against Western attempts to overthrow the Bolshevist regime, took the line of supporting all nationalist movements fighting for political independence. This policy lies at the root of its relations at that time with a number of Middle East states like Persia and Turkey. By the new treaty Russia cancelled all Persian financial obligations, waived its concessions, and gave up all its capitulatory rights. The Russians further declared the port installations of Enzeli (Pahlavi) and all roads, power stations, railways, and banks established by them to have become the property of Persia. The Caspian Sea was opened up for joint fishing and in 1928 the Soviet-Persian Company, mentioned in our discussion of Persia prior to the World War, was set up.[2] On the other hand, the Soviet Union reserved to itself the right of taking action in Persia against any powers endangering the safety of the Soviet Union.[3]

At that time major internal changes took place in Persia itself. Prompted by the disintegration of the ancient regime, the constant riots, the attempts at democratisation, Western influence including the principle of self-determination of nations based on national and economic consolidation—forces sprang up which demanded the realisation of the new ideals. To a large extent these forces—as in Turkey—utilised the arrangement arrived at with the Soviet Union and its active support in order to achieve their ends. The leader of the revolutionaries who upset the ancient regime was Riza Khan, an officer cadet trained by the Cossack unit, who within the shorts pace of time between 1921 and 1925 advanced from chief of

---

* Although since 1935 the name Iran was officially substituted for Persia, we retained the latter term which was in use for most of the inter-war period.
[1] *Treaty of Friendship between Persia and the R.S.F.S.R.* (Feb. 26th, 1921), League of Nations, *Treaty Series,* No. 268, 1922, pp. 401-413. Also see Appendix 26.
[2] League of Nations, *Treaty Series No. 2621,* Vol. 112, 1931, pp. 350-360. For text, see our Appendix 32.
[3] Cf. A. C. Millspaugh, *op. cit.,* pp. 20-1. Riza Shah had an utterly negative attitude to communism, but at the same time, like Atatürk, aimed at maintaining good and even friendly relations with the Soviet Union on a basis of mutual non-intervention.

general staff and minister of war to prime minister in 1923 and to the throne of the Shah in December 1925.[4]

As early as the beginning of his rise, in 1921, Riza chased out his former friend Ziya el-Din Tabatabai, his predecessor in the office of premier, who had tried to carry out certain badly needed agrarian reforms in a country afflicted by disastrous inequality in the distribution of its lands. Riza's conservatism in this respect was no less pronounced during the later years of his reign. He turned his back completely on his former comprehensive plans of reform which belonged to an earlier, romantic period of his life.

There is at least an external similarity between the administrative and social reforms of Riza Shah and those carried out at about the same time in Turkey. First of all he severely put down attempts at tribal mutiny, similar to the suppression of the Kurds by Atatürk. He further tried to restrict the decisive role played by religion. *Inter alia*, he instituted legislation on civil status and had a law passed by which lands and irrigation plants belonging to religious institutions could be nationalised. As opposed to Kemal Atatürk, however, he did not risk an all-out fight against religion, preferring a compromise whereby it was reserved its due share in the national life. His most important reforms were the publication of the Civil Code[5] and the Commercial Law[6] (in 1928) and the organisation of the judicial system according to the Swiss and French models, while upholding the principles of Muslim law according to the Shi'ite interpretation; the extension of the educational network; the abolition of titles; the adoption of family names; and the introduction of European dress. Persia, like Turkey, tried to abrogate the capitulations by a unilateral declaration (in 1918), but achieved their final abolition with the consent of the parties concerned only on May 10th, 1928,[7] after a number of countries had freely given up their capitulatory rights (China in 1920, Afghanistan and the Soviet Union in 1921).

Regarding labour relations, the law of 1936 was designed to provide regulations for buildings factories, hygienic and safety conditions, vocational training, workers' compensation, etc. However, the practical value of the law was negligible. The employers ignored it, while the workers were forbidden to strike and to organise into unions. The law itself was cancelled in 1941 following the removal of Riza Shah.[8]

2. ATTEMPTS AT ECONOMIC RECONSTRUCTION

The new regime's main concern was the army with whose help it had come to power. The military forces required strengthening for the preservation of peace and order inside the country as well as for purpose of national defence. The

---

[4] In that year the previous ruler, Ahmed Shah Kajar, was removed from office. Cf. A. C. Millspaugh, *The Financial and Economic Situation of Persia*, 1926, pp. 4-5.
[5] Cf. *Persian Civil Code* (translated by A. C. Trott), 1937.
[6] Persia, *Code de Commerce*, 1307 (1928).
[7] A. Moazzami, *op. cit.*, pp. 72-75.
[8] In the same year—1941—workers' unions became legal.

consolidation of the army and its increase from 40,000 to 90,000 men would not have been possible without the prior reorganisation of the country's financial structure. Persia's finances had become seriously undermined during the preceding period. While the country's reinforced political independence upon the accession of Riza Shah opened up new economic vistas, the development plans of the new regime first of all required a thorough reorganisation of public finances on a modern basis and stabilisation of the currency.

Owing to the lack of professional and scientific personnel, economists and other experts, Persia had to apply for help abroad. The outstanding foreign expert of that period was Shuster's fellow-countryman, Arthur C. Millspaugh,[9] who was in charge of Persia's finances during the years 1922-27. At his initiative a more uniform method was introduced for the collection of land taxes based on a legal redefinition of ownership. This measure, complemented by the transfer of fiscal authority from the various ministries to the Ministry of Finance, significantly increased the income of the treasury. However, frequent clashes ensued between the American mission on the one hand, and the big landlords, who had for years evaded taxes, the local military commanders and even various government offices, particularly the Ministry of Posts and Telegraphs, on the other hand.[10]

Under the conditions prevailing in Persia the mission and the treasury had the important task of providing for the supply of grains to all those cities and provinces to which supplies had to be made from distant centres of production, and in particular to Teheran. The supply of grain was of major political significance in view of the constant danger of hunger riots. The mission succeeded in doing away with obsolete taxes, such as abusive differential road tolls and tolls collected at city gates, and replaced them in 1926 by a comprehensive road toll (see p. 210). Further it improved the collection of other taxes and the administration of State property (lands and forests); it balanced the State budget and thus created a basis for a sounder economic activity.[11] Millspaugh also planned to shift the emphasis from taxes falling mainly on to the shoulders of the fellahin to other sources of revenue, like the opium, tobacco and match monopoly, and income tax.[12] Millspaugh's administration did not last because Riza altered his policy, and dismissed the American mission following a dispute on military expenditures.[13] The mission ceased to function at the moment it had managed to balance the budget and improve the collection of taxes and other government revenue (government revenue per

---

[9] See A. C. Millspaugh, *Americans in Persia*. After 20 years Millspaugh returned to Persia and served as financial adviser to the government between 1943-1945.

[10] A. C. Millspaugh, *op. cit.*, p. 23.

[11] Cf. *Sixth Quarterly Report... The Finances of Persia*, Ch. III.

[12] *Eighteenth Quarterly Report*, 1927, p. 16.

[13] One of the more unusual obstacles which the mission encountered in the collection of taxes was the fact that the Shah and his army used to pillage the villages by confiscating manpower, draught animals, crops and cash, thus reducing the taxability of the population to nil. This difference of opinion had not been the first dispute and Millspaugh expressly complained in his reports about the lack of co-operation on the part of the government and the local administration. Cf. *Seventh Report*, June 1924. For the causes of Millspaugh's removal from office, see also *Nineteenth Report*, pp. 11-12.

person in Persia was 3s. 4d. in 1888/9, and had risen to an annual average of 12s. 4d. by 1929/32).[14]

Public revenue continued to grow from 250 million *kran* in the budgetary year 1927/8 to 353 million in 1930/31, or to about £ 6 million (taking into account the fall in the value of the *kran*) sufficient to meet the expenditures.[15]

After the American mission had left a German specialist was appointed as financial expert while another foreign expert assisted in the foundation of the Melli Bank. Until 1928 the Imperial Bank of Persia founded by Baron de Reuther had managed the financial affairs of the government and issued the banknotes in circulation. The management of government finances passed gradually into the hands of the National Bank (Melli Bank) after its foundation in 1928, whilst the right to issue banknotes was granted to it only in 1930. Millspaugh points out that German influence, which became most marked at the beginning of the Second World War, had already started making itself felt in the days of Riza Shah in the 'twenties, when aviation concessions were granted to the Junkers Company and a large number of German experts were engaged.[16] Other foreign experts were active in the field of customs, communications and industry, although most of them had no wider powers, being employed mainly in administration and technical services.[17]

As a result of the measures introduced by Millspaugh and subsequently, Persia managed to balance its budget by means of special taxation and monopolies, despite considerable investments which were largely financed out of the ordinary budget. Obviously the rise in the income from oil royalties, especially since the new agreement of 1933, helped to make this possible. Thus the budget served as an important lever for the economy at large, whereas the often erroneous choice of patterns of investment, combined with other factors, frequently impeded the country's development efforts (see next chapter).

At the end of the period under review a considerable deficit occurred in the budget of 1939/40, due mainly to the outbreak of war and the increased expenses on security and communications (including transportation). Expenditure on security had also claimed an important share of about 20% in previous budgets. The general set-up of the budgetary expenses during the 'thirties was such that the items of security, communications and industry each took up 20% of the budget, i.e., all three together accounted for 60% of total expenditure, leaving only 40% for all other government functions, including health, education, agriculture and general administration. In the last budget, agriculture had received only 1.63% of the revenue. In this budget, of 1939/40, the share of communications was increased to 30% (this also being the main reason for the deficit) so that the above-mentioned three items constituted at least 75% of the total expenditure, if the rise in security expenses is also taken into account.

In the course of time also public revenue increased considerably, as compared with the beginning of the period, from approximately £ 5 million to £ 20 million

---

[14] A. T. Wilson, *op. cit.*, pp. 296-7.
[15] A. Tismer, *Die Persische Währungsreform*, Teheran, 1932, p. 14.
[16] Millspaugh, *op. cit.*, p. 38.
[17] *Ibid.*, p. 28.

(although the intervening devaluation of the pound sterling made this "real" increase somewhat smaller). The main change in the structure of the revenue budget was due to two major items which together made up 40% to 50% of the entire budget, namely oil royalties and the monopolies (including taxes on tea and sugar). The direct taxes levied on the peasants were reduced following Millspaugh's reform of 1926. Their condition, however, was not much improved since their share in indirect taxes and the monopoly charges was considerable, thus defying the declared target of Millspaugh's policy, not to mention the additional burden of the rental and the various payments imposed by the landlords.

TABLE XXI

Comparison between Receipts and Expenses of the Persian Budget for the Years 1924/5 and 1938/9
(in pounds sterling at market rate—in round figures)

Source of Revenue	Receipts 1924/5	Receipts 1938/9	Item	Expenditure 1924/5	Expenditure 1938/9
Customs	1,800,000	5,000,000	Security	2,000,000	5,000,000
Direct taxes	800,000	2,000,000	Public Debt	400,000	100,000
Grain taxes	350,000	—	Pensions	160,000	80,000
Oil royalties	340,000	3,000,000	Royal Court	100,000	65,000
Taxes on opium	1,000,000	1,000,000	Various Ministries[19]	2,340,000	14,755,000
Miscellaneous [18]	1,210,000	9,000,000			
	4,800,000	20,000,000		5,000,000	20,000,000

(Sources: *Quarterly Reports... of Finances*; *Bulletins de la Banque Melliè*, Iran).

The stabilisation of the currency was an important prerequisite for well-ordered finances and a stable economy. On the other hand, the large fluctuations in the value of the currency were themselves the result of a weak and unsteady economy. Owing to this chain reaction the efforts of the government in this direction inevitably met with only partial success. At the end of the First World War the Imperial Bank founded by the British kept its right to issue currency. The basic currency unit was the *kran*, whose relation to the pound sterling at the beginning of the 'twenties was 46-47 *kran* per one pound sterling ($10^{1}/_{2}$ *kran* to one American dollar and 54 *kran* to 100 French francs).[20] In view of the large fluctuations in the rate of the *kran* in terms of gold and foreign currency (some of the coins were used in the bazaars as metal scrap, sold by weight) a currency reform was carried out in

---

[18] The monopolies formed the largest item among "miscellaneous", amounting to £ 4.5 million in 1938/9.

[19] Government investments in new industries in 1938/9 amounted to nearly 7 million pounds sterling. Another outstanding expenditure in that year was on transport and communications to the amount of 2 million pounds, from which it increased steeply to 10 million in 1939/40.

[20] *Sixth Quarterly Report of the Administrator General of the Finances of Persia,* 1924, pp. 5-6. (10 *kran* nominally constituted one *tuman*.)

1930 and amended in 1932[21], which established the gold *riyal* as the new currency unit (divided into 100 *dinar*).[22] One hundred *riyal* were one *pahlevi* (in the original reform of 1930, 20 *riyal* were one *pahlevi*) equivalent to one pound sterling (i.e., this ratio was determined after the pound had left the gold standard in 1931). From then on the *riyal*, according to the rates fixed by the government, was to serve as the monetary unit for all transactions both local and foreign. Only the *pahlevi* and half a *pahlevi* were coined in gold; the remaining coins were minted in silver (a silver *riyal* "represented" a gold *riyal*) and in nickel. Simultaneously an agreement was concluded with the Imperial Bank by which, in accordance with the new legislation, the right of issuing banknotes was ceded to the National (Melli) Bank.

The National Bank was allowed to print up to 340 million *riyal* in banknotes over a period of 10 years. As from September 1932 the previous currency units were to become invalid. However the traditional difficulty arose in that the population refused to accept the new banknotes, preferring gold and silver coins.[23] During the 'thirties the National Bank concentrated in its hands most of the silver *krans* and *riyals* which together with its gold reserves served to cover (at a rate of about 80%) the banknotes in circulation. These in the meantime had increased three-fold and by 1939 amounted to over 800 million *riyal*, with about another 200 million held by the Bank.[24] Owing to the shortage of free gold reserves and foreign currency, difficulties in foreign trade ensued, constituting one of the major causes for the establishment of a far-reaching foreign trade government monopoly. It should be noted that the currency reform of 1932 and the simultaneous balancing of the government budgets both helped to strengthen the *riyal*, whose value in terms of pound sterling rose by 10-20% towards the end of the period.

Agriculture, the mainstay of the Persian population and the principal source of government revenue derived from direct and indirect taxes (perhaps apart from customs, in which the relative share of the urban population was greater), fell victim to two central trends after the war: a) the striving for military and political consolidation; b) industrialisation. These two trends required large funds—and hence heavy taxes—and since the bulk of investment funds and entrepreneurship had passed into the hands of the government, it was only natural that available resources were channelled in the directions referred to above.

Millspaugh, who was in fact personally responsible for the fiscal policy of the 'twenties, in his report of 1927[25] already pointed out the sad plight of the Persian village, stressing the fact that the main burden of taxes was shifted on to the

---

[21] Banque Nationale de Perse (Bank Melli), *Loi de l'Unité Monétaire Légale de Perse,* Téhéran, 1932.

[22] According to the Law of 1930, one gold *riyal* contained 0.3661191 grams of fine gold; in accordance with the amendment of 1932, the gold content of the *riyal* was reduced to 0.07322382 grams only. Even this regulation was observed only indirectly since gold minting was restricted, as a matter of fact, to one *pahlevi*, and half a *pahlevi*. H. L. Rabino di Borgomale, *op. cit.,* p. 18.

[23] An analysis of the state of Persian currency at that time and on the significance of currency reform may be found in Alfred Timser, *Die Persische Währungsreform,* Teheran, August, 1932 (mimeographed).

[24] *Bulletins de la Banque Mellié Iran,* 1939.

[25] *Eigthteenth Quarterly Report,* 1927, pp. 15-16.

shoulders of the fellah, while both social and economic considerations required the raising of his income and standard of living. With a minimum of irrigation in the more arid zones or in years of drought, the soil was undoubtedly fertile.[26] In certain crops like tobacco and opium Persia had achieved a considerable degree of specialisation. The cities provided a receptive market for grains. But the primitive roads and means of communication, the recurrent difficulties in the marketing of tobacco abroad, international campaigns to restrict the trade in and consumption of opium, and above all the lack of capital with all its consequences, including the inadequate technical standard of the fellah, all impeded and retarded the normal development of agriculture. The government undertook several rescue actions, but these proved insufficient, as is evidenced by the miserable portion allotted to agriculture in the State budget. The rosy picture of the goals and future of Persian agriculture as painted by Millspaugh, especially while still serving as financial administrator, was not merely disproved later on, but stood in complete contrast to the internal opinions expressed in his own reports to the Persian Minister of Finance.[27]

TABLE XXII

Average Yields in kg per Hectare in 1934/38

	Wheat	Barley	Cotton
Egypt	2010	1980	540
Persia	1200	1240	220
Sudan	760	1250	310
Turkey	990	1100	210

U.N. *Review of Economic Conditions in the M.E.*, 1951-1952, New York, 1953, p. 17, & FAO *Yearbooks*.

As the government was interested in the development of waste lands which had lain fallow for generations, it provided legislation by which title was granted to these lands after their rehabilitation. However, this legislation failed to provide even a minimum solution to the problem of the capital required for such rehabilitation. As a result title was therefore acquired mainly by landowners who had the required means available. (For the significance of this legislation from the social point of view, see below, Chapter 4.)

Several measures were adopted to promote agricultural credit. The Agricultural Bank, split from the Melli Bank in 1933, had at its disposal the funds received from the sale of part of the Crown lands in 1934. The new regime at one stroke unequivocally resolved the long-standing, painful problem of the Muslim economy, namely the lending of money against interest. The Civil Code was made to include a

---

[26] The fact that Persian soil was no less fertile than that of other countries can be seen from the following Table (it should be taken into account that in Egypt and the Sudan irrigated land is used for the cultivation of corn as well).

[27] Compare A. Millspaugh, *The Financial and Economic Situation of Persia*, 1926, pp. 10-11, and Report 1927, *loc. cit.*

clear provision stating that "The profit which is envisaged in a loan is a profit which is lawful and reasonable" (Article 637 of the Civil Code). Since, however, the bank granted loans only against securities in the form of land, of which the fellahin had little or none, most of the fellahin had to go on having recourse to moneylenders at exorbitant interest rates of 30 to 100% (while "regular" interest charged by banking institutions also amounted to 12-24%).[28]

The provision of regular agricultural supplies and the desired transition to a market economy as part of general economic development required an improved network of communications. Communications between the capital and the provinces also became essential for the purpose of improved economic administration and the integration of the provinces in the economic life of the country. To this were added military considerations. During the years 1927-1939 the Trans-Iranian Railway, of a length of 872 miles, was planned and built linking the southern shore of the Caspian Sea (at Bender Shah) with the Persian Gulf (at Bender Shahpur).

This major enterprise which according to estimates cost 30 million pounds sterling[29] was entirely financed by internal resources, derived especially from taxes on tea and sugar, under the monopoly law of May 30th, 1925.[30] This was not the only undertaking in the field of communications. Important foundations for future development had already been laid during the First World War, especially by the British Army in southern Persia. The network of roads, which was expanded considerably, was financed, especially until 1926, by various road tolls on goods, and from 1926 onwards by a comprehensive road toll (instead of the previous differential and scattered tolls) according to the Road Development Law of February of that year. Persia inherited from the period of the War 3,930 km of usable roads which by the end of the 'thirties were expanded to 24,000 km;[31] although even in the 'thirties most of these were second and third class roads, and only about a quarter were paved with stone or asphalt. A number of airways were likewise established from 1927 onwards, mainly by foreign investors and especially the German Junkers Company.

3. FORMATION OF STATE ECONOMY

Riza Shah's stake in industrialisation had a twofold result: on the one hand—a considerable neglect of agriculture, and on the other—an economic policy centred round government control and monopolies, guided by a special Ministry for

---

[28] R. N. Gupta, *Iran, An Economic Study*, The Indian Institute of International Affairs, New Delhi, 1947, pp. 62-3.

[29] According to another estimate, 150-200 million dollars, or 34-44 million pounds sterling. D. N. Wilber, *Persia, Past and Present*, New Jersey, 1958, p. 274.

[30] At the beginning of the 'thirties customs, duties on tea and sugar, and road tolls contributed over 50% of the total government revenue. Cf. A. T. Wilson, *op. cit.*, p. 302; and Appendix No. II, in *Thirteenth Quarterly Report of... Finances of Persia*, Dec. 1925, and also Appendix No. 3 in *Seventeenth Report*.

[31] *Bulletin de la Banque Mellié Iran*, No. 25, 1938.

National Economy. This policy aimed at both increased efficiency in the field of economic development and protection against foreign influence.

Nevertheless foreign enterprise continued to operate under concessions in two important branches, namely fishing in the Caspain Sea and oil. The Soviet Union succeeded in renewing the old Russian concession over the fishing rights in the Caspian Sea for a period of 25 years, though as from Ocotober 1927 the concession assumed a different character. The newly founded fishing company was a joint Russo-Persian venture with 50% capital participation of both governments and equal representation on the board of directors.[32] The actual contribution made by this company to the Persian economy was negligible. The concessions for the prospecting for and production of oil remained in foreign hands. This despite Riza Shah's policy of centralisation and nationalisation, and the liquidation of foreign privileges in other domains[33] either by abolition of the capitulations in 1928, or by the decree prohibiting the sale of rural property to foreigners in 1931 and the more extreme regulation by which land already in their possession—apart from immovables serving for purpose of residence of business—could be requisitioned.[34]

Policies favouring a State economy became more vigorous from 1931 onwards, when the attempts of the 'twenties to encourage private initiative were abandoned, largely as a result of the world depression and the difficulties encountered in foreign trade. The government moreover decided that the traditional crafts, even if given assistance, were no longer adequate to meet needs and that modern industrialisation was required. A start in this direction had already been made in the 'twenties, particularly by government support to the textile and sugar industry.[35] But a clear policy of industrialisation, monopolisation and control was drawn up only at the beginning of the 'thirties. Stringent official control was imposed on foreign trade (by a law of 1931 declaring a monopoly on foreign trade),[36] and the setting up of a number of State-owned industries was initiated.

Several large companies were founded, especially in the field of industry (the Imperial Company), foreign trade (the Central Company), and for the importation and marketing of cotton (The Cotton Goods Company), as well as a series of additional undertakings with government participation. As a result of government support to domestic industry, various sectors developed which previously had been unable to subsist. The sugar industry founded by a Belgian company as early as 1895, but liquidated owing to the Russian dumping of 1899, was restored in 1930. The plant established at Kabarisk near Teheran was based on both sugar cane and sugar beet, but its production was still at a low ebb (in 1935/6 the output reached only 2,200 tons). Only during the war did local production increase to 10,000 tons of raw sugar and another 10,000 tons of refined sugar. Among the other industries, comprising wool, silk, jute, soap, breweries, matches and tobacco, the textile industry with 23 enterprises, 120,000 looms and 7,000 employees was of major

---

[32] See Appendix 32.
[33] G. Lenczowski, *Russia and the West in Iran, 1918-1948,* New York, 1949, p. 79-80.
[34] L. P. Elwell-Sutton, *Modern Iran,* London, 1941, p. 84.
[35] A. C. Millspaugh, *The Financial and Economic Situation of Persia,* 1926, p. 19.
[36] A. Tismer, *op. cit.,* p. 15.

importance,[37] as well as the cement industry set up in 1932 with an annual production capacity of 72,000 tons, although its output was always much lower and peak production of 69,000 tons was achieved only in 1939.[38]

At the same time Riza Shah tried to revive Persian crafts, which had been severely hit during the period of the *Kajars*. For this purpose he set up special trade schools, in particular for carpet weaving, an industry which had to struggle against the severe competition of imitators in other countries, such as Turkey and the southern parts of Russia, and the products of China, India and others.[39] A special government corporation was put in control of carpet manufacture and marketing. Encouragement was likewise given to the bronze and dyeing industries.[40]

The annual investments of the Persian government in the establishment of new industries rose from a total of 78 million *riyal* in 1931, to 702 million in 1939, or from 19% of the total budget to 46%.[41] The impetus given to industry by the government also attracted private capitalists from among the landowners, the merchants and industrialists, although their investments failed to attain large dimensions. As against 38 private companies with a capital of 47.8 million *riyal* in 1931/2, 460 companies were operating in Persia by 1939/40, with a capital of 527.1 milion *riyal*, i.e., the entire capital of these companies at the end of the 'thirties was less than government investments in industry for one year.

In the field of foreign trade, which was decisively concentrated in the hands of the government,[42] the barter system played a most prominent role from the beginning of the 'thirties, especially in the commercial relations with the Soviet Union and with Germany, even though clearing agreements served as the official basis.[43] The system was adopted as a result of the expanded foreign trade activities during the 'twenties and the persistent gap in the trade balance of about 10 million pounds sterling annually towards the end of that decade. The deficit was only barely covered by the foreign exchange received from the oil company for royalties and the company's local expenditures.[44] This situation also led to a decline in the value of the *kran* to one-half or even one-third of its value, during the short interval between 1928 and 1930.

With respect to opium, a major export item, Persia found itself in a conflicting situation. While on the one hand it was desirous of improving its balance of payments, on the other hand the cultivation of this drug gave rise to various internal problems and international complications. Persia affords particularly favourable

---

[37] R. N. Gupta, *op. cit.*, pp. 74-5.
[38] K. Grunwald, "The Industrialisation of Persia", *The New East* (Hebrew), Vol. VIII, No. 30, p. 97.
[39] *Eighteenth Quarterly Report,* pp. 28-32.
[40] R. N. Frye, *Iran,* p. 79; Grunwald, *loc. cit.,* p. 95.
[41] Grunwald, *loc. cit.,* pp. 100-101.
[42] According to new regulations, export licences were given on the condition that the forthcoming revenues in foreign currency be deposited with the Central Bank. Imports were allowed in respect of 50% of this currency while the rest was transferred to the government sterling reserve fund. To the extent that the exporters did not use the export revenues for import purpose, they had to remit to the government 90% of the foreign currency received. Cf. A. Tismer, *op. cit.,* p. 9.
[43] *Bulletin de la Banque Nationale de Perse,* avril 1936, pp. 38-61.
[44] *Ibid.,* janvier 1934, p. 5.

conditions for the growing of opium, which fetches good prices on the market. At the beginning of the 'thirties it contributed 50% of the entire value of exports, excluding oil. But as part of the international anti-drug campaign and in view of the danger involved for the Persian population, the use of opium was legally restected to medical purposes only (Law of the Majlis of 1910). Later on a League of Nations committee recommended that Persia should gradually reduce the cultivation of opium while expanding the cultivation of cotton, wool, silk and sugar and promoting general economic development. Persia, however, made compliance with this recommendation conditional on various countries defreezing import quotas and reducing customs tariffs on other Persian goods (such as carpets). This condition was quite unrealistic in view of the world market situation towards the end of the 'twenties and the beginning of the 'thirties and the problem thus remained unsolved.[45]

As from the beginning of the financial year 1923/4 a certain degree of government control over foreign trade and encouragement of local production brought about a slight improvement in the trade balance. It should, however, be taken into account that most official publications on foreign trade included among exports the production of enterprises like the Anglo-Persian Oil Company and the Caspian Fisheries Company, through which even the picture of the 'twenties becomes considerably distorted owing to the extraterritorial nature of these two companies, and the consequent need to debit the Persian balance of payments with their receipts. Tismer's data (*ibid.,* p. 17) also fail to give an accurate picture. While deducting oil exports from the total exports he leaves the import figures unchanged despite the fact that they include considerable imports for the oil companies and others. According to his data the total imports in 1930/31 amounted to 810 million *kran* and exports (excluding oil) to 459 million. In 1931/32 the total imports decreased to 609 millions while the exports (excluding oil) rose to 633 million. Hence, keeping the above reservation in mind, the actual deficit in 1930/1 was smaller while the surplus in 1931/2 was in effect greater. At the same time a certain export of capital took place either by way of goods or by the accumulation of part of the royalties in London. An attempt to present the trade balance of Persia at the end of the period in a more accurate manner was made in the Report of the League of Nations.

TABLE XXIII

Persia's Foreign Trade, 1939 (in million riyals) [46]

				Export Surplus
Commodities imports	661	Commodities exports	804	+ 193
Imports of A.I.O.C., Caspian Fisheries and other foreign Companies	458	Exports of A.I.O.C. and Caspian Fisheries Company	1698	+ 1240
	1069		2502	+ 1433

---

[45] A. T. Wilson, *op. cit.,* pp. 55-60.
[46] U.N., *Economic Developments in the Middle East, 1945 to 1954,* p. 77.

The government derived considerable profits from its price policy with regard to imported goods and its customs policy ever since the abolition of the capitulatory restrictions in 1928. The system of monopolies which was tightened during the depression of the first half of the 'thirties (especially after February 1931) helped to balance both external (balance of payments) and internal (government budget) finances; but this was achieved, mainly through the monopolistic price structure, at the expense of the masses of consumers (especially after the import of rice and matches, which had become a government monopoly, was forbidden) and the small businessman.

Particular attention should be paid to Persia's oil industry. During Riza Shah's time, oil—the major potential for financing development—did not yet play the decisive role in the State revenue it assumed from the 'forties onwards, both because of the still rather low level of production—especially until the middle 'twenties—and also because of the low rate of royalties payable until the beginning of the 'thirties. On the other hand the important progress—especially in relative terms—made in this field should not be ignored. Whereas the total royalties paid to the Persian government for the eight years 1913-20 amounted to £ 1,325,552, by the end of the 'twenties the *annual* revenue from this source already reached an equivalent amount, while a further amount, at least equal to the above and according to some sources twice as much,[47] was spent by the company on wages and local purchases. During the beginning of the 'thirties the royalties constituted 15-20% of government revenue. Much significance should be attached to the indirect influence of the oil industry on economic concepts and attitudes of those who came in close contact with this industry, through whom it spread to other strata. Equally significant was the part played by the company in the field of health, education, vocational training, mechanisation and the adoption of a modern economic approach in other branches of the economy. The discovery and refining of oil on the spot also provided a possibility—at least for the future—of exploiting this relatively cheap source of power for development purposes.

The great importance of Persian oil from the second half of the 'twenties onwards also becomes evident from a comparison with total world production. In absolute terms the Persian output grew from 82,000 tons in 1913 to 1,124,000 in 1919, 3,774,000 in 1924, 5,809,000 in 1929, and 11,327,000 tons in 1939. Persia's share in world production during the same period increased from 0.15% in 1913 to 4.45% in 1939; while the world production index of oil (on a basis of 1913 = 100) increased to 477 in 1939, the Persian index rose to 13,799. It is clear that this jump is the natural result of the very modest start made by Persia, yet the fact that by the end of the period it provided almost 5% of the entire world production emphasises the importance of Persian oil not only in the national economy but on the world market as well. The great drawback was that of the estimated profits of about £ 200 million of the Anglo-Persian (and subsequently the Anglo-Iranian) Company during the years 1919-1930, Persia received only £ 10 million. Hence the cancelling of the

---

[47] G. Hartner, *Währung und Notenbankwesen Persiens,* Leipzig, 1932, p. 17, quoted by A. Tismer, *op. cit.,* p. 12.

concession by Riza Shah in 1932 and his refusal to renew it except after major concessions on the part of the company, granted in 1933, was no less important in its effects than the increase in production. Riza Shah's main demands were an increased amount of royalties and taxes payable, in addition to a decrease in the concession areas of the company. As a result, the Persian oil revenues rose from £ 1.1 million in 1931 to £ 4 million in 1940/1, which amounted to some 15% of government revenues and, together with oil companies' local disbursements, to over 60% of foreign exchange receipts.[48]

Oil might have solved the problem of capital supply for Persian economic development, but in Persia, even more than in other Middle Eastern countries, the backwardness of the regime, the social structure and educational and cultural standards, impeded economic progress. The patterns of investments, priorities and the direction of social reform were determined by a government which at that time did not yet appreciate the foremost importance of structural socio-economic transformation which, in a backward country, meant thorough agrarian reform and a change in educational and cultural values. Even where special priority was given, as to industry, no serious research into possibilities and desirable patterns of investment was as a rule carried out. Official sources even defended the view that research, selection and direction in this field were not necessary in countries which were at the beginning of their development, as distinct from developed countries.[49] This approach to the development of backward countries, which has since been completely discredited—especially after the Second World War—hardly helped the Persian economy to overcome the obstacles to accelerated growth.

4. BOTTLENECKS IN THE DEVELOPMENT PROCESS

In a backward country a certain advantage attached to the existence of an absolute ruler leading his country towards economic development, political independence and a European standard of education and culture. However the drawbacks of Riza Shah's political, social and economic methods outnumbered their advantages, and as a rule led to the failure of his efforts and a persistent lack of progress. The control exercised by the Shah over all aspects of life and public opinion, and the complete submission of the administration to the Shah, instilled terror into the population and paralysed initiative.

---

[48] The royalties paid to the Persian government during the years 1913-1920 amounted to an annual average of £ 165,500; £ 468,700 in 1921; £ 728,800 in 1925; £ 478,893 in 1929; £ 1,288,000 in 1930; £ 2,770,814 in 1939 and £ 4,000,000 in the financial year 1940/41. Cf. *Sixth Quarterly Report... of the Finances of Persia,* 1924, pp. 34-35; A. T. Wilson, *Persia,* London, 1932, pp. 95-100; L. Dudley Stamp, *Asia,* Methuen, London, ed. 1950, p. 156; Taghi Kaveh, *Einfluss der Iranischen Ölindustrie auf die wirtschaftliche Entwicklung des Iran* (doctoral thesis, mimeogr.), Nürnberg, 1957, pp. 53-54 and 73; U.N., *Economic Developments in the M.E., 1945-1954, passim,* & *Public Finance Information Papers—Iran,* 1951, p. 34.

[49] In this respect the *Bulletin of the Melli Bank* of June 1937 states on p. 2: "Quant à l'Iran, il est naturel que son industrie ne soit pas encore trop préoccuppée de ces questions".

The casting off of the foreign yoke made still heavier taxes on the local population inevitable, especially indirect taxes, which impoverished the in any case destitute masses. Various services were further required from the fellahin which were in fact identical with compulsory labour, as well as "gifts" of produce to the landowners. The abolition of the land tax in 1934 and its replacement by a tax on marketed produce constituted an important change in fiscal policy and a certain concession to the subsistence-farmers. But, on the other hand, the Civil Code and its supplmentary laws dealing, *inter alia*, with ownership and classification of land, and with the crop sharing among the factors of production, generally favoured the landlords. In reality, the protection given to the peasant and the leaseholder was even less than laid down by law.

The condition of the rural and urban labourers was worse than that of the peasants producers. With the continued decrease in the value of the *kran* during the 'twenties and the rise in the price of primary commodities, the purchasing power of the labourer's daily wage (3-4 *kran*, equivalent to 12-17d.) was reduced to a daily portion of bread, cheese and sometimes a piece of cotton cloth (according to the *British Consular Report* of 1928). Whereas during the period 1932-1936 the *kran* was strengthened in terms of foreign currency, the cost-of-living index gradually rose, especially during the second half of the 'thirties, from an average of 100 in 1936 to 149 points at the end of 1939. This deterioration of the purchasing power of currency affected mainly the urban classes. In the middle 'thirties, while a workman earned $3^{1}/_{2}$ *riyal*, a weaver 5 *riyal* and a servant only $1^{1}/_{2}$ *riyal*, the price of a pound of bread was $^{1}/_{4}$ *riyal,* a pound of mutton 1.06 *riyal*, a pound of rice 0.74 *riyal,* a pound of butter 3.08 *riyal* and the price of a fowl 3.80 *riyal*. It is not hard to imagine the state of a labourer's family of five or more which, according to an investigation, was shown to spend over 57% of its earnings on food.[50]

Despite his strong position, the Shah had to compromise with various internal factors, such as the religious leaders and the landlords. In Persia, to a larger extent than in several other Middle Eastern countries, the Beduin tribes succeeded in maintaining their status. The nomads constituted about one-quarter of the entire population and surpassed the fellahin in vitality and in intellectual capacities. They took a major share in both production and exports, in particular in the supply of meat, butter, wool, hides, camels, mules and horses.

The conservative nature of these factors was instrumental in shaping government policy on central social and economic problems, despite the gradual rise of a new class of capitalists who had become rich through commerce, monopolies and concessions. The Shah himself gradually expanded his private properties, especially by concentrating in his hands extensive estates[51] either through political confiscations or by way of purchase (in many cases identical with confiscation). As in other backward countries during the first stages of development, Riza Shah put great emphasis on construction, not only in the beneficial direction of

---

[50] *Bulletins de la Banque Mellié Iran,* 1936-1939.
[51] A contemporary of Riza also reports on a deposit of 20 million dollars in the private bank account of the Shah.

communications, for instance, but also in the less desirable field of public and private building, which in the first line served the needs of the Shah and the wealthy classes and only to a limited degree those of the masses of the urban and rural population. Here the exhibitionary propensities of the Shah undoubtedly played an important part, since by his building activities he was able to point to immediate and concrete achievements, evident to all.[52]

Riza Shah's opposition to foreign intrusion was also far from being unqualified. Foreign companies continued to play quite a prominent role in the country's economic life, and among them the share of British firms was outstanding. Foreign capital—not only in Persia but in other backward countries as well—was channelled mainly to the field of oil, commerce, transportation and insurance—but not to main production sectors, industry or agriculture.

In industry the State tried its hand at several projects, getting also, to a certain degree, the co-operation of local and even foreign capital. Instead, the neglect of agriculture and irrigation limited the country's chances of utilising its major natural assets, of building a sound economy, and raising the standard of living of the masses.

In comparison with two other major entities in the region, Egypt and Turkey—both still backward on the eve of World War II—Persia, with nearly the same population and a much vaster area, lagged significantly behind in physical and human infrastructure, in agricultural and industrial output, and in power supply.[53] The underutilisation of existing resources, inadequate exploration of potentials, poor experience in development techniques and the limited social scope of Riza's reforms prevented the achievement of the desired goal—an industrialised society. Obviously the time factor was of major importance, and the outbreak of the Second World War also interfered with the process of development.

---

[52] A. C. Millspaugh, *op. cit.*, p. 32.

[53] Cf. League of Nations, *International Statistical Yearbook 1939/40;* U.N., *op. cit.;* and national statistics of Egypt and Turkey, quoted in the Bibliography, below.

PART NINE

THE EGYPTIAN ECONOMY DURING THE TWENTIES AND THIRTIES

1. EGYPT'S POST-WAR PROBLEMS AND ECONOMIC POLICY

There was a considerable degree of uniformity in the Egyptian population from the religious and national point in view. Only the one million Christian Copts constituted a major exception, and the total number of all the other minorities did not exceed 300,000. The bulk of the population was rural, with quite a high proportion of town dwellers (about 30%) and only a tiny percentage of nomads (estimated in the census of 1937 at only about 12,000).

Since the end of World War I Egypt's particular problem was the fast population increase, with a birth rate of 4.4% and a death rate of 2.6-2.8% during the 'twenties and 'thirties. As a result of this natural increase the Egyptian population grew from 9.7 million in 1897 to 14.2 million in 1927 and 15.9 million in 1937[1] Consequently more and more people remained without land, while the number of these who owned less than one feddan increased from 942,530 in 1913 to 1,751,587 in 1939. At the same time the pressure on the cities increased, particularly the larger ones like Cairo and Alexandria. Disguised unemployment became deeply ensconced, since the city was able to absorb only part of the increased population while the rest had to share the agricultural income from constantly dwindling plots parcellated among the smallholders. Underemployment persisted not only owing to lack of alternative occupations to farming, but also because as long as the fellah escaped actual starvation, he preferred to work only half a year or even less,[2] instead of to intensify or supplement his agricultural activities.

The situation remained unchanged despite the fact that the standard of nutrition of the Egyptian population was at an absolute low. According to H. Wilson's report of 1921, almost the entire working population of Egypt suffered from malnutrition, as may be seen from the following Table: [3] (on p. 219)

The data indicate that not even the best-placed group reached the nutritional minimum in proteins and fats and their diet was satisfactory only as regards the carbohydrates and number of calories consumed. This, by the way, is also typical of other backward countries where corn and pulses constitute the central nutrients.

The population was content to remain in the villages under such conditions because in the course of generations of suffering and exploitation the fellah had learned to be satisfied with little and also because of the illiteracy of over 90% of the

---

[1] Cf. note 131 on p. 115. For the development and distribution of the Egyptian population from the national and religious point of view, prior to the First World War, cf. also M. Sabry, *L'Egypte Telle Qu'elle Est*, 1905, pp. 50-52.
[2] W. Cleland, *op. cit.*, p. 98.
[3] *Ibid*, pp. 75-7 and Table F.

TABLE XXIV

Food Cousumption in Egypt in 1921 (annual data)

Food components	Required minimum for a workers' family of 5	Available		
		In the poorest category (Lower Egypt)	In the intermediate category (Middle Egypt)	In the best-placed category (Upper Egypt)
Proteins	75,700 grams	42,300 grams	60,400 grams	62,500 grams
Fats	71,000 grams	56,800 grams	59,600 grams	57,800 grams
Carbohydrates	912,000 grams	835,600 grams	790,200 grams	1,006,100 grams
Calories	4,450,000	4,425,000	4,382,000	5,328,600

population as recently as the 'twenties and 'thirties. By 1927 only 4% of the population (including the "intellectuals" and their families) could read and write, while all the rest were total illiterates. Even at the beginning of the 'thirties only 21% of children of school age were receiving any education.[4]

The dividing line between the lettered and the illiterates also constituted one of the most distinctive lines of separation in Egyptian society, especially since it was identical with the frontier between under-nourishment and normal diet, sickness and health, apathy and sloth and a larger measure of daring and economic activity. Against this background, it will be easier to understand the lack of initiative shown during the inter-war period, when political conditions were equally to the disadvantage of development efforts.

The development of Egypt during the period between the two World Wars was still largely affected by the suppression of the anti-British riots of 1919[5] and the continued presence of the British according to the Declaration of February 28th, 1922, which granted formal independence to Egypt by putting an end to the British Protectorate proclaimed at the outbreak of the First World War.[6] This declaration, however, and the Anglo-Egyptian Treaty of 1922 entered into on pursuance of the recommendations of the Milner commission, reserved certain rights and influence to the British (especially until 1936), with respect to the maintenance of communications and transports, the defence of Egypt and the protection of the interests of foreigners and minorities. The Egyptian constitution passed on 18.4.1923, the establishment of houses of representatives and the grant of the general vote[7] proved of little avail in practice, both because of the ingrained tradition of despotism and the continued influence of the British. Hence the national aspirations of the period were not crowned with any much greater success than those of the mandated countries. Bargaining with the British centred round the

---

[4] *Ibid*, pp. 70-80.

[5] Cf. M. Sabry, *La Révolution Egyptienne*, Paris, 1919.

[6] Cf. *Journal Officiel Egyptien*, 19 décembre 1914; Fawzi Tadros, *La souveraineté Egyptienne et la Declaration du 28 février 1922*, Paris, Pedone, 1934.

[7] Ch. H. Pouthas, *Histoire de l'Egypte depuis la conquète Ottomane*, Librairie Hachette, 1948, p. 161.

four principal points of the Declaration of Independence of 1922:[8] the Suez Canal, the army of occupation, the capitulations and the Sudan. Some of these problems were settled by the treaty of August 26th, 1936, which laid down a policy of gradual limitation of the British forces and their evacuation from the Canal Zone by 1956, provided that Egypt by that time would be able to assume its defence.[9] The problem of the Sudan remained open, and the capitulations were annulled in 1937 by the Montreux Treaty, which also prepared the way towards the participation of foreigners in the fiscal burden (cf. below). Following the decisions of the Montreux conference (Clause 3 of the Treaty), the Mixed Courts were to be abolished only in 1949.[10]

A state of internal political instability continued to prevail. Frequent amendments were introduced in the constitution and governments were rapidly changed—a feature common to the entire Arab camp. The constant bargaining with the British and the internal political unrest distracted the Egyptians from social and economic development efforts.

Unlike the mandated countries, the economic policy of Egypt during the period in question was not dependent on foreign trustees, especially after 1922. However, the continuation of the capitulations until 1937 and Egypt's international financial obligations prevented her from adopting a sweeping economic policy, especially as regards industrialisation. It should be borne in mind that the extensive foreign investments before World War I were directed mainly towards services (including financial services) and building activities. The World War itself brought about economic upheavals of alternating booms and depressions, especially for the fellahin.[11] Upon the outbreak of the war, when Egypt was partially cut off from the cotton markets and had to supply cheap commodities to the Army through Greek and other contractors, the country was visited by a depression which fomented revolution. The civil authorities subsequently remedied the situation and business started to flourish at a high price level[12] so that many of the fellahin were able to get rid of their debts as their income increased. But the situation again deteriorated

---

[8] Ch. Issawi, *Egypt, An Economic and Social Analysis,* Oxf. Univ. Press, 1947, p. 171.

[9] Convention between the Government of the U.K. of Great Britain and Northern Ireland and the Egyptian Government Concerning the Immunities & Privileges to be enjoyed by the British Forces in Egypt (London, Aug. 26th, 1936), League of Nations, *Treaty Series,* No. 4032, 1937, pp. 434-443.

[10] Convention regarding the abolition of capitulations in Egypt, signed at Montreux, May 8th, 1937 (between Egypt and U.S.A., Belgium, Gt. Britain, Denmark, Spain, France, Greece, Italy, Ethiopia, Norway, Netherlands, Portugal, Sweden), L. of N., *Treaty Series,* No. 4202, 1937-8, pp. 37-103. Regarding the treaty of 1936, the problems which preceded it, its effect, and the Montreux Treaty of 8.5.1937, see, Albert Bourgeois, *La Formation de l'Egypte Moderne,* Le Traité Anglo-Egyptien du 27 Août 1936, et la Convention de Montreux du 8 Mai 1937, Paris 1939; A. N. Cumberbatch, *Egypt, Economic & Commercial Conditions in Egypt,* Overseas Economic Surveys, Oct. 1951, p. 2. As a result of these two agreements Egypt was admitted to the League of Nations in 1937. League of Nations, *Special Session of the Assembly,* May 26th, 1937.

[11] M. Sabry, *La Révolution Egyptienne,* Paris, 1919, pp. 13-17.

[12] The steep rise in prices which occurred after 1915 triggered the wholesale price index in Cairo and Alexandria (on a basis of I. 1913-VIII. 1914 = 100) up to 316 in 1920, and from then onwards a decline set in to 130 in 1923. League of Nations, *Memorandum on Currency and Central Banks,* 1913-1925, Vol. II, 1926, p. 103.

towards the end of the War when the confiscation and requisitioning of produce and livestock started affecting also the poorer classes and the small producers. Mobilisation to the Gallipoli and other fronts turned into a kind of corvée leading to desertion of the villages to escape the call-up, or to truancy from army camps after recruitment.[13] The Egyptian village after the War should have been the main object of social and economic rehabilitation.

Attempts to reconstruct Egypt's economy in the post-War I period registered a certain initial success by the emergence of three important and influential institutions: the Misr Bank; the Egyptian Federation of Industries; and, the Egyptian General Agriculture Syndicate. Their main purpose was to reorganise and dynamise the economy, considered dormant under the past Cromer regime, to lay foundations for a new bourgeoisie and organised private enterprise. Through cooperation, in the course of time, between national and resident foreign enterpreneurs, expectations were nourished of more intensive industrialisation and encouragement of domestic investments, including those by foreign capital, provided that government support (such as the later customs law of 1930) would come forth.

The interrelation between the agencies mentioned was reflected in their respective tasks and activities. The Misr Bank, set up in 1920, aimed at the encouragement and financing of private national industry and at the emergence and consolidation of an Egyptian bourgeoisie. Since big landowners were the dominant factor in industrial investments they were supposed to constitute the chief agents of transfer of capital from agriculture to industry and commerce, and of the diversification and modernisation required for restructuring the economy and escaping the trap of monoculture, with the assistance of the two industrial and agricultural institutions mentioned above.[14]

The financing of the plans proposed after the War by a commission headed by Sidky Pasha met with difficulties owing to shortage of resources and even more so owing of lack of qualified manpower.[15] In the course of time customs (since 1930) and taxes on foreigners (especially with the liquidation of the capitulations in 1937) were raised. More extensive investments started to be made in industry, and simultaneously the infrastructure was developed, especially to serve the industrial

---

[13] V. Chirol, *The Egyptian Problem*, pp. 130-141; 284-285.

[14] Issues of modernisation and industrialisation in that period are discussed in: "The Egyptian Revolution of 1919: New Directions in the Egyptian Economy", by R. L. Tignor; "Bank Misr and the Emergence of Local Bourgeoisie in Egypt", by M. Deeb—both published in *Middle Eastern Studies,* Vol. 12, No. 3, October, 1976; and in "Bank Misr and Foreign Capitalism", by R. L. Tignor, published in *International Journal of Middle East Studies,* 8 (1977).

[15] Side by side with the suffering and economic upheavals caused by the World War the accumulation of major resources should not be ignored which under a wise and development-minded policy might have served as funds for investment and economic regeneration. The British war expenditure in Egypt was estimated at £ 200 million; the price of cotton rose from £ 4 per kantar in 1916 to £ 20 in 1919 (on a considerably larger area); the trade balance in 1919 showed a surplus of £ 33 million; the State revenue increased at a larger rate than the rise of prices (and the decline in the value of the currency) while a large part of the Egyptian debt started being concentrated in the hands of Egyptians who invested their profits in debentures.

centres. The change which occurred during this period was reflected amongst other things in a considerable increase in the local consumption of cotton for industrial purposes from an annual average of about 56,000 kantar during 1920-29 to 513,000 kantar in 1935-39. This increase was accompanied by a policy of encouragement to the cultivation of cotton adopted as from 1930 in contrast to the restrictions imposed prior to that date.[16]

Egypt possibly suffered more severely from the world depression than the rest of the Middle East, being decisively dependent on export revenues from one major item, namely cotton. A considerable deterioration took place in the trade balance, and following the domestic impact of depression the surpluses in the State budget of the 'twenties disappeared or dwindled owing to the large decrease in government revenues. Accordingly a new economic policy of increased economic intervention by the State was required. Gradually conditions were created for an economic policy untrammelled by foreign restrictions. In 1930, with the lapse of the relevant international agreements, the country became free of customs restrictions, though the capitulations proper were abolished only in 1937. However the customs income, which already constituted a considerable proportion of total revenues, began to increase only after the end of the world depression and the revival of foreign trade. Only in 1939 did the government become free to raise land taxes above the limit fixed in the regulations of 1899. By the cancellation of the capitulations direct taxes could also be imposed on the foreigners operating or resident in Egypt.

Issawi points out[17] that the economic policy of the 'thirties acted mainly for the benefit of industrialists and landlords, while the masses of fellahin suffered considerable neglect. The industrialists benefited from the Customs Law of 1930; the landowners, though hit by the crisis, were assisted by loans of the Crédit Agricole, and by virtue of the resolutions of the parliament in 1931 received 1 million Egyptian pounds for purposes of rehabilitation and assistance, and another million Egyptian pounds against mortgages, further credit being approved in 1933. While the rental had declined as a result of the recession, the landowners, on the other hand, thanks to customs protection and the high domestic prices for wheat and rice, in turn profited at the expense of the city workers. The extreme inequality in this country—deeply ingrained in the distribution of property, especially land—was still further aggravated by a series of additional factors outlined above, by the widespread corruption of the ramified government services and the enormous gulf in wage scales, where a bank manager received £E. 5,000, a senior government official about £E. 1,500, and a lower official less than £E. 100 per year.

As distinct from most of the other Arab countries and from Persia and Turkey, Egypt's central problem during the present century, has been the density of its population. It is therefore only natural that its economic policy should attempt to tackle the problem from both ends—by endeavouring to halt the population increase and by opening up new sources of livelihood. Until recently Egypt failed to take any important action in the first direction and it is typical that a committee for

---

[16] Cf. Ch. Issawi, *Egypt, etc.*, p. 71; V. Chirol, *op. cit.*, pp. 288-391.
[17] Ch. Issawi, *op. cit.*, p. 173.

the reduction of production expenses of cotton in 1935 should have expressly recommended means *against* a decline in the population increase[18] on the assumption that this would prove harmful to agriculture. On the other hand certain efforts at promoting agriculture and industry were made, but the above-mentioned factors prevented any considerable progress in this field during the inter-war period.

The occupational structure of the Egyptian population at that time to a large extent revealed the potential direction of development policy.

TABLE XXV

The Occupational Structure of the Egyptian Population prior to the Outbreak of the Second World War.[19]

Agriculture	3.5 million
industry and mines	0.6 million
transportation	0.2 million
commerce, finance and insurance	0.5 million
public services	0.2 million
free professions	0.1 million
domestic service	0.2 million
Total active population	5.3 million

This structure necessitated extensive short-term aid for agriculture which provided a livelihood for nearly 65% of the working population. Another long-term conclusion to be drawn from this structure, especially in view of the existing limitations to Egyptian agriculture and the population increase, was the need for expansion of the industrial basis in order to absorb a much larger proportion of labour. These two conclusions were in fact hardly contradictory, but they required a much larger development effort than was actually put up by the economy.

2. PUBLIC FINANCING

As early as 1898 the National Bank of Egypt was founded by a group of British financiers headed by Sir Ernest Cassel and given a monopoly for the issue of banknotes. In 1914 the full status of legal tender was given to the notes issued by the National Bank, and in the absence of gold it was authorised to cover its notes with British treasury notes, so that an equivalence with the pound sterling was established. Despite the difference between the status of Egypt and that of the mandated countries their central banking principles were similar,[20] i.e., the bank's main concern was to lend stability to the currency by full coverage with gold, hard currency and gilt-edged securities, without using the reserves for an adequate expansion of local credit and investments in the national economy. Generally, the

---

[18] *Ibid.,* p. 196.
[19] *L'Egypte Indépendante,* Paris, 1938, p. 275.
[20] See below for the procedure of the Currency Boards in the mandated countries.

gold and foreign currency (especially sterling) reserve somewhat exceeded the amount of currency in circulation.[21]

The banknotes in circulation increased from £E. 2.7 million in 1913 (annual average) to 67.3 million in 1919. Then a considerable decline in circulation occurred, to £E. 33 million in 1925 and 18.8 million in 1932, followed by a rise to about 28 million in 1939. In that year the total money supply (including short-term deposits) amounted to £E. 63 million[22], thus reflecting the increasing role of banking during the 1930s.

Public financing in Egypt, as explained in the discussion of the economic policy, was adversely affected by the customs restrictions in force until 1930, the capitulations and restrictions with respect to foreigners in force until 1937, as well as by the effect of the world depression on the customs revenue even after greater freedom in the fixing of tariffs had been achieved. The rigid monetary structure likewise limited the government in its financial activities. Budget surpluses of up to £E. 17 million in 1919 were left over from the days of the World War, and apart from the short period when reserves were swallowed up by a considerable deficit in 1920, the budgets of the 'twenties were characterised by surpluses which gradually grew to £E. 40 million by 1930.[23] It is thus seen that not the scarcity of funds but the lack of State initiative—incapable of properly applying even these limited means—lay at the root of the country's sluggish pace of development. The crisis of the 'thirties seriously aggravated the situation since the traditional revenue was curtailed and a strong deflationary policy was needed in order to keep a balanced budget. Apart from 1931/2 and 1937/8, the Egyptian treasury in effect managed to maintain small but constant budget surpluses.

Three select budgetary years 1929/30 (peak year) 1933/4 (depression) and 1937/8 (the year preceding the Second World War), given below, may be indicative of three different financial and fiscal situations: (see p. 225)

Except in 1930/31 when government investments still stood at about £E. 7 million or 17% of the total expenditure budget (and when the only serious deficit occurred in the budget), both the current expenditures and government investments were reduced during the rest of the 'thirties (the latter to £E. 4.5 million or less than 15% of the total expenditures of 1933/4, i.e., both an absolute and a relative decrease). Only with the gradual revenue increase towards the end of the 'thirties did the expenditure and investment cuts become somewhat slighter.[24] There is no doubt that this trend was partially determined by the world crisis, but, in addition, Cromer's financial and fiscal policy still made itself felt. Since 1931/2, despite continuous annual budget surpluses, the reserves started dwindling owing to losses and expenses incurred by the Egyptian treasury, and not included in the budget, such as losses on

---

[21] League of Nations, *Memorandum on Currency and Central Banks, 1913-1925,* Vol. II, Geneva, 1926, pp. 42-3, 56-7.

[22] *Ibid.,* pp. 26-7, as well as later statistics of the League of Nations and Egypt. Until 1939 no reliable data are available as to the extent of current deposits.

[23] Ch. Issawi, *Egypt, etc.,* p. 139.

[24] League of Nations, *op. cit.,* p. 2.

TABLE XXVI
Egyptian Budgets, 1929/30-1937/8

Receipts (in million £E.) Item	1929/30	1933/4	1937/8 (estimate)
Land and house tax	5.97	6.39	6.27
Customs and excise [25]	13.26	13.99	18.15
Cotton tax	1.63	0.84	—
Telephone, telegraph, railways [26]	7.94	1.44	1.45
Miscellaneous	13.09	9.97	10.02
Total	41.89	32.63	35.89

Expenditure (in million £E.) Item	1929/30	1933/4	1937/8
Army, navy and police	5.20	4.76	6.34
Interests and payments on account of national debt	4.75	4.19	4.19
Telephone, telegraph & railways [26] (current expenses)	4.89	—	—
Ministry of Public Works	6.97	5.99	7.22
Ministry of Education [27]	2.92	3.10	3.99
Royal Court	0.74	0.61	0.42
Miscellaneous	15.66	11.90	14.83
Total	41.13	30.55	36.99

(Source: League of Nations, *Public Finance, 1928-1937*, xxxii, *Egypt*, Geneva, 1938, pp. 6-11.)

coinage, on the sale of cotton, or balances payable on account of treasury note coupons. Towards the end of the inter-war period however reserves again increased to some £ 35 million.[28]

At the end of the 'thirties the budget amounted to £E. 40 million, i.e., it returned to its nominal level of pre-depression period. (The Egyptian pound, as will be remembered, was in the meantime devalued following the pound sterling.) It should however be borne in mind that until 1933/4 the entire gross receipts of the railways, telephone and telegraph were included in the budget, while afterwards only the surpluses of these services were so included. The actual net income had accordingly increased by £E. 3.5 million. The receipts derived mainly from customs and excise (40%)[29] and taxes on land[30] and buildings (16%). Income tax yielded only 7%. In

---

[25] The proportion of the excise under this item has increased; part of the excise is further included among "Miscellaneous".

[26] 1933/34 is the first year in which only the surpluses of these services are shown in the above item (and hence it no longer appears in the expenditure budget).

[27] Including salaries of civil servants.

[28] *Ibid.*, pp. 3-5.

[29] The customs continued to yield a high absolute and relative budgetary revenue even during the slump, since the decline in the volume of imports was counterbalanced by the considerable increase in customs tariffs almost making good all the losses.

[30] These were paid at the rate of 28.64% of the value of the land rental.

constrast to the mandated territories the security expenditure was not great (less than 20%), yet one-third of the budget was spent on salaries to civil servants, of whom a large number were redundant, while only 10% each was spent on health and education. In the 'thirties, quite a considerable percentage (about 20%) was spent on public works, including, *inter alia*, expansion of the railway and road network, and water works in conjunction with the Nile. Only about 2% on the average was expended on agriculture.[31] The Public Debt Fund continued to receive certain revenues in order to pay dividends to bondholders (only a small proportion being paid up during the War), and effect payments on account of Egypt's obligations according to the Lausanne Treaty whereby Egypt undertook to discharge the Ottoman debts from the loans of 1855, 1891 and 1894 in respect of which the Egyptian tribute had been mortgaged. Egypt's total national debt towards the end of the 'thirties amounted to about £E. 88 million, i.e., somewhat less than the debt to foreign creditors alone on the eve of the First World War—and this (in 1938/9) in terms of devalued pounds.[32]

3. THE AGRICULTURAL SECTOR AND AGRARIAN POLICIES

From the 19th century until 1952 Egyptian agriculture had to contend with two related problems: the small size of its cultivated area as compared with the growing population and the extreme polarisation of ownership.

The total number of landowners rose from 1,600,000 before the outbreak of the First World War, to 2.5 million at the outbreak of the Second. A considerable proportion of the new owners came as a result of the population increase and the splitting-up of existing units among the heirs. Some of the peasants and the landless population also became landowners. While the number of landowners increased by about 55%, the cultivated area increased from 5.4 million feddan to only 5.8 million feddan, i.e. by less than 10%. Although cultivation became more intensive (both as regards the cropped area and unit yields) this was insufficient to close the gap and prevent the decrease in the size of the total and even the cropped area per farmer and

TABLE XXVII

Distribution of Landed Property in Egypt in 1936 [33]

Size of units in feddan	No. of owners	No. of feddan in their possession
1 feddan and less	1,677,536	688,600
1.1-5	564,700	1,148,018
5.1-10	84,617	561,348
10.1-20	39,643	528,362
20.1-49.9	21,799	657,000
50 and over	12,420	2,253,583
	2,400,715	5,836,912

[31] *The Economist,* Dec. 4th, 1937, (Egypt) pp. 12-14.

[32] *Ibid.,* p. 11; *Memento Economique, L'Egypte,* pp. 165 ff.

[33] See publication of the Jewish Agency for Palestine, Economic Research Institute, *Statistical Handbook of Middle Eastern Countries,* Jerusalem, 1945, p. 60; *Annuaire Egyptien,* 1948.

per capita.[34] The greatest increase was recorded with respect to units of less than 1 feddan, from 430,000 to 700,000 and from 1 million owners to 1.7 million. This increase obviously implied an enormous multiplicity of tiny plots with a much lower average size towards the end of the period than at its beginning. The total area of units of up to 1 feddan (and even up to 5 feddan—though here the increase was smaller) grew mainly as the result of splitting up of medium-sized units. According to some sources there was no decrease in the area owned by the larger landlords, most of them absentees, of over 50 feddan each,[35] whilst the area within the range of 5-50 feddan was reduced.

This state of affairs led to an increase in rental and an inflation in the price of land. During the 'twenties 500-1,000 dollars were paid per feddan (as against $ 250-450 during the depression at the beginning of the 'thirties)[36], as compared, for instance, with an average of 40.8 dollars in the U.S.A. in 1925, or 119 dollars in Iowa—the highest priced area in the U.S.A. (per acre, which is approximately equivalent to the feddan).[37]

It was estimated that at the same time a unit of 5-7 feddan was required for the employment and livelihood of a family of six. After deduction of the rental and/or taxes and other charges such a family had about £E. 14 left over, which had to suffice not only for their living expenses but also for the acquisition of indispensable new equipment and essential repairs.[38] It is clear that as the average size of the plot fell below this minimum, both income and standard of living went down. Only during the 'fifties of the present century were serious attempts made to change the agrarian set-up both as regards cultivated area—mainly by means of the High Dam south of Aswan—and land tenure—through agrarian reform.

During the 'thirties the distribution of the crop area among the various crops was approximately as follows (it should be borne in mind that the annual crop areas exceeded by 40% and more the physical area cultivated):[39]

---

[34] The area in hectares per person (for the entire population) is given below:

	Cultivated area per person	Crop area per person
1907	0.20	0.29
1927	0.16	0.26
1937	0.14	0.22

See U.N. *Economic Development in the M.E., 1945-54*, p. 27; cf. also W. Cleland, *The Population Problem in Egypt*, 1936, pp. vi-vii, and 31. Almost all scholars, economists as well as demographers, including one of the most outstanding authorities, W. Cleland, who points out the relative increase of the urban population in Egypt and the industrial "alternative" (pp. 66, 99), failed to investigate properly the changes which occurred in the size of *the crop area per farmer*. Indeed no exact data are available for that period on the occupational structure, but there was a clear trend towards a relative decline of agricultural earners. Such an investigation would have placed the development of the Egyptian economy in a more favourable light, provided there was a concomittant increase in production in non-agrarian sectors and that an increasing transition to a market economy had taken place. We have discussed this problem more extensively in our book on *The Economic Structure of the Middle East*.

[35] About 500,000 feddan were owned by foreign firms and individuals towards the end of the 'thirties, while another 700,000 feddan were *waqf* lands, most of which was private (*ahli*) *waqf*.

[36] Cf. *L'Egypte Indépendante*, Paris, 1938, p. 282.

[37] W. Cleland, *op. cit.*, p. 95.

[38] *L'Egypte Indépendante*, p. 285.

[39] *Ibid.*, p. 301.

TABLE XXVIII

Distribution of Crop Areas in Egypt during the Thirties

cotton	1,700,000 feddan
maize	1,500,000 feddan
clover	1,500,000 feddan
wheat	1,400,000 feddan
beans	500,000 feddan
rice	400,000 feddan
sorghum	300,000 feddan
barley	290,000 feddan
sugar cane	65,000 feddan
miscellaneous	400,000 feddan
	8,055,000 feddan

Cotton during that period remained the major agricultural product. It is however difficult to find any clear-cut increasing trend in area and total yields despite a certain inconsistent rise in unit yields. The average area under cotton during the years 1920-24 was 707,000 hectares with an average yearly yield of 277,700 tons ginned cotton, and 3.9 quintals (= 390 kg) per hectare. During the 1939/40 season, 708,000 hectares were cultivated with a total yield of 412,000 tons, or 5.8 quintals (580 kg) per hectare. This comparison shows a considerable rise both in total and per unit yields, even though the season 1939/40 registered a decline from the peak achieved in 1936/7, with an area of 831,000 hectares, a yield of 494.6 thousand tons, and 6 quintals (600 kg) per hectare.[40]

Cotton maintained its position in comparison with other crops as regards profitability,[41] but its share in the agricultural income gradually decreased from about 50% in the 'twenties to about 30% in the 'thirties.

This was partly due to the fluctuations in the price of cotton, but even more so to the economic policy, which encouraged breeding of livestock (about 5 million head including cattle, sheep, camels, horses and mules) and in particular the growing of grains, both by its price policy and protective customs, and by subsidies granted largely at the expense of the municipal taxpayer. As such the principle of multiple crops was correct, but the methods by which it was implemented were of doubtful value.

Issawi, in discussing Egypt's agrarian policy during the 'thirties, pointed out the good sense in removing the restrictions on the cultivation of cotton but objected to the stress laid on wheat and maize. In his opinion Egypt's soil was too rich and valuable to be wasted on grains. Instead he proposed to vary the crops by means of fruit, vegetables and dairy products, which require intensive cultivation and achieve

---

[40] *Annuaire Egyptien,* 1948.

[41] During the period 1935-39 the net income per feddan of cotton was £E. 9 per season, for rice £E. 4.850 and wheat and maize £E. 4.500. This calculation was made at a farm near Dikernes, but auxiliary data required in order properly to evaluate this income are missing (e.g. what is the income per working day on which these data are based, assuming that "net income" means the income which is left after payment of all other production factors apart from labour). Cf. C. Issawi, *op. cit.,* p. 64.

good prices.[42] Until the Second World War no serious advances were made in the proposed direction.

During the said period the height of the Aswan dam was increased, the Jebl el-Aulia dam was built in the Sudan (in 1937), and the network of smaller barrages and canals was expanded. Greater attention was also paid to drainage works, especially in the delta region, which suffered greatly from salination and swamps. The increase in the cultivated and cropped area and the high productivity per unit area became possible mainly through extensive use of water and fertilisers, in addition to the unusual input of labour. The use of fertilisers, mainly on a nitrogen basis, surpassed the standard of many developed countries, with about 60 kg per feddan harvested towards the end of the 'thirties as against 38 in Holland, 15 in Denmark and 8 in France.[43] The need for such concentrated fertilisation arose from the transition from one-time basin irrigation by flooding to perennial irrigation, which partially prevented the rich alluvium of the Nile from reaching the exhausted soil that rarely lay fallow, as well as from changes in the crop rotation.

In view of the polarisation of ownership and the high rate of the rental[44] the net income of the fellah was desperately low (cf. p. 227). At the same time the wages of agricultural labourers, which had fallen by at least 50%[45] during the slump, never seriously recovered afterwards. Towards the end of the 'thirties, the wage of an agricultural labourer varied between 2 and 4 piastres per day.

The situation in respect of agricultural credits during the first years after the War was disastrous. Gradually an improvement took place both through the expansion of the network of co-operatives which supplied relatively cheap credit and the foundation of the Banque de Crédit Agricole in 1931. By 1939, however, the total number of co-operative members did not exceed 78,000, while the credit of the Bank was chiefly utilised by the landlords.[46]

4. LIMITED RESULTS OF INDUSTRIALISATION AND OF THE DEVELOPMENT OF INFRASTRUCTURE

The census conducted in Egypt in 1937 showed that two-thirds of the industrial enterprises in Lower Egypt were founded during the preceding ten years. This was largely due to the government industrialisation policy especially since 1930, which was given an additional impetus by the spread of the depression, accompanied as it was by extreme protective customs.

---

[42] *Ibid.,* p. 71.

[43] As against an average of about 270,000 tons of fertilisers per year during the 'twenties, the consumption of fertilisers at the end of the 'thirties rose to 500,000 tons.

[44] The rental in its various forms ranged from one-fifth to three-fourths of the gross income, according to the relative rates of input of the fellah and the landlord. It should not be regarded as a rental in the accepted sense, but rather as payment for the input factors owned by the landlord (including the rental for the land leased).

[45] This decline in the nominal wages was indeed assuaged by a decline in the cost of living index, but not at the same rate, especially as the price of certain primary commodities rose following the protectionist government policy.

[46] Cf. Ch. Issawi, *op. cit.,* p. 79.

The change benefited mainly the textile mills—and particularly their chief centre at Mekhala-el-Kubra—which absorbed increasing quantities of domestic raw cotton. From the beginning of the 'twenties until the end of the thirties the local consumption of cotton increased from 2,500 tons to 25,000 tons, i.e., tenfold.

Part of the textile works enjoyed the backing of the Misr Bank whose large textile mill at Mekhala-el-Kubra employed 15,000 workers and served as a model of modern industrialisation in Egypt[47] although the working conditions proved appalling, in striking contradiction to the populist ideology of the founders of Bank Misr.[48]

The Misr Bank, whose paid-up capital grew from £E. 80,000 in 1920 to £E. 1 million in 1926, and to £E. 2 million in the 'forties, set up a series of subsidiary companies—17 in number—between the years 1920 and 1940, with a varying scope of business and different objectives. The main activity of these companies however centred round textiles, from production to the marketing and export stage. Other companies also engaged in insurance, navigation, fishing, mining, pharmaceuticals and commerce. The aggregate registered capital of these companies amounted to some £E. 55 million, and though the Misr Bank had been conceived as a purely Egyptian enterprise, opting only for foreign experts, less than 14 years later it went into partnership with foreign firms, in areas such as aviation, insurance as well as textiles.[49]

In Egypt, as in Syria, the Lebanon and Turkey, foodstuffs and textiles were the mainstay of the domestic industry, providing up to two-thirds of industrial output. The rapid development of certain industries served as a vivid testimonial to the fact that Egypt was capable of achieving self-sufficiency in those sectors where local raw materials were available and industrial processes lent themselves to relatively easy adaptation; to wit the sugar industry, which during the second half of the 'thirties produced some 140,000 tons of refined sugar from sugar cane, with sometimes up to 50,000 tons per year being left over for exports. Already certain further raw materials were known which might serve as a basis for an industrial breakthrough in new directions. These were oil, whose output increased from 102,000 tons in 1914 to 670,000 tons crude oil (of which 598,000 tons refined oil) in 1939; and phosphates whose output at the end of the 'thirties reached 500,000 tons and which were all exported as raw materials.[50] The development of the mineral resources, the expansion of the refineries and the establishment of a local fertiliser industry received increased attention only after the Second World War.

The industrial enterprises were mostly on a small scale. The following Table shows the number of enterprises and their employment figures according to censuses carried out in Egypt during the years 1927-1945:[51]

---

[47] *L'Egypte Indépendante*, pp. 332-4.
[48] R. L. Tignor, "Bank Misr and Foreign Capitalism", *International Journal of M. E. Studies*, 8 (1977), p. 167.
[49] *Ibid., passim.*
[50] *The Economist*, Dec. 4th, 1937, (Egypt), p. 14; *Memento Economique, L'Egypte*, p. 186-7; *L'Egypte Indépendante*, p. 321, and *passim*.
[51] Ministère de Finances, *Annuaire Statistique*; cf. W. Cleland, *op. cit.*, p. 99.

TABLE XXIX

Growth of Egyptian Industry, 1927-1945

	1927	1937	June 1942	June 1945
No. of enterprises	70,314	92,021	103,290	129,231
No. of employed	215,438	215,467	288,260	458,000

The above data include both industry and crafts. By the end of the said period only about 20,000 enterprises could be considered industrial undertakings; of these 13,000 employed less than 5 workers and only 40 over 500. The overwhelmingly small-scale industry is also reflected in the fact that of these 20,000 enterprises, 90% had an invested capital of less than £ 1,000 and only 2% of over £ 10,000. The preference of the Egyptians for investing their savings—if any—mainly in land resulted in a shortage of domestic capital for industry. On the other hand the local market preferred foreign industrial products. Thus the two factors of patterns of demand and deficient supply of capital combined to bar the development of local industry. Accordingly the progress of industrial development during the period under review was slow. Towards the end of the period industry contributed no more than 8-10% of the national income without as yet showing any serious prospects of absorbing the surplus of labour driven out from the village or keeping pace with the growth of the population.[52]

Inadequate investment per plant and per earner is among the important factors responsible for low productivity in industry. A comparison in Colin Clark's figures[53] between Egypt and a few other countries is shown below:

TABLE XXX

Productivity of Egyptian Industry (1937) in Comparison with Other Countries

Country	Net Income per earner in 1938, in I.U.	Net Income per working hour in I.U.	Investment per earner in 1935-39 in I.U.
Egypt (1937)	300	0.130	450
Japan	526	0.173	2,380 (1930)
The Jewish community in Palestine (1940)	600-650	0.280	1,850
Gr. Britain	870	0.765	6,600
U.S.A.	1,849	1.065	5,800

The combination of low industrial productivity with a small ratio of employment in this sector (about 10%) resulted in the small share of industry in the national income. As in many backward countries, an outside factor was needed to break the vicious circle of low investment, low productivity and low savings. The "outside"

---

[52] U.N., *The Development of Manufacturing Industry in Egypt, Israel and Turkey*, N.Y., 1958, p. 4.
[53] Colin Clark, *op. cit.*, pp. 266, 278 and *passim*.

factor might have been the government, by intervening in the allocation of resources and their efficient use, through industry-oriented policies in a country with population pressure and a growing disguised agricultural unemployment. But the government failed to meet the challenge.

The development and diversification of the national product and the creation of a wider basis for a market economy depended to a large extent on two complementary factors: communications and foreign trade.

Communications in Egypt were limited mainly to the narrow, densely populated strip along the Nile. While thus there was no connection between the Nile Valley and the expanses of the desert, quite a dense communications network sprang up in the settled part of the country. This was vital for the cultivation and marketing of cotton, which had assumed a central place in the economy as a cash crop, destined mainly for foreign markets. In the 19th century Egypt's rulers were prompted by additional considerations—such as industrialisation experiments, defence and conspicuity—to promote the development of canals and railways and to a lesser extent roads. As a result attention was drawn to the transport and communications sector. The railway line between Cairo and Alexandria was constructed as early as 1851, and by 1880 the lines reached 1,300 km in length. On the eve of World War I the entire network comprised 5,000 km, two-thirds being State-owned. This was quite a large network considering the still low level of economic activity and mobility of the population.[54] During the Second World War it was extended by approximately another 1,000 km.

At the end of the 'thirties, the main railways of Egypt operated between Shelal-Alexandria: 1,098 km; Cairo-Port Said: 237 km; Tanta-Damietta: 116 km; Cairo-Suez: 155 km; Port Said-Ismailia-Suez: 156 km; and Alexandria-Mersa-Matrukh: 312 km.[55]

The long section between Cairo and Aswan had a double line; on the other hand there was no direct railway connection between the ports of Alexandria and Port Said, and, except along the Mediterranean shore, there was no railway communication between the eastern and western part of the country. Despite differential tariffs favouring various export items, the railway services operated satisfactorily from the business point of view, and the annual balances of account showed quite considerable surpluses during the period under review.

The geographic structure of the country and the concentration of the population in certain areas led to a considerable duplication among various communication services. Accordingly those services which received the greatest attention and government support, namely the railways, developed particularly well. The roads and partly also the navigation routes (by the end of the 'thirties there were some 6,000 km of internal navigation routes on the Nile and along the canals, of which 1,700 km were fit for the passage of larger ships) largely ran parallel with the railways and were unable to compete with them, especially in view of the poor state of the roads and of the canals and Nile shipping installations. The river ports were

---

[54] Cf. Ch. Issawi, *Egypt, etc.,* 99-100.
[55] *L'Egypte Indépendante,* pp. 261-2.

of a low standard and there was no navigation route from east to west. Most of the roads, covering a total length of 9,000 km, were neglected and only about 1,000 km were paved. The total number of motor cars amounted to 30,000 and there was one car per 500 inhabitants in 1939, i.e., more than twice the rate, for instance, in Syria but only one-tenth of the world average (two years earlier).[56]

There was only a slight degree of co-ordination between the various services although the management of the government railways also had certain interests in the navigation companies and in motorised traffic. The Suez Canal combined its function as an international waterway with that of inland transportation, but this had already been discussed in a separate chapter.

5. THE STRUCTURE AND TRENDS OF FOREIGN TRADE

Egypt, which in the distant past and still at the beginning of the 19th century had been an important foreign supplier of grains, within a short time turned into a net importer of grains as a result of two principal factors: 1) the rapid growth of the population since the middle of the 19th century; 2) the increasing monocultural concentration on the cultivation of cotton. Denied large-scale capital imports after the First World War, the dependence of Egypt's import volume on export receipts became most marked, being in fact dependent on the receipts for one single export item, namely cotton. Whilst indeed the share of cotton among total export receipts declined from 92% in 1930 to 72% in 1939, the predominance of a single item still remained practically unparalleled as compared with most economies. In view of extensive exports and good cotton prices achieved in the 'twenties, imports also reached a high level and the trade balance was favourable throughout most of this decade.

In the years 1919-24 the average yearly imports amounted to £E. 68.8 million, and exports to £E. 74.1 million, i.e., an annual average surplus of £E. 5.3 million.[57] The world depression effected an extreme turnabout both in limiting trade generally and in the creation of serious deficits for several years, especially owing to deteriorating terms of trade from the second half of the 'twenties onwards. But the measures adopted by the government as from 1930 helped to improve the situation. The annual export and import averages during the period 1931-5 were balanced by import cuts, with average yearly imports of £ 29.9 million and exports of £ 30.4 million, i.e., a small average surplus of £ 0.5 million. During the years 1936-7 the average surplus increased to £ 2.0 million, but in 1938 deficits started recurring.[58] During the middle of the 'thirties Egypt expanded its policy of bilateral trade agreements in order to promote the exchange of goods by making easier the grant of import licences and fixing customs ceilings.[59]

---

[56] Cf. *The Economist,* Dec. 4th, 1937, (Egypt) pp. 17-23.
[57] M. A. Rifaat, *The Monetary System of Egypt,* London, 1935, p. 71.
[58] *Statistical Handbook of M.E. Countries,* Jerusalem, p. 67.
[59] Cf. Exchange of Notes between H.M. in the U.K. and the Egyptian Government Constituting an Agreement to Facilitate Commercial Relations between Egypt and Palestine (Aug. 18th, 1936), L. of N., *Treaty Series,* No. 4059, 1937, pp. 178-184.

An important change took place in the structure of foreign trade and especially of imports, as compared with the period preceding the First World War. While the share of foodstuffs in exports grew, their share in imports declined along with the increase of imported raw materials and industrial products during the 'thirties.[60]

TABLE XXXI

Structure of Egypt's Foreign Trade, 1913-1935
(in %)

Item	Imports		Exports	
	1913	1935	1913	1935
Foodstuffs	23.4	11.2	4.5	10.1
raw materials	25.2	29.8	93.1	87.4
industrial products	49.7	58.3	2.3	2.4
errors and amendments	1.7	0.7	0.1	0.1
	100.0	100.0	100.0	100.0

Undoubtedly, some of the changes in the foreign trade structure were considerably affected by the incidence of the world depression and did not simply result from changes in national product and development trends. At any rate it may be reasonably stated that the rise in the proportion of raw materials among imports and their fall among exports indicate increasing local industrial activity. Among industrial products, imports of which increased, capital goods for agriculture, industry and communications play a major part. Side by side with phosphates, cigarettes, cotton yarn, cotton cloth and grains, the central place among exports is taken by cotton—constituting 75% of total exports and the bulk of raw materials exported.

In fact the price index of cotton was identical with the total export price index. On the basis of 1913 = 100, it rose to 220 in 1925 and again declined to 148 in 1929. According to the basis of 1934 = 100, on the other hand, the index in the period 1930-33 was slightly over 90, rose to 113 in 1937 and decreased again to 92 in 1938.[61]

During the years of depression import prices also fell, but less than cotton prices. The measures taken by the government for the protection and encouragement of exports, especially after the removal of the capitulatory restrictions on customs, were of greater assistance to certain sections of the economy, such as industrialists and landlords, than to the economy as a whole.[62] The outbreak of the Second World War gave rise to new problems in the field of exports and foreign trade. While the movement of goods to and from Egypt encountered difficulties, a significant improvement occurred towards the end of World War II in the precarious state of

---

[60] *L'Egypte Indépendante, passim.*
[61] Ch. Issawi, *Egypt, etc.,* p. 117; *L'Egypte Contemporaine,* avril 1955.
[62] See p. 222 above.

the Egyptian balance of payments, whose debit on current account, including services and debt payments, was barely equilibrated during the inter-war period by Suez Canal and harbour dues, and British Army expenditure until 1935. Thanks to the Allies' expenditure in Egypt during the war, the country's reserves in foreign exchange grew considerably.[63]

---

[63] Serious attempts to draw up reliable accounts of the Egyptian balance of payments started in the second half of the 'forties only.

PART TEN

THE ECONOMY OF THE MANDATED TERRITORIES—SYRIA, LEBANON, IRAQ AND TRANSJORDAN—BETWEEN THE TWO WORLD WARS

1. ETHNIC AND DEMOGRAPHIC PROBLEMS AND THE POLITICAL STRUCTURE

I

A joint discussion of those Arab countries which were set up as mandated territories, out of the Ottoman succession, is made possible by virtue of the uniformity lent to them by their common origins as regards religion and race and the similarity of their socio-economic structure. If these, however, were the sole reasons for dealing with them conjointly, such a discussion should also have included Egypt, leaving aside a number of countries and Shaykhdoms of lesser significance at that time. It was the mandatory solution imposed at the termination of the First World War on a central group of Middle Eastern countries which provided them with a series of common problems and features until the Second World War. Responsible for this development were on the one hand the principles of mandatory rule laid down by the League of Nations and the actual policy of the mandate holders, and on the other the reaction of the local national movement. This national movement aimed at liberation from all political and economic dependence and though it reconciled itself temporarily to mandatory rule, at least in some of the countries, as in Iraq, Syria and the Lebanon, it urged an economic policy which would respond to their own image of the true interests of the respective countries and their peoples, and not to those of the mandatory governments.

It is not always possible to distinguish between the demands and the needs of the people and the economy as a whole, and claims advanced by particular groups, sometimes representing private economic interests, sometimes separatist national sects, and sometimes religious sects. The division within the Arab bloc was considerable, especially along the lines indicated, but as a rule those in charge of the mandated countries added still further to the spirit of separatism. It was indeed not easy to bridge the various conflicting interests, and every historian of Imperialism in the Middle East during that period must bear in mind the particularly fertile nature of the soil for a policy of division, and sometimes must lay the blame on the local population and its leaders rather than on their mandatories.

What impeded progress was the backward structure of society and the absence of a spirit of initiative and progress at least as in Republican Turkey or like the spirit which after the Second World War stirred up both the Western world and the peoples and local rulers of the Middle East. The inter-war period was in fact marked—leaving aside various declarations and promises—by the preservation of this rigid backward structure which was not much different towards the end of the period than at its beginning.

Highly typical was the debate which took place in this respect in 1928 at the

Mandate Commission of the League of Nations.[1] Lord Lugard asked whether the latest reforms in Turkey had had any reactions in Iraq; to this Bourdillon replied that there were none. Orts asked whether the "new spirit" and the anticlerical tendencies prevailing in Turkey had spread in Iraq; to this, too, Bourdillon answered in the negative.

The combination of the national-religious structure of the population and of the rigid occupational structure was among the most serious bottlenecks on the road to economic development, in addition to the economic policy, which will be discussed below.

II

The degree of division of the Syrian and Lebanese population was of particular strength in the region. In the first place, there was the sharply outlined division of the population among the various provinces, which also constituted separate administrative and political units (with a large measure of autonomy in local government, despite the decisive influence of the mandatories over such local government as well). According to the data of the League of Nations, partly based on censuses and partly on estimates derived from registrations of changes in personal status, the distribution of the population according to districts was as follows:[2]

TABLE XXXII

Distribution of the Population in the French Mandate Area, 1921-1938

	1921-3	1932	1938
Syria	986,000	1,562,000	2,044,000
Lebanon	710,000	836,000	850,000
Latakiya (the Alawi State)	261,000	340,000	372,000
Sanjak of Alexandretta	212,000	186,000	228,000
The Jebel Druze	50,000	64,000	71,000
Beduins	250,000	200,000	200,000
Total	2,469,000	3,188,000	3,765,000

As a result of this distribution, the density of the population in the Lebanon was 80-90 persons per sq. km, whereas in Syria it was only about 10. About one-third of the population of Syria and the Lebanon at this time lived in the cities, while the proportion of the urban population in the Alawi State and the Jebel Druze was negligible.[3]

---

[1] League of Nations, *Permanent Mandates Commission,* 14th Session, Oct./Nov. 1928, p. 172.
[2] L. of N., *The Mandates System,* Geneva, 1945, pp. 86-87. In view of the doubtful nature of the estimates and the low standard of the censuses (from which the population frequently escaped to other districts) the figures should be treated with considerable reservations.
[3] Crédit Foncier d'Algérie et de Tunisie, *Répertoire Economique et Financier de la Syrie et du Liban,* Paris, 1932, p. 48.

The division of the population among the districts was of unique significance under the particular conditions of the country. It should not be regarded as the usual territorial distribution obtaining everywhere. The French mandatory encouraged it by administrative and political means, with the justification that it corresponded to a large measure with religious or tribal division.

The area under the French Mandate was marked by profound religious division, especially in the Lebanon, half of whose population was Christian. Among the Muslims there were at least 5 different sects, among the Christians 10, while in addition there were Jews, Yazidis and others.

The French government interpreted the claim for maximum autonomy contained in the Mandate of June 24th, 1922 by encouraging the existence of a large number of administrative political units.[4] From time to time local economic circles, especially in the Syrian district, complained to the Mandates Commission of the League of Nations that this division was causing exaggerated administrative and other expenses.[5]

The religious structure implied that those who clamoured for greater unity would be the Muslims, who under a uniform framework were liable to receive a majority and gain decisive influence, while the Christians supported regional autonomy. When temporarily a Federation of local governments was formed (Damascus, Aleppo [united on January 1st, 1925], the Jebel Druze, and the Alawi State), Lebanon remained outside the Federation. The French representative at the League of Nations explained that Lebanon had *de facto* always, and from 1861 on also *de jure*, constituted a separate area distinct from other parts of the Ottoman Empire, according to the "Regulations for Governing the Lebanon" of June 19th, 1861, amended and supplemented by the "Organic Statute" of September 6th, 1864. The two documents, signed by the representatives of Turkey, Austria, France, Britain, Prussia and Russia, had granted widespread autonomy to the Lebanon under a Christian governor appointed by the Sultan.[6]

III

According to the population census in Iraq (conducted in the villages mainly by the primitive method of counting the number of houses and multiplying by an arbitrary number of persons) of 1933, the occupational-residential structure of the population of over 3 million consisted of 700,000 rural and 500,000 urban residents, as well as 1,800,000 nomads and semi-nomads.[7] Other sources give a more detailed figure of 3,214,173 by June 1935, but excluding some migrating tribes and absent residents. Therefore total population has been estimated at some 4 million in 1936.[8]

[4] League of Nations, *P.M.C.,* 25th Sess., May/June, 1934, p. 56.

[5] *Ibid.,* 26th Sess., Nov. 1934, p. 187; at this opportunity these circles also complained of discrimination against the Muslims.

[6] *Parliamentary Papers,* London, 1861, Vol. 68, pp. 683-686; *Crops de Droit Ottoman,* Vol. I, pp. 139-154.

[7] *Iraq Times,* 27.8.1933.

[8] Himadeh, *The Economic Regime of Iraq* (Arabic), 1938, pp. 10 ff., and the *Official Iraqi Guide* of 1936, p. 271.

The religious and national division in that country according to the census of 1919 was as follows:[9]

TABLE XXXIII

Religious and National Distribution of the Population of Iraq in 1919

Religious distribution:	
Shi'ites	1,494,015
Sunnites (incl. Kurds)	1,146,685
Jews	87,488
Christians	78,792
Others	43,302
Total	2,849,282

The national distribution according to the same source was:	
Arabs	2,206,192
Kurds	499,336
Persians	79,908
Turks	60,493
Indians	3,061
Europeans	292
Total	2,849,282

This religious-national division was among the decisive causes for the lack of political stability in Iraq. Tension continued throughout that period particularly owing to the aspirations of the Kurds for autonomy and British intervention on the side of the government. No less complicated was the problem of the Assyrians, despite their small number (less than 40,000). Their fears as Christians living under the Muslim regime turned out to be well-founded when at the beginning of the 'thirties thousands were slaughtered with the active assistance of the Iraq army.[10] Under the auspices of the League of Nations and with the consent of France, provision had to be made for the transfer of the remaining Assyrians and their resettlement in the Levant.[11]

In constrast to other Arab countries, the Shi'ites constituted a majority among the Muslims in Iraq even if the Kurds (who are not Arabs) are included among the Sunnites.

In spite of considerable, and to a certain degree successful, efforts on the part of the government during the 'twenties to promote the settlement of nomads in Iraq by means of improved communications, irrigation installations and living conditions,

---

[9] League of Nations, *Mandates*, Geneva, May 21st, 1928; cf. E. Main, *Iraq*, Allen and Unwin, London, 1935, p. 133. In the national statistics the Jews are divided up among the remaining national groups.
[10] Cf. R. S. H. Stafford, *The Tragedy of the Assyrians*, London, 1935, Ch. XI.
[11] Cf. League of Nations, *Settlement of the Assyrians of Iraq*, Geneva, 1936.

their proportion in the total population remained very high. Nevertheless tribal bonds gradually weakened as government authority penetrated to distant parts.[12]

IV

In Transjordan no population census was carried out during the said period. Official estimates put the number of the population at the beginning of the 'twenties at 200,000, in 1926 at 300,000,[13] and the same number again in 1938. During the 'thirties the rate of natural increase tended to rise, from 1.02% in 1934 to 2.76% in 1939, mainly due to the fall in the death rate to 1.76% in 1939, at a high birth rate of 4.5%. Therefore population figures for 1926 and 1938, above, are of course very rough estimates. This, in addition to the great mobility of the nomads, accounts for the identical figure in both years in spite of the significant natural increase. The overall density of the population was 3.4 persons per sq. km, and per cultivated area (4,600 sq. km) 67 persons per sq. km. The settled population (in town and village) was estimated at 55%, the nomads at 13%, and the semi-nomads at 32% (in 1943).

V

One of the results of this demographic structure in the mandated territories was the lack of political stability. While most of the stipulations of the Sévres Treaty of August 10th, 1920, with respect to Turkey were abandoned and subsequently replaced by the Lausanne Treaty, its provision with respect to the separation of the non-Turkish provinces from the body of the former Empire was duly carried out by the Western Powers with the approval of the League of Nations. Most of these provinces were given the status of mandated territories, temporarily subject to the effective rule of the mandatory countries.

In the mandated, or semi-mandated countries as in Iraq, the mandatory powers tried to set up local governments and even parliaments. According to the constitution of 1924 (as amended in 1925)[14] Iraq was "a sovereign, independent and free State" and though the Senate was appointed by the King, the House of Representatives was chosen in general elections where the vote was given to males only. However, under the existing social structure and under the conditions of the Mandate, the implementation of quite a liberal constitution remained illusory. Constant uprisings[15] and frequent changes of government highlighted the political instability of Iraq. Thus during the years 1921-33 the country had 15 governments, and in the short period 1933-36, 21 governments.[16] The declaration of full

---

[12] E. Dowson, *op. cit.*, p. 27.
[13] L. of N., *Mandates, Statistical Information,* Oct. 1933, p. 6.
[14] League of Nations, *Official Journal,* May 1929, pp. 802-817.
[15] Sir H. Dobbs, in L. of N., *P.M.C.,* 10th Sess., p. 45.
[16] Cf. G. Kirk, *A Short History of the Middle East*, p. 176.

independence and Iraq's admission to the League of Nations in 1932 failed to enhance the stability of the regime.

In Syria formal independence under the guidance of the mandatory power—France—was declared by the Sèvres Treaty. Syria was divided into 3 autonomous provinces, side by side with the Lebanon which continued its traditional autonomy likewise within the scope of the mandate.[17]

In 1926 a republic was declared in the Lebanon upon the arrival of the first civilian High Commissioner (after suppression of the Druze uprising). However the attempt to establish independent governments in Syria and the Lebanon in the course of the 'thirties failed owing to lack of co-operation between the local inhabitants and the French, despite the initialling of an agreement between Syria, the Lebanon and France in 1936 which envisaged Syrian and Lebanese independence within 3 years.[18]

Transjordan too was not left unscathed by the vicissitudes of fortune after the end of the First World War. After 400 years of Turkish rule the country was conquered by the British in 1917. During the four subsequent years it remained almost without any effective rule, although in 1920 Faysal, the King of Syria, served as nominal ruler. With the removal of Faysal from Syria by the French in July that year, a vacuum was again created in Transjordan. Three governments were set up in Ajlun, Belka and Kerak, which refused to amalgamate. Abdullah, the son of Hussayn, was appointed Emir of Transjordan by the British as late as March 1921, within the scope of the joint Mandate of Palestine and Transjordan. In 1922 Transjordan was in fact split off from Palestine, although the High Commissioner for Palestine was appointed over Transjordan as well through his representative in Amman. Until the Second World War the political status of Transjordan remained unchanged, except for the incorporation of the Maan-Aqaba district in June 1925, which was given up by Ali, the then ruler of the Hedjaz, in favour of his brother, Abdullah.

The lack of political stability in the mandated countries, the constant religious, tribal and national squabbles and the struggle among the pretenders for Arab Muslim leadership for various thrones (all under terms of dependency on mandatory powers) consumed most of the energy and time of the ruling classes. Only little energy and initiative were thus left over for economic efforts which hardly enjoyed a sumptuous tradition.

2. ECONOMIC POLICY AND REALITY

I

During the inter-war period the consciousness grew in several Middle Eastern countries that the utilisation of existing idle or only partially exploited production factors, both in labour potential and natural resources, might facilitate the expansion of investments and, consequently, render increase in income possible. In

---

[17] H. S. J. Lammens, *La Syrie,* 1921, pp. 262-264.
[18] League of Nations, *P.M.C.,* 33rd Sess., Nov. 1937, pp. 13-16.

turn, increased income might result in larger savings and investment funds without infringing upon consumption. Few economic surveys carried out during that period confirmed the existence of such resources, but showed that social and technological bottlenecks had interfered with their efficient exploitation in the past.

At the end of the First World War, considerable unemployment prevailed in the French and British mandated territories while the absence of progressive social legislation aggravated the state of the unemployed and their families. The increase in labour supply, accompanied by shortage of capital and credit facilities, on the one hand, and inadequate know-how, skills and economic organisation, on the other - resulted in continuous underemployment. Following the 1929 depression, unemployment in the French mandated territories alone increased to 150,000 men, i.e., nearly 20% of the entire labour force (apart from disguised unemployment).[19] Long-range employment-oriented development strategies were hardly part of the economic policy of the mandatory regimes.

This was a period of growing autarchic and protectionist tendencies all over the world, intensified on the outbreak of the world depression. At the same time the provisions of the mandates limited the freedom of the mandated countries in protecting their commerce.[20] With a large degree of justification a Beirut journal wrote: "No Member-State of the League of Nations Assembly in Geneva does, in fact, stick to free trade. But all the members of this Assembly demand the application of this system to Syria and the Lebanon."[21]

League of Nations circles expressed their concern about the economic paralysis which had overtaken the mandated territories. While pointing to certain steps taken by the mandatories by way of subsidies, limited credits and guarantees for local loans, they clearly opined that local development could not be financed out of the ordinary budget. The mandatories "must ensure the welfare and civilisation of the local population". This would require a considerable investment without immediate returns. Theoretically the necessary means could have been raised in financial circles—especially outside the area—interested in profits in the long run, or income from interest. These, however, were deterred from such investments by lack of confidence in the stability of the mandatory regimes, as were the mandatory governments themselves.[22] Suitable international guarantees were required, but by the time practical plans were worked out, the world crisis broke out and put an end to this solution.[23]

There was a difference in the approach of the French and the British to mandatory rule (as in their colonial policies). The French made long-range plans, and tried to ensconce themselves within their mandatory areas for protracted or even permanent domination with the aid of friendly local elements. Moreover in the

---

[19] *The Baghdad Times,* 15.11.1933; *Palestine Post,* 28.3.1934; L. of N., *P.M.C.,* 25th Sess., May/June 1934, pp. 88-9.

[20] See in Appendices, Clause 11 of the Iraqi Mandate, Clause 18 of the Palestine Mandate, and Clause 11 of the Syrian-Lebanese Mandate.

[21] Javy, in *Le Commerce du Levant,* Beyrouth, 17.9.1935.

[22] F. D. Lugard, *The Dual Mandate in British Tropical Africa,* 1923, p. 55.

[23] M. d'Andrade, in L. of N., *P.M.C.,* 2nd. Sess., pp. 197-8.

French dependencies legislation and administration emanated from the central imperial authorities. The British, on the other hand, acted on a short-term basis according to a method of trial-and-error. The British method revolved mainly round the initiative of the representative and his advisers within the area (colonial or mandated) according to the specific needs of each district, although His Majesty's Government reserved the right to cancel or amend laws of the local authorities.[24] However, as a result of the political conditions prevailing in the area and the general economic conception of the period, the economic consequences of the respective policies were hardly different in the two spheres of influence (Palestine forms an exception owing to factors over which the mandatory power had only partial control).

II

In the French mandated area the concern for economic matters found its chief expression in the establishment of an office called Service for Economic and Agricultural Affairs whose functions were land improvement, irrigation, fight against disease and expansion of silk and cotton cultivation.[25] In Syria and the Lebanon important foundations had been laid for agricultural and industrial development during the Egyptian conquest and the administration of Ibrahim Pasha in the 'thirties of the 19th century, when the cultivated area was expanded, credit terms ameliorated and agricultural improvements introduced while several industries were established, especially in the field of olive-oil, textiles and silk. After the War, several of these enterprises required rehabilitation and others expansion and development.[26]

Various development plans, since the days of the first Commissioner Gouraud until those of de Martel, did not advance beyond the theoretical stage for different causes, such as emigration from the country, abandonment of the land, lack of capital and political upheavals.[27] The demand for a more dynamic approach arose with the arrival of de Martel at the end of 1933.[28] The stress was laid on road, railway, port and irrigation development within the scope of a six year development

---

[24] Lord Lugard, in *The Dependencies of the British Empire and the Responsibilities they Involve*, 1928, p. 6: "This lack of uniformity, this absence of any desire to make them all conform to a stereotyped pattern, is a distinguishing feature of the British dependencies in contrast to their French and Portuguese neighbours". In his book: *The Dual Mandate in British Tropical Africa*, 1923, in part. pp. 59-60, 91, 278-9, Lugard explains at greater length the differences between the British and French conception both as he understands them and on the basis of French authorities like M. Leroy Beaulieu, or M. de Caix.

[25] Raymond O'Zoux, *Les Etats du Levant sous Mandat Français,* Larose-Paris, 1931, p. 67.

[26] For some ideas on this subject see, Arthur Ruppin, *Syrien als Wirtschaftsgebiet,* 1920, in particular pp. 217-227.

[27] E. Topf, *Die Staatenbildung in den Arabischen Teilen der Türkei seit dem Weltkriege nach Entstehung, Bedeutung und Lebensfähigkeit,* Hamburg, 1929, p. 45; P. K. Hitti, *Lebanon in History*, Macmillan & Co., London, 1957, p. 493.

[28] *L'Orient,* 23.11.1933.

plan.[29] Local circles also put forward claims of autarchy in view of similar trends in other parts of the world. It should be noted that such claims were voiced at the time in other parts of the Middle East as well, partly as a reaction to the world depression and partly as an expression of the desire for economic independence, understood mainly in mercantilistic terms.[30]

There was a pronounced difference between the economic reality of the 'twenties and beginning of the 'thirties, and the subsequent period. The strained internal political situation and the persistent uprisings until 1925 instilled a feeling of impotence and insecurity, deterring both local and French investors, who pressed for securities and government aid even for existing enterprises. In September 1930, a decree (No. 3267) was published to provide urgent aid to industry. Customs on raw materials, fuel and equipment were reduced. But little was done in practice and the mandatory government was continuously requested to adopt measures for the encouragement of agriculture and protection of industry.[31] A ban on the French Electric Company was declared in Syria and the Lebanon in 1931. The official reason was opposition to the high service prices. In fact the ban and the numerous strikes, followed by lockouts, were directed against the government which in the opinion of local circles protected foreign companies under the cloak of the mandate regulations.[32]

The world depression affected particularly those sectors which were more closely connected with marketing and commerce, both internal and external. Hence the main blow was dealt to the Lebanon, which had a higher degree of economic and commercial activity than the rest of the Mandate. During the period 1931-33, 118 official bankruptcies of various local businesses were declared.[33] The French authorities claimed that in Syria the more harmful effects of the crisis were prevented by virtue of its being a country of fellahin living on their own produce, though even there the market-economy sector and the economic life of the cities suffered. Such indeed seemed to be the situation at the beginning of the crisis.[34] But matters changed for the worse, later on, and silk production was so severely hit by the depression as almost to face total ruin in 1935.

Economic revival occurred only in 1937-8. The condition of agriculture improved and the government budget enjoyed greater stability thanks to regular income from taxes.[35] Industry developed and prices tended to rise after the low reached during the slump. Between 1937 and 1938 profits were estimated to have risen at an average rate of 50%. Exports, too, showed an upward trend but while they rose by 33% in volume their value rose by only 14% mainly because of the increase in heavy-weight exports and the decrease in low-weight, but remunerative exports. Despite increased exports, the commercial deficit grew owing to a still larger increase in imports. The

---

[29] *L'Orient*, 8.1.1934.
[30] *Le Commerce du Levant*, 12.9.1930; 26.4.1935; 27.8.1935.
[31] E. Topf, *op. cit.*, p. 49.
[32] League of Nations, *P.M.C.*, 20th Sess., June 1931, p. 33.
[33] *Commerce du Levant*, 1.1.1932; 19.2.1932; 14.1.1933.
[34] L. of N., *P.M.C.*, 20th Sess., June 1931, p. 32.
[35] L. of N., *P.M.C.*, 36th Sess., June 1939, p. 241.

deficit in 1936 was 239 million francs, rising to 543 million in 1937, and to 815 million in 1939.[36] The general situation both in the economic and in social and political spheres deteriorated again in 1939. Schools were closed down, the number of prisons multiplied, political apathy grew and nepotism increased.[37] In 1938 the number of beggars in Beirut was estimated at 10,000, most of whom came from the villages of Syria and the Lebanon. Substantial sums had to be spent on their return to their places of origin.[38] The French mandated territory entered upon the period of the Second World War with a weakened and badly handicapped economy.

III

The affairs of Iraq were likewise managed under the Mandate officially approved on 27.9.1924 as well as by an amical agreement between Britain and the King of Iraq, signed in Baghdad on October 10th, 1922.[39] From time to time Iraq was promised full independence and membership in the League of Nations. This latter promise was fulfilled in 1932. At the same time the capitulations were finally cancelled after being severely curtailed by the text of the Mandate. Even such limited political independence prompted the local government, together with British superintendents, to tackle various development projects and plans which might have considerably altered the history of Iraq during the last few decades had they been properly followed up. A financial agreement between Britain and Iraq of 25.3.1924, interpreting the treaty of 1922, defined the terms by which certain economic activities passed into the hands of the Iraqi government. According to this agreement Iraq further undertook to meet its obligations concerning its share in the Ottoman Debt.[40] Certain valuable assets were inherited from the period of the War, including: a civil administration, fairly satisfactory security conditions, a telephone, telegraph, railway and road network, and Basra port. This infrastructure was of the greatest significance in a country standing on the threshold of development.

The economic plans comprised housing, labour legislation, settlement of tribes, draining of swamps and prevention of disease, assistance to agriculture, exploitation of raw materials, preparations for the establishment of agricultural,

---

[36] *Haaretz,* 5.7.1939; L. of N., *P.M.C.,* 36th Sess., June 1939, p. 234.
[37] *Davar,* 4.7.1939.
[38] *Palestine Post,* 8.5.1938.
[39] Rappard at the Permanent Mandates Commission stated that Iraq might be compared to double-faced Janus—one face directed towards Geneva, bearing the expression of a Mandate, and the other directed towards Baghdad, bearing the expression of a treaty. *P.M.C.,* 7th Sess., Oct. 1924, p. 123.
[40] According to the principle formulated by the Lausanne Treaty (see chapters on Republican Turkey) the successor States, in addition to Turkey, had to bear their share in the Ottoman Debt. Iraq's share was at first put at 7 million Turkish gold pounds, and another 2.5 million Turkish pounds as interest and expenses. By virtue of the agreements providing for an alternative basis (other than gold) for calculating the debt, Iraq's share was subsequently reduced to £ 1.6 million. In 1927 Iraq redeemed £ 1,228,000 worth of Ottoman debentures and the balance of £ 383,000 was paid in 7 equal annual instalments, until the budgetary year 1933/4. *Special Report, etc., Progress of Iraq,* 1920-31, p. 127; L. of N., *Public Finance 1928-1937, lviii, Iraq,* 1938, p. 10.

national and mortgage banks, encouragement of production and exports, savings, communications and government control over basic sectors.[41] This was obviously much too wide and ill-defined a programme for a country still lacking in sufficient resources and qualified personnel, and backward in its institutional structure. The Mandatory together with the local government tried from time to time to recast these plans in a more practical and well-defined mould as regards scope and time of execution. Until the beginning of the 'thirties, matters did not go beyond investigations and recommendations of numerous commissions which visited the country, like the Hilton-Young Financial Commission (of 1930) which continued the work of a previous commission (of 1925), of which Hilton-Young and H. Vernon had likewise been members;[42] Munroe's Commission on matters of education and training; or the Mission of Sir E. Dowson.[43]

Hilton-Young's Reports dealt with the effect of the world depression on primary production countries generally and, in particular, Iraq, which was hit mainly as producer and exporter of grains, especially wheat and barley. Prices were falling rapidly because of the reduced demand during the prevailing depression and world unemployment and the flooding of the markets with agricultural produce.[44] To these general hardships were added various local misfortunes such as the recurring scourge of locusts and lack of water during drought seasons. At the end of the 'twenties the cultivated area and agricultural output were considerably enhanced by investments in communications and an increased number of pumps (1,057 new pumps in the three years preceding 1930). However the farming sector which had suffered during the slump both as regards yields and prices was unable to pay the high charges on input assumed during the period of relative prosperity.

In the rush after quick gains the land, too, was over-exploited during the period of prosperity. Insufficient attention was paid to the preservation of its fertility by letting part of it lie fallow, and by drainage works or fertilisation. The market for dates, one of Iraq's main export items, likewise deteriorated.

As a result of the crisis, the producers abandoned part of their lands and even harvests in the fields. Whilst toying with vain illusions of a rise in price after the depression, they stopped selling their produce and thus merely increased their losses from stocks since the slump continued. To be sure, those who suffered most from adverse export conditions were the large-scale producers and European merchants, while the masses of the fellahin generally lived in a state of subsistence economy. But they too suffered from the depression on the local market—which nonetheless

---

[41] *Iraq Times,* 5.4.1935; 28.10.1935.

[42] Iraq Government, *Reports on Economic Conditions and Policy and Loan Policy,* by Sir Edward Hilton-Young, June 1930, Baghdad, 1930.

[43] See April 1932 issues of *El-Ahali*; also Sir E. Dowson, *An Inquiry into Land Tenure and Related Question, Proposals for the Initiation of Reform,* Letchworth (for the Iraqi Government), December 1930.

[44] The Report attributes the aggravated situation to the fact that the Soviet Union, which during the years following the First World War had played a negligible part on the world grain market, suddenly reappeared and offered not only its current surpluses but also its hoarded supplies. Hilton-Young, *op. cit.,* p. 1.

absorbed a certain part of their produce—as well as from dwindling yields and from expenses which had become unbearable under the altered circumstances. The great potentials of irrigation by rivers were extremely underutilised and even by the middle of the 1930's only one-fifth of the irrigable area was cultivated. In effect, the yields per hectare in all major crops such as wheat (334 kgs), barley (609 kgs) and rice (1,112 kgs) fell by 50 or even 75 percent behind those of Turkey, Syria and Lebanon, and Egypt in 1934/5.[45]

The depression in agriculture went hand in hand with a general depression in commerce, construction and every field of economic initiative which was checked by limited purchasing power. Many businesses went bankrupt.[46] Government revenue was inevitably affected, reducing the chances of a revival of economic activity by State initiative. Economic policy generally—not only in Iraq—had not yet learned the lesson of the crisis, and was carried along on the wave of inaction and inert, idle expectation.

The reports of the various advisers contained optimistic though reserved forecasts of future developments. They prophesied a return to a normal state of economic activity, but without specifying the time required and on the assumption that prices would not return to their pre-crisis level. On the other hand they suggested that conclusions be drawn from the depression in order at least partially to prevent a similar occurrence in the future. One of the means to that end in their opinion was a greater variety in agricultural output (with the stress on industrial crops) and in the general national produce so as to prevent profound upheavals affecting a focal branch of the economy. Other proposals included modernised, more efficient and cheaper production methods, and a better organisation of communications and marketing in order, amongst others things, to reduce the deficit in the trade balance.

This deficit was apparently balanced by invisible exports and a renewed flow of capital to the country (which was quite considerable during the War and the British occupation, but then came to a halt). However, in the absence of reliable data, all conclusions were hardly more than conjecture and guess work insufficient for a determination of the available resources of the economy and the planning of their allocation.[47]

Those in charge of the economic policy of Iraq encountered the same difficulty which was, and still is, typical of other countries in the Middle East, namely the serious lack of *reliable* statistical data in almost every sphere: population, national product, balance of payments, consumption and savings.

In 1931, a Five Year Plan was drawn up, consisting of three parts: 1) Public buildings (hospitals, schools, post offices, law courts, prisons, police buildings, etc.); 2) Roads, bridges, and telephone equipment and lines; 3) Irrigation plans. The estimated expenditure was 270 *lakh* (the *lakh* up to that year being, besides the

---

[45] Cf. Himadeh, *The Economic Regime of Iraq*, pp. 63-71 & 171. For discussion of actual developments in Iraqi agriculture, see Chapter 5, II, below.
[46] Hilton-Young, *op. cit.*, Appendix, p. 15.
[47] *Report of the Financial Mission*, 1925, p. 19; and Hilton-Young, *op. cit.*, pp. 4-5.

basic unit of the rupee, the largest official currency unit, equivalent to 100,000 rupees, or £ 7,448[48]), i.e., slightly over £ 2 million.

Three further plans of £ 80,000 were designed mainly for industrial development.[49] In 1935 a "popular housing plan" was prepared for the building of 8,000 houses.

Another two new development plans, one for three years in 1936 and one for five in 1938, were put forward. The first was intended mainly to set up irrigation works, roads, public and industrial buildings and to grant loans and subsidies to existing and future enterprises. Its budget was over £ 4 million.[50] The second, with a budget of over £ 8 million, was intended to provide municipal credits and to finance new banks, railways, irrigation, communications, military equipment and buildings as well as industrial investments. The oil revenue was to serve as the principal source for the financing of both plans[51]

These plans had their origin in the repeated claims for greater variety both in agricultural and industrial development, since many had pointed to the past failures of Egypt owing to its exclusive dependence on cotton.

Attempts were also made at raising the professional and technical standard of the workers, by sending abroad trainees in agriculture and industry, by setting up agricultural and technical schools and inviting foreign experts in these fields.[52] The general standard of education gradually improved, but even by the end of the 'thirties the number of pupils did not exceed 10-15% of all children of school age. Below are some data on the number of pupils in the years 1936-8[53]:

TABLE XXXIV

School Network in Iraq in 1936-38

No. of pupils	1936	1937	1938
Elementary schools	74,000	88,000	93,000
Intermediate classes	6,500	9,500	11,500
High schools	1,250	1,450	2,750
Total	81,750	98,950	107,250

Several hundreds of additional students went to special schools or studied abroad. On the other hand many of these included in the data attended schools of an extremely low standard where their studies were confined to principles of religion and exegesis.

---

[48] Cf. below chapter on Currency and Public Finances; also see League of Nations, *Public Finance 1928-1937, LVIII, Iraq,* 1938, p. 8.
[49] *The Baghdad Times,* 2.6.1931.
[50] L. of N., *loc. cit.,* p. 10.
[51] *Türkische Post,* 9.7.1936; *Iraq Times,* 2.11.1935; *Palestine Post,* 9.5.1938.
[52] Articles in the October 1931 issues of *el-Iraq;* also *The Iraq Times,* 11.5.1934; *The Times of Mesopotamia,* 16.1.1933.
[53] Iraq Government, *Statistical Abstract,* Baghdad, 1939, p. 54.

In our discussion of the various economic sectors, we shall see to what degree the various plans were put into effect and how the development of the sectors in question was affected. The official summing-up shows that the total government investments during the years 1927-39 totalled 9 million dinar (= £ 9 m.) approximately, but there is little information available on the extent of private investments during that period.

IV

There was hardly any economic policy to speak of in Transjordan. It was not accidental that a cautious observer like Rappard defined Transjordan as a parasite State[54] existing on the permanent subsidy of Britain and the civil administration of Palestine. The British financial support was in the first place intended for the upkeep of the Arab Legion and the execution of public works. While helping to expand the country's economic activity the central objective of these works was military defence, as was the case with the Transjordanian section of the Haifa-Baghdad road.[55] No more than one-tenth of the budget expenditure was channelled to constructive activities in agriculture, education and health, the rest being swallowed up by defence and administration. No attempt was ever made at industrialisation or at the modernisation and intensification of agriculture, while only about 5% of the entire area of the country was under cultivation. The development of the educational network also failed to give promise of any pronounced change in the educational and technical level. The number of schools (including private schools) remained more or less fixed at 200 between the years 1927 and 1939, while the number of pupils rose from about 9,000 to close to 14,000 (i.e., 10-15% of all children of school age).

Transjordan during the inter-war period constituted an artificial body politic, lacking a solid economic backbone. Apart from the autarchic economy of the nomads and fellahin, the mandatory authorities maintained the nucleus of all other economic activities through the government budget and balance of payments. The initiative of these authorities as regards development was unaspiring especially since the country lacked any local incentive. The local rulers invested their energies in political and tribal intrigues, and only a few sparks of economic initiative in agriculture and industry (to be discussed in the following chapters) foretold of better things to come provided that new resources of capital and entrepreneurship were to be discovered.

3. CURRENCY AND PUBLIC FINANCES

I

Hilton-Young, in discussing Iraq's chances of obtaining international credits, counts among the necessary conditions: a) political stability; b) financial stability; and c) currency stability.[56] These obviously are almost ideal conditions which few

---

[54] L. of N., *P.M.C.*, 23rd Sess., p. 119.
[55] A. Konikoff, *Transjordan, An Economic Survey*, Jerusalem, 1943, pp. 116-117.
[56] Hilton-Young, *op. cit.*, Part 2, Loan Policy, p. 3.

countries, especially those requiring extensive credits, can boast of. On the other hand it is clear that stability in the above three spheres is desirable not only in order to acquire confidence so as to secure international credits, but also for the undisturbed growth of production and adequate implementation of development plans desigued to raise real *per capita* income. Having previously reviewed the political structure instituted after the First World War, we shall now see how the currency and financial machinery of the Middle East behaved during the period in question.

The legal currencies of the Middle Eastern countries belonged partly to the pre-war regimes and partly to the new regimes constituted thereafter. Even before the War, coins of various European powers had been in circulation in addition to the Turkish pound.

With the entry of the Allies into Syria and the Lebanon the Egyptian pound was declared to be legal tender on November 1st, 1918, while the Turkish paper pound became invalid.[57]

After November 19th, however, when the French assumed effective rule over the area in question it was decided (in April 1920) to issue a local currency based on the French franc. La Banque de Syrie et du Grand Liban (the name "Lebanon" was added only in 1924), which in 1919 succeeded the Ottoman Bank and its various branches in the French mandated territory served as the central bank (though not in the full sense) and its issue department was in charge of printing the Syrian and Lebanese pound. In fact, this bank, in later years also, constituted a subsidiary of the Ottoman Bank,[58] and its banking department gradually extended its activities to include credit and discounts, deposits and investments. French control over the central bank and the entire monetary system through the Office des Changes—similar in its functions to the British Currency Boards—is evident also from the fact that both official and private transactions were actually made in French francs and that most of the data on currency circulation were published in terms of francs. The circulation was 258 million francs (or about £S. 12.5 million) in January 1934 and 423 million francs (about £S. 21 million) in December 1936. 95% of the currency was covered by francs, but a fixed ratio was established between the local currency and the pound sterling. The Egyptian pounds, which were taken out of circulation and exchanged for new local pounds, served the French administration as foreign currency for international transactions. On the other hand Turkish paper pounds were exchanged at low rates on the local market and then exported to Turkey where during the transition period until the establishment of the Turkish Republic they were exchanged at a higher rate of profits and if possible against metal coins.

The official rate of exchange of the Syrian and Lebanese pound—fixed on January 23rd, 1924, at 20 French francs per one Syrian-Lebanese pound, and fluctuating on the free market in terms of the dollar between 50 and 125 cents per Syrian pound in the 'twenties—stood at 45 American cents, or 2s. 3d., in the

---

[57] S. B. Himadeh, *Monetary and Banking System of Syria*, 1935, pp. 50-55.
[58] *The Ottoman Bank in the Middle East; The Banque de Syrie et du Liban,* London, 1948.

'thirties, i.e., one pound sterling was equivalent to 8.83 Syrian or Lebanese pounds.[59] Almost until the end of the 'twenties the Syrian pound was subject to sharp fluctuations on the free market—either because of variations in the value of the franc on which it was based, or owing to internal economic factors and lack of confidence on the part of the population, due to acute changes in prices, and all efforts at its stabilisation remained in vain. Only following the new French currency policy, especially since June 1928, was the Syrian pound linked to the gold standard[60] by free conversion to the French franc at a ratio of 1 Syrian pound = 20 francs. From then on the Syrian pound remained stable thanks to the stability of the franc, until 1936, when the franc was taken off the gold standard. The two currencies were again stabilised in 1938, being linked to each other at 40% of the previous gold standard.

At the beginning of the 'thirties, when the Syrian-Lebanese pound became stabilised and was accepted as a means of exchange, clearing and fixing of prices, the Turkish gold pound was still widely used. Gradually used less in actual transactions, it started to be hoarded, together with gold bars, to such an extent that in the 'forties and 'fifties Syria (more than the Lebanon) despite the abatement of hoarding was still counted among the countries which had one of the highest gold hoarding rates in the area, without it being possible to determine the exact volume.[61]

In the arguments advanced against the currency system in Syria, where on the whole the situation was similar to that prevailing in other mandates in the Middle East and for some time also in Egypt, two main points were made: a) that the close ties and dependence on the franc (or the pound sterling) ensured the stability of the local currency as long as the mother currency remained stable; but as soon as the latter was undermined, the local currencies became subject to upheavals, even when the local economy remained undisturbed and the local Central Bank had sufficient gold reserves available; b) that by keeping a high ratio of deposits in the Bank of France (or of England) and the investment of most of the reserves serving as cover in foreign securities—in fact French (or British)—local economic activity was hamstrung and the country required more expensive credits than the returns received from investments in foreign securities.

In fact these arguments, and especially the second, laid bare a major weakness of the mandatory economic policy, namely the lack of a dynamic approach to development. On the other hand the link with the mother currency, during the period of transition from one political regime to another and during the first stages of a modern market economy, ensured relative uniformity and currency stability by means of a better founded and more experienced system (naturally, as long as the mother currency remained steady).

The obligations of Syria and the Lebanon with respect to the Ottoman Debt, in which they had a nominal share of 10,870,000 Turkish gold pounds (considerably reduced later on by the agreement of 1929), created difficulties in financing the

---

[59] *The Ottoman Bank,* etc., pp. 23, 33; *Le Commerce du Levant,* 13.11.1931.
[60] Cf. S. B. Himadeh, *op. cit.,* Ch. VII.
[61] Cf., *I.B.R.D., The Economic Development of Syria,* 1955, p. 18 and *passim.*

expenditure budget.[62] As a result France was forced to subsidise the ordinary budget of the country until 1923.[63] From then on, budget surpluses started to accumulate, especially since payments of the Ottoman Debt were stopped on the excuse that other Ottoman successor countries had failed to meet their obligations. The French representatives at the League of Nations stressed that these payments were kept in a blocked account until resumption of payment. By 1926 a reserve of 220 million francs had accumulated, on which the High Commissioner was authorised to draw a sum of 50 million for expenses connected with the damage caused by riots. Political instability prevented the achievement of financial and fiscal stability. Once it was curbed it also became possible to increase the collection of revenues and reduce expenditures resulting from such uprisings.[64]

The agreement of 1928 with Turkey regarding the liquidation of the Ottoman Debt stipulated that Turkey would bear 62.25% of the debt prior to 1912 and 76.54% after 1912. The share of Syria and the Lebanon was 8.17% of the debt before and 10.5% after 1912, but a further reduction to 7.5% of the total debt was demanded and obtained in 1929. In 1934 these countries finally discharged their obligations to the Debt Administration while the total national debt decreased from 63 million francs in 1934 to 37 million in 1935. League of Nations circles expressed their concern lest this rapid reduction of the indebtedness might have occurred at the expense of the development of the local economy which did not have any major financial resources at its disposal.[65] De Martel argued that in net figures Syria and the Lebanon had neither a national debt nor a budget deficit; on the contrary, a surplus of 30 million francs had again accumulated which might serve for development, especially of communications and irrigation.

The taxation method in Syria and the Lebanon was still similar to that obtaining in the Ottoman Empire, although collections were improved and the '*ushr* gradually gave place to a kind of proporty tax, especially after the new assessments of 1929. Income from customs constituted over half the entire revenue budget at the end of the 'twenties and beginning of the 'thirties. On the outbreak of the crisis the revenue began to decline. The customs tariff increase at that time, intended mainly for the protection of local produce and reduction of imports, to some degree compensated the treasury, whose income from sources other than customs started to grow again only after the gradual improvement of the economic situation.[66]

The organisation of the revenue was defective. An outstanding example was the "banderole" system in respect of tobacco and cigarettes, whereby the government collected taxes—40% in Syria and 25% in the Lebanon—against grant of the "banderole" on the wrapping of privately marketed tobacco and cigarettes. In Palestine, where the government had a monopoly, tobacco and cigarettes yielded an

---

[62] See below.

[63] French military expenditures in the mandated area decreased from 740 million francs in 1921 to 225 million in 1930.

[64] League of Nations, *P.M.C.*, 8th Sess., Feb. 1928, p. 41; 10th Sess., Nov. 1926, p. 124; 13th Sess., June 1928, p. 160.

[65] *P.M.C.*, 33rd. Sess., Nov. 1937, p. 40.

[66] *Le Commerce de Levant*, 18.3.1933.

amount equal to that in Syria despite the much smaller population (one-third). Even a parliamentary commission demanded the establishment of a State monopoly in the French mandated area.[67]

This mandated region in fact had two main budgets: I. The budget of "Interêts Communs"; II. The budget of the various States and the Federation. The income of the first budget was within the range of 200 million francs per annum towards the end of the 'twenties, and served to cover the expenses of the customs administration, the Ottoman Debt, common services, postal services and the navy. The rest was divided as follows among the provincial States:[68]

Lebanon	47%
Syria	37%
Alawi State	8%
Alexandretta	7%
Jebel Druze	2%

The second budget (which in fact was divided into at least 3 subsidiary budgets: budget of the Commissioner, of the States, and supplementary budget) showed an upward trend during the 'twenties up to about 400 million francs, but afterwards a steep decline set in which was halted only in the middle of the 'thirties.[69]

The budgetary revenue for the entire mandate area rose from 150 million francs in 1921 to 312 million in 1925, and 600 million in 1929. This last rise stemmed largely from the decline in the value of the currency. Owing to the depression and the deflationary policy (at a time when the Syrian pound and the franc enjoyed relative stability) the size of the budget was reduced during the first half of the 'thirties to two-thirds up to three-quarters of its 1929 level, increasing again only from 1936 onwards.

In addition to the high ratio of defence expenditure to total expenses (about 50%), a considerable proportion of the expenditures in the French mandated territories was allotted to public works (15-30% of the total). The health and education budget was rather low—at first about 10% and then only about 7% (together).[70]

Lively banking activity was maintained especially in the Lebanon. Side by side with the above-mentioned Bank of Syria and the Lebanon with 15 branches throughout the country, the following banks deserve special mention:

La Banque Française de Syrie, was founded in 1919 as a subsidiary company of Société Générale, whose main business was to finance industrial private initiative and public works. Together with the Banque de Syrie et du Grand Liban it participated in the financing of municipal investments and the investments of

---

[67] *Ibid.*, 8.2.1933.
[68] Due to rounding off of the figures the total amounts to 101%. Raymond O'Zoux, *op. cit.*, pp. 151-157.
[69] *Le Commerce du Levant*, 21.11.1930; 5.4.1935.
[70] L. of N., *Mandates, Statist. Information*, Oct. 1933, p. 7.

agricultural banks. Its main seat was in Paris and it maintained 4 branches in Syria and the Lebanon. Le Crédit Foncier d'Algérie et de Tunisie founded in 1880 maintained during the mandate 4 branches in Syria and took part mainly in public services, such as electricity and railways, as well as in hotels and a tobacco company. A branch of La Compagnie Algériénne founded in 1877 was opened in Beirut in 1931 and another branch in Tripoli in 1932, which was active mainly in the field of agricultural credits in the Lebanon.[71] Commercial credit transactions were carried out by the three branches of Banco di Roma in Syria and the Lebanon. Various local banks which being devoid of savings were limited in funds dealt mainly with short-term discounts. Out of the 50 different banking institutions only about 15 operated on a basis of deposits, and only 6 had a capital of 50,000 Turkish gold pounds (or 217,000 gold dollars) each.[72] The weakness of the local banking system encouraged the business of private moneylenders among the landlords, merchants and others who in consideration of their relatively high risks collected interest of up to 50%.

II

The British Occupation introduced the Indian rupee[73] in Iraq (just as at the same time in Palestine it introduced the use of the Egyptian pound, which may also serve as an indication of the direction of the British advance during the First World War). The Iraq Currency Board was established in London only in 1931 at the recommendation of E. Hilton-Young. A new currency was established, namely the dinar, equivalent to the pound sterling and divided into 1000 fils.[74] To the Currency Board in London two members were appointed by the Government of Iraq, two representatives of three banks (Eastern Bank, Ottoman Bank, Imperial Bank of Persia) by rotation, and one representative appointed by the Bank of England or the Finance Committee of the League of Nations.[75] Hilton-Young himself served as the first chairman of the Board.

Even before the new currency regulations came into force, an amendment was passed by which the Iraq currency would in future be based not on the gold standard but on the pound sterling. The result was that when the British pound sterling abandoned the gold standard and declined in value during the world crisis, the Iraqi dinar was simultaneously devalued.[76]

[71] "Dix Ans de Mandat", *Le Commerce du Levant*, 10.7.1931.
[72] S. B. Himadeh, *op. cit.*, p. 175.
[73] One rupee was equivalent to one shilling and $5^7/_8$d. 100,000 rupees constituted one lakh. Hence the following ratios may be worked out; 1 lakh = £ 7,448; £ 1 = Rs. 13.420. *Report of the Financial Mission*, 1925. Cf. *Report of the Iraq Currency Board*, 1943, p. 2.
[74] *Report of the Iraq Currency Board*, 1933, pp. 2-4. The ratio between the new and the previous currency was:
   1 rupee = 75 fils
   14 rupees = 1 dinar 050 fils
   40 rupees = 3 dinar
   100,000 rupees = 1 lakh = 7,500 dinar.
[75] *Iraq Currency Law No. 44 for the Year 1931*, Art. 14.
[76] Various local papers compared this interdependence, and the simultaneous devaluation together with

Gradually the currency in circulation rose from 2,086,185 dinar in April 1932 (when the new currency was officially introduced) to 2,248,185 dinar in March 1933, 3,084,365 dinar in March 1934, 3,064,321 dinar in 1935, 3,760,313 dinar in 1936, 4,868,311 dinar in 1937, 4,838,300 dinar in 1938 (when prices went down) and 4,773,296 dinar in March 1939.[77] Throughout that period the reserves of the Currency Board in London grew to a much larger extent than the currency in circulation owing to considerable receipts in pounds sterling (which served as reserves and cover) and the relatively limited economic activity in Iraq itself. A similar method was applied in Palestine. The monetary and consequently the economic policy of the British government in the mandated countries was severely rapped for not using the central bank or its substitute for purposes of economic development and expansion[78] and the investment of most of the reserves in British and Imperial securities (in 1939, according to the report of the Board, p. 7, only one out of 22 investments was in Iraq securities, to the amount of £ 25,000).

Not before 1935 did the Currency Board decide to pay out part of the profits to the Iraqi government, the first annual sum paid being no more than £ 15,000, while £ 75,000 were transferred to the reserve currency fund. In subsequent years, however, these sums increased to 40,000 dinar in 1935/6, 81,000 in 1936/7, 110,000 in 1937/38, and 60,000 in each of the years 1938/39 and 1939/40. The reserve currency fund in March 1939 stood at £ 4,280,981, thus nearly equalling the currency in circulation in Iraq.[79]

The revenue of the Iraqi government at the beginning of the 'twenties derived mainly from customs and excise (44%), and land taxes (31%) out of a revenue budget of about £ 4 million. This ratio changed in the course of years owing to the introduction of the *istihlak* (see below) and the increase in oil royalties, so that by 1931 (out of a budget of about £ 4.5 million) the customs and excise brought in 48%, land taxes 9.5% and the rest came from the *istihlak* and other income.[80]

The *'ushri* tax which remained in force during the first years after the War was not paid on *mulk* but only on *miri* lands. Already in 1925 severe complaints were voiced against the tax collectors and their methods. The *'ushr* was cancelled and instead the *istihlak* was introduced—a kind of produce tax at first levied on the producers and as from 1931 on the merchants, as a turnover tax. In contrast to the land taxes, the *istihlak* gradually increased. At the beginning of the 'thirties oil royalties started bringing in greater revenues so that in 1932, for instance, the ordinary government revenue was 3.5 million dinar and the income from royalties

---

the pound sterling, to the custom of the Babylonians, Egyptians and other ancient peoples of burying their dead king together with his servants and personal aides. *The Baghdad Times,* 4.12.1931.

[77] *Report of the Iraq Currency Board,* 1933-40. On the outbreak of the War the currency in circulation increased immediately to 6 million dinar and more in March 1940.

[78] *Near East India,* 4.1.1934; 16.5.1935; *Iraq Times,* 2.9.1939.

[79] *Report of the Iraq Currency Board,* 1936, pp. 4-6 and 1933-40.

[80] In certain regions, such as in the vicinity of river Hai (Shatt-el-Gharraf), the landowners and the peasants vied for the right to pay the land tax—to strengthen their ownership claims over the land. *P.M.C.,* 12th Sess., Oct./Nov. 1927, pp. 18-19; P. Ireland, *Iraq,* London, 1937, p. 440; E. Dowson, *op. cit.,* p. 71.

another 750,000 dinar. The budget of the *waqf* property, which under normal conditions might have served as a major source of income, hardly balanced during the 'thirties and amounted to 80-90,000 dinar. Income tax was first instituted on 1.4.1927, but by 1928 did not yet contribute more than 0.7% of the total government revenue,[81] rising to 3.5% in the revenue budget of 1938/9, of a total of 7.8 million dinar. The *istihlak* together with other agricultural taxes at the end of the period yielded over 10% of the revenue, while the most important items were customs (about 33%), various indirect taxes (excise, stamps and services) (about 25%), and oil royalties which already at the end of the 'twenties contributed about 15% of the total revenue budget and at the end of the 'thirties about 25% of the total revenues.[82]

The growth of principal sources of income during the period 1927-1939 was as follows (not all items are included and hence the total is not equal to the total budgets):[83]

TABLE XXXV
Development of Main Sources of Revenue of the Iraqi Budget, 1927-1939

Source of Revenue	Yearly average 1927/8-1933/4		1938/9	
	In dinars	in %	In dinars	in %
Income tax	67,000	1.6	316,000	4.0
Customs and export duties	1,565,000	37.2	2,620,000	33.4
Oil royalties	645,000	15.3	1,977,000	25.2
Istihlak and other revenue from agriculture	925,000	22.2	924,000	11.6

Considerable sums were spent on internal defence in most of the countries of the region, especially during the 'twenties, amounting to half the entire budget of Iraq,[84] apart from special subsidies made for this purpose by the mandatory government. Adding to this Iraq's obligations under the Ottoman Debt, estimated at 6,772,142 Turkish pounds in 1928, with average annual payments in 1927/8-1933/4 of 339,395 dinar (the debt was liquidated in 1934), the pressure on the budget was considerable. Education and agriculture, and the financing of other activities for the promotion of production and development[85] suffered as a result

---

[81] *The Baghdad Times*, 18.11.1932; *Iraq Times*, 1.7.1933; *Special Report*, etc., *Progress of Iraq, 1920-31*, pp. 88-9; *Iraq Government Statistical Abstract*, 1939, p. 79.
[82] League of Nations, *Public Finance, 1928-1937, LVIII, Iraq*, Geneva, 1938, pp. 4-6.
[83] *Statistical Abstract*, 1939, p. 83.
[84] *Ibid; The Iraq Times*, 5.6.1933; Hilton-Young, *op. cit.*, p. 12.
[85] League of Nations, *P.M.C.*, 12th Sess., Oct./Nov. 1927, p. 35; L. of N., *Mandates*, 1928, p. 3; *Le Commerce du Levant*, 24.4.1936; E. Dowson, *op. cit.*, p. 71; *Statistical Abstract*, 1939, p. 82.

El-Ahali, the opposition paper, complained in March 1932 of the faulty structure of the budget and the grant of tax facilities to the wealthy classes. According to the paper, the distribution of the expenditure was as follows: salaries 60%, pensions 30%, miscellaneous 6%, development 4%.

(when investments in the Baghdad-Mosul line alone, including the Baghdad brigde, and in two flood-prevention projects should have cost £ 2.5 million). Such was the situation despite the fact that the revenue collected in Iraq in 1920 was three and a half times as large as that of the Mesopotamian province (subsequently Iraq) in Turkish times (in 1911).[86] Yet the budget deficits during the years of the world depression (and the crisis in agriculture, which still formed an important tax reservoir) swallowed up part of the reserves accumulated at the beginning of the 'twenties (most of the reserves were used for payment of Iraq's share of the Ottoman Debt). In the course of the 'thirties the budget was occasionally balanced but this was achieved mainly by part of the oil royalty income intended for investments and development being transferred to the ordinary budget.[87]

Total government investments in Iraq at that time were estimated as follows:[88]

TABLE XXXVI

Government Investments in Iraq in the Years 1927-1939

Annual average for 1927/8-1933/4	—	210,000 dinar
1934/5	—	428,000 dinar
1935/6	—	1,237,000 dinar
1936/7	—	2,400,000 dinar
1937/8	—	2,373,000 dinar
1938/9	—	2,464,000 dinar

Throughout, complaints were voiced against the high salaries, especially of the British officials who saved part of their salaries and transmitted them to England. Only gradually was the number of British officials in the Iraqi government reduced from 871 in 1920 and 1,839 at the beginning of 1923, to 164 in 1928, and 78 in 1935. A 6% cut was made in the salaries of officials in 1936.[89]

Despite their deficient structure, Iraq succeeded in balancing its budgets during the 'twenties, especially by reducing expenditures for economic and social ends. For instance, the expenditures for public works (including irrigation) which in 1920/21 were about £ 819,000 (or over 20% of the total expenditure) were reduced in 1922-26 to £ 200-400,000 (or 5-10% of the expenditure). The health expenditure was treated in a similar manner, and only in education was the expenditure raised from £ 100,000 in 1920/21 to £ 180,000 in 1925/6 (still constituting only 4% of the total expenditure).[90] The effects became evident in the 'thirties when the revenue failed to keep pace with expenditures. The underdeveloped economic resources were unable to furnish the required income. The general development of the Iraqi budget is shown below, including oil royalties on the one hand and investment expenditures on the other.[91]

---

[86] *Report of the Financial Mission*, 1925.
[87] League of Nations, *Public Finance, 1928-1937, LVIII, Iraq*, Geneva, 1938.
[88] *Statistical Abstract*, 1939, p. 82.
[89] *El-Istiklal, El-Iraq, Al-Ahali, The Baghdad Times*, of December 1932; P. Ireland, *Iraq*, p. 437; *Special Report*, etc., *Progress of Iraq*, pp. 26, 292; L. of N., *Public Finance, 1928-37*, p. 8.
[90] L. of N., *Mandates*, Geneva, May 21st, 1928, pp. 2-3.
[91] Iraq Government, *Statistical Abstract*, Baghdad, 1939, p. 81.

TABLE XXXVII
The Budgets of Iraq for the Years 1927-1939

Year	Receipts	Expenditure	+ Surplus — Deficit
Average for 1927/8-1933/4	4,195,413	4,320,609	— 125,196
1934/5	5,023,081	4,220,502	+ 802,579
1935/6	5,357,502	5,648,592	— 291,090
1936/7	6,026,776	7,158,961	— 1,132,185
1937/8	6,916,697	7,542,148	— 625,451
1938/9	7,838,497	8,134,303	— 295,806

The banking system in Iraq was too weak to supply the needs of the economy by other than government channels. During the depression, when the discount rate in Iraq went down as compared with relatively high rates in Egypt and Palestine, the banks operating in Iraq directed their liquid funds to these countries.[92]

III

In Transjordan the legal currency was the Palestine pound, from September 1927 until 1949. The Palestine Currency Board, which had its seat in London, managed the currency affairs of both Transjordan and Palestine. The profits were divided by the Board between the two countries according to the size of their respective circulation. The currency circulation in Transjordan was small; in 1931/2 it was estimated at £P. 150,000 and in 1938/9 at £P. 400,000. This low rate of about £P. 1.3 per capita prior to the Second World War was due to the limited recourse to the market of the fellahin and the nomads who lived under conditions of economic self-sufficiency.

Britain in effect sustained Transjordan financially. At the beginning of the 'twenties British assistance amounted to one-third of the entire government expenditure. In 1924/5, for instance, the British subsidy was £ 77,500 as against a budget revenue of £ 203,000; in 1930/31 the subsidy was £ 108,700 as against a budget revenue of £ 260,000.[93] From the budgetary year 1937/8 onwards Britain increased its share in the Transjordanian budget, which until the Second World War approximated half a million pounds sterling.

About 35% of the local revenue derived from customs and excise. The share of other indirect taxes in the total income was likewise considerable. On the other hand direct taxes (from land, livestock, *verko* [municipal taxes] and income tax) brought in only negligible amounts. At the end of the 'thirties, for instance, only 1% of the government revenue derived from income-tax, first instituted in 1933.

---

[92] *The Baghdad Times,* 19.1.1933; *Iraq Times,* 1.7.1933.
[93] League of Nations, *Mandates, Statistical Information,* Oct. 1933, p. 6.

Throughout most of the period about 60-65% of the State revenue was spent on defence, about 20% on administration and only 15-20% on agriculture, irrigation, education and health. During the period under review Transjordan had no need of internal or external public debts, mainly thanks to British assistance. Most of British contributions to the Transjordan fiscus did not enter the official budget, e.g., 75-80% of the Arab Legion expenditure and a series of expenses on services, administration and public works. Even the annuities of Transjordan's share in the Ottoman Debt were taken over by Britain.[94]

4. TRANSPORT AND COMMUNICATIONS

I

Within the framework of infrastructure communications and transportation were a central factor in the process of economic development. Good communications provided greater security on roads and in settlements, facilitated the mobility of the labour force and linked the sources of production with the markets. Due to the fact that already before World War I foreign capital channelled a large proportion of its investments to communication services, especially railways and telegraph and telephone services, an important foundation was laid for further development at a later period. The First World War also brought about an extension of the road, rail and port network, which afterwards became the property of the successor States. However the various transport routes remained incomplete, like the Baghdad railway, while others were put out of action, like most of the Hedjaz railway. In addition it should be remembered that most of the communication network at that time served strategic purposes or the needs of isolated private concessions rather than the comprehensive economic interests of the countries concerned. New needs arose in the field of communications with the increasing consolidation of new national-economic units after the First World War.

II

In Syria and the Lebanon the total length of highways in 1920 was estimated at 730 km (230 km in Syria and 500 km in the Lebanon) but only about 470 km were in a more or less usable condition. Ten years afterwards, in 1930, the general network was expanded to 2,100 km, of which 1,300 km were in Syria, 590 in the Lebanon, 190 in the Alawi State and 20 km in the Jebel Druze. At the same time the railway network amounted to 700 km, including the Beirut-Aleppo-Tripoli line, the Beirut-Damascus line, and the local section of the Baghdad railway completed in May 1935 (along a stretch of 72 km) in the north of the country, and the section of the Hedjaz railway in the south.[95] This section, from Damascus southwards, was in the middle

---

[94] Cf. A. Konikoff, *op. cit.*, pp. 115-121.
[95] *Revue Economique et Financière*, Cairo, 28.11.1931; *Le Commerce du Levant*, 7.5.1935.

'twenties handed over to a railway company (D.H.P.) which managed the entire Syrian network (except the Baghdad line) held as a concession from the Ottoman government, and only thereafter were deficits on the Hedjaz line avoided.[96]

In the 'thirties the authorities tried further to rehabilitate and improve the communications network. They preferred to maintain and extend the network of roads rather than the railways, which required a high rate of investment, hardly profitable in an agricultural country without rainfall for 7 months each year. But motor traffic in Syria was still backward, as may be seen from the fact that at the beginning of the 'thirties there was one motor car per 160 inhabitants in the Lebanon and per 1,000 in Syria. Gradually the situation improved, but again mainly in the Lebanon.[97]

Only slight progress took place in the development of the merchant fleet and the volume of incoming and outgoing vessels. The coastal shipping had to compete for traffic with the increasingly developing roads along the shore. While the number of ships using the ports of Beirut and Tripoli increased between the 'twenties and the 'thirties and the total volume of goods handled by Beirut port came to an annual average of 2.5 million tons, the volume of trade in the ports of Alexandretta and Latakiya decreased.[98]

III

We have been already stressed the growing importance of the port of Basra inherited by Iraq from the period of the War. This port—at which 400,000 tons were loaded and unloaded in 1914 and 4 million tons in 1936 benefited from considerable improvements, including a modern silo. By the treaty of 1930 it was transferred to the Iraqi government against 30 annual payments to Britain. The reduction of port charges on ships using the port encouraged traffic and reduced the price of transportation.

The rivers were used only to a slight extent for transportation despite favourable basic conditions, until major improvements were made in Shatt-el-Arab, where the river bed was deepened to allow the passage of ships with a draught of up to 29 feet (instead of 15 feet previously).[99]

The state of Iraqi railways was unsatisfactory, despite the construction of the famous Baghdad Railway in Ottoman times, mainly owing to the lack of a connection between Mosul and Baghdad (until 1940). Under the pressure of foreign advisers the line was completed in the 'thirties[100] and the length of the Basra-Baghdad-Kirkuk line reached 2,300 km, constituting an addition of 850 km to main

---

[96] League of Nations, *P.M.C.*, 8th Sess., Feb. 1926, p. 39.
[97] *Le Commerce du Levant*, 19.9.1930; League of Nations, *P.M.C.*, 25th Sess., May/June 1934, p. 85.
[98] *Le Commerce du Levant*, 14.2.1939; G. T. Havard, *Report on Economic and Commercial Conditions in Syria and the Lebanon* (June 1936), H.M.S.O., London, 1936, p. 25.
[99] L. of N., *P.M.C.*, 21st Sess., Nov. 1931, p. 104; *The Iraq Times*, 3.3.1933.
[100] Hilton-Young, *op. cit.*, pp. 9-10.

lines between 1920 and 1940. The railways, like Basra port, were sold by the British to the Iraqi government in 1936.[101]

In Iraq as in the countries of the French mandate special attention was paid to the roads, which were in an extremely poor condition. The actual improvement, however, was not great. The length of the roads in Iraq was 5,900 km at the beginning of the 'twenties, 7,200 km at the beginning of the 'thirties and 8,000 km in 1939, but only 1,000 km of roads were paved (macadamised or covered with asphalt) so as to allow undisturbed use throughout the year.[102]

IV

Transjordan, which in the distant past had been a most important transit country, distinguished by excellent roads along its length and breadth, lost its political and economic importance during the last few centuries and its roads too became neglected and covered with desert sand. Camel caravans and other draught animals served the limited needs of the country. Apart from the Hedjaz railway existing since the beginning of the twentieth century, a start in the development of communications was made only during the First World War. Even at the beginning of the 'twenties, however, the length of paved roads fit for travel throughout the year did not exceed 30 km. There were another 220 km of second class roads. Until 1936 little was done to expand the road network and only 49 km of paved roads had been added till then. The connection between Haifa and Baghdad *via* Transjordan was started only on the eve of the Second World War when other by-roads were also paved. In 1944 the length of the paved roads in Transjordan totalled 600 km, apart from 2,000 km second class roads.

The relatively greatest progress took place in motor equipment. The number of cars grew from 130 in 1926 to 589 (apart from military vehicles) in 1938. The highest relative increase was in trucks, from 16 to 230. The population of Transjordan at the outbreak of the War numbered some 300,000, so that there was one car per 500 persons, the same as in Egypt and Iraq in that year.

In the railway network of Transjordan only slight progress was made during the inter-war period. The country was traversed by the Hedjaz railway which had been completed in Ottoman times (1908) down to Medina in the Arabian peninsula. While a section of 436 km (a narrow gauge of 1.05 metres) passed through Transjordan, only the 323 km between Nessibin on the Syrian border and Maan were partially operated since 1922, and fully since 1924.

On the other hand the long section between Maan and Medina was damaged during the First World War. The rails were neglected and partially dismantled and stolen, and this section was not rehabilitated owing to differences of opinion among

---

[101] British participation in the management of the railways was secured also thereafter. *Special Report,* etc. *Progress of Iraq, 1920-31,* pp. 157 and 177; *Türkische Post,* 18.4.1936.

[102] *The Iraq Times,* 29.7.1939; *Special Report,* etc., *Progress of Iraq, 1920-1931,* p. 139; Banco di Roma, *Iraq,* 1938, p. 73.

the Arab countries as to the distribution of the required finances and perhaps also out of political considerations. The traffic on the active part of the Hedjaz railway in Transjordan was slight, causing constant deficits until the Second World War. The railways suffered from the absence of two factors which might have contributed to their full utilisation and increased efficiency: a) adequate local commercial and economic activity; b) connection with Mecca and Medina, which would enable the exploitation of the railway for the purpose for which it was originally intended, namely the pilgrimage to the holy cities of Islam.[103] Differences of opinion also continued as to the ownership of the railway between Muslim religious factions, who claimed that the railway was a *waqf*, and the mandatory powers in the area who claimed that it was in the nature of State property.[104]

Sea communications in this area, which in the past had benefited greatly from the port of Aqaba in the south of the country, had come to a complete standstill since the Arab conquest. Even during the Mandate the port remained idle, if one disregards a number of shipping boats which set out from the impoverished village on the shore.

5. THE AGRARIAN SECTOR

I

In Syria and the Lebanon, as in the remaining Arab countries, the settlement of problems of land ownership and tenure required a great deal of care and attention. Most of the land in Syria, except the large estates, was cultivated under *mushā'* conditions. The mandatory authorities tried to amend the Ottoman Land Law by regulations of 1926, requiring new registration of immovables.[105] The provisions also aimed at the distribution of State lands among smallholders and ensuring continued cultivation of *mushā'* lands by one and the same family so as to permit improvements in crop rotation and cultivation methods.[106] The Code de la Propriété of 1930[107] attempted again to bring about certain far-reaching changes by enforcing compulsory registration, annulling most of the differences between *mulk* and *miri*, and allowing the donation of both *mulk* and *miri* lands to the *waqf* only with the consent of the government. The law further indicated the means by which cultivation should be encouraged and a credit supply assured to the cultivators. The actual changes achieved, however, were slight. Special difficulties were caused by the *waqf* lands. Their control was first taken over by the French High

---

[103] The case of the Hedjaz railway may serve as an example of the fact that just as the lack of infrastructure may prevent economic development, economic paralysis due to other factors may render the infrastructure ineffective and pointless.
[104] L. of N., *P.M.C.*, 29th Sess., pp. 120-1.
[105] Regulations Nos. 186, 189 of 15.3.1926. *L'Indicateur Libano-Syrien*, 1928-9.
[106] L. of N., *P.M.C.*, 29th Sess., May/June 1936, p. 113.
[107] *Recueil des Actes Administratifs du Haut Commissariat de la République Française en Syrie et au Liban*, Beirut, Vol. 11, pp. 57-115.

Commissioner, then transferred to the local governments and again returned to the High Commissioner, while the Ministry of the Interior was actually in charge of affairs. The *waqf*, according to the tradition taken over from the preceding period, was perhaps more susceptible to corruption than any other domain.[108]

Corruption was also rampant in another most vital aspect of agriculture, namely credits. As early as 1930 the Mandates Commission expressed its doubts as to whether the purpose of agricultural credits could be achieved as long as the banks failed to evolve a practical efficient system for granting loans to the smallholders. The French representatives admitted even at a later period that the customary method was to grant loans to the landlords who in turn transferred them to the fellahin at a much higher rate of interest than they themselves paid.[109] Thus the agricultural banks failed in their function in all the sub-states of this Mandate, and missed the purpose for which they were set up. The largest and most important of these banks, the Syrian successor of the Ottoman Agricultural Bank, was the Agricultural Bank of Syria with 25 branches and a considerable degree of autonomy. The remaining agricultural banks were hardly more than departments of the States' treasuries.[110] The resources available to the banks for the grant of loans were limited, and consisted mainly of credits received from the States (provinces) and foreign banks while only a tiny share derived from deposits; the banks' own capital was likewise small. The debts owed by the fellahin to their creditors grew and their chances of repayment were very slight.

Agricultural settlement was another problem which at that time preoccupied the authorities. Special experiments in the settlement of the Armenians had led to the establishment of a number of model villages in the vicinity of Antioch. The settlement of the Beduins posed particular problems, to a large extent owing to the strained relations between them and the State. The Beduins were prepared to settle down and engage partially in agriculture, but refused to give up their traditional rights and to submit to the written law which laid down ownership conditions, imposed the duties of taxation and registration and forbade the invasion of others' fields.[111]

The hardships of the climate, the unsatisfactory ownership conditions and the lack of capital exerted a severe pressure on agriculture, especially since little was done in the agrotechnical sphere. In the absence of other crops, the groundwater which grain crops failed to reach was not efficiently exploited. Plantations had to be expanded and afforestation work was needed.

Various develoment plans started being implemented and showed quite significant results at the beginning, especially until 1928. The cultivated area increased from 700,000 hectares in 1920 to 1,600,000 and more in 1928, and as a result the grain output rose from half a million to one million tons; the output of

---

[108] *L'Orient*, Beyrouth, 30.6.1932.
[109] League of Nations, *P.M.C.*, 18th Sess., June/July 1930, p. 201; 27th Sess., June 1935, p. 100.
[110] Cf. S. B. Himadeh, *op. cit.*, pp. 223-237.
[111] *P.M.C.*, 36th Sess., June 1939, p. 213.

wool from 20,000 to 50,000 bales; silk cocoons[112] from 1,100 to 3,500 tons; tobacco from 1,300 to 3,000 tons.[113] Thanks to the increased output the French mandated territory became an exporter instead of an importer of grain. On the other hand the extensive method of cultivation helped to preserve the traditional structure of the livestock, distinguished by its large number of sheep (2.1 million) and goats (1.7 million) as against a relatively limited number of cattle (350,000).[114]

With the depression, the rate of improvement slowed down, and the difficulties encountered by agriculture grew. Particularly serious was the situation in the Jebel Druze. Efforts were made by the French at setting up the agricultural credit bank—but most of the benefit accrued, as mentioned above, to the feudal landlords.

The yields during the years of depression were quite good as compared, for instance, with Arab agriculture in Palestine. The yields in Syria and Lebanon were 30-50% higher, yet marketing difficulties marred the advantages of good crops. Cotton and silk were particularly affected. Both crops, being distinct market products, were hit more severely than the rest[115]—cotton until 1935 and silk until 1936. The rehabilitation efforts of the government combined with the boom which developed gradually on the international market succeeded only as from then in improving the state of these two crops. Between 1934 and 1935 the cotton area increased from 13,000 to 32,000 hectares and fibre production from 3,500 to 24,000 tons. The receipts from tobacco exports increased thanks to improved prices, and the export of Lebanese fruit profited—though only temporarily—from the embargo imposed on Italy in 1935.[116]

Estimates of the cultivated area at the end of the 'thirties vary between 1,300,000 and 1,600,000 hectares, i.e., around the level towards the end of the 'twenties. As in many other countries no further rise was recorded at that time because the second half of the 'thirties were taken up by rehabilitation and healing the wounds of the depression rather than by further development.

The intensification of agriculture made gradual advances in Syria and the Lebanon with the penetration of capitalistic methods into the agricultural economy. Cash was increasingly used for the payment of the rental; private holdings and the capitalist farm system started to replace the old share-cropping and *mushā'* methods; and the use of chemical fertilisers rose tenfold between 1924 and 1939 (after going down during the crisis). On the other hand, while the prospects of development were enhanced, capitalistic methods and growing mechanisation greatly increased unemployment in the rural districts.

---

[112] During the war mulberry trees were burned as firewood and the government did much for the rehabilitation of this sector of the economy.
[113] *Le Commerce du Levant,* 31.7.1931; 21.3.1932.
[114] G. T. Havard, *op. cit.,* p. 28.
[115] See Chapter 2 above; also cf. G. T. Havard, *op. cit.,* p. 18.
[116] *Ibid.,* pp. 19-27.

II

In Iraq attempts were made as early as the 19th century to stabilise land tenure by the compulsory registration of lands, but to the extent that such regulations were followed ownership was accorded mainly to the landlords and tribal chiefs. The vast majority of the fellahin remained landless. A great deal of confusion continued to reign in land tenure conditions generally. It has already been mentioned that landlords and peasants sometimes vied with each other to pay taxes in order to obtain title to the land. The problem of land tenure continued to preoccupy the mandatory, and subsequently the local, authorities; from time to time land surveys and investigations were carried out by various commissions in order to arrive at a new settlement.

The picture obtained from the well-known investigation of Sir E. Dowson in 1929/30 was very grave: four-fifths of the land officially belonging to the State as *miri* land, was held illegally.[117] In Iraq the Ottoman law was not strictly observed in that State lands were divided into two quite distinct sub-categories: a) *miri*, in respect of which the State had not officially waived its rights of usufruct; b) *tapu*, lands in respect of which the rights of usufruct legally accrued to the owner. Dowson proposed the drawing-up of a detailed land register, the introduction of improvements in the application of the Ottoman Land Law, the establishment of special courts for the settlements of land disputes and changes in the ownership terms of *miri* land.[118] In pursuance of the Dowson report, commissions for the settlement of land questions were set up in 1932 which covered in their surveys two-thirds of the cultivated land, and led to the Law of Farmers' Rights and Duties of 1933. The Government re-classified the categories of land, in particular of *miri* (*miri tapu*—recognising the tenant's ownership; *miri lazma*—belonging to tribes who had to pay rent to the State for a certain period until their conversion into *miri tapu*; and *miri sīrf*—genuine State land). However, little was done to implement the recommendations of the surveys and of the Government's regulations, and the opportunity for carrying out a serious reform was allowed to go by.[119]

On the other hand certain improvements were made in cultivation and especially in irrigation methods. Dowson estimated the entire cultivated area at the end of the 'twenties at 78,000 sq. km and the area fit for cultivation at a further 14,500 sq. km, out of a total area of 453,500 sq. km. These figures are later corroborated, approximately, by Himadeh, but both of them point out that only one-fifth or perhaps one-tenth of the so-called cultivated area was actually sown every year.[120]

In the north of Iraq grain cultivation did not advance during the inter-war period. In the central and southern regions—which are more arid and dependent on irrigation—progress was slow too. Before the war the Hindya dam was the only major irrigation plant in operation. Further attempts were now made to control the

---

[117] E. Dowson, *op. cit.,* pp. 17 and 74-5.
[118] *Ibid.,* 17 and 76-7.
[119] Cf. S. Himadeh, *The Economic Regime in Iraq,* pp. 120-137.
[120] *Ibid.* pp. 63-71, and E. Dowson, *op. cit.,* p. 11.

waters of the Euphrates, both for their better exploitation and for the prevention of floods. An agreement was concluded with France (for Syria) for increased control of the Euphrates which extended also to Turkey, the source of this river. Two new projects were prepared for the construction of two dams—Habaniya on the Euphrates and Kut on the Tigris at an estimated expenditure of half a million pounds sterling each. These plans had already been suggested to the authorities of the Ottoman Empire in 1905 by Sir William Willcocks.[121] The Habbaniya dam was to protect the region of the lower Euphrates against spring floods and assure a summer supply of water to central Iraq. An ancient canal found on the site was used to divert the surplus water. The main object of the project was to safeguard rather than to increase harvests, so that it should be regarded as an emergency rather than as a development measure. The construction of the first stage of the dam was completed by the British between 1934 and 1939.[122] Supplementary irrigation was achieved by expanding the network of canals, which in 1921 comprised 88 miles of government canals and 543 miles or other canals, and by 1927/8 691 miles of government and 702 miles of other canals, serving as ample evidence of government initiative in this field.[123] The number of motor pumps was increased from 143 (with 1,500 H.P.) in 1921 to 2,500 (with 90,000 H.P.) in 1939, and the area thus irrigated from 190 to 7,000-8,000 sq. km.[124] The private pump owners and even more so the manufacturers were severly censured for the large profits they accumulated at the expense of the farmers.[125] Frequent disputes arose between the owners of pumps and irrigation plants and the land holders upon whose tenure rights the first were able to trespass by virtue of the influence they had in government offices. No solution to these disputes had yet been found.

The salination of certain areas, especially date plantations, created difficulties and reduced the prospects of expansion. Primitive traditional means were not sufficient to wash out and desalinate the ground and exterminate the diseases which spread with the swamps. The sufferings of agriculture were aggravated during the years of the world crisis which were accompanied by continuous drought. Prices of agricultural produce fell considerably and an improvement started to set in only from 1934 onwards.[126] Some rehabilitation efforts were made in the field of cotton and afforestation.[127] Coffee-growing experiments were also launched.

The turn for the better in Iraqi agriculture became noticeable in the second half of the 'thirties, with the end of the crisis and the larger flow of oil income which revived general investment and marketing activity. Cotton production—as

---

[121] Cf. Sir W. Willcocks, *The Irrigation of Mesopotamia,* 1917, Sections 9, 17 and *passim.*

[122] *Reuter Agency,* 12.9.1934; *Davar,* 3.4.1939; Ernest Main, "Water Supplies of Iraq", *Journal of Royal Asian Society,* April 1933, p. 266-9. The company which built the dam was Balfour Beatty & Co. which also constructed the electricity and water works in Jerusalem.

[123] *Palestine Post,* 27.7.1939; *P.M.C.,* 14th Sess., Oct./Nov. 1928, p. 163.

[124] E. Dowson, *op. cit.,* p. 29; *Iraq, Review of Commercial Conditions,* February 1945, p. 6.

[125] *Le Commerce du Levant,* 10.2.1934.

[126] A. Bonné in *Davar,* 16.4.1935; *The Baghdad Times,* 1.7.1931; A. Ruppin in *Davar,* 8.6.1932.

[127] In 1933 a mission of the Botanical and Geological Institute of the Hebrew University visited Iraq with the main objective of proposing a plan for the rehabilitation of the forests. *Haaretz,* 14.11.1933.

mentioned above—jumped from 5,000 bales in 1935 to 19,000 in 1939. Dates, at an output of 250,000 tons, continued to contribute 80% of the total world trade in this commodity. Tobacco production increased from a poor 21 tons in 1930/1 to 6,000 tons at the end of the 'thirties, though exportation was not yet possible. On the other hand fluctuations in yields and prices of grains continued. Thus, for instance, barley yields per hectare were 490 kg in 1933, 740 kg in 1934, 480 kg in 1935, and 680 kg in 1936.

These fluctuations also affected exports; about 200,000 tons of barley were exported each year, but the export of wheat was more limited and unstable. On the eve of the Second World War Iraqi agriculture still bore a subsistence character, as reflected in the composition of the crops—with cereals at the head (over 1 million tons)—and the structure of the livestock—with a high proportion of small cattle.[128]

III

In Transjordan as in Egypt both the cultivated and cultivable areas are concentrated around the river—along the eastern bank of the Jordan. Hence, as in Egypt, the cultivated area—4,600 sq. km in 1938—constituted only a small percentage (5.1%) of the total area. On the other hand the density of the population per sq. km of cultivated land in that year was 67 persons per sq. km in Transjordan against about ten times as much (about 660 per sq. km) in Egypt. But in Transjordan, in contrast to Egypt, the cultivated land was not adequately exploited; most of it was non-irrigated while the use of chemical fertilisers was negligible. In 1938 the irrigated area in Transjordan was about 260 sq. km or 5.6% of the total cultivated area while in Egypt it amounted to almost 100%, in the Lebanon about 52%[129]

The condition of the Transjordanian fellah was no better than that of his fellows in Egypt and Iraq, especially in droughty seasons. In 1931, for instance, a Transjordanian fellah who sowed 120 measures (840 kg) of wheat, reaped 401 measures (about 2,800 kg) of which he had to pay 371, as follows: 21.5% for lease of the land; 16.2% for camels and animal fodder; 16.4% for ploughing and harvesting; 8.1% tithe to the government; 37.8%—miscellaneous.[130] The influence landlords had over State legislation enabled them to delay until 1938 the enactment of the Water Settlement Law which was to their disadvantage in that it made the government responsible for the distribution of water. Even after it was passed the law was not implemented. Land tenure conditions were particularly stringent in the mountainous area in the northern part of the country,[131] as evidenced by the large number of small holdings, and the large estates owned by a few.

---

[128] *Iraq, Review of Commercial Conditions,* Feb. 1945, p. 6; Banco di Roma, *Iraq,* 1938, pp. 39-43.
[129] U.N. *Final Report of the United Nations Survey Mission for the Middle East,* Part II, 1949, p. 27.
[130] *Falastin,* 30.10.1931. Possibly "miscellaneous" includes at least part of the labour of the fellah's family.
[131] A. Konikoff, *op. cit.,* p. 41.

Wheat and barley were grown on about 80-85% of the area and average annual yields in 1935/39 were 100,700 tons of wheat and 50,500 tons of barley. The supply of these grains exceeded domestic demand and hence these two products constituted the main export items of Transjordan. On the remaining cultivated area tobacco and fruit were grown, but the extent of these crops was still limited during the period under review.

4. THE INDUSTRIAL SECTOR

I

The first estimates made of the natural resources which might form the basis for industrial development in Syria and the Lebanon had been optimistic. It was pointed out that the iron deposits—especially in the Lebanon, Latakiya and Alexandretta regions—had been used in Roman times to make the world-renowned Damascene steel; that the brown coal in the Lebanon and Anti-Lebanon was used during the occupation of Mehmed Ali and by the Germans during the war; and that chrome had been mined for a period of fifty years, as well as asphalt and sulphur, which were abandoned owing to decreased productivity and growing competition.[132] Prospecting for oil continued, especially east of Aleppo[133]

Employment estimates for industry (including crafts) in Syria and the Lebanon were 10-15% of the total employment in 1914 while some even arrived at a rate of 25% and more.[134] The higher estimates however include farmers exercising various crafts on a part-time basis as well as those engaged in building, fishing, the railways service, etc., and should hence be regarded as exaggerated. In all events this mandated territory harboured an important nucleus for further industrial development, though while new industries sprang up after the War, the traditional industries were in a process of decay. Industrial experiments were carried out from 1930 onwards and local industrialists forced the hands of the government and of the parliament to consider steps to facilitate and aid industrial progress. The syndicate of industrial corporations in the Lebanon went so far as to demand a "guided economy" (economie dirigée) and the compulsory purchase of local goods as long as they were not over 15% more expensive than foreign products. The first results of government assistance made themselves felt as from 1935, mainly as regards textiles.[135]

The hopes placed in mineral raw materials were disappointed. Industry based itself mainly on agricultural raw materials, producing foodstuffs (beverages, flour, oil) and textiles (cotton, silk). In most branches (including electricity and cement)

---

[132] *Türkische Post,* 20.4.1933.
[133] *Le Commerce du Levant,* 11.11.1933.
[134] Z. Abramowitz, I. Gelfat, *The Arab Economy in Palestine and the Middle East* (Hebrew), 1944, pp. 157-8.
[135] *Le Commerce du Levant,* 3.7.1931; 1.5.1936.

Lebanese production exceeded that of all the varioius provinces of Syria taken together.[136] Lebanese industry furthermore enjoyed considerable variety due to the accessibility of both raw materials and markets and the relatively higher level of general economic activity.

The state of the tobacco industry improved considerably after the abolition of the "banderole" system and the establishment of a monopoly on March 1st, 1935. Yet while some had objected to the previous system (see Chapter 2 above), the new system was opposed by both producers and consumers, especially because of the arbitrary price policy of the monopoly, which was not governmental but privately held by the Compagnie Libano-Syrienne de Tabacs.[137]

In the middle 'thirties, Japanese dumping seriously threatened local industry. The authorities however took no immediate steps and even failed to impose the maximum allowable customs tariff under the mandatory restriction. The argument that such protection would encourage non-profitable enterprises hardly seemed convincing under the existing backward conditions, and in the light of the urgent need for development and the desperate struggle for existence of both the newly established and traditional local industries—and above all in view of the customs policy adopted at that time by countries which had full freedom of decision.[138] Nevertheless the government did not sit idly by. In the 'twenties the *ad valorem* customs duties were raised to 25%, and after 1928 the specific tariff system was introduced which made a distinction between vital and less vital imports. A number of capital and production goods (machinery, spare parts, raw materials) were completely exempted from customs as from 1931, while duties on textiles competing with local products were gradually raised. While the depression in agriculture and the cheap manpower which flowed to the cities favoured industrialisation efforts, on the other hand the domestic market for industrial products was impaired by the condition of the rural consumer. Moreover, with increased Japanese dumping and only limited government protection, new difficulties arose. Whereas the new industries were able to hold out and even to expand, the traditional industries (cotton cloth, silk, leather, soap) declined in output and the number of employed fell to half the 1914 figure in 1937. Since the absolute majority of industrial earners were employed in the traditional industries, this resulted in a total decrease in the number (and proportion) of industrial earners, including artisans. The renewed industrialisation efforts of 1937-39 did not manage to show results within the short time until the outbreak of the War.

II

Our discussion of the economic policy of Iraq has shown that despite repeated attempts to carry out extensive development plans most of them remained on paper, and that the main stress was laid on infrastructure and agriculture.

---

[136] *Recueil de Statistiques de la Syrie et du Liban,* 1944.
[137] G. T. Havard, *op. cit.,* p. 4.
[138] *Palestine Post,* 12.8.1935.

Though certain legislative and institutional frameworks were created for the advancement of industry, the results were poor. A law for the encouragement of industry was published in 1929.[139] In 1935 it was extended so as to exempt new approved enterprises from income tax for a period of 6 years and to release raw materials from customs duties. Gradual industrial development was ewisaged, in line with the conditions of the country.[140] In 1935 an industrial and agricultural bank was established. The Five Year Plan of 1938 to the amount of 8 million pounds sterling mentioned above tried to combine industrial development with investments in roads, telephone and irrigation.[141] However, this programme petered out before the implementation stage had been reached as the War approached.

The projects for mineral prospecting and mining also led to disappointment. Concessions were generously dished out to various businessmen and companies, including Twitchell, Philby, and other British, Canadian and American firms, especially for mineral prospecting in the territories adjacent to Syria (apart from the oil concessions concentrated in the hands of the T.P.C.), none of which bore results.[142]

Apart from the arms factory in Baghdad set up in 1939, seventy larger enterprises operated at the end of the 'thirties, including 20 brick-yards, 8 tobacco and cigarette factories, 6 woollen cloth manufactories, 3 cotton gins, 3 soap factories, 4 breweries, 6 flour mills, as well as few tanneries, and a meat and fruit storage and refrigeration plant.[143] Cotton carding plants had difficulties in the supply of raw cotton, though when the local cotton output rose during the second half of the 'thirties, Iraq was able to export a certain amount of raw cotton. The building of cement factories proposed by various foreign firms never got beyond the project stage. About half of the total number of employed in industry were craftsmen, while most of the industrial enterprises, especially the tobacco factories, were on a small scale.

The structure of Iraqi imports, where in 1938/9 textile products constituted 20%, clothing 5%, sugar 7% and cement 3%, totalling 35% of the entire imports, might have afforded quite a convenient basis for replacing imports by local production,[144] even at the existing state and structure of the industry and the still rather low local demand. It is thus seen that—as has been shown in the chapter on Economic Policy and Reality—factors other than comparative advantage or demand, e.g., poor human and physical infrastructure, impact of the depression and inadequate planning, have intervened to prevent a more dynamic development of Iraqi industry.

---

[139] According to this law enterprises were given income tax reductions, release of machinery from customs duty, exemption from property tax, and remission of excise on industrial products. *Special Report*, etc., *Progress of Iraq,* 1920-31, p. 215; *Iraq, Review of Commercial Conditions,* Feb. 1945, p. 7.
[140] *Great Britain and the East,* 30.1.1936.
[141] *Palestine Post,* 11.4.1938.
[142] *Le Commerce du Levant,* 26.2.1935.
[143] *Le Commerce du Levant,* 17.1.1934, 26.3.1935; *Türkische Post,* 24.12.1934; *Palestine Post,* 11.10.1936; Banco di Roma, *Iraq,* pp. 7-8.
[144] Just as the expansion of the cigarette industry brought about a decrease in imports, from 66,000 dinar in 1925/6 to 32,000 dinar in 1935/6, and in like manner developments in a few other branches.

III

While none of the Arab countries had a well-developed industry during the interwar period, Transjordan was particularly badly off. Even home industries were few and limited to weaving, oil and flour production. Modern machinery started to be used only at the end of the 'thirties, especially in the oil plants and the tobacco industry.

The main industries of Transjordan during this period were: wines, alcohol and cigarettes. The production of arak in 1939 amounted to 39,426 litres, wine 8,265 litres and cognac 17,528 litres. In 1927 and 1928 two tobacco factories were set up whose total output in 1939 was 32,439 kg cigarettes and 39,556 kg cut tobacco. The manufacture of cigarettes was the only industry which covered practically the entire needs of the country and worked with modern methods and equipment, and managed to catch up with the constantly growing demand. Both factories were British-owned.[145]

The cement industry developed only after the Second World War, and to a certain extent also the textile industry.

The industrial backwardness of Transjordan was due to the same causes which operated in the rest of the Arab world: 1) a limited domestic market owing to the poor purchasing power of the nomadic population and the fellahin; 2) the lack of a major entrepreneurial class as potential industrial investors; 3) the low vocational and technical level of the workers; and 4) the lack of cheap electric power. The concession granted in 1926 to the Jewish Palestine Electric Corporation met with strong opposition and was therefore cancelled. Hence Transjordan had no central electricity grid. The few industries which used motor power had to employ local generators. Only one institution, the Government School for Arts and Crafts,[146] provided proper vocational training to a limited number of trainees (50-60 on a yearly average).

No data are availble on productivity and wage scales in Transjordanian industry at that time. The reports of the mandatory government merely point out that in the 'thirties wages rose considerably, but they still lagged behind those of the Arab workers in Palestine. They further indicate that child labour under the age of 12 was prohibited and that various additional restrictions were imposed to ameliorate the labour conditions of youth above this age.[147]

7. THE OIL SECTOR

In the mandated areas, oil played a major part only in one, namely Iraq. Though in Syria and the Lebanon prospecting continued—unsuccessfully—especially under the extensive concession granted to the "Petroleum Concession", it was not until

---

[145] Europa Publications, *Middle East,* 1950, p. 251, & A. Konikoff, *op. cit.,* Table XI and *passim.*
[146] Cf. A. Konikoff, *op. cit.,* pp. 73-4.
[147] *Annual Reports for the years 1935, 1938.*

the 'thirties, when the first pipelines of I.P.C. were laid to the Mediterranean, that the question of participation of the transit countries in the company's profits arose.

Iraq was the winner in the dispute with Turkey on the Mosul area, with the strong support of Britain and by decision of the League of Nations. The Turkish Petroleum Company (T.P.C.) which received its concession in October 1912—reconfirmed as regards the Mosul and Baghdad areas on March 14th, 1925—was reorganised pursuant to the Red Line Agreement of 1928 as the Iraq Petroleum Company (I.P.C.) in 1929.[148] In 1931 its concession was extended over the entire region east of the Tigris against £ 40,000 "dead rent" of which half was to be returned when production commenced and royalties at the rate of 4 shillings per ton would become payable to the government.[149]

A concession for the prospecting and exploitation of oil east of the Tigris and north of latitude 33⁰ was given to the British Oil Development Co. in 1932 (since 1942, Mosul Oil Fields, Ltd.) against a payment of dead rent until the starting of production, royalties at the rate of 4 shillings per ton on commencement of production, and allocation of 20% of the output for free use by the government.[150] In 1938, a concession on oil production in the Basrah area was given to subsidiary of the I.P.C., the Basrah Petroleum Company. A concession for the area on the Persian border, which was handed over to Ottoman Turkey by the agreement of 1914 (and hence called "transferred territories"), was held by the D'Arcy Company, but not exploited. Its terms were adapted to those of the other concessions granted in Iraq and in 1925/6 it was transferred to a subsidiary of the British Oil Development Co., called Khanaqin Oil Co. In Basrah a refinery was further established whose products were intended for the local market. Here, too, the government received 4 shillings per ton of crude oil produced.[151]

Until 1933 the output of oil in Iraq was insignificant, not exceeding 100,000 tons in 1933. The output did not increase considerably until the completion of the two pipelines of a diameter of 12" conveying the oil of the I.P.C. to Haifa and Tripoli, when it reached 3.55 million tons in 1935 and 4 million tons approximately at the outbreak of the Second World War, or about 2% of the total world production.[152]

---

[148] The composition of the I.P.C. and the participation in its share capital was as follows:

D'Arcy Exploration Co. (Anglo-Persian Oil Co.)	— 2 3 . 7 5 %
Anglo-Saxon Petroleum Co. (Royal Dutch/Shell Group)	— 2 3 . 7 5 %
Compagnie Française des Pétroles	— 2 3 . 7 5 %
Near East Development Corp. (American Group)	— 2 3 . 7 5 %
Participations and Investments Ltd. (M.C.S. Gulbenkian)	— 5 . 0 0 % .

Cf. *The Red Line Agreement* In the Appendix 33 as well as L. of N., *P.M.C.*, 14th Sess., Oct/Nov. 1928, p. 162.

[149] Generally "dead rent" meant a fixed one-time or repeated payment agreed upon in advance, which the concession-holder paid to the government granting the concession, prior to commencement of production and payment of royalties linked to output. Usually this rent was afterwards not deducted from the royalty account.

[150] *Petroleum Times* & *Palestine Post*, 22.12.1933.

[151] L. of N., *P.M.C.*, 12th Sess., Oct./Nov. 1927, p. 38.

[152] Iraq, *Review of Commercial Conditions,* Feb. 1945, p. 7; Banco di Roma, *Iraq*, 1938, pp. 47-50. Iraq at that time ranked seventh in world oil production and second after Persia (with 8 million tons) in the Middle East.

In 1928 the participants in the Iraq Petroleum Company signed the "red line agreement" according to which they undertook not to act independently "directly or indirectly for the production or refining of crude oil" in most of the territories of the former Ottoman Empire,[153] except through the intermediary or at least with the consent of the said company. The foundations were thus laid for the operation of the oil companies in Iraq and other parts of the Middle East, though development from the 'thirties onwards proved that competition and vested interests of governments and companies were stronger than any agreements or undertakings.

The actual income received by Iraq from oil royalties at that time was still limited but the Five Year Plan of 1931 already allocated £ 4 million derived from royalties to various development purposes. During the second half of the 'thirties the royalties received by the government under the concessions averaged £ 2 million per year, a sum which seems ridiculous as compared with the royalties paid as from the 'fifties, after the output increased and the terms of the concessions were changed, but nonetheless significant both for the Iraqi treasury and the balance of payments as a means of balancing their deficits.[154]

8. FOREIGN TRADE AND BALANCE OF PAYMENTS

I

The Customs Union between Syria and the Lebanon of 1930 provided a partial solution to their respective trading problems. It was intended thereby to abolish customs between these two countries, who would share in the revenue from this source.[155] This union however also gave rise to many misunderstandings and constant disputes (until its liquidation in 1950). Lebanon tried to justify its high share in the revenues (47%—which it wanted increased to 70%) by its high standard of living as against "the lack of any standard of living among the beduins and Druze of Syria" and the consequent larger consumption of imported commodities, with the bulk of Syrian exports going to the Lebanon. Indeed the level of imports per person in the Lebanon was much higher than in Syria. The average for the two countries—£ 3-3.5—was high but on internal distribution it was five times as high in the Lebanon as in Syria. Syria on its part demanded an increase of its share to 75% in view of the size of its territory and population.[156]

In Syria and the Lebanon, imports before the First World War were estimated at

---

[153] The boundaries of this area were marked in red on the map, and hence the name of the agreement.
[154] The full significance of oil to the Middle East economy came to the fore only in the 1940ies, within the framework of the comprehensive development programmes of the oil-producing countries after World War II, following increased output and the region's increased share in oil incomes. These developments as well as the impact of the 1973 oil upheaval are dealt with in our *The Economic Structure of The Middle East*, 1975.
[155] *Réglement Organique de la Conférence des Intérêts Communs,* Beyrouth, 14.5.1930.
[156] *Palestine Post,* 12.5.1937.

£ 6.6 million and exports at £ 3.3 million.[157] After the war, in the 'twenties, the gap increased, mainly owing to the rise in imports which in 1928 amounted to £ 10.6 million as against exports of £ 4.3 million.[158] The funds for balancing the constant deficits came from the invisibles in the current account and in particular the French military expenditure, tourism,[159] transit revenues (including oil as from 1935), and capital transfers by Syrian and Lebanese emigrants abroad.[160] Although after 1929 a considerable reduction took place in import expenditures because of a slight reduction in volume and in particular in price, export receipts similarly decreased. This was due to a marked deterioration in the terms of trade in that export prices fell much more than import prices. Between 1929 and 1935, the total value of foreign trade decreased by 50% but the volume of imports decreased by only 4% while the volume of exports rose by 85%.[161] At the end of the period, in 1939, when the value of imports again rose to £ 13 million and exports decreased to only £ 2 million,[162] the gap in the trade balance grew considerably.

France continued to be the first among the export and import countries of its mandated territories, followed by Britain, though sometimes Japan, which had climbed to a leading position in the trade with Syria and the Lebanon, jeopardised its rank.[163]

In discussing the economic policy we already mentioned that the Lebanon, which was more dependent than Syria on foreign trade, especially in its invisible exports, was more severely hurt by the depression than Syria. It is typical that the number of foreign holiday-makers in the Lebanon, which during the slump at the beginning of the 'thirties was in the range of 5-7,000 per year, rose to 18,000 and more towards the end of the 'thirties. While the existence of the customs union between Syria and Lebanon was of primary importance to the Lebanon in view of its high level of income in periods of relative prosperity, its disadvantages too were more serious in times of depression.

The main export items of Syria and the Lebanon were fruit and vegetables, wheat, wool, silk and cotton cloth, and among imports—cotton products and foodstuffs, machinery and equipment, iron and steel, oils and minerals. The yearly averages of exports in the 'thirties were 60% for foodstuffs and 20% for textiles (and another 5-10%, shoes and clothing). Among imports as well these three items together constituted about 50% (mainly cigarettes, beverages and sugar), while fuel and other capital and production goods made up only about 20%.

The interesting feature of this foreign trade structure was that not only 80-85% of exports consisted of agricultural produce and textiles, but that these items also

---

[157] In that period also Palestine was included in the concept of Syria. For detailed data see, A. Ruppin, *op. cit.*, pp. 238-280.

[158] Bulletin de l'Union Economique de Syrie, quoted in *Le Commerce du Levant*, 21.3.1932.

[159] L. of N., *P.M.C.*, 22nd Sess., Nov./Dec. 1932, p. 285.

[160] According to estimates, the revenue from this source in 1929 exceeded all export receipts on goods.

[161] G. T. Havard, *Report on Economic and Commercial Conditions in Syria and the Lebanon* (June 1936), H.M.S.O., London, 1936, p. 1.

[162] The Reports of the British Consul in Beirut; also L. of N., *P.M.C.*, 36th Sess., June 1939, p. 234.

[163] G. T. Havard, *op. cit.*, p. 8.

constituted a relatively high proportion of imports. The rather low share of capital and production goods among imports limited the prospects of development while some proportion of imported consumer goods could have been substituted by domestic production, thus saving foreign exchange for reducing deficits and/or increasing capital imports. It is nevertheless significant that the services and goods exported were of much greater variety than for instance in Egypt or Iraq, with industrial products, tourism and services assuming an important place in the balance of payments.

II

As early as the 'twenties, projects were from time to time put forward in Iraq to promote local and foreign trade by improved means of transportation by sea and by land, propaganda, exhibitions of local produce, and negotiations with other countries for purposes of mutual exchange. But little was actually done during that period, especially since stronger incentives for the protection of domestic production, on the one hand, and the expansion of foreign relations, on the other, arose only in the course of the 'thirties. These were provided jointly by the world depression, increased political independence, the admission of Iraq to the League of Nations, and attempts at lending greater variety to domestic industrial production.

On the other hand, just at the beginning of the 'thirties, the Iraqi economy was flooded with cheap products, especially Japanese-made, while Iraq was not yet at full liberty to take steps for retaliation or protection. The only loophole in the Anglo-Iraqi agreement and the mandatory restrictions (Clause 11) against discrimination in foreign trade, was Clause 16 of the Treaty[164] by which special agreements could be concluded with the neighbouring Arab countries. At that time most of the Iraq's exports were absorbed by Britain which in 1931/2, for instance, bought 60% of its grains, 70% of its skins, 90% of its raw cotton and 30% of its dried dates (all this apart from oil). The grain merchants[165] complained that Russia, Japan and Brazil flooded the Iraqi market with their products but bought only very little from it. Japan, for instance, from which Iraq purchased cotton and silk goods for 14 million rupees in 1931/2, altogether imported 191 cases of dried dates. Germany imposed high custom tariffs on Iraqi maize to prevent competition with German maize. Commercial ties with Persia, which were of importance to the Iraqi trade balance, suffered from the severe foreign currency restrictions imposed at that time in Persia.[166] Britain itself removed Iraq from the list of "most favoured countries" (which included the dominions and the colonies) while still reserving to

---

[164] See Appendices for these two clauses.

[165] The export of grains which in ordinary years amounted to 300-400,000 tons decreased as a result of the crisis and the abstention of foreign purchasers to 143,000 in 1935, and though it rose in 1936 to 324,000 and in 1937 to 425,000 tons, it again declined in 1938 to 239,000, and in 1939 rose only slightly to 267,000 tons. *Statistical Abstract*, 1939, p. 161. It should, however, be noted in respect of the above figures that fluctuations in exports were also affected by the degree of success of the harvest.

[166] Hilton-Young, *op. cit.*, p. 3.

itself a whole series of rights, privileges and posts of advisers to the Iraqi government.[167]

In a certain sense it was Iraq's good fortune that Japanese imports, especially of textiles, constituted serious competition for British Lancashire exports also, so that Britain supported the initiation of some protective measures which helped Iraq and to a certain extent Britain.[168] Britain had first place both in Iraqi imports and exports until 1939, followed by Japan and India (including Ceylon) as importers, and the U.S.A., India (including Ceylon) and Palestine (including Transjordan) as export markets.[169]

The measures taken by the government for the encouragement of local production and exports applied to both agricultural and industrial products. In 1931 and 1932 the customs on wheat and barley were raised from 11 to 15%, while the export-duty on dates was reduced from 3 to 1%, in order to encourage this sector which had acquired decisive importance among Iraqi exports until the enormous development of oil.[170] By other regulations customs duties on luxury items were increased and those on raw materials reduced; essential machinery was exempted from customs; and principles of reciprocity were set down.[171] Demands were put forward that trade agreements be based on the exchange method concurrently with efforts to improve the quality of exports. Little was done to this effect, on the one hand owing to the restrictions—first of the mandate and then of the treaties—and on the other, because of the low level of investments.[172]

As in other countries, export difficulties increased during the depression, and the value of exports, excluding oil, fell from 4.6 million dinar in 1927 to 2.6 million in 1931. Even by 1939 it had not returned to its previous level, reaching only 3.7 million dinar. The receipts from the export of dates were around 1 million dinar.

Throughout, the gap between exports and imports persisted, and though it followed the export curve its fluctuations were considerably higher. In 1927 the imports were 8.1 million dinar, in 1931—4.7 million and in 1939—8.1 million. All these figures are official data, and a considerable degree of inaccuracy is to be assumed especially in imports, in view of smuggling and other deals.

The balance sheet published by the government for 1938/9[173] illustrates the deficit on current account, its sources and its balancing by net capital imports.

---

[167] *Türkische Post*, 2.3.1932; *The Iraq Times*, 31.3.1933; *The Baghdad Times*, 21.4.1933.
[168] *The Times*, London, 28.5.1936.
[169] *Iraq*, February 1945, H.M.S.O., p. 28.
[170] The value of dates exported at the beginning of the 'thirties ranged between £ 1.5 million and 2 million. *The Baghdad Times*, 27.3.1932; E. Main, *op. cit.*, pp. 209-210.
[171] *The Baghdad Times*, 1.5.1933.
[172] One of the important constructive measures was an agreement signed in 1937 between the governments of Iraq and Palestine by which Iraq obtained better trade facilities with Palestine and was granted a free zone in Haifa port. *Palestine Post*, 22.2.1937.
[173] Iraq Government, *Statistical Abstract*, 1939, pp. 123, 161-2, 172. We were bound to adjust the figures for commodities debit (in the source, ID.9.1 m.) and for total (in the source, ID. 10,337,000), in order to correct, partly at least, the erroneous presentation of the Balance by the source.

TABLE XXXVIII

Iraq's Balance of Payments in 1938/9 (in dinars)

	Credit	Debit
Commodities	3,840,000	8,100,000
Interest and Dividends	100,000	50,000
Services and Royalties	3,797,000	1,140,000
Gold movement	163,000	47,000
Current account	7,900,000	9,337,000
Net capital imports (especially foreign investments and local expenses of foreign firms)	1,437,000	
Total	9,337,000	9,337,000

III

Throughout the history of Transjordan between the two World Wars its trade balance was unfavourble.[174] The trade deficit increased until it reached £P. 715,000 in 1939, when imports were £P. 1,295,000, and exports, including re-export, £P. 580,000. Most of the imports consisted of textiles. Durable finished products constituted 57% of the total imports in 1937; foodstuffs, beverages and tobacco constituted 27%.

The average yearly imports for 1937-9 were £P. 1,200,000, i.e., about £P. 4 per capita as against £E. 2.2 in Egypt, 2.8 dinars in Iraq, £ 3-3.5 in Syria and the Lebanon, and £P. 4.1 among the Arabs of Palestine.[175] The reason for the relatively high rate in Transjordan lies mainly in the low level of domestic production and the need to supply even the low local demand with foreign goods.

Not only was there a constant considerable deficit which throughout accompanied the evolution of foreign trade but almost all import items were consumer goods, especially textiles and foodstuffs. In the absence of producer and capital goods, serious changes in the structure and extent of production could be hardly expected.

Exports consisted mainly of grains, vegetables, fruit and some livestock. In 1937 livestock, foodstuffs, beverage and tobacco constituted 82.7% of the total exports.

Palestine was the largest single buyer of the Transjordanian exports (39% in 1937) and the trade balance of Transjordan with Palestine was always favourable. This state of affairs was due to the fact that the goods exchanged between the two countries were exempt from customs according to Clause 7 of the Treaty of 1928[176] between Britain and Transjordan, and to the supplement to this agreement of 1934.

---

[174] It should be taken into account that in Transjordan, more than in the other mandated territories, control of border movements was very defective and hence a large part of the traffic of goods does not appear in the statistical data.

[175] Cf. A. Bonné, *State and Economics in the Middle East*, London, 1948, p. 307—for Egypt; for other countries—our own calculations. The £, £E, £P and dinar were nearly identical in value.

[176] Hurewitz, *op. cit.*, II, pp. 156-9.

A similar treaty was signed between Transjordan and Syria in 1923, but when Transjordan realised that Syria was flooding its markets without absorbing Transjordanian goods, it applied for its cancellation in July 1937 as of February 1939. First among the suppliers of Transjordan was Japan as regards textiles, followed at the end of the period by Syria, Iraq and Palestine. Transjordan formed an exception among the countries of the region in that most of its trade—with the exception of Japan—was conducted with the neighbouring countries.

In the inter-war years no data were published on the Transjordanian balance of payments, but it may be safely stated that the movement of capital was not great. Invisible exports were negligible—a few thousand pounds from tourism and transit services between Palestine and Iraq, and Syria and Saudi Arabia. The deficit on current account was covered by British subsidies for the Arab Legion, British expenditures for public works (usually of a military nature) and the Palestinian government assistance. British non-military aid to Transjordan averaged £P. 90,000 in the years 1924/5-1935/6 and rose to £P. 101,000 in 1937/8. This aid was increased to £P. 404,000 in 1938/9 when the construction of the Baghdad-Haifa highway was commenced and the country incurred a significant rise in the deficit on current account.

SUMMARY

I

An ostensibly convenient method of analysing historical processes is that of "challenge and response." This macro-historical attempt at understanding major events within the realities of the area under review bears the image of the meeting—or clash—between East and West. But doubts arise with regard to three main aspects:

a) The history of the human race, and certainly that of more limited national or geographic sectors, is not summed up in large strokes leading either to success or to failure. A combination of millions of challenges and reactions shapes the trends of development, and frequently exogenic cataclysms intervene which entirely change the slope and direction of trends.

b) On applying the said method to the Middle East the emergence of the West appears as a challenge, while the East is believed to react with "response". In the long-range view of history this is certainly not correct, especially if the meaning of "challenge" is not limited exclusively to the cultural field.

Till the Crusades—and in Spain even afterwards—it was Muslim Arabic culture which laid siege to Christianity and constituted an immense challenge to the West. The Crusades themselves—and perhaps even the Inquisition—were a reaction to this challenge. And again, at least until the end of the 17th century, it was the Muslim-Ottoman East which constituted a challenge to Europe. The economic venture of Mehmed Ali (though he himself was influenced by Europe) and his military campaign in the North undoubtedly served as a challenge—and the European reaction did not fail to come. The opening of the Suez Canal in the 19th century and the discovery of Middle Eastern oilfields in the 20th century also constituted a decisive economic and political challenge which in turn gave rise to a chain reaction by the West and then by the East. On the other hand there is no doubt that, for instance, the wave of revolutions and movements for national and social economic regeneration which swept Turkey, Persia and Egypt between 1906 and 1909 was fed to a large extent by Russian revolutionary ideas and the national and social ideals of Western Europe; and although this wave ebbed away and ran off into the bywaters of the First World War, it helped to strengthen and mould the forces which after the War were to affect the modern history of the Middle East.

The historical events referred to above point to an interaction rather than to a unilateral direction of challenges.

c) The essence of the "challenge and response" approach as well as the dialectical method of analysis is that the challenge, clash or collapse, of civilisations, of regimes, of 'relations of production', and of other social or institutional structures usually results in a new, more advanced stage of social development, although as every developmental phase it embraces the vestiges of the previous phase and the nuclei of the next. This last aspect makes it possible to present the central question relevant to our problem, namely, do the society and economy of the East on the eve of the Second World War constitute a new stage in the development of the area? What is the nature of this phase, and do its sources indeed lie in the challenge of the West to the East? Or has nothing changed in the structure of this society, as compared for instance with the year 1800? And political independence, oil, the modern quarters in the Eastern cities, the thousands of tractors, the number of universities, and even the powerful multi-purpose schemes—are they only foam upon the water, underneath which religion, education, methods of government, public relations and production methods in country and even in town continue along the path of past generations, foreign to the spirit of modern industrial society? If the study of the Middle Eastern economy and society on the eve of World War II fails to reveal a structural change as compared with the beginning of the period, but if at the same time serious fissures are noted within this structure, then it is doubtful whether either of the two approaches, the "challenge and response" or the dialectical one, serves well the analysis of our problem.

On the other hand, the Middle East economy, during the period reviewed, certainly does not provide an example of a growth model that could be discussed in terms of dynamics, be it a "critical minimum effort", "growth poles", "stages" and "leading sector" model.[1] Not only was the development discontinuous, which might be compatible with any of these models, but the degree of the economic ebb and the impact of exogenous factors have been so great that they even bar the feasibility of following the strides of the economy in terms of business cycles inherent in the prevailing system.[2] Additional reasons render this method difficult. On the one hand, the Middle East economy has remained in a rather primitive, non-capitalist stage and its fluctuations have been largely dependent on natural causes rather than on economic forces. On the other hand, a number of economic sectors became involved in the network of international capitalism, which, up to a certain degree, both prevented industrial progress and infused into the oriental economy some, mainly infrastructural, elements of growth, these latter being again, due to their origin, exogenous factors of development. In spite of the wide range of development theories, no model has been presented so far which could adequately apply to the discontinuous, "jerky" progress and retreat of a backward region with a deeply traditional social set-up, the capitalist ventures into which were interested in speculatory profits rather than in domestic progress. If lack of adequate statistical series and data is added, the difficulty, if not impossibility, of employing the methods mentioned emerges clearly.

---

[1] The 'leading sector' model cannot as yet be applied even to the dominating oil sector, which still has to prove the pervasiveness of its linkages and impact on the structural economic trends in the Middle East.

[2] Cf. J. Schumpeter, *The Theory of Economic Development,* 1949, p. 63.

SUMMARY

II

In view of the qualifications mentioned, an adjusted type of structural analysis, i.e., an investigation of changes in the main components of the social and economic structure, with full weight given to the elements of both time and environment (cf. Introduction), seems to be the best procedure in the study of the economic history of an underdeveloped region.

How can we determine whether structural changes have indeed taken place in the economy of the Middle East during the last five generations—and if so, what were the trends of such changes and their factors?

One may try to draw up a comparison between the judgment of Weulersse, according to which Eastern society has perpetuated throughout generations "the same status of the land, the same social hierarchy, the same policy of the State, the same function of religion" as at the Ottoman conquest, and the actual condition of the Middle East on the eve of the Second World War. We might ask what new events had taken place in these domains: the agricultural, the social, the political and the religious. But before doing so, Weulersse's list of sectors must be amended so as to lend them the character of "structural components". Agricultural conditions, social hierarchy and religion undoubtedly belong among these components, while State policy is not by itself a structural element. On the one hand, it is a function of various structural factors; on the other, it might itself effect alterations in structural components, affecting their intensity and influence on historical processes.

As against that there are factors, impinging mainly on the social hierarchy mentioned above, but constituting structural factors by themselves. These are, chiefly as an amplification of the "statut de la terre", the production methods at large and the institutional and social structure of production relationships, as they have emerged and shaped themselves in the course of generations under the impact of internal regional factors, or through outside pressure or example.

We have tried to answer several questions of structural change by following the processes which have taken place in the field of land tenure; the changes in production; the financing of current expenditures and investments and the institutional services established for these purposes; the economic, juridical and political relations between the Middle East and the West as reflected in the capitulatory rights, concessions and international money market; and the attempts to achieve modernisation and consolidation of the economic and political framework with the aid of comprehensive reforms, mobilisation of foreign capital and know-how, or by an independent domestic economic, particularly industrial, effort with the State as the prime mover.

Let us now recapitulate briefly the changes in the main structural components.

With regard to the factor of *religion,* the reform movement in the Ottoman Empire of the 19th century undoubtedly had a distinctly secular character, as reflected in the secular civil legislation which restricted the rule of religious law and its influential interpreters. In Persia among religious circles themselves a reform movement sprang up, whose social goals went beyong the old hallowed order, fanatically preserved both by the official priesthood and the Shah. There, and especially in Turkey after the First World War, the secular trend continued, but a certain retrenchment took place in other countries of the region.

To the extent that Islam had an arresting effect on economic development, regression set in in the Arab provinces of the former Ottoman Empire upon its disintegration. In the chapter on the influence of religion it was pointed out that the Turkish way of thought was different from the Arab in having a more secular approach to social problems. With Arab emancipation from the Ottoman rule, religion was again released as a State factor, and at least in two countries within the area, Yemen and Saudi Arabia, it is easy to see the brakes it placed on technical and economic development.

The traditional *social structure* was too deeply ingrown for regulations and reforms like the *Tanzimat* to undermine it completely and replace it by another structure. Yet while oriental feudalism was not ready to submit to the orders of Mahmud II or of Mehmed Ali, and when Mamluk Beys, or Janissaries were physically exterminated, they were soon replaced by other Beys and *multazimin*—these classes on the other hand were unable to hold out against historical processes stronger than transitory and unrealistic measures and commands.

The profound changes in the political and military situation and in fighting methods, the increasing encroachment of modern economic and financial methods, both in the Empire and in Egypt—with the latter's monocultural cotton cultivation and the consequent dependence on the market—and finally the new central administrations, formed in the successor States, all these rendered superfluous many elements of the old structure—nomads, feudals and their agents, the tax collectors—that became essentially contradictory to the new development trends. The commercial and capitalistic element in production, distribution, investment and foreign trade increased. Relations between the State and the landlords ceased to be feudal.

On the other hand, the *village* remained the predominant factor within the national economies and the State had not yet taken revolutionary measures to change the methods of production in agriculture or alter existing ownership relations. Therefore deep within society the semi-feudal relations (and sometimes even serfdom) persisted between the landowners (who continued to be absentees) and the masses of the fellahin in Persia, Iraq, Syria, Egypt, Transjordan, and to a smaller extent, Turkey.

The *city* could not yet serve as a substitute for the village in performing central economic functions. Industrialisation was too feeble, even in inter-war Turkey, to be able to break down and overthrow the traditional society. Hence the village, represented by the landlord, the shaykh, or the go-between merchant, continued to exert pressure on national policy in combination with other counter-progressive factors, such as the vestiges of the capitulatory regime, the hesitant mandatory policy and the lack of adequate funds for new compreheusive investments.

However, certain fissures did appear in the traditional structure. The old duality of centralism and feudalism gave way to a new duality of a traditional subsistence economy and a slowly expanding capitalist market economy.

III

The economic criteria of backwardness or progressiveness of the national economy are the following: efficiency standards; national product *per capita* and in particular the per capita income of the poorer strata; the rate of investments; the relative share of the main economic sectors—agriculture, industry and services—in the national product and the related occupational structure; and the structure of foreign trade.

It is difficult to judge whether it is better for man, or whether a society is more virtuous, when the level of the above-mentioned criteria is high and when society assumes an industrial character. Experience teaches that even a technological and enlightened society (as regards know-how) does not manage to solve its internal, and even more its international problems peacefully and equitably, but despite the sighs heaved by various moralistic preachers it does not in this respect qualitatively fall behind traditional, either past or contemporary societies. At any rate it has at its disposal better means to feed men adequately, to clothe them and give them proper housing, to shorten working hours, improve health conditions (perhaps not as compared with the primordial "natural" society, but certainly as compared with what is going on today in backward areas). Existing social relations and political regimes prevent the reaping of full benefits from the economic and technical achievements. This still remains the bottleneck of modern society, as it was one of the central bottlenecks, for instance, in the Ottoman or Persian Empire.

But disregarding these unpleasant thoughts, we shall of necessity come back to the above criteria, applicable to modern society as far as the distinction between backward and advanced is concerned.

In our attempt to examine the state of the Middle East on the eve of the Second World War according to these criteria, there will be no escape from adopting relative data, i.e., comparing our area to more developed parts of the world. It is difficult, on the other hand, to draw up a comparison within the area itself between the beginning and end of the said five generations, apart from certain auxiliary data which will be mentioned in the course of our discussion.

Productivily per earner in the Middle East countries at the outbreak of the Second World War, according to Colin Clark's sources, fluctuated between 130 and 350 International Units per year, as compared with 1,429 in England and 2,093 in the United States. As a result, the *per capita income* in the Middle East was likewise only a fourth or a seventh of that in Western countries. In view of the unequal distribution of the income, due to a highly differentiated land ownership system (including the excessive rentals), and likewise to highly differentiated wages—as demonstrated with respect to several countries—the real income of most of the population remained below subsistence level.

SUMMARY

On the basis of an average per capita income, fluctuating throughout the region on the eve of World War II between 50 and 100 I.U., the real per capita income of the great mass of the poorer classes—in view of the very large area of inequality of the Lorenz curve—fell below the mark of 50 I.U. Furthermore, there are strong indications that while in Turkey, for instance, the real per capita income rose during the inter-war period, in Egypt it lagged behind or even declined.

With due regard to all reservations as to climate and to consumption habits and the conflicting views as to the nutritional value of various food items, it is difficult to ignore the fact that the consumption level in the Middle East was far lower than that of the West. Table XXXIX gives a relevant comparison between Egypt in 1937 and England and the United States.[3]

TABLE XXXIX

Per Capita Consumption of Food in Egypt, England and the U.S.A. in 1937

Per capita consumption	Egypt	England	U.S.A.
Meat, fish, fowl (kg)	20	187	90
Milk (litres)	73	88	217
Eggs (units)	44	200	228
Sugar (kg)	24	95	35
Potatoes (kg)	11	222	180
Vegetables (kg)	22	103	79

According to the data relating to Turkey in the 'thirties (see Table XX) it transpires that, in spite of the progress mentioned, the situation in food consumption was no better and in some respects even worse than in Egypt.

Even in calories consumption, whose main source is cereals which generally formed the staple of the Middle Eastern diet, the latter lagged seriously behind that of more developed areas.

TABLE XL

Average Daily Consumption of Calories in Different Countries in 1938/39

New Zealand	3,281
U.S.A.	3,249
England	3,005
Soviet Union	2,827
Turkey	2,619
Palestine	2,570
Syria and Lebanon	2,394
Egypt	2,199
Persia	1,966
Iraq	1,962
Transjordan	1,909
Korea	1,904

---

[3] Tables xxxix and xl are based partly on Colin Clark's data (*op. cit.*, Ch. VIII) and partly on publications of the World Health Organisation.

SUMMARY

The rate of investments is one of the major factors which determine productivity and income. Until foreign capital made its appearance in the Middle East by way of loans and investments, there was only one outstanding attempt on the part of the State to modernise the economic structure with the aid of large investments, squeezed out of the local population, namely Egypt under Mehmed Ali—and the causes of his failure have already been discussed. In the remaining periods and areas of this part of the world, the fruit of conquests and investments in previous ages was eaten up by wars, which in turn brought political and economic losses; by waste and corruption on the part of the rulers and their retinue; and in the best case—by abortive investments in luxurious buildings, military installations or enterprises whose economic profitability was not properly examined. The soil did not receive the fertilisers it needed, manpower was not adequately cared for, taxes were not used for constructive purposes; the economy was continuously pillaged and robbed. And when the inherited assets and the loot, from which the rulers had learned to live extravagantly, finally gave out, and instead of booty and taxes of conquest there came the ruinous expenses for armaments which were lost, soldiers who were killed and compensation for wars which ended in defeat—the political and economic structure was inevitably undermined. The irrigation system in Egypt perhaps continued to form an exception, but here the "population explosion" which started in the second half of the 19th century cancelled out its achievements. The fragile regional economy, devoid of new investments and shaken to the foundations by cruel taxes, tumbled rapidly on the heels of confrontation with foreign interests. Towards the end of the 19th century, just when a rather strong reform movement had sprung up in the Middle East, the stranglehold of power politics and international financial interests tightened round the neck of these territories. This fate overtook Persia and Egypt, but the greatest calamity overcame the Ottoman Empire, where the experiments of the *Tanzimat* were no longer able to prevent the disaster which had been looming over it for many years.

Actually, this collapse mainly affected the political and economic independence of these countries and did not make itself directly felt in the countryside, which remained rigidly frozen within its backwardness. Yet the traditional crafts were severely affected, without an extensive local industry rising up in their stead. As a result, the partially unemployed city proletariat grew. The debts and the foreign administration set up for their efficient collection inevitably cut down the real income of the masses out of whose taxes State obligations were met. At the same time these obligations resulted partly from new investments which Egypt and Ottoman Turkey, and at the end of the 19th century also Persia, started to make either directly with the aid of foreign credits or through foreign concessionaires who were prepared under certain conditions to invest their capital in local undertakings. Even at a short range several economic sectors benefited from the improvements which took place as a result of these investments, especially in communications and transport, while at a longer range these infrastructures might have become a major lever for the development of the productive sectors.

In particular the railways, as in a number of other countries, could have served as the leading sector of the economy by increasing the demand for raw materials (although both coal and iron required for their operation were in short supply within the region), and improving the supply of other sectors by reducing transportation costs and facilitating the access to the markets.

Until World War II, however, such positive effects did not make themselves felt to any significant degree, owing to the deficiency of complementary investments and in view of the faulty location of communication lines; and especially because a large part of the investments were not completed in time—such as the Baghdad line—or were abandoned and largely destroyed—like the Hedjaz railway—or became an extraterritorial sector with respect to the local economy, like the Suez Canal, and to a considerable degree the oilfields. The Ottoman and Egyptian Debt Administrations at the end of the 19th century served as a good example of European efficiency which implanted certain faint beginnings of a modern administration, but owing to the attitude of the creditors and the Western Powers and to local factors they were incapable of setting up a comprehensive statewide administration along modern lines.

Foreign capital was loath to come to the Middle East under the new conditions created after the First World War—apart from investments in oil which were still to a large extent extraterritorial. There was a dearth of domestic capital which proved hesitant in making industrial investments, preferring fast and high returns in other fields and adopting a method of distributing profits instead of reinvesting them and expanding the basis of production. The quick realisation of profits showed itself in the fact that in a country like Persia, for instance, the gap between locally distributed dividends and those of a number of high-income European countries gradually assumed major proportions. The dividend rates in Persia (excepting the oil companies!) rose from 9% in 1932 to 35% in 1936, and the averages for 1930/37 were as follows:[4]

TABLE XLI

Company Dividends (in % of the share capital) Distributed in Select Countries during 1930-37 (annual average)

Belgium	5.51%
England	6.60%
Czechoslovakia	7.96%
France	14.73%
Persia	27.00%

In Persia these trends were undoubtedly also the result of the prosperity and inflation which accompanied the period of investments—but at the same time they were a clear expression of the conditions typical of the Middle East.

The securities market was still in its swaddling clothes. The wider strata of the population could not serve as a serious source of financing, since the level of savings continued to be low, both because the low incomes fostered a high propensity to consume and because adequate saving habits were non-existent. Hoarding was in

---

[4] Banque Mellié Iran, *Bulletins,* fév. 1939.

effect still common, and the lack of confidence in banking institutions detracts from the comparative value of the data on savings deposits; yet, despite this reservation, it appears from the next Table[5] that the differences between the Middle East and more developed parts of the world at the end of the 'thirties were so pronounced that they are undoubtedly of great significance.

TABLE XLII

Per Capita Savings (in Dollars) in 1938

Country	Dollars
New Zealand	172.3
Sweden	163.4
Norway	152.0
Britain	131.1
U.S.A.	98.9
Canada	89.2
Holland	71.9
Italy	54.1
Czechoslovakia	52.3
Poland	8.4
Chile	6.7
Bulgaria	6.3
Greece	4.6
Egypt	3.0
Turkey	1.1
Persia	0.06

The governments, both in the independent countries and in the mandated territories, refrained from adopting a daring fiscal policy. Since the government potentially represented a central factor in the regeneration of the Eastern economy, some development experiments were practically doomed to failure when backed by inefficient and corrupt governments, as in Egypt, or governments devoid of a genuine desire for progress and interested above all in their selfish political and economic ends, like the foreign administrations and the mandatory governments.

The extent and the patterns of investments did not change much under the mandatory regime, which in a way was merely a new edition of the British administration in Egypt. While preventing financial disaster and instituting a more efficient and well-regulated administrative machine, it was unable with its

---

[5] Banque Mellié Iran, *Bulletins,* oct. 1939. More competent statistics, such as I.M.F., *International Financial Statistics,* employ a different classification of time deposits (both individual and corporate); consequently, a calculation on a *per capita* basis using their data would lead to different figures but not to different proportions nor to basically different conclusions. For instance, *per capita* deposits were at the end of 1938, in the U.S.A.-$ 114, in Gr. Britain-$ 101, in Sweden-$ 96, in Turkey-$ 4, in Egypt-$ 1.4 in Persia-$ 1.5, and in Iraq-$ 0.8.

conservative financial and economic policy to usher in a new period of modern industrial development.

The inter-war period, despite the above reservations, gave rise to new local initiative—private in the mandatory territories and in Egypt, public in Persia and Turkey. The process of renewed investments started to bear fruit even within the short period until the Second World War, in the form of industrial undertakings, improvements in irrigation and agriculture generally, and consequently in the rate of national produce and per capita income, which increased gradually, at least in Turkey.

The *relative shares of the different economic sectors in the national product and the occupational structure* also determine the total and per capita income and the structure of foreign trade. In this respect several notable changes took place. A more rapid increase of the population in the last two generations introduced a new structural element into Eastern society. Instead of the lack of manpower which sometimes became extremely pronounced during long periods of military adventure and corvée labour, the strong pressure of the growing population now made itself felt, accompanied—especially in Egypt—by disguised unemployment or the ejection of unemployed from the agricultural sector.

The population and the resources—the two main variables of the economic structure—did not grow proportionally, at least not in all countries. A larger degree of differentiation in the level of production and income evolved within the confines of the Middle Eastern countries themselves, but the most outstanding feature was the increasing gap between the area as a whole on the one hand and the more developed regions of the world on the other. The rich grew richer and the poor relatively poorer.

In all the countries of the Middle East, to a larger or smaller extent, there was a relative growth of the urban population while in some of them income from agriculture decreased to less than 50% of the total national income. Migration took place between the villages and the urban centres providing employment—either full or seasonal. The primary character of the exports, though substantially preserved to this day, was reduced, while agricultural and mineral raw materials gradually started to be processed by local industry. The only slight increase in the share of industry in employment and output, was due to the dwindling of the crafts, whose decline had continued for almost two hundred years, so that in certain instances, as in Syria and the Lebanon, the proportion of industrially employed (including artisans) had even decreased at the end of the period under review. Under the effect of the pressure exerted on the cities by former craftsmen, rural unemployed and the surplus population resulting from the natural increase, wages and income were kept at a low level, especially in the absence of trade unions. Certain industries, in particular foodstuffs and textiles, exploited this state of affairs in order successfully to compete with imported goods, and despite the existing limitations a certain degree of government protection was given, which was increased during the 'twenties and 'thirties of the twentieth century. Hence the relative share of these items among imports went down, but scarce domestic capital and initiative made it difficult to utilise the input of cheap labour and act as an industrial incentive as had happened in the industrial revolution in the West or in Japan. Of course this state of affairs was not due merely to the absence of a spirit of progress and technical know-how, but also to still prevailing external restrictions and foreign influence which did not sufficiently encourage, and sometimes even impeded, the existing drive for development.

IV

The factors which fostered or hindered development are so complex that it is almost impossible to isolate one central or even several factors and make them responsible for the region's continuous backwardness, with merely isolated spots of progress and development. To place the main responsibility on Western imperialism would be as misleading as to place it on the passive form of religion or the character of the population or the corruption of the rulers. It might easily be claimed, and many arguments may be adduced for the fact, that Mehmed Ali—the despot, the ignoramus, the lover of loot—was the most enlightened ruler of his time, attempting at one stroke to turn backward Egypt into a modern State with a modern economy. On the other hand it will not be difficult to find arguments to show that while the Western States and Western capitalists risked their capital in investments in the Ottoman or Persian Empire and exerted pressure for the protection of minorities and entire peoples, it was the Sultans, the Shahs and the Khedives who with their tyranny, corruption, unbridled greed and with the "aid" of a corrupt administrative machine put a spoke in the wheel of all attempts at Westernisation, 'treacherously' evaded the capitulatory restrictions, exploited the grant of concessions in order to enjoy selfish privileges and finally brought about the subjection and the disintegration of the Empire.

But all these are merely half-truths, which distort the trend of the processes themselves as well as their causes. As Marx rightly pointed out, capitalist exploitation and expansion must not be attributed to the iniquity of the capitalists. In the 19th century, the growing demand of industrialising countries for agricultural produce and raw materials combined with their search for markets caused by the growing output of finished goods and modern services. The presumptive danger of falling rates of profit induced European capital to look for better opportunities in capital-starved regions, thus effecting a renewed scramble for strategic positions in Africa and Asia. Here, the demand for capital and economic leadership, under conditions of local corruption and incompetence, threw the gates of the economy open to foreign domination. A balanced record and scrutiny of events in the course of a century preceding World War II shows a high degree of "co-operation" between destructive forces from within and without the region, working for economic stagnation and even disintegration.

Nevertheless, a distinct qualitative change in the conception of the State and its economic functions must be noted after the First World War. This change took place mainly in Turkey and to some degree in Persia, but in a certain respect it was brought about by the mandatory regimes. Taxation ceased to be the main economic activity of the State and was no longer, as in the past, directed towards increasing the power of despotic rulers, larger war expenditure and greater corruption. The better regulated administration in the mandated countries, the land surveys, censuses and statistical services made inroads upon the feudal elements and the old ownership relations, and led to the rise of a civil-servant and other new classes, which undermined the previous social and economic structure. A considerable degree of corruption, inefficiency and egoism on the part of the ruling classes was gradually removed and the practically absolute neglect of the primary needs of the masses was replaced by modest beginnings of development and welfare measures.

In some of the independent countries the government now tried to strengthen their political and economic independence by economic, and as far as possible, industrial development. Taxes and customs increasingly started to serve as instruments for economic protection and public savings for re-investment in new sectors.

Oriental society and economy on the threshold of the Second World War were in an obvious process of disintegration as a result of incipient structural changes in population, social stratification, legal situation, international status, and national and economic consciousness. On the other hand, in the field of consumption, production and investment, only the first signs of change were apparent. In a certain sense the area remained suspended between structural models which had become obsolete and new ones which had not yet consolidated. In the absence of a strong refreshing stream of social and economic revolution, the fissures in the traditional wall of society had not widened sufficiently to pull it down and lead to the remoulding of the social and economic structure. The old conservative forces had not yet laid down their arms.

APPENDICES

APPENDIX 1

*Interpretation of the Distinction between 'Ushr and Kharadj Lands
by Abū Yūsuf Ya'kūb (731-798)*

...In what concerns, Prince of believers, your question referring to the distinction between the land of *'ushr* and that of *kharadj*, all the land of Arab territory or of non-Arab one whose inhabitants became Muslim converts, belongs to them and constitutes *'ushuri* land, like (the city of) Medina whose inhabitants became Muslims to this end, and like Yemen. *'Ushuri* land is also that of idolatrous Arabs, from whom tithe cannot be accepted and who have no choice but between conversion to Islam and death, in spite of its conquest by the Imam. And this, because the Prophet, after having conquered the lands of the Arab populations, let them to them as they were, and they will remain *'ushuri* lands until the last day of Judgement.

Every habitation place of non-Arabs that was conquered by the Imam and left by him in the hands of the vanquished, is *kharadj* land, but it is *'ushuri* land if he distributed it among the conquerors. This is the evidence: the lands of non-Arabs conquered by 'Omar ben el-Khattab and left by him in the hands of the vanquished are *kharadj* lands. Therefore, all non-Arab land whose inhabitants became tributaries through peace treaties, is *kharadj* land.

(Source: *Kitab el-Kharadj lilQadi Abū Yūsuf Ya'kūb bin Ibrahim*, Cairo, 1933, (1346 A.H.), Second Edition, p. 69.)

APPENDIX 2

Treaty of 1454 between Venice and the Ottoman Empire

(Translated from copy found in Législation Ottomane by Aristarchi Bey,
Constantinople, 1874)

I, Great Lord and Great Emir, Sultan Mohamed Bey, swear by God, the Creator of Heaven and earth; by the Great Prophet Mahomet; by the seven martyrs sacred to all Mussulmans; by the 24 Prophets of God; by the Faith I confess; by my father's soul, by my soul, and by the sword I wear.

His most Illustrious and Most Excellent Lordship the Duke of Venice, desirous of concluding a new treaty of peace and friendship with my lordship, has sent here the glorious, most noble and honored gentleman, M. Batolomee Marcello, an ambassador worthy of his aforementioned lordship of Venice, to confirm anew the provisions of the treaty of Adrianople and to amend the said treaty by the addition of the provisions which shall appear in the following articles; I, Great Lord and Great Emir, Sultan Mohamed Bey, promise and swear by the aforesaid oaths that, even as peace and friendship existed in the past between us and his most illustrious lordship of Venice and his subjects, so have I concluded and do now conclude a good, pure, and faithful peace, on land and sea, with every city, land, island, or locality whatsoever, which does now or shall hereafter fly the standard of St. Mark; that none of my subjects nor any person subject to my jurisdiction shall annoy or hinder **or** permit to be annoyed or hindered the Commune of Venice, and that if any such act is committed, and protest made on account of it, I shall visit the guilty with the punishments appropriate to the offense. And his lordship of Venice shall do likewise with regard to my subjects.

Article 1. That neither of us shall harbor within our borders any person guilty of a crime against the State, nor any person guilty of theft, and if any such person shall arrive within the jurisdiction of either of us, he shall be forthwith given up to the other together with any goods he may have stolen.

Article 2. That it shall be permitted to the merchants of the two nations to visit the territories of the other, to go and return and carry on their trade freely by land or sea without let or hindrance.

Article 3. That the Duke of Nasso, with his subjects and dependents, shall be and are included within the provisions of this treaty, being considered as Venetian subjects not liable to the rendering of any service or the payment of any tribute to the Sublime Porte.

Article 4. That the vessels of either State visiting the other or of any of its dependencies, shall be welcome and unmolested.

Article 5. That the Venetians shall pay to my lordship 100 ducats for the right of entering Lepanto, as was the custom in the time of my father, and 200 ducats for the right of entering the lands on the borders of my Empire in Albania, that is to say, Scutari, Alessio, and Drivasto; they shall pay for the right of entering Scutari and Alessio 136 ducats, in all 436 ducats, which sum the governor (consul) of Constantinople shall be held to deliver to my lordship.

Article 6. That all Venetian slaves shall be given up without ransom, except that in case any slave shall have embraced the Mohametan religion, a ransom of 1,000 piastres shall be paid.

To these articles the following were later added, to wit:

Article 7. That in spite of the full liberty of trade guaranteed to the Venetians in all parts of the Ottoman Empire, they shall be required to pay a sum equal to 2 per cent of the value of all merchandise sold by them; and Turkish merchants carrying on trade in the Venetian dependencies shall be subject to a like tax.

Article 8. That all ships of whatever kind, whether proceeding to or returning from the Black Sea, shall put in at the port of Constantinople, where they shall be permitted to take on board whatever supplies they may need and then depart freely.

Article 9. That any goods originating in the Mediterranean or Black Sea, and belonging to a Christian nation may be carried anywhere and if sold, the tax of 2 per cent shall be collected; but the Venetians are forbidden to transport goods belonging to Mussulmans.

Article 10. That all the inhabitants of Pera, except the Genoese, shall be compelled to pay their debts, if any they owe to Venetians, except debts, goods, or things of value owed to a Venetian which my lordship may have confiscated by force.

Article 11. That his lordship of Venice shall continue to exercise those privileges of entrée which he has heretofore enjoyed with respect to the patriarchate of Constantinople.

Article 12. In case any ship shall be wrecked in territory belonging to my lordship, I shall cause a satisfactory account to be rendered of all goods and men saved; and under similar circumstances, his lordship of Venice shall do likewise.

Article 13. That in case a Venetian shall die, intestate and without heirs, within the dominions of my lordship, his property shall not be in any manner disturbed, but the governor (consul), the judge and the pacha of the district shall make an exact inventory of it and all his goods shall be placed under the care of the governor (consul), but if he should die in a district where there is no governor (consul), the goods shall be turned over to another Venetian, if such there be in the district, to be held at the disposition of his lordship of Venice.

Article 14. That neither of us shall give subsidies or aid to the enemies of the other.

Article 15. No enemy or traitor to the Sultan shall be received within any of the castles, cities, or fortresses which his lordship of Venice possesses in Rumania and Albania, nor shall such person receive any financial aid or be permitted to pass either by land or sea, and if this provision shall not be observed, the Sultan may, at discretion, make war against these lands and castles and such war shall not be considered an interruption of peace or a violation of this treaty. My lordship extends a like privilege to his lordship of Venice.

Article 16. That his lordship of Venice may, if he desires, send to Constantinople a governor (consul), with his suite, according to custom, which governor (consul), shall have the privilege of ruling over, governing and administering justice to the Venetians of every class and condition; and the Sultan engages to cause the pacha or military commander of Roumelia to accord to the said governor (consul), all assistance which he may require for the conduct of his office.

Article 17. My lordship agrees to repair or recompense for all damages accruing to the goods or persons of Venetians as a result of the operations of the Turks at the capture of Constantinople, provided that they be proved "idoneamente" (just and proper).

Article 18. That the Venetians may introduce into the Empire and put into circulation any kind of money coined or uncoined without paying any tax, provided that uncoined metal be presented at the mint and coined.

Article 19. That finally all debts which arose between the citizens of Constantinople and the Venetians prior to the capture of the city by the Turks, shall be and hereby are canceled and of no force.

Which things, both new and old, we have sworn to, signed, enacted, et cetera.

(Source: G. Bie Ravndal, *The Origin of the Capitulations and of the Consular Institutions*, 67th Congress, 1st Session, Senate, Doc. No. 34, Washington, 1921, pp. 92-3.)

APPENDIX 3

Capitulation with France

(Done at Constantinople, February 1535 (25 Chaban 941))

Be it known to everybody that in the year of Jesus Christ one thousand five hundred and thirty-five, in the month of February, and of Mohammed 941, in the moon of Chaban, Sire Jean de la Foret, privy councilor, and ambassador of the most excellent and most powerful prince Francis, by the grace of God most Christian King of France, accredited to the most powerful and invincible Grand Signior, Sultan Suleiman, Emperor of the Turks, and having discussed with the powerful and magnificient Signior Ibrahim, Serasker of the Sultan, the calamities and disadvantages which are caused by war, and, on the other hand, the good, quiet, and tranquillity derived from peace; and knowing how good it is to prefer the one (peace) to the other (war), each of them guaranteeing the above-mentioned monarchs, their superiors, they have negotiated and agreed upon the following chapters and conventions in the name and on the honor of the said monarchies which are the protectors of their component States and the benefactors of their subjects:

Article 1. They have negotiated, made, and concluded a valid and sure peace and sincere concord in the name of the above Grand Signior and King of France during their lives and for the kingdoms, dominions, provinces, castles, cities, ports, harbors, seas, islands, and all other places they hold and possess at present or may possess in the future, so that all subjects and tributaries of said sovereigns who wish may freely and safely, with their belongings and men, navigate on armed or unarmed ships, travel on land, reside, remain in and return to the ports, cities, and all other places in their respective countries for their trade, and the like shall be done for their merchandise.

Article 2. Likewise, the said subjects and tributaries of the said monarchs shall, respectively, be able to buy, sell, exchange, move, and transport by sea and land from one country to the other all kinds of merchandise not prohibited, by paying only the ordinary customs and ancient dues and taxes, to wit, the Turks, in the dominions of the King, shall pay the same as Frenchmen, and the said Frenchmen in the dominions of the Grand Signior shall pay the same as the Turks, without being obliged to pay any other new tribute, impost, or storage due.

Article 3. Likewise, whenever the King shall send to Constantinople or Pera or other places of this Empire a bailiff – just as at present he has a consul at Alexandria – the said bailiff and consul shall be received and maintained in proper authority so that each one of them may in his locality, and without being hindered by any judge, cadi, soubashi, or other, according to his faith and law, hear, judge, and determine all causes, suits, and differences, both civil and criminal, which might arise between merchants and other subjects of the King. Only in case the orders of the said bailiffs and consuls should not be obeyed and that in order to have them executed they should appeal to the soubashi or other officer of the Grand Signior, the said soubashis or other officers shall lend them the necessary aid and compulsory power. But the cadi or other officers of the Grand Signior may not try any difference between the merchants and subjects of the King, even if the said merchants should request it, and if perchance the said cadis should hear a case their judgment shall be null and void.

Article 4. Likewise, in a civil case against Turks, tributaries, or other subjects of the Grand Signior, the Merchants and subjects of the King can not be summoned, molested, or tried unless the said Turks, tributaries, and subjects of the Grand Signior produce a writing from the hand of the opponent, or a "heudjet" (document) from the cadi, bailiff, or consul, outside of which writing or heudjet no other testimony of a Turk, tributary, or other person shall be valid nor received in any part of the States and dominions of the Grand Signior, and the cadis, soubashis, or other persons may not hear or try the said subjects of the King without the presence of their dragoman.

Article 5. Likewise, in criminal cases the said merchants and other subjects of the King may not be called before the cadi or other officers of the Grand Signior by Turks, tributaries, or others, and said cadis may not try them, but must immediately refer them to the Sublime Porte (the official residence of the Grand Vizier) and in the absence of the Porte, to the principal lieutenant of the Grand Signior, where the testimony of the subject of the King and of the tributary of the Grand Signior shall be valid one against the other.

Article 6. Likewise, as regards religion, it has been expressly promised, concluded, and agreed that the said merchants, their agents, and servants, and all other subjects of the King shall never be molested nor tried by the cadis, sandjak-beys, or soubashis, or any person but the Sublime Porte only, and they can not be made or regarded as Turks (Mohammedans) unless they themselves desire it and profess it openly and without violence. They shall have the reight to practice their own religion.

Article 7. Likewise, when one or more subjects of the King, having made a contract with a subject of the Grand Signior, taken merchandise, or incurred debts, afterwards depart from the State of the Grand Signior without giving satisfaction, the bailiff, consul, relatives, factor, nor any other subject of the King shall for this reason be in any way coerced or molested, nor shall the King be held responsible. Only His Majesty shall cause full justice to be done to the plaintiff as regards the person and goods of the debtor if they be found within his Kingdom and dominions.

Article 8. Likewise, the said merchants, their agents, and servants, and other subjects of the King, their ships, boats, or other equipments, artillery, ammunition, and mariners shall not be seized, coerced, or used by the Grand Signior or other person against their pleasure and desire for any service or duty either on sea or land.

Article 9. Likewise, all merchants and subjects of the King in all parts of the Empire of the Grand Signior shall be allowed to freely dispose of their property by testament, and having died either a natural or violent death, all their effects—money as well as other goods—shall be distributed according to the testament; if they die intestate, the effects shall be turned over to the heir or his representative by and with the authority of the bailiff or consul at places where there may be one or the other, and where there is neither bailiff nor consul the said effects shall be protected by the cadi or the locality under authority of the Grand Signior, having first of all made an inventory in the presence of witnesses; but where said bailiff or consul are present no cadi, beitulmaldji, or other person shall take possession of the effects, and if they should be in the hands of one of them and the bailiff or consul should demand them they must at once and without contradiction be entirely turned over to the said bailiff or consul or their representative, to be later handed to whom they belong.

Article 10. Likewise as soon as the present treaty shall have been ratified by the Grand Signior and the King, all persons and subjects shall be set free and liberated who may, respectively, be bought slaves, prisoners of war, or otherwise detained, both in the hands of the said sovereigns or of their subjects, galleys, ships, and all other places and countries owing allegiance to the said sovereigns, on the demand and statement of the ambassador, bailiff, or consul of the King, or persons delegated by them; and if any of the said slaves should have changed his faith and religion he shall nevertheless be free. And, especially, henceforth reciprocally neither the Grand Signior nor the King, their captains, soldiers, tributary subjects, or mercenaries, shall or may in any manner, on sea or land, take, buy, sell, or detain as a slave any prisoner of war. But if a pirate or other person of the country of one of the said sovereigns should attempt to capture or destroy the goods or persons owing allegiance to the other sovereign, the sovereign of the country where the malefactor is found must and should be obliged to punish him as a disturber of the peace and to make an example to others, and also to return to the injured party whatever may be found to have been taken from him by the malefactor. If the said malefactor should escape without being caught and punished at once, he shall be banished from his country with his accomplices, and all their goods shall be confiscated by the sovereign who shall also cause the malefactor and his companions to be punished if they should ever be in his power; and out of the said confiscation shall be paid the damages, and the injured party shall to that end have recourse to the protectors of the present peace, who shall be the Serasker on the part of the Sultan, and the "grand-maître" of France on the part of the King.

Article 11. Likewise when the navies of the said Grand Signior and King, respectively, meet vessels of the subjects of the other, they shall be obliged to lower the sails and hoist the flags of their ruler, in order to be recognized thereby and not be detained or otherwise molested by said navy or any unit thereof; but if any wrong or damage be inflicted upon them, the ruler to whom the navy belongs shall be obliged to make immediate reparation. When private ships of the subjects of said rulers meet shall each hoist the flag of its ruler, salute each other by firing one gun, and reply truthfully when asked who they are. But after having spoken and recognized each other one shall not forcibly enter or visit the other, nor hinder it under any pretext whatsoever.

Article 12. Likewise when a vessel belonging to subjects of the King arrives, by accident or otherwise, in the ports or on the coasts of the Grand Signior, it shall receive food and other necessaries against a reasonable payment, without being obliged to discharge and pay duties, and it shall be allowed to go wherever it pleases; and having come to Constantinople, it shall be ready to leave after having obtained and paid for the heudjet (permit) of the emin (official), and having been searched and visited by the said emin, they must not be visited at any other place, except the castles of the straits of Gallipoli, without, however, paying anything there or elsewhere, in the name of the Grand Signior or his officers, for the departure.

Article 13. Likewise, if any ship belonging to the subjects of one of the said sovereigns should, by accident or otherwise, suffer shipwreck within the dominions and the jurisdiction of the other sovereign all persons escaping from such danger shall remain free and be allowed to collect all their belongings; if all should have died in the shipwreck the goods which shall have been saved shall be consigned to the said bailiff, or consul, or their representative, to be returned to whom they may belong; and the captain general of the sea, the sandjak-bey, soubashi, cadi, or other officer or subject of the Grand Signior shall not, under penalty of punishment, take or claim anything, and they must give facilities and assistance to those who shall be charged with the recovery of the goods.

Article 14. Likewise if a subject of the Grand Signior should lose a slave who has such subject, claiming that the slave had lived and served on a ship or in a house of a subject of the King, can not force the subject of the King to do anything but search his ship or house, and if the slave should be found there, the person who received him should be duly punished by his bailiff or consul and the slave returned to his master. If the slave was neither in their ship nor in their house, said subjects of the King shall not and can not be molested in this connection.

Article 15. No subject of the King who shall not have resided for 10 full continuous years in the dominions of the Grand Signior shall or can be forced to pay tribute, Kharadj, Avari, Khassabiye, nor to guard neighboring land, storehouses of the Grand Signior, work in an arsenal, nor perform any other forced service. In the dominions of the King reciprocal rights shall be granted to the subjects of the Grand Signior.

The King of France has proposed that His Holiness the Pope, the King of England, his brother and perpetual ally, and the King of Scotland should be entitled to adhere to his treaty of peace, if they please, on condition that when desirous of doing so they shall within eight months from date send their ratifications to the Grand Signior and obtain his.

Article 16. Likewise the Grand Signior and the King of France shall within six months exchange the confirmation of the present treaty in valid and due form, with the promise to observe it, and the order to all their lieutenants, judges, officers, and subjects to observe it without bad faith and in all its points; and in order that nobody should plead ignorance, this treaty, after the confirmations have been exchanged, shall be published at Constantinople, Alexandria, Marseille, Narbonne, and other principal cities and ports of the jurisdiction, kingdoms, and states of the said sovereigns.

(Source: G. Bie Ravndal, *op. cit.*, pp. 94-6.)

APPENDIX 4

Capitulations between Great Britain and the Ottoman Empire

Constantinople 1675 (Main Clauses)

Article 1. That the English nation and merchants, and all other merchants sailing under the English flag, with their ships and vessels, and merchandise of all descriptions, shall and may pass safely by sea, and go and come into our Dominions, without any the least prejudice or molestation being given to their persons, property, or effects, by any person whatsoever, but they shall be left in the undisturbed enjoyment of their privileges, and be at liberty to attend to their affairs.

Article 2. That if any of the English coming into our Dominions by land be molested or detained, such persons shall be instantly released, without any further obstruction being given to them.

Article 3. That English ships and vessels entering the ports and harbours of our Dominions shall and may at all times safely and securely abide and remain therein, and at their free will and pleasure depart therefrom, without any opposition or hindrance from any one.

Article 4. That if it shall happen that any of their ships suffer by stress of weather, and not be provided with necessary stores and requisites, they shall be assisted by all who happen to be present, whether the crews of our Imperial ships, or others, both by sea and land.

Article 5. That being come into the ports and harbours of our Dominions, they shall and may be at liberty to purchase at their pleasure, with their own money, provisions and all other necessary articles, and to provide themselves with water, without interruption or hindrance from any one.

Article 7. That the merchants, interpreters, brokers, and others, of the said nation, shall and may, both by sea and land, come into our Dominions, and there trade with the most perfect security; and in coming and going, neither they nor their attendants shall receive any the least obstruction, molestation, or injury, either in their persons or property, from the Beys, Cadis, sea-captains, soldiers, and others, our slaves.

Article 8. That if an Englishman, either for his own debt, or as surety for another, shall abscond, or become bankrupt, the debt shall be demanded from the real debtor only; and, unless the creditor be in possession of some security given by another, such person shall not be arrested nor the payment of such debt be demanded of him.

Article 10. That if any one shall calumniate an Englishman, by asserting that he has been injured by him, and producing false witnesses against him, our judges shall not give ear unto them, but the cause shall be referred to his Ambassador, in order to his deciding the same, and that he may always have recourse to his protection.

Article 11. That if an Englishman, having committed an offence, shall make his escape, no other Englishman, not being security for him, shall, under such pretext, be taken or molested.

Article 12. That if an Englishman, or subject of England, be found to be a slave in our States, and be demanded by the English Ambassador or Consul, due inquiry and examination shall be made into the causes thereof, and such person being found to be English, shall be immediately released, and delivered up to the Ambassador or Consul.

Article 13. That all Englishmen, and subjects of England, who shall dwell or reside in our Dominions, whether they be married or single, artisans or merchants, shall be exempt from all tribute.

Article 14. That the English Ambassadors shall and may, at their pleasure, establish Consuls in the ports of Aleppo, Alexandria, Tripoli, Barbary, Tunis, Tripoli of Syria and Barbary, Scio, Smyrna, and Egypt, and in like manner remove them, and appoint others in their stead, without any one opposing them.

Article 15. That in all litigations occurring between the English, or subjects of England, and any other person, the judges shall not proceed to hear the cause without the presence of an interpreter, or one of his deputies.

Article 16. That if there happen any suit, or other difference or dispute, amongst the English themselves, the decision thereof shall be left to their own Ambassador or Consul, according to their custom, without the judge or other governors our slaves, intermeddling therein.

Article 17. That our ships and galleys, and all other vessels, which may fall in with any English ships in the seas of our Dominions, shall not give them any molestation, nor detain them by demanding any thing, but shall show good and mutual friendship the one to the other, without occasioning them any prejudice.

Article 18. That all the Capitulations, Privileges, and Articles, granted to the French, Venetian, and other Princes who are in amity with the Sublime Porte, having been in like manner, through favour, granted to the English, by virtue of our special Command, the same shall be always observed according to the form and tenor thereof, so that no one in future do presume to violate the same, or act in contravention thereof.

Article 19. That if the corsairs or galliots of the Levant shall be found to have taken any English vessels, or robbed or plundered them of their goods and effects, also if any one shall have forcibly taken any thing from the English, all possible diligence and exertion shall be used and employed for the discovery of the property, and inflicting condign punishment on those who may have committed such depredations; and their ships, goods, and effects, shall be restored to them without delay or intrigue.

Article 21. That duties shall not be demanded or taken of the English or the merchants sailing under the flag of that nation, on any piastres and sequins they may import into our sacred Dominions, or on those they may transport to any other place.

Article 22. That our Beglerbegs, Judges, Defterdars, and Masters of the mint, shall not interpose any hindrance or obstacle thereto by demanding either dollars or sequins from them, under the pretence of having them recoined and exchanged into other money, nor shall give them any molestation or trouble whatever with regard thereto.

Article 23. That the English nation, and all ships belonging to places subject thereto, shall and may buy, sell, and trade in our sacred Dominions and (except arms, gunpowder, and other prohibited commodities) load and transport in their ships every kind of merchandise, at their own pleasure, without experiencing any the least obstacle or hindrance from any one; and their ships and vessels shall and may at all times safely and securely come, abide, and trade in the ports and harbours of our sacred Dominions, and, with their own money, buy provisions and take in water, without any hindrance or molestation from any one.

Article 24. That if an Englishman, or other subject of that nation, shall be involved in any lawsuit, or other affair connected with law, the judge shall not hear nor decide thereon until the Ambassador, Consul, or Interpreter, shall be present; and all suits exceeding the value of four thousand Aspers shall be heard at the Sublime Porte, and nowhere else.

Article 26. That in case any Englishman, or other person subject to that nation, or navigating under its flag, should happen to die in our sacred Dominions, our fiscal and other officers shall not, upon pretence of its not being known to whom the property belongs, interpose any opposition or violence, by taking or seizing the effects that may be found at his death, but shall be delivered up to such Englishman whoever he may be, to whom the deceased may have left them by his will: and should he have died intestate, then the property shall be delivered up to the English Consul, or his representative, who may be there present: and in case there be no Consul, or Consular Representative, they shall be sequestered by the judge, in order to his delivering up the whole thereof, whenever any ship shall be sent by the Ambassador to receive the same.

Article 27. That all the privileges and other liberties already conceded, or hereafter to be conceded to the English and other subjects of that nation sailing under their flag, by divers Imperial Commands, shall be always obeyed and observed, and interpreted in their favour, according to the tenor and true intent and meaning thereof; neither shall any fees be demanded by the fiscal officers and judges in the distribution of their property and effects.

Article 30. That the English merchants having once paid the customs at Constantinople,

Aleppo, Alexandria, Scio, Smyrna, and other ports of our sacred Dominions, not an Asper more shall be taken or demanded from them at any other place, nor shall any obstacle be interposed to the exit of their merchandise.

Article 31. That having landed their merchandise imported by their ships into our sacred Dominions, and paid in any port the customs thereon, and beging obliged, from the impossibility of selling the same there, to transport them to another port, the Commandants or Governors shall not, on the landing of such merchandise, exact from them any new custom or duty thereon, but shall suffer them, freely and unrestrictedly, to trade, without any molestation or obstruction whatsoever.

Article 32. That no excise or duty on animal food shall be demanded of the English, or any subjects of that nation.

Article 34. That the English merchants, and other subjects of that Nation, shall and may, according to their condition, trade at Aleppo, Egypt, and other ports of our sacred Dominions, on paying (according to ancient custom) a duty of three per cent on all their merchandise, without being bound to the disbursement of an Asper more.

Article 35. That, in addition to the duty hitherto uniformly exacted on all merchandise, laden, imported, and transported in English ships, they shall also pay the whole of the consulage to the English Ambassadors and Consuls.

Article 36. That the English merchants, and all others sailing under their flag, shall and may, freely and unrestrictedly, trade and purchase all sorts of merchandise (prohibited commodities alone excepted), and convey them, either by land or sea, or by way of the River Tanaïs, to the countries of Muscovy or Russia, and bring back from thence other merchandise into our sacred Dominions, for the purposes of traffic, and also transport others to Persia and other conquered countries.

Article 37. That such customs only shall be demanded on the said goods in the conquered countries as have always been received there, without any thing more being exacted.

Article 38. That should the ships bound for Constantinople be forced by contrary winds to put into Caffa, or any other place of those parts, and not be disposed to buy or sell any thing, no one shall presume forcibly to take out or seize any part of their merchandise, or give to the ships or crews any molestation, or obstruct the vessels that are bound to those ports; but our Governors shall always protect and defend them, and all their crews, goods, and effects, and not permit any damage or injury to be done to them: and should they be desirous of purchasing, with their own money, any provisions in the places where they may happen to be, or of hiring any carts or vessels (not before hired by others), for the transportation of their goods, no one shall hinder or obstruct them therein.

Article 39. That custom shall not be demanded or taken on the merchandise brought by them in their ships to Constantinople, or any other port of our sacred Dominions, which they shall not, of their own free will, land with a view to sale.

Article 40. That on their ships arriving at any port, and landing their goods and merchandise, they shall and may, after having paid their duties, safely and securely depart, without experiencing any molestation or obstruction from any one.

Article 41. The English ships coming into our sacred Dominions, and touching at the ports of Barbary and of the Western Coast, used oftentimes to take on board pilgrims and other Turkish passengers with the intention of landing them at Alexandria, and other ports of our sacred Dominions; on their arrival at which ports the Commandants and Governors demanded customs of them on the whole of their goods before they were landed, by reason of which outrage they have forborne receiving any more pilgrims; the more so as they were forced to take out of the ships that were bound to Constantinople the merchandise destined for other places, besides exacting the duties on those that were not landed: all English ships, therefore, bound to Constantinople, Alexandria, Tripoli of Syria, Scanderoon, or other ports of our sacred Dominions, shall in future be bound to pay duties, according to custom, on such goods only as they shall, of their own free will, land with a view to sale; and for such merchandise as they shall not discharge, no custom or duty shall be demanded of them, neither shall the least molestation or hindrance be given to them, but they shall and may freely transport them wherever they please.

Article 42. That in case any Englishman, or other person navigating under their flag, should happen to commit manslaughter, or any other crime, or be thereby involved in a lawsuit, the Governors in our sacred Dominions shall not proceed to the cause until the Ambassador or Consul shall be present, but they shall hear and decide it together, without their presuming to give them any the least molestation, by hearing it alone, contrary to the Holy Law and these Capitulations.

Article 43. That notwithstanding it is stipulated by the Imperial Capitulations that the merchandise laden on board all English ships proceeding to our sacred Dominions shall moreover pay over consulage to the Ambassador or Counsul for those goods on which customs are payable, certain Mahometan merchants, Sciots, Franks, and ill-disposed persons, object to the payment thereof; wherefore it is hereby commanded, that all the merchandise, unto whomsoever belonging, which shall be laden on board their ships, and have been used to pay custom, shall in future pay the consulage, without any resistance or opposition.

Article 44. That the English and other merchants navigating under their flag, who trade to Aleppo, shall pay such customs and other duties on the silks brought and laden by them on board their ships, as are paid by the French and Venetians, and not one Asper more.

....

Article 46. That in case any of the interpreters shall happen to die, if he be an Englishman proceeding from England, all his effects shall be taken possession of by the Ambassador or Consul; but should he be a subject of our Dominions, they shall be delivered up to his next heir; and having no heir, they shall be confiscated by our fiscal officers.

And it was expressly commanded and ordained, that the above-mentioned Articles and Privileges should, in future, be strictly observed and performed, according to the form and tenor thereof.

Article 47. That whereas the Corsairs of Tunis and Barbary having, contrary to the tenor of the Capitulations and our Imperial Licence, molested the merchants and other subjects of the King of England, as also those of other Kings in amity with the Sublime Porte, and plundered and pillaged their goods and property, it was expressly ordained and commanded, that the goods so plundered should be restored, and the captives released: and that if after such commands, the Tunisians and Algerines should, contrary to the tenor of our Capitulations again molest the said merchants, and pillage their goods and property, and not restore the same, but convey them to the countries and ports of our sacred Dominions, and especially to Tunis, Barbary, Modon, or Coron, the Beglerbegs, Governors, and Commandants of such places should, in future, banish and punish them, and not permit them to sell the same.

Article 48. That it is written and registered in the Capitulations, that the Governors and officers of Aleppo and other ports of our sacred Dominions, should not, contrary to the tenor of the said Capitulations, forcibly take from the English merchants any money for their silk, under the pretence of custom or other duty, but that the said merchants should pay for the silk by them purchased at Aleppo, the same as the French and Venetians do, and no more. Notwithstanding which, the Commandants of Aleppo have, under colour of custom and duty, demanded *two and a half per cent* for their silk, and thereby taken their money: wherefore we command that this matter be investigated and inquired into, in order that such money may be refunded to them by those who have taken the same; and for the future, the duty exacted from them shall be according to ancient custom, and as the Venetians and French were accustomed to pay, so that not a single asper more be taken by any new imposition.

Article 49. That the merchants of the aforesaid nation, resident at Galata, buy and receive divers goods, wares, and merchandises, and after having paid to our customer the duties thereon, and received a *Teskéré*, ascertaining their having paid the sum, preparatory to loading such goods in due time on board their ships, it sometimes happens that in the interim the customer either dies, or is removed from his station and his successor will not accept the said *Teskéré*, but demands a fresh duty from the said merchants, thereby molesting them in various ways; wherefore we do command, that on its really and truly appearing that they have once paid the duties on the goods purchased, the customer shall receive the said *Teskéré* without demanding any fresh duty.

Article 50. That the merchants of the aforesaid nation, after having once paid the duties, and received the *Teskéré*, for the camlets, mohair, silk, and other merchandise purchased by them at Angora, and transported to Constantinople and other ports of our sacred Dominions, and having deposited such goods in their own warehouses, have been again applied to for duties thereon; we do therefore hereby command that they shall no longer be molested or vexed on that head, but that when the said merchants shall be desirous of loading such goods on board their ships, and on its appearing by the *Teskéré* that they have already paid the duties thereon, no fresh custom or duty shall be demanded for the said goods, provided that the said merchants do not blend or intermix the goods which have not paid custom with those which have.

Article 51. That the merchants of the aforesaid nation, having once paid the customs on the merchandise imported into Constantinople and other ports of our sacred Dominions, and on those exported therefrom, as silks, camlets, and other goods, and being unable to sell the said goods, are under the necessity of transporting them to Smyrna, Scio, and other ports; on their arrival there the Governors and Custom-house Officers of such ports shall always accept their *Teskérés*, and forbear exacting any further duty on the said merchandise.

Article 52. That for the goods which the merchants of the nation aforesaid shall bring to Constantinople, and other ports of our sacred Dominions, and for those they shall export of our sacred Dominions, and for those they shall export from the said places, the *Mastarriagi* of Galata and Constantinople shall take their *Mastarria*, according to the old canon and ancient usage; that is to say, for those merchandises only whereon it was usually paid; but for such merchandises as have not been accustomed to pay the same, nothing shall be taken contrary to the said canon, neither shall any innovations be made in future with regard to English merchandise, nor shall one asper more be taken than is warranted by custom.

Article 53. That the merchants of the aforesaid nation shall and may always come and go into the ports and harbours of our sacred Dominions, and trade, without experiencing any obstacle from any one, with the cloths, kerseys, spice, tin, lead, and other merchandise they may bring, and, with the exception of prohibited goods, shall and may, in like manner, buy and export all sorts of merchandise, without any one presuming to prohibit or molest them; and our customers and other officers, after having received the duties thereon, according to ancient custom and the tenor of these sacred Capitulations shall not demand of them any thing more, touching which point certain clear and distinct Capitulations were granted, to the end that the Beglerbegs and other Commandants, our subjects, as also the Commandants and Lieutenants of our harbours might always act in conformity to these our Imperial Commands, and let nothing be done contrary thereto.

Article 57. That notwithstanding it is stipulated by the Capitulations that the English merchants, and other subjects of that nation, shall and may, according to their rank and condition, trade to Aleppo, Egypt, and other parts of our Imperial Dominions, and for all their goods, wares, and merchandise, pay a duty of *three per cent* only, and nothing more, according to ancient custom, the customers having molested the English merchants, with a view to oppress them and the subjects of that nation, on their arrival with their goods laden on board their ships, whether conveyed by sea or land, at our ports and harbours, under pretence of the goods so brought by them not belonging to the English; and that for goods brought from England they demanded *three per cent* only; but for those brought by them from Venice and other ports, they exacted more; wherefore, on this point, let the Imperial Capitulations granted in former times be observed, and our Governors and officers in no wise permit or consent to the same being infringed.

Article 58. That whereas it is specified in the Capitulations, that in case an Englishman should become a debtor or surety, and run away or fail, the debt shall be demanded of the debtor; and if the creditor be not in the possession of some legal document given by the surety, he shall not be arrested, nor such debt be demanded of him; should an English merchant, resident in another country, with the sole view of freeing himself of the payment of a debt, draw a bill of exchange upon another merchant, living in Turkey, and the person to whom the same is payable, being a man of power and authority, should molest such merchant who had contracted no debt to the drawer, and oppress him, contrary to law and the sacred Capitulations, by contending that the bill was drawn upon him, and that he was bound to pay the debt of the other merchant: now, We do hereby expressly command, that no such molestation be given in future; but if such merchant shall accept the bill, they shall proceed in manner and form therein pointed out; but should he refuse to accept it, he shall be liable to no further trouble.

Article 59. That the interpreters of the English Ambassadors, having always been free and exempt from all contributions and impositions whatever, respect shall in future be paid to the Articles of the Capitulations stipulated in ancient times, without the fiscal officers intermeddling with the effects of any of the interpreters who may happen to die, which effects shall be distributed amongst his heirs.

Article 60. That the aforesaid King, having been a true friend of our Sublime Porte, his Ambassador, who resides here, shall be allowed ten servants, of any nation whatsoever, who shall be exempt from impositions, and in no manner molested.

Article 61. That if any Englishman should turn Turk, and it should be represented and proved, that besides his own goods, he has in his hands any property belonging to another person in England, such property shall be taken from him and delivered up to the Ambassador or Consul, that they may convey the same to the owner thereof.

Article 62. That for every piece of cloth, called *Londra*, which, from ancient times, was always brought by the English ships to Alexandria, there should be taken in that place a duty of forty paras; for every piece of kersey six paras; for every bale of hare-skins six paras; and for every quintal of tin and lead, Damascus weight, fifty-seven paras and a half.

Article 63. That on afterwards transporting the said goods from Alexandria to Aleppo, there should be demanded, by the custom-house officers of Aleppo, for every piece of *Londra* eighty paras; for a piece of kersey eight paras and two aspers; for every bundle of hare-skins eight paras and two aspers; and for every Aleppo weight of tin and lead one para.

Article 64. That on the goods purchased by the aforesaid nation at Aleppo, there should be paid for transport duty, on every bale of unbleached linen, cordovans, and *Chorasani-hindi*, two dollars and a half; for every bale of cotton yarn one dollar and a quarter; for every bale of galls one quarter; for every bale of silk ten osmans; and for rhubarb and other trifles, and various sorts of drugs, according to a valuation to be made by the appraiser there should be taken a duty of *three per cent*.

Article 65. That on carrying the said goods to Alexandria, and there loading them on board their ships, there should be taken for transport duty, on every bale of unbleached linen and cordovans one dollar and a half; for every bale of *Chorosani-hindi* and cotton-yarn, three quarters, for every bale of galls one quarter; and for rhubarb and other trifles, and various sorts of drugs, after a valuation made thereof, there should be taken three quarters of a piastre; and that for the future no demand whatever to the contrary should be submitted to.

Article 66. That all commands issued by the Chamber contrary to the above-mentioned Articles should not be obeyed; but for the future, every thing be observed conformably to the tenour of the Capitulations and the Imperial Signet.

Article 67. It being stipulated by the Capitulations that the English merchants shall pay a duty of *three per cent* on all goods by them imported and exported, without being bound to pay an asper more; and disputes having arisen with the customers on this head, they shall continue to pay duty as heretofore paid by them at the rate of *three per cent* only, neither more nor less.

Article 68. That for the *Londra* and other cloths manufactured in England, whether fine or coarse, and of whatsoever price, imported by them into the ports of Constantinople and Galata, there shall be taken, according to the ancient canons, and as they have always hitherto paid, one hundred and forty-four aspers, computing the dollar at eighty aspers, and the leone at seventy, and nothing more shall be exacted from them; but the cloths of Holland and other countries, viz. serges, *Londrina* scarlets, and other cloths, shall pay, for the future, that which hitherto has been the accustomed duty; and at Smyrna likewise shall be paid, according to ancient custom, calculated in dollars and leones, for every piece of *Londra* or other cloth of English fabric, whether fine or coarse, one hundred and twenty aspers, without an asper more being demanded, or any innovation being made therein.

Article 69. It being registered in the Imperial Capitulations that all suits wherein the English are parties, and exceeding the sum of four thousand aspers shall be heard in our Sublime Porte, and nowhere else:

That if at any time the Commanders and Governors should arrest any English merchant, or other Englishman, on the point of departure by any ship, by reason of any debt or demand upon him, if the Consul of the place will give bail for him, by offering himself as surety until such suit shall be decided in our Imperial Divan, such person so arrested shall be released, and not imprisoned or prevented from prosecuting his voyage, and they who claim any thing from him shall present themselves in our Imperial Divan, and there submit their claims, in order that the Ambassador may furnish an answer thereto. With regard to those for whom the Consul shall not have given bail, the Commandant may act as he shall think proper.

Article 70. That all English ships coming from the ports of Constantinople, Alexandria, Smyrna, Cyprus, and other ports of our sacred Dominions, shall pay three hundred aspers for anchorage duty, without an asper more being demanded from them.

Article 71. That should any Englishman coming with merchandise, turn Turk, and the goods so imported by him be proved to belong to merchants of his own country, from whom he had taken them, the whole shall be detained, with the ready money, and delivered up to the Ambassador, in order to his transmitting the same to the right owners, without any of our judges or officers interposing any obstacle for hindrance thereto.

Article 72. That no molestation shall be given to any of the aforesaid nation buying camlets, mohairs, or grogram yarn, at Angora and Beghbazar, and desirous of exporting the same from thence, after having paid the duty of *three per cent*, by any demand of customs for the exportation thereof, neither shall one asper more be demanded of them.

Article 74. That the King, having always been a friend to the Sublime Porte, out of regard to such good friendship, His Majesty shall and may, with his own money, purchase for his own kitchen, at Smyrna, Salonica, or any other port of our sacred Dominions, in fertile and abundant years, and not in times of dearth or scarcity, two cargoes of figs and raisins, and after having paid a duty of *three per cent* thereon, no obstacle or hindrance shall be given thereto.

Article 75. That it being represented to Us that the English merchants have been accustomed hitherto to pay no custom or scale duty, either on the silks bought by them at Brussa and Constantinople, or on those which come from Persia and Georgia, and are purchased by them at Smyrna from the Armenians; if such usage or custom really exists, and the same be not prejudicial to the Empire, such duty shall not be paid in future: and the said Ambassador having requested that the aforegoing Articles might be duly respected and added to the Imperial Capitulations, his request was acceded to; therefore in the same manner as the Capitulations were heretofore conceded by our Imperial *Hatti-sheriff*, so are they now in the like manner renewed by our Imperial Command; wherefore, in conformity to the Imperial Signet, We have again granted these sacred Capitulations, which We command to be observed, so long as the said King shall continue to maintain that good friendship and understanding with our Sublime Porte, which was maintained in the happy time of our glorious Ancestors, which friendship We, on our part, accept; and adhering to these Articles and Stipulations, We do hereby promise and swear, by the one Omnipotent God, the Creator of Heaven and Earth, and of all creatures, that We will permit nothing to be done or transacted contrary to the tenour of the Articles and Stipulations heretofore made, and these Imperial Capitulations; and accordingly every one is to yield implicit faith and obedience to this our Imperial Signet, affixed in the middle of the month of Gemaziel, in the year 1086.*

* Corresponding with the year (A.D.) 1675.

(Source: *Treaties, & c. between Turkey and Foreign Powers, 1535-1855*, London 1855, pp. 247-268.)

APPENDIX 5

Treaty of Commerce and Navigation between The United States and the Ottoman Porte

Signed at Constantinople, May 7th, 1830. (Article 1-Article 9)

Article 1. Merchants of the Sublime Porte, whether Mussulmans or Rayahs going and coming in the Countries, Provinces, and Ports, of the United States of America, or proceeding from one Port to another, or from the Ports of The United States to those of other Countries, shall pay the same Duties and other Imposts that are paid by the most favoured Nations; and they shall not be vexed by the exaction of higher Duties; and in travelling by sea and by land, all the privileges and distinctions observed towards the Subjects of other Powers, shall serve as a rule, and shall be observed towards the Merchants and Subjects of the Sublime Porte. In like manner, American Merchants who shall come to the well defended countries and Ports of the Sublime Porte, shall pay the same Duties and other Imposts, that are paid by Merchants of the most favoured friendly Powers; and they shall not, in any way, be vexed or molested. On both sides, travelling Passports shall be granted.

Article 2. The Sublime Porte may establish *Shahbenders* (Consuls) in the United States of America; and The United States may appoint their Citizens to be Consuls or Vice Consuls, at the commercial places in the Dominions of the Sublime Porte, where it shall be found needful to superintend the affair of commerce, these Consuls, or Vice-Consuls, shall be furnished with *Berats* or *Firmans;* they shall enjoy suitable distinction, and shall have necessary aid and protection.

Article 3. American Merchants established in the well-defended States of the Sublime Porte, for purposes of commerce, shall have liberty to employ *Semrars* (Brokers) of any Nation, or religion, in like manner as Merchants of other friendly Powers; and they shall not be disturbed in their affairs, nor shall they be treated, in any way, contrary to established usages. American Vessels arriving at, or departing from, the Ports of the Ottoman Empire, shall not be subjected to greater visit, by the Officers of the Custom House, and the Chancery of the Port, than Vessels of the most favoured Nation.

Article 4. If litigations and disputes should arise between Subjects of the Sublime Porte and Citizens of the United States, the parties shall not be heard, nor shall judgment be pronounced, unless the American Dragoman be present. Causes in which the sum may exceed 500 piastres, shall be submitted to the Sublime Porte, to be decided according to the laws of equity and justice. Citizens of the United States of America, quietly pursuing their Commerce, and not being charged or convicted of any crime or offence, shall not be molested; and even when they may have committed some offence they shall not be arrested and put in prison by the Local Authorities, but they shall be tried by their Minister or Consul, and punished according to their offence; following, in this respect, the usage observed towards other Franks.

Article 5. American Merchant Vessels that trade to the Dominions of the Sublime Porte, may go and come in perfect safety with their own Flag, but they shall not take the Flag of any other Power, nor shall they grant their Flag to the Vessels of other Nations and Powers, not to the Vessels of Rayahs. The Minister, Consuls, and Vice Consuls of the United States shall not protect, secretly or publicly, the Rayahs of the Sublime Porte, and they shall never suffer a departure from the principles here laid down and agreed to by mutual consent.

Article 6. Vessels of War of the two Contracting Parties shall observe towards each other demonstrations of friendship and good intelligence, according to naval usage; and towards Merchant Vessels they shall exhibit the same kind and courteous manner.

Article 7. Merchant Vessels of the United States, in like manner as Vessels of the most favoured Nations, shall have liberty to pass the Canal of the Imperial Residence, and go and come in the Black Sea, either laden or in ballast; and they may be laden with the produce, manufactures, and effects, of the Ottoman Empire, excepting such as are prohibited, as well as of their own Country.

Article 8. Merchant Vessels of the two Contracting Parties shall not be forcibly taken for the shipment of troops, munitions, and other subjects of War, if the Captains or Proprietors of the Vessels shall be unwilling to freight them.

Article 9. If any Merchant Vessel of either of the Contracting Parties should be wrecked, assistance and protection shall be afforded to those of the Crew that may be saved; and the merchandise and effects which it may be possible to save and recover, shall be conveyed to the Consul nearest to the place of the wreck, to be by him delivered to the Proprietors.

(Source: *Treaties, & c. between Turkey and Foreign Powers, 1535-1855*, London, 1855, pp. 698-9.)

APPENDIX 6

Imperial Ottoman Firman for the Protection of English Steam Vessels Destined to Navigate the River Euphrates, dated December 29th, 1834

To their Excellencies the Viziers, Pashas of three tails, to the illustrious Miri Mirans, Pashas of two tails, to the learned Judges, to the Wainadas, Captains of Ports, and other Magistrates of places situated on both banks of the Euphrates, health.

On receiving the imperial command, you will know as follows: The Ambassador Extraordinary and Plenipotentiary of Great Britain at Constantinople, Lord Ponsonby, one of the most illustrious personages among the Christian nations, has presented at our Sublime Porte an official note, by which he intimates that the British Government requires permission to cause to navigate by turns two boats on the river Euphrates which flows at a small distance from the city of Bagdad, for the purpose of facilitating commerce.

We in consequence issued to our very illustrious governor of Bagdad and Bussora, Ali Reza Pasha, an order to furnish our Sublime Porte with information of the proposed navigation.

Although the answer of the Pasha had not arrived, the Ambassador made representations on this point, informing our Sublime Porte (that) the British Government awaited our reply.

For this reason we have and do permit two steam boats to navigate the Euphrates by turns, and this navigation is to continue as long as, conformably to what has been represented to us, it may prove useful to the two powers, and no inconvenience result therefrom, and it is to this purpose that an official rule has been transmitted to the British Ambassador.

A firman couched in the same terms has been addressed to the Pasha of Bagdad and Bussora.

Sublime Porte. Le 13 juillet.

(Source: C. U. Aitchison, *A Collection of Treaties, Engagements and Sanads*, 1909, Vol. XIII, pp. 16-17.)

APPENDIX 7

Convention of Commerce and Navigation between Her Majesty and the Sultan of the Ottoman Empire. Signed at Balta-Liman, near Constantinople, August 16th, 1838

(The main part only)

Article 1. All rights, privileges, and Immunities which have been conferred on the subjects or ships of Great Britain by the existing Capitulations and Treaties, are confirmed now and for ever, except in as far as they may be specifically altered by the present Convention: and it is moreover expressly stipulated, that all rights, privileges, or immunities which the Sublime Porte now grants, or may hereafter grant, to the ships and subjects of any other foreign Power to enjoy, shall be equally granted to, and exercised and enjoyed by, the subjects and ships of Great Britain.

Article 2. The subjects of Her Britannic Majesty, or their agents, shall be permitted to purchase at all places in the Ottoman Dominions (whether for the purposes of internal trade or exportation) all articles, without any exception whatsoever, the produce, growth, or manufacture of the said Dominions; and the Sublime Porte formally engages to abolish all monopolies of agricultural produce, or of any other articles whatsoever, as well as all *Permits* from the local Governors, either for the purchase of any article, or for its removal from one place to another when purchased; and any attempt to compel the subjects of Her Britannic Majesty to receive such *Permits* from the local Governors, shall be considered as an infraction of Treaties, and the Sublime Porte shall immediately punish with severity Vizirs and other officers who shall have been guilty of such misconduct, and render full justice to British subjects for all injuries or losses which they may duly prove themselves to have suffered.

Article 3. If any article of Turkish produce, growth, or manufacture, be purchased the British merchant or his agent, for the purpose of selling the same for internal consumption in Turkey, the British merchant or his agent shall pay, at the purchase and sale of such articles, and in any manner of trade therein, the same duties that are paid, in similar circumstances, by the most favoured class of Turkish subjects engaged in the internal trade of Turkey, whether Mussulmans or Rayahs.

Article 4. If any article of Turkish produce, growth, or manufacture, be purchased for exportation, the same shall be conveyed by the British merchant or his agent, free of any kind of charge or duty whatsoever, to a convenient place of shipment, on its entry into which it shall be liable to one fixed duty of nine per cent. *ad valorem* in lieu of all other interior duties.

Subsequently, on exportation, the duty of three per cent., as established and existing at present, shall be paid. But all articles bought in the shipping ports for exportation, and which have already paid the interior duty at entering into the same, will only pay the three per cent. export duty.

Article 5. The regulations under which Firmans are issued to British merchant vessels for passing the Dardanelles and the Bosphorus, shall be so framed as to occasion to such vessels the least possible delay.

Article 6. It is agreed by the Turkish Government, that the regulations, established in the present Convention, shall be general throughout the Turkish Empire, whether in Turkey in Europe or Turkey in Asia, in Egypt, or other African possessions belonging to the Sublime Porte, and shall be applicable to all the subjects, whatever their description, of the Ottoman Dominions: and the Turkish Government also agrees not to object to other foreign Powers settling their trade upon the basis of this present Convention.

Article 7. It having been the custom of Great Britain and the Sublime Porte, with a view to prevent all difficulties and delay, in estimating the value of articles imported into the Turkish Dominions, or exported therefrom, by British subjects, to appoint, at intervals of fourteen years, a Commission of men well acquainted with the traffic of both countries, who have fixed by a tariff the sum of money in the coin of the Grand Signior, which should be paid as duty on each article; and the term of fourteen years, during which the last adjustment of the said tariff was to remain in force, having expired, the High Contracting Parties have agreed to name conjointly fresh Commissioners to fix and determine the amount in money which is to be paid by British subjects, as the duty of three per cent upon the value of all commodities imported and exported by them; and the said Commissioners shall establish an equitable arrangement for estimating the interior duties which, by the present Treaty, are established on Turkish goods to be exported, and shall also determine on the places of shipment where it may be most convenient that such duties should be levied.

The new tariff thus established, to be in force for seven years after it has been fixed, at the end of which time it shall be in the power of either of the parties to demand a revision of that tariff; but if no such demand be made on either side, within the six months after the end of the first seven years, then the tariff shall remain in force for seven years more, reckoned from the end of the preceding seven years; and so it shall be at the end of each successive period of seven years.

Article 8. The present Convention shall be ratified, and the ratification shall be exchanged at Constantinople within the space of four months.

In witness whereof, the respective Plenipotentiaries have signed the same, and have affixed their seals thereunto.

Done at Balta-Liman, near Constantinople, on the sixteenth day of August, one thousand eight hundred and thirty-eight.

(L.S.) Ponsonby.

(Signed in Turkish Original)
(L.S.) Mustapha Reshid
(L.S.) Mustapha Khianee
(L.S.) Mehmed Nouree.

(Source: *Parliamentary Papers*, 1839, Vol. L, pp. 291-295.)

APPENDIX 8

The Hatti Sherif of Gülhane

November 3rd, 1839

All the world knows that in the first days of the Ottoman Monarchy, the glorious precepts of the Koran and the laws of the empire were always honored.

The empire in consequence increased in strength and greatness, and all its subjects, without exception, had risen in the highest degree to ease and prosperity. In the last one hundred and fifty years a succession of accidents and divers causes have arisen which have brought about a disregard for the sacred code of laws and the regulations flowing therefrom, and the former strength and prosperity have changed into weakness and poverty; an empire in fact loses all its stability as soon as it ceases to observe its laws.

These considerations are ever present to our mind, and ever since the day of our advent to the throne the thought of the public weal, of the improvement of the state of the provinces, and of relief to the (subject) peoples, has not ceased to engage it. If, therefore, the geographical position of the Ottoman provinces, the fertility of the soil, the aptitude and intelligence of the inhabitants, are considered, the conviction will remain that by striving to find efficacious means, the result, which by the help of God we hope to attain, can be obtained within a few years. Full of confidence, therefore, in the help of the Most High, and certain of the support of our Prophet, we deem it right to seek by new institutions to give to the provinces composing the Ottoman Empire the benefit of a good administration.

These institutions must be principally carried out under three heads, which are:
1. The guarantees insuring to our subjects perfect security for life, honor, and fortune.
2. A regular system of assessing and levying taxes.
3. An equally regular system for the levying of troops and the duration of their service.

And, in fact, are not life and honor the most precious gifts to mankind? What man, however much his character may be against violence, can prevent himself from having recourse to it, and thereby injure the government and the country, if his life and honor are endangered? If, on the contrary, he enjoys in that respect perfect security, he will not depart from the ways of loyalty, and all his actions will contribute to the good of the government and of his brothers.

If there is an absence of security as to one's fortune, everyone remains insensible to the voice of the Prince and the country; no one interests himself in the progress of public good, absorbed as he is in his own troubles. If, on the contrary, the citizen keeps possession in all confidence of all his goods, then, full of ardor in his affairs, which he seeks to enlarge in order to increase his comforts, he feels daily growing and doubling in his heart not only his love for the Prince and country, but also his devotion to his native land.

These feelings become in him the source of the most praiseworthy actions.

As to the regular and fixed assessment of the taxes, it is very important that it be regulated; for the state which is forced to incur many expenses for the defense of its territory cannot obtain the money necessary for its armies and other services except by means of contributions levied on its subjects. Although, thanks be to God, our empire has for some time past been delivered from the scourge of monopolies, falsely considered in times of war as a source of revenue, a fatal custom still exists, although it can only have disastrous consequences; it is that of venal concessions, known under the name of "Iltizam".

Under that name the civil and financial administration of a locality is delivered over to the passions of a single man; that is to say, sometimes to the iron grasp of the most violent and avaricious passions, for if that contractor is not a good man, he will only look to his own advantages.

It is therefore necessary that henceforth each member of Ottoman society should be taxed for a quota of a fixed tax according to his fortune and means, and that it should not be possible that anything more could be exacted from him. It is also necessary that special laws should fix and limit the expenses of our land and sea forces.

(Further on the Hatt deals mainly with legal and religious issues.)

(Source: Report for 1880, by Ed. A. Van Dyck, Part I. The Capitulations, in *The Executive Documents, Senate of the U.S.*, 1881, Vol. 3, No. 3, Appendix XII, pp. 106-108.)

APPENDIX 9

The Hatti Hümayun by Sultan Abdul Mejid relative to Privileges and Reforms in Turkey (1856)

(Excerpts)

...Let it be done as herein set forth.

To you, my Grand Vizier, Mehemed Emin Aali Pasha, decorated with my Imperial Order of the Medjidiyé of the first class, and with the Order of Personal Merit; may God grant to you greatness, and increase your power.

It has always been my most earnest desire to insure the happiness of all classes of the subjects whom Divine Providence had placed under my imperial sceptre, and since my accession to the Throne I have not ceased to direct all my efforts to the attainment of that end.

...The guarantees promised on our part by the Hatti-Humaïoun of Gul-Hané, and in conformity with the Tanzimat, to all the subjects of my Empire, without distinction of classes or of religion, for the security of their persons and property, and the preservation of their honor, are to-day confirmed and consolidated, and efficacious measures shall be taken in order that they may have their full entire effect.

...All commercial, correctional, and criminal suits between Mussulmans and Christians, or other non-Mussulman subjects, or between Christians or other non-Mussulmans of different sects, shall be referred to Mixed Tribunals.

...The equality of taxes entailing equality of burdens, as equality of duties entails that of rights, Christian subjects, and those of other non-Mussulman sects, as it has been already decided, shall, as well as Mussulmans, be subject to the obligations of the Law of Recruitment. The principle of obtaining substitutes, or of purchasing exemption, shall be admitted. A complete law shall be published, with as little delay as possible, respecting the admission into and service in the army of Christian and other non-Mussulman subjects.

...As the laws regulating the purchase, sale, and disposal of real property are common to all the subjects of my Empire, it shall be lawful for foreigners to possess landed property in my dominions, conforming themselves to the laws and police regulations, and bearing the same charges as the native inhabitants, and after arrangements have been come to with foreign Powers.

The taxes are to be levied under the same denomination from all the subjects of my Empire, without distinction of class or of religion. The most prompt and energetic means for remedying the abuses in collecting the taxes, and especially the tithes, shall be considered. The system of direct collections shall gradually, and as soon as possible, be substituted for the plan of farming, in all the branches of the revenues of the State. As long as the present system remains in force all agents of the Government and all members of the Medjlis shall be forbidden under the severest penalties, to become lessees of any farming contracts which are announced for public competition or to have any beneficial interest in carrying them out. The local taxes shall, as far as possible, be so imposed as not to affect the sources of production or to hinder the progress of internal commerce.

Works of public utility shall receive a suitable endowment, part of which shall be raised from private and special taxes levied in the Provinces, which shall have the benefit of the advantages arising from the establishment of ways of communication by land and sea.

A special law having been already passed, which declares that the budget of the revenue and the expenditure of the State shall be drawn up and made known every year, the said law shall be most scrupulously observed. Proceedings shall be taken for revising the emoluments attached to each office.

...Steps shall be taken for the formation of banks and other similar institutions, so as to effect a reform in the monetary and financial system, as well as to create funds to be employed in augmenting the sources of the material wealth of my Empire.

Steps shall also be taken for the formation of roads and canals to increase the facilities of communication and increase the sources of the wealth of the country. Everything that can impede commerce or agriculture shall be abolished. To accomplish these objects means shall be sought to profit by the science, the art, and the funds of Europe, and thus gradually to execute them.

(Source: *Parliamentary Papers*, 1856, LXI, pp. 348-351.)

APPENDIX 10

The Ottoman Land Code

(1858)

(Excerpts)

I. Land Law

1. Land in Turkey is divided into five classes:
    i. Arazi Memluké. Lands held in fee simple, freehold lands.
    ii. Arazi Mirié. Crown lands, belonging to the state exchequer.
    iii. Arazi Mevkufé. Lands possessed in mortmain, but tenanted by a kind of copyhold.
    iv. Arazi Metruké. Lands abandoned without cultivation or ostensible owner.
    v. Arazi Mevat. Dead lands, uncultivated and unappropriated.
2. Arazi Memluké is of four kinds:
    i. Building sites within the town or village, and places on the border of such town or village, of at most half a donum in extent considered as the complement of habitation.
    ii. Land separated from Arazi Mirié which has been given into the possession of a person to be held freehold by patent from the Crown and to be possessed with all the conditions of freehold proprietorship in accordance with the permission of the Sheri (Religious Law).
    iii. Arazi Ushrié. Places given into the possession and distributed among the conquerors at the time of the conquest.
    iv. Arazi Kharajié. Places left in the hands of the original non-Moslim owners at the same time.

Kharaj Arazi is of two classes:

One is Kharaj Mukaseme, from the produce of which land, according to its capability, one-tenth to one-half has been fixed to be taken.

The other is Kharaj Muwazzaf, on which land, by way of limitation, a fixed sum of money is assigned to be paid.

The servitude of all Arazi Memluké, that is the land itself and its proprietorship, belongs to the owner: like other property and goods it can be inherited, and it is subject to the privisions of Vakf, mortgage (Rehn), gift and pre-emption.

When Arazi Ushrié and Kharajié belongs to the Beit ul Mal by the death of the owner without heirs, it acquires the effect of Arazi Mirié.

The procedure to be followed with regard to the four kinds of Arazi Memluké having been explained in the Kutb Fikhié (Books of Religious Law), the provisions of Arazi Memluké will not be treated on in this law.

3. The servitude of Arazi Mirié belongs to the Beit ul Mal. The places of which the transfer and gift comes to the Government are arable fields, pastures, yaylaks, kishlaks, woods, &c., which formerly, in case of sale or vacancy, were held with the permission and through the gift of the possessors of Timars and Ziamets, who were considered the owners of the soil, and for some time with the permission and through the gift of the Multezims and Muhassils. Subsequently, on account of these being abolished, as at present, they are held by the permission and through the gift of the person appointed by the Government as official for this purpose, and a title-deed with the Tughra at the top is given to the owner.

Tapu is the Muajele (immediate payment) given in exchange for the right to possess, and is collected by the official for the Government.

4. Arazi Mevkufé is of two classes:

i. Is land which while being really Arazi Memluké has been made Vakf in accordance with the Sheri. The servitude and all the rights of possession of this kind of Arazi Mevkufé being that which concerns the Vakf, the provisions of the law do not apply to it; and as it is necessary that they should be treated in accordance with the conditions, whatever they may be, of the bequeather only, this class of Arazi Mevkufé will not be treated on in this law.

ii. Is land separated from Arazi Mirié which has been made Vakf by the Sultans or by others with the permission of the Sultan, as the Vakfiet of this kind of land only means that the Government dues, such as the tithes and taxes, of a piece of land separated from Arazi Mirié have been assigned to some object by the Sultan, this kind of Arazi Mirié is not real Vakf (Evkaf Sahiha). Most of the Arazi Mevkufé in the Imperial dominions is of this category; and the servitude of this Takhsisat category of Arazi Mevkufé, like simple Arazi Mirié, being that which concerns the Beit ul Mal, the legal procedure which will be explained and stated hereafter will be carried out entirely regarding it. But in the same way as the fees on sale and inheritance, and the equivalent value of vacant (Bedel Mahlulat) simple Arazi Mirié belong to the Government, so also in this kind of Arazi Mevkufé they belong to the Vakf. As the provisions which will be stated hereafter with regard to Arazi Mirié shall also be applied to this category of Arazi Mevkufé, whenever the term Arazi Mevkufé is used in this law, this "Takhsisat" category of Arazi Mevkufé is meant. But there is also a kind of this category of Arazi Mevkufé of which, while the tithes and taxes belong to the Government in the same way as its servitude belongs to the Beit ul Mal, only the rights of possession have been assigned to some object, or its servitude belonging to the Beit ul Mal, the tithes and taxes together with the rights of possession have been assigned to some object. The provisions and procedure of the law do not apply to the sale and inheritance of this kind of Arazi Mevkufé, which are possessed and cultivated only on behalf of the Vakf, either by itself or by way of letting, and the profits derived therefrom shall be expended on the thing or person in whose favour it is stipulated.

5. Arazi Metruké is of two classes:
  i. Are places which have been left for the public. Public roads are of this category.
  ii. Are places which are left and assigned to the inhabitants in general of a village or town, or of several villages or towns. Pasture lands (meras) assigned to the inhabitants of towns or villages are of this category.

6. Arazi Mevat is waste (Khali) land which is not in the possession of anybody, and, not having been left or assigned to the inhabitants, is distant from town or village so that the loud voice of a person from the extreme inhabited spot cannot be heard, that is about a mile and a half to the extreme inhabited spot, or a distance of about half an hour.

7. This Land Law is divided into three books:
Book I. Arazi Mirié.
Book II. Arazi Metruké and Arazi Mevat, in which book Mountains (Jibal Mubah) will also be treated.
Book III. Muteferikat (Diverse).

Article 78. If a person has possessed Arazi Mirié and Mevkufé for ten years without disturbance his prescriptive right (Hak Karar) becomes proved, and whether he has a title-deed or not such land cannot be looked upon as Mahlul, but a new Tapu Sened should be given to him gratis. But if he admits that such land was Mahlul and he took it without right, no consideration will be paid to the passage of time, but the land will be offered to him for its Tapu value, and if he refuses it will be sold by auction to the candidate.

II. Tapu Law

1. The Mal Memours, that is to say, the Defterdars, Malmudirs, and Kaza Mudirs, being authorised to confer Arazi Mirié in the provinces, they are in the position of the owner of the land.

2. The Mudirs of Agriculture have no special concern in matters of alienation, inheritance, and transfer of the said land, and they will only have the same authority as other members in their quality of members of the Council.

3. When a person desires to alienate his land to another, he must get a certificate bearing the seals of the Imam and Mukhtar of his quarter or village, stating that he is really the owner of such land, the true amount of how many piastres he is going to alienate it for, the Kaza and village in which it is situate, its boundaries, and the number of donums. When the alienor and alienee, or their legal agents, come to the Mejlis of the Country, the certificate brought by them will be taken and kept, and after the fees of the alienation have been paid, their statements will be taken in the presence of the Mudir of the Country if it is at the head-quarters of a Kaza, and the Mal Memours if it is at the head-quarters of a Liva or Vilayet; and the process of its registration will be carried out, and the title-deed in hand will be taken, if at the head-quarters of a Kaza and sent with a Mazbata and the said fees to the head-quarters of the Liva, to which it is attached, in order to have an annotation written in the margin, or, if it is an old one, for it to be changed and the old one kept. There the Mazbata of the Kaza will be kept and the registration carried out, and in accordance therewith another Mazbata will be prepared and sent to the Defter Khané. If it is at the head-quarters of the Liva, the Mazbata will be at once prepared and sent to the Defter Khané. If the alienor has no old title-deed, the nature of his possession should be stated in the Mazbatas prepared as above...

(Source: *The Ottoman Land Code*, translated from the Turkish by F. Ongley, London, 1892.)

APPENDIX 11

Treaty of Commerce and Navigation between Her Majesty and the Sultan

Signed at Kanlidja, April 29th, 1861

(Ratifications exchanged at Constantinople, July 9th, 1861)

Her Majesty the Queen of the United Kingdom of Great Britain and Ireland, on the one part, and His Majesty the Emperor of the Ottomans, on the other part being equally animated by the desire of extending the commercial relations between their respective dominions, have agreed, for this purpose, to conclude a (treaty) of Commerce and Navigation, and have named as their respective Plenipotentiaries, that is to say:

Her Majesty the Queen of the United Kingdom of Great Britain and Ireland, the Right Honourable Sir Henry Lytton Bulwer, a Member of Her Britannic Majesty's Most Honourable Privy Council, Knight Grand Cross of the Most Honourable Order Treaty of the Bath, and Her Majesty's Ambassador Extraordinary and Plenipotentiary to the Sublime Porte;

And His Majesty the Emperor of the Ottomans, His Highness Mehemed Emin Aali Pasha, President of the Council of the Tanzimat, and Acting Minister for Foreign Affairs, decorated with the Orders of the Medjidié and Merit of the First Class, Grand Cross of the Imperial Order of the Legion of Honour, of Saint Stephen of Austria, of the Red Eagle of Prussia, of Saint Alexander Newsky of Russia, and several other Foreign Orders;

Who, after having communicated to each other their respective full powers, found in good and due form, have agreed upon the following Articles:

Article 1. All rights, privileges, and immunities which have been conferred on the subjects or ships of Great Britain by the existing Capitulations and Treaties are confirmed now and for ever, with the exception of those clauses of the said Capitulations which it is the object of the present Treaty to modify; and it is moreover expressly stipulated, that all rights, privileges, or immunities which the Sublime Porte now grants or may hereafter to grant to, or suffer to be enjoyed by, the subjects, ships, commerce, or navigation of any other foreign Power, shall be equally granted to and exercised and enjoyed by, the subjects, ships, commerce, and navigation of Great Britain.

Article 2. The subjects of Her Britannic Majesty, or their agents, shall be permitted to purchase, at all places in the Ottoman dominions and possessions (whether for the purposes of internal trade or of exportation) all articles without any exception whatsoever, the produce or manufacture of the said dominions and possessions; and the Sublime Porte having, in virtue of the Second Article of the Convention of Commerce of the 16th of August, 1838, formally engaged to abolish all monopolies of agricultural produce or of any articles whatsoever, as well as all permits (teskérés) from the local Governors, either for the purchase of any article, or for its removal from one place to another, when purchased, any attempt to compel the subjects of Her Britannic Majesty to receive such permits from the local Governors shall be considered as an infraction of Treaties and the Sublime Porte shall immediately punish with severity and Viziers or other officers who shall have been guilty of such misconduct, and shall render full justice to British subjects for all injuries or losses which they may duly prove themselves to have suffered thereby.

Article 3. If any article of Turkish produce or manufacture be purchased by British merchants or their agents, for the purpose of selling the same for internal consumption in Turkey, the said British merchants or their agents shall pay, at the purchase and sale of such articles, and in any manner of trade therein, the same duties that are paid in similar circumstances by the most favoured class of Ottoman subjects, or of foreigners engaged in the internal trade of Turkey.

Article 4. No other or higher duties or charges shall be imposed in the dominions and possessions of either of the Contracting Parties, on the exportation of any article to the dominions and possessions of the other, than such as are or may be payable on the exportation of the like article to any other foreign country; nor shall any prohibition be imposed on the exportation of any article from the dominions and possessions of the either of the two Contracting Parties to the dominions and possessions of the other, which shall not equally extend to the exportation of the like article to any other country.

No charge or duty whatsoever will be demanded on any article of Turkish produce or manufacture purchased by British subjects or their agents, either at the place where such article is purchased, or in its transit from that place to the place whence it is exported, at which it will be subject to an export duty not exceeding eight per cent. calculated on the value at the place of shipment, and payable on exportation; and all articles which shall once have paid this duty shall not again be liable to the same duty, however they may have changed hands, within any part of the Ottoman dominions.

It is furthermore agreed that the duty of eight per cent above mentioned will be annually reduced by one (1) per cent., until it shall be in this manner finally reduced to a fixed duty of one (1) per cent. *ad valorem*, destined to cover the general expenses of administration and control.

Article 5. No other or higher duties shall be imposed on the importation into the dominions and possessions of Her Britannic Majesty, of any article the produce or manufacture of the dominions and possessions of His Imperial Majesty the Sultan, from whatever place arriving, whether by sea or by land, and no other or higher duties shall be imposed on the importation into the dominions and possessions of His Imperial Majesty, of any article the produce or manufacture of Her Britannic Majesty's dominions and possessions, from whatever place arriving, than are or may be payable on the like article the produce or manufacture of any other foreign country; nor shall any prohibition be maintained or imposed on the importation of any article the produce or manufacture of the dominions and possessions of either of the Contracting Parties into the dominions and possessions of the other, which shall not equally extend to the importation of the like articles being the produce or manufacture of any other country.

His Imperial Majesty further engages that, save as hereinafter excepted, he will not prohibit the importation into his dominions and possessions of Her Britannic Majesty, from whatever place arriving; and that duties to be imposed on any article the produce or manufacture of the dominions or possessions of Her Britannic Majesty imported into the dominions or possessions of His Imperial Majesty, shall in no case exceed one fixed rate of eight (8) per cent. *ad valorem*, or a specific duty, fixed by common assent equivalent thereto.

Such rate shall be calculated upon the value of such articles at the wharf, and shall be payable at the time of their being landed, if brought by sea, or at the first Customhouse they may reach, if brought by land.

If these articles, after having paid the import duty of eight (8) per cent., are sold either at the place of their arrival or in the interior of the country, neither the buyer nor the seller shall be charged with any further duty in respect to them and if such articles should not be sold for consumption in Turkey, but should be re-exported within the space of six months, the same shall be considered as merchandise in transit by land, and be treated as is stated in Article 12; the Administration of the Customs being bound to restore at the time of their re-exportation to the merchant, who shall be required to furnish proof that the goods in question have paid the import duty of eight (8) per cent., the difference between that duty and the duty levied on goods in transit by land, as set forth in the Article above cited.

Article 6. It is understood that any Article the produce or manufacture of a foreign country, intended for importation into the United Principalities of Moldo-Wallachia, or into the Principality of Servia, which shall pass through any other part of the Ottoman dominions, will not be liable to the payment of Customs duty until it reaches those Principalities; and, on the other hand, that any article of foreign produce or manufacture passing through these Principalities, but destined for some other part of the Ottoman dominions, will not be liable to the payment of Customs duty until such article reaches the first Custom-house under the direct administration of the Sublime Porte.

The same course shall be followed with respect to any article the produce or manufacture of those Principalities, as well as with respect to any article the produce or manufacture of any other portion of the Ottoman dominions, intended for exportation: such articles will be liable to the payment of Customs duties the former to the Custom-house of the aforesaid Principalities, and the latter to the Ottoman Custom-house, the object being, that neither import nor export duties shall in any case be payable more than once.

Article 7. The subjects of one of the Contracting Parties shall enjoy, in the dominions and possessions of the other, equality of treatment with native subjects in regard to warehousing, and also, in regard to bounties, facilities, and drawbacks.

Article 8. All articles which are or may be legally importable into the dominions and possessions of Her Britannic Majesty, in British vessels, may likewise be imported in Ottoman vessels, without being liable to any other or higher duties or charges, of whatever denomination, than if such articles were imported in British vessels; and reciprocally, all articles which are or may be legally importable into the dominions and possessions of His Imperial Majesty the dominions and possessions of His Imperial Majesty the Sultan in Ottoman vessels, may likewise be imported in British vessels, without being liable to any other or higher duties or charges, of whatever denomination, than if such articles were imported in Ottoman vessels. Such reciprocal equality of treatment shall take effect without distinction, whether such articles come directly from the place of origin or from any other country.

In the same manner, there shall be perfect equality of treatment in regard to exportation, so that the same export duties shall be paid, and the same bounties and drawbacks allowed, in the dominions and possessions of either of the Contracting Parties, on the exportation of any article which is or may be legally exportable whether such exportation shall take place in Ottoman or in British vessels, and whatever may be the place of destination, whether a port of either of the Contracting Parties or of any third Power.

Article 9. No duties of tonnage, harbour, pilotage, lighthouse, quarantine, or other similar or corresponding duties, of whatever nature, or under whatever denomination, levied in the name or for the profit of Government, public functionaries, private individuals, corporations, or establishments of any kind, shall be imposed in the ports of the dominions and possessions of either country upon the vessel of the other country, which shall not equally under the same conditions be imposed in the like cases on national vessels in general. Such equality of treatment shall apply reciprocally to the respective vessels, from whatever port or place they may arrive, and whatever port or place they may arrive, and whatever may be their place of destination.

Article 10. All vessels which according to British law are to be deemed British vessels, and all vessels which according to Ottoman law are to be deemed Ottoman vessels, shall for the purposes of this Treaty be deemed British and Ottoman vessels, respectively.

Article 11. No charge whatsoever shall be made upon British goods being the produce or manufacture of the British dominions or possessions, whether in British or other ships, nor upon any goods the produce or manufacture of any other foreign country carried in British ships, when the same shall pass through the Straits of the Dardanelles or of the Bosphorus, whether such goods shall pass through those Straits in the ships that brought them, or shall have been transhipped to other vessels; or whether, after having been sold for exportation, they shall for a certain limited time be landed in order to be placed in other vessels for the continuance of their voyage.

In the latter case the goods in question shall be deposited at Constantinople, in the magazines of the Custom-house, called *Transit* magazines; and in any other places where there is no *entrepôt*, they shall be placed under the charge of the Administration of the Customs.

Article 12. The Sublime Porte desiring to grant by means of gradual concessions all facilities in its power to transit by land, it is stipulated and agreed that the duty of three (3) per cent. levied up to this time on articles imported into Turkey, in their passage through Turkey to other countries, shall be reduced to two (2) per cent. payable, as the duty of three per cent. has been paid hitherto, on arriving in the Ottoman dominions; and at the end of eight years to be reckoned from the day of the exchange of the ratifications of the present Treaty, to a fixed and definite tax of one (1) per cent., which shall be levied, as is to be the case with respect to Turkish produce exported, to defray the expense of registration.

The Sublime Porte at the same time declares that it reserves to itself the right to establish, by a special enactment, the measures to be adopted for the prevention of fraud.

Article 13. Her Britannic Majesty's subjects, or their agents, trading in goods the produce or manufacture of foreign countries, shall be subject to the same taxes, and enjoy the same rights, privileges, and immunities as foreign subjects dealing in goods the produce or manufacture of their own country.

Article 14. An exception to the stipulations laid down in the 5th Article shall be made in regard to tobacco, in any shape whatsoever, and also in regard to salt, which two articles shall cease to be included among those which the subjects of Her Britannic Majesty are permitted to import into the Ottoman dominions.

British subjects, however, or their agents, buying or selling tobacco or salt for consumption in Turkey, shall be subject to the same regulations, and shall pay the same duties, as the most favoured Ottoman subjects trading in the two articles aforesaid; and furthermore, as a compensation for the prohibition of the two articles above-mentioned, no duty whatsoever shall in future be levied on those articles when exported from Turkey by the subjects of Her Britannic Majesty.

British subjects shall, nevertheless, be bound to declare the quantity of tobacco and salt thus exported, to the proper Custom-house authorities, who shall, as heretofore, have the right to watch over the export of these articles, without thereby being entitled to levy any tax thereon on any pretence whatsoever.

Article 15. It is understood between the two High Contracting Parties, that the Sublime Porte reserves to itself the faculty and right of issuing a general prohibition against the importation into the Ottoman dominions of gunpowder, cannon, arms of war, or military stores; but such prohibition will not come into operation until it shall have been officially notified, and will apply only to the articles mentioned in the decree enacting the prohibition. Any of these articles which have not been so specifically prohibited shall, on being imported into the Ottoman dominions, be subject to the local regulations, unless Her Britannic Majesty's Embassy shall think fit to apply for a special license, which license will in that case be granted, provided no valid objection thereto can be alleged.

Gunpowder, in particular, when allowed to be imported, will be liable to the following stipulations:

1st. It shall not be sold by subjects of Her Britannic Majesty in quantities exceeding the quantities prescribed by the local regulations.

2ndly. When a cargo or a large quantity of gunpowder arrives in an Ottoman port on board a British vessel, such vessel shall be anchored at a particular spot to be designated by the local authorities, and the gunpowder shall thence be conveyed, under the inspection of such authorities, to depôts or fitting places designated by the government, to which the parties interested shall have access under due regulations.

Fowling-pieces, pistols, and ornamental or fancy weapons, as also small quantities of gunpowder for sporting, reserved for private use, shall not be subject to the stipulations of the present article.

Article 16. The firmans required for British merchant vessels on passing through the Dardanelles and the Bosphorus, shall always be delivered in such manner as to occasion to such vessels the least possible delay.

Article 17. The captains of British merchant-vessels, with goods on board destined for the Ottoman Empire, shall be obliged, immediately on their arrival at the port to which they are bound, to deposit in the Custom-house of the said port a true copy of their manifest.

Article 18. Contraband goods will be liable to confiscation by the Ottoman Treasury; but a report or *procès-verbal* of the alleged act of contraband must, as soon as the said goods are seized by the authorities, be drawn up and communicated to the Consular authority of the foreign subject to whom the goods said to be contraband shall belong; and no goods can be confiscated as contraband, unless the fraud with regard to them shall be duly and legally proved.

Article 19. All merchandize, the produce or manufacture of the Ottoman dominions and possessions, imported into the dominions and possessions of Her Britannic Majesty, shall be treated in the same manner as the like merchandize the produce or manufacture of the most favoured nation.

All rights, privileges, or immunities which are now or may hereafter be granted to, or suffered to be enjoyed by the subjects, ships, commerce, or navigation of any foreign Power in the British dominions or possessions, shall be equally granted to, and exercised and enjoyed by, the subjects, ships, commerce, and navigation of the Ottoman Porte.

Article 20. The present Treaty, when ratified, shall be substituted for the Convention concluded between the two High Contracting Parties on the 16th of August, 1838, and shall remain in force for twenty-eight years from the day of the exchange of the ratification, each of the High Contracting Parties being, however, at liberty to give to the other, at the end of fourteen years (that time being fixed, as the provisions of this Treaty will then have come into full force), notice for its revision, or for its determination at the expiration of a year from the date of that notice, and so again at the end of twenty-one years.

The present Treaty shall receive its execution in all and everyone of the provinces of the Ottoman Empire, that is to say, in all the possessions of His Imperial Majesty the Sultan situated in Europe or in Asia, in Egypt and in the other parts of Africa belonging to the Sublime Porte, in Servia, and in the United Principalities of Moldavia and Wallachia.

The Sublime Porte declares that she is ready to grant to other foreign Powers who may seek to obtain them, the commercial advantages contained in the stipulations of the present Treaty.

Article 21. It is always understood that Her Britannic Majesty does not pretend, by any Article in the present Treaty, to stipulate for more then the plain and fair construction of the terms employed, nor to preclude in any manner the Ottoman Government from the exercise of its rights of internal administration, where the exercise of those rights does not evidently infringe upon the privileges accorded by the present Treaty, to British subjects or British merchandize.

Article 22. The High Contracting Parties have agreed to appoint, jointly, Commissioners for the settlement of a Tariff of Custom-house duties, to be levied in conformity with the stipulations of the present Treaty, as well upon merchandize of every description, being the produce or manufacture of the British dominions and possessions imported into the Sultan's dominions and possessions imported, as upon articles of every description the produce or manufacture of the dominions and possessions of the Sultan, which British subjects or their agents are free to purchase in any part of the Ottoman dominions and possessions for exportation to Great Britain or to any other country.

The new Tariff to be so concluded shall remain in force during seven years, dating from the first of October, one thousand eight hundred and sixty-one.

Each of the Contracting Parties shall have the right, a year before the expiration of that term, to demand the revision of the Tariff. But if, during the seventh year, neither the one nor the other of the Contracting Parties shall avail itself of this right, the Tariff then existing shall continue to have force of law for seven more years, dating from the day of the expiration of the seven preceding years; and the same shall be the case with respect to every successive period of seven years.

Article 23. The present Treaty shall be ratified, and the ratifications shall be exchanged at Constantinople in two calendar months, or sooner if possible, and shall be carried into execution from the first of October, one thousand eight hundred and sixty-one.

Done at Kanlidja, on the twenty-ninth day of April, one thousand eight hundred and sixty-one.

(L.S.) Henry L. Bulwer.
(L.S.) Aali.

(Source: *Tracts on Trade, Finance, etc., 1857-66*, Printed at the office of the *Levant Herald*, Constantinople.)

APPENDIX 12

Decree of 28 Muharrem, 1299 (December 8 (20), 1881)

(Main Clauses)

The Imperial Ottoman Government, in pursuance of the declarations made by their representative at the Congress of Berlin at the session of the 11th July, 1878, and in accordance with the engagement which they entered into by their note of the 3rd October, 1880, have, in a subsequent note of the 23rd October, 1880, invited the holders of bonds of the Ottoman Public Debt to choose a certain number of delegates to proceed as soon as possible to Constantinople for the purpose of coming to a direct agreement with the Imperial Government as to an equitable and practical settlement of the Ottoman Public Debt as well as to the means of resuming the service of the interest and sinking fund on that debt.

The holders of the aforesaid debt have responded to that invitation by appointing as their representatives:

    The English and Dutch holders:
      The Right Honourable Robert Bourke.
    The French holders:
      M. Valpey, late Political Sub-Director at the French Ministry for Foreign Affairs.
    The Austro-Hungarian holders:
      His Excellency Baron de Mayr, late Envoy Extraordinary and Minister Plenipotentiary of Austria-Hungary at Washington.

The German holders:
M. Primker, Judicial Councillor.
The Italian holders:
M. Mancardi, ex-deputy, late Director-General of the Public Debt of Italy.

The said delegates of the holders presented themselves at the Sublime Porte in August and September of the current year.

The Imperial Government on their side have appointed a special commission instructed to treat with the delegates and composed of:

His Excellency Server Pasha, President of the Council of State, President of the Commission;

His Excellency Munir Bey, Minister of Finance;

His Excellency Ohannés Effendi Tchamitch, President of the Audit Department;

His Excellency Wettendorff Bey, Under-Secretary of State at the Imperial Ministry of Finance;

Gescher Effendi, Legal Adviser at the Ministry of Foreign Affairs; and

Bertram Effendi, Mustechar of the Customs Administration.

The deliberations of the aforesaid commission commencing on the 1st September and continued during the months of September, October, November, and December of the current year having resulted in a complete understanding between the Imperial Commissioners and the delegates, as recorded in the minutes of the proceedings of the Commission bearing the signatures of both parties:

The Government, on the basis of that understanding, hereby decree as follows:

Article 1. (a) The capital balances remaining due on each of the loans enumerated in the annexed table, increased by the nominal amount of the provisional bonds, called Ramazan bonds, issued for a moiety of the bonds drawn in conformity with the decree of the 6th October 1875 (30th Ramazan, 1202), are reduced to the mean rates of issue hereinafter specified:

		Per cent
Loan 1858	to	85
„ 1860	„	57.375
„ 1862	„	68
„ 1863-4	„	69.62216
„ 1865	„	64.775
„ 1869	„	56.725
„ 1872	„	98.50
„ 1873	„	50.235
General Debt to		45.84
Turkish lottery bonds to		41.00545

(b) The capital reduced to these rates is increased in principal by 10 per cent., representing the interest of the aforesaid loans, and the premiums on the European Turkish Railways as on the privisional bonds called Ramazan, issued for the moiety of the interests and premiums in conformity with the decree of the 6th October, 1875.

(c) The amount for which the interest and premiums in arrear participate in this increase of 10 per cent, not including the Ramazan certificates for interest and premiums, the settlement of which forms the subject of article 2 below, is added to the capital of each loan, reduced in conformity with paragraph (2), which raises the rates of reduction of each loan to the definitive rates in round figures indicated as follows:

		Per cent
Loan 1858	to	93.15
,, 1860	,,	62.90
,, 1862	,,	74.50
,, 1863-4	,,	76.30
,, 1865	,,	71
,, 1869	,,	62.40
,, 1872	,,	107.75
,, 1873	,,	55.25
General Debt to		50.25
Turkish lottery bonds to		45.09

(d) The bonds of the above-mentioned loans bearing the unpaid coupons from April 1876 to March 1882, inclusively, will be consequently reduced to an amount corresponding with the rates indicated for each of the loans mentioned in paragraph (c).

The privisional Ramazan certificates issued for a moiety of the bonds drawn in conformity with the decree of the 6th October 1875, and mentioned in paragraph (a) above, will, with the exception of those of the Turkish lottery bonds drawn with premiums, be converted at the rates specified in paragraph (c) into bonds of the loans to which they belong.

N.B. The sum of £st. 31,508,000 indicated in the annexed table as capital balance of the European Turkish Railways Loan—Turkish lottery bonds—comprises the nominal capital, viz. 400 fr. per bond of the bonds drawn with premiums and unpaid. The difference between the nominal amount of this capital and the amount for which these bonds are drawn is included in the amount assigned to arrears of interest.

Article 2. The amount for which the provisional Ramazan certificates issued for a moiety of the interest and premiums—nominal capital deducted—in conformity with the decree of the 6th October, 1875, participate in the increase of 10 per cent. mentioned in paragraph (b) of the preceding article shall be regulated by conversion into bonds of the loans to which they belong, the nominal amount of these certificates being reduced in the proportion adopted for the total of the interest, and being calculated upon the figures enumerated in column (11) of the annexed table, which gives the following rates:

Certificates of interest for the loans:		Per cent
	1858	23.26
	1860	15.29
	1862	18.12
	1863-4	18.553
	1865	17.26
	1872	17.20
	General Debt	14.78
	Turkish lottery bonds	19.18

Notwithstanding the certificates issued for the coupons of the 1872 loan shall be converted at the above rates into bonds of one of the loans in Group II, which will be mentioned subsequently (article 12).

Article 3. Accordingly the reduced amount of the Ottoman Debt, as a result of the present arrangement, will be composed:

(i) Of the amount of the bonds of each loan still in circulation, reduced to the rates indicated in paragraph (c) of article 1.

(ii) Of the amount of the bonds given in exchange for the provisional certificates issued for a moiety of the bonds (paragraph (d) of Article 1).

(iii) Of the amount of the bonds given in exchange for the provisional certificates issued for a moiety of the interest or premiums (article 2).

The annexed table, which forms part of the present Iradé, contains all the figures relative to the reduction and settlement of the Ottoman Debt.

Notwithstanding the figures specified in the table, with the exception of the rates mentioned in article 1, shall not prejudice the definitive fixing of the amounts which make up the debt in the event of error or omissions in the calculations, the Council of Administration spoken of hereinafter being entrusted, after an understanding with the Government, with the rectification of any errors that may have occurred.

Article 8. For the service of the Debt determined by article 3, the Government cede by these presents, absolutely and irrevocably, from the 1st (13th) January 1882, and until the complete extinction of the said debt:

1. The revenues of the monopolies and indirect taxes which form the subject of the convention of the 10th (22nd) November 1879, which is abrogated from the 1st (13th) January 1882, in virtue of the convention annexed to the present decree, viz.:

(a) Of the monopolies of tobacco and salt produced or consumed in the vilayets of the empire enumerated in the list annexed to the convention of the 10th (22nd) November 1879, and appended to this decree, annex 2, not including cigars, snuffs, chewing tobacco, and imported tombeki, and with the exception of the tithe and the customs duties on tobacco.

(b) Of the stamp duty (varakai-sahiha);

Of the mirié and rouhsatié duties on spirits in the vilayets of the empire enumerated in the said list, except the customs duties levied on spirits;

Of the duty on fish in Constantinople and its suburbs, according to the detail which figure in the list relating thereto; and

Of the silk tithe of the suburbs of Constantinople, as also of Adrianople, Brusa, and Samsun, according to the detail stated in the list relating thereto.

2. The silk tithes:

Of Tokat, a dependency of the Samsun administration.

Of Kavala, Yenidjeh, Eskidje, Dede Agatch, dependencies of the Adrianople administration.

Of Sarouhan, a dependency of the Sarouhan administration.

Of Yenikeui of Chile, a dependency of the Constantinople administration.

Of Kartal, Guebzé and Daridja, dependencies of the Ismidt administration.

As also the duty on fish:

Of Banados, a dependency of the Rodosto administration.

Of Gallipoli, a dependency of the Gallipoli administration.

Of Yalova, a dependency of the Kara Mussal administration.

Of Seyki, Mudania, Guemlek, Kurchunlu, Armudlu, Kapu, Dagh, Marmora, Pasha-Liman, Erdek, Panderma, and Lake of Manias, dependencies of the Brusa administration.

3. The surplus of the customs receipts resulting from a modification in the tariffs in the event of a revision of the commercial treaties.

4. The surplus of revenue which will result from the general application of the tax on professions as compared with the actual receipts from the temettu tax.

The means by which the revenues mentioned in paragraphs 3 and 4 will be secured to the holders of the debt shall form the subject of special provisions.

5. The tribute of the principality of Bulgaria.

So long as this tribute shall not have been fixed by the representatives of the signatory Powers of the Treaty of Berlin, the Government shall replace it from the 1st (13th) January, 1882, by an annual sum of £T. 100,000 to be levied on the tobacco tithe.

Once the said tribute is fixed, should the Sublime Porte think fit to assign it in whole or in part to some other purpose, the amount thus disposed of shall be replaced by an equivalent sum to be levied on the tobacco tithe, and, in case this should not be sufficient, on some other revenue equally secure.

6. The surplus revenues of the island of Cyprus.

Should the surplus revenue of the island of Cyprus not be at the disposal of the Imperial Government it will be replaced from the 1st (13th) January 1882, by an annual sum of £T. 130,000.

The Council of Administration (article 15) shall have the right to apply the surplus of the tobacco tithe, after deduction of the £T. 100,000 which are to replace the tribute of the principality of Bulgaria, to the payment of the aforesaid £T. 130,000 which are to replace the surplus revenues of the island of Cyprus; for the amount remaining uncovered on this sum, the Ministry of Finance shall furnish to the council half-yearly drafts on the General Customs Administration.

7. The revenue from Eastern Rumelia, now fixed at £T. 240,000, plus the arrears from the 1st (13th) March, 1880, subsequent increases of which this revenue is susceptible by the terms of article 5 of the organic statute, and the sum of £T. 5,000, representing the net annual proceeds of the customs of the said province. The Council of Administration (article 15) shall receive the aforesaid sums through the medium of the Imperial Ottoman Bank, in the safes of which they shall be deposited.

In the event of delay in the payments at the due dates, the Imperial Government shall use all diligence to see that the said province resumes the fulfilment of its engagements.

8. The proceeds from the duty on the tombeki up to a sum of £T. 50,000.

In order to ensure the receipt of this sum by the Council of Administration, the Ministry of Finance shall issue to the council half-yearly drafts on the General Customs Administration.

9. All the sums accruing to the Imperial Government as the contributive portions of Servia, Montenegro, Bulgaria, and Greece to the debt mentioned in article 3 according to the provisions of the Treaty of Berlin and article 10 of the Convention of Constantinople of the 24th May 1881.

Article 9. The revenues specified in paragraphs 1, 2 and 8, as also the tobacco tithe mentioned in paragraphs 5 and 6 of the preceding article, shall be administered in accordance with existing laws and regulations and the revenues mentioned in paragraphs 3 and 4 (surplus of customs and tax on professions) in accordance with the provisions to be enacted for that purpose.

Notwithstanding, the Council of Administration shall have the right to decide upon all modifications and improvements which may be introduced in the existing system of monopolies or contributions mentioned in Nos. 1 and 2 or the tobacco tithe mentioned in Nos. 5 and 6 of the preceding article, in case the said tithe should be applied to the service of the debt in pursuance of the provisions of the same article relating thereto, without going beyond the limits of the existing laws and regulations and without imposing fresh charges on Ottoman subjects.

For all other modifications or improvements to be introduced in the system, or in the taxes of the aforesaid monopolies or contributions or any other revenues ceded to the bondholders, except the revenues mentioned in paragraphs 3, 4 and 8 of the preceding article (surplus of customs, tax on professions, and tombeki), a previous arrangement must be come to between the Imperial Government and the council. Likewise, the tariffs and regulations relative to the ceded revenues, with the exception, however, of the revenues mentioned in paragraphs 3, 4 and 8 of the preceding article, may be modified only by mutual agreement between the Government and the council.

The Government undertake to inform the council within six months at the latest of their acceptance or refusal of the proposals which have been submitted to them on this subject by the council.

The Government shall make known at an early date their decision with regard to the proposals made to them by the present council of the six Indirect Contributions as to stamp duty.

With regard to the tobacco and salt monopolies, the Government shall not oppose in principle arrangements for working the tobacco and salt by means of a *régie* subject, in the matter of the details to be promulgated with this object, to the previous agreement mentioned above.

As regards the tobacco, any profits which may be derived from its working by way of a *régie* shall be divided between the Government, the bondholders, and the company that works it under conditions to be fixed by the parties concerned.

Should the Government desire to abolish the tithes, the duty on fish, or the duty on spirits ceded to the bondholders, they would have the right to do so on condition that they replace the duties that are to be abolished by another equivalent revenue and with the adherence of an absolute majority of the members of the council. The possible increase in the revenues that are to be abolished shall be taken into consideration when the equivalent is fixed.

It is understood that the collection and administration of the equivalent revenues shall be entrusted to the council as stated hereinafter.

Article 10. The net proceeds of the revenues indicated in article 8 shall be devoted wholly, on the 1st (13th) September and the 1st (13th) March of each year, from the 1st (13th) January 1882, to the payment of interest and sinking fund of the Debt.

Notwithstanding, there shall be deducted each year preferentially from the portion of these proceeds derived from the six Indirect Contributions a sum of £T. 590,000 to ensure until their complete extinction the service of the 5 per cent privileged bonds, issued in representation of a maximum amount of £T. 8,170,000 in execution of the annexed convention concluded between the Imperial Government and the signatories of the convention of the 10th (22nd) November, 1879.

The first payment shall be made on the 1st (13th) September 1882, so that the sum to be distributed on that date will represent a period of eight months.

The interest and sinking fund shall be calculated on the total of the registered bonds.

The application of the sums accruing to the Turkish lottery bonds shall be made in conformity with the provisions of Article 13.

Matured coupons and drawn bonds shall be payable abroad, and in Constantinople by the establishments which have been entrusted with this service from the beginning. The Council of Administration shall take all the necessary steps to ensure the remittance to foreign countries of the encashed revenues with a view to the payment of the coupons and redeemed bonds. The remittances for this purpose shall be made through the agency of the Imperial Ottoman Bank, which continues to be entrusted with the service of the Ottoman debt. The council shall come to an understanding with the said establishments as to the amount of the commission which they shall be given.

The service of the privileged bonds shall be undertaken by the Imperial Ottoman Bank, which shall take a commission of $\frac{1}{2}$ per cent on the amount of the coupons and redeemed bonds.

The risks of exchange arising from the necessity of remitting to foreign countries the necessary funds for the aforesaid service shall be borne by the Council of Administration, subject to agreements to be subsequently reached between the council and the Bank.

The council shall issue new coupon sheets in case of necessity.

It shall be entitled to invest provisionally the encashed proceeds, until they are required for payment at the due dates for interest and sinking fund.

It shall determine in due course, in conformity with the principles established above, the rates of interest and redemption payable half-yearly, so that the amounts due on the 1st (13th) September and the 1st (13th) March are always punctually paid.

It shall have the right to reserve out of the amounts available for the service of interest and fractions necessary for equalising the amount of interest in the ensuing half-years.

Article 11. There shall be assigned every year to the service of the interest four-fifths of the net proceeds of the revenues ceded to the bondholders, not including the contributive portions of Servia, Montenegro, Bulgaria and Greece, and after deduction of the sums representing interest on the redeemed bonds.

But from the net proceeds of the said revenues there shall first be deducted the sum necessary to pay 1 per cent. interest calculated on the reduced capital (column 21 of the table), in conformity with article 10.

The interest shall never exceed 4 per cent. on the said capital. If the sum available for the service of the interest divided by the amount representing $\frac{1}{4}$ per cent. on the said reduced capital of the debt happens to leave a fraction, such fraction shall be reserved for the service of the interest for the following half-year.

The interest shall be paid upon the matured coupons of all loans without distinction in proportion to the available revenues.

Article 12. There shall be assigned every year for the sinking fund one-fifth of the net proceeds of the revenues ceded to the bondholders, not including the contributive portions of Servia, Montenegro, Bulgaria, and Greece, but increased by the amount representing interest upon the redeemed bonds, as stated in the preceding article.

Notwithstanding, if the net proceeds of the said revenues do not exceed 1 per cent. calculated on the reduced capital (column 21 of the annexed table) in conformity with article 10, the necessary difference shall be deducted from the fifth applicable to redemption.

The sinking fund to be served out of the proceeds of the above-mentioned revenues shall not exceed 1 per cent. on the said reduced capital.

If the proceeds of the said revenues should exceed 4 per cent. on the said capital for interest and 1 per cent. on the said capital for sinking fund, or 5 per cent., in all, the surplus shall be paid to the Treasury.

If the sum available for sinking fund leaves a remainder which does not permit the redemption of a round number of bonds, this remainder shall be reserved in order to be applied to the service of redemption for the ensuing half-year.

For the service of the sinking fund derived from the fifth of the proceeds of the above-mentioned revenues, augmented by the interest on the redeemed bonds, the loans shall be combined in groups constituted as follows:

Group I Loans of 1858 and 1862
,, II ,, ,, 1860, 1863-4 and 1872
,, III ,, ,, 1865, 1869, and 1873
,, IV ,, ,, 1865, 1869, and 1873
,, IV General debt and Turkish lottery bonds.

After payment of 1 per cent. on the aforesaid reduced capital as interest, the surplus up to $\frac{1}{4}$ per cent. of the said reduced capital shall be applied to the redemption of Group I, after that of Group II, after the latter of Group III, finally of Group IV.

If the sum available annually for sinking fund should exceed $\frac{1}{4}$ per cent. on the said reduced capital, the surplus up to $\frac{1}{2}$ per cent. on the said capital shall be applied to the redemption of Group II, unless the said Group II is already in possession of the first $\frac{1}{4}$ per cent. In this case the sum exceeding $\frac{1}{4}$ per cent., up to $\frac{1}{2}$ per cent., passes to Group III, unless Group III is already in possession of the first $\frac{1}{4}$ per cent., in which case the sum exceeding $\frac{1}{4}$ per cent., up to $\frac{1}{2}$ per cent., passes to Group IV.

If the sum available for sinking fund should exceed $\frac{1}{2}$ per cent., on the reduced capital, the excess up to $\frac{3}{4}$ per cent on this capital shall be applied to the redemption of Group III, unless the said Group III is already in possession of a quota of redemption of $\frac{1}{4}$ per cent. In this case this third $\frac{1}{4}$ per cent. passes to Group IV, unless the said Group IV is already in possession of $\frac{1}{4}$ per cent. in which case the sum exceeding $\frac{1}{2}$ per cent. up to $\frac{1}{4}$ per cent. on the said capital shall be divided in equal shares between Groups III and IV.

If the sum available for sinking fund should exceed $\frac{3}{4}$ per cent., on the said capital, the surplus goes to Group IV, unless the said Group IV is already in possession of the quota of redemption of $\frac{1}{4}$ per cent., in which case the sum exceeding $\frac{3}{4}$ per cent. is divided in equal shares between the groups that remain to be extinguished.

After the extinction of the first three groups, the sum available for sinking fund will operate for the advantage of the fourth.

In addition to the said fifth of the proceeds of the above-mentioned revenues there shall be applied to the service of the sinking fund the sums which Servia, Montenegro, Bulgaria and Greece will contribute to the service of the Debt mentioned in article 3.

These sums, whether in capital or interest, shall be applied to the redemption of all the loans in proportion to their amount resulting from the registration of the bonds, and if the conversion of the Debt should be eventually accomplished they shall be applied to the redemption of a portion of the converted Debt, all the bonds being treated on the same footing.

Every sum representing interest on the redeemed bonds shall augment the sinking fund. Redemption shall always be effected by purchase or drawing half-yearly, according to the decision of the Council of Administration.

The payment of the drawn bonds shall take place at the end of each half-year, beginning on the 1st (13th) September, 1882.

The redemption of the bonds, whether effected by purchase or drawings shall take place at rates not exceeding the following figures:

(a) 66.66 per cent. of the capital when the interest paid is 1 per cent.;

(b) 75 per cent. of the capital when the interest is more than 1 per cent., but less than 3 per cent.;

(c) 100 per cent. of the capital when the interest paid reaches 3 per cent. or more.

Article 15. A Council of Administration is established to represent the bondholders, and to act in their interests.

This council has its head office at Constantinople.

The said council shall be composed as hereinafter stated:

One member, representing the English bondholders, who also represents the Dutch bondholders, and who is to be appointed by the Council of Foreign Bondholders of London, or in default of it by the Governor of the Bank of England, or in default of him by a resolution adopted at a public meeting of English and Dutch bondholders in London;

One member representing the French bondholders;

One menber representing the German bondholders;

One member representing the Austro-Hungarian bondholders; who are to be appointed by the syndicates of the financial houses of Paris, Berlin and Vienna, which have adhered to the communication of the Imperial Ottoman Government of the 23rd October, 1880, and, if necessary, their choice shall be approved by a general meeting of the French, German, and Austro-Hungarian bondholders in each of the three capitals designated above.

One member representing the Italian bondholders, who is to be appointed by the Roman Chamber of Commerce, constituted in the syndicate of the chambers of commerce of the kingdom, and, if necessary, its choice shall be approved by a general meeting of the Italian bondholders in Rome.

One member representing the Ottoman bondholders, who is to be appointed by a general meeting of the latter, assembled at Constantinople at the invitation of the prefect of the city.

One member representing the holders of the bonds provided for by the annexed convention, who will be appointed by the Imperial Ottoman Bank, or in default of it by a resolution adopted at a public meeting of the said bondholders in Constantinople.

This latter member shall sit in the council only until the complete extinction of the said bonds.

Vacancies which may occur in the council shall be filled according to the same formalities.

The appointments of the members representing the English, Dutch, French, German, Austro-Hungarian, and Italian bondholders shall be notified by the representatives of the Sublime Porte in London, Paris, Berlin, Vienna, and Rome. The appointment of the Ottoman member, as well as that of the member representing the bonds mentioned in the annexed convention, shall be notified to the Minister of Finance of the Ottoman Empire.

Every employé in the service of the Imperial Ottoman Government, whether a foreigner or an Ottoman subject, who shall be appointed a member of the council shall be bound to resign his public functions for the whole duration of his office.

If the authorities who have the appointment of the council in England, Germany, Austria-Hungary, France, and Italy should appoint a member who is fulfilling at that time a diplomatic, consular or military mission in the Ottoman Empire, such member must likewise resign his public functions. He shall be treated as regards salary on the same footing as members of the council coming from abroad.

The members of the council shall be appointed for five years, and they shall sit until the installation of the new council.

They may be re-elected on the expiration of their mandate.

If a member of the council should happen to fail in his duties, his recall shall be pronounced by the authorities from whom he holds his mandate, but, according to circumstances, upon the proposal or with the approval of the council.

The salaries of the members of the council are fixed as follows:

2,000 *l.* to each of the representatives of the foreign bondholders coming from abroad.

1,200 *l.* to each of the representatives of the foreign bondholders or Ottoman bondholders who may be chosen from among the residents of the Ottoman Empire.

1,200 *l.* to the Imperial Ottoman Commissioner (article 18).

No salary is assigned to the member representing the holders of the bonds provided for in the annexed convention, but he is granted an annual fixed sum, 500 *l.* for his attendance at the meetings.

These salaries shall be reckoned from the date of the arrival of each member of the council in Constantinople.

The general meetings which shall take place in pursuance of the above provisions for the appointment of the first council shall be convoked in each country for the delegate then representing the bondholders of the said country.

When it is a question of filling up a vacancy in the council, the meeting of the bondholders shall be convened by the Council of Administration.

In both cases the meetings shall be held in conformity with the forms prescribed by the authority which shall have convoked them, and the resolutions of these meetings shall be confined to the object which shall have given rise to their convocation.

In view of the number and far greater importance of the Ottoman bonds held in England and France, the annual presidency of the council shall devolve alternately during a period of five years, and according to the order fixed by the first selection of the council, upon the English and French representatives.

In the event of this situation becoming essentially modified after a first period of five years, the council shall elect its president.

In the event of and during the absence of the president, or if and as long as he is temporarily prevented from acting, the presidency shall be undertaken by the senior member of the council.

The members of the council shall each have a vote. Resolutions shall be taken by a majority of votes. In case of a tie, the president shall have a casting vote.

The first meeting of the council shall take place immediately after the appointment of its members.

Two months after the publication of the present decree, the presence of three members regularly appointed shall be sufficient to permit the council to enter upon its functions and proceed to business.

When the council is complete, the presence of three members at least shall be necessary for the regular dispatch of business.

During the existence of vacancies caused by the recall of members of the council or for other reasons, the council shall retain the right of taking all decisions in conformity with its constitutive powers.

The council shall cease to act only on the complete extinction of the loans to which the present decree applies.

Article 16. The Council of Administration shall have the direct administration, collection, and encashment on behalf of the bondholders and by means of agents holding its authority of the revenues and other resources enumerated in article 8, sections 1, 2, 5, 6, 7, and 9, including the tobacco tithe in the cases provided for by sections 5 and 6 of the said article, excepting, however, as regards the said tithe the obligation of rendering an account thereof to the Government, and paying annually to the Exchequer the surplus over and above the £T. 100,000 which shall take the place of the Bulgarian tribute, and eventually of the £T. 130,000 which shall take the place of the surplus revenue of the island of Cyprus.

It shall likewise leave the encashment of the £T. 50,000 ceded on the proceeds of the tombeki duties (paragraph 8 of article 8) and of the revenues mentioned in paragraphs 3 and 4 of the said article.

The amount of the six Indirect Contributions shall be collected in cash in conformity with the regulation in force as regards the fiscal agencies of the State ("Meskukiat Nizamnamessi") promulgated on the 1st March 1296.

It shall realise the value of the ceded revenues and other resources, and shall apply the whole amount thereof, after deduction of the costs of administration and collection, to the service of the interest and sinking fund of the bonds provided for by the annexed convention and of the debt fixed by article 3 in conformity with the distribution adopted.

The council shall have the right to farm or lease to third parties any of the ceded revenues; but in any case it shall remain directly responsible to the Imperial Government.

The council shall appoint a director-general of the administration who shall have, under the authority of the council, the management of affairs. He shall represent the council as regards third parties for the execution of any decisions, and in legal proceedings if required, subject to obtaining the necessary authorisation for appearing before the courts or other jurisdictions either as plaintiff or defendant in the name of the administration of the ceded revenues.

The council shall likewise appoint and dismiss the other employés of the administration of the ceded revenues.

The said employés shall be considered as State officials in the exercise of their duties. The Government shall take into favourable consideration every recommendation of the council as regards their rank, advancement, and promotion in the Ottoman hierarchy.

As regards duties, contributions, and taxes, the administration of the ceded revenues and its employés shall be treated on the same footing as the administrations of the State and its employés.

As regards employés of the State who shall enter the service of the Council of Administration, their position shall be fixed by a special regulation. The provisions of this regulation shall apply equally to the employés of the State who are already in the service of the administration of the six Indirect Contributions. It is understood that this regulation shall not prejudice the right of the council to appoint and dismiss any official to this administration—a right which is already exercised, in fact, by the present administration.

As regards the indemnities and other extraordinary disbursements provided for in article of the convention of the 22nd November, liability shall rest with the council.

The Government shall afford the council in the exercise of its administration all general assistance compatible with the existing public institutions and, with a view to a repression of contraband trade, they undertake to apply against it the penalties enacted by law.

In case of delay in the payments of the revenue from Eastern Roumelia, the council shall have the right to apply to the Sublime Porte and to demand the necessary measures for recovery of the arrears.

The Government shall afford to the Administration of the Council the military protection indispensable for the security of its head office and its local branches.

The Government shall continue to the council the gratuitous use of the premises which they have already placed at the disposal of the actual administration of the six Indirect Contributions.

The removable stamps and stamped papers necessary for the council's transactions shall be supplied by the Government under the supervision and at the expense of the latter.

Independently of the State employés entrusted with the policing and supervision of the service to be undertaken by the State, the council may appoint auxiliary employés responsible to none but itself, as well as secret inspectors whose duty shall be to prevent frauds punishable in conformity with the laws.

The secret inspectors of the administration shall receive, like those of the Government, the usual portion of the fines and double duties to be paid by delinquents.

The council shall make regulations concerning the resolutions and dispatch of business.

It shall sign the bonds to be issued in conformity with the annexed convention to discharge the debts of the signatories of the said convention indicated in article 10.

Article 17. The Council of Administration shall be bound to draw up and present to the Ministry of Finance two months before the commencement of each budgetary year a budget indicating the estimates of the council as to receipts and expenditure, especially as to the sums which shall be applied during the course of the said year to the service of the bonds provided for in the annexed convention and for the service of the Debt established by article 3.

This budget must conform to the existing regulations, and shall be approved by the Imperial Government within two months.

It shall be inserted in the general budget of the Empire.

The Ministry of Finance shall forward to the council a certified extract from the aforesaid budget concerning the administration of the ceded revenues.

The council shall be found to present every month, in accordance with the information which it shall have received, and according to the rules and usages in force, to the Imperial Ministry of Finance a statement showing all the receipts and general encashments effected out of the revenues and resources in question, as well as the payments made in the same month.

The council shall have likewise to submit at the close of each financial year its definitive general account to the above-mentioned Ministry.

The council shall present each half-year to the Ministry of Finance the necessary account showing the remittances made to Europe on account of the service of the Debt established by article 3 and the payments made to the bondholders.

The Council shall cause to be published monthly, in all the capitals, where registration shall take place, a summary of the receipts and payments made during the preceding month.

Such statement shall show:

1. The amount of receipts realised out of the proceeds of each of the six Indirect Contributions as also of every other revenue ceded to the bondholders.
2. The total sum of the payments made for the general charges of administration.
3. The sums paid on account of the bonds provided for in the annexed convention.
4. The funds transmitted to Europe for the service of the Debt mentioned in article 2.
5. And the cash existing at Constantinople and in the provinces at the end of the month.

The publication of the monthly table shall take place not later than one month after the termination of the month to which it refers.

The council shall likewise publish every year, for the information of the bondholders, an account of its administration.

Article 18. The administration of the ceded revenues shall be submitted to the control of the Imperial Government. This control shall be exercised by a Commissioner and by comptrollers appointed by the Government and accredited to the said administration.

The Imperial Commissioner must be invited to each sitting of the council.

He shall have a consultative voice.

Every communication of the Government to the council and *vice versa* shall be made through the said commissioner.

The functions of each comptroller shall be determined by the Imperial Government.

The commisioner and every comptroller within his province shall have the right to take cognisance of the administration of the council and its employés, to examine the books and other documents relating thereto, and to proceed to the verification of the moneys in its safes in the presence of a delegate of the council at Constantinople and of the head official in the provincial agencies, but they may under no circumstances interfere in the administration. The council at Constantinople and its provincial employés—the latter in the presence of the heads of the local agencies, who may not refuse their assistance—shall be bound to give to the commissioner and to the comptrollers of the Government all the information necessary for the exercise of the control.

The salaries and travelling expenses of the comptrollers, as also in general the expenses arising from the policing and supervision of the services to be undertaken by the State, shall be paid by the Imperial Government. The salary of the commissioner shall be paid by the council.

Article 19. Every dispute that may arise between the Imperial Government and the council as to the interpretation and execution of the present decree shall be submitted to the judgment of four arbitrators appointed by both, who shall choose an umpire to decide between them should occasion arise.

The arbitrators decision shall be binding and without appeal.

Article 20. In the event of the Government quashing or suspending the present arrangement, the bondholders shall re-enter into their full rights established by the original loan contracts in so far as their bonds shall not already have been redeemed in conformity with the provisions of the present decree.

The securities given to the bondholders by the original loan contracts shall remain appropriated to the safeguarding of the said rights until the loans to which these securities are appropriated by the respective contracts are completely extinguished in conformity with the provisions of the present decree.

Article 21. The Imperial Government shall communicate to the Powers without delay the present decree, which shall come into force from the date of its publication, except as regards the administration of the ceded revenues, which shall commence from the 1st (13th) January, 1882.

In the event of the members of the Council of Administration not being assembled at Constantinople on the 1st (13th) January, 1882, the present administration of the six indirect contributions shall continue after that date to administer the said contributions in the name of the council until the latter is ready to enter upon its functions, in order that in this way there may be no interruption in the progress of the administration of the ceded revenues.

(Source: Decree of Muharrem, *Parliamentary Papers*, 1911, Vol. CIII, pp. 672-690.)

APPENDIX 13

The Baghdad Railway Convention, March 5th, 1903

Between his Excellency Zihni Pasha Minister of Commerce and Public Works, acting in the name of the Imperial Ottoman Government, of the first part; M. Arthur Gwinner, president of the board of directors, Dr. Kurt Zander, director-general, and M. Edouard Huguenin, assistant director-general of the Ottoman Anatolian Railway, acting in the name and on behalf of the Ottoman Anatolian Railway Company at Constantinople, of the second part, it has been decided as follows:

Article 1. The Imperial Ottoman Government grant the concession for the construction and working of an extension of the line from Konia to Bagdad and Busra, passing through, or as near as possible to, the towns of Karaman, Eregli, Kardash-Beli, Adana, Hamidieh, Osmanieh, Bagtcheb, Kazanali, Killis, Tel-Habesh, Harran, Ras-ul-Ain, Nisibin, Avniat, Mosul, Tekrit, Sadidjeh, Bagdad, Kerbela, Nedjef, Zobeir, and Busra, as well as the following branches:

1. From Tel-Habesh to Aleppo.
2. From a neighbouring point on the main line, to be agreed upon, to Ufra.

The Imperial Ottoman Government will not grant a guarantee, under any form, for the construction of this branch line, about 30 kilom. in length, not any appropriation for working expenses, but the gross receipts of every description from the branch line shall belong excusively to the concessionnaires.

3. From Sadidheh to Khanikin.
4. From Zobeir to a point on the Persian Gulf to be agreed upon between the Imperial Ottoman Government and the concessionnaires, as well as everything appertaining to the said lines. The main line and its branches shall follow a route to be approved by the Imperial Ottoman Government—to the Ottoman Anatolian Railway Company on the following conditions:

Article 2. The duration of this concession shall be ninety-nine years. A similar period shall be adopted for the lines of Angora and Konia, and shall commence to run from the date of the issue of the firman and the exchange of the present convention.

As regards the new lines, this period of ninety-nine years shall commence to run seperately for each section from the date on which the Imperial Government shall have issued the Government bonds to the concessionnaires in accordance with article 35 of the present convention.

Article 3. These lines, taken collectively, are divided, as regards the submission of the final plans and designs, into sections of 200 kilom. in length. The concessionnaires shall, within three months from the date of the issue of the firman granting the concession and the exchange of the present convention and specification (and after the conditions of article 35 have been fulfilled), submit to the Ministry of Public Works, after the survey has taken final shape, and in accordance with the terms of the specification full plans and designs of the first section of 200 kilom. in length, starting from Konia and passing through, or as near as possible to, Karaman and Eregli, i.e., along the contemplated route of the Bagdad line. As regards the other sections, the plans and designs relating thereto shall be submitted within eight months from the date on which the concession for each section commences in pursuance of the provisions of article 35 which relate to each section.

The plans and designs must be examined by the Ministry, and, according to circumstances, approved as they stand, or modified if necessary, within three months from the date of their submission. After that period, if the Imperial Government have not notified their decision to the concessionnaires, the latter may consider the designs which they have submitted as having been approved, and they shall proceed to put the work in hand. If the Imperial Government introduce such modifications into the designs as will involve a delay of more than one month in the approval of the plans, the period allowed for construction shall be extended by a period equal to the delay caused by the examination of those modifications and approval of the plans.

The special assignments intended for the first section of 200 kilom. starting from Konia and passing through or as near as possible to Karaman and Eregli, are set forth in Annex I (Financial Convention), which forms an integral part of the present convention.

Article 4. The concessionnaires undertake to commence work on the first section, at their own expense, risk, and peril, within three months from the date of approval of the plans and designs of those first 200 kilom., and likewise to complete it not later than two years from that same date.

The concessionnaires undertake to commence work within three months from the date of approval of the plans and designs of the other sections, and to complete the whole of the lines and branches within eight years from the date of the issue of the firman and the exchange of the present convention. Notwithstanding, any period of delay in carrying out the terms of article 35, for any section, that is to say any period of delay in the issue of the bonds by the Imperial Government to the concessionnaires, shall be added to the said period of eight years. The works must be carried out in accordance with standard practice and the terms of the annexed specifications, as well as with the approved plans and designs; notwithstanding, in case of *vis major*, the periods for completion shall be extended by a period equal to that of the interruption of the work, provided that the concessionnaires immediately notify the local authorities as well as the Ministry of Public Works.

The term *vis major* shall be understood to include the case of a war between European Powers, as also a radical change in the financial situation of Germany, England, or France.

Article 5. The Ministry of Public Works shall control the works by one or more commissioners both during execution, on completion of the works, and before their reception. This control shall likewise apply to the working of the line and the maintenance of the works during the period of concession.

The concessionnaires shall deposit each year, to the order of the Ministry of Public Works, and in respect of expenses of control, a sum of 270 gold piasters per kilometre, payable monthly, from the date fixed for the commencement of the works until the termination of the concession.

Article 6. The enterprise being of public utility, land necessary for the building of the railway and everything appertaining thereto, quarries, and gravel-pits for ballast necessary for the railway and belonging to private persons shall be taken over in accordance with the law on expropriation, whenever it has not proved possible to come to an understanding between the concessionnaires and the owners for the purchase of such land.

The Government shall expropriate and hand over to the concessionnaires land necessary for the building of the line and everything appertaining thereto after the location of the railway has been approved and staked out. The land shall be handed over by the Government within two months.

The land necessary for temporary occupation during the work shall be handed over to the concessionnaires by the local authorities on condition that the former shall indemnify the owners.

If in the said land necessary for the building of the railway and everything appertaining thereto there should be land called **Arazii-Emirie-Halie**, it shall be handed over free of charge to the concessionnaires.

If within a zone 15 kilom. each side of the railway there should be land called Arazii-Emirie-Halie which contains quarries and gravel-pits for ballast, the concessionnaires may work them free of charge, during the period of construction, provided that they close them down on the completion of the work; should the concessionnaires desire to make use of these quarries and gravel-pits during the period of working they shall conform to the regulations governing the matter and pay the specified royalty.

The temporary occupation of such land during the work of construction shall likewise be granted to them free of charge.

Article 7. The railway shall be built for a single line; but land shall be acquired in view of the construction of a second line. As soon as the gross kilometric receipts shall have reached 30,000 fr. per annum, the Imperial Government shall have the right to demand the construction of the second line which the concessionnaires will be bound to build at their own expense.

Article 8. Manufactured material for the permanent way and the materials, iron, wood, coal, engines, carriages and waggons, and other stores necessary for the initial establishment as well as the general enlargement and development of the railway and everything appertaining thereto which the concessionnaires shall purchase in the Empire or import from abroad shall be exempt from all inland taxes and customs duties. The exemption from customs duties shall also be granted for the coal necessary for working the line which is imported from abroad by the concessionnaires until the gross receipts of the line and its branches reach 15,000 fr. per kilometre. Likewise, during the entire period of the concession the land, capital, and revenue of the railway and everything appertaining thereto shall not be taxed, neither shall any stamp duty be charged on the present convention or on the specification annexed thereto, the additional conventions, or on any subsequent instruments, or for the service of the Government bonds to be issued; nor on the amounts encashed by the concessionnaires on account of the guarantee for working expenses, nor shall any duty be levied on their shares, preference shares, and bonds, nor on the bonds which the Imperial Ottoman Government shall issue to the concessionnaires.

The concessionnaires shall be liable to stamp duty for all their transactions other than those for which exemption is granted to them in the present article.

The concessionnaires shall form an Ottoman joint-stock company, under the name of "Imperial Ottoman Bagdad Railway Company," which shall take the place of the Ottoman Anatolian Railway Company in all that concerns the new line from Konia to the Persian Gulf with its branches, and which shall be governed by the annexed statutes.

The Ottoman Anatolian Railway Company undertakes never to cede or transfer to any other company the existing lines from Haidar-Pasha to Angora and to Konia.

The Imperial Ottoman Bagdad Railway Company which will be formed undertakes likewise not to cede or transfer the lines to be constructed from Konia to Bagdad and to Busra and their branches.

Article 9. The building and other materials necessary for the construction and working of this line and its branches, as also the officials and workmen, shall be conveyed, but only during the period of construction and under the supervision of the Ministry of Marine, on the Shatt-el-Arab, the Tigris, and Euphrates, in steam or sailing ships, or other craft which shall be acquired or hired by the company.

Material thus conveyed shall be exempt from customs duty, taxes, etc.

Article 10. The wood and timber necessary for the construction and working of the railway may be cut in the forests of the neighbouring districts which belong to the State, in accordance with the regulations relating thereto.

Article 11. As soon as the concessionnaires shall have notified to the Ministry of Public Works the completion of the work on one section the latter shall cause an inspection of the works already completed to be made by a technical commission appointed for that purpose, and shall accept them provisionally if approved; one year after they have been provisionally passed, a second inspection of the works shall be made by a technical commission, and, should it be reported that the works have been carried out in accordance with standard practice and the terms of the specification, the Ministry of Public Works shall pronounce their final acceptance as a result of the commission's report.

The concessionnaires shall have the right to open the lines to traffic in successive sections after they have been accepted provisionally. The length of the completed sections, from Konia, Adana, Bagdad, Busra, as also from the different intermediate points, shall be at least 40 kilom. and shall finish at a station.

Article 12. Should the Imperial Government decide upon the construction of branches joining the railway which forms the subject of this convention with the sea at a point situated between Mersina and Tripoli in Syria, they shall grant the concession for the said branches exclusively to the concessionnaires, provided, however, that the rights already granted to the Damascus-Hamah Railway Company and extensions are safeguarded.

Notwithstanding, should the concessionnaires, within a maximum period of one year from the date of the notification made to them by the Imperial Government, not agree to construct the branch or branches in question in accordance with the clauses and terms of the present concession, or, having agreed to do so, fail to execute them within the time agreed on by the Imperial Government and the concessionnaires, the latter shall forfeit all rights to the said branches, and the Imperial Government may grant the concession for them to third parties.

The concessionnaires shall, further, have the preferential right on equal terms to construct the following branches:

(a) Towards Marash.
(b) Towards Aintab.
(c) Towards Birijik.
(d) Towards Mardin.
(e) Towards Erbil.
(f) From the Diala towards Salakié and Tuz-kharmati.
(g) From El-Badj to Hit.

This preferential right for the seven branches specified above is dependent for its validity on the following conditions:

Should the Imperial Government decide definitely to grant the concession of one of these branches to third parties, the concessionnaires shall be obliged, within nine months from the date of the notification made to them by the Ministry of Commerce and Public Works, to inform the Imperial Ottoman Government whether they desire to take up that concession upon the conditions accepted by the third parties mentioned above.

Article 13. The concessionnaires shall have the right to establish and work tile and brick works on the line with the permission of the local authorities. Machinery and tools for the use of the said works shall enjoy the same exemption as that granted to the material and tools for the railway. The coal consumed in those works shall be exempt from customs duty.

The works shall revert free of charge to the State on the expiration of the concession.

Article 14. During the entire period of the concession, the concessionnaires shall be bound at their own expense to maintain in perfect condition the railway and everything appertaining thereto, as well as its fixtures and rolling stock, in default of which the procedure provided for by article 16 of the specifications shall be adopted.

Article 15. The concessionnaires are bound to conform, as regards the policing and safety of the line, to the laws and regulations now in force, or to be enacted hereafter in the Ottoman Empire.

The Imperial Government shall take all necessary measures for the maintenance of order along the line and in the construction yards.

In the case of interruption of the traffic on part or whole of the line through the fault of the concessionnaires, the Imperial Government shall take, at the expense, risk, and peril of the concessionnaires, all necessary steps in accordance with article 16 of the specification with a view to ensuring the temporary working of the line.

Article 16. The concessionnaires shall have the right to levy tolls in accordance with the tariff of the specification from the date on which each section of the railway is provisionally accepted until the expiration of the concession.

Article 17. The transport of officers and men, both naval and military, travelling collectively or separately, whether in time of war or peace, as well as that of war material and stores, prisoners and convicts, State officials, and mails, shall be effected in accordance with the terms of Chapter V of the specification.

Article 18. As guarantee for the fulfilment of the present engagements the concessionnaires, shall, within three months from the day on which they receive official notice of the issue of the firman granting the concession, deposit as security in a bank at Constantinople, approved by the Government, a sum of £T. 30,000 either in cash or Government bonds, or the bonds of an Ottoman joint-stock company, or else guaranteed by the State at the current price.

If the deposit is made in bonds the bank shall obtain an undertaking that any deficiency caused by a fall in the price shall be made good. Immediately after the deposit of the security the firman granting the concession shall be issued to the concessionnaires.

The security shall be returned only when the works have been finally accepted and in proportion to the length of the sections opened to traffic; if within the three months above mentioned the concessionnaires do not make the said deposit, they shall, without any previous summons, forfeit all concession rights.

In the event of its proving impossible to carry out the terms of article 35, the concessionnaires shall have the right to recover their security without any formality or obligation to ask the previous consent of the Government.

Article 19. The Imperial Ottoman Government reserve the right of withdrawing at any time the concession of the line from Konia to Busra and branches on payment to the concessionnaires, for the remaining period of the concession, of an annual sum equivalent to 50 per cent. of the average gross receipts for the five years preceding the year in which the concession is withdrawn, provided always that the said annual sum is not less than 12,000 fr.

per kilometre. In this case the Imperial Ottoman Government shall repay in one payment the whole of the Government bonds issued to the concessionnaires which have not been previously redeemed, and from the annual sum to which, under the present article, the concessionnaires are entitled there shall be deducted the annuity of the said loans, viz., 11,000 fr. per kilometre. The Government shall guarantee to the concessionnaires the regular payment at the specified periods of the balance due to them on account of the withdrawal of the concession, which shall form the subject of a special convention.

The lines and everything appertaining therefo shall then be handed over to the Government, and the Government shall then proceed to purchase the existing rolling stock and fixtures, materials, and stores, in accordance with article 19 of the specification.

In the event of the concession for the railway being withdrawn, and should the Imperial Government not deem it desirable to work it through their own officials, they shall not grant the right of working it to another company, but undertake to cause it to be worked on lease by the concessionaires.

Article 20. On the expiration of the concession for each section the Imperial Government shall acquire all rights of the concessionnaires over the railway and everything appertaining thereto, as well as in regard to plant and material, and shall become entitled to all the proceeds derived therefrom.

The lines and everything appertaining thereto shall be handed over free of all debt and liability to the Imperial Government, and the latter shall effect the purchase of plant and stores in accordance with article 20 of the specification.

Article 21. The railway employés and officials shall wear the uniform approved and adopted by the Imperial Government; they shall all wear the fez, and shall as far as possible be selected among Ottoman subjects.

Five years after the date of the opening of each section to traffic the whole of the executive working staff, except the higher officials, shall be exclusively composed of Ottoman subjects.

Article 22. The concessionnaires may work any mines which they shall discover within a zone of 20 kilom. each side of the middle of the line, provided that they conform with the laws and regulations relating thereto, but this shall not give them a privilege or monopoly.

They may likewise cut wood in the forests adjoining the line, either for timber or for charcoal, on application to the competent authorities and if they conform to the regulations governing the matter.

Article 23. The concessionnaires shall have the right to build at their own expense at Bagdad, Busra, and at the terminus of the branch from Zobeir, harbours with all necessary arrangements for bringing ships alongside the quay and for the loading, unloading, and warehousing of goods.

The plan of these harbours shall be submitted within eight years at the latest from the date of exchange of the present convention, and the works on each harbour shall be finished within twelve years at the latest from the date at which the work is begun on the section adjacent to each harbour respectively.

A scale of tariffs shall be annexed to the plans.

The three ports shall form an integral part of the railway, and the net receipts derived therefrom shall be carried to the account of the gross receipts of the railway.

On expiration of the concession these harbours and everything appertaining thereto shall revert free of charge to the State.

Should the concessionnaires fail to construct any one of these harbours within the above-mentioned period, the Imperial Government shall be entitled to grant the concession to third parties.

In any case the concessionnaires may during the period of construction of the railway establish at these three points, as well as at the port of Kostambul, temporary structures for the unloading of materials for the railway.

These structures shall, if the Imperial Government require it, be demolished on the completion of the works.

Article 24. The concessionnaires shall be entitled to set up and open, wherever the need is felt, on the land belonging to the railway depôts and warehouses which shall be available for use by the public.

These depôts, warehouses, and other plant shall become the property of the Government on the expiration of the concession in accordance with article 20 of the specification.

The Government shall have a share of 25 per cent. in the net receipts of these depôts and warehouses.

Article 25. The concessionnaires shall be entitled to use on the lines free of charge natural hydraulic power, the right of using which is not already appropriated, or which will be created, for the purpose of generating electricity for the driving of trains, for their lighting, or for other purposes in the working of the railway. The plans and designs of the works which are to be carried out for this purpose shall be submitted for the approval of the Ministry of Commerce and Public Works.

Should use be made of this electric power, 50 per cent. of the savings under this head in the working expenses shall be carried to the credit of the Imperial Ottoman Government.

All plant of this kind shall revert free of charge to the State on the expiration of the concession.

Article 26. The Government shall be entitled to construct at their own expense entrenchments and works of defence on the points of the main line or its branches and wherever they shall deem it necessary.

Article 27. Works of art and antiquities discovered during construction shall be subject to the regulations relating thereto.

Nevertheless the concessionnaires shall be exempt from the formality of presenting an application and obtaining permission for research.

Article 28. The concessionnaires shall be bound to submit to the Ministry of Public Works a monthly statement of all receipts; these statements shall be drawn up in the manner prescribed by article 17 of the specification.

Article 29. The railway being considered as divided into sections of 200 kilom. in length, should the concessionnaires, except in an established case of *vis major*, not have commenced the works within the appointed time, or should they not complete the work on one section within the appointed time or should they interrupt the traffic, or should they not, on any one section, fulfil the other principal engagements under the present convention, the Imperial Government shall issue a summons to the concessionnaires stating the undertakings which remain to be fulfilled by them and should they within a period of eighteen months from the date of the summons not have taken such steps as are necessary, they shall forfeit their concessionary rights for every section of the line in regard to which they shall have been found in default, and procedure provided for by article 18 of the specification shall be adopted.

It is agreed that, so long as the main line between Konia and Bagdad is not entirely completed, the concessionnaires may not open to traffic the parts of the line from Bagdad to Busra which they may have constructed.

During the period in which the sections between Bagdad and Busra are not open to traffic the concessionnaires shall refund to the Imperial Government, at the dates when the annual instalments fall due, the annuity of 11,000 fr. per kilometre for interest on and redemption of the bonds which the Imperial Government shall have issued to them for the said sections and they shall not, of course, receive anything on account of working expenses; but these clauses do not in any was prejudice the other rights of the concessionnaires on the line from Bagdad to Busra.

The forfeiture of the concession for one or several sections of the railway shall not prejudice the right of the concessionnaires as regards the remaining sections of the new lines, nor as regards the whole of the old lines.

Article 30. The concessionnaires shall construct free of charge at the points selected by the Government the necessary premises for the offices of the Imperial Railway Commissioners and of the customs, postal, and police officials.

The concessionnaires shall construct at important stations, after arrangement with the Ministry of Commerce and Public Works, two rooms with water-closet for the postal service.

Article 31. The concessionnaires may instal at their own expense on the whole extent of the line telegraph poles and wires; this line shall not be used for private correspondence which has no connection with the working of the railway.

The Imperial Government reserve to themselves the right of control at all times by inspectors appointed by the Ministry of Posts and Telegraphs of all telegraphic correspondence carried over the wires of the company.

The Government shall be entitled to make use of the poles belonging to the railway for the the erection of one or, if necessary, two telegraphic wires, and the poles on the railway shall be erected so that they are capable of supporting these two additional wires, as well as those of the company. In case of need the Government shall have the right of erecting, at their own expense, other poles throughout the extent of the line or, in case of breakage or interruption of their lines, placing telegraphists in the stations for the transmission of important and urgent official telegrams on the telegraph lines of the railway, provided always that the railway service is not obstructed.

Article 32. The concessionnaires shall be entitled to convey by their own means of transport and without paying any tax to the postal administration of the Empire correspondence and bags concerning exclusively the railway service; but on condition that they shall submit them, according to rule, to the control of the officials of the postal administration. Private letters of the staff shall be subject to postage. The concessionnaires shall only carry letters of this nature on their lines on condition that they comply with the terms of the inland postal regulations in force within the Empire. They shall also be entitled to carry free of charge stores, such as coal, lubricants, and materials and plant required for the construction, maintenance, and working of the railway, both on the existing lines and on those lines which form the subject of the present convention.

Article 33. The Imperial Government undertake that the service of the line connecting Haidar-Pasha with Sirkedji and the bridge of Karakeuï shall be carried on by the Mahsoussé Administration, by means of three new boats, of an average service speed of at least 14 miles (of 1,855 metres) per hour.

If within one year from the date of exchange of the present convention the Mahsoussé Administration should not organise the service under the above-mentioned conditions, the concessionnaires shall have the right to carry passengers and goods between the two points, provided that they select the crews of these boats from retired officers and men of the Imperial fleet, or from cadets of the Imperial Naval School who are eligible for commissions.

The boats of the concessionnaires shall carry on their service in the place and instead of those of the Mahsoussé Company while being exclusively appropriated to the said transport service, and the concessionnaires shall pay yearly to that administration a sum equal to 5 per cent. of the gross receipts derived from the transport of passengers and goods carried on by them between the above-mentioned points.

From the balance of the gross receipts there shall be deducted:
1. Working expenses;
2. An annuity of 8.30 per cent. of the initial capital appropriated to the acquisition of boats;

after deduction of the said sums, the remainder shall be carried to the account of the gross receipt of the new guaranteed lines.

The amount of initial capital shall be determined after the boats have been purchased.

It is understood that if the gross receipts of one year do not allow of the above-mentioned expenses being met the company shall have no claim upon the Imperial Government.

It may, however, make good the deficit from the receipts of the following years.

The boats of the concessionnaires, being considered as a section of the Mahsoussé, shall enjoy the same rights as the latter.

Article 34. The concessionary company and the company about to be formed by it being Ottoman joint-stock companies, all disputes and differences which may arise, either between the Imperial Government and the concessionnaires or the company, or between the concessionnaires or the company and private persons, as a result of the execution or interpretation of the present convention and the specification attached thereto, shall be carried before the competent Ottoman courts.

The new company, being Ottoman, must correspond with the State departments in the Turkish language, which is the official language of the Imperial Ottoman Government.

Article 35. The Imperial Government guarantee to the concessionnaires an annuity of 11,000 fr. per kilometre constructed and worked, and also a contract sum of 4,500 fr. per annum for working expenses in respect of each kilometre worked.

This annuity of 11,000 fr. shall be met by an Ottoman State loan bearing interest at 4 per cent. with a sinking fund of 0.087538 per cent., redeemable during the period of the concession. Consequently the concessionnaires will be entitled to a nominal sum of 269,110 fr. 65 c. of this State loan for each kilometre constructed and opened to traffic, and the concessionnaires shall be debarred from demanding other amounts on this head from the Imperial Ottoman Government.

The total nominal amount of Government bonds accruing to the concessionnaires by the terms of the foregoing arrangement shall be issued to them by the Imperial Ottoman Government on the signature of each special convention for each section; but the concessionnaires shall make good to the Imperial Ottoman Government the sums which the latter have paid during the period of construction for the service of the bonds issued to the concessionnaires, viz., till the date on which each section of the railway is provisionally accepted. These sums shall be placed by the concessionnaires in the hands of the Public Debt for the account of the Imperial Ottoman Government.

The Imperial Government reserve the right of modifying at any moment the system of payment of the kilometric annuity of 11,000 fr. fixed in the first paragraph of the present article, after redemption of the bonds issued in respect of the said annuity.

As soon as the growth of the traffic and receipts and the financial situation permit the issue by the concessionnaires themselves of bonds of their own to replace the Government bonds which have been issued to them by the Imperial Government, the concessionnaires shall come to an agreement with the Imperial Government for the purpose of carrying out this arrangement.

For the first section of 200 kilom. beyond Konia the face value of the bonds to be issued by the Imperial Ottoman Government to the concessionnaires is fixed at 54,000,000 fr. But as soon as this section is finally accepted and the length of the completed line is fixed, the exact nominal value of the bonds accruing to the concessionnaires for that section shall be calculated at the rate of 269,110 fr. 65 c. per kilometre. Any surplus over this nominal amount shall be calculated at the issue price, plus interest at 4 per cent. accrued up to the date of payment, and the sum thus ascertained shall be paid in cash by the concessionnaires into the Imperial Treasury. The calculation shall be made at a min mum of $81\frac{1}{2}$ per cent.

The Ottoman Anatolian Railway Company guarantees to the Imperial Ottoman Government the construction of the aforesaid first section of 200 kilom. until the work on this section is completed.

In the event of the Imperial Ottoman Government deeming it necessary, they may also require the Ottoman Anatolian Railway Company to guarantee other sections, and the Ottoman Anatolian Railway Company shall have the right so to do.

The contract sum of 4,500 fr. per annum for working expenses in respect of each kilometre opened to traffic will be guaranteed to the concessionnaires by a special convention for each section simultaneously with the convention regulating the annuity of 11,000 fr.

As regards the first section of 200 kilom. beyond Konia, the above-mentioned contract sum of 4,500 fr. per kilometre per annum is secured to the concessionnaires on the surplus of the guarantees already assigned to the lines of the Ottoman Anatolian Railway Company.

The service of the Government bonds which are to be issued for the aforesaid kilometric annuity of 11,000 fr. shall be secured on the special appropriations agreed on with the Imperial Government before work is begun on each section.

The Imperial Ottoman Bagdad Railway Company, on its part, further pledges, irrevocably and inalienably, to the holders of the said bonds the line from Konia to the Persian Gulf and its branches with their rolling stock. Similarly, and for the same purpose, it assigns its share in the receipts from this line after payment of the working expenses, but the bondholders shall not be entitled to intervene in the administration of the company.

The aforesaid share of the receipts, after deducting working expenses—both the said share and the amount of expenses to be determined by the company's books—shall be paid annually, if need be, by the company to the Administration of the Ottoman Public Debt for the service of the bonds. The Imperial Ottoman Government shall refund to the company any sums that the latter may have supplied under this head for the service of the bonds issued. The Imperial Ottoman Government further assign, irrevocably and inalienably, to the holders of the aforementioned Government bonds their share of the gross receipts of the said line.

If the gross kilometric receipts of the line exceed 4,500 fr. but do not exceed 10,000 fr., the surplus above 4,500 fr. shall belong entirely to the Government.

If the gross kilometric receipts exceed 10,000 fr., the portion up to 10,000 fr. being always divided as stated above, 60 per cent. of the surplus over and above the 10,000 fr. shall pass to the Imperial Government, and 40 per cent. to the Company.

It is agreed that if the gross kilometric receipts do not reach 4,500 fr. the sum required to make good the deficiency in this amount shall be paid to the concessionnaires by the Government at the same time as the annuity of 11,000 fr. from the special assignments to be agreed on between the Imperial Government and the concessionnaires before the fulfilment by the concessionnaires of the clauses of the present convention relative to each section.

The above assignments shall be collected and paid through the agency of the Administration of the Ottoman Public Debt.

As regards the Government bonds to be issued for the construction of the different sections of the railway, the receipts accruing to the Imperial Government shall be pooled in such a manner that the amount available shall be assigned to the whole of the said bonds in proportion to the original nominal value of each issue.

Immediately after the payment of the coupons and the sinking fund of the Government bonds issued, the surplus of the receipts accruing to the Imperial Ottoman Government shall be paid to the latter annually after the completion of the formalities provided for by article 40 of the present convention.

Article 36. For the purpose of determining the average of the kilometric receipts of the new Bagdad lines, all the receipts from every portion of the new lines, together with the net receipts referred to in articles 23 and 33 of the present convention, shall be pooled as and when the new lines are opened to traffic.

The average of the gross kilometric receipts thus obtained shall serve as the basis for ascertaining the total of the sums to be paid in accordance with article 35.

Article 37. The concessionnaires undertake to carry out at their own expense all the improvements on the old lines from Haidar-Pasha to Angora and Eskishehr to Konia required for the introduction of an express train service, but the expenditure involved shall not exceed a sum of 8,000,000 fr.

In return for this expenditure and for the new extraordinary charges for working expenses involved in the introduction of the express train service, the Imperial Government assign to the concessionnaires:

1. An annuity of 350,000 fr. for thirty years for interest and sinking fund in respect of the capital sum of 8,000,000 fr. mentioned above.

This annuity shall be paid from the commencement of the works of improvement.

2. An annuity of 350,000 fr. for the establishment of the express trains.

This latter annuity shall not become payable till the main line reaches Aleppo.

The annuities provided for in the present article shall be paid to the Ottoman Anatolian Railway Company out of the existing assignments for the guarantees of the old railway system and in the same manner as the latter.

Article 38. The concessionnaires undertake to construct and work, as soon as the Imperial Government shall require them to do so, on the conditions of the present convention, a branch line starting from the Konia-Busra line and ending at Diarbekr and Kharput.

Article 39. The proposed junction of the Damascus-Hamah line and its extensions with the railway system forming the subject of the present convention shall take place at Aleppo.

Article 40. The concessionnaires shall submit to the Ministry of Public Works, in the course of the month of January of each year, an account of the receipts, after it has been audited and approved by the Imperial Commission, and this shall be the basis on which the sums accruing to the Imperial Government and the company shall be determined in conformity with article 35 of the present convention.

As soon as the amount of the Government's share of these receipts is determined, the Imperial Ottoman Bagdad Railway Company shall remit it to the Administration of the Ottoman Public Debt for the account of the service of the Government bonds, and the latter shall deliver in cash to the Imperial Government any surplus which remains available over and above the sums required for the payment of the coupon which matures on the 1st July of the current financial year.

The Imperial Government, on their part, undertake to inform the Administration of the Public Debt within two months of the presentation of the account of receipts for a financial year of the amount of the sums acknowledged to be due to the company for immediate payment.

Article 41. The concessionnaires shall have the right to establish between Hamidieh and the port of Kostambul a temporary branch line for the transport of the plant and materials required for the railway. It is nevertheless understood that after the completion of the works which form the subject of the present convention the concessionnaires shall, if the Imperial Government signify their demand for it, have to remove the rails from this temporary branch line.

It is understood that during this temporary working the Imperial Government will not pay either annuity or working expenses for the said branch line.

Article 42. The land and the quarries which are expropriated in virtue of article 6 of the present convention shall be such area as is strictly necessary for the works of the railway and everything appertaining thereto, and may not be of greater extent. The expropriations shall be carried out under the supervision of the Ministry of Public Works.

Article 43. All the plant and materials required for the construction of the new lines and everything appertaining thereto referred to in article 8 of the convention, being free of all taxes and customs duties, shall, on arrival, be inspected in the usual manner by the Customs officials.

Article 44. The stores and warehouses to be constructed on the station premises in accordance with article 24 of the convention shall be used only for the storage of goods to be transported.

Such warehouses and stores shall be built in accordance with designs which will be submitted by the concessionaires and approved by the Ministry of Public Works.

Article 45. The concessionnaires must erect, at their own expense and up to a total outlay of 4,000,000 fr., such military stations as may be deemed necessary by the Ministry of War. The number, the site, and the arrangements of these military stations and everything appertaining thereto shall be settled by agreement between the concessionnaires and the Ministry of War.

Article 46. The concessionnaires undertake to pay annually a sum of £T. 500 to the Poorhouse as soon as the main line is opened to traffic.

(Source: *Parliamentary Papers*, No. Cd. 5635, Vol. C III (1911), No. 1, pp. 37-48.)

APPENDIX 14

Ottoman Circular announcing the Abrogation of the Capitulations

The Imperial Ottoman Government, in its sentiments of hospitality and sympathy towards the subjects of the friendly Powers, had in former times determined in a special manner the rules to which foreigners coming to the Orient to trade there should be subject, and had communicated those rules to the Powers. Subsequently those rules, which the Sublime Porte had decreed entirely of its own accord, were interpreted as privileges, corroborated and extended by certain practices, and were maintained down to our days under the name of ancient treaties (or Capitulations). Meanwhile these privileges, which on the one hand were found to be in complete opposition to the juridical rules of the century and to the principle of national sovereignty, constituted on the other hand an impediment to the progress and the development of the Ottoman Empire, just as they gave birth to certain misunderstandings in its relations with the foreign Powers; and thus they form an obstacle to the attainment of the desired degree of cordiality and sincerity in those relations.

The Ottoman Empire, surmounting all resistance, continues to march in the path of renaissance and reform which it entered upon in 1255 by the Hatti-Humayoun of Gul-Hané, and, in order to assure for itself the place which was due it in the family of the civilized peoples of Europe, it accepetd the most modern juridical principles and did not deviate from the program of supporting the edifice of the State on these foundations. The establishment of the constitutional régime demonstrates with what happy success the efforts of the Ottoman Government in the way of progress were crowned.

However, as consequences deduced from the Capitulations, the intervention of foreigners in the exercise of judiciary power, which constitutes the most important basis of the sovereignty of the State; the limitation of the legislative power, by the claim put forth that many laws could not be applied to foreigners; the fact that a criminal who has committed an offense against public security is screened from the application of the laws on the sole ground of his being of foreign nationality; or again the fact that public action is compromised by the necessity of respecting in regard to the foreign delinquent all sorts of restrictions and conditions; the fact finally that, according to the nationality of the contracting parties, a difference arising from a single contract admits of a different forum and mode of procedure—all these facts and other similar restrictive privileges constitute an insurmountable barrier to all organization of tribunals begun with a view to assuring in the country the perfect working of justice.

Likewise, that consequence of the Capitulations which renders foreigners exempt and free from taxes in the Ottoman Empire renders the Sublime Porte powerless not only to procure the necessary means for providing for the carrying out of reforms, but even for satisfying current administrative needs, without having recourse to a loan. In the same order of ideas, the obstacles raised to the increase of indirect taxes result in raising the quota of direct taxes and in overburdening the Ottoman taxpayers. The fact that foreigners trading in the Ottoman Empire and enjoying there all sorts of immunities and privileges are less heavily taxed than Ottomans constitutes at the same time a manifest injustice and an infringement of the independence and dignity of the State. The Imperial Government, in spite of all these obstacles, was zealously pursuing its efforts at reform when the unforeseen outbreak of the general war brought the financial difficulties in the country to the last degree of acuteness, endangering the accomplishment of all the work which had been begun or the undertaking of which had been decided upon. Now the Sublime Porte is convinced that the only means of salvation for Turkey is to bring into being this work of reform and of development as soon as possible, and it is likewise convinced that all the steps that it takes in this direction will meet with the encouragement of all the friendly Powers.

It is on the basis of this conviction that the decision has been taken to abrogate, reckoning from October 1, 1914, the Capitulations, which up to the present have constituted a hindrance to all progress in the Empire, as well as all privileges and toleration accessory to these Capitulations or resulting from them, and to adopt as the basis of relations with all States the general principles of international law.

While having the honor of communicating the present decision, which as it is to open an era of happiness for the Ottoman Empire will for this reason, I have no doubt, be received with satisfaction by the American Government. I consider it my duty to add that the Sublime Porte, inspired exclusively in its decision by the higher interests of the Ottoman land, does not nourish, in abrogating the Capitulations, any unfriendly thought in regard to any Power and that it is quite disposed to enter upon negotiations with a view to concluding with the American Government treaties of commerce on the basis of the general principles of public international law.

(Source: *Foreign Relations of the United States*, 1914, pp. 1092-93.)

APPENDIX 15

Second Act of Concession and Specification for the Construction and Management of the Great Maritime Suez Canal and Supplementary Works (with the Modifications up to July 1875), January 5th, 1856

§ I. Obligations

Article 1. The Society founded by our friend M. Ferdinand de Lesseps, in virtue of our grant of the 30th of November, 1854, must execute at its own expense, risk, and peril, all works and constructions necessary for the establishment.

1st. A Canal for the navigation of large vessels, between Suez on the Red Sea, and the gulf of Pelusium in the Mediterranean.

2nd. A Canal of irrigation, for the navigation of the Nile, joining the river to the Maritime Canal above-mentioned.

3rd. Two branches for irrigation and alimentation derived from the preceding Canal and bearing their waters in the two directions of Suez and of Pelusium.

The works to be conducted in such a manner as to be finished in six years' time, except in the case of unavoidable hindrances and delays.

Article 2. The Company are to have all facillities for executing the works with which it is charged, by itself and with administrative powers *(in regie)*, or to cause them to be executed by contractors by means of adjudication or otherwise. In all cases four-fifths at least of the workmen employed in these works are to be Egyptians.

Article 3. The Canal for the navigation of large vessels shall be of the depth and width fixed by the programme of the scientific International Commission.

In conformity with this programme it shall start from the port itself of Suez; use the basin, so called, of the Bitter Lakes and of Lake Timsah; and will fall into the Mediterranean, at a point of the gulf of Pelusium to be determined by the final plans drawn up by the Company's engineers.

Article 4. The Canal of irrigation destined for the navigation of the rivers as laid down with conditions of the said programme, is to take its rise near the city of Cairo, follow the valley (Ouady) Toumilat (old land of Gessen or Goshen) and fall into the great Maritime Canal at Lake Timsah.

Article 5. The arms of the said Canal are to branch off from the main body of water, above the outlet into Lake Timsah; at which point they will be directed on one side towards Suez, on the other towards Pelusae, parallel to the great Maritime Canal.

Article 6. Lake Timsah will be converted into an inland port able to receive vessels of the largest tonnage.

The Company will be bound, moreover, if necessary, 1st to construct an harbour att he entrance of the Maritime Canal to the gulf of Pelusium. 2nd. To improve the port and roadstead of Suez, so as also to afford shelter to vessels.

Article 7. The Maritime Canal and ports belonging to it, as well as the Canal of junction with the Nile and that of derivation, will always be kept in good order by the Company and at its own expense.

Article 8. The owners of property on the bank of the river wishing their land to be irrigated by artificial supplies from the Canals constructed by the Company, may obtain grants from it for this purpose by means of an indemnity or duty, the amount of which shall be fixed by the conditions of Article 17, hereinafter mentioned.

Article 9. We reserve the right to appoint on the Board of Management a special commissioner, to be paid by the Company and who will represent the rights and interests of the Egyptian Government in the execution of the provisions of this present deed.

If the Society's Board of Management be established elsewhere than in Egypt, the Company will be bound to be represented at Alexandria by a superior agent provided with all powers necessary to secure the furtherance of the work and the relations of the Company with our Government.

§ II. Concessions

Article 10. In return for the construction of the Canals and the additional works mentioned in the foregoing articles, the Egyptian Government allows the Company, without tax or duty, to enjoy the use of all land not belonging to private individuals which they may require.

Also the use of all land as yet uncultivated not belonging to private individuals, which will be watered and cultivated at the Company's expense and trouble, with this difference: 1st. That the portions of land included in this last category shall be exempt from taxes for ten years only dating from their connexion with the undertaking. 2nd. That after that term, and until the expiration of the grant, they shall be liable to the obligations and taxes to which the land of the other Egyptian provinces is liable under the same circumstances. 3rd. That the Company can, afterwards, by its own acts or by its assigns, keep possession of this land and the artificial supply of water necessary for its fertilization on undertaking to pay to the Egyptian Government the taxes imposed upon the land under the same conditions.

Article 11. To determine the extent and limits of the land granted to the Company, under the conditions of the Sections 1 and 2 of Article 10 above quoted, reference is to be made to the plans hereto annexed; it being understood that the lands granted for the construction of the Canals and dependencies free of tax or duty in conformity with Section 1 are shown coloured black, and the lands granted for cultivation by payment of certain dues in conformity with Section 2, are therein shown coloured blue.

All deeds to be considered null and void made subsequent to our firman of 30th November, 1854, which will either vest rights of indemnity against the Company in private individuals which have not yet existed with respect to those lands, or rights of indemnity more extensive than they have yet enjoyed.

Article 12. The Egyptian Government will make over, if occasion arise, to the Company any private property the possession of which may be necessary to the execution of the work and the administration of the grants provided the Company pay a just indemnity to the owners.

Indemnity for temporary occupation, or of definitive expropriation is to be regulated amicably as far as possible; in case of disagreement, it will be fixed by a tribunal of arbitration proceeding summarily and composed: 1st, of an arbitrator chosen by the Company; 2nd, of and arbitrator chosen by the parties interested, of a 3rd arbitrator nominated by us.

The decisions of the tribunal of arbitration to be immediately executory and without appeal.

Article 13. The Egyptian Government invests the privileged Company, for the whole term of the grant, with power to work any mines and quarries that are public property free of duty, tax, or indemnity, and extract all materials necessary for the purposes of constructing and maintaining the works and establishments belonging to the undertaking.

It frees the Company, moreover, from all Custom-house dues, of export or import, on the importation into Egypt of all merchandize and materials whatsoever from abroad for the needs of the Company's different works in course of construction or management.

Article 14. We declare solemnly, for ourselves and our successors subject to the ratification of H.I.M. the Sultan, the Great Maritime Canal of Suez to Pelusium and the ports belonging to it, open at all times, as neutral passages, to every merchant vessel crossing from one sea to the other, without any distinction, exclusion, or preference of persons or nationalities, in consideration of the payment of the dues, and the performance of regulations established by the universal privileged Company for the use of the said Canal and its dependencies.

Article 15. In consequence of the principle laid down in the foregoing article, the universal privileged Company cannot, in any case, give to any vessel, Company, or private individual, any advantage or favour not given to all other vessels, Companies, or individuals on the same conditions.

Article 16. The duration of the Company is fixed at 99 years, counting from the completion of the works and the opening of the Maritime Canal to large vessels.

At the expiration of this period, the Egyptian Government will resume possession of the Canal constructed by the Company, on condition, in this case, that the Government take over the material and provisions in use for the Maritime Service of the undertaking, and pay the Company the value fixed, either by amicable arrangement or official estimate.

Nevertheless, should the Company retain the concession by successive period of 99 years, the previous deduction for the benefit of the Egyptian Government stipulated by Article 18 hereafter shall be increased for the second period to 20 per cent., for the third period to 25 per cent. and so on, at an increase of 5 per cent. for each period, such deductions not to exceed 35 per cent. of the net profits of the undertaking.

Article 17. In order to indemnify the Company for the expense of construction, maintenance and management placed to its account by these present, we authorize it, henceforth, and for the term of its possession, as may be determined by paragraphs 1st and 3rd of foregoing Article, to establish and collect for the right of passing through the Canals and the ports belonging, navigation, all pilotage, towage, or anchorage dues, according to tariffs to be modified by the Company at all times; but under this strict condition:

1st. The dues to be levied without exception or favour upon all vessels under like conditions;

2nd. The tariff to be published three months before being put into force in all the capitals and principal ports of commerce of the countries concerned;

3rd. For the special navigation dues the maximum of ten francs a ton for vessels, and ten francs a head for passengers not to be exceeded.

The Company may, also, for all artificial supplies of water granted on demand by private individuals, in virtue of Article 8 above-mentioned collect, according to a tarif to be fixed by itself, a duty proportionate to the quantity of water used and the extent of ground watered.

Article 18. At the same time, since grants of land and other advantages have been bestowed upon the Company by the foregoing Articles, we reserve, for the benefit of the Egyptian Government, a deduction of 15 per cent. upon the net profits of each year settled and allotted by the general meeting of shareholders.

Article 19. The list of Founder-Members who have assisted by their labours, exertions, and their capital the realization of the undertaking before the foundation of the Society will be determined by us.

After the deduction for the Egyptian Government stipulated in Article 18 above-mentioned, 10 per cent. of the net annual products of the undertaking is to be allotted to the Founder-Members, their heirs or assigns.

Article 20. Independently of the time necessary for the execution of the works, our friend and representative, M. Ferdinand de Lesseps will preside over and direct the Society as first founder, for ten years, dating from the time when the period of the enjoyment of the grant of 99 years begins, by the terms of Article 16 above-mentioned.

Article 21. The statutes of the Society thus created under the denomination of Universal Company of the Maritime Canal of Suez are hereby approved; this present approbation being valid as an authorization of constitution, in the usual form of "Sociétés Anonymes", dating from the day on which the capital of the Company shall have been entirely made up.

Article 22. As a testimony of the interest we attach to the success of the enterprise, we promise the Company the hearty co-operation of the Egyptian Government, and by these presents expressly invite all functionaries and agents of the departments of our administration to afford it their aid and protection under all circumstances.

Our engineers, Linant-Bey and Mougel-Bey, whom we place at the Company's disposal for the direction and management of the works required by it, will have the supervision of workmen and be charged with the execution of regulations concerning the setting up of the works.

Article 23. All the provisions of our ordinance of the thirtieth November, one thousand eight hundred and fifty-four are revoked, with others which will be found to be in opposition to the clauses and conditions of the present specification which will only be law for the grant for which it applies.

Executed at Alexandria, January 5th, 1856.

(Source: Percy Fitzgerald, *The Great Canal at Suez*, London, 1876, Vol. I, pp. 297-306.)

APPENDIX 16

Decree for the Establishment of a Treasury of the Public Debt in Egypt, May 2nd, 1876

We, the Khedive of Egypt, desiring to take definitive and opportune measures for obtaining the unification of the different debts of the State and those of the Daira Sanieh, and also desiring the reduction of the excessive charges resulting from these debts, and wishing to bear solemn testimony to our firm intention to secure every guarantee to all persons interested, have resolved to establish a special Treasury charged with the regular service of the public debt, and to appoint to its management foreign Commissioners, who at our request will be indicated by the respective Governments as fit officials to fill the post to which they will be appointed by us in the quality of Egyptian officials, and under the following conditions. Having consulted our Privy Council, we have decreed, and do hereby decree, as follows:

Article 1. A Treasury of the Public Debt is established, charged with receiving the funds necessary for the interest and the redemption of the debt, and with applying them to this object exclusively.

Article 2. The officials, the local Treasuries, or the special Administrations, after collecting, receiving, or accumulating the revenues specially devoted to the payment of the debt, are or shall be in future charged to pay them into the Central Treasury or to keep them at the disposal of the Intendants of Public Expenditure ("Ordonnateurs des Dépenses de l'Etat"). The Intendants of Public Expenditure are, by virtue of the present Decree, bound to pay these revenues on account of the State Treasury into the special Treasury of the Public Debt, which will be considered in this respect as a special Treasury. These officials, treasuries and administrations can only procure a valid discharge by means of the vouchers which will be delivered to them by the said treasury of the Public Debt. Any other order or voucher will not be valid. These same officials, treasuries or administrations will every month send to the Minister of Finance a statement of the receipts or collections made by themselves directly or paid in by the receivers of the revenues specially devoted to the debt and the payments made into the special Treasury of the Public Debt. The Minister of Finance will communicate these statements to the Administration of the Treasury of the Public Debt.

The Treasury of the Public Debt shall receive from the Daira Sanieh the entire sum necessary for the interest and redemption of the amount of its unified debt, and it shall likewise receive the funds for the yearly payment due to the English Government, and representing the interest on the Suez Canal shares.

Article 3. If the payments of the revenue devoted to the debt be insufficient to meet the half-yearly charges, the special Public Debt Department will demand from the Treasury, through the intermediary of the Minister of Finance, the sum required to complete the half-yearly payments; the Treasury will have to deliver this sum a fortnight before the payments are due. If the funds in hand constitute a surplus over the amount necessary for the payment of the interest and the sinking fund, the special Treasury of the Public Debt will pay this surplus at the end of each year to the general Treasury of the Exchequer. The Treasury of the Public Debt will submit its accounts, which will be examined and reported upon according to law.

Article 4. The suits which the Treasury and its Directors, on its behalf, acting in the name and in interests of the creditors, mostly of foreign nationality, may consider they have to bring against the financial administration represented by the Minister of Finance in so far as regards the guardianship of the guarantees of the debt which we have confided to the said Treasury, will be brought in the terms of their jurisdiction before the new tribunals which, in conformity with the agreement entered into with the Powers, have been instituted in Egypt.

Article 5. The Commissioners selected as stated above will have the direction of the special Treasury of the Public Debt. They will be appointed by us for five years, and will sit in Cairo. Their functions may be continued after the five years have expired, and in case of the death or resignation of one of them the vacancy will be filled by us in the manner of the original appointment. They may intrust one of themselves with the functions of President, and the latter will notify his nomination to the Minister of Finance.

Article 6. The cost of exchange insurance, and conveyance of specie abroad as well as the commission for the payment of the coupons, will be borne by the Government. The Directors of the Treasury will come to a previous arrangement with the Ministers of Finance with regard to all these operations, but the Minister will decide whether the despatch of these sums is to be effected in specie or by letters of exchange.

Article 7. The Treasury will not be allowed to employ any funds, disposable or not, in operations of credit, commerce, industry, & c.

Article 8. The Government will not be able, without an agreement with the majority of the Commissioners directing the Treasury of the Public Debt, to effect in any of the taxes specially devoted to the Debt any changes which might result in a diminution of the revenue from these taxes. At the same time, the Government may farm out one or several of these taxes, provided that the contract entered into insure a revenue at least equal to that already existing, and may also conclude Treaties of commerce introducing modifications in the Customs duties.

Article 9. The Government undertakes not to issue any Treasury bonds, and not to contract any other loan of any nature whatsoever. This same engagement is entered into in the name of the Diara Sanieh. Nevertheless, in case the Government, from urgent national reasons should find itself placed under the necessity of having recourse to credit, it may do so within the limits of strict necessity and without doing anything to affect the employment of revenues set apart for the Treasury of the Public Debt, or to cause their diversion from their destination. These totally exceptional loans can only be contracted after an agreement on the subject with the Commissioners directing the Treasury.

Article 10. In order that the arrangements stated in the preceding article shall not place obstacles in the way of the Administration, the Government may open a running account with a bank to facilitate its payments by anticipations to be regulated in accordance with the year's receipts. The debit or credit balance will be settled at the end of each year. This current account must never be overdrawn during the year by more than 50,000,000 fr.

Done at Cairo, the 2nd of May, 1876. (Signed) Ismail.

(Source: *Parliamentary Papers*, 1876, Vol. 83, pp. 65-66 or, as corrected, 71-72.)

APPENDIX 17

Convention between Great Britain, Germany, Austria-Hungary, Spain, France, Italy, the Netherlands, Russia, and Turkey, respecting the Free Navigation of the Suez Maritime Canal. Signed at Constantinople, October 29th, 1888

Article 1. The Suez Maritime Canal shall always be free and open, in time of war as in time of peace, to every vessel of commerce or of war, without distinction of flag.

Consequently, the High Contracting Parties agree not in any way to interfere with the free use of the Canal, in time of war as in time of peace.

The Canal shall never be subjected to the exercise of the right of blockade.

Article 2. The High Contracting Parties, recognizing that the Fresh-Water Canal is indispensable to the Maritime Canal, take note of the engagements of His Highness the Khedive towards the Universal Suez Canal Company as regards the Fresh-Water Canal; Which engagements are stipulated in a Convention bearing date the 18th March, 1863, containing an *exposé* and four Articles.

They undertake not to interfere in any way with the security of that Canal and its branches, the working of which shall not be exposed to any attempt at obstruction.

Article 3. The High Contracting Parties likewise undertake to respect the plant, establishments, buildings, and works of the Maritime Canal and of the Fresh-Water Canal.

Article 4. The Maritime Canal remaining open in time of war as a free passage, even to the ships of war of belligerents, according to the terms of Article 1 of the present Treaty, the High Contracting Parties agree that no right of war, no act of hostility, nor any act having for its object to obstruct the free navigation of the Canal, shall be committed in the Canal and its ports of access, as well as within a radius of 3 marine miles from those ports, even though the Ottoman Empire should be one of the belligerent Powers.

Vessels of war of belligerents shall not revictual or take in stores in the Canal and its ports of access, except in so far as may be strictly necessary. The transit of the aforesaid vessels through the Canal shall be effected with the least possible delay, in accordance with the Regulations in force, and without any other intermission than that resulting from the necessities of the service.

Their stay at Port Said and in the roadstead of Suez shall not exceed twenty-four hours, except in case of distress. In such case they shall be bound to leave as soon as possible. An interval of twenty-four hours shall always elapse between the sailing of a belligerent ship from one of the ports of access and the departure of a ship belonging to the hostile Power.

Article 5. In time of war belligerent Powers shall not disembark nor embark within the Canal and its ports of access either troops, munitions, or materials of war. But in case of an accidental hindrance in the Canal, men may be embarked or disembarked at the ports of access by detachments not exceeding 1,000 men, with a corresponding amount of war material.

Article 6. Prizes shall be subjected, in all respects, to the same rules as the vessels of war belligerents.

Article 7. The Powers shall not keep any vessel of war in the waters of the Canal (including lake Timsah and the Bitter Lakes).

Nevertheless, they may station vessels of war in the ports of access of Port Said and Suez, the number of which shall not exceed two for each Power.

This right shall not be exercised by belligerents.

Article 8. The Agents in Egypt of the Signatory Powers of the present Treaty shall be charged to watch over its execution. In case of any event threatening the security or the free passage of the Canal, they shall meet on the summons of three of their number under the presidency of their Doyen, in order to proceed to the necessary verifications. They shall inform the Khedivial Government of the danger which they may have perceived, in order that Government may take proper steps to insure the protection and free use of the Canal. Under any circumstances, they shall meet once a year to take note of the due execution of the Treaty.

The last-mentioned meetings shall take place under the presidency of a Special Commissioner nominated for that purpose by the Imperial Ottoman Government. A Commissioner of the Khedive may also take part in the meeting, and may preside over it in case of the absence of the Ottoman Commissioner.

They shall especially demand the suppression of any work or the dispersion of any assemblage on either bank of the Canal, the object or effect of which might be to interfere with the liberty and the entire security of the navigation.

Article 9. The Egyptian Government shall, within the limits of its powers resulting from the Firmans, and under the conditions provided for in the present Treaty, take the necessary measures for insuring the execution of the said Treaty.

In case the Egyptian Government should not have sufficient means at its disposal, it shall call upon the Imperial Ottoman Government, which shall take the necessary measures to respond to such appeal; shall give notice thereof to the Signatory Powers of the Declaration of London of the 17th March, 1885; and shall, if necessary, concert with them on the subject.

The provisions of Articles 4, 5, 7 and 8 shall not interfere with the measures which shall be taken in virtue of the present Article.

Article 10. Similarly, the provisions of Articles 4, 5, 7 and 8 shall not interfere with the measures which His Majesty the Sultan and His Highness the Khedive, in the name of His Imperial Majesty, and within the limits of the Firmans granted, might find it necessary to take for securing by their own forces the defence of Egypt and the maintenance of public order.

In case His Imperial Majesty the Sultan, or His Highness the Khedive, should find it necessary to avail themselves of the exceptions for which this Article provides, the Signatory Powers of the Declaration of London shall be notified thereof by the Imperial Ottoman Government.

It is likewise understood that the provisions of the four Articles aforesaid shall in no case occasion any obstacle to the measures which the Imperial Ottoman Government may think it necessary to take in order to insure by its own forces the defence of its other possessions situated on the eastern coast of the Red Sea.

Article 11. The measures which shall be taken in the cases provided for by Articles 9 and 10 of the present Treaty shall not interfere with the free use of the Canal. In the same cases, the erection of permanent fortifications contrary to the provisions of Article 8 is prohibited.

Article 12. The High Contracting Parties, by application of the principle which forms one of the bases of the present Treaty, agree that none of them shall endeavour to obtain with respect to the Canal territorial or commercial advantages or privileges in any international arrangements which may be concluded. Moreover, the rights of Turkey as the territorial Power are reserved.

Article 13. With the exception of the obligations expressly provided by the clauses of the present Treaty, the sovereign rights of His Imperial Majesty the Sultan, and the rights and immunities of His Highness the Khedive, resulting from the Firmans, are in no way affected.

Article 14. The High Contracting Parties agree that the engagements resulting from the present Treaty shall not be limited by the duration of the Acts of Concession of the Universal Suez Canal Company.

Article 15. The stipulation of the present Treaty shall not interfere with the sanitary measures in force in Egypt.

Article 16. The High Contracting Parties undertake to bring the present Treaty to the knowledge of the States which have not signed it, inviting them to accede to it.

Article 17. The present Treaty shall be ratified, and the ratifications shall be exchanged at Constantinople within the space of one month, or sooner if possible.

In faith of which the respective Plenipotentiaries have signed the present Treaty, and have affixed to it the seal of their arms.

Done at Constantinople, the 29th day of the month October, in the year 1888.

(Signatures)

(Source: *Parliamentary Papers*, 1889, LXXXVII, Commercial No. 2, C. 5623, pp. 796-799.)

APPENDIX 18

Homestead Exemption Law (Five Feddans Law)

Articles 2 and 4 of Law No. 31 of 1912; "Official Journal" of December 4th, No. 139

Article 2. The agricultural holdings of farmers who do not own more than 5 feddans of land cannot be seized for debt. This exception from seizure includes the dwelling-house of such farmers and their dependencies, as well as the draft animals, and the agricultural implements necessary for the cultivation of the said land. Such exemption applies to the claims of mortgage creditors and those who are secured by a pledge or a right of affectation, but not to privileged creditors.

Article 4. The provisions of Article 2. shall not affect the rights of creditors whose security is registered at the time of the coming into force of this law, nor those of unsecured creditors whose document of title has obtained an official date before that time.

(Source: *Parl. Papers*, 1913, Cd. 6682, Vol. LXXXI, pp. 259-260.)

APPENDIX 19

The Grants and Privileges made by Shah Abas unto Mr. Cannocke in the behalf of the King of England

(text adjusted by Shah Sefi, 1629)

Article 1. That in the behalf of the supreme Majesty of King James there might continually reside at the court of Shah Abas an ambassador; and at what time soever as the Majesty of the King of England shall, for the better establishing of amity, benevolence and correspondency desire an ambassador from hence, we shall gladly send one, who being arrived in his country shall conserve and keep those amorous links and bands of friendship, love, unity and benevolence.

Article 2. At what time soever as the said English nation shall arrive with their ships to any of the ports belonging to the King of Persia, or shall travel by land with their merchandises, the Governors of the said ports or places wheresoever they come shall not exact from them one farthing more than the accustomed duties which my own subjects pay.

Article 3. Whatsoever is necessary, as victuals, munition, etc., shall be sold unto the said nation for the furnishing their shipping at the same rates and prices my own subjects pay.

Article 4. If by chance there happen any torment or tempestuous storm where the English ships shall ride, and that any of the said ships suffer shipwreck (which God forbid), no man whatsoever shall pretend anything thereof, but shall suffer the said nation in the best manner they can to save their goods and make the most of all things thereof. If any person take anything thereof, they shall restore it again.

Article 5. Whatsoever goods the said nation shall import (into?) our dominions, they may carry it to whatsoever place in my country they please, buying and selling freely, nobody molesting them, or offer(ing?) them any force or violence.

Article 6. They shall buy whatsoever short of merchandise they list, nobody hindering them.

Article 7. They shall live in their own laws and religion, and no man compel them by violence to turn Mussellmen; for as religion is a work which proceeds from the conscience and mind, which pleads between the creature and the Creator, so nobody but the high Majesty of God hath power to penetrate the said conscience; and God it is above unto whom all men are to render an account of their salvation. But if any of the said nation shall voluntarily turn Mussellman, he shall live in any part of my dominion he lists, possessing quietly what belongs unto him.

Article 8. They shall keep whatsoever sort of arms or weapons in their houses; and if in their travels any person shall steal anything from them, and they in defence thereof kill him, the governors of that jurisdiction shall not molest them for it; but if they apprehend the thief and carry him before the magistrate, he shall in their presence give him punishment.

Article 9. At what time soever any ambassador shall come from the high Majesty of the King of England, he hath power to constitute in any part of my dominions agents and factors for the negotiating their business; and our governors and supreme ministers of such places shall respect them and assist them in all occasions.

Article 10. If any of their people shall commit any disorders, they shall be carried before the said Ambassador to have chastisement.

Article 11. In whatsoever part any of the said nation shall reside, and anybody offer them force or violence, they shall acquaint the governor of those parts thereof. If he deny them justice, they shall appeal unto the Ambassador which is in my Court, and he informing our Royal Person thereof, We shall severely chastise such abuses.

Article 12. If in any part whatsoever there shall be any servant or interpreter of the said nation in whom they themselves put trust and confidence, they[1] (shall?) give credence unto and respect him in the like manner as if he were one of the said nation.

Article 13. If from any parts of Turkie, or other places whatsoever, any man shall bring any slaves of the English nation, if he be not turned Mussellman, he shall be delivered unto the said nation, they paying only the price he cost.

Article 14. If any of the said nation die in any part of my dominions, that no man offer to take one farthing of his goods, but that the said Ambassador dispose thereof as he see good, and that the corpse of the said deceased be interred in places where other Christians bury.

Article 15. If the said English shall not find vent for such commodities as they bring, according to their content, they may transport it through my country into any other parts whatsoever, paying only the accustomed duties my own subjects pay, and as they do in Constantinople and Alepo and other parts of Turkie.

If anything be stolen from them on the way the governors of those parts shall make search for the thief; and, finding him, shall restore the said goods; if not, the said governors shall make good what was stolen.

Article 16. If between the said nation and our subjects happen any difference or discord in

---

[1] the governors?

buying or selling, they shall repair unto the Justice who shall do them right according to the ancient laws of this land. But if the said difference pass or exceed twenty tomans, the Justice, shall send them to the Ambassador to be decided, that he in presence of our Justices might do whatsoever shall be conformable to honourable and noble laws.

Article 17. If any of the said nation shall marry a wife of any of those Christians in our country, if he have any issue, and should die, leaving the said children destitute of friends to protect them, they shall in such cases be delivered to the disposure of the Ambassador.

Article 18. That no soldier, merchant, rustic or whatsoever person in my dominions, nay, the said English themselves, shall not break these conditions, for that the high Majesty of Shah Abas, the conqueror of the world, hath accepted and allowed thereof.

Given in the moon Ziadja, 1038.

(Source: *Letters received by the East India Company from its Servants in the East*, edited by William Foster, B.A., London, 1902. Vol. VI, Appendix, pp. 294-297.)

APPENDIX 20

Anglo-Persian Commercial Treaty, January 28th, 1801

(Farman from Futteh Ali Shah for certain commercial privileges granted to the English)

Article 1. The merchants of the high contracting States are to travel and carry on their affairs in the territories of both nation in full security and confidence, and the rulers and governors of all cities are to consider it their duty to protect from injury their cattle and goods.

Article 2. The traders and merchants of the kingdom of England or Hindoostan that are in the service of the English Government shall be permitted to settle in any of the Seaports or cities of the boundless empire of Persia (which may God preserve from calamity) that they prefer; and no government duties, taxes, or requisitions shall ever be collected on any goods that are the actual property of either of the governments; the usual duties on such to be taken from purchasers.

Article 3. Should it happen that either the persons or property (of merchants) are injured or lost by thieves or robbers, the utmost exertions shall be made to punish the delinquents and recover the property. And if any merchant or trader of Persia evades or delays the payment of a debt to the English Government, the latter are authorized to use every possible mode for the recovery of their demands, taking care to do so in communication and with the knowledge of the ruler or governor of the place, who is to consider it as his duty to grant, on such occasion, every aid in his power. And should any merchants of Persia be in India, attending to their mercantile concerns, the officers of the English Government are not to prevent them carrying on their affairs, but to aid and favour them, and the above-mentioned merchants are to recover their debts and demands in the mode prescribed by the customs and laws of the English Government.

Article 4. If any person in the empire of Persia die indebted to the English Government, the ruler of the place must exert his power to have such demand satistied before those of any creditor whatever. The servants of the English Government, resident in Persia, are permitted to hire as many domestic natives of that country as are necessary for the transaction of their affairs; and they are authorised to punish such, in cases of misconduct, in the manner they judge most expedient, provided such punishment does not extend to life or limb; in such cases the punishment to be inflicted by the ruler or governor of the place.

Article 5. The English are at liberty to build houses and mansions in any of the ports or cities of Persia that they choose, and they may sell or rent all such houses or mansions at pleasure. And should ever a ship belonging to the English Government be in a damaged state in any of the ports of Persia, or one of Persia be that condition in an English harbour, the Chiefs and rulers of the ports and harbours of the respective nations are to consider it as their duty to give every aid to refit and repair vessels so situated. And if it happens that any of the vessels of either nation are sunk or shipwrecked in or near the ports or shores of either country, on such occasions whatever part of the property is recovered shall be restored to their owners or their heirs, and a just hire is to be allowed by the owners to those who recover it.

Final Article. Whenever any native of England or India, in the service of the English Government, resident in Persia, wishes to leave that country, he is to suffer obstruction from no person, but to be at full liberty to do so, and to carry with him his property.

The Articles of the Treaty between the two States are fixed and determined. That person who turns from God turns from his own soul.

Additional Article. It is further written in sincerity that on iron, lead, steel, broadcloth, and purpetts that are exclusively the property of the English Government, no duties whatever shall be taken from the sellers; a duty not exceeding one per cent, to be levied upon the purchasers. And the duties, imports, and customs which are at this period established in Persia and India (on other goods) are to remain fixed and not to be increased.

The high in rank Hajee Kulleel Khan Mullick-oo-Tijjar is charged and entrusted with the arrangement and settlement of the remaining points relative to commerce.

Seal of Hajec
Ibrahim Han.

Seal of Captain
(Sd.) John Malcolm, Envoy.

(Source: C. U. Aitchison, *A Collection of Treaties, Engagements and Sanads*, Calcutta, 1909, Vol. XII, pp. 44-46.)

APPENDIX 21

Treaty of Friendship and Commerce between the United States and Persia

Signed at Constantinople December 13th, 1856
(Ratifications exchanged at Constantinople, June 13th, 1857)

In the name of God, the Clement and the Merciful.

The President of the United States of North America, and His Majesty as exalted as the planet Saturn; the Sovereign to whom the sun serves as a standard; whose splendour and magnificence are equal to that of the skies; the Sublime Sovereign, the monarch whose armies are as numerous as the stars: whose greatness calls to mind that of Jeinshid; whose magnificence equals that of Darius; the Heir of the Crown and Throne of the Kayanians, the Sublime Emperor of all Persia, being both equally and sincerely desirous of establishing relations of friendship between the two Governments, which they wish to strengthen by a Treaty of friendship and commerce, reciprocally advantageous and useful to the citizens and subjects of the two High Contracting Parties, have for this purpose named for their Plenipotentiaries:

The President of the United States of North America, Carroll Spence, Minister Resident of the United States near the Sublime Porte; and His Majesty the Emperor of all Persia, His Excellency Emin-ul-Molk Farrukh Khan, Ambassador of His Imperial Majesty the Shah, decorated with the portrait of the Shah, with the great Cordon Blue, and Bearer of the Girdle of Diamonds, etc.

And the said Plenipotentiaries, having exchanged their full powers, which were found to be in proper and due form, have agreed upon the following Articles:

Article 1. Good understanding between Persia and the United States. There shall be hereafter sincere and constant good understanding between the Government and citizens of the United States of North America and the Persian Empire, and all Persian subjects.

Article 2. Reception and Treatment of Ambassadors or Diplomatic Agents. The Ambassadors or Diplomatic Agents whom it may please either of the two High Contracting Parties to send and maintain near the other, shall be received and treated, they and all those composing their missions, as the Ambassadors and Diplomatic Agents of the most favoured nations are received and treated in the two respective countries; and they shall enjoy there in all respects the same prerogatives and immunities.

Article 3. Protection of Travellers, Merchants and Other Residents. The citizens and subjects of the two High Contracting Parties travellers, merchants, manufacturers, and others, who may reside in the territory of either country, shall be respected and efficiently protected by the authorities of the country and their agents; and treated in all respects as the subjects and citizens of the most favoured nation are treated.

Right to Import, Export, and Trade in all kinds of Produce and Manufactures. They may reciprocally bring by land or by sea into either country, and export from it, all kinds of merchandise and products, and sell, exchange, or buy, and transport them to all places in the territories of either of the High Contracting Parties. It being, however, understood that the merchants of either nation who shall engage in the internal commerce of either country shall be governed, in respect to such commerce, by the laws of the country in which such commerce is carried on.

Internal Commerce. And in case either of the High Contracting Powers shall hereafter grant other privileges concerning such internal commerce to the citizens or subjects of other Governments, the same shall be equally granted to the merchants of either nation engaged in such internal commerce within the territories of the other.

Article 4. Payment of Duties on Merchandise Imported or Exported. Taxes. The merchandise imported or exported by the respective citizens or subjects of the two High Contracting Parties shall not pay in either country on their arrival or departure other duties than those which are charged in either of the countries on the merchandise or products imported or exported by the merchants and subjects of the most favoured nation, and no exceptional tax, under any name or pretext whatever, shall be collected on them in either of the two countries.

Article 5. Consular Jurisdiction in Persia: Suits and Disputes between Persian Subjects and United States Citizens. All suits and disputes arising in Persia between Persian subjects and citizens of the United States shall be carried before the Persian tribunal to which such matters are usually referred at the place where a Consul or Agent of the United States may reside, and shall be discussed and decided according to equity in the presence of an employé of the Consul or Agent of the United States.

Jurisdiction. Suits and Disputes between United States Citizens. All suits and disputes which may arise in the empire of Persia between citizens of the United States shall be referred entirely for trial and for adjudication to the Consul or Agent of the United States residing in the province wherein such suits and disputes may have arisen, or in the province nearest to it, who shall decide them according to the laws of the United States.

Jurisdiction. Suits and Disputes between United States Citizens and Subjects of other Foreign Powers. All suits and disputes, occurring in Persia between the citizens of the United States and the subjects of other foreign Powers shall be tried and adjudicated by the intermediation of their respective Consuls or Agents.

Jurisdiction. Trials in the United States of Disputes between Persian Subjects, or between them and United States Citizens or Foreigners. In the United States Persian subjects, in all disputes arising between themselves, or between them and citizens of the United States or foreigners, shall be judged according to the rules adopted in the United States respecting the subjects of the most favoured nation.

Jurisdiction. Trials for Criminal Offences. Persian subjects residing in the United States, and citizens of the United States residing in Persia, shall, when charged with criminal offences, be tried and judged in Persia and the United States in the same manner as are the subjects of the most favoured nation residing in either of the above-mentioned countries.

Article 6. Effects of Deceased Subjects or Citizens. In case of a citizen or subject of either of the Contracting Parties dying within the territories of the other his effects shall be delivered up integrally to the family or partners in business of the deceased, and in case he has no relations or partners his effects in either country shall be delivered up to the Consul or Agent of the nation of which the deceased was a subject or citizen, so that he may dispose of them in accordance with the laws of his country.

Article 7. Protection of Subjects and Citizens and their Commerce. For the protection of their citizens or subjects, and their commerce respectively, and in order to facilitate good and equitable relations between the citizens and subjects of the two countries.

Right to appoint Diplomatic Agents and Consuls at certain places. The two High Contracting Parties reserve the right to maintain a Diplomatic Agent at either seat of Government, and to name each three Consuls in either country. Those of the United States shall reside at Tehran, Bender-Bushire, and Tauris, those of Persia at Washington, New York, and New Orleans.

Consular Privileges, etc. The Consuls of the High Contracting Parties shall reciprocally enjoy in the territories of the other, where their residences shall be established, the respect, privileges, and immunities granted in either country to the Consuls of the most favoured nation.

Persian Subjects not to be Protected by United States Diplomatic Agent or Consuls. The Diplomatic Agent or Consuls of the United States shall not protect, secretly or publicly, the subjects of the Persian Government, and they shall never suffer a departure from the principles here laid down and agreed to by mutual consent.

Trading Consuls. And it is further understood, that if any of those Consuls shall engage in trade they shall be subjected to the same laws and usages to which private individuals of their nation engaged in commercial pursuits in the same place are subjected.

Employment of Domestics by United States Diplomatic and Consular Agents to be limited. And it is also understood by the High Contracting Parties that the Diplomatic and Consular Agents of the United States shall not employ a greater number of domestics than is allowed by Treaty to those of Russia residing in Persia.

Article 8. Duration of Treaty. And the High Contracting Parties agree that the present Treaty of Friendship and Commerce, cemented by the sincere good feeling and the confidence which exists between the Governments of the United States and Persia, shall be in force for the term of ten years from the exchange of its ratification; and if, before the expiration of the first ten years neither of the High Contracting Parties shall have announced, by official notification to the other, its intention to arrest the operation of said Treaty, it shall remain binding for one year beyond that time, and so on until the expiration of twelve months, which will follow a similar notification, whatever the time may be at which it may take place, and the Plenipotentiaries of the two High Contracting Parties further agree to exchange the ratifications of their respective Governments at Constantinople in the space of six months, or earlier if practicable.

In faith of which the respective Plenipotentiaries of the two High Contracting Parties have signed the present Treaty, and have attached their seals to it.

Done in duplicate in Persian and English the 13th day of December 1856, and of the Hijereh the 15th day of the moon of Rebiul Sany, 1273, at Constantinople.

(L.S.) Carroll Spence
(L.S.) Eminul Molk Farrukh Khan.

(Source: C. U. Aitchison, *A Collection of Treaties*, etc., 1909, Vol. XII, pp. lxxxii-lxxxvi.)

APPENDIX 22

Concession of the Tobacco Régie in Persia, March 8th, 1890

The monopoly of buying, selling, and manufacturing all the tootoon and tobacco in the interior or exterior of the Kingdom of Persia is granted to Major Talbot by us for fifty years from the date of the signing of this Concession, in accordance with the following stipulations:

Article 1. The concessionnaires will have to pay 15,000 l. per annum to the exalted Imperial Treasury whether they benefit or lose by this business, and this money shall be paid every year, five months after the beginning of the year.

Article 2. In order merely to ascertain the quantities of tootoon and tobacco produced in the protected provinces (of Persia) the concessionnaires will keep a register of the cultivators who wish to work under the conditions of this Concession, and the Persian Government will issue strict orders to the local Governors to compel the cultivators of tobacco and tootoon to furnish such a registration.

Permission for sale, & c., of tootoon, tobacco, cigars, cigarettes, snuff, & c., is the absolute right of the concessionnaires, and no one but the proprietors of this Concession shall have the right to issue the above-mentioned permits.

The Guilds of the sellers of tobacco and tootoon who are engaged in this trade will remain permanent in their local trade and transactions, on condition of possessing permits which will be given to them by the concessionnaires.

Article 3. After deducting all the expenses appertaining to this business and paying a divedend of 5 per cent. on their own capital to the proprietors of this Concession, one quarter of the remaining profit will yearly be paid to the exalted Imperial Treasury, and the Persian Government will have the right to inspect their (the concessionnaires') yearly books.

Article 4. All the materials necessary for this work which the proprietors of this Concession import into the protected provinces (Persia) will be free of all customs duties, taxes, & c.

Article 5. Removal and transfer of tootoon and tobacco in the protected provinces (of Persia) without the permission of the proprietors of this Concession is prohibited, except as such quantities as travellers may have with them for their own daily use.

Article 6. The proprietors of this Concession must purchase all the tootoon and tobacco that are produced in the protected provinces and pay cash for it. They purchase all the tobacco, & c., fit for use that is now in hand, and the price that is to be given to the owner or the producer will be settled in a friendly manner between the producer or the owner and the proprietors of this Concession, but in case of disagreement between the parties the case will be referred to and Arbitrator accepted by both sides, and the decision of the Arbitrator will be final and will be carried out.

Article 7. The Persian Government engages not to increase the revenues, taxes, and customs that are now levied on tootoon, tobacco, cigars, cigarettes, and snuff for fifty years from the date of the signing of the Concession, and the proprietors also undertake that all the customs that the Persian Government now obtains from tobacco shall be continued as they are.

Article 8. Any person or persons who shall attempt to evade (the rules) of these Articles will be punished by the Government, and any person or persons found to be secretly in possession of tobacco, tootoon, & c., for sale or trade, will also be fined and severely punished by the Government. The Government will give its utmost help and support in all the business of the proprietors of this Concession, and the proprietors of this Concession undertake in no way to go beyond their own rights consistent with these Articles.

Articles 9. The proprietors of this Concession are permitted, should they wish, to transfer all their rights, Concessions, undertakings, & c., to any person or persons, but, prior to this, they must inform the Persian Government.

Article 10. The producer or owner of tootoon and tobacco, whenever his crop of tobacco and tootoon is gathered, shall at once inform the nearest agent of the proprietors of this Concession of the quantity, in order that the proprietors of this Concession may be able to carry out the engagement in above-mentioned Article 6, and to purchase it quickly.

Article 11. The proprietors of this Concession have no ritht to purchase lands, except to the necessary extent, for storehouses and abodes, and what may be necessary to carry out this Concession.

Article 12. The cultivators, in accordance with certain conditions which will be made in conjunction with the Government, are entitled to be given an advance to a limit for their crop.

Article 13. If, from the date for the signing of this Concession until one year, a Company to carry it out is not formed, and the work does not begin, this Concession will be null and void, except that war or such like may prevent the formation of a Company.

Article 14. In case of misunderstanding arising between the Persian Government and the proprietors of this Concession, that misunderstanding shall be referred to an Arbitrator accepted by both sides and in case of the impossibility of consent to the appointment of an Arbitrator, the matter will be referred to the arbitration of one of the Representatives, resident at Teheran of the Government of the United States, Germany, or Austria, to appoint an Arbitrator, whose decision shall be final.

Article 15. This Concession is exchanged in duplicate with the signature of His Imperial Majesty, registered in the Foreign Ministry, between Major Talbot and the Persian Government, and the Persian text of it is to be recognized.

(Source: *Parliamentary Papers*, 1892, Vol. 79, pp. 211-213.)

APPENDIX 23

Agreement of May 28th, 1901, between the Government of this Imperial Majesty the Shah of Persia and William Knox D'Arcy, now held by the Anglo-Persian Oil Company, Limited

Between the Government of His Imperial Majesty the Shah of Persia, of the one part, and William Knox d'Arcy, of independent means, residing in London at No. 42, Grosvenor Square (hereinafter called "the Concessionnaire"), of the other part;

The following has by these presents been agreed on and arranged—viz.:

Article 1. The Government of His Imperial Majesty the Shah grants to the concessionaire by these presents a special and exclusive privilege to search for, obtain, exploit, develop, render suitable for trade, carry away and sell natural gas petroleum, asphalt and ozokerite throughout the whole extent of the Persian Empire for a term of sixty years as from the date of these presents.

Article 2. This privilege shall comprise the exclusive right of laying the pipe-lines necessary from the deposits where there may be found one or several of the said products up to the Persian Gulf, as also the necessary distributing branches. It shall also comprise the right of constructing and maintaining all and any wells, reservoirs, stations and pump services, accumulation services and distribution services, factories and other works and arrangements that may be deemed necessary.

Article 3. The Imperial Persian Government grants gratuitously to the concessionaire all uncultivated lands belonging to the State which the concessionnaire's engineers may deem necessary for the construction of the whole or any part of the above-mentioned works. As for cultivated lands belonging to the State, the concessionnaire must purchase them at the fair and current price of the province.

The Government also grants to the concessionnaire the right of acquiring all and any other lands or buildings necessary for the said purpose, with the consent of the proprietors, on such conditions as may be arranged between him and them without their being allowed to make demands of a nature to surcharge the prices ordinarily current for lands situated in their respective localities.

Holy places with all their dependencies within a radius of 200 Persian archines are formally excluded.

Article 4. As three petroleum mines situated at Schouster, Kassre-Chirine, in the Province of Kermanschahan, and Daleki, near Bouchir, are at present let to private persons and produce an annual revenue of two thousand tomans for the benefit of the Government, it has been agreed that the three aforesaid mines shall be comprised in the Deed of Concession in conformity with Article 1, on condition that, over and above the 16 per cent mentioned in Article 10, the concessionnaire shall pay every year the fixed sum of 2,000 (two thousand) tomans to the Imperial Government.

Article 5. The course of the pipe-lines shall be fixed by the concessionaire and his engineers.

Article 6. Notwithstanding what is above set forth, the privilege granted by these presents shall not extend to the provinces of Azerbadjan, Ghilan, Mazendaran, Asdrabad and Khorassan, but on the express condition that the Persian Imperial Government shall not grant to any other person the right of constructing a pipe-line to the southern rivers or to the South Coast of Persia.

Article 7. All lands granted by these presents to the concessionnaire or that may be acquired by him in the manner provided for in Articles 3 and 4 of these presents, as also all products exported, shall be free of all imposts and taxes during the term of the present concession. All material and apparatuses necessary for the exploration, working and development of the deposits, and for the construction and development of the pipelines, shall enter Persia free of all taxes and Custom-House duties.

Article 8. The concessionnaire shall immediately send out to Persia and at his own cost one or several experts with a view to their exploring the region in which there exist, as he believes, the said products, and, in the event of the report of the expert being in the opinion of the concessionnaire of a satisfactory nature, the latter shall immediately send to Persia and at his own cost all the technical staff necessary, with the working plant and machinery required for boring and sinking wells and ascertaining the value of the property.

Article 9. The Imperial Persian Government authorises the concessionnaire to found one or several companies for the working of the concession.

The names' "statutes" and capital of the said companies shall be fixed by the concessionnaire, and the directors shall be chosen by him on the express condition that, on the formation of each company, the concessionnaire shall give official notice of such formation to the Imperial Government, through the medium of the Imperial Commissioner, and shall forward the "statutes", with information as to the places at which such company is to operate. Such company or companies shall enjoy all the rights and privileges granted to the concessionnaire, but they must assume all his engagements and responsibilities.

Article 10. It shall be stipulated in the contract between the concessionnaire, of the one part, and the company, of the other part, that the latter is, within the term of one month as from the date of the formation of the first exploitation company, to pay the Imperial Persian Government the sum of £ 20,000 sterling in paid-up shares of the first company founded by virtue of the foregoing article. It shall also pay the said Government annually a sum equal to 16 per cent of the annual net profits of any company or companies that may be formed in accordance with the said article.

Article 11. The said Government shall be free to appoint an Imperial Commissioner, who shall be consulted by the concessionnaire and the directors of the companies to be formed. He shall supply all and any useful information at his disposal, and he shall inform them of the best course to be adopted in the interest of the undertaking. He shall establish, by agreement with the concessionnaire, such supervision as he may deem expedient to safeguard the interests of the Imperial Government.

The aforesaid powers of the Imperial Commissioner shall be set forth in the "statutes" of the companies to be created.

The concessionnaire shall pay the Commissioner thus appointed an annual sum of £ 1,000 sterling for his services as from the date of the formation of the first company.

Article 12. The workmen employed in the service of the company shall be subject to His Imperial Majesty the Shah, except the technical staff, such as the managers, engineers, borers and foremen.

Article 13. At any place in which it may be proved that the inhabitants of the country now obtain petroleum for their own use, the company must supply them gratuitously with the quantity of petroleum that they themselves got previously. Such quantity shall be fixed according to their own declarations, subject to the supervision of the local authority.

Article 14. The Imperial Government binds itself to take all and any necessary measures to secure the safety and the carrying out of the object of this concession of the plant and of the apparatuses, of which mention is made, for the purposes of the undertaking of the company, and to protect the representatives, agents and servants of the company. The Imperial Government having thus fulfilled its engagements, the concessionnaire and the companies created by him shall not have power, under any pretext whatever, to claim damages from the Persian Government.

Article 15. On the expiration of the term of the present concession, all materials, buildings and apparatuses then used by the company for the exploitation of its industry shall become the property of the said Government, and the company shall have no right to any indemnity in this connection.

Article 16. If within the term of two years as from the present date the concessionnaire shall not have established the first of the said companies authorised by Article 9 of the present agreement, the present concession shall become null and void.

Article 17. In the event of there arising between the parties to the present concession any dispute or difference in respect of its interpretation or the rights or responsibilities of one or the other of the parties therefrom resulting, such dispute or difference shall be submitted to two arbitrators at Teheran, one of whom shall be named by each of the parties, and to an umpire who shall be appointed by the arbitrators before they proceed to arbitrate. The decision of the arbitrators or, in the event of the latter disagreeing, that of the umpire shall be final.

Article 18. This Act of Concession, made in duplicate, is written in the French language and translated into Persian with the same meaning.

But, in the event of there being any dispute in relation to such meaning, the French text shall alone prevail.

Tehran, Sefor 1319 of the Hegire that is to say, May 1901.

(Source: League of Nations, *Official Journal*, December 1932, pp. 2305-2307.)

APPENDIX 24

Convention between the United Kingdom and Russia relating to Persia, Afghanistan and Thibet Signed at St. Petersburgh, August 31st, 1907, and ratified September 23rd, 1907

(Part concerning Persia only)

Convention

His Majesty the King of the United Kingdom of Great Britain and Ireland and of the British Dominions beyond the Seas, Emperor of India, and His Majesty the Emperor of All the Russians, animated by the sincere desire to settle by mutual agreement different questions concerning the interests of their States on the Continent of Asia have determined to conclude Agreements destined to prevent all cause of misunderstanding between Great Britain and Russia in regard to their questions referred to, and have nominated for this purpose their respective Plenipotentiaries, to—wit:

His Majesty the King of the United Kingdom of Great Britain and Ireland and of the British Dominions beyond the Seas, Emperor of India, The Right Honourable Sir Arthur Nicolson, His Majesty's Ambassador Extraordinary and Plenipotentiary to His Majesty the Emperor of all the Russians; (and His Majesty the Emperor of All the Russians) the Master of his Court Alexander Iswolsky, Minister for Foreign Affairs;

Who having communicated to each other their full powers, found in good and due form, have agreed on the following:

Arrangement concerning Persia

The Governments of Great Britain and Russia having mutually engaged to respect the integrity and independence of Persia, and sincerely desiring the preservation of order throughout that country and its peaceful development, as well as the permanent establishment of equal advantages for the trade and industry of all other nations;

Considering that each of them has, for geographical and economic resons, a special interest in the maintenance of peace and order in certain provinces of Persia adjoining, or in the neighbourhood of, Russian frontiers on the one hand, and the frontiers of Afghanistan and Baluchistan on the other hand; and being desirous of avoiding all cause of conflict between their respective interests in the above-mentioned provinces of Persia;

Have agreed on the following terms:

I

Great Britain engages not to seek for herself, and not to support in favour of British subjects, or in favour of the subjects of third Powers, any Concessions of a political or commercial nature—such as Concessions for railways, banks, telegraphs, roads, transport, insurance, etc.—beyond a line starting from Kas'r-i-Shirin, passing through Isfahan, Yezd, Kakhk, and ending at a point on the Persian frontier at the intersection of the Russian and Afghan frontiers, and not to oppose, directly or indirectly, demands for similar Concessions in this region which are supported by the Russian Government. It is understood that the above-mentioned places are included in the region in which Great Britain engages not to seek the Concessions referred to.

II

Russia on her part engages not to seek for herself and not to support, in favour of Russian subjects, or in favour of the subjects of third Powers, any Concessions of a political or commercial nature—such as Concessions for railways, banks, telegraphs, roads, transport, insurance, & c.—beyond a line going from the Afghan frontier by way of Gazik, Birjand, Kerman, and ending at Bunder Abbas, and not to oppose, directly or indirectly, demands for similar Concessions in this region which are supported by the British Government. It is understood that the above-mentioned places are included in the region in which Russia engages not to seek the Concessions referred to.

III

Russia, on her part, engages not to oppose without previous arrangement with Great Britain, the grant of any Concessions whatever to British subjects in the regions of Persia situated between the lines mentioned in Articles I and II.

Great Britain undertakes a similar engagement as regards the grant of Concessions to Russian subjects in the same regions of Persia.

All Concessions existing at present in the regions indicated in Articles I and II are maintained.

IV

It is understood that the revenues of all the Persian customs, with the exception of those of Farsistan and of the Persian Gulf, revenues guaranteeing the amortization and the interest of the loans concluded by the Government of the Shah with the "Banque d'Escompte et des Prêts de Perse" up to the date of the signature of the present Agreement, shall be devoted to the same purpose as in the past.

It is equally understood that the revenues of the Persian customs of Farsistan, and of the Persian Gulf, as well as those of the fisheries on the Persian shore of the Caspian Sea and those of the Posts and Telegraphs, shall be devoted, as in the past, to the service of the loans concluded by the Government of the Shah with the Imperial Bank of Persia up to the date of the signature of the present Arrangement.

V

In the event of irregularities occurring in the amortization or the payment of the interest of the Persian loans concluded with the "Banque d'Escompte et des Prêts de Perse" and with the Imperial Bank of Persia up to the date of the signature of the present Agreement, and in the event of the necessity arising for Russia to establish control over the sources of revenue guaranteeing the regular service of the loans concluded with the first-named bank, and situated in the region mentioned in Article II of the present Agreement, or for Great Britain to establish control over the sources of revenue guaranteeing the regular service of the loans concluded with the second-named bank, and situated in the region mentioned in Article I of the present Agreement, the British and Russian Governments undertake to enter beforehand into a friendly exchange of ideas with a view to determine, in agreement with each other, the measures of control in question and to avoid all interference which would not be in conformity with the principles governing the present Arrangement.

(Source: W. M. Shuster, *The Strangling of Persia*, New York, 1912, pp. xxiv-xxviii.)

APPENDIX 25

Treaty of Friendship between Russia and Turkey, Moscow, March 16th, 1921
(Ratifications exchanged at Kars, September 13th, 1921)

The Government of the Russian Socialist Federal Soviet Republic and the Government of the Grand National Assembly of Turkey, sharing as they do the principles of the liberty of nations, and the right of each nation to determine its own fate, and taking into consideration, moreover, the common struggle undertaken against imperialism, foreseeing that the difficulties arising for the one would render worse the position of the other, and inspired by the desire to bring about lasting good relations and uninterrupted sincere friendship between themselves, based on mutual interests, have decided to sign an agreement to assure amicable and fraternal relations between the two countries, and have for this purpose appointed as their representatives:

Article 1. Each of the contracting parties agrees not to recognise any peace treaty or other international agreement imposed upon the other against its will. The Government of the R.S.F.S.R. agrees not to recognise any international agreement relating to Turkey which is not recognised by the National Government of Turkey, at present represented by the Grand National Assembly.

The expression "Turkey" in the present treaty is understood to mean the territories included in the Turkish National Pact on the 28th January, 1920, elaborated and proclaimed by the Ottoman Chamber of Deputies in Constantinople, and communicated to the press and to all foreign Governments.

The north-east frontier of Turkey is fixed as follows: A line which begins at the village of Sari, situated on the coast of the Black Sea, goes over the mountain Khedis Mga, then by the line of watershed of the mountains Shavshet Dagh and Kapni Dagh, after which it follows the northern border of the sanjaks of Ardahan and Kars, then the thalweg of the Rivers Arpa-Chai and Araxes to the mouth of the Lower Kara Su. (A detailed description of the frontier and connected matters is given in Annex I (A) and (b) and on the attached map signed by both contracting parties.)

Article 2. Turkey agrees to cede to Georgia the right of suzerainty over the town and the port of Batum, and the territory situated to the north of the frontier mentioned in Article 1, which formed a part of the district Batum, on the following conditions:

(a) The population of the localities specified in the present Article shall enjoy a generous measure of autonomy, assurring to each community its cultural and religious rights, and allowing them to enact agrarian laws in according with the wishes of the population of the said districts.

(b) Turkey will be granted free transit for all Turkish imports and exports through the port of Batum, without payment of taxes and customs duties and without delays. The right of making use of the port of Batum without special expenses is assured to Turkey.

Article 3. Both contracting parties agree that the Nakhichevan district, with the boundaries shown in Annex 1 (C) to the present treaty, shall form an autonomous territory under the protection of Azerbaijan, on condition that the latter cannot transfer this protectorate to any third State. In the Nakhichevan region, which forms a triangle enclosed within the Araxes Valley and the line of the mountains Daghna (3,829), Veli Dagh (4,121), Bagarsik (6,587), Kemurlu Dagh (6,930), the boundary of the above-mentioned district beginning at the Kemurlu Dagh (6,930), passing over Serai Bulak Dagh (8,071) and the station of Ararat, and finishing at the junction of the Kara Su and the Araxes, will be determined by a commission composed of delegates of Turkey, Azerbaijan and Armenia.

Article 4. The contracting parties, establishing contact between the national movement for the liberation of the Eastern peoples and the struggle of the workers of Russia for a new social order, solemnly recognise the right of these nations to freedom and independence, also their right to choose a form of government according to their own wishes.

Article 5. In order to assure the opening of the Straits to the commerce of all nations, the contracting parties agree to entrust the final elaboration of an international agreement concerning the Black Sea to a conference composed of delegates of the littoral States, on condition that the decisions of the above-mentioned conference shall not be of such a nature as to diminish the full sovereignty of Turkey or the security of Constantinople, her capital.

Article 6. The contracting parties agree that the treaties concluded heretofore between the two countries do not correspond with their mutual interests, and therefore agree that the said treaties shall be considered as annulled and abrogated.

The Government of the R.S.F.S.R. declares that it considers Turkey to be liberated from all financial and other liabilities based on agreements concluded between Turkey and the Tsarist Government.

Article 7. The Government of the R.S.F.S.R., holding that the Capitulations régime is not compatible with the full exercise of sovereign rights and the national development of any country, declares this régime and any rights connected therewith to be null and void.

Article 8. The contracting parties undertake not to tolerate in their respective territories the formation and stay of organisations or associations claiming to be the Government of the other country or of a part of its territory and organisations whose aim is to wage warfare against the other State.

Russia and Turkey mutually accept the same obligation with regard to the Soviet Republic of the Caucasus.

"Turkish territory," within the meaning of this Article, is understood to be territory under the direct civil and military administration of the Government of the Grand National Assembly of Turkey.

Article 9. To secure uninterrupted communication between the two countries, both contracting parties undertake to carry out urgently, and in agreement one with the other, all necessary measures for the security and development of the railways lines, telegraph and other means of communication, and to assure free movement of persons and goods between the two countries. It is agreed that the regulations in force in each country shall be applied as regards the movement, entry and exit of travellers and goods.

Article 10. The nationals of both of the contracting parties residing on the territory of the other shall be treated in accordance with the laws in force in the country of their residence, with the exception of those connected with national defence, from which they are exempt. The nationals of the contracting parties will be exempt from the provisions of the present Article as regards family rights, rights of succession and juridical capacity. These latter rights shall be settled by a special agreement.

Article 11. The contracting parties agree to treat the nationals of one of the parties residing in the territory of the other in accordance with the most-favoured-nation principles.

This Article will not be applied to citizens of the Soviet Republics allied with Russia, nor to nationals of Mussulman States allied with Turkey.

Article 12. Any inhabitant of the territories forming part of Russia prior to 1918, and over which Turkish sovereignty has been acknowledged by the Government of the R.S.F.S.R., in the present treaty, shall be free to leave Turkey and to take with him all his goods and possessions or the proceeds of their sale. The population of the territory of Batum, sovereignty over which has been granted to Georgia by Turkey, shall enjoy the same right.

Article 13. Russia undertakes to return, at her own expense within three months, to the north-east frontier of Turkey all Turkish prisoners of war and interned civilians in the Caucasus and in European Russia, and those in Asiatic Russia within six months, dating from the signature of the present treaty. The details concerning the repatriation of these prisoners will be fixed by a special agreement, which will be concluded immediately after the signature of the present treaty.

Article 14. The contracting parties agree to conclude in as short a time as possible a consular agreement and other arrangements regulating all economic, financial and other questions which are necessary for the establishment of friendly relations between the two countries, as set forth in the preamble to the present treaty.

Article 15. Russia undertakes to take the necessary steps with the Transcaucasian Republics with a view to securing the recognition by the latter, in their agreement with Turkey, of the provisions of the present treaty which directly concern them.

Article 16. The present treaty shall be subject to the formality of ratification. Ratifications shall be exchanged as soon as possible at Kars. With the exception of Article 13, the present treaty shall come into force at the moment of the exchange of ratifications.

(Source: *British and Foreign State Papers*, 1923, Part II, Vol. 118, pp. 990-994.)

APPENDIX 26

Treaty of Friendship between Persia and the Russiàn Socialist Federal Soviet Republic, signed at Moscow, February 26th, 1921

Article 1. In order to confirm its declarations regarding Russian policy towards the Persian nation, which formed the subject of correspondence on the 14th January, 1918, and the 26th June, 1919, the R.S.F.S.R. formally affirms once again that it definitely renounces the tyrannical policy carried out by the colonising Governments of Russia which have been overthrown by the will of the workers and peasants of Russia.

Inspired by this principle, and desiring that the Persian people should be happy and independent and should be able to dispose freely of its patrimony, the Russian Republic declares the whole body of treaties and conventions concluded with Persia by the Tsarist Government, which crushed the rights of the Persian people, to be null and void.

Article 2. The R.S.F.S.R. expresses it reprobation of the policy of the Tsarist Governments of Russia, which, on the pretext of ensuring the independence of the peoples of Asia, concluded, without the consent of the latter, treaties with European Powers, the sole object of which was to subjugate those peoples.

This criminal policy, which infringed upon the independence of the countries of Asia and which made the living nations of the East a prey to the cupidity and the tyranny of European robbers, is abandoned unconditionally by Federal Russia.

Federal Russia, therefore, in accordance with the principles laid down in Article 1 and 4 of this Treaty, declares its refusal to participate in any action which might destroy or weaken Persian sovereignty. It regards as null and void the whole body of treaties and conventions concluded by the former Russian Government with third parties in respect of Persia or to the detriment of that country.

Article 3. The two Contracting Powers agree to accept and respect the Russo-Persian frontiers, as drawn by the Frontier Commission in 1881.

At the same time, in view of the repugnance which the Russian Federal Government feels to enjoying the fruit of the policy of usurpation of the Tsarist Government, it renounces all claim to the Achouradeh Islands and to the other island on the Astrabad Littoral, and restores to Persia the village of Frouzeh and the adjacent land ceded to Russia in virtue of the Convention of the 28th May, 1893.

The Persian Government agrees for its part that the Russian Sarakhs, or "old" Sarakhs, and the land adjacent to the Sarakhs River, shall be retained by Russia.

The two High Contracting Parties shall have equal rights of usage over the Atrak River and the other frontier rivers and waterways. In order finally to solve the question of the waterways In order finally to solve the question of the waterways and all disputes concerning frontiers or territories, a Commission, composed of Russian and Persian representatives, shall be appointed.

Article 4. In consideration of the fact that each nation has the right to determine freely its political destiny, each of the two Contracting Parties formally expresses its desire to abstain from any intervention in the internal affairs of the other.

Article 5. The two High Contracting Parties undertake:

1. To prohibit the formation or presence within their respective territories of any organisations or groups of persons, irrespective of the name by which they are known, whose object is to engage in acts of hostility against Persia or Russia, or against the allies of Russia.

They will likewise prohibit the formation of troops or armies within their respective territories with the aforementioned object.

2. Not to allow a third party or any organisation, whatever it be called, which is hostile to the other Contracting Party, to import or to convey in transit across their countries material which can be used against the other Party.

3. To prevent by all means in their power the presence within their territories or within the territories of their allies of all armies or forces of a third party in cases in which the presence of such forces would be regarded as a menace to the frontiers, interests or safety of the other Contracting Party.

Article 6. If a third party should attempt to carry out a policy of usurpation by means of armed intervention in Persia, or if such power should desire to use Persian territory as a base of operations against Russia, or if a foreign Power should threaten the frontiers of Federal Russia or those of its allies, and if the Persian Government should not be able to put a stop to such menace after having been once called upon to do so by Russia, Russia shall have the right to advance her troops into the Persian interior for the purpose of carrying out the military operations necessary for its defence. Russia undertakes, however, to withdraw her troops from Persian territory as soon as the danger has been removed.

Article 7. The considerations set forth in Article 6 have equal weight in the matter of the security of the Caspian Sea. The two High Contracting Parties therefore have agreed that Federal Russia shall have the right to require the Persian Government to send away foreign subjects, in the event of their taking advantage of their engagement in the Persian navy to undertake hostile action against Russia.

Article 8. Federal Russia finally renounces the economic policy pursued in the East by the Tsarist Government, which consisted in lending money to the Persian Government, not with a view to the economic development of the country, but rather for purposes of political subjugation.

Federal Russia accordingly renounces its rights in respect of the loans granted to Persia by the Tsarist Governments. It regards the debts due to it as void, and will not require their repayment. Russia likewise renounces its claims to the resources of Persia which were specified as security for the loans in question.

Article 9. In view of the declaration by which it has repudiated the colonial and capitalist policy which occasioned so much bloodshed, Federal Russia abandons the continuation of the economic undertakings of the Tsarist Government, the object of which was the economic subjugation of Persia. Federal Russia therefore cedes to the Persian Government the full ownership of all funds and of all real and other property which the Russian Discount Bank possesses on Persian territory, and likewise transfers to it all the assets and liabilities of that bank. The Persian Government nevertheless agrees that in the towns where it has been decided that the Russian Socialist Republic may establish consulates, and where buildings exist belonging to the Discount Bank, one of these buildings, to be chosen by the Russian Government, shall be placed at the disposal of the Russian Consulate, free of charge.

Article 10. The Russian Federal Government, having abadoned the colonial policy, which consisted in the construction of roads and telegraph lines more in order to obtain military influence in other countries than for the purpose of developing their civilisations, and being desirous of providing the Persian people with those means of communication indispensable for the independence and development of any nation, and also in order to compensate the Persian people as far as possible for the losses incurred by the sojourn in its territory of the Tsarist armies, cedes free of charge to the Persian Government the following Russian installations:

(a) The high-roads from Enzeli to Tehran, and from Kazvin to Hamadan, and all land and installations in connection with these roads.

(b) The railroad Djoulfa-Tauris-Sofian-Urmia, with all installations, rolling-stock and accessories.

(c) The landing-stages, warehouses, steamships, canals, and all means of transport of the lake of Urmia.

(d) All telegraph and telephone lines established in Persia by the Tsarist Governments, with all movable and immovable installations and dependencies.

(e) The port of Enzeli and the warehouses, with the electrical installation, and other buildings.

Article 11. In view of the fact that the Treaty of Turkomantchai, concluded on the 10th February, 1828 (old style), between Persia and Russia, which forbids Persia, under the terms of Article 8, to have vessels in the waters of the Caspian Sea, is abrogated in accordance with the principles set forth in Article 1 of the present Treaty, the two High Contracting Parties shall enjoy equal rights of free navigation on that sea, under their own flags, as from the date of the signing of the present Treaty.

Article 12. The Russian Federal Government, having officially renounced all economic interests obtained by military preponderance, further declares that, apart from the concessions which form the subject of Articles 9 and 10, the other concessions obtained by force by the Tsarist Government and its subjects shall also be regarded as null and void.

In conformity with which the Russian Federal Government restores, as from the date of the signing of the present Treaty, to the Persian Government, as representing the Persian people, all the concessions in question, whether already being worked or not, together with all land taken over in virtue of those concessions.

Of the lands and properties situated in Persia and belonging to the former Tsarist Government, only the premises of the Russian Legation at Tehran and at Zerguendeh with all movable and immovable appurtenances, as well as all real and other property of the Consulates and Vice-Consulates, shall be retained by Russia. Russia abandons, however, her right to administer the village of Zerguendeh, which was arrogated to itself by the former Tsarist Government.

Article 13. The Persian Government, for its part, promises not to cede to a third Power, or to its subjects, the concessions and property restored to Persia by virtue of the present Treaty, and to maintain those rights for the Persian nation.

Article 14. The Persian Government, recognising the importance of the Caspian fisheries for the food supply of Russia, promises to conclude with the Food Service of the Russian Socialist Federal Soviet Republic immediately upon the expiry of the legal period of these existing engagements, a contract relating to the fisheries, containing appropriate clauses. Furthermore, the Persian Government promises to examine, in agreement with the Government of the Russian Socialist Federal Soviet Republic, the means of at once conveying the produce of the fisheries to the Food Service of Soviet Russia pending the conclusion of the above contract.

Article 15. In accordance with the principle of liberty of conscience proclaimed by Soviet

Russia, and with a desire to put an end, in Moslem countries, to religious propaganda, the real object of which was to exercise political influence over the masses and thus to satisfy the rapacity of the Tsarist Government, the Government of Soviet Russia declares that the religious settlements established in Persia by the former Tsarist Governments are abolished. Soviet Russia will take steps to prevent such missions from being sent to Persia in the future.

Soviet Russia cedes unconditionally to the nation represented by the Persian Government the lands, property and buildings belonging to the Orthodox Mission situated at Urmia, together with the other similar establishments. The Persian Government shall use these properties for the construction of schools and other institutions intended for educational purposes.

Article 16. By virtue of the communication from Soviet Russia dated the 25th June, 1919, with reference to the abolition of consular jurisdictions, it is decided that Russian subjects in Persia and Persian subjects in Russia shall, as from the date of the present Treaty, be placed upon the same footing as the inhabitants of the towns in which they reside; they shall be subject to the laws of their country of residence, and shall submit their complaints to the local Courts.

Article 17. Persian subjects in Russia and Russian subjects in Persia shall be exempt from military service and from all military taxation.

Article 18. Persian subjects in Russia and Russian subjects in Persia shall, as regards travel within the respective countries, enjoy the rights granted to the most favoured nations other than countries allied to them.

Article 19. Within a short period after the signature of the present Treaty, the two High Contracting Parties shall resume commercial relations. The methods to be adopted for the organisation of the import and export of goods, methods of payment, and the customs duties to be levied by the Persian Government on goods originating in Russia, shall be determined, under a commercial Convention, by a special Commission consisting of representatives of the two High Contracting Parties.

Article 20. Each of the two High Contracting Parties grants to the other the right of transit for the transport of goods passing through Persia or Russia and consigned to a third country.

The dues exacted in such cases shall not be higher than those levied on the goods of the most favoured nations other than countries allied to the Russian Socialist Federal Soviet Republic.

Article 21. The two High Contracting Parties shall open telegraphic and postal relations between Russia and Persia within the shortest possible period after the signature of the present Treaty.

The conditions of these relations shall be fixed by a postal and telegraphic Convention.

Article 22. In order to consolidate the good relations between the two neighbouring Powers and to facilitate the realisation of the friendly intentions of each country towards the other, each of the High Contracting Parties shall, immediately after the signature of the present Treaty, be represented in the capital of the other by a Plenipotentiary Representative, who shall enjoy the rights of extra-territoriality and other privileges to which diplomatic representatives are entitled by international law and usage and by the regulations and customs of the two countries.

Article 23. In order to develop their mutual relations, the two High Contracting Parties shall establish Consulates in places to be determined by common agreement.

The rights and duties of the Consuls shall be fixed by a special Agreement to be concluded without delay after the signature of the present Treaty. This Agreement shall conform to the provisions in force in the two countries with regard to consular establishments.

Article 25. The present Treaty is drawn up in Russian and Persian. Both texts shall be regarded as originals and both shall be authentic.

Article 26. The present Treaty shall come into force immediately upon signature.

(Source: League of Nations, *Treaty Series*, No. 268, 1922, pp. 401-413.)

APPENDIX 27

Article 22 of the Covenant of the League of Nations, June 28th, 1919

1. To those colonies and territories which as a consequence of the late war have ceased to be under the sovereignty of the States which formerly governed them and which are inhabited by peoples not yet able to stand by themselves under the strenuous conditions of the modern world, there should be applied the principle that the well-being and development of such peoples form a sacred trust of civilisation and that securities for the performance of this trust should be embodied in this Covenant.

2. The best method of giving practical effect to this principle is that the tutelage of such peoples should be entrusted to advanced nations who by reason of their resources, their experience or their geographical position can best undertake this responsibility, and who are willing to accept it, and that this tutelage should be exercised by them as Mandatories on behalf of the League.

3. The character of the mandate must differ according to the stage of the development of the people, the geographical situation of the territory, its economic conditions and other similar circumstances.

4. Certain communities formerly belonging to the Turkish Empire have reached a stage of development where their existence as independent nations can be provisionally recognised subject to the rendering of administrative advice and assistance by a Mandatory until such time as they are able to stand alone. The wishes of these communities must be a principal consideration in the selection of the Mandatory.

5. Other peoples, especially those of Central Africa, are at such a stage that the Mandatory must be responsible for the administration of the territory under conditions which will guarantee freedom of conscience and religion, subject only to the maintenance of public order and morals, the prohibition of abuses such as the slave trade, the arms traffic and the liquor traffic and the prevention of the establishment of fortifications or military and naval bases and of military training of the natives for other than police purposes and the defence of territory, and will also secure equal opportunities for the trade and commerce of other Members of the League.

6. There are territories, such as South-West Africa and certain of the South Pacific Islands, which, owing to the sparseness of their population, or their small size, or their remoteness from the centres of civilisation, or their geographical contiguity to the territory of the Mandatory, and other circumstances, can be best administered under the laws of the Mandatory as integral portions of its territory, subject to the safeguards above mentioned in the interests of the indigenous population.

7. In every case of mandate, the Mandatory shall render to the Council an annual report in reference to the territory committed to its charge.

8. The degree of authority, control or administration to be exercised by the Mandatory shall, if not previously agreed upon by the Members of the League, be explicitly defined in each case by the Council.

9. A permanent Commission shall be constituted to receive and examine the annual reports of the Mandatories and to advise the Council on all matters relating to the observance of the mandates.

(Source: League of Nations, *The Mandates System*, Origin-Principles-Application, Geneva, April 1945, pp. 22-23.)

APPENDIX 28

Select Articles from Mandate for Syria and the Lebanon

(24 July, 1922)

Article 5. The privileges and immunities of foreigners, including the benefits of consular jurisdiction and protection as formerly enjoyed by Capitulations or usage in the Ottoman Empire, shall not be applicable in Syria and the Lebanon. Foreign consular tribunals shall, however, continue to perform their duties until the coming into force of the new legal organisation provided for in Article 6.

Unless the Powers whose nationals enjoyed the afore-mentioned privileges and immunities on August 1st 1914, shall have previously renounced the right to their re-establishment, or shall have agreed to their non-application during a specified period, these privileges and immunities shall at the expiration of the mandate be immediately re-established in their entirety or with such modifications as may have been agreed upon between the Powers concerned.

Article 6. The Mandatory shall establish in Syria and the Lebanon a judicial system which shall assure to natives as well as to foreigners a complete guarantee of their rights.

Respect for the personal status of the various peoples and for their religious interests shall be fully guaranteed. In particular, the control and administration of Wakfs shall be exercised in complete accordance with religious law and the dispositions of the founders.

Article 11. The Mandatory shall see that there is no discrimination in Syria or the Lebanon against the nationals, including society and associations, of any State Member of the League of Nations as compared with its own nationals, including societies and associations, or with the nationals of any other foreign State in matters concerning taxation or commerce, the exercise of professions or industries, or navigation, or in the treatment of ships or aircraft. Similarly, there shall be no discrimination in Syria or the Lebanon against goods originating in or destined for any of the said States; there shall be freedom of transit, under equitable conditions, across the said territory.

(Source: U.N., *Terms of League of Nations Mandates*, New York, Oct. 1946.)

APPENDIX 29

Select Articles of Anglo-Iraqi Treaty (later [in 1924] included in Mandate for Iraq)

Article 11. There shall be no discrimination in Iraq against the nationals of any State, Member of the League of Nations, or of any State to which His Britannic Majesty has agreed by treaty that the same rights should be ensured as it would enjoy if it were a Member of the said League (incluring companies incorporated under the laws of such State), as compared with British nationals or those of any foreign State in matters concerning taxation, commerce or navigation, the exercise of industries or professions, or in the treatment of merchant vessles or civil aircraft. Nor shall there be any discrimination in Iraq against goods originating in or destined for any of the said States. There shall be freedom of Transit under equitable conditions across Iraq territory.

Article 16. So far as it is consistent with his international obligations, His Britannic Majesty undertakes to place no obstacle in the way of the association of the State of Iraq for Customs or other purposes with such neighbouring Arab States as may desire it.

(Source: Treaty between His Britannic Majesty and His Majesty the King of Iraq, Oct. 10th, 1922, in U.N., *Terms of League of Nations Mandates*, N.Y., Oct. 1946.)

APPENDIX 30

Article 18 of the Mandate for Palestine

July 24th, 1922

The Mandatory shall see that there is no discrimination in Palestine against the nationals of any State Member of the League of Nations (including companies incorporated under its laws) as compared with those of the Mandatory or of any foreign State in matters concerning taxation, commerce or navigation, the exercise of industries or professions, or in the treatment of merchant vessels or civil aircraft. Similarly, there shall be no discrimination in Palestine against goods originating in or destined for any of the said States, and there shall be freedom of transit under equitable conditions across the mandated area.

Subject as aforesaid and to the other privisions of this mandate, the Administration of Palestine, may, on the advice of the Mandatory, impose such taxes and customs duties as it may consider necessary, and take such steps as it may think best to promote the development of the natural resources of the country and to safeguard the interests of the population. It may also, on the advice of the Mandatory, conclude a special Customs agreement with any State the territory of which in 1914 was wholly included in Asiatic Turkey or Arabia.

(Source: League of Nations, *Mandate for Palestine*, Geneva, Sept. 16th, 1922, in U.N., *Terms of League of Nations Mandates*, N.Y., Oct. 1946.)

APPENDIX 31

Text of the Chester Concession

(1923)

Part. I Clauses Concerning the Railroads

Between Feyzy Bey, acting in the name of the Government of the Turkish Grand National Assembly, under reserve of ratification by a special law, of the one part, and Messrs. Kennedy and Chester, acting in the name of the Ottoman American Development Society, established under the laws of the State of Delaware, U.S.A., of the other part, it is agreed as follows:

Article 1. The concession is accorded by the Government of the Turkish Grand National Assembly to the Ottoman American Development Society, which accepts it, of constructing and operating, under the conditions of the present agreement and its annexes, the railroad lines below enumerated, which shall be approved by the Department of Public Works, and which shall have a gauge of 1.435 meters:

A. A line leaving Sivas and passing through Karpout, Erghna, Dearbekir and Bitlis, to end at Van;

B. A line leaving the environs of Karpout to Youmourtalik, traversing the Valley of Djelhoun;

C. A line beginning at a point to be determined from line A, and passing through Mosul and Kerkut, ending at Suleymanie.

Article 2. The duration of this concession is for ninety-nine years from the date of ratification of this agreement.

Article 3. The Ottoman American Development Society, within thirty days after its notification of definite acceptance of the concession, is obligated as a guarantee of execution of its engagement to increase its deposit in the Commercial Bank of Italy to the sum of 70,000 Turkish pounds. This sum will be returned to it after the construction and acceptance of the first 200 kilometers. The company is privileged to deposit this guarantee in any other bank, except the Ottoman bank, but in case that this bank shall be a foreign bank the society is under obligation to obtain from the Embassy of the country in which this bank is located a letter declaring that any disputes which may arise on the subject of this sum of money shall be carried for settlement before the tribunals of the Turkish Grand National Assembly. In case the guarentee deposit shall not be brought to the sum of 70,000 Turkish pounds within the month provided for, the initial guarantee of 50,000 pounds shall be acquired by the Government of the Turkish Grand National Assembly. Also, in case the Ottoman American Development Society does not constitute, in the manner provided by the present agreement, a Turkish company, the guarantee of 70,000 Turkish pounds shall be acquired by the Government of the Turkish Grand National Assembly.

Article 4. The Ottoman American Development Society binds itself to establish in the six months that shall follow the ratification of the present agreement a Turkish stock company, subject to the present and future laws of the Turkish Grand National Assembly, and whose laws and by-laws shall be accepted by the aforesaid Government. The Ottoman American Development Society agrees to put at the disposition of Turkish investors during a period of thirty days, counting from the publication in Turkish journals of the capital, half of the securities issued by the Turkish stock company thus constituted. After that period the company shall be free to dispose of securities not acquired by Turkish subjects.

Article 5. The Turkish stock company is bound within the periods below mentioned to furnish four copies of the estimates and maps prepared under the conditions required by the present agreement to the Commissioner of Public Works:

1. The projects and plans of line B for a section of 200 kilometers shall be delivered every four months. The projects and plans of the first section that is to start from Youmourtalik are to be delivered within a period of no more than twelve months from the ratification of the convention.

2. The projects and plans of the other lines are to be delivered in a period of nine months after the delivery of the projects and the plans provided for line B.

3. The Department of Public Works shall examine and return these plans approved within a period of three months after the date of their delivery. Following this period of three months the company will consider the plans approved, and will enter upon their execution. If reasons arising from force majeure prevent the company from completing its plans in the periods granted it shall immediately notify the Department of Public Works, which will have the power to grant additional delays.

Article 6. The company binds itself to begin the work of construction of line B within six months following the expiration of the periods granted for the delivery and acceptance of the plans, and to terminate them in the three years following these same periods. The work connected with the other lines is to begin in the two years following the stipulated periods, and to be completed within a period of seven years.

Article 7. The Department of Public Works shall appoint technical experts to examine the plans and constructions, the administration and operation of lines, as well as their maintenance in condition. In order to cover the cost of this supervision the company agrees to pay to the Department of Public Works monthly, dating from the ratification of the agreement, an annual sum of 270 gold piastres per kilometer conceded.

Article 8. Since these are works of public utility, the lands and buildings necessary for the construction of the railroad lines and the Port of Youmourtalik, which belong to private persons, shall be expropriated at the expense of the company, and in accordance with the Turkish laws governing expropriation. These operations shall be concluded within the two months following each request for expropriation.

The quarries and sand pits necessary for the constructions shall be delivered up to the company, which shall remunerate the owners. Such of these properties as belong to the State shall be given without compensation, and for the whole period of the concession.

Article 9. The lines shall be single track. Nevertheless, the lands will be expropriated on the same basis as if the lines were double track. As soon as the revenues of the company, as set forth in Article 22, shall be sufficient to provide for the interest and the amortization of the securities issued for the construction of the first line and of those to be issued for the construction of the second line, the Government shall have the right to demand this latter construction, and the company agrees to do this at its own expense.

Article 10. The materials, machines, coal and so forth, necessary for the various constructions of the company and purchased in the country itself or imported from abroad, shall be exempt from customs or any other tax. The coal imported for the operation of the lines described in Article 1 shall be exempt from customs tax during a period of twenty years, dating from the ratification of the present agreement. For the entire duration of the concession the lines and ports constructed by the society, as well as its capital and revenues, shall be exempt from all impost.

Article 11. The company shall have the right to obtain all the wood supplies necessary for its constructions and for their maintenance from the public forests, provided it conforms to the regulations laid down ad hoc, and pays the usual charges.

Article 12. As soon as the company shall notify the Government of the construction of a section, the Department of Public Works shall name a technical commission charged to examine the constructions and accept them provisionally if this seems justified. A year after this provisional acceptance a technical commission shall examine anew the constructions to see if they comply with the provisions of the contract of construction, and after this inspection shall compile its report, on the basis of which the definite acceptance will take place. These technical commissions will consist at the most of eight members, and their traveling expenses shall be paid by the company.

Article 13. The company is under obligation to maintain all its constructions in good condition for the entire duration of the concession, and in case it fails in this, it shall come under the application of Article 25 of the construction contract.

Article 14. The company must obey all laws, alike present and future, relating to the policing and maintenance of the mines which it shall operate.

Article 15. In the case, where, through the fault of the company, transportation shall be interrupted upon all or parts of the railroad lines, or of the port, the Government shall take provisional measures in virtue of Article 2 of the construction contract. If within nine months the company shall not prove that it is able to resume and ensure the services thus interrupted, it shall be deprived of its rights in conformity with Article 27 of the present agreement. The only exception will be in the case of force majeure, officially established.

Article 16. From the moment of provisional acceptance the company shall be empowered to collect upon the sections that have been constructed rates for transportation and other rates in accordance with the tariffs established by the construction contract.

Article 17. In times of peace, as in times of war, the company shall conform to part VI. of the construction contract as regards the transportation individually or collectively of soldiers and material of war, as well as of prisoners or condemned, and of functionaries and mail sacks.

Article 18. Without in any way creating a right of monopoly, the company shall have the right to construct the railroad lines necessary to link to the principal lines the mines which it shall operate in virtue of the present agreement. These secondary lines shall be returned free of charge to the Government at the expiration of the duration of the concession.

The company may build across Turkish territory the pipe lines necessary for the technical and economic development of petroleum wells. For the right of way of these pipe lines the same rules shall be applied to the territory which they traverse as those which are provided for the construction of the railroad lines.

Article 19. Without creating a right of monopoly and within the limits of present and future regulations, the company shall have the right of utilizing the natural hydraulic forces upon which no previous claim has been acquired, in order to extract the electric current necessary for the operation of the railroad lines and the mines. The company, in compliance with the regulations bearing on this subject, shall have the right of selling this current to third parties.

Plans for these installations must be delivered to the Department of Public Works before any construction is undertaken. At the ending of the concession these installations will be turned over without charge to the Government. In any case where the Government might elect to avail itself of its right of redemption of the railroad lines, it shall pay the company for these constructions a price agreed on by two technical experts, of whom one shall be designated by the Government and the other by the company. In the event that these two experts are unable to reach an agreement they shall designate a third, whose decision shall be conclusive. If the two experts cannot agree upon the choice of this third arbitrator he shall be chosen by the Chief Magistrate of the Turkish Court of Cassation. In case of redemption of the railroad lines, however, those of the electrical installations that are connected with the mines shall remain the property of the company until the termination of the period provided in Article 2.

Article 20. The company has the right to construct a port at Youmourtalik. This port shall be built in such a way as to permit ships to draw up alongside of piers and so that cargoes can be loaded and discharged directly and be given warehouse facilities at the port. The company, within five years following the ratification of this agreement, must furnish the plans bearing on this construction, and must terminate the work within the seven years following that date. The plan furnished by the society must also include the tariffs applying to the port. As the port is considered as forming part of the railway line, its gross revenues shall be incorporated with the gross revenues of the railroads, and it shall be restored without charge to the Turkish Government on the termination of the concession.

If within the stipulated periods the plan for the port is not delivered to the Turkish Government, or if the construction is not made, the Government reserves to itself the right to have the construction effected by a third party. Nevertheless, the company shall have the right to avail itself of Youmourtalik and to create there installations necessary for receiving the materials essential for its constructions. But if the port is constructed by a third party, the company will have to remove at its own expense all installations that may have been constructed by itself.

Article 21. The company must construct all the lines provided for in Article 1, and operate them at its own risk, without demanding any guarantee or pecuniary aid from the Government. In return, all the revenues of the railway lines and of their ramifications shall belong to the company for the duration of the concession, except in case of redemption.

Article 22. The Government of the Turkish Grand National Assembly, after the expiration of a period of thirty years, dating from the ratification of this agreement, shall have the right to redeem the railways and the port, excluding the mines and the installations connected with them. In case of redemption it will pay an annual sum equivalent to the annual average of the net revenues of the five years last preceding the date of redemption, and will continue these payments up to the termination of the concession.

The net revenues shall be determined by deducting from the gross revenues of the railways and the port the cost of maintenance of the lines, of materials and the expenses of operation. The payments devoted to interest and the amortization of capital are not included in these expenses. In all cases, the Government will guarantee the payment of a sum equal to at least 7,500 gold francs per kilometer, and if the money employed for the payment of interest and the amortization of capital shall exceed this sum, it will make up the difference. The Government reserves to itself the right to pay back in one sum the capital invested. The cession of the railway lines and the port, as well as of the electrical installations, will be regulated by Article 30 of the construction contract.

Article 23. At the termination of the concession, the Government of the Turkish Grand National Assembly shall acquire all the rights of the company to the lines, ports and their adjuncts, as well as to the mines and all the establishments and materials pertaining to them. It will have the enjoyment of all their revenues. This substitution will be regulated by Article 28 of the construction contract.

Article 24. The company shall choose its functionaries, employes and laborers from among Turkish subjects, and with this in view it shall establish schools for the training of this personnel. The company may, nevertheless, employ foreigners in its higher positions, provided that it communicates their names to the Department of Public Works. It may also employ technical experts and specialists of foreign nationality. The employes of the railroad shall wear uniforms approved by the Government. The company is authorized to bring Turkish emigrants from other countries to work on its constructions.

Article 25. The Government of the Turkish Grand National Assembly shall have the right to construct fortifications at its own expense anywhere on the railway lines or at the port.

Article 26. Archaeological discoveries which may be made in the course of the work shall be subject to existing regulations.

Article 27. In case the company shall suspend the operation of lines without being able to claim prevention by force majeure, it shall be deprived of all its rights in the railway line and the port, as well as in its mines, and shall come under the application of Article 28 of the construction contract.

Furthermore, if the company does not, within the periods provided and in conformity with Article 6, begin the plans and the construction of one of the sections of the Karpout-Youmourtalik line, or if, after having begun them, it shall not succeed in finishing them, or still further if, after having finished the Karpout-Youmourtalik line, it does not begin the leveling of the land embraced in the first 150 kilometers of the Sivas-Van line, it shall be deprived of all its rights, and Article 28 of the construction contract shall be applied to it. These penalties shall be taken within a period of six months following the date of the official notification by the Government of the defaults that have been proved, and in case the company does not make good the defaults during that period. In case the company, after having constructed the Karpout-Youmourtalik line and effected the required work on the Sivas-Van line, within the periods prescribed by Article 6, shall not have met the conditions bearing on the other portions, it shall lose all its rights connected with the parts that have not been constructed, and all the installations on these lines, as well as the mines, shall revert to the Government.

Article 28. The company pledges itself to construct, in the stations and places designated by the Government, posts for Government inspectors as well as for the military authorities and representatives of the customs, the postal authorities and the police.

Article 29. The company shall have the right to install along the whole extent of its railway lines telegraph and telephone lines for service and signal purposes, but it shall not, on any account, use these lines for private communications. The Government has the right at any time to inspect the correspondence going over these lines. The Government has the right to avail itself of the telegraph poles of the company in order to suspend upon them its own lines. These poles must be strong enough to sustain this additional burden. The Government shall have the power also for its own needs to erect poles along the railway lines, and to use for its own communications the lines of the company in case the Governmental lines shall have been disabled by accident, and provided this can be done without crippling the operation of the service.

Article 30. The company shall have the right to transport free of cost correspondence relating to the operation of the mines and railroads. Private letters shall be subject to charges. The company shall have the right to transport free the personnel necessary for the operation of the railway lines, but this does not apply to the personnel and materials of the mines. The materials necessary for putting the mines in operation and carrying on their operation, and the product of the mines, shall be subject to transportation charges in accordance with the general tariff of rates.

Article 31. The company is authorized to construct any railway line in prolongation of the lines mentioned in Article 1. It must, however, conform in these constructions to all the conditions imposed on the principal lines, and must obtain an authorization from the Government. In any case where the Government shall desire to construct junction lines, the company shall have for a period of 20 years the right of priority on equivalent conditions. It must notify the Government within six months following the announcement of the proposed construction whether or not it wishes to avail itself of this right.

Article 32. In case the Government should desire to construct roads, railway lines or canals that would cross the railway lines of the company, the latter shall abstain from opposition, provided that these constructions do not involve it in expense or cause it any injury.

Article 33. The Government, while reserving the rights acquired by third parties and the rights secured by the stipulations of Article 40, accords to the Turkish stock company, which is to be formed in virtue of the present agreement, the right of operation of all mines indicated within a zone of 20 kilometers on each side of the railway line that is to be constructed in accordance with this agreement. These mines comprise those explored by the concessionary or his authorized agents, those discovered by third parties after the ratification of this agreement, those at present operated by the State, and those which are abandoned by their owners. The term "mines" used in this agreement includes all the mining beds, mineral waters, oil lands and all quarries and sand-pits. If the Government should modify the route proposed by the company, the latter shall have the right, within the period of one year, to demand the substitution in the vicinity of the modified route of the concessions that were attached to the initial route, provided that this latter shall conform to the general provisions of the contract.

Article 34. The company shall operate the mines described in Article 33 in accordance with existing laws and regulations, and this right of operation shall terminate at the same time as the railway concession.

The company shall be subject to existing taxes, but shall be exempt from any increases which may follow the ratification of the present contract. On the other hand, it will profit by all tax diminutions.

The company shall have the benefit of all facilities and exemptions provided by the mining regulations.

Article 35. The company is exempt from the obligation of asking for a permit to operate mines which it may discover in the zone of concession. As soon, however, as it shall commence the operation of a mine it must notify the Department of National Economy, and must remit to it two copies of a chart of the mine on a scale of 1,500.

Article 36. As soon as the route of line B shall be approved, the company shall have the right to begin development work in the zone attached to this route. The company, however, shall not have the power to transport, or to profit from, the minerals produced before the branch of the road connecting with this mine shall be constructed.

Article 37. The company must operate the conceded mine under conditions that are technically satisfactory. Except in case of force majeure the company shall lose its right over all mines which it shall leave unoperated for a period of more than two years.

Article 38. Without a monopoly being hereby created, the company is authorized to create establishments for working its extracted mine products.

Article 39. The company must remit every six months to the Departments of National Economy and Public Works a report upon the mines in operation.

Article 40. Dating from the twenty-first year, following the ratification of the present agreement, the company shall have no right over the mines which shall be discovered after that date by third parties in the zone of concession.

Article 41. Should the Government impose a consumption tax on oil or any other mineral product, the company shall pay these taxes.

Article 42. After deducting from the gross revenues derived from operation of mines and railroads: (1) costs of operation; (2) annual payment of interest and payment for the amortization of the capital involved; (3) reserve; (4) a dividend of 12 per cent. to share-holders, the balance shall be shared in the proportion of 30 per cent. to the Government and 70 per cent. to the company.

Article 43. Government lands necessary for the operation of the mines will be ceded without cost to the company; and, as regards lands held by private owners, the company shall conform to the regulations governing expropriations and mines.

Article 44. The putting in force of the agreement begins after the two years accorded to the concessionary, counting from the date of ratification, in which to accept or refuse the concession.

Article 45. Differences of opinion arising between the Government and the company concerning the application and interpretation of this agreement and the construction contract must be settled by the Turkish Council of State. Disputes between the company and individuals shall be submitted to the Turkish tribunals. Correspondence between the company and the Government shall be carried on in the Turkish language, and operation services shall also be couched in the Turkish tongue.

SUPPLEMENTARY AGREEMENT CONCERNING THE RAILROADS OF EASTERN ANATOLIA

It is agreed as follows between Feyzy Bey, Commissioner of Public Works, acting in the name of the Government of the Turkish Grand National Assembly, subject to ratification by the said Assembly, party of the first part, and Messrs. Chester and Kennedy, acting in the name of the Ottoman American Development Society, party of the second part:

Article 1. The Government of the Turkish Grand National Assembly grants to the Ottoman American Development Society, which accepts it, the concession to construct and operate, in conformity with the provisions of the principal agreement, of the present supplementary agreement, and of the construction contract:

a. A line beginning at Samsun and passing through Havze, Amassia and Zilé, ending at Sivas;

b. A line, leaving line (a) at Moussa-Keuy and ending at Angora;

c. A line starting from Tchalti, upon line (a) of the principal agreement, and ending at Erzerum;

d. A line starting from a point on the Tchalti-Erzerum line and ending at a point on the shores of the Black Sea.

All these lines shall have a gauge of 1.435 meters, and shall be constructed along a route designated and approved by the Department of Public Works.

Article 2. The duration of the concession is ninety-nine years, dating from the putting in force of this supplementary agreement.

Article 3. The Government of the Turkish Grand National Assembly shall transfer, on payment of their price, to the Ottoman American Development Company, documents relating to the Samsun-Sivas line, to the Port of Samsun and to the Angora-Sivas line. It will also transfer, under due recompense, the leveling and excavating works, the workshops, fixtures, stationary machinery and rolling stock already existing.

Article 4. The company shall notify the Department of Public Works within a period of six months, dating from the ratification of the present agreement by the Turkish Grand National Assembly, whether or not it agrees to the construction of the Samsun-Sivas line, of the Port of Samsun, and of the Moussa-Keuy-Angora line. In case of acceptance, the company shall begin work on the Samsun-Sivas line within a period of one month, counting from the date of acceptance, and shall begin work on the Angora-Moussa-Keuy line within a period of six months, counting from the same date.

The company shall communicate its acceptance of the Tchalti-Erzerum line within a period of two years, dating from ratification. The company shall announce its acceptance of line D within a period of three years, and, provided it accepts, it shall begin the work within two years following this acceptance, and shall terminate it in three years in readiness for operation.

Article 5. The Ottoman American Development Society shall pay to the Turkish Government the price of the concessions agreed upon in Article 3.

Article 6. The angagements entered into under this supplementary agreement shall be executed by the Ottoman American Development Society or by the Turkish Stock Company which is to be substituted for it in virtue of Article 4 of the principal agreement.

Article 7. The Samsun-Sivas line is to be finished in the three years following the beginning of the work, and the Angora-Moussa-Keuy line in four years. One year after the construction of the Sivas-Tchalti branch of line A of the principal agreement, the company shall begin the construction of the Tchalti-Erzerum line, and shall finish it in four years.

Article 8. The company agrees, at its own risk, to construct a port at Samsun in conformity with the original project, or with the introduction of admissible modifications. This port shall possess wharves large enough to permit ships to draw up alongside of them, and installations, machinery and rolling stock necessary for the embarkation or disembarkation of passengers and for the direct loading and discharging of cargoes.

Article 9. The period granted for the construction of the port is four years, dating from the ratification of this agreement.

Article 10. A special agreement and construction contract shall be drawn up and exchanged on the matter of this port.

Article 11. Without hereby implying a monopoly, the company, which shall have the right to carry on coasting trade in the Lake of Van, shall have the power to locate the terminus of line A of the principal agreement at a point upon this lake to be determined.

Article 12. The company shall have the power to notify the route of line B of the principal agreement in order to link this line at a point to be chosen on the Bagdad line, and to leave it at another point. In the event that the Government should approve this modification, it will do whatever is necessary in order to enable the company to derive profit from the section of the Bagdad line thus borrowed.

Article 13. The company shall have an option for seven years, counting from the date of ratification of the present supplementary agreement, to construct the following further lines:

E. a line extending from Erzerum to Bayezid and to the Persian frontier. (The material already in existence upon this line is to be ceded upon payment of its value);

F. a line from Sivas to Cesarea;

G. a line from Hadji, Chefaatli (on the line Angora-Moussa-Keuy) to Cesarea;

H. a line from Cesarea to Oulou Kichla;

I. a line starting from the vicinity of Hadji Bairam upon the line Samsun-Sivas, passing through Tchoroum and Songourlou to end in the vicinity of Tchereki on the Angora-Moussa-Keuy line.

Article 14. The construction and operation of all these lines are subject to the conditions of the principal agreement and the construction contract.

Article 15. This agreement has been made as a supplement to the principal agreement as established for the construction of the Sivas-Van line and of a line running from a point on this first line to Mosul, Kerket and Suleymanie, and of a line from another point to Youmourtalik.

TEXT OF LAW CONFIRMING THE CHESTER PROJECT

Article 1. The preliminary agreement, the principal agreement, the supplementary agreement and the technical agreement established between Feyzy Bey, Commissioner of Public Works, and Messrs. K. Kennedy and A. Chester, representing the Ottoman American Development Society, constituted in conformity with the laws of the State of Delaware, having in view the construction and operation of railroads and ports and the operation of mines found within a zone of twenty kilometers on each side of the railroad lines to be constructed, are here-with adopted.

Article 2. The Department of Public Works is charged with the execution of the present law.

Jan. 29, 1923.

(Source: *The Current History Magazine,* New York, 1923, Vol. 18, pp. 395 and 485-9.)

MAP OF THE CHESTER CONCESSION

The heavy black lines show the extent of the Chester Concession, consisting of railroad lines and mining and petroleum rights for twenty kilometres on each side of the right of way. The shaded area is the Mosul district, claimed by the Turks but held by the Arabs under British mandate. Rich mineral resources, including gold, iron, lead, copper, zinc, tin, mercury, cobalt, manganese, nickel, coal, silver and platinum allegedly abound, particularly in the region extending southeastward from the Black Sea and bordering on Soviet Russia. Where the area of the concession runs into the Mosul district, it reaches the territory about which much controversy has arisen.

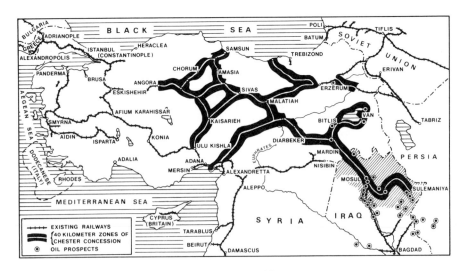

APPENDIX 32

Soviet Caspian Sea Fisheries Concession in Persia

October 1st, 1927

Article 1. By the present Agreement the Persian Government grants on the following conditions, to a special mixed commercial and industrial Company organised by the Persian Government and the Government of the Union of Soviet Socialist Republics, a concession to catch and prepare fish along the Persian South-Caspian coast within the boundaries defined in Article 2 of the present Agreement.

In the present Agreement, the above-mentioned mixed Company shall be termed "the Company".

Article 2. The boundaries of the fisheries for which the Company is granted a concession shall coincide with the boundaries of the concession formerly granted by the Persian Government to Lianozov Brothers. The rivers running into the sea within the boundaries of the concession shall be excluded therefrom. The line where they flow into the sea shall be the boundary between these rivers and the waters of the concession.

The mouths of the following rivers shall form an exception:

(a) Safid-Rud, the two arms of which (Safid-Rud and Mussa-Chay), being shallow, prevent fishing at the mouth. For this reason the Company shall be entitled to fish in these arms as far as the limits where the former fisheries of Lianozov Brothers are at present situated at the mouth.

(b) Babol, in the district of Meshed-i-Sar, in view of the shallow water at the mouth. The Company shall also be entitled to fish at this place within the limits of the former fisheries of Lianozov Brothers.

(c) The river Gorgan with its arms Kara-Su, up to the boundary of the former fisheries of Lianozov Brothers.

If the mouths of rivers within the limits of the concession change their course with the lapse of time, or the rivers form new arms, the fishing rights granted to the Company shall be applicable to the new courses and arms.

Note: With regard to the fishing-places within the limits mentioned in this Agreement, the Company is not restricted except by the provisions of the present Agreement.

Article 3. In order to regulate the fishing work of the Company, the following provisions are adopted:

(a) All scaleless fish (Haram) within the limits of the concession belong to the Company, and the Company's fishermen or private fishermen must sell them to the Company at prices which the Company shall from time to time fix in advance.

(b) All scaled fish (Halal) may be caught by private fishermen as well as by the Company's fishermen; they belong to the fishermen, who may sell them to anyone they choose, including the Company.

(c) In order that the Company and private fishermen of Persian nationality may not hinder each other's work, fishing areas shall be allotted to private fishermen for three-year periods by agreement between the Persian Government and the Management of the Company. The Company, for its part, undertakes to lay down and publish every three years the rules and conditions governing the admission of private fishermen to the waters where fishing is carried on directly by the Company.

Article 4. The duration of the concession granted to the Company shall be 25 years from the date when the present Agreement comes into force. On the expiry of this period of 25 years, the obligations of the Persian Government arising out of Article 14 of the Treaty of February 26, 1921, shall be considered terminated. If the Persian Government does not wish to renew the Company's concession to the above-mentioned fisheries, the Company shall be considered dissolved, and its property shall be divided equally between the two parties, with the exception of the plots of land assigned free of charge to the Company by the Persian Government under Article 17 of the present Agreement. These plots shall revert to the Persian Government. The Persian Government undertakes, if the Company's concession is not renewed, not to grant a concession in respect of these fisheries to any third Power and its nationals for a period of 25 years thereafter. It undertakes to exploit them exclusively through the appropriate agencies of the Persian Government, and not to engage any specialists other than Persian subjects for the exploitation of these fisheries.

Article 5. The Persian and Soviet Governments shall have equal shares of 50% in the Company.

Article 6. In order to improve the organisation of the fisheries, to purchase the necessary fishing gear and appliances, and to defray the costs of exploiting the fisheries, the Company shall form a total capital which must not exceed three million tomans. Should this capital be found to be too high, the Parties shall create a total capital commensurate with actual requirements, one half being paid by the Persian Government and the other half by the Government of the Union of Soviet Socialist Republics. Both Parties shall pay in their shares at dates agreed upon between them, as required for the development of the undertaking. The payment due for the catch of previous years, which, according to Article 13 of the present Agreement, must be made to the Persian Government, shall be placed to the account of the Persian Government's share in the total capital required for exploitation. If the Persian Government does not pay its share in cash, the procedure established by Article 7 of the present Agreement shall be followed. In that case, the following sums, which should have been paid to the Persian Government, shall be paid to the Soviet Government to be offset against the amounts due to that Government by the Persian Government:

(a) Payment for the grant of the concession, in accordance with Article 13.

(b) 50% of the net profits, in accordance with Article 9.

The Persian Government shall, however, be entitled, at any time it thinks fit, to effect and complete, in cash, the payment of its outstanding contributions. In that case the sums mentioned in points (a) and (b) of this Article shall be paid to the Persian Treasury. After the Persian Government has paid its share of the total capital required for exploitation, the sums mentioned in points (a) and (b) of this Article shall be paid direct to the Persian Government.

Article 7. If the sums mentioned in Article 6 are insufficient to cover the Persian Government's share of the capital which is found to be actually necessary in accordance with Article 6, and if the Persian Government does not pay the remainder of its share, this part of the Persian Government's share shall be paid by the Soviet Government after a notification ad hoc has been made by the Persian Government to the Government of the Union of Soviet Socialist Republics. After the Persian Government has been informed by the Soviet Government that the payment has been made, it shall pay 8% interest per annum on the amount advanced by the Soviet Government from the date of payment until the Persian Government's contributions to the above-mentioned capital has been made in full. With regard to the apportionment of the Company's profits, the Soviet Government shall not be entitled, even in cases provided for in the present Article, to receive a higher proportion of the Company's net profits than that specified in Article 9 of the present agreement, *i.e.*, 50%.

It is understood that the payment by the Persian Government of the above-mentioned 8% shall not be taken into account in the apportionment of the profits in accordance with Article 9 of the present Agreement.

Article 8. The annual payment made by the Company to the Persian Government for the grant of the concession in accordance with the present Agreement shall be effected as follows:

(1) 80,000 tomans per annum from the gross receipts of the Company as a payment for the concession rights;

(2) 15% of the remaining gross profit, which, after deduction of administrative and working expenses, shall be regarded as the Company's net profit.

The above-mentioned sums are not reckoned in the profit to which the Persian Government, as a shareholder in the Company, is entitled in accordance with Article 9 of the present Agreement.

Article 9. The whole of the net profit obtained from the Company's operations shall be divided equally—*i.e.*, 50% to each Party—between the Persian and Soviet Governments, share-holders in the Company.

Note: The Company undertakes to dispose of the products of the fisheries at the most favourable price on the Soviet, Persian or foreign markets, selecting the market where the prices are most remunerative.

Article 10. The Board of Mangement of the Company, directing all its business and having its head office in Teheran, shall consist of six members appointed for one year. Three members shall be appointed by the Persian Government and three by the Soviet Government. The rulings and decisions of the Board of Management shall be given by a majority of votes.

The members of the Board of Mangement shall be appointed by both Parties not later than one month after the date when the present Agreement comes into force. The Chairman of the Board shall be one of its Persian members and shall be appointed by the Persian Government.

If, within thirty days after the expiry of the above-mentioned period of one month, either Party has not appointed any or all of the members of the Board, the Board shall, until those members are appointed, be regarded as competent to decide all questions with the members already appointed.

Article 11. Both Parties agree that, in addition to Soviet specialists, Persian specialists who are Persian nationals shall be widely used at the fisheries, for which purpose the Company undertakes to organise suitable training for Persian specialists in its work. As specialists of Persian nationality become available, they shall be engaged by the company and shall take the place of Soviet specialists. The remaining employees, labourers and fishery workmen, not requiring special knowledge, must be Persian nationals.

All employees of the Company must act and work in accordance with the instructions approved by the Board of the Company. At the same time, the Parties agree that the Company shall not have the right to engage other persons than Persian nationals and Soviet citizens.

Article 12. The Company shall be subject to all laws, decrees and regulations by the Persian Council of Ministers for Persian companies, that are, or may hereafter be, in force in Persia. The Persian Government has the right, within the limits of these laws, decrees and regulations, to supervise the operations of the Company.

Article 13. From the year 1923, *i.e.*, after the year 1922, for which accounts have already been settled by a payment of 50,000 tomans, until the present Agreement comes into force, the Government of the Union of Soviet Socialist Republics shall pay to the Persian Government 50,000 tomans per annum for the exploitation of the fisheries.

In return for this the Persian Government shall waive payments of the outstanding Customs duties and other taxes on the fishery products exported and the fishing gear imported during those years.

Article 14. The Company's working year shall begin on October 1st, that month corresponding to the Persian month of Mehr. The Company shall settle its accounts with the Persian and Soviet Governments for each year not later than the beginning of the following month of April, which corresponds to the Persian month of Farvardine.

Article 15. In order to avoid loss of time, the Company may start exploiting the fisheries immediately the capital necessary for beginning its work is paid up and the Company has notified the Persian Government that it is starting its work. The Parties shall pay the shares of the capital due from them at dates decided by the Board of the Company. If the Persian Government does not pay its share at the date fixed by the Board of Management of the Company, the Soviet Government shall pay this share in the manner specified in Article 12 of the present Agreement.

Article 16. The Government of Persia and of the Union of Soviet Socialist Republics shall grant complete exemption from Customs duties and other taxes levied on imports and exports, and also the right of free transit and coasting trade, for appliances, gear, products and other supplies required by the Company for operating the fisheries, and for all kinds of fish products obtained from the fisheries. In all cases, however, the above-mentioned articles shall not be exempt from Customs inspection. The Customs Administrations of both Parties, whilst carrying out the laws, regulations and provisions relating to Customs inspection, shall render every assistance to the Company in order to facilitate the above-mentioned importation and exportation.

Article 17. The Persian Government agrees to place at the disposal of the Company, free of cost, in the Concession area, such plots of land as are required for the fishery buildings, and auxiliary plant. The Company undertakes to effect a settlement to the private owners of plots of land required for the above-mentioned buildings and plant.

Article 18. The Governments of Persia and of the Union of Soviet Socialist Republics shall, each within its own spheres, render such assistance as may be necessary, for the work of the Company.

In particular, the Persian Government shall assist the Company both in preventing any illicit fishing in the waters leased by the latter and in ensuring that the Haram fish are really delivered to the Company.

Article 19. As the maintenance of order in the concession area is in the hands of the Persian Government, it agrees to render the Company such assistance as may be needed to carry into effect the provisions of the present Agreement, and to guard the warehouses and other fishery buildings.

Article 20. The present Agreement shall be ratified by both Parties in accordance with the provisions of their laws. Ratification must take place in both countries as early as possible.

The Agreement shall come into force on the date of the exchange of ratifications, which shall take place at Tehran.

Article 21. The present Agreement has been drawn up and signed in the Persian, Russian and French languages, and each of the signatory Parties receives one copy in each language; all three copies shall be regarded as authentic for the interpretation of the Agreement. In case of a dispute as to the interpretation of the Agreement, the French text shall be followed.

Done at Moscow, October 1, 1927.
L. Karakhan.   Ali Gholi Khan Ansari.
(Source: League of Nations, *Treaty Series*, 1931, Vol. CXII, N. 2621, pp. 350-355.)

APPENDIX 33

The Group (Red Line) Agreement of the Turkish (Iraq) Petroleum Company

July 31st, 1928

An agreement made the Thirty-first day of July 1928 *between d'Arcy Exploration Company Limited* a Company incorporated under the Companies Acts 1908 to 1917 whose registered office is situate at Britannic House Finsbury Circus in the City of London (hereinafter called "the D'Arcy Company") of the first part *the Anglo-Saxon Petroleum Company Limited* a Company incorporated under the Companies Acts 1862 to 1900 whose registered office is situate at St. Helens Court Leadenhall Street in the City of London (hereinafter called "the Anglo-Saxon Company") of the second part *Compagnie Française des Pétroles* a Société Anonyme incorporated under the laws of France whose siège social is situate at No. 63 Avenue Victor Emmanuel III Paris in the Republic of France (hereinafter called "the French Company") of the third part *Near East Development Corporation* a Company incorporated under the laws of the State of Delaware U.S.A. whose principal office is situate at 26 Broadway New York U.S.A. (hereinafter called "the American Company") of the fourth part *Participations and Investments Limited* a Company incorporated under the laws of the Dominion of Canada whose principal office is situate at Dominion Bank Building, King Street, Toronto (hereinafter called "the Participations Company") of the fifth part and *Turkish Petroleum Company Limited* a Company incorporated under the Companies (Consolidation) Act 1908 whose registered office is situate at No. 97 Gresham Street in the City of London (hereinafter called "the Turkish Company") of the sixth part.

Whereas the Turkish Company was incorporated on the 31st day of January 1911 under the Companies (Consolidation) Act 1908.

And whereas the capital of the Turkish Company is now £ 2,000,000 divided into 2,000,000 shares of £ 1 each the whole of which are issued.

And whereas immediately prior to the execution hereof the shares of the Turkish Company were held as follows: *(see next page)*

And whereas on the 14th day of March 1925 a Convention (hereinafter called the "Iraq Concession" which expression shall include any extension or modification thereof) was entered into between the Government of Iraq of the one part and the Turkish Company of the other part, whereby the said Government granted to the Turkish Company the exclusive

Name of Shareholder	Serial Number of Shares held	Total Number of Shares held
The Anglo-Saxon Petroleum Co. Ltd.	20,001 - 56,000 601,001 - 790,000 1,300,001 - 1,525,000	450,000
Calouste Sarkis Gulbenkian	59,001 - 60,000 595,751 - 601,000 1,250,001 - 1,256,250	12,500
D'Arcy Exploration Co. Ltd.	80,004 - 156,000 160,001 - 558,985 1,525,001 - 1,999,982	949,964
Lloyds Bank City Office Nominees Ltd.	56,001 - 59,000 156,001 - 160,000 559,001 - 580,000 580,001 - 595,750 1,256,251 - 1,281,250 1,281,251 - 1,300,000	87,500
Sir John Buck Lloyd	80,002 558,991 - 558,995 1,999,983 - 1,999,988	12
Compagnie Française des Pétroles	1 - 20,000 60,000 - 80,000 790,001 - 1,000,000 1,000,001 - 1,250,000	500,000
Sir John Cadman	80,003 558,996 - 559,000 1,999,989 - 1,999,994	12
Arthur Charles Hearn	80,001 558,986 - 558,990 1,999,995 - 2,000,000	12
		2,000,000

right to explore prospect drill for extract and render suitable for trade petroleum naphtha natural gases and ozokerite and the right to carry away and sell the same and the derivatives thereof within the areas upon the terms and subject to the provisions and conditions in the Iraq Concession described or contained.

And whereas it has been agreed that the American Company and the Participations Company shall respectively become shareholders in the Turkish Company in manner hereafter appearing.

And whereas from time to time the questions have arisen between the parties hereto or some of them in connection with or arising out of the Turkish Company or its undertaking or business or the engagements or rights of the parties in connection therewith.

And whereas with a view to settling such questions and to codifying for the future their rights and obligations the parties hereto have agreed to enter into these presents.

Now in consideration of the premises it is hereby agreed and declared as follows:

Preliminary

1. (i) Each of the parties hereto of the first five parts hereby contracts with each of the other of such parties and with the Turkish Company that they will observe and will procure their respective Associated Companies (as hereinafter defined) to observe the provisions of this Agreement and each of the said parties shall be responsible for any breach or non-observance of this Agreement committed by any Associated Company of such party in the same manner and to the same extent as if such breach or non-observance had been committed by such party itself.

(ii) The provisions of this Agreement other than clauses 5 (i) and 26 hereof shall apply only to the area (hereinafter called "the defined area") bordered in red on the map attached hereto* as explained by the notes and descriptions set out on such map.

(iii) In this Agreement the expression "Associated Company" as regards each of the parties hereto of the first five parts means and includes:

(a) Any Company over which such party either alone or in conjunction with any other party or parties hereto and/or in conjunction with one or more Associated Companies of any party hereto can now or hereafter exercise control either directly or indirectly and whether such control be exercisable by means of the possession of a majority of votes or of the right of appointing directors or by contract or in any manner whatsoever whether similar to the above or not.

(b) As regards the American Company each of the Companies specified in Schedule A hereto.

(c) Any Company over which any Associated Company of such party either alone or in conjunction with any one or more Associated Companies of any party hereto can now or hereafter exercise control either directly or indirectly and whether such control be exercisable by means of the possession of a majority of votes or of the right of appointing directors or by contract or in any manner whatsoever whether similar to the above or not.

(iv) The Turkish Company hereby contracts with each of the other parties hereto that it will observe and will procure any General Operating Company formed as hereafter mentioned and any company over which it can now or hereafter exercise control either directly or indirectly and whether such control be exercisable by means of the possession of a majority of votes or of the right of appointing directors or by contract or in any manner whatsoever whether similar to the above or not (all of which Companies are intended to be included in the expression "Associated Company" as applied to the Turkish Company) to observe the provisions of this Agreement, and the Turkish Company shall be responsible for any breach or non-observance of the provisions of this Agreement committed by any Associated Company of the Turkish Company in the same manner and to the same extent as if such breach or non-observance had been committed by the Turkish Company.

A Company shall cease to be an Associated Company of any party hereto within the meaning of these presents if and when and so long as it shall cease to fulfil the conditions contained in this clause and as regards the American Company the Companies specified in Schedule A hereto as Associated Companies of that Company shall cease to be such if and so long as they are not directly or indirectly interested in the American Company.

Provided always that no party hereto shall be held responsible for any breach or non-observance of this Agreement by an Associated Company of such party if such party can shew that it has used its utmost endeavours to prevent such breach or non-observance.

Distribution of Capital of the Turkish Company

2. The share capital of the Turkish Company as at the date hereof shall be redistributed among the parties of the first five parts in the proportions following that is to say:

* Cf. below, Map of the Middle East on the Eve of World War II.

	% of Such Capital
The D'Arcy Company (hereinafter called Group A)	23.75
The Anglo-Saxon Company (hereinafter called Group B)	23.75
The French Company (hereinafter called Group C)	23.75
The American Company (hereinafter called Group D)	23.75
The Participations Company (hereinafter called Group E)	5.00
	100.00

Groups A, B, C, D, and E are hereinafter collectively called the "Groups".

3. (i) For the purpose of the last preceding clause immediately upon the execution of this Agreement:

(a) The D'Arcy Company shall deliver or procure to be delivered to the American Company duly executed and certified transfers of 474,964 shares of the Turkish Company now registered in the name of the D'Arcy Company and 36 like shares now registered as to 12 in the name of the said Sir John Cadman, as to 12 in the name of the said Sir John B. Lloyd and as to 12 in the name of the said A. C. Hearn, against payment by the American Company of the sum of £ 490,265 5s. 9d. on the First day of August 1928 and will execute and do or procure to be executed and done all documents deeds acts and things necessary for effectually vesting the said shares in the American Company.

(b) The French Company shall deliver to the Anglo-Saxon Company a duly executed and certified transfer of 25,000 shares of the Turkish Company against payment by the Anglo-Saxon Company of the sum of £ 25,948 1s. 3d. on the First day of August 1928 and will execute and do or procure to be executed and done all documents deeds acts and things necessary for effectually vesting the said share in the Anglo-Saxon Company.

(c) The Participations Company shall procure to be delivered to itself duly executed and certified transfers of 87,500 shares of the Turkish Company now registered in the name of Lloyds Bank City Office Nominees Limited and of 12,500 like shares now registered in the name of Calouste Sarkis Gulbenkian against payment to him of the sum of £ 103,210 3s. 11d. on the First day of August 1928 and will execute and do and procure to be executed and done all documents deeds acts and things necessary for effectually vesting the said shares in the Participations Company.

Board of Directors and General Meetings of the Turkish Company

4. (i) Groups A, B, C, and D (each herein termed a "Major Group") shall each be entitled to appoint two Directors on the Board of the Turkish Company and Group E (herein termed "a Minor Group") shall be entitled to appoint one Director.

Provided always that as and when by reason of transfer of shares or by new issues of share capital or otherwise the basic proportion (as hereinafter defined) for the time being of any Major Group falls below 11.875 per cent. the right of representation of such Major Group shall be reduced from two Directors to one Director.

Provided further that should the basic proportion for the time being of any Major Group fall below 5.9375 per cent. such Major Group shall cease to have the rights attaching to a Major Group and shall thereafter only be entitled to such rights as attach to a Minor Group and shall be treated as a Minor Group for all purposes of this Agreement and of the Articles of Association of the Turkish Company.

(ii) In the event of the basic proportion for the time being of any Group falling below 2.5 per cent. such Group shall lose the right of representation by any Director on the Board of the Turkish Company.

(iii) The phrase the "basic proportion" or the "basic proportions", shall wherever used in this Agreement mean the proportion which from time to time the aggregate nominal value of all Ordinary Shares in the Turkish Company and all General Operating Companies (as hereinafter defined) held by each Group bears to the total nominal value of all such Ordinary Shares held by all the Groups. For the purposes of this Agreement a share shall be deemed to be an Ordinary Share if it entitles the holder to dividends at an unlimited rate and Shares which any Group is entitled to subscribe and has subscribed (even if not then allotted) shall be treated for the purposes of this clause as held by such Group. Shares having no nominal value shall be deemed to be of a nominal value equal to the price at which they were first issued by the Company of whose capital they form part.

(iv) Any appointment or removal of Directors by any Group shall be made in writing left at the registered office of the Turkish Company signed by or on behalf of the Group.

(v) In addition to the Directors to be appointed by the Groups one Director may be appointed by the Government of Iraq and the Board may elect not exceeding two persons one to be Chairman of the Board and/or one to be a Managing Director of the Turkish Company.

(vi) All the Directors shall enjoy the same rights and privileges and the Chairman shall not have a casting vote.

(vii) The Articles of Association of the Turkish Company shall forthwith be altered so as to provide that Resolutions at Board Meetings can only be carried if the Directors or one of the Directors appointed by at least three of the Major Groups vote in favour thereof and that no Resolution at a General Meeting of Shareholders shall be carried unless the votes attaching to the Shares then held by at least three of the Major Groups be cast in favour of it.

Operating Companies under the Turkish Company

5. (i) The Turkish Company except as herein otherwise expressly provided shall not be concerned engaged or interested directly in acquiring exploring testing and proving oilfields and operations incidental thereto except within the defined area and a separate Company or Companies shall be constituted to work any field or fields within such area which it shall in accordance with this Agreement be decided to develop or to provide pipe lines storage or other facilities in connection therewith and any such Company is hereinafter referred to as an Operating Company. Neither the Turkish Company nor any Operating Company shall except as herein expressly provided be engaged or interested in the refining or marketing of oil either within or outside the defined area.

(ii) The Turkish Company in exercising its right under the Iraq Concession to select plots shall select plots the area of each of which shall not exceed 8 square miles, and each of which shall if geologically advisable be such that the length thereof shall not exceed twice the breadth.

6. (i) Such Operating Companies shall be of two kinds—General and Special—and shall only be formed with the approval of the Turkish Company and shall immediately after incorporation be made by the Turkish Company to execute under seal a covenant with the Turkish Company and each Group undertaking to be bound by this Agreement so far as applicable to such Company and in particular (in the case of a General Operating Company) to deliver free of cost to the D'Arcy Company any oil produced by such Operating Company the delivery of which to the D'Arcy Company as royalty oil fails to be procured by the parties hereto under Clause 12 hereof and no Company which has not entered into such covenant shall be entitled to be treated as an Operating Company or be eligible for any of the purposes of this Agreement as an Operating Company.

(ii) Prior to the formation of any such Operating Company the Turkish Company shall determine the amount and character of the payment or other form of interest which it shall receive from such Operating Company in consideration of the cession to it by the Turkish Company of its rights properties or concessions or any part thereof provided that the Turkish Company shall make provision for the delivery of the Royalty Oil (if any) due to the D'Arcy Company in respect of selected plots under Clause 12 hereof and provided further that in respect of any plots under Article 6 of the Iraq Concession no other consideration for such cession shall be receivable by the Turkish Company than the amount of the bid by tender paid over to the Turkish Company by the Government of Iraq under the provisions of that Article.

(iii) General Operating Companies shall be so constituted that the voting control at General Meetings thereof shall be vested in the Turkish Company and the Turkish Company shall not in any circumstances part with such control. Special Operating Companies shall as far as legally possible be so constituted that the power to appoint the Directors thereof shall be vested in the Turkish Company.

(iv) The right to subscribe to the first issue of ordinary share capital of Operating Companies shall be offered to the Groups in the basic proportions and shares refused by any of the Groups in those proportions and according to their desire to take up such shares and so on until all the Groups have been satisfied. Subsequent issues of such ordinary share capital shall be made in accordance with the provisions of clause 9 (i) hereof.

7. (i) A "General Operating Company" shall be
(a) Any Operating Company for the purposes of the exploitation of any of the first 24 plots to be selected under Article 5 of the Iraq Concession; (b) Any Operating Company formed for the exploitation of plots under Article 6 of the Iraq Concession or of other concessions in cases in which all the Groups are associated; (c) any Operating Company formed for the construction of pipe lines of storage facilities of port works of refineries or other purposes common to the Turkish Company and all the Groups.

(ii) A "Special Operating Company" shall be one formed in cases in which all the groups may not wish to participate for the exploitation of plots under Article 6 of the Iraq Concession or of other concessions or for other purposes not common to all the Groups.

8. (i) In the election of Directors of every General Operating Company the Turkish Company shall always appoint such persons as to secure that the Board of Directors of that Company shall include persons nominated by the Major and Minor Groups respectively equal in number to their respective nominees on the Board of the Turkish Company if such Groups wish to exercise the right and in the election of Directors of every Special Operating Company the Turkish Company shall if such Groups wish to exercise this right always appoint such persons as to secure that the Board of Directors of that Company shall consist of persons nominated by the Group or Groups participating in the Special Operating Company substantially in proportion to their participation but so that on the Board of Directors of every Special Operating Company there shall always be at least one Director nominated by each Group participating therein on condition that such Group's shareholding interest is not less than 2.5 per cent. of the issued capital of such Special Operating Company.

(ii) The provisions above referred to in clause 4 (vi) and (vii) with regard to method of voting at Board Meetings shall so far as is legally possible equally apply to any General Operating Company as well as to the Turkish Company.

Issues of Capital and Transfers

9. (i) The provisions in the new Articles of Association of the Turkish Company set out in Schedule C hereto with regard to the offer of shares on any increase of capital to existing

shareholders shall so far as legally possible be incorporated in the constitution of every Operating Company.

(ii) Subject to the making of the transfers of shares referred to in clause 3 hereof the provisions in the said new Articles of Association containing restrictions on transfers of shares shall be maintained and provisions in similar terms containing restrictions on transfers of shares shall so far as legally possible be incorporated in the constitution of every Operating Company.

(iii) No person or Company shall be permitted to become a shareholder in the Turkish Company or any Operating Company except on the basis that such person or Company acknowledges that the Turkish Company or such Operating Company is bound by this Agreement.

Concessions and Production

10. (i) All the parties hereto agree that the Turkish Company or a nominee of the Turkish Company shall except as hereinafter mentioned have the sole right to seek for or obtain oil concessions within the defined area and each of the Groups hereby covenants and agrees with the Turkish Company and with the other Groups that excepting only as herein provided or authorized such Group will not nor will any of its Associated Companies either personally or through the intermediary of any person firm company or corporation seek for or obtain or be interested directly or indirectly in any such oil concession or be interested directly or indirectly in the production of oil within the defined area or in the purchase of any such oil otherwise than through the Turkish Company or an Operating Company under the Turkish Company. *Provided* always that as regards any plot offered for competition under Article 6 of the Iraq Concession if the Groups are unanimous in determining to tender for a lease of such plot then a tender for such plot shall be made by a nominee on behalf of the said Groups and if such tender is successful the lease of such plot when acquired shall be transferred forthwith to a General Operating Company in which each Group shall be entitled to be offered its participation in accordance with clause 6 hereof and such General Operating Company shall be entitled to own and operate the said plot free from the restrictions in this sub-clause. If the Groups are not unanimous in determining to tender for a lease of any plot then if any one or more Groups is in favour of so tendering a nominee of such Group or Groups shall be at liberty to tender for a lease of such plot and if successful in obtaining such a lease such Group or Groups shall procure such nominee forthwith to transfer the same to an Operating Company in which each Group shall be entitled to be offered its participation in accordance with clause 6 hereof.

Provided further that as regards any area other than plots under Article 6 of the Iraq Concession if the Turkish Company does not determine to apply for any oil concession then if any two Groups are in favour of so applying the Turkish Company shall be bound forthwith to grant permission to a nominee of those Groups to seek for and obtain such concession on the terms that if successful such Groups shall forthwith transfer the same to an Operating Company in which each Group shall be entitled to be offered its participation in accordance with clause 6 hereof.

(ii) Without prejudice to any other remedy any lease concession or other interest that may be obtained by any Group in breach of the provisions of this Agreement and all the interest of any person or company or corporation intended to be bound by this Agreement in any such lease concession or interest shall be held in trust for a Special Operating Company in which the Groups (other than the Group committing the breach) shall be entitled to participate in accordance with clause 6 hereof.

11. The American Company and any of its Associated Companies shall as regards any

plot offered for competition under Article 6 of the Iraq Concession be entitled to apply for and obtain a lease thereof and if successful it shall, notwithstanding anything contained in clause 10 hereof, not be bound to transfer such plot to an Operating Company but shall be entitled to retain and develop or dispose of the same for its own account. But the American Company or any of its Associated Companies before so acting shall thirty days before the date fixed for the closing of the tenders give notice in writing to the Turkish Company that it intends to avail itself of the provisions of this clause and shall then within ten days thereafter be entitled to receive similar notice from such of the other Groups as propose to put in tenders pursuant to clause 10 hereof. If the American Company or any of its Associated Companies avails itself of its rights under this clause then it shall notwithstanding anything in this Agreement contained forfeit any right it otherwise might have had to the offer of a participation in any such plot which shall be transferred to a separate Special Operating Company to be formed to operate this particular plot alone.

Royalty Oil

12. (i) The parties hereto agree (but as regards the Groups only so far as their powers as shareholders of the Turkish Company and any General Operating Company or through the right to nominate Directors permit) to procure the delivery free of cost to the D'Arcy Company but subject to the provisions hereinafter contained of ten per cent. (hereinafter called royalty oil) of all crude oil produced by any General Operating Company from 24 plots in Iraq each identical with a plot of such General Operating Company such plots to be selected by the D'Arcy Company at its option either within one month after the ultimate date at which the Turkish Company itself shall make its final selection of 24 plots under Article 5 of the Iraq Concession or within one month after the order is given by the Turkish Company through a General Operating Company for the construction of a pipeline to the Mediterranean and up to either of those dates the D'Arcy Company may relinquish any plot previously selected and may select in place thereof any other plot worked or taken up by any General Operating Company. Provided that if the D'Arcy Company shall relinquish any plot previously selected and select in place thereof any other plot, the D'Arcy Company shall be debited with any royalty oil it may have received from the plot first selected against any royalty oil it would have been entitled to from the plot so substituted if it had originally selected such plot.

(ii) Delivery of royalty oil shall be made in respect of each selected plot at the gathering station or stations for such plot and not at the wells' mouth it being the intention of the parties hereto that the royalty oil shall be drawn from each selected plot in proportion to the oil produced therefrom and that the cost of producing such oil and transporting the same to the nearest available gathering station shall be borne by the Turkish Company or any one or more General Operating Companies as the case may be but that the cost of transporting such oil from the gathering station to any other destination shall be borne by the D'Arcy Company.

(iii) In calculating the royalty oil to be delivered to the D'Arcy Company there shall be deducted from the total oil produced from each selected plot:

(a) All water and foreign substances provided that neither the Turkish Company nor any General Operating Company shall be under any obligation to separate such water and foreign substances or any of them from such oil and

(b) All oil lost up to the point of delivery to the D'Arcy Company including all oil which the Turkish Company or any General Operating Company working the plot from which it is produced may be bound to supply free in compensation for damage to native wells caused by operations on such plot.

(c) All oil produced by any General Operating Company in Iraq and used in connection with the operations on any such plot up to the point of delivery to the D'Arcy Company.

(iv) Royalty oil shall rank proportionately with all other oil produced by General Operating Companies in respect of rights to and cost of transport or other facilities provided by the Turkish Company or by any General Operating Company.

Working Agreement

13. (i) The Turkish Company hereby agrees with each of the Groups that it will offer or procure the Operating Company producing or purchasing the same to offer all crude oil whether purchased by the Turkish Company or produced or purchased by any Operating Company which is available for sale (exclusive of the royalty oil deliverable to the D'Arcy Company under the provisions hereinbefore contained) to the Groups for purchase by them upon the terms and conditions following that is to say:

(a) The Turkish Company shall be responsible for the division of all such oil amongst the Groups and shall in this connection supervise the relations between the Groups and conduct all correspondence and keep all accounts and for so doing shall receive the sums referred to in sub-clauses (iii) (b) (4) (iv) (b) and (v) hereof.

(b) Such oil shall be offered to the Groups in the basic proportions as existing when the offer is made but oil from any Special Operating Company shall be offered to those Groups which have contributed to the subscribed ordinary share capital of such Special Operating Company in the proportion in which such Groups are interested in such Special Operating Company.

(c) Delivery shall (subject to pipe-line facilities being available and subject to the provisions of this Agreement) be made in cargo lots if so desired at each Group's option either on board a vessel or vessels or into such Group's own storage tanks either at the Mediterranean terminal of the pipe-line or in case the Turkish Company through a General Operating Company shall provide a pipe-line to any other terminal or terminals then at such terminal or terminals or partly at one and partly at the other as nearly as possible in proportion to the quantities available at such terminals. Provided always that if the pipe-line capacity is available and subject to the rights of other users delivery may be effected at each Group's option wholly at any available terminal or in such proportions at different terminals subject as aforesaid as each Group may desire.

(d) On or before the first day of each quarter of the year the Turkish Company shall notify each of the Groups of the estimated quantity of crude oil and/or refined products (if any) and of the source from which the oil will be derived in each case which the Group notified will be entitled to purchase during (a) the quarter beginning three calendar months after the due date for giving such notice and (b) each of the three succeeding quarters.

(e) Not later than fifteen days after the first day of each quarter or the receipt of such notice whichever shall be the later each Group shall notify the Turkish Company of the quantity (not exceeding the amount so offered) and particulars of the source of production of the oil which such Group will purchase during the next succeeding quarter notifying at the same time the approximate dates places and methods of delivery desired which quantity shall be as nearly as possible equally spread over the quarter. Any Group which fails to notify the Turkish Company in accordance with this sub-paragraph of the quantity which it elects to purchase shall be deemed to have declined such quantity. Provided always that so far as the Participations Company is concerned the period within which such Group shall notify the Turkish Company as aforesaid shall be 18 days instead of 15 days and in the event of the four Major Groups declining the whole of the oil offered to them the Turkish Company shall forthwith notify the Participations Company.

(f) Payment for all quantities delivered during any calendar month shall be due and payable on the last day of the following calendar month to the Turkish Company in London or other place agreed by the Turkish Company in sterling or other currency agreed by the Turkish Company. The Turkish Company will effect the distribution of the payments to the Operating Companies concerned. Any payment in arrear shall carry interest at the rate of £ 10 per centum per annum.

(g) Any Group which at any time is in arrear in its payments under this clause or otherwise in default under this agreement (including in particular default under clause 12) shall without prejudice to any other remedies lose its right to receive oil under this clause so long as it is in arrear or in default and also during the remainder of the quarter during which such default occurred and during the whole of the quarter in which such arrears are paid off or default made good and shall forfeit all quantities it would have been entitled to purchase or receive during such period which quantities shall be offered to the other Groups not in arrear or default.

(h) Any Group which has failed during any quarter to take delivery of the quantity which it notified the Turkish Company it would take shall automatically forfeit the right to receive any balance of which it has not taken delivery and shall be debited with any loss sustained by the Turkish Company or any Operating Company as a result of its failure to take delivery.

(i) The Turkish Company shall as soon as reasonably possible offer or procure to be offered to the Groups which have accepted their full quotas any quantities not accepted in accordance with sub-paragraph (e) or forfeited in accordance with sub-paragraphs (g) and (h) of this sub-clause or any oil in excess of the estimate under sub-paragraph (d) of this sub-clause and each Group shall notify the Turkish Company within ten days after receipt of such offer of the maximum quantity of such additional oil that it is willing to purchase during the following quarter and so on until all the Groups shall have been satisfied and the provisions of the foregoing sub-paragraphs shall apply as nearly as possible to any offer or acceptance of any quantities under this sub-paragraph.

(ii) In case there shall remain for delivery during the next succeeding quarter after complying with the provisions of sub-paragraphs (e) to (i) inclusive of sub-clause (i) of this clause any surplus oil which none of the Groups is willing to purchase then and in that case only the Turkish Company shall be at liberty to dispose of such surplus to any other person or persons and in case the Turkish Company shall find it impossible to sell such surplus at a price arrived at in accordance with the provisions of sub-clause (iii) hereof then such surplus shall before being sold to any other person or persons at any lower price be offered at such lower price to the Groups in the basic proportions and the provisions of sub-clause (i) shall apply to such subsequent offer as nearly as may be.

(iii) The price at which the crude oil produced by each General Operating Company and available for division among all the Groups shall be offered under sub-clause (i) of this clause in the first instance to the Groups shall be determined half-yearly in the following manner:

(a) For the first two quarters in each calendar year the cost f.o.b. seaboard terminal for the first half of the previous year shall be the basis and for the last two quarters of each calendar year the cost f.o.b. seaboard terminal for the second half of the previous year shall be the basis. Provided that until the above scale can be applied the basis shall be a figure to be estimated by the Board of the Turkish Company and calculated as nearly as possible to be the cost f.o.b. seaboard terminal for the quarter in question. The price shall in each case be calculated for each General Operating Company separately.

(b) The cost f.o.b. at the seaboard terminal referred to in paragraph (a) above shall include:

(1) The cost of production to each General Operating Company of the oil at the gathering station on the field including royalties and the cost of production of royalty oil (where applicable) and overhead expenses.

(2) The cost of services rendered by General Operating Companies such as transport by

the main pipe-lines—storage facilities at the gathering stations and at the terminal—anchorage for steamers—pumpage and port works—dehydrating plant—common refinery and similar facilities which for the purpose of this Agreement it may be agreed to provide for ends common to the Turkish Company and all the Groups such cost to be determined in the manner set out below.

(3) Charges for services if any rendered by Special Operating Companies or third parties.

(4) An additional sum to be fixed by the Board of the Turkish Company not exceeding 5/— per ton.

In determining for the purposes of this clause the cost of production at a gathering station and the cost of the service above mentioned allowance shall be made for reasonable depreciation and repayment of capital having regard to the probable life of the fields, plant and other installations together with interest at £ 6 per centum per annum on the amount shown in the capital account year by year.

The accounts of the Turkish Company and its General Operating Companies shall be audited annually by the same Auditors who shall be Chartered Accountants and who in addition to the usual audit shall determine and certify the cost f.o.b. at the seaboard terminal as above mentioned and their certificate shall be final.

(iv) (a) The rights of user of the Groups of the available capacity of any particular common facility such as is contemplated in sub-clause (iii) (b) (2) above.

(i) When the Groups are associated in any General Operating Company shall be in the proportions in which they are from time to time in fact taking the oil.

(ii) When any of the Groups are associated in any Special Operating Company shall be a right attaching to such Special Operating Company which right shall extend only to the balance of any such available capacity after the requirements (as determined under sub-clause (i) above) of all the Groups when associated in any General Operating Company have been met and shall for each such Special Operating Company be in the proportion which the oil production of that Special Operating Company bears to the aggregate oil production of all Special Operating Companies who can make commercial use of any such particular common facility and within any such Special Operating Company its facilities shall be available to the participants therein in the proportion in which they are from time to time in fact taking such oil.

(b) The basis of charge to any Special Operating Company for the use of the above common facilities and the additional sum as in sub-clause (iii) (b) (4) above shall be determined by the Turkish Company prior to the formation of each Special Operating Company provided that for all Special Operating Companies operating in Iraq the additional sum shall be identical and for all Special Operating Companies there shall be an identical basis of charge for the use of identical common facilities.

(v) The Turkish Company or a General Operating Company shall alone have the right to purchase on any field any crude oil available for purchase. The price at which crude oil purchased by the Turkish Company or any General Operating Company shall be offered to the Groups shall be the cost to the Turkish Company or such Operating Company at the place of delivery plus cost of delivery therefrom to f.o.b. vessel or terminal storage tanks as referred to in sub-clause (i) (c) plus an additional sum not exceeding 2/6 per ton. such cost to be certified by the Auditors of the Turkish Company, whose certificate shall be final.

Pipe-Line

14. (i) As soon as sufficient oil production has been secured to justify in the opinion of the Board of the Turkish Company the construction of a trunk pipe-line the Turkish Company shall proceed through one or more of its General Operating Companies with the

construction of a pipe-line to a Mediterranean port including the necessary gathering lines.

(ii) In the event of the pipe-line facilities reserved for the transportation of oil by lessees pursuant to Article 6 of the Iraq Concession falling materially short of the production obtained by lessees and requiring transportation through the said pipe-line system and if there should be no General Operating Company willing or able to find the capital required to build additional pipe-line facilities then any Special Operating Company or any Group who may desire that the additional pipe-line facilities shall be provided may require the Turkish Company through a General Operating Company to proceed as rapidly as reasonably possible with the construction of such additional facilities provided that any such Special Operating Company or Group provides the whole of the capital required on a basis which will not subject the Turkish Company or its General Operating Company as the case may be to any liability in connection therewith in excess of the net profits to arise from the use of such additional pipe-line facilities the whole of which net profits shall be applied in payment of interest on and repayment of the said capital. Such additional pipe-line facilities shall when provided be reserved by the Turkish Company or its General Operating Company exclusively when required for the transportation of oil belonging to the Special Operating Company or Group which shall have supplied the capital until such capital with interest and a premium of twenty-five per centum shall have been repaid in full. The additional pipe-line facilities shall be the property of the said General Operating Company but the capital advanced with the said premium thereon shall if required by the Special Operating Company or Group providing the same or by the Turkish Company be secured by a first charge thereon until repaid by the General Operating Company out of the net profits as aforesaid.

15. (i) The location of the Mediterranean terminal of the trunk pipe-line shall be selected by the Turkish Company at a place where sufficient land can be acquired by a General Operating Company upon which to construct its own seaboard terminal and upon which to construct its own seaboard terminal and upon which land each of the Groups for itself or for one or more of its Associated Companies may if desired and according to the basic proportions of such Group but adequately for normal commercial requirements in each case take leases of land for their respective refineries or storage plants. The ownership of all such land shall at all times be retained by the Turkish Company or a General Operating Company.

(ii) The Turkish Company shall through a General Operating Company provide at the Mediterranean terminal of its pipe-line reasonable and adequate facilities having regard to the production including storage tanks suitable loading facilities anchorage for steamers awaiting loading and pipe-line facilities connecting the individual plants (if any) of the Groups with the pipe-line terminal and with the terminal wharves and loading berths of the Operating Companies.

(iii) The privisions of this clause shall apply *mutatis mutandis* to any other terminal of a trunk pipe-line which may be constructed by the Turkish Company through a General Operating Company.

Refining

16. (i) Within the area in which the Turkish Company is under an obligation to refine or supply oil for local markets under the Iraq Concession the Turkish Company or a General Operating Company shall alone have the right to refine oil in such area but the Turkish Company or a General Operating Company shall not refine in excess of the consumption of such area and one of the Groups nor any of their Associated Companies shall be at liberty to refine oil in such area and each of the Groups agrees with the other parties hereto and each of them that (excepting only as herein expressly provided) such Group will not nor will any of its Associated Companies directly or indirectly be engaged or interested (except through the

Turkish Company or an Operating Company) in the refining of oil in such area but nothing herein contained shall preclude any of the Groups or any of their Associated Companies from owning or operating refineries at the terminus of any main pipe-line at a point accessible to Tank ships.

(ii) With the consent in writing of all the Major Groups for the time being the Turkish Company may through a General Operating Company erect and operate refineries at any point accessible to Tank ships.

(a) for the refining of such oil as may be offered to the Groups under the provisions of clause 13 hereof and as may not be from time to time purchased by them or any of them and/or

(b) for the refining of oil on account of any or all the Groups but so that all Groups shall have the same rights in the basic proportions to have oil refined for their account.

(iii) All products refined under the preceding sub-clause (ii) (a) shall in the first instance be offered on equal terms to the Groups in the basic proportions.

Except as above authorized or in fulfillment of any obligation under any concession to be granted to it, neither the Turkish Company nor any Operating Company shall be concerned engaged or interested directly or indirectly in the refining of oil.

Marketing

17. Within the area in which the Turkish Company is under an obligation to supply oil for local markets under the Iraq Concession the Turkish Company or a General Operating Company shall alone have the right to market in such area the oil or the products of the oil obtained under the Iraq Concession and none of the Groups nor any of their Associated Companies shall be at liberty to market any such oil or any product thereof in such area and each of the Groups agrees with the other parties and each of them that neither it nor any of its Associated Companies will directly or indirectly except through the Turkish Company or a General Operating Company be engaged or interested in the marketing of such oil and products in such area.

Except as above authorized or in fulfilment of any obligation under any concession to be granted to it neither the Turkish Company nor any Operating Company shall be concerned engaged or interested directly or indirectly in the marketing of oil.

Assignment of Interest

18. (i) None of the Groups shall be entitled to assign its interest under this Agreement, unless

(a) such assignment shall relate to the whole of the interest hereunder of the Group (hereinafter called "the Assignor Group") assigning its interest.

(b) such assignment shall be to a Company (hereinafter called the "Assignee-Company") the shareholders in which are at the date of assignment identical with the shareholders for the time being in the Assignor Group, and

(c) the Assignee Company shall contemporaneously with such assignment enter into a contract with all the parties hereto other than the Assignor Group and with each of them agreeing to be bound by all the provisions of this Agreement in the same way as if it had been a party hereto in the place of the Assignor Group, and

(d) the Assignor Group shall contemporaneously with such assignment as aforesaid transfer to the Assignee Company all shares, debentures or other securities or interests whatsoever of the Assignor Group of and in the Turkish Company and every Operating Company and the parties hereto may refuse to recognise the title of any assignee in respect of any assignment unless all the provisions of this sub-clause shall have been complied with.

Provided always that in the event of any Group desiring to assign its whole interest under this Agreement on terms which comply with the foregoing conditions the other Groups shall waive any right they may have under the Articles of Association of the Turkish Company or any Operating Company in connection with such assignment to purchase the share of the Assignor Group in the Turkish Company or any Operating Company and Provided further that nothing in this Agreement contained shall be deemed in any way to restrict the right of any holder of shares in any Company a party hereto to transfer such shares.

(ii) In case the Turkish Company shall assign any part of its concession rights it shall obtain from the assignee a formal undertaking entered into with the parties hereto and with each of them to accede to and become bound by the provisions of this Agreement.

Miscellaneous Provisions

19. (i) The Turkish Company and all General Operating Companies shall on request furnish to each of the Groups all such geological reports and information as may come into its or their possession relating to the subject matter of this Agreement and shall not communicate to any Group information of any kind without on request giving the like information to each and every one of them and like duties shall rest upon all Special Operating Companies with regard to such Groups as participate therein.

(ii) It is hereby agreed that so far as arrangements can properly be made without prejudicing the rights of the Turkish Company or any of its Operating Companies or any of the parties hereto the business of the Turkish Company and its Operating Companies shall so far as reasonably possible be so conducted as to avoid multiple taxation.

Force Majeure

20. (i) If any party hereto by reason of any cause whatsoever beyond the control of such party commits any breach of this Agreement such party and any party or parties hereto liable jointly with such party shall to the extent to which breach is due to such cause be relieved from liability therefor.

(ii) No cause shall be deemed beyond the control of any party if it was within the control of such party's Associated Companies or in the case of the Turkish Company of the Turkish Company's General Operating Companies.

Articles of Association

21. The Groups shall use all their voting power and influence and rights for the purpose of procuring

(a) The adoption of the new Article of Association of the Turkish Company set out in Schedule C hereto.

(b) The incorporation in the constitution of every General Operating Company of the Turkish Company of provisions of a like character so far as legally possible to those contained in Articles 3, 4, 8, 9, 11, 12, 13, 34, 35, 36, 56, 62, 74, 88, 89, 97, 98, 99 and 100 of the Articles of Association of the Turkish Company and such as shall enable this Agreement to be carried into effect.

(c) The incorporation in the constitution of every Special Operating Company of the Turkish Company of provisions of a like character so far as legally possible to those contained in articles 11, 12, 13, 35 and 36 of the Articles of Association of the Turkish Company and such as shall enable this Agreement to be carried into effect.

(d) That at no time without the consent of all the Groups shall Articles 3, 4, 8, 9, 11, 12, 13, 34, 35, 36, 56, 62, 69, 70, 71, 74, 88, 89, 97, 98, 99 and 100 of the Articles of Association of the Turkish Company or the corresponding Articles of any General Operating Company of the Turkish Company be modified or amended.

Duration

22. This Agreement shall remain in force so long as the Turkish Company shall continue in existence and/or so long as any concessions granted or hereafter to be granted to the Turkish Company or any of its Operating Companies continue to remain in force and shall be deemed to be separate contract in respect of the obligations imposed on the parties hereto in reference to each separate year.

Jurisdiction and Interpretation

23. (i) The parties hereto are for the purposes of this Agreement to be deemed to be domiciled in the City of London at the addresses following:

The D'Arcy Company at Britannic House, Finsbury Circus, London E.C. 2.

The Anglo-Saxon Company at St. Helen's Court, Leadenhall Street, London, E.C. 3.

The French Company at the office of Messrs. Denton, Hall & Burgin, Solicitors, or of their successors in business.

The American Company at the office of Messrs. Piesse & Sons, Solicitors, or their successors in business.

The Participations Company at the office of Messrs. Freshfield, Leese & Munns, Solicitors, or of their successors in business.

The Turkish Company at 97 Gresham Street, London, E.C. 2. and the parties hereto hereby submit to the jurisdiction of the English Courts and agree that any summons writ or other process and any notice requiring to be served on them respectively may be served at the said respective addresses and that the persons named are respectively authorised to accept service and that such service shall be deemed to be good service on them respectively.

(ii) Provided always that any party hereto may at any time and from time to time during the currency of this Agreement by notice in writing to the Turkish Company change the name and address of the party above-mentioned as authorised to accept on its behalf by substituting therefor the name of some other party at an address within the City or County of London in England and after any such notice has been served this Agreement shall be read as if the name of such party and address had been substituted for that above-mentioned as regards the party giving the said notice.

(iii) Any summons writ or other process or any notice requiring to be served on any party may be served by delivering the same or by posting the same in London in a prepaid registered letter addressed to the said party at the aforesaid address and the same shall be deemed to have been served on the day after that on which it was so posted.

24. This Agreement shall be construed according to and be governed by English Law.

Arbitration

25. If any question or dispute shall arise between the parties hereto or between any one or more of them or between any one or more of them on the one hand and other or others of them on the other hand in anyway arising out of or in connection with this Agreement or as to the true meaning or construction thereof or as to the rights or liabilities of any of the parties hereto and if it shall be decided by the parties at variance to resolve their difference by arbitration then such question or dispute shall be referred to the decision of a sole arbitrator to be agreed upon or failing agreement to be nominated by a judge of the High Court of Justice in England and the decision of such arbitrator shall be final and binding upon all parties to the arbitration. The provisions of the Arbitration Act 1889 and of any statutory modification thereof in force shall apply to any such arbitration.

Waiver of Claims

26. As from the date hereof this Agreement shall be deemed to contain all the existing

contractual rights of any party hereto against any other party or other parties hereto in connection with the defined area and/or in connection with the Turkish Company and each party hereto waives as against every other party hereto any claim whatsoever which it or he may have or claim to have arising out of or in connection with any pre-existing contract or arrangement or alleged contract or arrangement in connection with such area and/or the Turkish Company.

In Witness whereof the parties hereto have respectively executed these presents the day and year first above written.

(Source: *U.S., 84th Congress, House of Representatives, Committee on the Judiciary, Subcommittee No. 5*, part 2, pp. 1004-1033).

BIBLIOGRAPHY

I. Sources, Documents, Official Publications, Contemporary Studies, Diaries, Reports, Statistics

Abou Yousof Ya'koub, *Le Livre de l'Impôt Foncier (Kitab El-Kharad)* traduit et annoté par E. Fagnan, Paris, 1921.
— *Kitab el-Kharadj lilQadi Abū Yūsuf Ya'kūb bin Ibrahim,* Cairo, 1933 (1346 A.H.), Second Edition.
Administration de la Dette Publique Ottomane, *Compte-Rendu* (ou *Rapport*) *du Conseil d'Administration,* Constantinople, 1881-1920.
Aitchison, C.U., *A Collection of Treaties, Engagements and Sanads,* relating to India and neighbouring countries, 13 vols., Calcutta, 1909.
Ali Bey Ismail, *Les Conséquences Financières de l'occupation de l'Egypte par l'Angleterre,* Discours prononcé le 24 septembre 1910 devant le Congrès National Egyptien tenu à Bruxelles.
Ali Haydar Midhat, *Life of Midhat Pasha,* London, 1903.
Ali Haydar Midhat Bey, *Midhat-Pacha, sa vie—son oeuvre,* Paris, 1908.
Anderson, Arthur, *Observations on the Practicability and Utility of Opening a Communication between the Red Sea and the Mediterranean,* London, 1843.
Annuaire Egyptien, 1948.
Annuaire Statistique de l'Egypte, Ministère des Finances, 1916-1921/2.
Archiv für Eisenbahnwesen, herausgegeben im Königlich Preussischen Ministerium der Öffentlichen Arbeiten, Berlin, 1914. Die Eisenbahnen der asiatischen Türkei. Von Hecker, Pp. 744, 1057, 1283, ff.

Banque Mellié Iran, *Bulletins,* 1934-1939.
Banque Nationale de Perse (Bank Melli), *Loi de l'Unité Monétaire Légale de Perse,* Téhéran, 1932.
Behind the Veil in Persia—English Documents, C. L. van Langehuysen, Amsterdam (ditto in German, *Englische Dokumente zur Erdrosselung Persiens,* Der Neue Orient, Berlin), 1917.
Bie Ravndal, G., *The Origin of the Capitulations and of the Consular Institutions,* 67th Congress, 1st Session, Senate, Doc. No. 34, Washington, 1921.
Bilkur, Şefik, *National Income of Turkey,* Ankara, 1949.
Blue Book: Persia, No. 1, 1909.
Bowring, John, *Report on Egypt and Candia, Parliamentary Papers,* Vol. XXI, 1840.
British and Foreign State Papers, London.
Brydges, Sir Harford Jones, *An Account of the Transactions of H.M.'s Mission to the Court of Persia,* to which is appended *A Brief History of the Wahaubi,* London, 1834.

(The) Capitulations and Articles (between Gr. Britain and the Ottoman Empire), Constantinople, 1663, & London, 1679.
Chardin, J., *A New and Accurate Description of Persia and other Eastern Nations,* 2 Vols., London, 1724.
Chesney, F. R., *Narrative of the Euphrates Expedition,* London, 1868.
— *Reports on the Navigation of the Euphrates,* 1833.
— *The Expedition for the Survey of the Rivers Euphrates and Tigris,* London, 1850.
C.H.P., *Üçüncü Büyük Kongre Zabıtları, 10-18 Mayıs 1931,* Devlet Matbaası, 1931.
Clician Vassif Effendi, *A., Son Altesse Midhat-Pacha Grand Vizir,* Paris, 1909.
Clot Bey, A. B., *Aperçu Général sur l'Egypte,* Fortin, Masson et Cie., Paris, 1840.
(Le) Comité Ottoman d'Union et de Progrès, *Assassinat de Midhat Pacha,* d'après les Documents Officiels de la Jeune Turquie, Genève, 1898.
(La) Constitution Ottomane du 7 Zilhidjé 1293 (23 décembre 1876), Expliquée et annotée par A. Ubicini, Paris, 1877.
Courthope-Munroe, C. H., *General Report on the Trade and Economic Conditions of Turkey for the Year 1919,* London, 1920.

Crédit Foncier d'Algérie et de Tunisie, *Répertoire Economique et Financier de la Syrie et du Liban,* Paris, 1932.
Cromer, Lord, *Abbas II,* Macmillan & Co., London, 1915.
— *Modern Egypt,* 2 vols., Macmillan & Co., London, 1908.
Cumberbatch, A. N., *Egypt, Economic and Commercial Conditions in Egypt,* Overseas Economic Surveys, October, 1951.

Deny, J., *Sommaire des Archives Turques du Caire,* Société Royale de Géographie d'Egypte, 1930.
Description de l'Egypte, ou recueil des observations et des recherches qui ont été faites en Egypte pendant l'expédition de l'armée française, 24 vol., ed. 1821-29.
Direction Générale des Contributions Indirectes, *Statistique du Commerce Extérieur de l'Empire Ottoman pendant l'année 1326* (1910/11), Constantinople, 1328.
Direction Générale de la Presse, *La Turquie Contemporaine; La Turquie Economique.*
— *Politique des Chemins de fer en Turquie Républicaine,* Ankara, 1938.
Djabarti, Cheikh Abd-El-Rahman El-, *Merveilles Biographiques et Historique ou Chroniques,* I-IX, Le Caire, 1888-1896.
Douin, G., *L'Egypte de 1802 à 1804,* Correspondance des Consuls de France en Egypte, recueillie et publiée par G.D., 1925.
— *L'Egypte de 1805-1807,* Correspondance etc., 1926.
— *L'Egypte de 1828 à 1830,* Correspondance etc., Rome, 1935.
Dowson, Sir E., *An Inquiry into Land Tenure and Related Questions,* Letchworth, 1930.
Duhamel, Colonel, (Consul Général de Russie en Egypte), *Tableau Statistique de l'Egypte en 1837,* Denkschriften der russischen geographischen Gesellschaft, I, 1847.

Empire Ottoman, Ministère des Finances, *Loi, 25 Mai 1327, portant fixation du Budget Général de l'Exercise 1327,* Constantinople, 1911.
Esad, Mehmed, *Précis historique de la destruction du corps des Janissaires par le Sultan Mahmoud en 1826,* traduit du Turc par A. P. Caussin de Perceval, Paris, 1833.

Fisher, Stanley, *Ottoman Land Laws,* Oxford, 1919.
Forster, William (ed.), *Letters received by the East India Company from its Servants in the East,* London, 1902.

Garnett, Lucy M., *Turkey of the Ottomans,* London, 1911.
— *Turkish Life in Town and Country,* 1904.
Gazi Mustafa Kemal Tarafindan, *Nutuk,* Istanbul, 1938.
General Directory of Statistics, *Small Statistical Abstract of Turkey,* Ankara, 1947.
Gesellschaft zur Erforschung der Türkischen Geschichte, *Geschichte der Türkischen Republik,* Istanbul, 1935.
Gökalp, Ziya, *Türkçülüğün Esasları,* Istanbul, 1939 ed.

Hakluyt, Richard, *The Principal Navigations, Voiages, Traffiques and Discoveries of the English Nation,* 3 vols., London, 1598-1600.
Havard, G. T., *Report on Economic and Commercial Conditions in Syria and the Lebanon* (June 1936), Dept. of Overseas Trade, H.M.S.O., London, 1936.
Hertslet, Edward, *Treaties concluded between Great Britain and Persia and between Persia and other Foreign Powers,* wholly or partially in force on the 1st April 1891, London 1891.
Hilton-Young, E., *Reports on Economic Conditions and Policy and Loan Policy,* Baghdad, 1930.
Hurewitz, J. C., *Diplomacy in the Near and Middle East,* 2 vols., Princeton, 1956.

Imperial Ottoman Debt, *Decree dated December 8/20, 1881, with its Annexes* (in French and English), London, Council of Foreign Bondholders.
L'Indicateur Libano-Syrien, 1928-9.
International Monetary Fund, *International Financial Statistics.*
Iraq Currency Board, *Reports,* since 1933.
Iraq Currency Law No. 44 for the Year 1931, Baghdad.

Iraq Government, Ministry of Economics, *Statistical Abstract,* Baghdad, 1939.
Iraq, Review of Commercial Conditions, February 1945, H.M.S.O., London.
İstatistik Yıllığı, Ankara.

Jewish Agency for Palestine, Economic Research Institute, *Statistical Handbook of Middle Eastern Countries,* Jerusalem, 1945.
Journal des Tribunaux Mixtes, *Les Juridictions Mixtes d'Egypte 1876-1926,* Alexandrie, fév. 1926.
Journal Officiel Egyptien, Le Caire.

(The) Koran.

Lamba, Henry, "Khédivat d'Egypte", *Code Administratif Egyptien,* Paris, 1911.
Lane, Edward William, *An Account of the Manners and Customs of the Modern Egyptians,* London, 1860 (5th edition).
Lanzoni, Adriano, "La Mesopotamia economica", 1910, reproduced in Ch. Issawi (ed.), *The Economic History of the Middle East 1800-1914,* Ch. 6.
Layard, A. H., *Turkish Budgets and Turkish Finance,* (Private & Confidential), 1869.
League of Nations, Economic Intelligence Service, *Public Finance* 1928-1937, LVIII, *Iraq,* Geneva, 1938.
— *Enquiry into Clearing Agreements,* Geneva, 1935.
— *Greek Refugees Settlement.*
— *International Statistical Yearbooks.*
— *Mandates, Statistical Information concerning Territories under Mandate,* Geneva, May 21st, 1928; & Oct. 1933.
— *Memorandum on Currency and Central Banks,* 1913-1925, Vol. II, Geneva, 1926.
— *Official Journal,* Geneva.
— *Permanent Mandates Commission,* Minutes.
— *Question of Frontier between Turkey and Iraq,* Geneva, 1925.
— *Settlement of Bulgarian Refugees,* Rapporteur: Commander Hilton Young, Geneva, Sept. 21st, 1926.
— *Settlement of the Assyrians of Iraq,* Geneva, Feb. 29th, 1936.
— *The Mandates System,* Origin-Principles-Application, Geneva, April 1945.
— *The Transition from War to Peace Economy,* Report of the Delegation on Economic Depressions, Geneva, Part 1, 1943, Part 2, 1945.
— *Treaty Series.*
(La) Législation Turque, Edition Rizzo & Son, Galata, Constantinople.
(De) Lesseps, F., *Lettres, journal et documents pour servir à l'histoire du Canal de Suez,* Paris, 1875-81.
Linant de Bellefonds, A., *Principaux travaux,* etc., Le Caire, 1872-3.
Lingeman, E. R., *Turkey, Economic and Commercial Conditions in Turkey.* Overseas Economic Surveys, September 1947, London, H.M.S.O., 1948.
Loi sur l'Encouragement de l'Industrie, Loi No. 1055 de 28 mai 1927, J. A. Rizzo, Stamboul, 1929.
Lucovich, M. Antoine, *Episode de l'Histoire contemporaine. La Société Agricole et Industrielle d'Egypte,* Paris, 1865.
Lugard, Lord, *The Dependencies of the British Empire and the Responsibilities they Involve,* Birbeck College (University of London), 1928.
— Sir F. D., *The Dual Mandate in British Tropical Africa,* Edinburgh and London, 1923.

Makal, Mahmut, *Bizim Köy,* Varlık Yayınevi, Istanbul.
Malcolm, John, *Sketches of Persia,* 2 Vols., London, 1828.
Malcolm, Napier, *Five Years in a Persian Town,* John Murray, London, 1905.
Midhat Pacha, *La Turquie, son passé, son avenir,* Paris, 1878.
Millspaugh, A. C., *Americans in Persia,* Washington, 1946.
— *The Financial and Economic Situation of Persia, 1926,* New York, July 1, 1926.
Milner, Viscount, *England in Egypt,* London, 1904.
Moltke, Helmuth von, *Briefe über Zustände und Begebenheiten in der Türkei aus den Jahren 1835 bis 1839,* Berlin, 1893.

— *Der russisch-türkische Feldzug in der europäischen Türkei 1828 und 1829,* Berlin, 1845.
Moustafa Kamel, *Egyptiens et Anglais,* Paris, 1906.

Nansen, Fridtjof, *Report on the Work of the High Commission for Refugees,* League of Nations, Geneva, Sept. 4, 1923.
Noradounghian, G., *Recueil d'Actes Internationaux de l'Empire Ottoman,* recueillis et publiés par, 4 vols., Paris, 1897-1903.

D'Ohsson Mouradgea, Ignatius, *Tableau Général de l'Empire Othoman,* Paris, 1790.
(The) Ottoman Bank in the Middle East: the Banque de Syrie et du Liban, London, 1948.
(The) Ottoman Land Code, translated from the Turkish by F. Ongley, William Clowes and Sons, London, 1892.

Parliamentary Papers, London.
(Le) Percement de l'Isthme de Suez, Enfantin (1853-1855). F. de Lesseps (1855-1869). [Resumé Historique], E. Dentu, Paris, 1869.
Persia, *Code de Commerce,* 1307-1928, Imp. Madjless.
— *Persian Civil Code* (Articles 1 to 1335), 1937, translated by A. C. Trott.
— *Quarterly Reports of the Administrator General of the Finances,* Teheran, 1923-1928.
Press Dept. of the Ministry of the Interior, *The Development of National Banking in Turkey,* Ankara, 1938.

Question of the Frontier between Turkey and Iraq (Report submitted to the Council of the League of Nations by the Commission instituted by the Council Resolution of Sept. 30th, 1924), 1925.

Recueil des Actes Administratifs du Haut Commissariat de la République Française en Syrie et au Liban, Beirut.
Recueil des Firmans Impériaux Ottomans adressés aux valis et aux Khédives d'Egypte, 1597-1904, Le Caire, 1934.
Recueil de Statistiques de la Syrie et du Liban, 1944.
Réglement Organique de la Conference des Intérêts Communs, Beyrouth, 14.5.1930.
Report by Mr. Cave on the Financial Condition of Egypt, Parliamentary Papers, 1876, Vol. LXXXIII.
Report of the Financial Mission (Iraq), 1925.
Report on the Financial Condition of Turkey, by Mr. Foster and Lord Hobart, dated December 7, 1861, presented to both Houses of Parliament by Command of H.M., 1862.
Reports of Lord Hobart on *Turkish Finances,* London, 1863.
Reports of the Baghdad Railway Company.
Reports of H.M. Agent and Consul-General on the Finances, Administration and Condition of Egypt and the Sudan in 1905, H.M.S.O., London, 1906.
(The) Republican People's Party Programme, Ankara, May 1935.
Resmi Gazete, Ankara.

Salmon, Mr., *Modern History: or, The Present State of All Nations,* 3 Vols., London, 1744-5.
Senior, Nassau W., *A Journal kept in Turkey and Greece, in the autumn of 1857 and the beginning of 1858,* London, 1859.
— *Conversations and Journals in Egypt and Malta,* London, 1882.
Shuster, Morgan, *The Strangling of Persia,* New York, 1912.
Slade, A. (Muchaver Pacha), *Records of Travels in Turkey, Greece,* etc., London, 1854.
Smuts, General, *The League of Nations, A Practical Suggestion,* London, 1918.
(La) Société des Nations et les Mandats.
Special Report, *Progress of Iraq, 1920-31.*
(Van den) Steen de Jehay, *De la situation légale des Sujets Ottomans non-Musulmans,* Bruxelles, 1906.
Sublime Porte, *Budget 1863-64,* Constantinople, 1863, *Ditto.* 1875-76, Constantinople, 1875. *Ditto,* 1880-81, Constantinople, 1880.
Sümerbank, Ankara.

BIBLIOGRAPHY

T. C. İktisat Vekâleti, Sanayi Tetkik Heyeti, *2inci 5ylılık Sanayi Planı,* 1936.

The Proposed Imperial (Medjidieh) Ottoman Railway, its purposes and prospects (printed for private circulation only), 1857.

Tracts on Finance, *La Turquie et sa dette,* E. Dentu, Paris, 1881.

Tracts on Trade, Finance, etc., 1857-66, Printed at the office of the *Levant Herald,* Constantinople, 1862.

Treaties, & c. between Turkey and Foreign Powers, 1535-1855, compiled by the librarian and keeper of the papers, Foreign Office, London, 1855.

Treaty between the United Kingdom and Iraq and Turkey, regarding the settlement of the frontier between Turkey and Iraq, Angora, June 5th, 1926. Treaty Series No. 18 (1927), H.M.S.O., London, 1927.

Treaty of Peace with Turkey and other instruments, Treaty Series, No. 16 (1923), London.

Turkish Information Office, *Facts on Turkey,* New York.

(La) Turquie en chiffres, Ankara, 1937.

Türkiye İş Bankasının bu Yılı 1924-34.

Türkiye Ziraat Bankası, *Nizamnamei Esası,* 1929.

Türkofis, *L'Industrie Minière de la Turquie,* Istanbul, 1935.

Ubicini, M. A., *Letters on Turkey,* London, 1856.

U.N., *Economic Developments in the Middle East, 1945-1954,* New York, 1955.

— *Final Report of the U.N. Survey Mission for the Middle East,* Lake Success, 1949.
— *Monthly Bulletins of Statistics.*
— *Public Finance Information Papers-Iran,* N.Y., 1951.
— *Reviews of Economic Conditions in the M.E.* (Yearly).
— *Terms of Legue of Nations Mandates,* New York, Oct. 1946.
— *The Development of Manufacturing Industry in Egypt, Israel and Turkey,* N.Y. 1958.

U.S. Department of State, *Foreign Relations of the U.S.,* Washington (1914 papers).

— *67th Congress, 1st Session, Senate, Doc. No. 34.*
— *84th Congress, House of Representatives, Committee on the Judiciary Subcommittee No. 5,* part. 2.

Van Dyck, Ed. A., *The Capitulations,* in the *Executive Documents, Senate of the U.S.,* Vol. 3, N. 3, 1881.

Verhaeghe, Leon, *Recueil des Rapports des Secrétaires de Légation de Belgique,* Bruxelles, 1872.

Young, George (ed.), *Corps de Droit Ottoman, Recueil des Codes, Lois, Règlements, Ordonnances, et Actes les plus importants du Droit Intérieur, et d'Etudes sur le Droit Coutumier de l'Empire Ottoman,* 7 vols., Oxford, 1905-6.

Zolltariffgesetz und Zolltariff der Türkischen Republik, Konstantinopel, 1929.

II. Journals and Periodicals

Asian and African Studies, Jerusalem.
Aussenwirtschaft, Bern.
(The) Baghdad Times, Baghdad.
(Le) Commerce du Levant, Beyrouth.
(The) Contemporary Review, London.
Current Discussion, New York.
Davar, Tel-Aviv.
Deutsche Vierteljahrsschrift, Stuttgart and Tübingen.
(The) Economic History Review, Cambridge.
(The) Economist, London.
L'Economiste d'Orient, Istanbul.
L'Egypte Contemporaine, Le Caire.

El-Ahali, Baghdad.
El-Istikal, Baghdad.
El-Iraq, Baghdad.
Falastin, Jaffa.
Foreign Agriculture, Washington.
Great Britain and the East, London.
Haaretz, Tel Aviv.
Handelsblatt des Berliner Tageblatts, Berlin.
International Journal of Middle East Studies, Combridge Univ. Press.
(The) Iraq Times, Baghdad.
(Der) Islam, Strassburg.
Kadro, Istanbul.
Journal Asiatique, Paris.
Journal de Constantinople, Istanbul.
Journal of the Royal Central Asian Society, London.
Middle East Economic Digest, London.
(The) Middle East Journal, Washington.
Middle Eastern Studies, London.
Milliyet, Istanbul.
(Der) Nahe Osten, Istanbul.
Near East and India, London.
(The) New York Times Current History Magazine, New York.
L'Orient, Beyrouth.
Oriente Moderno, Roma.
Palestine Post, Jerusalem.
Petroleum Times, London.
Progress, London.
Revue de la Faculté des Sciences Economiques de l'Université d'Istanbul, Istanbul.
Revue Economique et Financière, Cairo.
Studia Islamica, Paris.
The Times, London.
The Times of Mesopotamia, Baghdad.
Türk Ekonomisi, Ankara.
Türkische Post, Istanbul.

III. Articles and General Works

Abramowitz, Z., Gelfat, I., *The Arab Economy in Palestine and the Middle East* (Hebrew), Tel-Aviv, 1944.
Académie Diplomatique Internationale, *Dictionnaire Diplomatique,* Paris.
d'Allemagne, H. R., *Les Saint-Simoniens, 1827-1837,* Paris, 1930.
Ananich, B.V., "Russia and the d'Arcy Concession" (in Russian), reproduced in Ch. Issawi (ed.), *The Economic History of Iran 1800-1914.*
Anhegger, Robert, *Beiträge zur Geschichte des Bergbaus im Osmanischen Reich,* 2 Bände und Nachtrag, Istanbul, 1943-5.
Aubin, Eugène, *La Perse d'aujourd'hui,* Paris, Librairie Armand Colin, 1908.
Ayalon, David, *Gumpowder and Firearms in the Mamluk Kingdom,* Vallentine, Mitchell, London, 1956.
— *L'Esclavage du Mamelouk,* Oriental Notes and Studies, Jerusalem, 1951.
Ayni, H. T., *Borsa Rehberi,* Istanbul, 1928.

Baer, G., *A History of Landownership in Modern Egypt, 1800-1950,* Oxford University Press, London, 1966.
— *Egyptian Guilds in Modern Times,* The Israel Oriental Society, Jerusalem, 1964.
— *Introduction to the History of Agrarian Relations in the Middle East* (Hebrew), Jerusalem.

— "The Structure of Turkish Guilds and its Significance for Ottoman Social History", *in Proceedings of the Israel Academy of Sciences and Humanities,* IV, 10, Jerusalem.
Banco di Roma, *Iraq,* 1938.
Barkan, Ö. L., "La Loi sur la distribution des terres aux agriculteurs et les problèmes essentiels d'une réforme agraire en Turquie", *R.F.S.E. de l'Université d' Istanbul,* oct. 1944-jan. 1945.
Becker, C. H., "Steuerpacht und Lehnswesen", *Der Islam,* V. Strassburg.
Belin, M., "Essai sur l'histoire économique de la Turquie, d'après les écrivains originaux", *Journal Asiatique,* mai-juin 1864, août-sept. 1864, oct.-nov. 1864, déc. 1864.
— "Etude sur la Propriété Foncière en pays musulmans et spécialement en Turquie", *Journal Asiatique,* oct.-nov. 1861, fév.-mars 1862, avril-mai 1862.
— "Du Régime des fiefs militaires dans l'Islamisme", *Journal Asiatique,* mars-avril 1870.
Beloff, Max, *The Foreign Policy of Soviet Russia, 1929-1941,* Oxford University Press, 1949.
Birge, J. K., *A Guide to Turkish Area Study,* Washington, 1949.
Blaisdell, D. C., *European Financial Control in the Ottoman Empire,* Columbia University Press, 1929.
Bonné, Alfred, *State and Economics in the Middle East,* London, 1948.
Bourgeois, Albert, *La Formation de l'Egypte Moderne,* Paris, 1939.
Braudel, Fernand, *La Méditerannée et le Monde Méditerranéen a l'époque de Philippe II,* Librairie Armand Colin, Paris, 1949.
Brockelmann, Carl, *History of the Islamic Peoples,* translated by J. Carmichael and M. Perlman, Routledge & Kegan Paul, London, 1949.
Buell, Raymond Leslie, "Oil Interests in the Fight for Mosul", *The New York Times Current History,* XVII, No. 6, March 1923.

Centre d'Etudes de Politique Etrangère, Collection du Monde Islamique, Tome I, *L'Egypte Indépendante,* par le groupe d'études de l'Islam, Paris, 1938.
Chirol, Valentine, *The Egyptian Problem,* Macmillan & Co., London, 1920.
— *The Middle Eastern Question or Some Political Problems of Indian Defence,* London, 1903.
Clark, Colin, *The Conditions of Economic Progress,* Macmillan & Co., London, 1951.
Cleland, W., *The Population Problem in Egypt,* 1936.
Clerget, M., *Le Caire,* 1934.
Cook, M. A. (ed.), *Studies in the Economic History of the Middle East,* from the rise of Islam to the present day, Oxford University Press, London, 1970.
Crabités, Pierre, *Ismail, the Maligned Khedive,* London, 1933.
Creasy, Edward S., *History of the Ottoman Empire,* 1878.
(La) Crise Financière Ottomane devant les Capitulations, August Ghio, Ed., Paris, 1876.
Crouchely, A. E., "A Century of Economic Development, 1837-1937", *L'Egypte Contemporaine,* Le Caire, 1939.
— *The Economic Development of Modern Egypt,* London, 1938.
— *The Investment of Foreign Capital in Egyptian Companies and the Public Debt,* Cairo, 1936.
Curzon, G. N., *Persia and the Persian Question,* London, 1892.

Deeb, M., "Bank Misr and the Emergence of Local Bourgeoisie in Egypt", *Middle Eastern Studies,* Vol. 12, No. 3, October 1976.
Dicey, Edward, *England and Egypt,* Chapman & Hall, London, 1881.
— "The Future of Egypt", in *Current Discussion,* Vol. I, New York, 1878.
Dikmen, M. O., "Entwicklung der türkischen Umsatzsteuer", *R.F.S.E. de l'Université d'Istanbul,* oct. 1943.
Dodwell, Henry, *The Founder of Modern Egypt.* A Study of Muhammad 'Ali, Cambridge, at The University Press, 1931.
Dominian, Leon, *The Frontiers of Language and Nationality in Europe,* published for the American Geographical Society of New York, London & New York, 1917.
Douin, G., *Histoire du Règne du Khédive Ismail,* Société Royale de Géographie d'Egypte, 3 Tomes, Rome and Cairo, 1933-36.
— *L'attaque du Canal de Suez (3 Février 1915),* Paris, 1922.
Du Velay, A., *Essai sur l'Histoire Financière de la Turquie,* Paris, 1903.

Earle, E. M., *Turkey, The Great Powers and the Baghdad Railway,* London, 1923.
(The) Eastern Question Association, *Papers on the Eastern Question,* London, 1877.
Edib, Halidé, *Memoirs of Halidé Edib,* J. Murray, London, 1926.
— *The Turkish Ordeal,* John Murray, London, 1928.
— *Turkey Faces West,* New Haven, Yale University Press, 1930.
Elwell-Sutton, L. P., *Modern Iran,* George Routledge & Sons, London, 1941.
Encyclopaedia of the Social Sciences.
Encyclopaedia of Islam (also *Enzyklopaedie des Islams*).
Engelhart, E., *La Turquie et le Tanzimat,* Paris, 1884.
Erginay, A., *Le Budget Turc,* Genève, 1948.

Fahmy, M., *La Révolution de l'Industrie en Egypte et ses Conséquences Sociales au 19e Siècle (1800-1850),* E. J. Brill, Leiden, 1954.
Fatemi, Nasrollah Saifpour, *Oil Diplomacy,* Powderkeg in Iran, Whittier Books Inc. New York, 1954.
Fitzgerald, Percy, *The Great Canal at Suez,* 2 vols., London, 1876.
Fry, Richard N., *Iran,* Allen and Unwin, London, 1954.

Gibb, H. A. R., *Modern Trends in Islam,* The University of Chicago Press, Second Impression, 1950.
Gibb, H. A. R., and Bowen, H., *Islamic Society and the West,* R.I.I.A., Oxford University Press, Vol. I, Parts I & II, 1950-57.
Gilbar, G.G., "Demographic developments in late Qajar Persia, 1870-1906", reprint from *Asian and African Studies,* Vol. 11, No. 2-1976, Jerusalem Academic Press, 1977.
— "The big merchants (tujjar) and the Persian constitutional revolution of 1906", *Asian and African Studies,* Vol. 11, No. 3, Jerusalem, 1977.
Goblot, Henri, "Le problème de l'eau en Iran", *Orient,* 1962, reproduced in Ch. Issawi (ed.), *The Economic History of Iran 1800-1914.*
Graves, P. P., *Briton and Turk,* Hutchinson & Co., London, 1941.
(el-) Gritly, Ali, *History of Industry in Egypt* (Arabic), Cairo, 1952.
Groseclose, Elgin, *Introduction to Iran,* Oxford University Press, New York, 1947.
Grunwald, K., "The Industrialisation of Persia", *The New East* (Hebrew), Vol. VIII, No. 2 (30), 1957.
— *Türkenhirsch,* A Study of Baron Maurice de Hirsch, Entrepreneur and Philantropist, Jerusalem, 1966.
Gupta, R. N., *Iran, An Economic Study,* The Indian Institute of International Affairs, New Delhi, 1947.

Hagemeister, Jules de, *Essai sur les Ressources Territoriales et Commerciales de l' Asie Occidentale,* St. Petersbourg, 1839.
(von) Hammer, Joseph, *Geschichte des Osmanischen Reiches,* Pesth, 1834.
Hanotaux, Gabriel, *Histoire de la Nation Egyptienne,* Paris, 1931.
Hartmann, Martin, *Der Islamische Orient,* 3 Bände, Berlin-Leipzig, 1899-1910.
Heaton, H., *Economic History of Europe,* Harper & Brothers, New York, 1948.
Heffening, Willi, *Das islamische Fremdenrecht bis zu den islamisch-fränkischen Staatsverträgen,* Hannover, 1925.
Helfferich, Karl, *Die Deutsche Türkenpolitik,* Berlin, 1921.
Henderson, W. O., *The Lancashire Cotton Famine, 1861-1865,* Manchester University Press, 1934.
Hershlag, Z.Y., *The Economic Structure of the Middle East,* Brill, Leiden, 1975.
— *Turkey, An Economy in Transition,* Van Keulen, The Hague, 1959.
— *Turkey, The Challenge of Growth,* Brill, Leiden, 1968.
Heyd, Uriel, *Foundations of Turkish Nationalism,* Luzac & Harvill, London, 1950.
Himadeh, S. B., *Monetary and Banking System of Syria,* Beirut, 1935.
Himadeh, S., *The Economic Regime of Iraq(in Arabic), American University of Beirut, 1938.*
(al-) Hitta, Ahmad Ahmad, *The Economic History of Egypt in the 19th Century* (Arabic), Cairo, 1957.
Hitti, P. K., *History of the Arabs,* London, 1951.
— *Lebanon in History,* London, 1957.
Hourani, A. H., *Syria and Lebanon,* 1946.

I.B.R.D., *The Economic Development of Iraq,* Baltimore, 1952.
— *The Economic Development of Syria,* Baltimore, 1955.
Institut National de la Statistique et des Etudes Economiques, *Memento Economique, l'Egypte,* Presses Universitaires de France, 1950.
Ireland, P., *Iraq,* London, 1937.
Issawi, Ch., *Egypt, An Economic and Social Analysis,* Oxford University Press, 1947.
— (ed.)*The Economic History of Iran 1800-1914,* The University of Chicago Press, 1971.
— (ed.) *The Economic History of the Middle East 1800-1914,* A Book of Readings, The University of Chicago Press, 1966.
Izeddin, Nejla, *The Arab World, Past, Present and Future,* Chicago, 1953.

Jäschke, Gotthard, *Die Türkei in den Jahren 1935-41,* Leipzig, 1943.
Jewish Agency, *Middle East Handbook,* Jerusalem, 1945.
Juynboll, Th. H., "Kharadj", *The Encyclopedia of Islam.*

Kaveh, Taghi, *Einfluss der Iranischen Ölindustrie auf die wirtschaftliche Entwicklung des Iran* (doctoral thesis, mimeogr.), Nürnberg 1957.
Keynes, J. M., *The End of Laissez Faire,* at the Hogarth Press, 1926.
Khadduri, M., *War and Peace in the Law of Islam,* Baltimore, 1955.
Khadduri, M., and Liebesny H. J. (ed.), *Law in the Middle East,* The M.E. Institute, Washington, D.C., 1955.
Kingsbury, J. B. and Aktan, Tahir, *The Public Service in Turkey, Organization, Recruitment and Training,* Brussels, 1955.
Kirk, George, *A Short History of the Middle East,* London, 1955.
Konikoff, A., *Transjordan, An Economic Survey,* Jerusalem, 1943.
Kotb, Sayed, *Social Justice in Islam,* Translated from the Arabic by John B. Hardie, Washington, 1953.
Kramers, J. H., "Tanzimat", *The Encyclopedia of Islam,* Vol. IV.
Kutay, Cemal, *Celâl Bayar,* III, 1937; IV, 1938.

Ladas, S. P., *The Exchange of Minorities: Bulgaria, Greece and Turkey,* New York, 1932.
Lafont, F. et Rabino, H.-L., *L'Industrie Séricicole en Perse,* Montpellier, 1910.
Lahitah, Muhammad Fahmi, *The Economic History of Egypt in Modern Times* (Arabic), Cairo, 1944.
Lambton, Ann K. S., *Landlord and Peasant in Persia,* Oxford University Press, London, 1953.
Lammens, H. S. J., *La Syrie,* Beirut, 1921.
Landes, David S., *Bankers and Pashas,* Heinemann, London, 1958.
Lenczowski, G., *Russia and the West in Iran, 1918-1948,* New York, 1949.
Lesage, C., *L'achat des actions de Suez,* Paris, 1906.
Lewis, Bernard, ,,Some Reflections on the Decline of the Ottoman Empire", *Studia Islamica,* Larose-Paris, 1958, IX, pp. 111-127.
— *The Arabs in History,* London, 1950.
— *The Emergence of Modern Turkey,* Oxford University Press, London, 1961 & 1968.
— "The Islamic Guilds", *The Economic History Review,* Vol. VIII, Nov. 1937.
— *Turkey To-Day,* Hutchinson & Co., London and Melbourne.
Lockhart, "The Emergence of the Anglo-Persian Oil Company, 1901-14", reproduced in Ch. Issawi (ed.), *The Economic History of Iran 1800-1914.*
Longrigg, H.L., *Four Centuries of Modern Iraq,* Oxford, at Clarendon Press, 1925.
— *Iraq, 1900 to 1950,* A Political, Social and Economic History, Oxford University Press, Third Impression, 1968.
Løkkegaard, J., *Islamic Taxation in the Islamic Period,* Copenhagen, 1950.
Lybyer, A. H., *The Government of the Ottoman Empire in the Time of Suleiman the Magnificent,* Harvard Economic Studies, Vol. XVIII, Cambridge, Mass., 1913.
Lynch, H. F. B., *The Importance of Persia,* A Lecture to the Persia Society, June 14th, 1912, London.

Mabro, Robert, *The Egyptian Economy 1952-1972,* Clarendon Press, Oxford, 1974.
Mabro, Robert and Radwan, Samir, *The Industrialization of Egypt 1939-1973,* Clarendon Press, Oxford, 1976.

Mackie, J. B., "Turkish Industrialisation", *R.C.A.J.,* July 1939.
McCarthy, Justin M., "Nineteenth-Century Egyptian Population", *Middle Eastern Studies, Special Issue, The Middle Eastern Economiy, Vol. 12, No. 3, October 1976.*
McCoan, J. C., *Egypt As It Is,* Cassel, Petter & Galpin, London, 1877.
— *Egypt under Ismail,* Chapman and Hall, London, 1889.
Main, E., *Iraq,* Allen & Unwin, London, 1935.
— "Water Supplies of Iraq", *J.R.C.A.S.,* April 1933.
Malcolm, John, *History of Persia* (Modern), edited and adapted by M. H. Court, Lahore, 1888.
Marlowe, John, *Anglo-Egyptian Relations, 1800-1953,* The Cresset Press, London, 1954.
Maunier, Réné, *Bibliographie économique, juridique et sociale de l'Egypte Moderne* (1798-1916), Le Caire, 1918.
Mazuel, Jean, *L'Oeuvre Géographique de Linant de Bellefonds,* Le Caire, 1937.
Mears, E. G. (ed.) *Modern Turkey,* New York, 1924.
Menemencioğlu, Nermin, "The Progress of Turkey", *Progress,* Winter, 1950/51, London.
Middle East, Europa Publications, 1950.
Miller, William, *The Ottoman Empire and its Successors, 1801-1927,* Cambridge University Press, 1934 edition.
Mitrani, David, "Land Tenure", *Encyclopaedia of the Social Sciences,* Vol. 9.
Moazzami, Abdollah, *Essai sur la Condition des Etrangers en Iran,* Librairie du Recueil Sirey, Paris, 1937.
Mommsen, Theodor, *Gesammelte Schriften,* Weidmann, Berlin, 1905-10.
Morawitz, Ch., *Les Finances de la Turquie,* Paris, 1902.
Morley, John, *The Life of Richard Cobden,* London, 1905.
Moustafa Khan Fateh, *The Economic Position of Persia,* P. S. King & Son, London, 1926.
Mukdim, O., *Handicrafts in Turkey,* Geneva, 1955.
Mulhall, M. G., "Egyptian Finance", *The Contemporary Review,* London, Oct. 1882.

Nahas, J. F., *Situation Economique du Fellah Egyptien,* Paris, 1901.
Neumark, F., "Betrachtungen zur Türkischen Aussenhandels und Währungspolitik", *Aussenwirtschaft,* Bern, März 1947.

Owen, E.R.J., *Cotton and the Egyptian Economy 1820-1914,* Oxford, 1969.
O'Zoux, Raymond, *Les Etats du Levant sous Mandat Français,* Larose-Paris, 1931.

Pélissié du Rausas, G., *Le Régime des Capitulations dans l'Empire Ottoman,* Arthur Rousseau, Paris, 1902 (2 vols., 4 parts).
Poliak, A. N., *Feudalism in Egypt, Syria, Palestine, and the Lebanon, 1250-1900,* Royal Asiatic Society of Great Britain and Ireland, 1939.
Pomiankowski, Joseph, *Der Zusammenbruch des Ottomanischen Reiches,* Amalthea Verlag, Wien, 1928.
Pouthas, Ch. H., *Histoire de l'Egypte depuis la conquète Ottomane,* Librairie Hachette, 1948.
Pressel, Wilhelm von, *Les Chemins de Fer en Turquie d' Asie,* Zurich, 1902.

Rabino di Borgomale, H. L., *Coins, Medals, and Seals of the Shâks of Iran (1500-1941),* 1945.
Ramsaur, Ernest Edmondson, *The Young Turks,* Prelude to the Revolution of 1908, Princeton University Press, 1957.
Rifaat Bey, *The Awakening of Modern Egypt,* Longmans, London, 1947.
Rifaat M. A., *The Monetary System of Egypt,* London, 1935.
Robertson, H. M., *Aspects of Rise of Economic Individualism,* Cambridge University Press, 1933.
Rohrbach, Paul, *Die Bagdadbahn,* Berlin, 1902.
— *Die Wirtschaftliche Bedeutung Westasiens,* Zweite Auflage, Frankfurt a.M., 1908.
Ross, Sir E. Denison, "The Making of Modern Turkey", *Journal of Royal Central Asian Society,* April 1937.
Rothstein, T., *Egypt's Ruin, A Financial and Administrative Record,* London, 1910.
Roux, J. C., *L'Isthme et le Canal de Suez,* Paris, 1901.
Ruppin, Arthur, *Syrien als Wirtschaftsgebiet,* Zweite, durchgesehene Auflage, Berlin/Wien, 1920.

Sabry, M., *La Révolution Egyptienne,* Librarie J. Vrin, Paris, 1919.
— *L'Egypte, Telle Qu'elle Est,* Gand, Imprimerie V. van Doosselacre, 1905.
— *L'Empire Egyptien sous Mohamed-Ali et la Question d'Orient (1811-1849),* Paris, Librairie Orientaliste Paul Geuthner, 1930.
— *L'Empire Egyptien sous Ismail et l'Ingérence Anglo-Française (1863-1879),* Paris, Librarie Orientaliste Paul Geuthner, 1933.
Sarc, Ö. C., "The Demand for Sugar in Turkey", *R.F.S.E.,* Istanbul, avr.-juill. 1944.
— "Economic Policy of The New Turkey", *The Middle East Journal,* Washington, October 1948.
— "Tanzimat ve Sanayimiz" ("The Tanzimat and Our Industry"), reproduced in Ch. Issawi (ed.), *The Economic History of the M.E. 1800-1914,* 1966, pp. 48-59.
Schumpeter, Joseph, *The Theory of Economic Development,* Harvard University Press, 1949.
Shotwell, J. T., and Deak, F., *Turkey at the Straits,* Macmillan, New York, 1940.
Stafford, R. S. H., *The Tragedy of the Assyrians,* G. Allen & Unwin, London, 1935.
Stamp, L. Dudley, *Asia,* Methuen, London, 1950.
Stratford de Redcliffe, *Turkey,* reprint from *The Nineteenth Century,* June and July 1877, in *Current Discussion,* Vol. I, New York, 1878.
Sykes, Percy, *History of Persia,* 1951 edition.

Tadros, Fawzi, *La souveraineté Egyptienne et la Déclaration du 28 février 1922,* Paris, Pedone, 1934.
Tawney, R. H., *Religion and the Rise of Capitalism,* New York, 1947.
Tekin Alp (M. Cohen), *Türkismus and Pantürkismus,* Weimar, 1915.
The Life of the late General F. R. Chesney, by His Wife and Daughter, London, 1885.
Tignor, Robert L., "Bank Misr and Foreign Capitalism", *International Journal of Middle East Studies,* Vol. 8, No. 2, Cambridge University Press, 1977.
— "The Egyptian Revolution of 1919: New Directions in the Egyptian Economy", *Middle Eastern Studies,* Vol. 12, No. 3, October 1976.
Tismer, Alfred, *Die Persische Währungsreform,* Teheran, August 1932 (mineographed).
Topf, E., *Die Staatenbildung in den Arabischen Teilen der Türkei seit dem Weltkriege nach Entstehung, Bedeutung und Lebensfähigkeit,* Hamburg, 1929.
Turner, G. D., *Lecture on main events, Oct. 1912-Oct. 1913,* to Persia Society, London, Oct. 1913.

Urguhart, David, *The Military Strength of Turkey,* London, 1869.
— *Turkey and Its Resources,* London, 1833.

Vaucher, G., "La Livre égyptienne de sa création par Mohamed Aly à ses recentes modifications", *L'Egypte Contemporaine,* Tome XLIe, 1950.
Vitali, Salty, *Industriewirtschaft der modernen Türkei,* Verlag Konrad Triltsch, Würzburg, 1934.

Weulersse, Jacques, *Paysans de Syrie et du Proche-Orient,* Gallimard, 1946.
Wilber, D. N., *Iran, Past and Present,* New Jersey, 1958.
Willcocks, W., *Egypt Fifty Years Hence,* Cairo, 1902.
— *Sixty Years in the East,* Edinburgh and London, 1935.
— *The Irrigation of Mesopotamia,* New York, 1911.
— and Craig, J. I., *Egyptian Irrigation,* Third Edition, 2 vols., London, 1913.
Wilson, A. T., *Persia,* London, 1932.
Wittek, Paul, *The Rise of the Ottoman Empire,* London, 1938.
Woodhouse, Henry, "American Oil Claims in Turkey," *The New York Times Current History Magazine,* Vol. XV, New York, March 1922.
— "The Chester Concession as an Aid to New Turkey", *The New York Times Current History Magazine,* XVIII, New York, 1923.
Wurm, C. F., "Der Projectierte Canal von Suez", *Deutsche Vierteljahrsschrift,* Stuttgart und Tübingen, 1844.

INDEX

Abbas I 100, 103, 120
Abbas II 118, 124
Abdu, Muhammad 118, 165
Abdul Aziz 32, 36, 37, 55, 64
Abdul Hamid I 14n, 21
Abdul Hamid II 32, 36-38, 52, 56, 60, 68, 76
Abdullah, Emir of Transjordan 241
Abdullaev, Z. Z. 148n
Abdul Mejid 31, 32, 55n
Abou Yousof Ya'koub (Abū Yūsuf Ya'kūb bin Ibrahim) 13n, 23n, 34n, 42n
Abramowitz, Z. 268n
Absenteeism 17, 42, 82, 145, 170, 227
Abu Hanifa 34, 42n, 43n
Acre 82, 93n, 95
Adana 76
Aden 169
Administration, corruption of,
  see: Ottoman Empire, Persia
Adrianople 24n, 29
Afghanistan 154, 204
Aga Muhammad 157
Africa 8, 80, 97n, 111, 112, 165n, 289
Aga Muhammad 157
  see: Land reform
Agriculture 24n, 46n, 71, 73, 80, 89, 166, 175n, 281, 282
  banks and credit 49, 61, 71, 87, 123, 181, 182, 192, 198, 209, 210, 222, 229, 243, 254, 262, 263, 284
  cooperatives 198, 229
    see also: Cooperatives
  cropped area 86, 88, 123, 198, 226, 229
  cultivated area 72, 85, 86, 88, 100, 103, 113, 119, 123, 125, 127, 181, 182, 197, 198, 202, 226, 227, 229, 243, 246, 249, 263, 264, 265, 267, 268
  cultivation methods 69, 71, 85, 87, 125, 144, 145, 262, 265
  exports 29, 69, 71-73, 75n, 79, 127, 148, 197, 198, 213, 233, 246
  fertilisers' consumption 87, 128, 167, 229, 264, 267
  improvements 68, 69, 71, 88, 119, 181, 198, 243, 262, 282
  income 69, 86, 127, 198-202, 218, 227, 228, 288
  irrigated area 85, 266, 267
  monoculture 87, 127, 221, 233, 282
  monopolies 84, 87, 95, 100
    see also: Monopolies

natural disasters 185, 197
prices 29, 71, 79, 84, 86n, 89, 95, 123, 182, 186, 187, 197, 213, 229, 246, 266
  see also: Prices
production 71, 72, 73, 77, 86n, 87, 127, 246
schools 71n, 181, 248
size of farm unit 71, 84, 197, 227
soil quality 69, 72, 86n, 87, 119, 127, 141, 144, 209, 228, 246
structure of production 72, 86, 87, 145, 146, 228, 267
subsistence farming 73, 79
taxation
  see: Taxation, Peasants
yields 69, 72, 88, 96, 182n, 197, 198, 202, 209, 226, 228, 246, 247, 264
See also: Cotton, Dates, Grain, Irrigation, Land, Livestock, Peasants, Silk, Sugar, Tobacco, Wool, and under individual countries
Ahmed I 24
Ahmed Shah 160, 204n
Aitchison, C. U. 150n, 151n, 152n, 154n
Ajlun 241
Aktan, T. 189n
Alawi State 237, 238, 253, 259
Alay Bey 11
Albanians 25, 83
Aleppo 8n, 73, 77, 238, 259, 268
Alexandretta 26n, 94n, 253, 260, 268
Alexandria 8n, 77, 89, 91, 92n, 93, 94, 96n, 102, 114, 115, 117, 120, 129, 130, 184, 218, 220n, 232
  port 81, 90, 101n, 109
Ali Bey Ismail 108n
Ali Riza Pasha 35
Ali (Hussayn's son) 241
Al-Jabarti
  see: El Djabarti
Alp, T. (M. Cohen) 22n
Amiens, agreement of 82
Amn 13n
Amsterdam 154n, 184
Ananich, B. V. 153n
Anatolia 11, 20n, 30, 50, 53, 60, 72, 73, 74, 76, 77, 171, 173, 175n, 177, 195, 201
Anatolian Railway Company 50, 52, 71, 77
  see also: Baghdad railway
Anderson, A. 130n
André, L. E. A. 104
Anglo-Iranian Oil Company 154, 213, 214

Anglo-Iraqi Treaty 275, APPENDIX 29
Anglo-Persian Treaty APPENDIX 20
Anglo-Russian Treaty 1907 54, 154, APPENDIX 24
Anhegger, R. 49n, 74n
Ankara 50, 51n, 77, 178, 181
Antioch 263
Aqaba 241, 262
Arabi Pasha 117
Arabian Peninsula (Arabia) 11, 12, 60, 72, 129, 169, 261
Arabs 1, 12, 13n, 23-25, 30, 44, 82n, 129n, 151, 152n, 156, 165, 168, 239, 241
  attitude to Zionism 167
Aras (river) 150
Arbabi (land) 156
Ardahan 37
Armenians 9n, 19, 23, 48, 63, 147, 173, 184, 263
Armistice
  see: Mudania, Mudros
Army 24n, 29, 36, 83, 100, 117, 190, 203-205, 220
  exemption taxes *see*: *Bedel*
  expenditure on 12, 55, 56, 60, 64, 83, 97, 105, 106, 120, 125, 143, 158, 189, 192, 205, 206, 226, 252n, 253, 256, 259, 290
  military considerations in economic development 52, 83, 210
  service in 31, 32, 35, 37, 57n, 71, 83, 88, 91, 95, 100n, 115, 140, 165, 181, 205, 221
  Westernization of 29, 68
  see also: Military industry
Asnaf 19
Asia 10n, 51, 77, 150, 289
Assyrians 23, 239
Aswan 232
  dam 119, 123, 227, 229
Atatürk, Kemal 14, 31n, 38, 48, 70, 172, 173, 184, 188, 190, 191, 204
Atf 93
Atrek river 150
Aubin, E. 156n, 159n
Austria-Hungary 92, 93n, 108, 132, 136
  and Ottoman Empire 45, 47, 48, 50, 62n, 66, 68, 69, 70, 78, 80, 117n, 165, 238
Avarisi (tax) 15n
Aviation
  see: Communication and transport
Ayalon, D. 81n
Aydın 50, 51, 76, 78
Ayni, Ali 55n
Ayni, H. T. 176n
Azerbaijan 152, 156, 161
Aziziyeh el-Misriyeh 101
  see also: Mejidiyeh

Bab 157, 158
Backwardness, causes of 1, 3, 17, 21, 24, 71, 141, 144, 166, 289
Baer, G. 16n, 82n, 84n, 92n
Baghdad 8n, 35, 50, 77, 152, 184, 245, 249, 257, 260, 270, 272
  railway 50, 51, 54, 68, 77, 175n, 259, 260, 286, APPENDIX 13
Baha Allah 157
Bahais 157
Baker, S. 112
Bakhtiari 155, 156
Balance of payments
  see: External trade, and under individual countries
Balance of trade
  see: External trade, and under individual countries
Balfour, Lord 168n
Balkans 37, 76
  wars 26n, 39, 53, 79
Balta-Liman Convention 99n, APPENDIX 7
Baluchis 156
Banco di Roma 254, 261n
Bandrole system 252, 269
Banking (and banks) 20, 22, 24, 32, 49, 52n, 55, 60, 61, 63, 64, 65, 69, 104, 196, 287
  Bank of England 254
  Central bank 70, 124, 125, 193, 194, 212, 223, 250, 251, 255
  Deutsche Bank 49, 50, 51n, 52, 68, 77
  Imperial Bank of Persia 141, 144n, 147, 152, 161, 206, 208, 254
  National Bank of Egypt 125, 137, 223
  Ottoman Bank 49, 50, 54, 60, 64n, 66, 70, 193, 250, 254
  see also under individual countries
Baring, E.
  see: Cromer
Barkan, Ö. L. 180n, 191n, 197n
Bashiktash 74
Basra 245, 260, 261, 272
Bast 19n, 157, 158, 159
Batum 37
Bayazıt 77
Beaulieu, M. L. 243n
Becker, C. H. 11n
Bedel 13, 32, 57n
Beduin
  see: Nomads
Beirut 77, 184, 242, 245, 254, 259, 260
Belgium 25n, 26n, 47, 141, 142n, 145, 147n, 152, 155, 160n, 161, 211, 220n
Belin, M. 9n, 11n, 12n, 14, 15n, 16n, 19n, 32n, 40n, 41n, 43n, 46n, 55n, 56n, 61n
Belka 241

INDEX

Beloff, M. 188n
Bender Abbas 154
Bender Rig 153n
Bender Shah 210
Bender Shahpur 210
Berlin 50, 154n
  Congress & Treaty of 2, 37, 65, 66, 67
Beyler Bey 11
Bie Ravndal, G. 46n, 52n
Bilkur, Ş. 200n
Birge, J. K. 194n
Birjand 154
Bismarck 110
Black Sea 79
Blaisdell, D. C. 52n, 59n, 64n, 66n, 69n, 72n
Bombay 94n, 138
Bonné, A. 167n, 266n, 277n
Bosnia 9n, 30, 64
Bosphorus 74, 77, 110n, 130
Bourdillon, B. H. 237
Bourgeois, A. 44n, 220n
Bowen, H. 9n, 13n, 15n, 18n, 19n, 41n
Bowring, J. 20n, 86n, 87n, 90, 92n, 94n, 95n, 97, 99n
Braudel, F. 1, 8n, 46n
Britain 101, 169, 200
  and Africa 112, 121
  and Egypt 82, 83, 89, 92, 93, 101, 103, 106-110, 116, 117, 120-125, 136, 220n, 223
  and Iraq 35, 169, 176, 177, 245, 247, 257, 260, 261, 272, 275
  and Ottoman Empire 37, 46, 52n, 54, 56, 64-70, 73, 76, 78, 81, 136, 165, APPENDIX 6, 11
  and Persia 143-162, 203, 207, 210, 217, APPENDIX 20
  and Suez Canal 51, 76n, 93, 106, 107, 111n, 123, 130-137, 220
  and Syria & Lebanon 238, 274
  and Transjordan 241, 271, 277
  and Turkey 173, 175-177, 189n, 195n
  army expenditure 120, 221n, 235
  capitulations 45-47, 151
  concessions 50, 151-152
  economic aid 7, 150, 158, 161, 170, 177, 180, 181, 183, 202, 273, 274
  investments & loans 49, 60, 62-65, 68, 76, 104, 105, 123, 153, 184n, 193
  road to India 51, 76, 83, 93, 101n, 131, 168,
    see also: Egypt
  trade 46, 72, 79, 80, 93
Brockelmann, C. 8n
Brusa 24n, 72
Buchanan, F. 160n
Budgets 22, 26, 53, 55-57, 65, 124, 165
  reforms 37, 56, 58, 66n, 68, 99, 144n

  revenue & expenditure 8, 13, 14, 16, 32, 33, 36, 42, 52, 55-60, 63-67, 78, 83, 95, 97-99, 100, 102, 106-110, 113, 119n, 121, 128, 143, 160, 169, 176, 179, 192, 193, 205-208, 210, 212, 214, 215, 222, 224-226, 242, 252, 253, 255-259
  see also: Army, Taxation, and under individual countries
Buell, R. L. 177n
Bulak 87, 89, 90, 92n
Bulgaria (and Bulgarians) 9n, 23, 48, 65, 177, 178
Burma Oil Company 154
Bushir 152
Butros-Pasha Ghali 122
Byzantine 1, 7, 13n, 20n, 25, 44

Cabotage
  see: Communications and transport
Cairo 19n, 20n, 24n, 73, 82n, 83, 89, 91, 93, 114, 115, 118, 218, 220n, 232
Caisse de la Dette Publique 104, 108, 109, 117, 120, 121, 126, 129, 135, 226, 286, APPENDIX 16
Caliph (Khalif) 23-25, 83n, 172, 173, 179
Canada 175n
Canals
  see: Communications, Irrigation
Cape of Good Hope 8, 73, 94, 138
Capital 52, 60n, 71, 75, 83, 86n, 96, 100n, 104n, 106, 124, 147, 166, 170, 179, 181, 184, 186, 189, 191, 198, 209, 213, 216, 230, 234, 242, 243, 254, 263, 269
  accumulation 3, 7, 20, 63, 149
  consumption 7
  foreign 7, 29, 49, 51-53, 66, 69, 74, 88, 99, 101, 104n, 111, 113, 174-176, 179, 184n, 186, 189, 211, 217, 221, 233, 247, 249, 259, 281, 285, 286, 289
  see also: Investment, Debt, Concessions
  internal 96, 101, 192, 202, 217, 231, 286
  supply of 3, 104, 215, 231
  see also: Investment
Capitalism 27n, 90, 221n, 280, 283, 289
Capitulations 26, 33n, 38, 39, 43-46, 48, 49, 52n, 59, 65, 73, 78, 97n, 99n, 142, 150, 151, 169, 281, 282, 289, APPENDIX 3, 4
  see also under individual countries
  capitulatory courts *see*: Jurisdiction
  outside the M.E. 43
  restrictions, evasion and abolition 48, 168, 169, 172, 175, 203, 211, 214, 220, 221, 222, 234, 245, APPENDIX 14
Carolingian Empire 8
Carlowitz, treaty of 8

Carpet industry 73, 75, 147, 148, 212, 213
Caspian Fisheries Company 211, 213, APPENDIX 32
Caspian Sea 144, 152, 203, 210, 211
Cassel, Ernst 223
Caucasus 37, 150
Caussin de Perceval, A. P. 10n
Cave Commission 106n, 107, 108, 111n, 112n
Çelebi, E. 20n
Cement industry 185, 195, 212, 268, 270, 271
Çernavoda 76
Cevdet Pasha 34
"Challenge and response" approach 279, 280
Chardin, J. 140n, 144n, 156n
Charles V 45
Chemical industry 194
Chesney, F. R. 76, 93n, 94n, 130, 131, 147n
Chester concession 53, 175, 176n, APPENDIX 31
China 72, 115n, 146, 148, 204, 212
Chirol, V. 83n, 93n, 100n, 119n, 124n, 142, 143n, 145n, 147n, 153n, 157n, 161n, 221n
Christians 13n, 14, 20, 25, 26, 33n, 37, 45, 151, 168, 238
  persecution of 2, 48, 168, 239
Çiftlik 12, 43, 84
Çirak (Mübtedi) 20
Circassian Mamluks 45
City 18-24, 42, 89, 146, 173, 177, 244, 280
  and village 18, 72, 124, 155, 156, 171, 218, 269
  characteristics 18, 170, 171, 282
  development and decline 18, 36, 96, 101, 171
  taxes, customs and duties 99, 192
Clark, C. 199n, 201n, 231, 283, 284n
Cleland, W. 116n, 218n, 227n
Clerget, M. 20n
Clician Vassif Effendi, A. 34n
Clot Bey, A. B. 86n, 89n, 90n, 91, 93n, 94n
Coal
  see: Mining
Cobden, R. 96n
Codification 25, 33, 34, 40, 179, 180, 204, 209
  see also: Law
Colbert, J. B. 45
Commercial policy
  see: Customs, External trade, and under individual countries
Communications and transport 22, 39, 49, 52, 71-73, 76, 79, 93, 101, 134, 138, 169, 184n, 259, 285
  aviation 210, 230
  cabotage 54, 175
  canals 77, 132n, 133, 232, see also: Suez Canal
  investment 51, 61, 76, 104, 111, 140, 246
  navigation 35, 36, 39, 45n, 47n, 50, 76n, 77, 92, 94, 137, 152, 170, 175, 230, 232, 233, 262

ports 19, 47, 49, 50, 54, 77-79, 83, 111, 133, 137, 138, 175n, 195, 203, 232, 235, 243, 245, 259-262
post, telegraph & telephone 31, 39, 77, 78, 100, 103, 109, 111, 121n, 128, 152, 159, 183, 205, 225, 245, 247, 253, 259
railway, see: Railways
roads and road transport 42, 77, 85, 93, 100n, 152, 203, 205, 209, 210, 226, 232, 233, 243, 245, 247-249, 259, 260, 261
see also: Concessions, Suez Canal, and under individual countries
Comparative advantage 73, 75, 128
Concessions 32, 38, 43n, 45, 47, 49, 50, 52, 53, 68, 259, 281, 285, 289
  abolition and expropriation 54, 64, 175n, 203, 214, 215
  banking 60, 61, 147, 152
  fishing 152, 211
  mining 57n, 74, 147, 152, 153, 175
  municipal services 184n
  oil 153, 154, 175, 211, 214, 215, 270, 271-273, APPENDIX 23
  transport and communication 51, 59, 64, 68, 69, 77, 103, 152, 159, 175, 206, 260
  see also: Caspian Fisheries Company, Railways, Suez Canal, Tobacco, and under individual countries
Constantinople 20n, 24, 46n, 60-62, 82, 177
  see also: Istanbul
Constantinople Agreement 37, 117n, 136
Constanza 76
Constitution
  in Egypt 219, 220
  in Iraq 240
  in Ottoman Empire 13, 36, 37n, 38
  in Persia 158
  in republican Turkey 179, 190
Consumption 4, 24, 39, 73, 90n, 146, 147, 167, 209, 219, 242, 247, 269, 273, 284, 290
Cooperatives 61, 181n, 201
  see also: Agriculture
Copts 90n, 122, 218
Cordier, M. 137
Corvée 88, 91, 95, 100, 101n, 114, 115, 119, 131-133, 140, 216, 221, 288
Cossack brigade 152n, 159n, 203
Cost of living
  see: Prices
Cotton 72, 73, 85, 86, 90, 91, 93, 96, 104, 105, 114, 124, 127, 146, 194, 211, 213, 216, 220, 222, 223, 228, 233, 234, 243, 264, 268-270, 275, 282
  exports 72, 87, 93, 101, 127, 148, 222, 225, 228, 232-234
  local consumption 222, 230
  output and yields 73, 87, 100, 127, 185, 264

prices 87, 99, 102, 105, 123, 125, 127, 221, 228, 233, 234
profitability 86, 228
role in the economy 72, 87, 88, 101, 102, 127, 248
Courthope-Munroe, C. H. 70n, 174n
Crabités, P. 101n, 105n, 111n, 112n, 113n, 132n, 133n, 135n
Craig, J. I. 86n
Crawford, R. F. 53
Creamer, D. 167n
Creasy, E. S. 10n, 28n, 30n
Credit 32, 49, 60, 61, 63, 64, 70, 102, 104, 107, 112, 119, 121, 149, 156, 166, 181, 223, 242, 248, 250, 251, 285
see also: Agriculture, Banking
Crimean War 54, 56, 60, 63
Cromer, Lord 96n, 108n, 109n, 110n, 112, 115n, 117, 118
  economic policy 119-122, 220, 224
Crouchley, A. E. 82n, 83n, 84n, 87n, 89n, 90, 91n, 92, 96n, 97n, 99n, 101n, 104n, 105, 106, 111n, 115n, 122n, 123n, 125n, 127n
Crusaders 45, 279
Cumberbatch, A. N. 220n
Cumberland, W. W. 59n, 175n
Currency 10, 55, 60, 124, 225, 248, 250
  amount in circulation 62, 125, 174, 193, 194, 208, 224, 250, 255, 258
  dearth of 17
  debasement 55, 61
  depreciation 8n, 29, 61, 62, 69n, 70n, 97, 136, 143, 147, 193, 197, 207, 212, 216, 221n, 225, 226, 253, 254
  foreign currency 62, 63, 96, 124, 207, 208, 212, 216, 224, 250
  gold reserves 70, 208, 223, 224, 251
  instability 60, 174, 193, 223
  issuance 49, 55, 60, 62, 70, 125, 152, 193, 206, 207, 208, 223, 250
  local currencies in circulation 61, 62, 87, 114n, 208, 212, 216, 247
  metallic base 55, 96, 124, 152
  paper currency 55, 61, 62, 70, 125, 144n
  reforms 61, 62, 96, 97, 124, 143n, 207, 208, 251
  see also under individual countries
Currency Boards 223n, 250, 254, 255, 258
Curzon, G. N. 142n, 143n, 144n, 146n, 147n, 151n, 155n, 158n, 168n
Customs 14, 15n, 35, 39, 45, 48, 53, 57n, 59, 62, 79n, 80, 93n, 108, 141, 142, 149, 151, 153, 155, 161, 167, 169, 175, 180, 189, 191, 194, 196, 206, 208, 210, 213, 221-224, 233, 234, 244, 253, 270, 276, 290

ad valorem 45, 48, 67, 143n, 151, 189n, 269
earmarked for debt service 67, 107-109, 143, 153
exemption from 51, 183, 269, 270n, 276, 277
protective 46, 47, 166, 194, 222, 228, 229, 252, 269, 275, 276
revenue from 47, 97, 121n, 141, 143, 192, 214, 222, 224, 252, 255, 256, 258
specific 45n, 48, 143n, 189n, 190, 269
union 273
Cyprus 37, 57n, 169
Cyrus 151

Daira 105, 108, 109
d'Allemagne, H. R. 132n
Damascus 24n, 73, 77, 184, 238, 259, 268
Damietta 85, 89, 232
d'Andrade, M. 242n
Danube 35, 50, 61
D'Arcy, W. K. 153, 154, 272
Dardanelles 30, 130, 168, 173
Darius 129, 140
Dates 35n, 246, 266, 267, 275, 276
Deak, F. 45n
De Blignières, M. 109
Debt, external 52, 56, 77, 96, 99, 100, 105-107
  conflict with creditors 103, 107, 110, 116, 119n, 120, 126
  growth or decrease of 55, 58, 100, 101, 104, 106, 110, 112, 113, 121, 193, 199
  liquidation of 110
  service of 105, 107-112, 120-122, 128, 135, 192, 235
  size of 101, 105, 106, 108, 109, 111, 121, 122, 162n, 192, 226
  see also: Caisse de la Dette Publique, Muharrem Decree, Ottoman Debt Administration, and under individual countries
Debt, internal 100, 189, 193
  see also: *Mukabele*
De Caix, M. R. 243n
Deeb, M. 221n
Defence expenditures
  see: Army
Defterdar 12n, 56n
De Lesseps, F. 104n, 109, 114, 131-134, 136, 137
De Martel, D. 243, 252
De Morgan, M. 153
Deniz Bank 193
Denmark 47, 181n, 220n
Deny, J. 83n, 106n
Depression 72, 99, 103, 105, 111, 123n, 128, 146, 147, 197, 220, 246, 269

the great depression 182, 186-188, 190, 193, 198, 200, 211, 214, 222, 224, 225, 227, 229, 233, 234, 242, 243, 247, 252, 253, 254, 257, 258, 264, 266, 274-276
Derby, Lord 135
Derebeys 15, 30
De Redcliffe, S. 57n, 62n, 92n
De Reuter, J. 152, 154, 206
Dervieu, E. 103, 104, 113, 135n
Deutsche Bank
  see: Banks
Dhimmis 13
Dicey, E. 106n, 110n, 114n, 117n, 125n
Dikmen, M. O. 180n
Disguised unemployment
  see: Unemployment
Disinvestment 107
  see also: Capital
Disraeli 135, 136
Diwani (land) 156
Dobbs, H. 240n
Dodwell, H. 81n, 83n, 92n
D'Ohsson, M. 9n, 14n, 24n, 25n, 34n, 42n
Dominian, L. 51n, 54n, 77n
Dönme 53
Douin, G. 83n, 87n, 89n, 90n, 96n, 99n, 101n, 102n, 105n, 112n, 113n, 124n, 136n
Dowson, E. 35n, 240n, 246, 255n, 256n, 265, 266n
Druse 25, 241
"Dual Control" 104, 108, 110, 117, 120
Duhamel, Colonel 90n
Du Velay, A. 38n, 50n, 66n

Earle, E. M. 51n, 52, 68n, 73n, 80n, 175n
Eastern Question Association 7n, 32n
East India Company 46
Economic aid
  see under individual countries
Economic development 1, 4, 22, 32, 52, 59, 60, 71, 94, 169, 170, 210, 211, 213-215, 237, 243, 244, 250, 255, 259, 262n, 282, 287, 289, 290
  see also under individual countries
Economic inequality 201, 222
Economic policy and leadership 29, 216, 236, 237, 241, 242, 251, 255
  see also under individual countries
Economic reform 25, 39, 165, 237
  see also under individual countries
Edib, Halidé 28n, 33n, 38n, 173n, 174n, 180n
Education 36, 172, 280
  expenditure on 33, 60, 100, 119
  foreign schools 52n, 60
  high 33, 37n, 94, 120

illiteracy 96, 120n, 218, 219
number of schools and pupils 33, 94, 112n, 120n, 248, 249
primary 33, 37, 94, 120
secondary 31, 33n
technical & vocational 33, 94, 204, 212, 214, 248
see also under individual countries
Egypt 20n, 24n, 44n, 63, 140, 159, 165, 217
  agriculture 72, 81, 84-87, 91, 95, 96, 99, 100, 111, 113, 123-128, 131n, 209n, 218, 221, 223, 226-229, 232-234, 267
  and Ottoman Empire 27, 29, 30, 36, 40, 45, 80, 81, 83, 92, 102, 103, 110, 113n, 115n, 116, 117, 122, 124, 131
  balance of payments 111, 122, 128, 221n, 235
  banking and credit 88n, 100-103, 107, 118, 124, 125, 223, 224
  British rule 27, 108, 110, 116-118, 120, 123, 126, 127, 128, 129, 219
  budget 82, 83, 95, 97-102, 105, 107, 108, 110, 113, 119-122, 128, 221-226
  capitulations 43, 47, 48, 92, 97n, 102, 103, 116, 149, 169, 220, 224, 234
  communication and transport 93, 94, 101-103, 111, 128, 130, 139, 219, 230-234
  concessions 102, 103
  currency 96, 97, 124, 125, 223, 224, 251
  economic development 81, 82n, 96, 101, 113, 120, 121, 129, 219, 220, 223, 234
  economic policy 92, 100, 101n, 102, 113, 118, 121, 218, 220, 222, 224, 228
  education 94, 112n, 119, 120, 218, 219, 226
  external debt 96, 99-102, 105, 107-113, 116, 118, 122, 129, 221n, 226, 235
    see also: Caisse de la Dette Publique, Debt, external
  external trade 80n, 90-93, 97n, 101, 111, 128, 129, 230-234
  feudalism 11, 12n, 16n, 81, 82, 84
  foreign intervention 92, 99, 100n, 102, 108, 110, 113, 116, 130
  French occupation 13n, 82, 89, 96, 131, 150
  health 85n, 87, 102, 115, 127, 219, 226
  industry 73, 83, 88, 90-92, 95, 96n, 99, 127, 128, 220-223, 229-234
  investment 85, 104n, 108, 112, 118, 121, 220, 221, 223, 224, 231
    foreign 53, 88, 102, 104n, 132n
  labour force 83, 91, 95, 96n, 115, 135, 221
  land ownership & tenure 42n, 81, 84, 85, 86n, 100, 103, 108, 109, 114, 124, 125, 126, 197, 226, 227, 229
    see also under: Land
  mining 127, 230

national income and product 139, 231, 232, 234
national movement 117, 118, 122, 124, 128
population 81-83, 88-90, 95, 105, 112-115, 121n, 125n, 139, 218, 232
route to Far East & India 81, 83, 94, 101n, 137
social & occupational structure 84-85, 223
standard of living 82, 227
taxation 11, 17n, 81, 82, 96, 105, 110, 113, 114, 121, 125, 126, 137, 220, 221, 227
tribute to Sultan 64, 65, 82, 106n, 226
El-Afghani, Jemal el-Din 118, 159, 165
El-Azhar University 118
Eldem, V. 197n, 200n
El-Djabarti 19n, 24n, 82n, 85n, 88n, 89n
Electricity 49, 184n, 195, 203, 217, 254, 268, 271
El-Gritly, A. 91n
El-Hizb el-Watani 118
Elwell-Sutton, L. P. 159n, 211n
Emigration 18, 243
 see also: Migration
Employment 20, 75, 83, 91, 115, 132, 139, 187, 227, 288
 see also: Labour, and under individual countries
Enfantin, B. P. 132
Engelhart, E. 31n
Engineering industry 195
English Levant Co. 46
Entrepreneurship 7, 17n, 51, 166, 169, 180, 241, 288
Enzeli 203
Ereğli 195
Erginay, A. 192n
Erzurum 77, 174, 180, 195
Esad, Mehmed 29n
Etatism 172, 179, 186, 187, 190, 191, 194, 196, 197, 199, 200
Ethiopia 220n
Eti Bank 193
Eton, W. 55n
Euphrates 36, 76n, 77, 93n, 94n, 130n, 147n, 266
Europe 3, 7, 8, 9, 19n, 43n, 50, 76n, 81, 83, 89, 91, 97n, 101, 103, 104, 107, 111, 119, 123n, 137, 146, 147, 158, 159
 see also: West
 and Ottoman Empire 2, 8, 10, 21, 22, 28, 34, 37, 45, 46, 63, 64, 73, 77, 80, 81
 feudalism in 9
 guilds in 19, 20, 21, 89
Evkaf, see: *Waqf*
Exchange rate 56, 62, 196, 207, 250
Export duties (*reftiyè*) 14, 46n, 48, 57n, 100, 142, 143n, 276

Exports, see: External trade
External trade 8, 15n, 22, 45-47, 49, 51, 75, 92, 97n, 211, 222, 282, 283, 288
 geographical patterns 68, 79, 80, 91, 93, 148, 153, 198, 274, 276
 government monopoly of 208, 211
 structure of 75, 80, 91, 96, 148, 187, 190, 195, 198, 199, 212, 213, 223, 234, 274
 terms of trade 233, 274
 value of exports & imports and balance of trade 79, 80n, 96, 111, 128, 142, 147-149, 187, 213, 225, 233, 234, 274, 276
 see also: Agriculture, Cotton, Grain, Industry, Oil, Tobacco
Eyub 75
Eyubi Effendi 55n

Fagnan, E. 13n
Fahmy, M. 84n, 89-92, 95n, 99n
Fashoda incident 118
Fath Ali Shah 150, 157, 158
Fateh, M. K. 140n, 144n, 155n
Fatemi, N. S. 153n, 154
Faysal 241
Fayum 86, 115n
Fellahin, see: Peasants
Fetwa (Futuwwa) 20n, 118, 156
Feudalism 9, 10, 12, 17, 180, 282, 283
 see also under inidividual countries
 Western & Eastern compared 8, 10, 11, 16, 17
Fief and fief holders 11, 12, 14n, 15, 16, 30, 31, 40, 41n, 43, 81, 84
Finkenstein agreement 150
Firman 13n, 25n, 29n, 47, 83n, 93n, 99n, 101n, 103, 106n, 117n, 134n, 151
Fiscal policy, see: Budget, Taxation
Fisher, S. 40n
Fishing 57n, 67, 203, 230
Fitzgerald, P. 131n, 133n, 135n, 139n
"Five Feddan Law" 123, APPENDIX 18
Five year Plans 188, 189, 191, 193-196
Food processing industry 73, 75, 148, 185, 268, 288
Foreign debt, see: Debt, external
Foreign exchange 34, 61, 144n
Foreign trade, see: External trade
Foster-Hobart mission 56, 60
Fournel, H. J. M. 130, 131n, 132n
France 3, 50, 65, 90, 104n, 121, 150, 168
 and Egypt 83, 87, 92, 93, 99, 103, 108, 109, 116-118, 130-137, 220n
 and Iraq 265
 and Ottoman Empire 28, 47, 49, 52n, 53, 54, 62n, 64, 66-70, 74, 78, 83, 165
 and Persia 149, 150, 152
 and Syria & Lebanon 169, 238, 241, 274

INDEX 419

and Turkey 173, 175, 176, 179
capitulations 26, 45, 46, 48, 50
investments & loans 49, 60, 64, 65, 68, 103, 104, 123n, 184n, 244
mandatory rule 238, 239, 242, 250, 252
trade 80
François I
French Electric Company 244
Frye, R. N. 212n
Fuad Pasha 56, 62

Galata bankers 60, 63
Galata Seray 33
Gallipoli 221
Garnett, L. M. 19n, 23n, 48n, 55n
Gass, O. 167n
Gazi, Mustafa Kemal 172n, *see* also: Atatürk
Gedik 19n
Gelfat, I. 268n
Genoa 46
Geneva 37n
Germany 3, 168, 268
 and Egypt 89, 110, 115n, 123, 131, 136
 and Ottoman Empire 30, 52n, 53, 54, 66-69, 74, 78, 117n, 124, 181n
 and Persia 150, 154, 155, 161n, 162n, 206, 210
 and Turkey 198
 capitulations 48
 concessions 50, 52, 68, 77
 in first world war 165, 175
 investments and loans 50, 51, 68, 70, 184n, 193
 trade 68, 79, 80
 see also: Prussia
Gibb, H. A. R. 9n, 13n, 15n, 18n, 19n, 41n, 195n
Gilbar, G. G. 140n, 158n
Gizeh 89
Gladstone, W. E. 117
Glass industry 75, 89, 148, 155, 184, 194, 195
Goblot, H. 145n
Gökalp, Ziya 39n, 165, 172
Gold 7, 8, 14, 20, 43, 62, 70, 79, 96, 124, 125, 152, 207, 208, 223, 251, 254
Gorst, E. 121, 122
Goschen, G. J. 104, 108
Goshen, Land of 132n
Gouraud, H. J. E. 243
Graig, J. I. 87n
Grain 85, 86, 142, 182, 205, 209, 234, 263
 area under 72, 86, 182n, 268
 exports 72, 95, 148, 182, 233, 246, 264, 267, 268, 275n, 277
 imports 182, 233, 264
 output, production and yields 72, 127, 145, 246, 265, 267, 268

prices 87n, 95, 123, 142, 145, 222, 228, 246, 267
Grand Vizier 25, 28n, 31, 34n, 36, 56, 62
Graves, P. P. 175n, 189n
Greece (and Greeks) 3n, 9n, 19, 28n, 29n, 31n, 32n, 38n
 and Egypt 83n, 92n, 116, 220
 and Ottoman Empire 40, 70n, 74
 and Turkey 173, 174, 176, 184, 189, 202
 investments and loans 63
 occupations of 71, 178
 persecution of 23, 48
 population exchange with Turkey *see* under: Turkey (republican)
 war against Turkey *see* under: Turkey (republican)
Greenwood, F. 135n
Gresham's law 96
Grey, F. 160n
Groseclose, E. 146n, 152n
Grunwald, K. 36n, 50n, 212n
Guilds 18-24, 89, 91, 92, 165, 171, 183
Gulistan agreement 150
Gumruk see: Customs
Gupta, R. N. 210n, 212n

Hagemeister, Jules de 141n
Haham Bashi (Chief Rabbi) 25, 26
Haifa 249, 272, 276n
Hakluyt, R. 45n
Hamdan 152
Hanotaux, G. 86n
Hartmann, M. 23n, 53n, 76n
Hartner, G. 214n
Hatti Hümayun 2, 13, 26, 31n, 32, 33, 38, 43, 47, 57n, 58n, 66n, 77, 113n, 116, APPENDIX 9
Hatti Sherif of Gülhane 2, 15, 31-33, 40, APPENDIX 8
Havard, G. T. 260n, 264n, 269n, 274n
Haydar Pasha 50, 77
Health 36, 65, 167, 177, 243
 see also under individual countries
Heaton, H. 17n
Hedjaz 37, 241, 260
Hedjaz railway 76, 259, 261, 262, 286
Heffening, W. 13n, 44n
Hekekyan, Y. 99n
Helfferich, K. 68n
Hemming, W. 13n
Henderson, W. O. 72n, 101n, 102n
Herat 154
Herodotus 129
Hersnlag, Z. Y. 166n, 172n, 176n, 182n, 185n, 186n, 191n, 194n
Hertslet, E. 151n

Herzegovina 65
Heyd, U. 39n
Hilton-Young, E. 246, 247n, 249, 254, 256n, 260n, 275n
Himadeh, S. B. 24n, 118n, 238n, 247n, 250n, 251n, 254n, 263n, 265
Hindya dam 265
Hines, W. D. 194
Hirsch, Baron, Concession of 36, 50, 76
Hitti, P. K. 82n, 243n
Hizb el-Umma 118
Holland, *see*: Netherlands
Holmes, J. 32n, 65n
Hotz & Co. 153n
Hourani, A. H. 48n
Hudja 84
Hukuki (ruzumi) 15
Hurewitz, J. C. 48n, 136n, 150n, 151n, 152n, 167n, 277n
"Hürriyet" 32n
Hussayn (Sheriff of Mecca) 125, 165
Hussayn (son of Ismail) 124

Ianei askeriïè, *see*: *Bedel*
Ibn-Tahri-Birdi 82n
Ibrahim Bey 19n
Ibrahim Pasha 31, 93, 243
I.B.R.D. (International Bank for Reconstruction & Development) 77n, 251n
Iltizam, see: *Multazimin*
Imam 157
Immigration 115n *see* also: Migration
Imperial Bank of Persia, *see*: Banks
Imperialism 289
Import duties
  see: Customs
Imports
  see: External trade
Income
  see: Agriculture, Industry, National income
India 62n, 76, 78n, 94, 117, 123, 138, 140, 142n, 148, 150, 159, 212, 254
Indian Ocean 129
Industrial revolution 3, 191, 289
Industry (and industrialization) 10, 21, 22, 29, 53, 73-75, 83, 87-89, 91-96, 166, 171, 280, 282, 283, 288, 290
  employment in 20, 75, 89-91, 127, 128n, 148, 184, 185, 197, 199, 211, 230, 268-270
  exports 73, 75, 79, 104n, 148
  foreign competition 47, 73-75, 91, 92, 128, 148, 155, 194, 269
  government aid 36, 53, 74, 268, 269
  government participation 53, 75, 91, 92, 114, 166, 191, 194, 196, 207n, 211, 212

income 75, 78, 200
investment 104, 207n, 212, 221, 248, 286
monopolies 73, 89, 90, 185
number & size of enterprises 75, 185, 230, 231, 269, 270
output (production) 73, 75, 79, 90-92, 105, 185, 196, 198, 200, 212, 269
private 75, 89, 146, 184, 196, 212, 221
productivity of labour 75, 231
structure 74, 75, 96n, 185, 270
traditional 72, 73, 75, 79, 89, 92, 147, 148, 211, 268, 269, 285
see also: Cement, Chemical, Food processing, Glass, Iron & steel, Leather, Military, Paper, Sugar, Textile (industries)
Inflation, *see*: Prices
Infrastructure 29, 77, 100, 112, 217, 221, 245, 259, 262n, 269
Initiative, *see*: Entrepreneurship
Inönü, Ismet 175, 188n
Insurance 152, 184, 217, 230
Interest 61, 63-65, 69, 91n, 107, 111, 122, 188, 197, 198, 209, 210, 242, 245
  attitude of Islam to 23, 24, 99, 118, 156, 209
  rates of 61, 69, 82, 85, 103, 105, 124, 135, 153, 156, 193, 210, 254, 262
Investment 3, 7, 63, 71, 86n, 100, 108, 156, 166, 179, 241, 242, 251, 255, 257, 281-283, 285, 286, 288-290
  amount of 53, 103, 104n, 196
  foreign 49, 51-54, 64, 69, 74, 76, 88, 103, 166, 168, 170, 176, 186, 210, 220, 244, 259
    see also under: Capital, foreign, Concessions
  in public works 111, 196, 226
  patterns of 52, 104n, 206, 215, 287
  see also: Capital, Communications, Industry, Irrigation, Suez Canal
Iqta (muqataʾa) 16n, 17
Iraq 35, 36, 63, 77n, 94n, 140, 157, 177
  agriculture 245-248, 256, 257, 267, 269, 270, 276
  and Ottoman Empire 35
  backwardness of 237
  balance of payment 247, 273, 276, 277
  banking 246, 248, 254, 258, 270
  budget 247, 248, 255-257, 273
  capitulations 48, 245
  communications and transport 159, 239, 245, 246, 247, 248, 257, 260, 270, 275
  currency 247-249, 254, 255
  development plans 245, 247, 269, 270, 273
  economic policy & development 245, 247, 256, 257, 269, 270, 276
  education 246-248, 256, 257
  external trade 246, 270, 275, 276

health   245, 247, 257, 266
industry & mining   75, 248, 270, 276
irrigation   239, 257, 265, 266, 270
investment   249, 257, 266, 276
land ownership & tenure   11, 255n, 265
mandatory rule   169, 236, 239, 276
national product   247
oil   248, 255-257, 270-273, 276
population   238-240, 247
share in Ottoman debt   70n, 245, 256, 257
standard of living   36
taxation   255, 256
Iraq Petroleum Company   176, 177, 270, 272, 273
Ireland, P.   255n
Iron & steel industry   194, 195, 197, 199
see also: Mining
Irrigation   36, 71, 100, 101, 123, 134, 144, 145, 149, 161, 204, 209, 243, 247, 248, 259, 285
canals   85-87, 93, 95, 101, 111, 119n, 121, 139, 144, 145, 229, 266
dams & barrages   85, 119, 121, 145, 229, 266
improvements in   2, 35, 84-86, 88, 111, 113, 119, 127, 167, 170, 229, 265, 288
Iş Bank   184, 193, 196
Isfahan   147, 157
Iskenderun
see: Alexandretta
Islam   1, 21, 24, 25, 76, 159, 165, 172, 180, 238, 282
and economic development   23
and the west   118
see also: West
attitude to inequalities in wealth   14, 23
attitude to non-Muslims   12n, 13n, 23, 44
compared to other religions   22, 26
conversion to   12n, 14, 25, 53n
Islamic Law   12n, 15, 23-25, 34, 40, 42n, 44n, 49, 99, 118, 204
Islamic State   12n, 24, 44
Shi'ites   146, 156, 157, 204
Sunnites   20n, 34, 42n, 239
Ismail   83n, 99, 101-117, 120, 123-130, 135n
Ismailia   134n, 232
Ismailia canal   119, 139
Ismet Bey   53n
Israel   166n
Issawi, Ch.   3n, 72n, 73n, 75n, 84n, 125n, 145n, 146n, 148n, 153n, 154n, 162n, 220n, 222, 224n, 228, 229n, 232n, 234n
Istanbul   20, 21n, 25, 26, 33, 37n, 38, 46n, 50, 61, 71n, 73, 74, 76-78, 116, 118, 157, 173, 181
see also: Constantinople
Istihlak (tax)   255, 256
Italy   72, 104n, 264

and Egypt   92n, 108, 116, 136, 220n
and Ottoman Empire   52n, 66, 69, 70
and Turkey   173
capitulations   45, 47, 48
trade   80
Izeddin, N.   119n
Izmir (Smyrna)   3, 19, 37, 50, 51, 72, 75-78, 173, 174, 177, 191n
Izmit   51n

Jamalzadeh, M. A.   148n, 162n
Janissaries   8-11, 15, 19, 21, 25, 28-30, 282
Japan   72, 159, 174
Jarablus   77
Jarib (tax)   35n
Jäschke, G.   188n, 193n
Javid Bey   53, 58, 68
Javy   242n
Jebel Druze   237, 238, 253, 259, 264
Jews   33n, 44n, 53n, 151, 168, 238, 239
and Islam   13n
and Ottoman Empire   25, 63
in Palestine   167
millet of   26
occupations   19, 20, 147, 184
persecution of   48n
see also: Minorities, Palestine
Jihad   1, 14n, 22, 165
Jizya
see: Taxation
Jomard, E.   82n
Jonescu, M.   71n
Joubert, M.   108
Jurisdiction   36
capitulatory   34, 45, 116, 150
civil   116n
mixed courts   116, 129, 151, 220
religious   25, 44, 116n
Juynboll, Th. H.   14n

Kabarisk   211
Kahyas   21
Kajar   143, 157, 212
Kamel, Ali Bey   121n, 129n
Kamel, Mustafa   118
Kanun   15
"Kanun"   159
Kapı Kulları   9, see also: *Kullar*
Karabük   194, 195, 197
Kararname   62
Karim, Khan   140
Kars   37
Karun river   145
Kasaba   50, 76, 78
Kashan   147

Katabtche 141
Kaulla, A. 77
Kavalla 83
Kaveh, T. 215n
Kazwi 156
Kemmerer, E. W. 194
Kerak 241
Kerman 154, 157
Kermanshah 152, 154, 158
Keynes, J. M. 187
Khadduri, M. 12n, 13n, 34n, 40n, 44n
Khalfa 20
Khalissa 156
Khanaqin 152
Kharadj 12-15, 40, 81, 82, 106, 125, 126, APPENDIX 1
Kilometric guarantees
  see: Railways
Kingsbury, J. B. 189n
Kirk, G. 118n, 168n, 240n
Kirkuk 260
Kitchener, Lord 121-124
Kleber, J. B. 82
Koçu Bey 8
Konikoff, A. 249n, 259n, 267n, 271n
Konya 50
Köprülü 55n
Koran 12-15, 23, 24, 44, 120n, 156, 157
Kotb, Sayed 23n
Kramer, J. H. 31n
Kran 143, 144, 147, 149n, 207, 208, 212, 213, 216
Kreuger, Ivar 193
Küçük-Kainarca, treaty of 46n, 55n, 61, 81
Kullar 10, 11n, 58n
Kum 146
Kurds 25, 156, 204, 239
Kut Dam 266
Kutay, C. 193n, 194n

Labour 141, 145n, 156, 241, 269, 289
  conditions 90, 96n, 133, 200, 204, 271, 285
  force 83, 91, 95, 135, 171, 199, 242, 248, 259
  in industry and agriculture 124, 185, 197, 223, 229, 231
  shortage of manpower 71, 88, 131n, 178, 288
  utilisation of 35, 86, 179
  see also: Corvée, Wages, and under individual countries
Ladas, S. P. 178n
Lafont, F. 146n, 156n
Lambton, A. K. 142n
Lammens, H. S. J. 241n
Land 3, 10, 12, 15, 105, 167, 178

crown lands (state lands) 14, 57n, 143, 156, 205, 209, 265
law 33, 40, 41, 43, 125, 262, 265, APPENDIX 10
ownership & tenure 9, 11, 17, 23, 28, 30, 35, 40-43, 81, 84, 85, 103, 109, 119, 155, 156, 165-167, 170, 180, 190, 197, 205, 216, 218, 262, 263, 267, 281, 283
  see also under individual countries
prices 119, 167, 227
reform 17n, 30, 40, 81, 84, 85, 95, 109, 126, 170, 178, 180, 181, 191, 197, 204, 215, 227, 265
registration 9, 35, 43, 84, 161, 170, 171, 180, 262, 263, 265
sale to foreigners 47, 49, 103, 211
surveys 43, 84, 119, 265, 290
  see also: Feudalism, Rent, Taxation, and under individual countries
Landes, D. S. 88n, 103n, 110n, 133n
Lane, E. W. 20n, 90n
Lanzoni, A. 72n
Latakiya 260
Laurent, M. C. 53
Lausanne, Treaty of 48, 54, 62, 70, 172-177, 179, 184n, 189, 226, 240, 245n
Law 2, 25, 31, 33, 37, 52n, 116, 123, 174, 179, 181, 183-185, 190, 191, 195, 196, 204, 208, 210, 213, 216
  see also: Jurisdiction, Land
Layard, A. H. 56n, 58, 62n, 64n
League of Nations 168, 169, 176n, 177, 187n, 198n, 203n, 213, 217n, 220n, 224n, 236, 237, 239-242, 244n, 245, 248n, 252, 254, 256-258n, 260n, 262n, 263n, 272, 275, APPENDIX 27
Leather industry 75, 89, 114, 146, 185, 269
Lebanon 86
  agriculture 243, 254, 262, 264, 267
  banking & currency 250, 253, 254
  budget 253
  capitulations 48
  commercial policy 242
  communications & transport 259, 260
  economic development & policy 274
  external trade 244, 273, 274
  feudalism 12n, 81n
  industry and mining 75, 243, 253, 268, 269
  land ownership & tenure 262
  mandatory rule 169, 236, 238, 241
  population 171, 237, 238
  share in Ottoman Debt 70n, 251, 252
  standard of living 273
  taxation 252
  trade 244
  Western influence 31

Lenczowski, G. 211n
Lesage, C. 107n, 134n, 135n
Lewis, B. 8n, 18n-21n, 31n, 32n, 191
Liakhov, Colonel 159
Liddel, H. G. 13n
Liebesny, H. J. 34n, 40n, 44n
Linant de Bellefonds, A. 130
Lingeman, E. R. 184n
Liquidation Law 110, 125
List, F. 172
Livestock 14, 41, 48, 102, 104, 146, 195, 221, 228, 258, 264, 266
Living standards
  see under individual countries
Loans see: Debt
Lockhart, L. 154n
Løkkegaard, J. 13n
London 94, 135n, 258
Lorenz curve 284
Lorini, E. 148n
Louis IX 45
Longrigg, H. S. 35n
Lucovich, M. A. 113
Lugard, Lord 237, 242n, 243n
Lynch, H. F. B. 144n
Lurs 156
Lybyer, A. H. 10n

Maan 241, 261
Mabro, D. 90n, 95n
Macedonia 67n, 72
Mackie, J. B. 195n
Mahmud II 10n, 14n, 29, 30, 31, 32, 47, 61
Mahmudia canal 93
Main, E. 239n, 266n, 276n
Majlis 149n, 157n, 159, 160, 203, 213
Makal, Mahmut 201
Malcolm, J. 140n, 141n, 143n, 144n, 146n, 150, 157n
Malcolm, N. 157n
Malet, E. Sir 117
Malta 85n, 100n
Mamluks 45, 81, 82, 83, 88, 282
Manpower
  see: Labour
Mandatory rule 166, 168, 287
  British and French compared 242, 243
  capitulations 48, 169
  commercial policy 242
  economic development 166, 242
  land policy 166
  League of Nations Permanent Mandates Commission 170, 236, 238, 245n, 263
  see also under individual countries
Marlowe, J. 108n

Marseille 94n
Marx, Karl 289
Masriyeh 96
Massignon, L. 18, 20n
Matruka 42
Mawwat 42
Mazuel, J. 86n, 130n
McCarthy, J. M. 115n
McCoan, J. C. 106n, 109n-116n, 126n, 127n, 134n
Means of payment see: Banking, Currency
Mears, E. G. 30n, 33n, 47n, 52n, 59n, 60n, 62n, 67n, 72n, 75n, 78n-80n, 168n, 173n-175n
Mecca 14n, 76, 262
Meclis-i Ahkam-i Adliye 32
Medina 76, 261, 262
Mediterranean (Sea) 76, 129, 130, 132, 138, 173, 232, 272
Mehmed Ali 4, 16n, 27, 29, 73, 81-100, 102, 106n, 108-110, 112n, 120, 124, 127, 129-131n, 172, 268, 279, 282, 285, 289
Mehmed Ali Shah 154
Mehmed Çelebi 12n
Mehmed Esad 10n
Mejelle 25, 34, 43, 180
Mejidiyeh 101 see also: *Aziziyeh el-Misriyeh*
Mekhala-el-Kubra 230
Melli Bank 152, 206, 208, 209
Menemencioğlu, N. 179n
Mercantilism 172, 244
Mersa-Matrukh 232
Mersin 50, 76
Meshed 146, 154
Midhat, Ali Haydar 34n, 36n
Midhat Pasha 10n, 15n, 23n, 34-37, 61, 181n
Migration 140, 288 see also: Emigration, Immigration
Military industry 75, 88-91, 147, 270
Miller, W. 2n
Millets 25, 26, 33, 34, 44, 60, 151n
  see also: Minorities
Milli istihlak 22
Millspaugh, A. C. 149n, 151n, 161, 203n-209, 211n, 217n
Milner, Visc. 102n, 105n, 108n, 112, 117n, 120, 219
Mining and minerals 43, 49, 53, 75, 195
  chrome 74, 196, 268
  coal 43, 50, 74, 91, 93, 101n, 153, 195, 196, 268, 286
  copper 73, 74, 147, 195n, 196
  development 74, 76, 196
  iron 74, 90, 147, 196, 268, 286
  output 74, 196, 198

424 INDEX

phosphates 128, 230, 234
precious metals 43, 74, 147, 152
surveys 161
taxes on 74 *see* also: Concessions, Monopolies, and under individual countries
Minorities 3, 21, 32, 38-41, 43, 44, 156, 178, 189, 218, 219, 289
  economic position of 22, 39, 147, 184
  occupations 20, 24, 26
  persecution of 7, 23, 177, 178
  self-government and jurisdiction 25, 26, 34, 116n, 151
  see also: Armenians, Christians, Greeks, Jews
Mint 18
Miri 11, 12, 16, 17, 40-43, 87n, 105, 108, 180, 255, 262, 265
Mirza Ali Muhammad 156, 159
Misr Bank 221, 230
Mitrani, D. 40n
Mochaver, F. 162n
Moazzami, A. 44n, 151n, 162n, 204n
Models of economic growth 280
Moldavia 29, 71n, 72, 80n
Moltke, H. von 28n, 29n, 61, 92n
Mommsen, T. 44n
Monetary policy 62, 70, 96, 193 *see* also: Banking, currency
Money, Money Supply
  see: Currency
Mongols 20n, 143n
Monopolies 29, 70, 84, 88, 92, 95, 97n, 99, 109, 174, 192, 196, 205, 253
  abolition of 47, 91-93, 96, 99, 100
  of various products & services 21, 60, 67, 93, 101, 113, 269
  price structure of 63, 90, 214, 269
  see also: Industry, Tobacco
Montenegro 65
Montreux, Convention of 48, 220
Morawitz, Ch. 8n, 11n, 12n, 26n, 37n, 38n, 41n, 45n, 55n, 64n, 66n, 67n, 69n, 71n, 75, 77n, 78n, 79n
Morley, J. 96n
Mornard, M. 161
Mosul 77, 176, 177n, 257, 260, 272
Mt. Athos 57n
Mudania armistice 173
Mudros armistice 69
Mufti 118, 156
Muhammad 9n, 12, 14n, 21, 23, 24
Muhammad Ali Shah 159, 160
Muhammad Shah 158
Muharrem Decree 50, 52, 66, 67, 70, APPENDIX 12
Muhtasib 21

Mujtahid 156
Mukabele 85, 105-108, 110, 125
Mukdim, O. 22n, 183n
Mulhall, M. G. 111n, 113n
Mulk 11, 12, 40, 41, 81, 180, 255, 262 *see* also: *ʾUshri*
Multazimin 16, 17, 74, 81, 82, 84, 282 *see* also: Tax farming
Munich 159
Munroe's Commission 246
Muqasama 12 *see* also: *Kharadj*
Murad, I 11n
Murad III 10, 14n
Murad IV 8, 55n
Murad V 36
Mushāʾ 17, 264
Mustafa II 16n
Mustafa IV 29
Mustaʾmin 13n
Mustawfi 141, 161
Muwazzaf 12, 14
Muzafer el-Din, Shah 153, 158

Nadir Shah 140, 146n
Nahas, J. F. 100n, 123n
Nansen, F. 177
Napoleon I 3, 83, 130, 150 *see* also: Egypt
Napoleon III 133, 135
Naqabat 19
Nasr el-Din Shah 152, 154, 157, 158
Nasser, Abdul 165n
Nathan, R. 167n
National Bank of Egypt
  see: Banks
Nationalisation 54, 74, 84, 175, 184n, 193, 196, 204, 211
National income 7, 42, 99n, 199 *see* also: National product, and under individual countries
Nationalism 26, 165, 166, 167n, 168, 189
National movements 73, 157n, 203, 236, 279
  see also under individual countries
National product 63, 199, 283, 288 *see* also under individual countries
Nauss, M. 142, 161n
Navarino 83n, 90
Navigation *see*: Communications
Nazis 150
Necho 129
Negroes 115n
Nessibin 261
Netherlands 45, 46, 66, 136, 137, 145, 153n, 220n
Neumark, F. 190n
Nile 86, 91, 95, 102, 112, 115n, 130, 133, 134, 226, 232

Nile irrigation 85, 96, 131n, 229
Nizam el-Mulk 11
Nizam jedid 28
Nomads 18, 35, 36, 82n, 115n, 155, 170, 171, 216, 218, 238-240, 245, 249, 258, 263, 271, 282
Noradounghian, G. 31n, 37n, 38n, 46n, 64n, 117n
Norway 220n
Nouzouli (avarisi) 15n
Nubar Pasha 109, 116, 119n, 133
Nuri, C. 178n

Occupational structure 3, 18-20, 199, 202, 237, 238, 283, 288
see also: Labour, and under individual countries
Oil 3, 73, 167, 286
 companies 213-215, 272, 273
 discovery 168, 214, 279
 exports 153, 213, 272, 276
 imports 153, 213
 income and royalties 149, 162, 177, 206, 207, 212-215, 255-257, 266, 272, 273
 investment 179
 output (production) 138, 153, 211, 214, 215, 230, 272, 273
 pipelines 138, 272
 prospecting 152, 153, 211, 268
 refining 142, 214, 230, 272, 273
 transit revenue 274
 transport of 137
 see also: Concessions, and under individual countries
Omar 129
Ongley, F. 40n
Opium 24, 29, 146, 148, 161, 205, 209, 212, 213
Oppenheim, H. 103, 104, 106, 113, 135n
Orts, P. 237
Othman 11
Ottoman Bank
 see: Banks
Ottoman Committee of Union and Progress 37n
 see also: Young Turks
Ottoman Debt 38, 47, 53, 63, 70, 176, 226, 245n, 252, 253
 amount of 58n, 63, 64, 66, 67, 70, 176
 creditors 47, 48, 63-70, 173, 176
 foreign supervision 65
 service of 58, 63-65, 68, 69, 176
 settlement and liquidation of 70, 173, 252
 see also: Muharrem Decree
Ottoman Debt Administration 48, 50, 52, 56, 57n, 58, 59, 62, 63n, 66-71, 76, 78, 179, 252, 286
Ottoman Empire 7, 14, 18, 21, 22, 26n, 37, 51, 54, 76, 93, 99, 101n, 105, 117n, 140, 159, 165, 167, 169, 170, 172, 174, 178, 190, 202, 238, 285, APPENDIX 2
 administration 7, 12, 22, 25, 28, 36, 38, 53, 58, 61, 63, 66n, 74, 76
 agriculture 63, 65, 71-73, 79
 and Suez Canal 136
 banking 61
 budgets 8, 10, 56-59, 63, 66, 78 see also: Budget
 capitulations 2, 34n, 43, 45, 48, 59, 149, 151, 168
 communication and transport 45, 50, 76, 78
 concessions 22, 49, 50, 52, 74, 77, 155
 currency 8n, 62, 70
 decline and disintegration of 2, 3, 7-9, 20, 26, 39, 44, 46, 55
 economic structure 26, 34n, 41
 education 27, 31, 37
 external trade 47, 79, 80
 feudalism 9, 15, 181
 industry 39, 73, 75, 184
 law & jurisdiction 33, 37, 38
 loss of territories 30, 37, 80
 mining 49, 63, 74
 population 3, 37, 63
 reforms 2, 3, 22, 27-39, 73, 161, 281
 taxation 9, 11, 15, 48, 63, 252
 wars 26n, 30n, 38, 39, 75
Owen, E. R. J. 87n
O'Zoux R. 243n, 253n

Palestine 30, 166, 243, 271, 274n
 agriculture 167, 264
 capitulations 45, 48
 currency 254, 255, 258
 external trade 233n, 277, 278
 feudalism 12n, 81n, 167
 industry 167
 Jewish settlement 151, 167
 mandate rule 169, 241, APPENDIX 30
 population 253
 State revenue 252
 trade agreements with Arab countries 276
Palestinians 167
Palmerston, Lord 38n, 131
Pape, W. 13n
Paper industry 75, 148, 194, 195
Paris 254
 Peace Conference 38
 treaty of 2, 38n, 154
Parliament (Ottoman) 36, 37, 53 see also: Majlis
Peasants 12n, 18, 30, 41n, 43, 83, 94, 109, 125, 155, 156, 171, 181
 and the government 11, 35, 43, 71, 84, 87, 88, 95, 100, 105

burden of taxes & rent on 8, 13n, 16-18, 29, 30, 59, 71, 82, 86n, 87, 96, 114, 126, 140, 142, 145, 156, 172, 180, 205, 207-209
character of 4, 144, 145n, 178
conditions of 9, 82, 86n, 105, 114, 119, 123, 124, 156, 170, 172, 181, 201, 207, 216, 218, 220, 222, 246, 249, 267
income of 71, 82, 87, 114, 145, 180, 182, 185, 209, 210, 229
self sufficiency 258
subjection to usury 24, 61, 71, 82, 85, 124, 210
see also: Taxation, Village
Pélissié du Rausas, G. 33n, 45n, 102n
Persia (Iran) 2, 19n, 27, 44n, 54, 129, 140
agriculture 144-149, 206, 208, 209, 213, 217
and Ottoman Empire 62n, 140, 147, 148, 150n, 157
and Turkey 212
balance of payment 143, 148, 212-214
banking and credit 141, 149, 152, 203
budget 140-147, 153, 158-161, 205-209, 212, 214, 215
capitulations 2, 43, 149, 150, 151, 162, 169, 203, 204, 214
cities 146, 159, 205, 209
communications and transport 141, 142, 147, 152, 159, 161, 203, 206, 207, 209, 210, 217
concessions 144, 146, 149, 151-156, 158, 159, 206, 216, APPENDIX 19 & 22
constitution 154, 158, 159
corruption of administration 141, 142, 149
currency 152, 205, 207, 208, 212
democratic party 150, 155
development plans 169, 205
education 158, 204, 206, 214, 215
external debt 141, 153, 162
external trade 145-149, 153, 158, 208, 209, 211-214, 216
feudalism 156
foreign intervention & influence 147, 217
health 140, 146, 206, 213, 214
industry 146-148, 155, 166, 206, 208, 210-212, 215, 217
investment 140, 141, 144, 145n, 148, 149, 156, 206, 208, 210, 212, 215
land ownership & tenure 144, 145, 156
mining 147, 152
monopolies 147, 205-207, 210, 211, 214, 216
national product 143
oil 147-149, 153, 154, 162, 206, 212, 214, 215, 217
see also: Oil
population 140, 142, 156, 159, 205n
reforms 2, 141, 158, 161, 203, 204, 207, 215, 217

reform movement 160, 281
social structure 155
standard of living 148, 209, 217
taxation 140-144, 149, 153, 156, 161, 205-208, 210, 215, 216
treaty with England, APPENDIX 20
treaty with Russia 143n, APPENDIX 26
wars 140, 143, 144n, 150, 155
Westernization 204
Persian Gulf 50, 76, 77, 94, 138, 152, 210
Poland 43n
Poliak, A. N. 12n, 13n, 81n
Poliakov, L. 152
Pomiankowski, J. 62n
Population 40, 72, 85, 94, 115n, 116, 127n, 216, 238-240
birth & death rates 218, 240
census of 35, 115n, 127n, 161, 218, 237-240, 290
decrease of 82, 140, 146, 155
density of 222, 232, 237, 240, 267
growth of 88, 96n, 115, 116n, 125n, 166, 182, 199, 202, 218, 222, 223, 226, 231, 233, 240, 285, 288
religious and national distribution 13, 71, 238, 239
rural 4, 18, 81, 121n, 125n, 155, 202, 217, 228, 231, 238, 240
urban 18, 22, 91, 166, 171, 216-218, 222, 227n, 237, 238, 240
see also: Nomads, and under individual countries
Porte see: Sultan
Ports
see: Communications and transport
Port Said 130n, 138, 232
Portugal 220n, 243n
Post and telegraph
see: Communications and transport
Potsdam Treaty 162n
Pouthas, H. 219n
Powers (Great Powers)
see: West, Europe
Pressel, W. von 50, 51n, 76n, 77n, 79n
Prices 73, 90n, 96, 135, 183, 185, 251
cost of living index 216, 229n
decline of 102, 105, 123, 143, 185-187, 197, 234, 255
effect of monopolies on 29, 84, 87
fixed by guilds 20
of primary products 29, 74, 229n
of various commodities and services 90n, 91, 102, 114, 115, 124, 146, 216, 244
regulated by government 84, 87n, 88, 89, 95, 192, 194, 199, 200, 214

rise of   8, 95, 102, 112, 119, 125, 136, 145, 174, 197, 199, 216, 220, 221n, 227, 244, 286
wholesale price index   220
see also: Agriculture, Cotton, Depression, Grain, Inflation, Land, Silk, Silver, Sugar, Tobacco
Productivity *see*: Labour, Industry
Protestantism   23, 26
Prussia   45, 47, 93n, 238 *see* also: Germany
Ptolemy II   129
Public utilities   61, 74
Punjab Land Alienation Act   123
Purchasing power   114, 127, 139, 216, 247, 271
Pyramids, battle of   83

Qadi   21, 24, 25, 41
Qaima   61, 62 *see* also: Treasury notes
Qanats   144, 145
Qansuh Ghoury   45

Rabino di Borgomale, H. L.   144n, 146n, 156n, 208n
Radwan, S.   90n, 95n
Railways   39, 49, 51, 53, 54, 59, 68, 76-79, 94n, 101n, 103, 107, 109, 111, 113, 121n, 127, 128, 132n, 152, 153, 155, 170, 175n, 184, 193, 195, 225, 226, 232, 233, 243, 245, 248, 254, 257, 259-262, 285
  investment in   64, 69, 76, 77, 100, 104, 121, 259
  kilometric guarantees   51, 52, 59, 69, 77
  ownership of   64, 193
  Trans-Iranian   210
  see also: Baghdad railway, Concessions, Hedjaz railway
Ramadan   14n
Ramsaur, E. E.   32n
Rappard, W. E.   168n, 245n, 249
Raw materials   8, 47, 53, 68, 74, 80, 89, 91, 93, 96, 104n, 128, 147, 155, 168, 183, 186, 187, 190, 191, 194, 195, 197, 198, 230, 234, 244, 245, 269, 276, 285, 289
Rayas   9n
Red Line Agreement   272, 273, APPENDIX 33
Red Sea   81, 115n, 129, 130, 132, 134 *see* also: Suez Canal
Reftiyè
  see: Export duties
Religion   1, 2, 4, 19, 27n, 33, 147, 157, 158, 236, 280, 281
  and State   84, 204, 216
  influence on the masses   156, 167
  movements   20, 118, 157
  status of religious minorities   31, 151, 157
Rent   3, 8, 17, 57n, 222, 265

Republican Party (in Turkey)   180, 189-191n, 202
Reshid Pasha   31, 34, 35, 36
Riaz Pasha   109
Rifaat Bey   129n
Rifaat, M. A.   233n
Riza Shah   172, 203-205, 210-212, 214-217
Roads *see*: Communications and transport
Robertson, H. M.   27n
Rohrbach, P.   51n, 145n, 153n
Romans   10, 17n, 44, 268
Rosetta   85, 89, 93
Ross, E. D.   173n
Rothstein, T.   110n, 111n, 120n, 129n
Rothschilds   109, 110, 135
Roux, J. C.   130n
Ruffin   83n
Rumania   174
Ruppin, A.   243n, 266n, 274n
Rusçuk   50, 76
Russia   37, 43n, 159, 168
  and Egypt   90n, 92, 93n
  and Iraq   246n
  and Ottoman Empire   23n, 26n, 28n, 37, 38n, 46n, 54, 65, 66n, 78, 117n, 238
  and Persia   142n, 145-155, 157n, 162n, 203, 211, 212, APPENDIX 26
  and Suez Canal   132, 136
  and Turkey   173, 186, 188, 194, APPENDIX 25
  capitulations   26, 45, 47, 48, 151, 203
  concessions   146, 152, 203, 211
  economic and technical aid   188
  loans   153, 158, 188, 193
Ruzname   106
Ruzumi
  see: *Hukuki*

Sabians   13n
Sabry, M.   84n, 86n, 93n, 95n, 101n, 103n, 106, 112n, 119n, 130n, 218n-220n
Sadir   143
Safawids   140
Said   84, 92, 100, 101, 106n, 111n, 116, 131, 132, 134, 138
Saint-Simon, C. H.   132n
Sakiye   86
Salahaddin   16n
Salat (Namaz)   14n
Salisbury, Lord   119n
Salmon, Mr.   9n
Salonika   19, 77
Samarra   77
Samos   57n
Samson   79
Sanjak Bey   11

San Stefano, treaty of 37
Sarc, Ö. C. 73n, 192n, 197n
Sarrafs 63
Saudi Arabia 169, 282
Savings 63, 184, 192, 231, 242, 246, 247, 254, 287, 290
Schumpeter, J. 280n
Schwarz P. 13n
Scott, R. 13n
Scutari, 51n, 73
Sefi, Shah 151n
Selim I 1, 10n
Selim III 14n, 16, 28, 29
Seljuks 1, 11, 12
Senior, N. W. 3n, 7n, 29n, 31n, 32n, 38n, 85n, 88n, 95n, 97n, 99n, 100n, 115n, 131n
Serbia 30, 35, 65, 74, 80n
Sèvres, treaty of 48, 54, 70, 172, 173, 240, 241
Shaduf 86
Sharia 15, 25, 34, 116n, 159n
Shatt el-Arab 260
Shaykh 19-21, 35, 123n, 170, 282
ul-Islam 25, 29, 156, 179
Shelal 232
Shi?ites
  see under: Islam
Shiraz 157
Shotwell, J. T. 45n
Shuster, W. M. 141-143, 149n, 152n-155, 157n, 158n, 160-162n, 205
Sidky Pasha 221
Silihars 11n
Silk 29, 67, 69, 72, 73, 75, 86, 90, 91, 145-148, 185, 211, 213, 243, 244, 264, 268
Silver 7, 8, 14, 20, 43, 61, 62, 74, 96, 124, 143, 152, 208
Sipahis 8-11, 15
Sivas 174, 180, 195
Slade, A. 28n-30n
Slaves 20, 95, 112, 133, 156
Smuts, General 168
Smyrna *see*: Izmir
Soviet Union *see*: Russia
Spain 47, 136, 220n
Stafford, R. S. H. 239n
Stamp, L. D. 215n
State capitalism 89
Steeg, L. 30n
Subaşi 11
Sudan 48, 86, 96n, 97, 106, 112, 118, 122n, 209n, 220, 229
Suez 93, 94, 134, 138, 232
Suez Canal 94, 100, 113, 122, 124, 168, 233, 286
  and Egypt's external debt 106, 135
  capital and shares of the Company 107, 132

Company 131-138
concession of 104n, 130-136, APPENDIX 15
construction of 102, 114, 115n, 129, 131-133, 139
effect on Egypt's economy 102, 129-134, 137-139, 235
Egypt's compensation to the Company 135, 139n
Egypt's investment and share in the Company 112n, 132-135, 138
freedom of navigation 136, APPENDIX 17
history of canal idea 129, 130
improvement in 137n, 139
income & dividends 108, 135-138
investment in 103, 111n, 132, 135, 136
nationalisation of 134, 138, 139
opening of 135, 279
opposition to construction 107
physical data 137n
sale of Egypt's share 106, 107, 135, 138
toll-fee 136n, 138
traffic 137
value to international trade 137, 138
Sugar 85, 86, 89, 90, 104, 105, 123, 127, 128, 142, 145, 148, 153, 155, 184, 185, 194, 197, 207, 210, 211, 213, 230, 270
Suleiman the Magnificent 7n, 10, 14n, 45
Sultan 3, 7, 9-11, 24-31, 35, 36, 38, 41n, 42, 44-48, 51, 52, 55, 57n, 58n, 63, 64, 66, 76-78, 81, 83, 84, 92, 93, 95, 103, 106, 110, 116, 124, 131, 133, 134, 172, 173, 179, 238
Sümerbank 184, 193
Sunna, Sunnis
  see: Islam
Sweden 74, 193, 220n
Switzerland 45, 179
Sykes, P. 153n, 161n, 162n
Syria 1n, 30, 150, 273
  agriculture 72, 243, 254, 260, 261, 263, 264, 269
  and Egypt 81, 85n, 95, 115n
  and Ottoman Empire 35, 37
  balance of payments 244, 245, 274, 275
  banking and credit 24n, 118, 250, 253, 254, 263
  budget 60, 244, 252, 253
  capitulations 48
  communication & transport 252, 259, 260
  currency 250, 251
  economic development & policy 242, 243, 244, 252, 263, 264, 269
  education 245, 253
  Egyptian conquest 31, 243
  external debt 252
  external trade 244, 273, 274, 275

INDEX

feudalism 12n, 81n, 264
health 253
industry & mining 75, 243, 244, 253, 268, 269
investment 244, 250, 253, 260
land ownership & tenure 262
mandatory rule 169, 236, APPENDIX 28
population 82, 171, 237, 253, 273
share in Ottoman debt 70n, 251, 252
standard of living 273
taxation 244, 252, 263
trade 244
Western influence 31

Tabatabai, Ziya el-Din 204
Tabriz 147, 150, 152, 154
Tadros, F. 219n
Talleyrand-Périgord, Ch.-M. de 83n
Talmud 44n
Tanta 232
Tanzimat 13n, 15, 16, 25, 28, 31-34, 37-40, 55, 73n, 103n, 282, 285
Tapu 16n, 41, 42, 43, 265
Tariff
 see: Customs
Tarsus 50, 76
Tawa'if 19
Tawney, R. H. 27n
Taxation 11, 12, 14, 15, 30, 31, 35, 40, 42n, 48, 55n, 57n, 59, 60, 65, 68, 74, 76-78, 81, 82, 84, 86n-88, 93n, 96, 97, 119, 149, 169, 190, 289, 290
 arbitrariness & fraud in collection 16
 collection methods (incl. farming) 3, 9-11, 15-17, 19, 21, 26, 28, 31, 32, 35, 40, 41n, 43, 47, 59, 68, 81, 88, 89, 110, 121, 141-143, 158, 160, 161, 205, 252, 255, 282
 collective responsibility for payment of 17
 consumption taxes 29, 192
 crop tax 14
 excise 14, 15, 21, 48, 57n, 67, 78, 225, 255, 256, 258
 exemption from 11, 42, 48, 51, 53, 84, 133, 153, 183
 in cash 59, 82, 141, 142
 income and direct taxes 14, 63, 192, 205, 208, 222, 225, 256, 258, 270n
 indirect taxes 56, 63, 208, 216, 256, 258
 in kind 16, 17, 82, 141, 142
 in towns 15, 19, 57n
 land taxes 14, 15n, 29, 30, 41, 43, 48, 53, 78, 87, 97, 105, 106, 108, 119, 121n, 133, 142, 143, 180, 183, 205, 216, 222, 225, 255, 258
 on foreigners 48, 110, 120, 220-222
 on mines 14, 15, 57n
 on minorities 57n, 192
 per capita 60, 121

poll tax (*jizya*) 9n, 13-15n, 48, 57n, 93n
property taxes 14, 183, 192, 252
reserved for debt service 52, 59, 65-69, 107, 109, 110
special taxes 58n, 103, 206
stamp taxes 57n, 67, 76, 120, 161, 183, 256
symbol of suzerainty 10, 30
turnover tax 192, 255
 see also: Budget, and under individual countries
Teheran 147, 152, 155, 157, 159, 205, 211
Tekâlifi 'urfiye 15
Tel-el-Kebir 117
Terms of trade
 see: External trade
Tewfiq 108, 110, 117
Textile 73, 75, 87, 89, 90, 92n, 96, 101, 148, 185, 194, 195, 211, 230, 243, 268-271, 276, 278, 288
Thrace 177
Tignon, R. L. 221n, 230n
Tigris 36, 76n, 147n, 266, 272
Tilsit, treaty of 150
Timar 12n
Tirnovo 73
Tismir, A. 206n, 208n, 211n-214n
Tithe
 see: Kharadj, 'Ushr
Tobacco 24, 47, 121n, 182, 184n, 209, 211, 254, 270, 271
 concessions 146, 152, 156
 exports 72, 75, 148, 197, 209, 264, 267, 277
 imports 96, 128, 156
 monopoly 50, 60, 67, 152, 179, 182, 185, 205, 252, 269
 prices of 185, 264
 production 75, 182, 185, 264, 267, 268
 taxes on 78, 108, 161, 252
Topf, E. 243n, 244n
Toprak 198
Tourism 22, 254, 274, 275
Trabzon 77, 195
Trade 7, 19, 20, 24, 32, 43n, 49, 52, 54, 79, 80, 93, 100, 129, 130, 143, 147, 150, 167, 169, 216, 217, 221
 diversion of transit trade 8, 73, 94
 see also: External trade, and under individual countries
Trade unions 183, 204, 288
Trans-Caucasia 150, 152
Transjordan
 agriculture 249, 259, 267, 268
 balance of payments 249, 277, 278
 British aid 249, 258, 259, 278
 budget 249, 258, 259
 communications & transport 249, 261, 262
 currency 258

430   INDEX

economic policy 249
education 249, 259
external debt 259
external trade 277, 278
health 249, 259
industry 249, 271
mandatory rule 169, 241
population 249, 260, 267
share in Ottoman debt 259
taxation 258
transport *see*: Communications and transport
Treasury (of state)
  see: Budget
Treasury, lack of differentiation between inner and State 7n, 55, 113
Treasury bonds 105, 108, 119n, 121, 125
Treasury notes 61, 62, 223 *see also*: Currency, Qaima
Treaties, international 2, 8n, 30n, 45, 48, 73, 150, 169, 203
  see also: Amiens, Anglo-Iraqi, Anglo-Russian, Berlin, Capitulations, Carlowitz, Finkenstein, Gulistan, Kuçuk-Kainarca, Lausanne, Mandatory rule, Montreux, Paris, Potsdam, San Stefano, Sèvres, Tilsit, Turkman-Chai, Constantinople
Tripoli 8n, 254, 259, 260, 272
Tuman 143, 207n
Turkey (republican) 21, 31n, 42n, 70, 169, 171, 203, 217, 236, 282
  agriculture 30, 61, 172, 180-182, 184, 186-188, 191, 192, 195, 197-202
  area 26n
  balance of payments 189-191, 194, 198, 199, 202
  banking and credit 178, 184, 191-193, 196
  budget 173, 176, 179, 189, 192, 193
  capitulations 48, 172, 173, 175
  communications and transport 78, 191, 193, 202
  concessions 74, 173, 175, 179
  corruption of administration 189
  currency 63, 173
  development plans 169, 183, 188-198
  economic policy and development 22, 166, 172, 174, 178-180, 182, 185, 186-199, 202
  effects of the great depression 182, 185-187, 197, 200
  external debt 173, 176, 192, 199
  external trade 175, 184, 186, 187, 189-191, 195, 198, 199
  foreign aid 174
  industry 53, 75, 166, 172, 180, 182-186, 190-202
  investments 173, 176, 179, 181, 183, 185, 187, 192-197

  mining 74, 183-185, 191, 193, 195, 196, 198
  national income 186, 187, 191, 199-201
  nationalism 39, 174, 180n
  occupational structure 26, 178
  oil 176n, 177, 179, 195
  population 178, 194, 197, 202
  population exchange with Greece 174, 177-179, 181, 202
  reforms 172, 179, 200, 204, 237
  standard of living 186, 187, 190-200, 202
  taxation 14, 180, 183, 192, 193, 199
  trade 174n, 178, 184
  war against Greece 75, 172-178, 182, 189
Turkman-Chai, treaty of 2, 150, 151
Türkofis 74n, 196n, 199
Turks 2, 3, 12, 19, 20, 25, 47, 48, 54, 69, 79, 156, 165, 173, 188
  attitude to Islam 25, 34, 44
Turkstroj 188
Turner, G. D. 144n

Ubicini, M. A. 12n, 16n, 25n, 26n, 30n, 31n, 36n, 38n, 41n, 56, 57n, 61n, 72n, 73n, 80n
ʾUlema 4, 24, 25, 28, 152, 156
Unemployment 46, 171, 187, 198, 218, 232, 242, 246, 264, 288
United States (of America) 101, 102, 168, 200
  and Egypt 116, 220n
  and Ottoman Empire 52, APPENDIX 5
  and Persia 146, 151, 152, 154, 160, 161, 203, 205, APPENDIX 21
  and Suez Canal 132, 137
  and Turkey 173, 175, 176, 194
  capitulations 45, 47, 151
  concessions 53
  loans 193
Urbanization *see*: City
Urquhart, D. 9n, 15n
ʾUshr, ʾUshri, ʾUshuri (tithe) 12, 14, 15, 40, 41, 48, 49, 59, 66n, 68, 74, 78, 79, 93n, 106, 125, 126, 172, 180, 252, 255, 267, APPENDIX 1
Usta 20
Usury 24, 61, 118, 156 *see also*: Peasants, Interest

Van den Steen de Jehay, F. 25n
Varna 50, 76
Vatican 45
Vaucher, G. 97n, 124n, 125n
Venice 45, 46
Vergi (Verko) 14, 59, 258
Vernon, H. 246
Vienna 8, 46, 50, 76
Village 43, 73, 75, 84, 92, 95, 100, 141, 156, 165, 170, 173, 177, 181, 205n, 245

characteristics of   17, 18, 22, 26, 71, 89, 120n, 170, 201, 282
desertion of   17n, 18, 24, 29, 221
taxation   29, 82, 95, 99n, 100n, 119, 143, 208
see also: Peasants
Vitaly, S.   53n
Von Hammer J.   7n, 9n, 10n, 12n, 17n, 25n, 28n

Wages and salaries   8, 60, 75, 76, 82, 89, 90, 95, 114, 127, 128n, 132, 133, 139, 141, 161, 171, 192, 214, 216, 222, 225, 226, 229, 256n, 257, 271, 288
Wahabis   30, 83n
Wallachia   29, 80n
Waqf, Evqaf   14, 24, 34, 41-43, 55n, 82, 84, 106, 124, 142, 156, 180, 227n, 256, 262, 263
Wars, economic consequences of   7, 14, 39, 46n, 55n, 56, 65, 73, 75, 79, 129n, 143, 145, 150, 177, 179, 182, 183, 285
West   3, 19, 31, 130, 188
  and East   1-3, 7, 27, 31, 32, 35, 38, 39, 44, 47, 49, 52, 78, 93n, 102, 109, 116, 118, 147, 149, 165, 166, 168-171, 203, 279, 280, 281
  economic relations with the East   22, 39, 47, 54, 73, 119n, 161, 167, 168, 189n
  intervention in Ottoman Empire   23, 64-67n, 168, 172, 173
Westernization   28, 33, 39, 52, 100, 101, 112, 113, 165, 166, 172, 180, 289
  see also: Europe
Weulersse, J.   1, 281
Wilber, D. N.   210n
Willcocks, W.   86n, 87n, 114n, 119, 126, 145, 266
William IV   76
Wilson, A. T.   144n, 145n, 147n, 148n, 151, 153n, 206n, 210n, 213n, 215n
Wilson H.   218
Wilson Rivers, Ch.   109
Wittek, P.   8n
Woodhouse, H.   53, 175n

Wool   73, 89, 91, 146, 148, 185, 194, 211, 213, 216, 264, 270
World War I   3-5, 13, 22, 23, 25, 26, 38, 39, 43, 48, 49, 52n-54, 56, 58, 60, 62, 64, 69-71, 73-75, 77-80, 110, 116-118, 124, 126-129, 131, 136, 137n, 144, 145, 148, 150, 151, 160-162, 165-169, 172, 179, 183, 185, 203, 207, 218, 219, 232, 233, 236, 241, 243, 246, 250, 254, 255, 261, 268, 273, 286
  compensation and reparations   176
  economic consequences of   72, 75, 78, 125, 147, 162, 166, 170, 173, 174, 184, 189, 206, 210, 220, 221, 224, 242, 245, 259, 260
World War II   3, 4, 42n, 129n, 136, 137, 139, 165, 168, 169, 179, 184n, 188, 192-194, 196, 201n, 206, 211, 215, 217, 219, 223, 226, 229, 230, 232, 234, 236, 241, 245, 248, 261, 262, 267, 269-273n, 280, 281, 283, 284, 286, 288-290
Wurm, C. F.   130n

Yazidis   238
Yemen   169, 282
Yeni çeri
  see: Janissaries
Yezd   154
Young, G.   25n, 33n
Young, H.   177n
Young Turks   13, 21, 22, 32, 36-39, 43, 48, 53, 56, 58, 68, 79, 122, 172, 183
  see also: Ottoman Committee of Union & Progress
Yugoslavia   174
Yuzluk   96

Zaglul, Saad   118
Zakat   14, 23
Zionism   167
Zonguldak   194, 195
Zoroastrians   13n